SOCIAL PSYCHOLOGY
EXPERIMENTATION, THEORY, RESEARCH

SOCIAL PSYCHOLOGY
EXPERIMENTATION, THEORY, RESEARCH

Edited by

WILLIAM S. SAHAKIAN

Suffolk University

INTEXT EDUCATIONAL PUBLISHERS

College Division of Intext

Scranton   San Francisco   Toronto   London

The Intext *Series in*

PSYCHOLOGY

Consulting Editor

HAROLD J. VETTER
Loyola University of New Orleans

ISBN 0-7002-2418-1 (hard)

ISBN 0-7002-2387-8 (soft)

Library of Congress Catalog Card Number: 77-183724

TO

my son

RICHARD LEWIS SAHAKIAN

who left me with the fondest of warm memories
to ward off the chill of any winter's night

PREFACE

There are some social psychologists living today who have had the exciting experience of watching their science mature from a state of infancy, a singular event in any professional's life. Some have marked the birth of this new science in 1908, the publication date of the first textbooks containing "social psychology" in their titles: *An Introduction to Social Psychology* by a psychologist, William McDougall; and *Social Psychology: An Outline and Source Book* by a sociologist, Edward Alsworth Ross.

Actually, the birth of experimental social psychology can be traced to 1897, the publication date of Norman Triplett's paper on experimental findings pertaining to competition. Some will argue that social psychology was originally sired by Hegel (1770–1831), Wundt (1832–1921) or Lazarus (1824–1903) and his colleague Steinthal (1823–1899); or some may even contend that the honor belongs to Aristotle (384-322 BC), owing to his studies on attitude.

This text seeks to do more than provide an interesting assortment of literature in the field of social psychology. Its intent is to encompass systematically the scope of social psychology, but even more important to provide the most influential contributions to the field to date, emphasizing the more recent offerings. Accordingly, this volume is a suitable text delineating the field as well as providing the course's content, versatile enough to enable the instructor either to deliver his own lectures or else to discuss the classics contained herein.

To augment the versatility of the book, a dual table of contents has been supplied, one for those who prefer the traditional analytical approach and another for those who travel the systems and theory road. In the author's experience, this is the initial appearance of a dual table of this order in any social psychology text.

WILLIAM S. SAHAKIAN

Beacon Hill
Boston, Massachusetts
January, 1972

CONTENTS
ANALYTICALLY ARRANGED

CONTENTS
ARRANGED BY THEORIES

THEORIES OF ATTITUDE MEASUREMENT

EARLY THEORIES OF GROUP PROCESSES

CURRENT THEORIES OF GROUP PROCESSES

THEORIES OF ACHIEVEMENT AND MOTIVATION

ENVIRONMENTAL INFLUENCE THEORIES OF SOCIAL BEHAVIOR

ROLE THEORY

Social psychology is the scientific study of the experience and behavior of individuals in relation to social-stimulus situations.

Muzafer Sherif
Psychology: A Study of a Science

Social psychologists regard their discipline as
an attempt to understand and explain how the thought, feeling, and behavior of individuals are influenced by the actual, imagined, or implied presence of others.

Gordon W. Allport
The Handbook of Social Psychology

1 · PRECURSORS OF MODERN SOCIAL PSYCHOLOGY

ARISTOTLE

*Social Psychology of Attitudes**

Rhetoric may be defined as the faculty of observing in any given case the available means of persuasion. This is not a function of any other art. Every other art can instruct or persuade about its own particular subject-matter; for instance, medicine about what is healthy and unhealthy, geometry about the properties of magnitudes, arithmetic about numbers, and the same is true of the other arts and sciences. But rhetoric we look upon as the power of observing the means of persuasion on almost any subject presented to us; and that is why we say that, in its technical character, it is not concerned with any special or definite class of subjects.

Of the modes of persuasion some belong strictly to the art of rhetoric and some do not. By the latter I mean such things as are not supplied by the speaker but are there at the outset—witnesses, evidence given under torture, written contracts, and so on. By the former I mean such as we can ourselves construct by means of the principles of rhetoric. The one kind has merely to be used, the other has to be invented.

Of the modes of persuasion furnished by the spoken word there are three kinds. The first kind depends on the personal character of the speaker; the second on putting the audience into a certain frame of mind; the third on the proof, or apparent proof, provided by the words of the speech itself. Persuasion is achieved by the speaker's personal character when the speech is so spoken as to make us think him credible. We believe good men more fully and more readily than others: this is true generally whatever the question is, and absolutely true where exact certainty is impossible and opinions are divided. This kind of persuasion, like the others, should be achieved by what the speaker says, not by what people think of his character before he begins to speak. It is not true, as some writers assume in their treatises on rhetoric, that the personal goodness revealed by the speaker contributes nothing to his power of persuasion; on the contrary, his character may almost be called the most effective means of persuasion he possesses. Secondly,

*Aristotle, "Rhetorica," in W. D. Ross (ed.), *The Works of Aristotle* (Oxford: Oxford University Press), 1924.

1

persuasion may come through the hearers, when the speech stirs their emotions. Our judgements when we are pleased and friendly are not the same as when we are pained and hostile. It is towards producing these effects, as we maintain, that present-day writers on rhetoric direct the whole of their efforts. This subject shall be treated in detail when we come to speak of the emotions. Thirdly, persuasion is effected through the speech itself when we have proved a truth or an apparent truth by means of the persuasive arguments suitable to the case in question.

There are, then, these three means of effecting persuasion. The man who is to be in command of them must, it is clear, be able (1) to reason logically, (2) to understand human character and goodness in their various forms, and (3) to understand the emotions—that is, to name them and describe them, to know their causes and the way in which they are excited. It thus appears that rhetoric is an offshoot of dialectic and also of ethical studies. Ethical studies may fairly be called political; and for this reason rhetoric masquerades as political science, and the professors of it as political experts—sometimes from want of education, sometimes from ostentation, sometimes owing to other human failings. As a matter of fact, it is a branch of dialectic and similar to it, as we said at the outset. Neither rhetoric nor dialectic is the scientific study of any one separate subject: both are faculties for providing arguments. This is perhaps a sufficient account of their scope and of how they are related to each other.

— · — · — · — — · — · — · — · — · —

WILHELM WUNDT

Folk Psychology: Language, Myth, and Custom*

The word 'Völkerpsychologie' (folk psychology) is a new compound in our [the German] language. It dates back scarcely farther than to about the middle of the nineteenth century. In the literature of this period, however, it appeared with two essentially different meanings. On the one hand, the term 'folk psychology' was applied to investigations concerning the relations which the intellectual, moral, and other mental characteristics of peoples sustain to one another, as well as to studies concerning the influence of these characteristics upon the spirit of politics, art, and literature. The aim of this work was a characterization of peoples, and its greatest emphasis was placed on those cultural peoples whose civilization is of particular importance to us—the French, English, Germans, Americans, etc. These were the questions of folk psychology that claimed attention during that period, particularly, to which literary history has given the name "young Germany." The clever essays of Karl Hillebrand on *Zeiten, Völker und Menschen* (col-

*Wilhelm Wundt, *Elements of Folk Psychology*, trans. Edward Leroy Schaub (New York: Macmillan, 1916), pp. 1–10.

lected in eight volumes, 1885 ff.) are a good recent example of this sort of investigation. We may say at the outset that the present work follows a radically different direction from that pursued by these first studies in folk psychology.

Practically coincident with the appearance of these earliest studies, however, was a radically different use of the term 'folk psychology.' The mental sciences began to realize the need of a psychological basis; where a serviceable psychology did not exist, they felt it necessary to establish an independent psychological foundation for their work. It was particularly in connection with the problems of philology and mythology, and at about the middle of the century, that the idea gradually arose of combining into a unified whole the various results concerning the mental development of man as severally viewed by language, religion, and custom. A philosopher and a philologist, Lazarus and Steinthal, may claim credit for the service of having introduced the term 'folk psychology' to designate this new field of knowledge. All phenomena with which mental sciences deal are, indeed, creations of the social community. Language, for example, is not the accidental discovery of an individual; it is the product of peoples, and, generally speaking, there are as many different languages as there are originally distinct peoples. The same is true of the beginnings of art, of mythology, and of custom. The natural religions, as they were at one time called, such as the religions of Greece, Rome, and the Germanic peoples, are in truth, folk religions; each of them is the possession of a folk community, not, of course, in all details, but in general outline. To us this fact has come to appear somewhat strange, because in our age these universal mental creations have already long transcended the limits of a single people. Though this is true, it does not imply that the folk community is not really the original source of these mental creations. Now, in the works of Lazarus and Steinthal and in the *Zeitschrift für Völkerpsychologie und Sprachwissenschaft* edited by them and appearing in twenty volumes from 1860 on, the conception had not as yet, it is true, received the precise definition that we must give it to-day. Nevertheless, a beginning was made, and the new venture was successfully launched along several different lines. Some uncertainty still prevailed, especially with regard to the relation of these studies to philosophy, and as to the method which psychology must follow when thus carried over into a new field. It was only gradually, as the psychological point of view gained ground in the special fields of research, that this condition was improved. To-day, doubtless, folk psychology may be regarded as a branch of psychology concerning whose justification and problem there can no longer be dispute. Its problem relates to those mental products which are created by a community of human life and are, therefore, inexplicable in terms merely of individual consciousness, since they presuppose the reciprocal action of many. This will be for us the criterion of that which belongs to the consideration of folk psychology. A language can never be created by an individual. True, individuals have invented Esperanto and other artificial languages. Unless, however, language had already existed, these inventions would have been impossible. Moreover, none of these languages has been able to maintain itself, and most of them owe their existence solely to elements borrowed from natural languages. How, again, could a religion have been created by an individual? There have, indeed, been religions whose founders were individual men: for example, Christianity, Buddhism, and Islamism. But all these religions rest on earlier foundations; they are elaborations of religious motives arising within particular folk communities. Thus, then, in the analysis of the higher mental processes, folk psychology is an indispensable supplement to the psychology of individual consciousness. Indeed, in the case of some questions the latter already finds itself obliged to fall back on the principles of folk psychology. Nevertheless, it must not be forgotten that just as there can be no folk community apart from individuals who enter into reciprocal relations within it, so also does folk psychology, in turn, presuppose individual psychology, or, as it is usually called, general psychology. The former, however, is an important supplement to the latter, providing principles for the interpretation of the more complicated processes of individual consciousness. It is true that the attempt has frequently been made to investigate the complex functions of thought on the basis of mere introspection. These attempts, however, have always been unsuccessful. Individual consciousness is wholly incapable of giving us a history of the development of human thought, for it is conditioned by an earlier history concerning which it cannot of itself give us any knowledge. For this reason we must also reject the notion that child psychology can solve these ultimate problems of psychogenesis. Among cultural peoples, the child is surrounded by influences inseparable from the processes that arise spontaneously within its own consciousness. Folk psychology, however, in its investigation of the various stages of mental development still exhibited by mankind, leads us along the path of a true psychogenesis. It reveals well-defined primitive conditions, with transitions leading through an almost continuous series of intermediate steps to the more developed and higher civilizations. Thus, folk psychology is, in an important sense of the word, *genetic psychology.*

In view of the general nature of the task of the science, objection has sometimes been raised to its being called folk psychology. For, the study is concerned, not merely with peoples but also with more restricted, as well as with more comprehensive, social groups. Family, group, tribe, and local community, for example, are more restricted associations; on the other hand, it is to the union and reciprocal activity of a number of peoples that the highest mental values and attainments owe their origin, so that, in this case, folk psychology really becomes a psychology of mankind. But it is self-evident that, if it is not to fade into indefiniteness, a term such as 'folk psychology' must be formulated with reference to the most important conception with which it has to deal. Moreover, scarcely any of the proposed emendations are practicable. *'Gemeinschaftspsychologie'* (community psychology) may easily give rise to the misconception that we are concerned primarily with such communities as differ from the folk community; *'Sozialpsychologie'* (social psychology) at once reminds us of modern sociology, which, even in its psychological phases, usually deals exclusively with questions of modern cultural life. In an account of the total development of mental life, however—and this is the decisive consideration—the 'folk' is the most important collective concept and the one with which all others are associated. The 'folk' embraces families, classes, clans, and groups. These various communities are not excluded from the concept 'folk,' but are included within it. The term 'folk psychology' singles out precisely the folk as the decisive factor underlying the fundamental creations of the community.

When this point of view is taken, the question, of course, arises whether the problem thus assigned to folk psychology is not already being solved by ethnology, the science of peoples, or whether it ought not to be so solved. But it must be borne in mind that the greatly enlarged scope of modern ethnology, together with the increased number and the deepened character of its problems, necessarily precludes such a psychological investigation as falls to the task of folk psychology. I may here be allowed to refer to one who, perhaps more than any other recent geographer, has called attention to this extension of ethnological problems—Friedrich Ratzel. In his treatise on anthropography and in a number of scattered essays on the cultural creations of peoples, Ratzel has shown that ethnology must only account for the characteristics and the habitats of peoples, but must also investigate how peoples originated and how they attained their present physical and mental status. Ethnology is the science of the origin of peoples, of their characteristics, and of their distribution over the earth. In this set of problems, psychological traits receive a relatively subordinate place. Apparently insignificant art products and their modifications may be of high importance in the determination of former migrations, fusions, or transferences. It is in this way that ethnology has been of valuable service to history, particularly in connection with prehistoric man. The central problem of ethnology concerns not only the present condition of peoples, but the way in which they originated, changed, and became differentiated. Folk psychology must be based on the results of ethnology; its own psychological interest, however, inclines it to the problem of mental development. Though of diverse origins, peoples may nevertheless belong to the same groups as regards the mental level to which they have attained. Conversely, peoples who are ethnologically related may, psychologically speaking, represent very different stages of mental culture. The ethnologist, for example, regards the Magyars and the Ostiaks of Obi as peoples of like origin. Psychologically, they belong to different groups: the one is a cultural people, the other is still relatively primitive. To the folk psychologist, however, 'primitive' always means the psychologically primitive—not that which the ethnologist regards as original from the point of view of the genealogy of peoples. Thus, folk psychology draws upon ethnology, while the latter, in turn, must invoke the aid of the former in investigating mental characteristics. The problems of the two sciences, however, are fundamentally different.

In fulfilling its task, folk psychology may pursue different methods. The course that first suggests itself is to single out one important phenomenon of community life after another, and to trace its development after the usual pattern of general psychology in its analysis of individual consciousness. For example, an attempt is made to trace the psychological development of language by the aid of the facts of linguistic history. This psychology of language is then followed by a study of the development of art, from its beginnings among primitive races down to its early manifestations among cultural peoples, at which point its description is taken up by the history of art. Myth and religion are similarly investigated as regards the development of their characteristics, their reciprocal relations, etc. This is a method which considers in longitudinal sections, as it were, the total course of the development described by folk psychology. For a somewhat intensive analysis this is the most direct mode of procedure. But is has the objection of severing mental development into a number of separate phases, whereas in reality these are in constant interrelation. Indeed, the various mental expressions, particularly in their earlier stages, are so intertwined that they are scarcely separable from one another. Language is influenced by myth, art is a factor in myth development, and customs and usages are everywhere sustained by mythological conceptions.

But there is also a second path of investigation, and it is this which the present work adopts. It consists—to retain the image used above—in taking transverse instead of longitudinal sections, that is, in regarding the main stages of the development with which folk psychology is concerned in their sequence, and each in the total interconnection of its phenomena. Our first task, then, would be the investigation of *primitive man*. We must seek a psychological explanation of the thought, belief, and action of primitive man on the basis of the facts supplied by ethnology. As we proceed to more advanced stages, difficulties may, of course, arise with regard to the delimitation of the various periods; indeed, it will scarcely be possible to avoid a certain arbitrariness, inasmuch as the processes are continuous. The life of the individual person also does not fall into sharply distinct periods. Just as childhood, youth, and manhood are stages in a continuous growth, so also are the various eras in the development of peoples. Yet there are certain ideas, emotions, and springs of action about which the various phenomena group themselves. It is these that we must single out if the content of folk psychology is to be classified, with any measure of satisfaction, according to periods. Moreover, it should be particularly noticed that in starting our discussion with primitive man, as we naturaly must, the term 'primitive' is to be taken relatively, as representing the lowest grade of culture, particularly of mental culture. There is no specific ethnological characteristic that distinguishes this primitive stage from those that are more advanced; it is only by reference to a number of psychological traits, such as are indicative of the typically original, that we may determine that which is primitive. Bearing in mind this fact, we must first describe the external traits of primitive culture, and then consider the psychological factors of primitive life.

Of the second period in the development of civilization, we may safely say that in many respects it represents a newly discovered world. Historical accounts have nothing to say concerning it. Recent ethnology alone has disclosed the phenomena here in question, having come upon them in widely different parts of the earth. This period we call the *totemic age*. The very name indicates that we are concerned with the discovery of a submerged world. The word 'totem,' borrowed from a distant American tongue, proves by its very origin that our own cultural languages of Europe do not possess any word even approximately adequate to designate the peculiar character of this period. If we would define the concept of totemism as briefly as possible, it might perhaps be said to represent a circle of ideas within which the relation of animal to man is the reverse of that which obtains in present-day culture. In the totemic age, man does not have dominion over the animal, but the animal rules man. Its deeds and activities arouse wonder, fear, and adoration. The souls of the dead dwell within it; it thus becomes the ancestor of man. Its flesh is prohibited to the members of the group called by its name, or, conversely, on ceremonial occasions, the eating of the totem-animal may become a sanctifying cult activity. No less does the totemic idea affect the organization of society, tribal division, and the forms of marriage and family. Yet the elements that reach over from the thought-world of this period into later times are but scanty fragments. Such, for example, are the sacred animals of the Babylonians, Egyptians, and other ancient cultural peoples, the prophetic significance attached to the qualities or acts of animals, and other magical ideas connected with particular animals.

Totemic culture is succeeded—through gradual transitions—by a *third* period, which we will call the *age of heroes and gods*. Initial steps towards the latter were already taken during the preceding period, in the development of a rulership of individuals within the tribal organization. This rulership, at first only temporary in character, gradually becomes permanent. The position of the chieftain, which was of minor importance in the totemic age, gains in power when the tribal community under the pressure of struggles with hostile tribes, assumes a military organization. Society thus develops into the *State*. War, as also the guidance of the State in times of peace, calls out men who tower far above the stature of the old chieftains, and who, at the same time, are sharply distinguished from one another through qualities that stamp them as typical personalities. In place of the eldest of the clan and the tribal chieftain of the totemic period, this new age gives rise to the *hero*. The totemic age possesses only fabulous narratives; these are credited myths dealing, not infrequently, with animal ancestors who have introduced fire, taught the preparation of food, etc. The hero who is exalted as a leader in war belongs to a different world, a world faithfully mirrored in the heroic song or epic. As regards their station in life, the heroes of Homer are still essentially tribal chieftains, but the enlarged field of struggle, together with the magnified characteristics which it develops, exalt the leader into a hero. With the development of poetry, the forms of language also change, and become enriched. The epic is followed by formative and dramatic art. All this is at the same time closely bound up with the origin of the State, which now displaces the more primitive tribal institutions of the preceding period. When this occurs, different customs and cults emerge. With national heroes and with States, national religions come into being; and, since these religions no longer direct the attention merely to the immediate environment, to the animal and plant world, but focus it primarily upon the heavens, there is developed the idea of a higher and more perfect world. As the hero is the ideal man, so the god becomes the ideal hero, and the celestial world, the ideally magnified terrestrial world.

This era of heroes and gods is finally succeeded by a *fourth* period. A national State and a national religion do not represent the permanent limits of human striving. National affiliations broaden into humanistic associations. Thus there begins a development in which we of the present still participate; it cannot, therefore, be referred to otherwise than as an age that is coming to be. We may speak merely of an advance *toward* humanity, not of a development *of* humanity. This advance, however, begins immediately with the fall of the barriers that divide peoples, particularly with regard to their religious views. For this reason, it is particularly the transcendence of the more restricted folk circle on the part of religions that constitutes one of the most significant events of mental history. The national religions—or, as they are generally, though misleadingly, called, the natural religions—of the great peoples of antiquity begin to pass beyond their original bounds and to become religions of humanity. There are three such world religions—Christianity, Islamism, and Buddhism—each of them adapted in character and history to a particular part of mankind. This appears most clearly in the contrast between Christianity and Buddhism, similar as they are in their endeavour to be world religions. The striving to become a world religion, however, is also a symptomatic mental phenomenon, paralleled externally by the extension of national States beyond the original limits set for them by the tribal unit. Corresponding to this expansion, we find those reciprocal influences of cultural peoples in economic life, as well as in custom, art, and science, which give to human society its composite character, representing a combination of national with universally human elements. Hellenism and the Roman Empire afford the first and, for Occidental mental development, the most important manifestations of these phenomena.

How immense is the chasm between the secret barter of primitive man who steals out of the primeval forest by night and lays down his captured game to exchange it, unseen by his neighbors, for implements and objects of adornment, and the commerce of an age when fleets traverse the seas, and eventually ships course through the air, uniting the peoples of all parts of the world into one great commercial community! We cannot undertake to delineate all aspects of this development, for the latter includes the entire history of mankind. Our concern is merely to indicate the outstanding psychological factors fundamental to the progression of the later from that which was original, of the more perfect from the primitive, partly under the pressure of external conditions of life and partly as a result of man's own creative power.

— · — · — · — · — · — · — · — · — · — · — · —

EMILE DURKHEIM

*Collective Conscience**

DEFINITION OF THE COLLECTIVE CONSCIENCE

The totality of beliefs and sentiments common to average citizens of the same society forms a determinate system which has its own life; one may call it the *collective* or *common conscience.* No doubt, it has not a specific organ as a substratum; it is, by definition, diffuse in every reach of society. Nevertheless, it has specific characteristics which make it a distinct reality. It is, in effect, independent of the particular conditions in which individuals are placed; they pass on and it remains. It is the same in the North and in the South, in great cities and in small, in different professions. Moreover, it does not change with each generation, but, on the contrary, it connects successive generations with one another. It is, thus, an entirely different thing from particular consciences, although it can be realized only through them. It is the psychical type of society, a type which has its properties, its conditions of existence, its mode of development, just as individual types, although in a different way. Thus understood, it has the right to be denoted by a special word. The one which we have just employed is not, it is true, without ambiguity. As the terms, collective and social, are often considered synonymous, one is inclined to believe that the collective conscience is the total social conscience, that is, extend it to include more than the psychic life of society, although, particularly in advanced societies, it is only a very restricted part. Judicial, governmental, scientific, industrial, in short, all special functions are of a psychic nature, since they consist in systems of representations and actions. They, however, are surely outside the common

*Reprinted with permission of The Macmillan Company from *The Division of Labor in Society* by Emile Durkheim, pp. 79–80, 129–130, 152. Copyright 1947 by The Free Press.

conscience. To avoid the confusion[1] into which some have fallen, the best way would be to create a technical expression especially to designate the totality of social similitudes. However, since the use of a new word, when not absolutely necessary, is not without inconvenience, we shall employ the well-worn expression, collective or common conscience, but we shall always mean the strict sense in which we have taken it.

We can, then, to resume the preceding analysis, say that an act is criminal when it offends strong and defined states of the collective conscience.[2]

TWO TYPES OF SOLIDARITY

Since negative solidarity does not produce any integration by itself, and since, moreover, there is nothing specific about it, we shall recognize only two kinds of positive solidarity which are distinguishable by the following qualities:

1. The first binds the individual directly to society without any intermediary. In the second, he depends upon society, because he depends upon the parts of which it is composed.

2. Society is not seen in the same aspect in the two cases. In the first, what we call society is a more or less organized totality of beliefs and sentiments common to all the members of the group: this is the collective type. On the other hand, the society in which we are solidary in the second instance is a system of different, special functions which definite relations unite. These two societies really make up only one. They are two aspects of one and the same reality, but none the less they must be distinguished.

3. From this second difference there arises another which helps us to characterize and name the two kinds of solidarity.

The first can be strong only if the ideas and tendencies common to all the members of the society are greater in number and intensity than those which pertain personally to each member. It is as much stronger as the excess is more considerable. But what makes our personality is how much of our own individual qualities we have, what distinguishes us from others. This solidarity can grow only in inverse ratio to personality. There are in each of us, as we have said, two consciences: one which is common to our group in its entirety, which, consequently, is not ourself, but society living and acting within us; the other, on the contrary, represents that in us which is personal and distinct, that which makes us an individual.[3] Solidarity which comes from likenesses is at its maximum when the collective conscience completely envelops our whole conscience and coincides in all points with it. But, at that moment, our individuality is nil. It can be born only if the community takes smaller toll of us. There are, here, two contrary forces, one centripetal, the other centrifugal, which cannot flourish at the same time. We cannot, at one and the

---

[1] The confusion is not without its dangers. Thus, we sometimes ask if the individual conscience varies as the collective conscience. It all depends upon the sense in which the word is taken. If it represents social likenesses, the variation is inverse, as we shall see. If it signifies the total psychic life of society, the relation is direct. It is thus necessary to distinguish them.

[2] We shall not consider the question whether the collective conscience is a conscience as is that of the individual. By this term, we simply signify the totality of social likenesses, without prejudging the category by which this system of phenomena ought to be defined.

[3] However, these two consciences are not in regions geographically distinct from us, but penetrate from all sides.

same time, develop ourselves in two opposite senses. If we have a lively desire to think and act for ourselves, we cannot be strongly inclined to think and act as others do. If our ideal is to present a singular and personal appearance, we do not want to resemble everybody else. Moreover, at the moment when this solidarity exercises its force, our personality vanishes, as our definition permits us to say, for we are no longer ourselves, but the collective life.

The social molecules which can be coherent in this way can act together only in the measure that they have no actions of their own, as the molecules of inorganic bodies. That is why we propose to call this type of solidarity mechanical. The term does not signify that it is produced by mechanical and artificial means. We call it that only by analogy to the cohesion which unites the elements of an inanimate body, as opposed to that which makes a unity out of the elements of a living body. What justifies this term is that the link which thus unites the individual to society is wholly analogous to that which attaches a thing to a person. The individual conscience, considered in this light, is a simple dependent upon the collective type and follows all of its movements, as the possessed object follows those of its owner. In societies where this type of solidarity is highly developed, the individual does not appear, as we shall see later. Individuality is something which the society possesses. Thus, in these social types, personal rights are not yet distinguished from real rights.

MECHANICAL AND ORGANIC SOLIDARITY

Not only, in a general way, does mechanical solidarity link men less strongly than organic solidarity, but also, as we advance in the scale of social evolution, it grows ever slacker.

The force of social links which have this origin vary with respect to the three following conditions:

1. The relation between the volume of the common conscience and that of the individual conscience. The links are as strong as the first more completely envelops the second.

2. The average intensity of the states of the collective conscience. The relation between volumes being equal, it has as much power over the individual as it has vitality. If, on the other hand, it consists of only feeble forces, it can but feebly influence the collective sense. It will the more easily be able to pursue its own course, and solidarity will be less strong.

3. The greater or lesser determination of these same states. That is, the more defined beliefs and practices are, the less place they leave for individual divergencies. They are uniform moulds into which we all, in the same manner, couch our ideas and our actions. The *consensus* is then as perfect as possible; all consciences vibrate in unison. Inversely, the more general and indeterminate the rules of conduct and thought are, the more individual reflection must intervene to apply them to particular cases. But it cannot awaken without upheavals occurring, for, as it varies from one man to another in quality and quantity, everything that it produces has the same character. Centrifugal tendencies thus multiply at the expense of social cohesion and the harmony of its movements.

GABRIEL TARDE

*Laws of Imitation**

By imitation I mean every impression of an inter-physical photography, so to speak, willed or not willed, passive or active. If we observe that wherever there is a social relation between two living beings, there we have imitation in this sense of the word (either of one by the other or of others by both, when, for example, a man converses with another in a common language, making new verbal *proofs* from very old negatives), we shall have to admit that a sociologist was justified in taking this notion as a look-out post.

I might have been much more justly criticised for having overstretched the meaning of the word *invention*. I have certainly applied this name to all individual *initiatives*, not only without considering the extent in which they are selfconscious—for the individual often innovates unconsciously, and, as a matter of fact, the most imitative man is an innovator on some side or other—but without paying the slightest attention in the world to the degree of difficulty or merit of the innovation in question. This is not because I have failed to recognize the importance of this last consideration. Some *inventions* are so easy to conceive of that we may admit the fact that they have arisen of themselves, without borrowing, in almost all primitive societies, and that their first accidental appearance here or there has little significance. Other discoveries, on the contrary, are so difficult that the happy advent of the genius who made them may be considered a pre-eminently singular and important chance of fortune. Well, in spite of all this, I think that even here I have been justified in doing some slight violence to common speech in characterising as inventions or discoveries the most simple innovations, all the more so because the easiest are not always the least fruitful nor the most difficult the least useless. What is really unjustifiable, on the other hand, is the elastic meaning that is given by many naturalistic sociologists to the word *heredity*. They use this word indifferently to express the transmission of vital characteristics through reproduction and the transmission of ideas and customs, of social things, by ancestral tradition, by domestic education, and by custom-imitation.

Let me add that a neologism from the Greek would have been the easiest thing in the world to conceive of. Instead of saying *invention* or *imitation* I might have readily forged two new words. Now let me dismiss this petty and uninteresting quibble. I have been sometimes charged with exaggeration, and this is a more serious thing, in the use of the two notions in question. It is rather a commonplace criticism, to be sure, and one which every innovator must expect even when he has erred on the side of too much reserve in the expression of his thoughts. We may be sure that if a Greek philosopher had undertaken to say that the sun might possibly be as big as the Peloponnesus, his best friends

*Gabriel Tarde, *Laws of Imitation*, trans. Elsie Clews Parsons (New York: Henry Holt, 1903), pp. xiv–xix, 2–4, 86–88, 213–216.

would have been unanimous in recognising the fact that there was something true at the bottom of his ingenious paradox, but that he was evidently exaggerating. In general, my critics did not consider the end which I had in view. I desired to unfold the purely sociological side of human facts, intentionally ignoring their biological side, although I am well aware that the latter is inseparable from the former. My plan allowed me to indicate, without developing to any extent, the relations of the *three principal forms of universal repetition*, especially the relation of heredity to imitation. But I have said enough, I think, to leave no doubt as to my views on the importance of race and physical environment.

Besides, if I say that the distinctive character of every social relation, of every social fact, is to be imitated, is this saying, as certain superficial readers have seemed to believe, that in my eyes there is no social relation, no social fact, no social cause, but imitation? One might as well say that every function of life could be reduced to reproduction and every vital phenomenon to heredity because in every living being everything is a matter of generation and inheritance. Social relations are as manifold, as numerous, and as diverse, as the objects of the desires and ideas of man, and as the helps or hindrances that each of these desires and ideas lends or presents to the similar or dissimilar tendencies and opinions of others. In the midst of this infinite complexity we note that these varied social relations (talking and listening, beseeching and being beseeched, commanding and obeying, producing and consuming, etc.) belong to two groups; the one tends to transmit from one man to another, persuasively or authoritatively, willingly or unwillingly, a belief; the other, a desire. In other words, the first group consists of various kinds or degrees of instruction; the second, of various kinds or degrees of command. And it is precisely because the human acts which are imitated have this dogmatic or commanding character that imitation is a social tie, for it is either dogma or power which binds men together. (People have seen only the half of this truth, and seen that badly, when they have said that social facts were distinguished by their constrained and coercive character. In saying this, they have failed to recognize the spontaneity of the greater part of popular credulity and docility.)

Therefore I think I have not erred through exaggeration in this book; and so I have reprinted it without eliminating anything. I have sinned rather through omission. I have said nothing at all about a form of imitation which plays a big rôle in societies, particularly in contemporary societies, and I shall make haste here to make good this omission. There are two ways of imitating, as a matter of fact, namely, to act exactly like one's model, or to do exactly the contrary. Hence the necessity of those divergences which Spencer points out, without explaining, in his law of progressive differentiation. Nothing can be affirmed without suggesting, no matter how simple the social environment, not only the idea that is affirmed, but the negation of this idea as well. This is the reason why the supernatural, in asserting itself through theologies, suggests naturalism, its negation. (See Espinas on this subject.) This is the reason why the affirmation of idealism gives birth to the idea of materialism; why the establishment of monarchy engenders the idea of republicanism, etc.

Let us say, then, from this wider point of view, that a society is a group of people who display many resemblances produced either by imitation or by *counter-imitation*. For men often counter-imitate one another, particularly when they have neither the modesty to imitate directly nor the power to invent. In counter-imitating one another, that is to say, in doing or saying the exact opposite of what they observe being done or said, they are becoming more and more assimilated, just as much assimilated as if they did or said precisely what was being done or said around them. Next to conforming to custom in the matter of funerals, marriages, visits, and manners, there is nothing more imitative than fighting against one's natural inclination to follow the current of these things, or than pretending to go against it. In the Middle Ages the *black mass* arose from a counter-imitation of the Catholic mass. In his book on the expression of the emotions, Darwin very properly gives a large place to the need of *counter-expression.*

When a dogma is proclaimed, when a political programme is anounced, men fall into two unequal classes; there are those who are enthusiastic about it and those who are not enthusiastic. There is no manifestation which does not recruit supporters and which does not provoke the formation of a group of non-supporters. Every positive affirmation, at the same time that it attracts to itself mediocre and sheep-like minds, arouses somewhere or other in a brain that is naturally rebellious,—this does not mean naturally inventive,—a negation that is diametrically opposite and of about equal strength. This reminds one of *inductive currents* in physics. But both kinds of brains have the same content of ideas and purposes. They are associated, although they are adversaries, or, rather, because they are adversaries. Let us clearly distinguish between the imitative propagation of questions and that of solutions. Because a certain solution spreads in one place and another elsewhere, this does not prevent the problem from having spread in both places. Is it not evident that in every period, among people in constant communication, particularly in our own day because international relations have never before been so manifold, is it not evident that the calendar of social and political debates is always the same? And is not this resemblance due to a current of imitation that may itself be explained by a diffusion of wants and ideas through prior contagions of imitation? Is not this the reason why labour questions are being agitated at the present moment throughout Europe? No opinion is discussed by the press, about which, I repeat, the public is not daily divided into two camps, those who agree with the opinion and those who disagree. But the latter as well as the former admit that it is impossible to be concerned for the time being with anything other than the question which is thus forced upon them. Only some wild and undisciplined spirit will ruminate, now and then, in the whirl of the social sea in which he is plunged, over strange and absolutely hypothetical problems. Such men are the inventors of the future.

We must be very careful not to confuse counter-imitation with invention, its dangerous counterfeit. I do not mean that the former is worthless. Although it fosters the spirit of partisanship, the spirit of either peaceful or warlike division between men, it introduces them to the wholly social pleasure of discussion. It is a witness to the sympathetic origin of contradiction itself; the back currents themselves are caused by the current. Nor must we confuse counter-imitation with systematic non-imitation, a subject about which I should also have spoken in this book. Non-imitation is not always a simple negative fact. The fact of not imitating when there is no contact—no social contact through the practical impossibility of communication—is merely a non-social relation, but the fact of not imitating the neighbour who is in touch with us, puts us upon a footing of really anti-social relations with him. The refusal of a people, a class, a town or a village, of a

savage tribe isolated on a civilised continent, to copy the dress, customs, language, industry, and arts which make up the civilisation of the neighbourhood is a continual declaration of antipathy to the form of society in question. It is thereby declared absolutely and
forever alien. Similarly, when a people deliberately undertakes not to reproduce the
examples of its forefathers in the matter of rights, usages, and ideas, we have a veritable
disassociation of fathers and sons, a rupture of the umbilical cord between the old and
the new society. Voluntary and persistent non-imitation in this sense has a purgative rôle
which is quite analagous to that filled by what I have called the *logical duel.* Just as the
latter tends to purge the social mass of mixed ideas and volitions, to eliminate inequalities
and discords, and to facilitate in this way the synthetic action of the *logical union*; so
non-imitation of extraneous and heterogeneous models makes it possible for the harmonious group of home models to extend and prolong themselves, to entrench themselves in
the custom-imitation of which they are the object; and for the same reason non-imitation
of anterior models, when the moment has come for civilising revolution, cuts a path for
fashion-imitation. It no longer finds any hindrance in the way of its conquering activity.

Our starting-point lies here in the re-inspiring initiatives which bring new wants,
together with new satisfactions, into the world, and which then, through spontaneous and
unconscious or artificial and deliberate imitation, propagate or tend to propagate, themselves, at a more or less rapid, but regular, rate, like a wave of light, or like a family of
termites. The regularity to which I refer is not in the least apparent in social things until
they are resolved into their several elements, when it is found to lie in the simplest of
them, in combinations of distinct inventions, in flashes of genius which have been accumulated and changed into commonplace lights. I confess that this is an extremely
difficult analysis. Socially, everything is either invention or imitation. And invention
bears the same relation to imitation as a mountain to a river. There is certainly nothing
less subtle than this point of view; but in holding to it boldly and unreservedly, in
exploiting it from the most trivial detail to the most complete synthesis of facts, we may,
perhaps, notice how well fitted it is to bring into relief all the picturesqueness and, at the
same time, all the simplicity of history, and to reveal historic perspectives which may be
characterised by the freakishness of a rock-bound landscape, or by the conventionality of
a park walk. This is idealism also, if you choose to call it so; but it is the idealism which
consists in explaining history through the ideas of its actors, not through those of the
historian.

    If we consider the science of society from this point of view, we shall at once see that
human sociology is related to animal sociologies, as a species to its genus, so to speak.
That it is an extraordinary and infinitely superior species, I admit, but it is allied to the
others, nevertheless. M. Espinas expressly states in his admirable work on *Sociétés animales*, a work which was written long before the first edition of this book, that the
labours of ants may be very well explained on the principle "*of individual initiative
followed by imitation.*" This initiative is always an innovation or invention that is equal
to one of our own in boldness of spirit. To conceive the idea of constructing an arch, or a
tunnel, at an appropriate point, an ant must be endowed with an innovating instinct equal

to, or surpassing, that of our canal-digging or mountain-tunnelling engineers. Parentheti-
cally it follows that imitation by masses of ants of such novel initiatives strikingly belies
the spirit of mutual hatred which is alleged to exist among animals.[1] M. Espinas is very
frequently impressed in his observation of the societies of our lower brethren by the
important rôle which is played in them by individual initiatives. Every herd of wild cattle
has its leaders, its influential heads. Developments in the instincts of birds are explained
by the same author as "individual inventions which are afterwards transmitted from
generation to generation through direct instruction."[2] In view of the fact that modification of instinct is probably related to the same principle as the genesis and modification
of species, we may be tempted to enquire whether the principle of the imitation of
invention, or of something physiologically analogous, would not be the clearest possible
explanation of the ever-open problem of the origin of species. But let us leave this
question and confine ourselves to the statement that both animal and human societies
may be explained from this point of view.

It is for this reason, perhaps, that so-called rough diamonds, people who strongly
rebel against assimilation and who are really unsociable, remain timid during their whole
life. They are but partially subject to somnambulism. On the other hand, are not people
who never feel awkward and embarrassed, who never experience any real timidity upon
entering a drawing room or a lecture hall, or any corresponding stupor in taking up a
science or art for the first time (for the trouble produced by entrance into a new calling
whose difficulties frighten one and whose prescribed methods do violence to one's old
habits, may be perfectly well compared to intimidation), are not such people sociable in
the highest degree? Are they not excellent copyists, *i.e.*, devoid of any particular avoca-
tion or any controlling ideas, and do they not possess the eminently Chinese or Japanese
faculty of speedily adapting themselves to their environment? In their readiness to fall
asleep, are they not somnambulists of the first order? Intimidation plays an immense part
in society under the name of Respect. Everyone will acknowledge this, and, although the
part is sometimes misinterpreted, it is never in the least exaggerated. Respect is neither
unmixed fear nor unmixed love, nor is it merely the combination of the two, although it
is a *fear which is beloved* by him who entertains it. Respect is, primarily, the impression
of an example by one person upon another who is psychologically *polarised*. Of course we
must distinguish the respect of which we are conscious from that which we dissemble to
ourselves under an assumed contempt. But taking this distinction into account, it is
evident that whomsoever we imitate we respect, and that whomsoever we respect we imitate or tend to imitate. There is no surer sign of a displacement of social authority than
deviations in the current of these examples. The man or the woman of the world who
reflects the slang or undress of the labourer or the intonation of the actress, has more

---

[1] Among the higher species of ants, according to M. Espinas, "*the individual develops an astonishing initiative*" [*Des Sociêtês animales*, p. 223; Alfred Espinas, Paris; 1877. The italics are M. Tarde's.—
Tr.] How do the labours and migrations of ant-swarms begin? Is it through a common, instinctive,
and spontaneous impulse which starts from all the associates at the same time and under the pressure
of outward circumstances which are experienced simultaneously by all? On the contrary, a single ant
begins by leaving the others and undertaking the work: then it strikes its neighbours with its antennae
to summon their aid, and the contagion of imitation does the rest.

[2] [*Ibid*., p. 272–*Tr.*]

respect and deference for the person copied than he or she is himself or herself aware. Now what society would last for a single day without the general and continuous circulation of both the above forms of respect?

But I must not dwell any longer upon the above comparison. At any rate, I hope that I have at least made my reader feel that to thoroughly understand the essential social fact, as I perceive it, knowledge of the infinitely subtle facts of mind is necessary, and that the roots of even what seems to be the simplest and most superficial kind of sociology strike far down into the depths of the most inward and hidden parts of psychology and physiology. *Society is imitation and imitation is a kind of somnambulism.* This is the epitome of this chapter. As for the second part of the proposition, I beg the reader's indulgence for any exaggeration I may have been guilty of. I must also remove a possible objection. It may be urged that submission to some ascendency does not always mean following the example of the person whom we trust and obey. But does not belief in anyone always mean belief in that which he believes or seems to believe? Does not obedience to someone mean that we will that which he wills or seems to will? *Inventions are not made to order,* nor are discoveries undertaken as a result of persuasive suggestion. Consequently, to be credulous and docile, and to be so as pre-eminently as the somnambulist and the social man, is to be, primarily, imitative. To innovate, to discover, to awake for an instant from his dream of home and country, the individual must escape, for the time being, from his social surroundings. Such unusual audacity makes him super-social rather than social.

★ ★ ★

IMITATION OF THE SUPERIOR BY THE INFERIOR

The profoundly subjective character that is taken on from the earliest times by human imitation, the privilege which it has of binding souls together from their very centres, involves, as may be seen from what has preceded, the growth of human inequality and the formation of a social hierarchy. This was inevitable, since the relation of model to copy developed into that of apostle to neophyte, of master to subject. Consequently, from the very fact that imitation proceeded from the inside to the outside of the model, it had to consist in a *descent* of example, in a descent from the superior to the inferior. This is a second law that is partly implied in the first, but it needs separate examination.

Moreover, let us be sure that we understand the exact bearing of the considerations in hand as well as of those that have preceded. In the first place, we know that they are based on the hypothesis that the influence of prestige, of alleged superiority, is neither partly nor wholly neutralised by the action of logical laws. However lowly or even despised may be the author or introducer of a new idea of relatively striking truth or utility, it always ends by spreading through the public. Thus the evangel of slaves and Jews spread throughout the aristocratic Roman world because it was more adapted than polytheism to answer the main problems of the Roman conscience. Thus at a certain period in ancient Egypt the use of the horse was introduced from Asia in spite of the Egyptians' contempt for Asiatics, because for many kinds of work the horse was obviously preferable to the mule, which had been in use up to that time. There are innumerable examples of this kind. Similarly, the most objective of examples, a word detached from its meaning, a religious rite from its dogma, a peculiarity of custom from the want which it expresses, a work or art from the social ideal which it embodies, may readily spread in a strange environment whose ruling needs and principles find it to their advantage to replace their usual methods of expression by this new one which is perhaps more picturesque, or more clear, or more forcible.

In the second place, even when the action of logical laws does not intervene, it is not only the superior who causes himself to be copied by the inferior, the patrician by the plebeian, the nobleman by the commoner, the cleric by the layman, and, at a later period, the Partisian by the provincial, the townsman by the peasant, etc., it is also the inferior who, in a certain measure, much less, to be sure, is copied, or is likely to be copied, by the superior. When two men are together for a long time, whatever may be their difference in station, they end by imitating each other reciprocally, although, of the two, the one imitates much the more, the other much the less. The colder body imparts its heat to the warmer. The haughtiest country gentleman cannot keep his accent, his manners, and his point of view from being a little like those of his servants and tenants. For the same reason many provincialisms and countrified expressions creep into the language of cities, and even capitals, and slang phrases penetrate at times into drawing rooms. This influence from the bottom to the top of a scale characterises all classes of facts. Nevertheless, on the whole, it is the generous radiation of the warm body towards the cold, not the insignificant radiation of the cold body towards the warm, that is the main fact in physics and the one which explains the final tendency of the universe towards an everlasting equilibrium of temperature. Similarly, in sociology, the radiation of examples from above to below is the only fact worth consideration because of the general levelling which it tends to produce in the human world.

1. Now let me endeavour to elucidate the truth which we are discussing. There is nothing more natural than that those who love each other should copy each other, or, rather, as this phenomenon always begins by being onesided, that the *lover* should copy the *beloved*. But in proof of the depth which is reached by the action of imitation in man's heart we see people aping one another everywhere, even in their fights. The conquered never fail to copy their conquerors if only to prepare for their revenge. When they borrow the military organisation of their conquerors they are careful to say and they sincerely think that their sole motive is a utilitarian calculation. But we shall find this explanation inadequate, if we compare this fact with a considerable number of correlated facts in which the sentiment of utility plays no part whatsoever.

For example, the conquered do not merely borrow the superior weapons, the longer range guns, and the more admirable methods of their conqueror; they also take from him many of his insignificant military peculiarities and habits, whose acclimatisation, granted that it were possible, would raise difficulties wholly out of proportion to its feeble advantages. During the thirteenth century Florence and Sienna, who were always at war with each other, arrayed troops against each other that were not only organised in the same way, but that were also preceded by that strange cart (*carroccio*) and singular bell (*martinella*) which were at first peculiar to Lombardy, that is, to what was for a long time the most powerful part of Italy (so much so that *Lombard* and *Italian* had the same meaning), and which were then imported with certain modifications to Florence, whence, thanks to the prestige of that flourishing city, they spread to its hostile neighbours. And yet the cart was an encumbrance and the bell a real danger. Why, then, should both Florence and Sienna have copied those peculiarities instead of keeping to their own customs? For the same reason that the lower classes of society, that is, the defeated, or the sons of the defeated, in civil wars, copy the dress, the manners, the speech, the vices, etc., of the upper classes. It will not be said, in this instance, that the imitation is a military operation in view of revenge. It is simply the satisfaction of a special fundamental need in social life the final consequence of which is the preparation through many conflicts of conditions of future peace.[3]

[3]It seems that before the Japanese came into communication with China they possessed a syllabic writing, or several, in fact, of much greater usefulness and convenience than the Chinese writing; but as soon as this youthful and pre-eminently suggestible people felt the prestige of the superiority which they attributed to the mandarins, they adopted Chinese writing to the hindrance of their own progress.

— · — · — · — · — · — · — · — · — · — · — · —

GUSTAVE LE BON

*The Crowd**

In its ordinary sense the word "crowd" means a gathering of individuals of whatever nationality, profession, or sex, and whatever be the chances that have brought them together. From the psychological point of view the expression "crowd" assumes quite a different signification. Under certain given circumstances, and only under those circumstances, an agglomeration of men presents new characteristics very different from those of the individuals composing it. The sentiments and ideas of all the persons in the gathering take one and the same direction, and their conscious personality vanishes. A collective mind is formed, doubtless transitory, but presenting very clearly defined characteristics. The gathering has thus become what, in the absence of a better expression, I will call an organised crowd, or, if the term is considered preferable, a psychological crowd. It forms a single being, and is subjected to the *law of the mental unity of crowds.*

It being impossible to study here all the successive degrees of organisation of crowds, we shall concern ourselves more especially with such crowds as have attained to the phase of complete organisation. In this way we shall see what crowds may become, but not what they invariably are. It is only in this advanced phase of organisation that certain new

*Gustave Le Bon, *The Crowd: A Study of the Popular Mind* (London: T. Fisher Unwin, 1896), pp. 25-26, 29-38, 159, 194-196; original French, *La psychologie des foules* (1895).

and special characteristics are superposed on the unvarying and dominant character of the race; then takes place that turning already alluded to of all the feelings and thoughts of the collectivity in an identical direction. It is only under such circumstances, too, that what I have called above the *psychological law of the mental unity of crowds* comes into play.

The most striking peculiarity presented by a psychological crowd is the following: Whoever be the individuals that compose it, however like or unlike be their mode of life, their occupations, their character, or their intelligence, the fact that they have been transformed into a crowd puts them in possession of a sort of collective mind which makes them feel, think, and act in a manner quite different from that in which each individual of them would feel, think, and act were he in a state of isolation. There are certain ideas and feelings which do not come into being, or do not transform themselves into acts except in the case of individuals forming a crowd. The psychological crowd is a provisional being formed of heterogeneous elements, which for a moment are combined, exactly as the cells which constitute a living body form by their reunion a new being which displays characteristics very different from those possessed by each of the cells singly.

It is more especially with respect to those unconscious elements which constitute the genius of a race that all the individuals belonging to it resemble each other, while it is principally in respect to the conscious elements of their character—the fruit of education, and yet more of exceptional hereditary conditions—that they differ from each other. Men the most unlike in the matter of their intelligence possess instincts, passions, and feelings that are very similar. In the case of everything that belongs to the realm of sentiment—religion, politics, morality, the affections and antipathies, etc.—the most eminent men seldom surpass the standard of the most ordinary individuals. From the intellectual point of view an abyss may exist between a great mathematician and his bootmaker, but from the point of view of character the difference is most often slight or nonexistent.

Different causes determine the appearance of these characteristics peculiar to crowds, and not possessed by isolated individuals. The first is that the individual forming part of a crowd acquires, solely from numerical considerations, a sentiment of invincible power which allows him to yield to instincts which, had he been alone, he would perforce have kept under restraint. He will be the less disposed to check himself from the consideration that, a crowd being anonymous, and in consequence irresponsible, the sentiment of responsibility which always controls individuals disappears entirely.

The second cause, which is contagion, also intervenes to determine the manifestation in crowds of their special characteristics, and at the same time the trend they are to take. Contagion is a phenomenon of which it is easy to establish the presence, but that it is not easy to explain. It must be classed among those phenomena of a hypnotic order, which we shall shortly study. In a crowd every sentiment and act is contagious, and contagious to such a degree that an individual readily sacrifices his personal interest to the collective interest. This is an aptitude very contrary to his nature, and of which a man is scarcely capable, except when he makes part of a crowd.

A third cause, and by far the most important, determines in the individuals of a crowd special characteristics which are quite contrary at times to those presented by the isolated individual. I allude to that suggestibility of which, moreover, the contagion mentioned above is neither more nor less than an effect.

To understand this phenomenon it is necessary to bear in mind certain recent physiological discoveries. We know today that by various processes an individual may be brought into such a condition that, having entirely lost his conscious personality, he obeys all the suggestions of the operator who has deprived him of it, and commits acts in utter contradiction with his character and habits. The most careful observations seem to prove that an individual immerged for some length of time in a crowd in action soon finds himself—either in consequence of the magnetic influence given out by the crowd, or from some other cause of which we are ignorant—in a special state, which much resembles the state of fascination in which the hypnotised individual finds himself in the hands of the hypnotiser. The activity of the brain being paralysed in the case of the hypnotised subject, the latter becomes the slave of all the unconscious activities of his spinal cord, which the hypnotiser directs at will. The conscious personality has entirely vanished; will and discernment are lost. All feelings and thoughts are bent in the direction determined by the hypnotiser.

★ ★ ★

We see, then, that the disappearance of the conscious personality, the predominance of the unconscious personality, the turning by means of suggestion and contagion of feelings and ideas in an identical direction, the tendency to immediately transform the suggested ideas into acts; these we see, are the principal characteristics of the individual forming part of a crowd. He is no longer himself, but has become an automaton who has ceased to be guided by his will.

Moreover, by the mere fact that he forms part of an organised crowd, a man descends several rungs in the ladder of civilisation. Isolated, he may be a cultivated individual; in a crowd, he is a barbarian—that is, a creature acting by instinct. He possesses the spontaneity, the violence, the ferocity, and also the enthusiasm and heroism of primitive beings, whom he further tends to resemble by the facility with which he allows himself to be impressed by words and images—which would be entirely without action on each of the isolated individuals composing the crowd—and to be induced to commit acts contrary to his most obvious interests and his best-known habits. An individual in a crowd is a grain of sand amid other grains of sand, which the wind stirs up at will.

It is for these reasons that juries are seen to deliver verdicts of which each individual juror would disapprove, that parliamentary assemblies adopt laws and measures of which each of their members would disapprove in his own person. Taken separately, the men of the Convention were enlightened citizens of peaceful habits. United in a crowd, they did not hesitate to give their adhesion to the most savage proposals, to guillotine individuals most clearly innocent, and, contrary to their interests; to renounce their inviolability and to decimate themselves.

★ ★ ★

The conclusion is to be drawn from what precedes is, that the crowd is always intellectually inferior to the isolated individual, but that, from the point of view of feelings and of the acts these feelings provoke, the crowd may, according to circumstances, be better or worse than the individual. All depends on the nature of the suggestion to which the crowd is exposed. This is the point that has been completely misunderstood by writers who have only studied crowds from the criminal point of view. Doubtless a crowd is often criminal, but also it is often heroic. It is crowds rather than isolated individuals that may be induced to run the risk of death to secure the triumph of a creed or an idea, that may be fired with enthusiasm for glory and honour, that are led on—almost without bread and without arms, as in the age of the Crusades—to deliver the tomb of Christ from the infidel, or, as in '93, to defend the fatherland. Such heroism is without doubt somewhat unconscious, but it is of such heroism that history is made. Were peoples only to be credited with the great actions performed in cold blood, the annals of the world would register but few of them.

★ ★ ★

The hero whom the crowd acclaimed yesterday is insulted to-day should he have been overtaken by failure. The reaction, indeed, will be the stronger in proportion as the prestige has been great. The crowd in this case considers the fallen hero as an equal, and takes its revenge for having bowed to a superiority whose existence it no longer admits. While Robespierre was causing the execution of his colleagues and of a great number of his contemporaries, he possessed an immense prestige. When the transposition of a few votes deprived him of power, he immediately lost his prestige, and the crowd followed him to the guillotine with the self-same imprecations with which shortly before it had pursued his victims. Believers always break the statues of their former gods with every symptom of fury.

Prestige lost by want of success disappears in a brief space of time. It can also be worn away, but more slowly by being subjected to discussion. This latter power, however, is exceedingly sure. From the moment prestige is called in question it ceases to be prestige. The gods and men who have kept their prestige for long have never tolerated discussion. For the crowd to admire, it must be kept at a distance.

★ ★ ★

Juries, like all crowds, are profoundly impressed by prestige, and President des Glajeux very properly remarks that, very democratic as juries are in their composition, they are very aristocratic in their likes and dislikes: "Name, birth, great wealth, celebrity, the assistance of an illustrious counsel, everything in the nature of distinction or that lends brilliancy to the accused, stands him in extremely good stead."

The chief concern of a good counsel should be to work upon the feelings of the jury, and, as with all crowds, to argue but little, or only to employ rudimentary modes of reasoning. An English barrister, famous for his successes in the assize courts, has well set forth the line of action to be followed:

> While pleading he would attentively observe the jury. The most favourable opportunity has been reached. By dint of insight and experience the counsel reads the effect of each phrase on the faces of the jurymen, and draws his conclusions in consequence. His first step is to be sure which members of the

jury are already favourable to his cause. It is short work to definitely gain their adhesion, and having done so he turns his attention to the members who seem, on the contrary, ill-disposed, and endeavors to discover why they are hostile to the accused. This is the delicate part of his task, for there may be an infinity of reasons for condemning a man, apart from the sentiment of justice.

These few lines resume the entire mechanism of the art of oratory, and we see why the speech prepared in advance has so slight an effect, it being necessary to be able to modify the terms employed from moment to moment in accordance with the impression produced.

The orator does not require to convert to his views all the members of a jury, but only the leading spirits among it who will determine the general opinion. As in all crowds, so in juries there are a small number of individuals who serve as guides to the rest. "I have found by experience," says the counsel cited above, "that one or two energetic men suffice to carry the rest of the jury with them." It is those two or three whom it is necessary to convince by skilful suggestions. First of all, and above all, it is necessary to please them. The man forming part of a crowd whom one has succeeded in pleasing is on the point of being convinced, and is quite disposed to accept as excellent any arguments that may be offered him.

— · — · — · — · — · — · — · — · — · — · —

WILLIAM McDOUGALL

Social Psychology: An Instinct Interpretation*
and
The Group Mind†

INSTINCTS DEFINED

In treating of the instincts of animals, writers have usually described them as innate tendencies to certain kinds of action, and Herbert Spencer's widely accepted definition of instinctive action as compound reflex action takes account only of the behaviour or movements to which instincts give rise. But instincts are more than innate tendencies or dispositions to certain kinds of movement. There is every reason to believe that even the most purely instinctive action is the outcome of a distinctly mental process, one which is incapable of being described in purely mechanical terms, because it is a psycho-physical

*William McDougall, An Introduction to Social Psychology (Boston: John W. Luce, 1908, 1912), pp. 26-29; xiv, 92-96, 159-163.

†William McDougall. The Group Mind, 2nd ed. (New York: G. P. Putnam's Sons, 1920), pp. 10-28.

process, involving psychical as well as physical changes, and one which, like every other mental process, has, and can only be fully described in terms of, the three aspects of all mental process—the cognitive, the affective, and the conative aspects; that is to say, every instance of instinctive behaviour involves a knowing of some thing or object, a feeling in regard to it, and a striving towards or away from that object.

We cannot, of course, directly observe the threefold psychical aspect of the psycho-physical process that issues in instinctive behaviour; but we are amply justified in assuming that it invariably accompanies the process in the nervous system of which the instinctive movements are the immediate result, a process which, being initiated on stimulation of some sense organ by the physical impressions received from the object, travels up the sensory nerves, traverses the brain, and descends as an orderly or co-ordinated stream of nervous impulses along efferent nerves to the appropriate groups of muscles and other executive organs. We are justified in assuming the cognitive aspect of the psychical process, because the nervous excitation seems to traverse those parts of the brain whose excitement involves the production of sensations or changes in the sensory content of consciousness; we are justified in assuming the affective aspect of the psychical process, because the creature exhibits unmistakable symptoms of feeling and emotional excitement; and, especially, we are justified in assuming the conative aspect of the psychical process, because all instinctive behaviour exhibits that unique mark of mental process, a presistent striving towards the natural end of the process. That is to say, the process, unlike any merely mechanical process, is not to be arrested by any sufficient mechanical obstacle, but is rather intensified by any such obstacle and only comes to an end either when its appropriate goal is achieved, or when some stronger incompatible tendency is excited, or when the creature is exhausted by its persistent efforts.

Now, the psycho-physical process that issues in an instinctive action is initiated by a sense-impression which, usually, is but one of many sense-impressions received at the same time; and the fact that this one impression plays an altogether dominant part in determining the animal's behaviour shows that its effects are peculiarly favoured, that the nervous system is peculiarly fitted to receive and to respond to just that kind of impression. The impression must be supposed to excite, not merely detailed changes in the animal's field of sensation, but a sensation or complex of sensations that has significance or meaning for the animal; hence we must regard the instinctive process in its cognitive aspect as distinctly of the nature of perception, however rudimentary. In the animals most nearly allied to ourselves we can, in many instances of instinctive behaviour, clearly recognise the symptoms of some particular kind of emotion such as fear, anger, or tender feeling; and the same symptoms always accompany any one kind of instinctive behaviour, as when the cat assumes the defensive attitude, the dog resents the intrusion of a strange dog, or the hen tenderly gathers her brood beneath her wings. We seem justified in believing that each kind of instinctive behaviour is always attended by some such emotional excitement, however faint, which in each case is specific or peculiar to that kind of behaviour. Analogy with our own experience justifies us, also, in assuming that the persistent striving towards its end, which characterises mental process and distinguishes instinctive behaviour most clearly from mere reflex action, implies some such mode of experience as we call conative, the kind of experience which in its more developed forms is properly called desire or aversion, but which, in the blind form in which we sometimes have it and which is its usual form among the animals, is a mere impulse, or craving, or

uneasy sense of want. Further, we seem justified in believing that the continued obstruc-
tion of instinctive striving is always accompanied by painful feeling, its successful progress
towards its end by pleasurable feeling, and the achievement of its end by a pleasurable
sense of satisfaction.

An instinctive action, then, must not be regarded as simple or compound reflex
action if by reflex action we mean, as is usually meant, a movement caused by a sense-
stimulus and resulting from a sequence of merely physical processes in some nervous arc.
Nevertheless, just as a reflex action implies the presence in the nervous system of the
reflex nervous arc, so the instinctive action also implies some enduring nervous basis
whose organisation is inherited, an innate or inherited psycho-physical disposition, which,
anatomically regarded, probably has the form of a compound system of sensori-motor
arcs.

We may, then, define an instinct as an inherited or innate psycho-physical disposition
which determines its possessor to perceive, and to pay attention to, objects of a certain
class, to experience an emotional excitement of a particular quality upon perceiving such
an object, and to act in regard to it in a particular manner, or, at least, to experience an
impulse to such action.

It must further be noted that some instincts remain inexcitable except during the
prevalence of some temporary bodily state, such as hunger. In these cases we must
suppose that the bodily process or state determines the stimulation of sense-organs within
the body, and that nervous currents ascending from these to the psycho-physical disposition maintain it in an excitable condition.

★ ★ ★

THE PRINCIPAL INSTINCTS AND THE PRIMARY EMOTIONS OF MAN

The instinct of flight and the emotion of fear—The instinct of repulsion and the
emotion of disgust—The instinct of curiosity and the emotion of wonder—The instinct of
pugnacity and the emotion of anger—The instincts of self-abasement (or subjection) and
of self-assertion (or self-display), and the emotions of subjection and elation (or negative
and positive self-feeling)—The parental instinct and the tender emotion—The instinct of
reproduction—The gregarious instinct—The instinct of acquisition—The instinct of construction.

★ ★ ★

SENTIMENTS

We have seen that a sentiment is an organised system of emotional dispositions
centred about the idea of some object. The organisation of the sentiments in the developing mind is determined by the course of experience; that is to say, the sentiment is a
growth in the structure of the mind that is not natively given in the inherited constitution. This is certainly true in the main, though the maternal sentiment might almost seem
to be innate; but we have to remember that in the human mother this sentiment may, and
generally does, begin to grow up about the idea of its object before the child is born.

The growth of the sentiments is of the utmost importance for the character and conduct of individuals and of societies; it is the organisation of the affective and conative life. In the absence of sentiments our emotional life would be a mere chaos, without order, consistency, or continuity of any kind; and all our social relations and conduct, being based on the emotions and their impulses, would be correspondingly chaotic, unpredictable and unstable. It is only through the systematic organisation of the emotional dispositions in sentiments that the volitional control of the immediate promptings of the emotions is rendered possible. Again, our judgments of value and of merit are rooted in our sentiments; and our moral principles have the same source, for they are formed by our judgments of moral value.

In dealing with the emotions, we named and classed them according to their nature as states of affective consciousness and as tendencies to action; and we may attempt to name and classify the sentiments also according to the nature of the emotional dispositions that enter into the composition of each one. But since, as we have seen, the same emotional dispositions may enter into the composition of very different sentiments, we can carry the naming and classification of them but a little way on this principle, and we have accordingly but very general names for the sentiments. We have the names love, liking, affection, attachment, denoting those sentiments that draw one towards their objects, generally in virtue of the tender emotion with its protective impulse which is their principal constituent; and we have the names hate, dislike, and aversion, for those that lead us to shrink from their objects, those whose attitude or tendency is one of aversion, owing to the fear or disgust that is the dominant element in their composition. The two names love and hate, and the weaker but otherwise synonymous terms liking and dislike, affection and aversion, are very general; each stands for a large class of sentiments of varied, though similar, composition; the character common to the one class being the fundamental tendency to seek the object and to find pleasure in its presence, while that of the other class is the tendency to avoid the object and to be pained by its presence.

We must, I think, recognise a third principal variety of sentiment which is primarily the self-regarding sentiment, and is, perhaps, best called respect. Respect differs from love in that, while tender emotion occupies the principal place in love, it is lacking, or occupies an altogether subordinate position, in the sentiment of respect. The principal constituents of respect are the dispositions of positive and negative self-feeling; and respect is clearly marked off from love by the fact that shame is one of its strongest emotions.

It may be asked—If respect is thus a sentiment that has for its most essential constituents these self-regarding emotions, how can we properly be said to entertain respect for others? The answer is, I think, that we respect those who respect themselves, that our respect for another is a sympathetic reflexion of his self-respect; for unless a man shows self-respect we never have respect for him, even though we may admire some of his qualities, or like, or even love, him in a certain degree. The generally recognised fact that we may like without respecting, and may respect without liking, shows very clearly the essentially different natures of these two sentiments, love and respect.

The older moralists frequently made use of the expression "self-love," and in doing so generally confounded under this term two different sentiments, self-love and self-respect. Self-love is fortunately a comparatively rare sentiment; it is the self-regarding sentiment of the thoroughly selfish man, the meaner sort of egoist. Such a man feels a tender emotion for himself, he indulges in self-pity; he may have little positive self-feeling and may be incapable of shame.

Besides the sentiments of these three main types, love, hate, and respect, which may be called complete or full-grown sentiments, we must recognise the existence of sentiments of all degrees of development from the most rudimentary upward; these may be regarded as stages in the formation of fully-grown sentiments, although many of them never attain any great degree of complexity or strength. These we have to name according to the principal emotional disposition entering into their composition.

The sentiments may also be classified according to the nature of their objects; they then fall into three main classes, the concrete particular, the concrete general, and the abstract sentiments—e.g., the sentiment of love for a child, of love for children in general, of love for justice or virtue. Their development in the individual follows this order, the concrete particular sentiments being, of course, the earliest and most easily acquired. The number of sentiments a man may acquire, reckoned according to the number of objects in which they are centred, may, of course, be very large; but almost every man has a small number of sentiments—perhaps one only—that greatly surpass all the rest in strength and as regards the proportion of his conduct that springs from them.

Each sentiment has a life-history, like every other vital organisation. It is gradually built up, increasing in complexity and strength, and may continue to grow indefinitely, or may enter upon a period of decline, and may decay slowly or rapidly, partially or completely.

When any one of the emotions is strongly or repeatedly excited by a particular object, there is formed the rudiment of a sentiment.

★   ★   ★

SYMPATHY AND THE SYMPATHETIC INDUCTION OF EMOTION

Sympathy is by some authors ascribed to a special instinct of sympathy, and even Professor James has been misled by the confused usage of common speech and has said "sympathy is an emotion." But the principles maintained in the foregoing chapter will not allow us to accept either of these views. The word "sympathy," as popularly used, generally implies a tender regard for the person with whom we are said to sympathise. But such sympathy is only one special and complex form of sympathetic emotion, in the strict and more general sense of the words. The fundamental and primitive form of sympathy is exactly what the word implies, a suffering with, the experiencing of any feeling of emotion when and because we observe in other persons or creatures the expression of that feeling or emotion.

Sympathetic induction of emotion is displayed in the simplest and most unmistakable fashion by many, probably by all, of the gregarious animals; and it is easy to understand how greatly it aids them in their struggle for existence. One of the clearest and commonest examples is the spread of fear and its flight-impulse among the members of a flock or herd. Many gregarious animals utter when startled a characteristic cry of fear; when this cry is emitted by one member of a flock or herd, it immediately excites the flight-impulse in all of its fellows who are within hearing of it; the whole herd, flock, or covey takes to flight like one individual. Or again, one of a pack of gregarious hunting animals, dogs or wolves, comes upon a fresh trail, sights the prey, and pursues it, uttering a characteristic yelp that excites the instinct of pursuit in all his fellows and brings them yelping behind him. Or two dogs begin to growl or fight, and at once all the dogs within sound and sight stiffen themselves and show every symptom of anger. Or one beast in a herd stands arrested, gazing in curiosity on some unfamiliar object, and presently his fellows also, to whom the object may be invisible, display curiosity and come up to join in the examination of the object. In all these cases we observe only that the behaviour of one animal, upon the excitement of an instinct, immediately evokes similar behaviour in those of his fellows who perceive his expressions of excitement. But we can hardly doubt that in each case the instinctive behaviour is accompanied by the appropriate emotion and felt impulse.

Sympathy of this crude kind is the cement that binds animal societies together, renders the actions of all members of a group harmonious, and allows them to reap some of the prime advantages of social life in spite of lack of intelligence.

How comes it that the instinctive behaviour of one animal directly excites similar behaviour on the part of his fellows? No satisfactory answer to this question seems to have been hitherto proposed, although this kind of behaviour has been described and discussed often enough. Not many years ago it would have seemed sufficient to answer, It is due to instinct. But that answer will hardly satisfy us to-day. I think the facts compel us to assume that in the gregarious animals each of the principal instincts has a special perceptual inlet (or recipient afferent part) that is adapted to receive and to elaborate the sense-impressions made by the expressions of the same instinct in other animals of the same species—that, *e.g.*, the fear-instinct has, besides others, a special perceptual inlet that renders it excitable by the sound of the cry of fear, the instinct of pugnacity a perceptual inlet that renders it excitable by the sound of the roar of anger.

Human sympathy has its roots in similar specialisations of the instinctive dispositions on their afferent sides. In early childhood sympathetic emotion is almost wholly of this simple kind; and all through life most of us continue to respond in this direct fashion to the expressions of the feelings and emotions of our fellow-men. This sympathetic induction of emotion and feeling may be observed in children at an age at which they cannot be credited with understanding of the significance of the expressions that provoke their reactions. Perhaps the expression to which they respond earliest is the sound of the wailing of other children. A little later the sight of a smiling face, the expression of pleasure, provokes a smile. Later still fear, curiosity, and, I think, anger, are communicated readily in this direct fashion from one child to another. Laughter is notoriously infectious all through life, and this, though not a truly instinctive expression, affords the most familiar example of sympathetic induction of an affective state. This immediate and unrestrained responsiveness to the emotional expressions of others is one of the great charms of childhood. One may see it particularly well displayed by the children of some savage races (especially perhaps of the negro race), whom it renders wonderfully attractive.

Adults vary much in the degree to which they display these sympathetic reactions, but in few or none are they wholly lacking. A merry face makes us feel brighter; a melancholy face may cast a gloom over a cheerful company; when we witness the painful emotion of others, we experience sympathetic pain; when we see others terror-stricken or hear their scream of terror, we suffer a pang of fear though we know nothing of the cause of their emotion or are indifferent to it; anger provokes anger; the curious gaze of the passer-by stirs our curiosity; and a display of tender emotion touches, as we say, a tender chord in our hearts. In short, each of the great primary emotions that has its characteristic and unmistakable bodily expression seems to be capable of being excited by way of this immediate sympathetic response. If, then, the view here urged is true, we must not say, as many authors have done, that sympathy is due to an instinct, but rather that sympathy is founded upon a special adaptation of the receptive side of each of the principal instinctive dispositions, an adaptation that renders each instinct capable of being excited on the perception of the bodily expressions of the excitement of the same instinct in other persons.

It has been pointed out on a previous page that this primitive sympathy implies none of the higher moral qualities. There are persons who are exquisitely sympathetic in this sense of feeling with another, experiencing distress at the sight of pain and grief, pleasure at the sight of joy, who yet are utterly selfish and are not moved in the least degree to relieve the distress they observe in others or to promote the pleasure that is reflected in themselves. Their sympathetic sensibility merely leads them to avoid all contact with distressful persons, books, or scenes, and to seek the company of the careless and the gay. And a too great sensibility of this kind is even adverse to the higher kind of conduct that seeks to relieve pain and to promote happiness; for the sufferer's expressions of pain may induce so lively a distress in the onlooker as to incapacitate him for giving help. Thus in any case of personal accident, or where surgical procedure is necessary, many a woman is rendered quite useless by her sympathetic distress.

★　★　★

THE GROUP MIND

Since, then, the social aggregate has a collective mental life, which is not merely the sum of the mental lives of its units, it may be contended that a society not only enjoys a collective mental life but also has a collective mind or, as some prefer to say, a collective soul.

The tasks of Group Psychology are, then, to examine the conception of the collective or group mind, in order to determine whether and in what sense this is a valid conception; to display the general principles of collective mental life which are incapable of being deduced from the laws of the mental life of isolated individuals; to distinguish the principal types of collective mental life or group mind; to describe the peculiarities of those types and as far as possible to account for them. More shortly, Group Psychology has, first, to establish the general principles of group life (this is general collective psychology); secondly, it has to apply these principles in the endeavour to understand particular examples of group life. Group Psychology, thus, conceived, meets at the outset a difficulty which stands in the way of every attempt of psychology to leave the narrow field of highly abstract individual psychology. It finds the ground already staked out and occupied by the representatives of another science, who are inclined to resent its intrusion as an encroachment on their rights. The science which claims to have occupied the field of Group Psychology is Sociology; and it is of some importance that the claims of these sciences should be reconciled, so that they may live and work harmoniously together. I have no desire to claim for Group Psychology the whole province of Sociology. As I conceive it, that province is much wider than that of Group Psychology. Sociology is essentially a science which has to take a comprehensive and synthetic view of the life of mankind, and has to accept and make use of the conclusions of many other more special sciences of which psychology, and especially Group Psychology, is for it perhaps the most important. But other special sciences have very important if less intimate contributions to make to it. Thus, if it be true that great civilisations have decayed owing to changes of climate of their habitats, or owing to the introduction of such diseases as malaria into them, then Climatology and Epidemiology have their contributions to make to Sociology. If peculiarities of diet or the crossing of racial stocks may profoundly affect the vigour of peoples, Physiology must have its say. General Biology and the science of Genetics are bringing to light much that must be incorporated in Sociology. Economics, although needing to be treated far more psychologically than it commonly has been, has its special contribution to make. These are only a few illustrations of the fact that the field of Sociology is very much wider and more general than that of Group Psychology, however important to it the conclusions of the narrower science may be.

In this book it will be maintained that the conception of a group mind is useful and therefore valid; and, since this notion has already excited some opposition and criticism and is one that requires very careful definition, some attempt to define and justify it may usefully be made at the outset; though the completer justification is the substance of the whole book. Some writers have assumed the reality of what is called the "collective consciousness" of a society, meaning thereby a unitary consciousness of the society over and above that of the individuals comprised within it. This conception is examined . . . and provisionally rejected. But it is maintained that a society, when it enjoys a long life and becomes highly organised, acquires a structure and qualities which are largely independent of the qualities of the individuals who enter into its composition and take part for a brief time in its life. It becomes an organised system of forces which has a life of its own, tendencies of its own, a power of moulding all its component individuals, and a power of perpetuating itself as a self-identical system, subject only to slow and gradual change.

In an earlier work, in which I have sketched in outline the program of psychology,[1] I wrote: "When the student of behaviour has learnt from the various departments of psychology . . . all that they can teach him of the structure, genesis, and modes of operation of the individual mind, a large field still awaits his exploration. If we put aside as unproven such speculations as that touched on at the end of the foregoing chapter (the view of James that the human mind can enter into an actual union of communion with the divine mind) and refuse to admit any modes of communication or influence between minds other than through the normal channels of sense-perception and bodily movement, we must nevertheless recognise the existence in a certain sense of over-individual or collective minds. We may fairly define a mind as an organised system of mental or

[1] *Psychology, the Study of Behavior*, Home University Library, London, 1912.

purposive forces; and, in the sense so defined every highly organised human society may properly be said to possess a collective mind. For the collective actions which constitute the history of any such society are conditioned by an organisation which can only be described in terms of mind, and which yet is not comprised within the mind of any individual; the society is rather constituted by the system of relations obtaining between the individual minds which are its units of composition. Under any given circumstances the actions of the society are, or may be, very different from the mere sum of the actions with which its several members would react to the situation in the absence of the system of relations which render them a society; or, in other words, the thinking and acting of each man, in so far as he thinks and acts as a member of a society, are very different from his thinking and acting as an isolated individual."

This passage has been cited by the author of a notable work on Sociology,[2] and made by him the text of a polemic against the conception of the group mind. He writes: "This passage contains two arguments in favour of the hypothesis of super-individual 'collective' minds, neither of which can stand examination. The 'definition' of a mind as 'an organised system of mental or purposive forces' is totally inadequate. When we speak of the mind of an individual we mean something more than this. The mind of each of us has a unity other than that of such a system." But I doubt whether Mr. MacIver could explain exactly what kind of unity it is that he postulates. Is it the unity of soul substance? I have myself contended at some length that this is a necessary postulate or hypothesis,[3] but I do not suppose that MacIver accepts or intends to refer to this conception. Is it the unity of consciousness or of self-consciousness? Then the answer is that this unity is by no means a general and established function of the individual mind; modern studies of the disintegration of personality have shown this to be a questionable assumption, undermined by the many facts of normal and abnormal psychology best resumed under Dr. Morton Prince's term "co-consciousness."

The individual mind is a system of purposive forces, but the system is by no means always a harmonious system; it is but too apt to be the scene of fierce conflicts which sometimes (in the graver psychoneuroses) result in the rupture and disintegration of the system. I do not know how otherwise we are to describe the individual mind than as a system of mental forces; and, until MacIver succeeds in showing in what other sense he conceives it to have "a unity other than that of such a system," his objection cannot be seriously entertained. He asks, of the alleged collective mind: "Does the system so created think and will and feel and act?"[4] My answer, as set out in the following pages, is that it does all of these things. He asks further: "If a number of minds construct by their interactivity an organisation 'which can only be described in terms of mind,' must we ascribe to the construction the very nature of the forces which constructed it?" To this I reply—my point is that the individual minds which enter into the structure of the group mind at any moment of its life do not construct it; rather, as they come to reflective self-consciousness, they find themselves already members of the system, moulded by it, sharing in its activities, influenced by it at every moment in every thought and feeling and action in ways which they can neither fully understand nor escape from, struggle as they

[2]*Community*, by R. M. MacIver, London, 1917.
[3]In *Body and Mind*, London, 1911.
[4]*Op. cit.*, p. 76.

may to free themselves from its infinitely subtle and multitudinous forces. And this system, as MacIver himself forcibly insists in another connection, does not consist of relations that exist external to and independent of the things related, namely the minds of individuals; it consists of the same stuff as the individual minds, its threads and parts lie within these minds; but the parts in the several individual minds reciprocally imply and complement one another and together make up the system which consists wholly of them; and therefore, as I wrote, they can "only be described in terms of mind." Any society is literally a more or less organised mental system; the stuff of which it consists is mental stuff; the forces that operate within it are mental forces. MacIver argues further "Social organisations occur of every kind and every degree of universality. If England has a collective mind, why not Birmingham and why not each of its wards? If a nation has a collective mind, so also have a church and a trade union. And we shall have collective minds that are parts of greater collective minds, and collective minds that intersect other collective minds." By this my withers are quite unwrung. What degree of organisation is necessary before a society can properly be said to enjoy collective mental life or have a group mind is a question of degree; and the exponent of the group mind is under no obligation to return a precise answer to this question. My contention is that the most highly organised groups display collective mental life in a way which justifies the conception of the group mind, and that we shall be helped to understand collective life in these most complex and difficult forms by studying it in the simpler less elaborated groups where the conception of a group mind is less clearly applicable. As regards the overlapping and intersection of groups and the consequent difficulty of assigning the limits of groups whose unity is implied by the term group mind, I would point out that this difficulty arises only in connection with the lower forms of group life and that a parallel difficulty is presented by the lower forms of animal life. Is MacIver acquainted with the organisation of a sponge, or of the so-called coral "insect," or with that of the Portuguese man-o'-war? Would he deny the unity of a human being, or refuse to acknowledge his possession of a mind, because in these lower organisms the limits of the unit are hard or impossible to assign? MacIver goes on: "The second argument is an obvious fallacy. If each man thinks and acts differently as a member of a crowd or association and as an individual standing out of any such immediate relation to his fellows, it is still each who thinks and acts; the new determinations are determinations still of individual minds as they are influenced by aggregation ... But this is merely an extreme instance of the obvious fact that every mind is influenced by every kind of environment. To posit a super-individual mind because individual minds are altered by their relations to one another (as indeed they are altered by their relations to physical conditions) is surely gratuitous."[5] To this I reply—the environment which influences the individual in his life as a member of an organised group is neither the sum of his fellow members as individuals, nor is it something that has other than a mental existence. It is the organised group as such, which exists only or chiefly in the persons of those composing it, but which does not exist in the mind of any one of them, and which operates upon each so powerfully just because it is something indefinitely greater, more powerful, more comprehensive than the mere sum of those individuals. MacIver feels that "it is important to clear out of the

[5] *Op. cit.*, p. 77.

way this misleading doctrine of super-individual minds corresponding to social or communal organisations and activities," and therefore goes on to say that "there is no more a great 'collective' mind beyond the individual minds in society than there is a great 'collective' tree beyond all the individual trees in nature. A collection of trees is a wood, and that we can study as a unity; so an aggregation of men is a society, a much more determinate unity; but a collection of trees is not a collective tree, and neither is a collection of persons or minds a collective person or mind. We can speak of qualities of tree in abstraction from any particular tree, and we can speak of qualities of mind as such, or of some particular kind of mind in relation to some type of situation. Yet, in so doing, we are simply considering the characteristic or like elements of individual minds, as we might consider the characteristic or like elements discoverable in individual trees and kinds of trees. To conceive because of these identities, a 'collective' mind as existing *beside* those of individuals or a collective tree beside the variant examples is to run against the wall of the Idea theory." Now, I am not proposing to commit myself to this last-named theory. It is not because minds have much in common with one another that I speak of the collective mind, but because the group as such is more than the sum of the individuals, has its own life proceeding according to laws of group life, which are not the laws of individual life, and because its peculiar group life reacts upon and profoundly modifies the lives of the individuals. I would not call a forest a collective tree; but I would maintain that in certain respects a forest, a wood, or a copse, has in a rudimentary way a collective life. Thus, the forest remains the same forest though, after a hundred or a thousand years, all its constituent trees may be different individuals; and again the forest as a whole may and does modify the life of each tree, as by attracting moisture, protecting from violent and cold winds, harbouring various plants and animals which affect the trees, and so on.

But I will cite an eloquent passage from a recent work on sociology in support of my view. "The bonds of society are in the members of society, and not outside them. It is the memories, traditions, and beliefs of each which make up the social memories, traditions, and beliefs. Society like the kingdom of God is within us. Within us, within each of us, and yet greater than the thoughts and understandings of any of us. For the social thoughts and feelings and willings of each, the socialised mind of each, with the complex scheme of his relation to the social world, is no mere reproduction of the social thoughts and feelings and willings of the rest. Unity and difference here too weave their eternal web, the greater social scheme which none of us who are part of it can ever see in its entirety, but whose infinite subtlety and harmony we may more and more comprehend and admire. As a community grows in civilisation and culture, its traditions are no longer clear and definite ways of thinking, its usages are no longer uniform, its spirit is no longer to be summed up in a few phrases. But the spirit and tradition of a people become no less real in becoming more complex. Each member no longer embodies the whole tradition, but it is because each embodies some part of a greater tradition to which the freely-working individuality of each contributes. In this sense the spirit of a people, though existing only in the individual members, more and more surpasses the measure of any individual mind. Again, the social tradition is expressed through institutions and records more permanent than the short-lived members of a community. These institutions and records are as it were stored social values (just as, in particular, books may be called stored social knowledge), *in themselves nothing*, no part of the social mind, but the instruments of the communication of traditions from member to member, as also from the dead past to the living present. In this way too, with the increase of these stored values, of which members realise parts but none the whole, the spirit of a people more and more surpasses the measure of any individual mind. It is these social forces within and without, working in the minds of individuals whose own social inheritance is an essential part of their individuality, stored in the institutions which they maintain from the past or establish in the present, that mould the communal spirit of the successive generations. In this sense too a community may be called greater than its members who exist at any one time, since the community itself marches out of the past into the present, and its members at any time are part of a great succession, themselves first moulded by communal forces before they become, so moulded, the active determinants of its future moulding." An admirable statement! "The greater social scheme which none of us can see in its entirety"—"the spirit of a people" which "more and more surpasses the measure of any individual mind"—"the communal spirit of the successive genera-tions"—"the community" which is "greater than its members who exist at any one time"; all these are alternative designations of that organised system of mental forces which exists over and above, though not independently of, the individuals in each of whom some fragment of it is embodied and which is the group mind. And the writer of this statement is Mr. R. M. MacIver; the passage occurs in the section of his book designed to "clear out of the way this misleading doctrine of super-individual minds." In the same section he goes on to say that "every association, every organised group, may and does have rights and obligations which are not the rights and obligations of any or all of its members taken distributively but only of the association acting as an organised unity. . . . As a unity the association may become a 'juristic person,' a 'corporation,' and from the legal standpoint the character of unity so conceived is very important. . . . The 'juristic person' is a real *unity*, and therefore more than a *persona ficta*, but the reality it possesses is of a totally different order of being from that of the persons who establish it." But, perversely as it seems to me, MacIver adds, "the unity of which we are thinking is not mechanic or organic or even psychic." I cannot but think that, in thus denying the organic and psychic nature of this unity, MacIver is under the influence of that unfortu-nate and still prevalent way of thinking of the psychic as identical with the conscious which has given endless trouble in psychology; because it has prompted the hopeless attempt, constantly renewed, to describe the structure and organisation of the mind in terms of conscious stuff, ignoring the all-important distinction between mental activity, which is sometimes, though perhaps not always consciousness, and mental structure which is not. The structure and organisation of the spirit of the community is in every respect as purely mental or psychic as is the structure and organisation of the individual mind.

MacIver very properly goes on to bring his conclusions to the pragmatic test, the test of practical results. He writes: "These false analogies . . . are the sources of that most misleading antithesis which we draw between the individual and society, as though soci-ety were somehow other than its individuals. . . . Analyse these misleading analogies, and in the revelation of their falsity there is revealed also the falsity of this essential opposi-tion of individual and society. Properly understood, the interests of 'the individual' are the interests of society."[6] But is it true that the interests of the individual are identical with the interests of society? Obviously not. We have only to think of the condemned criminal; of the mentally defective to whom every enlightened society should deny the right of procreation; of the young soldier who sacrifices his health, his limbs, his eyesight, or his life, and perhaps the welfare of his loved ones, in serving his country. It is true that the progress of society is essentially an approximation towards an ideal state in which this identification would be completed; but that is an ideal which can never be absolutely realised. Nor is it even true that the interests of society are identical with the interests of the majority of its members existing at any one time. It is, I think, highly probable that, if any great modern nation should unanimously and whole-heartedly embark upon a thorough-going scheme of state-socialism, the interests of the vast majority of individuals would be greatly promoted; they would be enabled to live more prosperously and comfortably with greater leisure and opportunity for the higher forms of activity. It is, however, equally probable that the higher interests of the nation would be gravely endangered, that it would enter upon a period of increasing stagnation and diminishing vitality and, after a few generations had passed away, would have slipped far down the slope which has led all great societies of the past to destruction.

The question may be considered in relation to the German nation. As will be pointed out in a later chapter, the structure of that nation was, before the Great War, a menace to European civilisation. If the Germans had succeeded in the aims and had conquered Europe or the world, their individual interests would have been vastly promoted; they would have enjoyed immense material prosperity and a proud consciousness of having been chosen by God to rule the rest of mankind for their good. And this would have confirmed the nation in all its vices and would have finally crushed out of it all its potentialities for developing into a well-organised nation of the higher type, fitted to play an honourable part in the future evolution of mankind. The same truth appears if we consider the problem of the responsibility of the German nation for the War. So long as that people might retain its former organisation, which, I repeat, rendered it a menace to the civilisation and culture of the whole world, its antagonists could only treat it as a criminal and an outlaw to be repressed at all costs and punished and kept down with the utmost severity. But, if it should achieve a new organisation, one which will give preponderance to the better and saner elements and traditions still preserved within it, then, although it will consist of the same individuals in the main, it will have become a new or at least a transformed nation, one with which the other nations could enter into moral relations of amity or at least of mutual toleration, one which could be admitted to a place in the greater society which the League of Nations is to become. In other words, the same population would in virtue of a changed organisation, have become a different nation.

Although MacIver, in making his attack upon the conception of the group mind, has done me the honour to choose me as its exponent, I do not stand alone in maintaining it. I am a little shy of citing in its support the philosophers of the school of German "idealism," because, as I have indicated in the Preface, I have little sympathy with that school. Yet, though one may disapprove of the methods and of most of the conclusions of a school of thought, one may still adduce in support of one's opinion such of its

[6]*Op. cit.*, p. 90.

principles as seem to be well founded. I may, then, remind the reader that the conception of the State as a super-individual, a superhuman quasi-divine personality, is the central conception of the political philosophy of German "idealism." That conception has, no doubt, played a considerable part in bringing upon Europe its present disaster. It was an instance of one of those philosophical ideas which claim to be the product of pure reason, yet in reality are adopted for the purpose of justifying and furthering some already existing interest or institution. In this case the institution in question was the Prussian state and those, Hegel and the rest, who set up this doctrine were servants of that state. They made of their doctrine an instrument for the suppression of individuality which greatly aided in producing the servile condition of the German people. Yet the distortions and exaggerations of the political philosophy of German "idealism" should not prejudice us against the germ of truth which it contains; and the more enlightened British disciples of this school, from T. H. Green onwards, have sought with much success to winnow the grain from the chaff of the doctrine; and I cannot adduce better support for the conception of the group mind than the sentences in which a recent English writer, a sympathetic student of German "idealism," sums up the results of this winnowing process.[7] Discussing the deficiencies of the individualist philosophy of the English utilitarian school, he writes: "Not a modification of the Benthamite premises, but a new philosophy was needed; and that philosophy was provided by the idealist school, of which Green is the greatest representative. That school drew its inspiration immediately from Kant and Hegel, and ultimately from the old Greek philosophy of the city-state. The vital relation between the life of the individual and the life of the community, which alone gives the individual worth and significance, because it alone gives him the power of full moral development; the dependence of the individual, for all his rights and for all his liberty, on his membership of the community; the correlative duty of the community to guarantee to the individual all his rights (in other words, all the conditions necessary for his, and therefore for its own, full moral development)—these were the premises of the new philosophy. That philosophy could satisfy the new needs of social progress, because it refused to worship a supposed individual liberty which was proving destructive of the real liberty of the vast majority, and preferred to emphasise the moral well-being and betterment of the whole community, and to conceive of each of its members as attaining his own well-being and betterment in and through the community. Herein lay, or seemed to lie, a revolution of ideas. Instead of starting from a central individual, to whom the social system is supposed to be adjusted, the idealist starts from a central social system, in which the individual must find his appointed orbit of duty. But after all the revolution is only a restoration; and what is restored is simply the *Republic* of Plato."[8] The same writer reminds us that "both Plato and Hegel thus imply the idea of a moral organism"; and he adds, "It is this conception of a moral organism which Bradley urges. It is implied in daily experience, and it is the only explanation of that experience. 'In fact, what we call an individual man is what he is because of and by virtue of community, and communities are not mere names, but something real.' Already at birth the child is what he is in virtue of communities; he has something of the family character, something of the national char-

---

[7] E. Barker, *Political Thought in England from Herbert Spencer to the Present Day*, Home University Library, London, 1915.

[8] *Op. cit.*, p. 11.

acter, something of the civilised character which comes from human society. As he grows, the community in which he lives pours itself into his being in the language he learns and the social atmosphere he breathes, so that the content of his being implies in its every fibre relations of community. He is what he is by including in his essence the relations of the social State. . . . And regarding the State as a system, in which many spheres (the family, for instance) are subordinated to one sphere, and all the particular actions of individuals are subordinated to their various spheres, we may call it a moral organism, a systematic whole informed by a common purpose or function. As such it has an outer side—a body of institutions; it has an inner side—a soul or spirit which sustains that body. And since it is a moral organism—since, that is to say, its parts are themselves conscious moral agents—that spirit resides in those parts and lives in their consciousness. In such an organism—and this is where it differs from an animal organism, and why we have to use the word moral—the parts are conscious: they know themselves in their position as parts of the whole, and they therefore know the whole of which they are parts. So far as they have such knowledge, and a will based upon it, so far is the moral organism self-conscious and self-willing. . . . Thus, on the one hand, we must recognise that the State lives; that there is a nation's soul, self-conscious in its citizens; and that to each citizen this living soul assigns his field of accomplishment."[9] On a later page of the same book we read— "All the institutions of a country, so far as they are effective, are not only products of thought and creations of mind: they *are* thought, and they *are* mind. Otherwise we have a building without a tenant, and a body without a mind. An Oxford college is not a group of buildings, though common speech gives that name to such a group: it is a group of men. But it is not a group of men in the sense of a group of bodies in propinquity: it is a group of men in the sense of a group of minds. That group of minds, in virtue of the common substance of an uniting idea, is itself a group-mind. There is no group-mind existing apart from the minds of the members of the group; the group-mind only exists in the minds of its members. But nevertheless it exists. There is a college mind, just as there is a Trade Union mind, or even a 'public mind' of the whole community; and we are all conscious of such a mind as something that exists in and along with the separate minds of the members, and over and above any sum of those minds created by mere addition."[10]

The political philosophers of the idealist school have not stood alone in recognising the reality of the group mind. Some of the lawyers, notably Maitland, have arrived at a very similar doctrine; and I cannot better summarise their conclusions than Barker has done in the following passage in the book from which I have already cited so freely. "The new doctrine," he writes, "runs somewhat as follows. No permanent group, permanently organised for a durable object, can be regarded as a mere sum of persons, whose union, to have any rights or duties, must receive a legal confirmation. Permanent groups are themselves persons, group-persons, with a group-will of their own and a permanent character of their own; and they have become group-persons of themselves, without any creative act of the State. In a word, group-persons are real persons; and just because they are so,

[9]*Op. cit.,* pp. 62–64.

[10]*Op. cit.,* p. 74. I consider Mr. Barker's brief statement of the nature of the group mind entirely acceptable, and it has given me great pleasure to find myself in such close harmony with it. It will perhaps give further weight to the fact of our agreement, if I add that the whole of this book, including the rest of this introductory chapter, was written before I took up Mr. Barker's brilliant little volume.

and possess such attributes of persons as will and character, they cannot have been made by the State."[11]

I am not alone, then, in postulating the reality of the group mind. And I am glad to be able to cite evidence of this, because I know well that very many readers may at first find themselves repelled by this notion of a group mind, and that some of them will incline to regard it as the fantastic fad of an academic crank.

I would say at once that the crucial point of difference between my own view of the group mind and that of the German "idealist" school (at least in its more extreme representatives) is that I repudiate, provisionally at least, as an unverifiable hypothesis the conception of a collective or super-individual consciousness, somehow comprising the consciousness of the individuals composing the group. I have examined this conception in the following chapter and have stated my grounds for rejecting it. The difference of practical conclusions arising from this difference of theory must obviously be very great.

Several books dealing with collective psychology have been published in recent years. Of these perhaps the most notable are G. le Bon's *Psychology of the Crowd*, his *Evolution psychologique des peuples;* Sighele's *La foule criminelle;* the *Psychologie collective* of Dr. A. A. Marie; and Alfred Fouillée's *La Science sociale contemporaine.* It is noteworthy that, with the exception of the last, all these books deal only with crowds or groups of low organisation; and their authors, like almost all others who have touched on this subject, are concerned chiefly to point out how participation in the group life degrades the individual, how the group feels and thinks and acts on a much lower plane than the average plane of the individuals who compose it.

On the other hand, many writers have insisted on the fact that it is only by participation in the life of society that any man can realise his higher potentialities; that society has ideals and aims and traditions loftier than any principles of conduct the individual can form for himself unaided; and that only by the further evolution of organised society can mankind be raised to higher levels; just as in the past it has been only through the development of organised society that the life of man has ceased to deserve the epithets "nasty, brutish, and short" which Hobbes applied to it.

We seem then to stand before a paradox. Participation in group life degrades the individual, assimilating his mental processes to those of the crowd, whose brutality, inconstancy, and unreasoning impulsiveness have been the theme of many writers; yet only by participation in group life does man become fully man, only so does he rise above the level of the savage.

The resolution of this paradox is the essential theme of this book. It examines and fully recognises the mental and moral defects of the crowd and its degrading effects upon all those who are caught up in it and carried away by the contagion of its reckless spirit. It then goes on to show how organisation of the group may, and generally does in large measure, counteract these degrading tendencies; and how the better kinds of organisation render group life the great ennobling influence by aid of which alone man rises a little above the animals and may even aspire to fellowship with the angels.

[11] *Op. cit.*, p. 175.

EDWARD ALSWORTH ROSS

Nature and Scope of Social Psychology*

SOCIAL PSYCHOLOGY TREATS OF SOCIAL PLANES
AND CURRENTS

Social psychology, as the writer conceives it, studies the psychic planes and currents that come into existence among men in consequence of their association. It seeks to understand and account for those uniformities in feeling, belief, or volition—and hence in action—which are due to the interaction of human beings, *i.e.*, to *social* causes. No two persons have just the same endowment. Looking at their heredity, we should expect people to be far more dissimilar and individual than we actually find them to be. The aligning power of association triumphs over diversity of temperament and experience. There ought to be as many religious creeds as there are human beings; but we find people ranged under a few great religions. It is the same in respect to dress, diet, pastimes, or moral ideas. The individuality each has received from the hand of nature is largely effaced, and we find people gathered into great planes of uniformity.

In shifting attention from the agreements in which men rest, such as languages, religions, and cultures, to the agitations into which they are drawn, it is natural to change the metaphor from *plane* to *current*. The spread of the lynching spirit through a crowd in the presence of an atrocious criminal, the contagion of panic in a beaten army, an epidemic of religious emotion, and the sympathetic extension of a strike call up the thought of a *current*, which bears people along for a time and then ceases.

RELATION OF SOCIAL PSYCHOLOGY
TO SOCIOLOGY PROPER

Social psychology differs from sociology proper in that the former considers planes and currents; the latter, groups and structures.[1] Their interests bring men into coöperation or conflict. They group themselves for the purpose of coöperating or struggling, and they devise structures as a means of adjusting interests and attaining practical ends. Social psychology considers them only as coming into planes or currents of uniformity, not as uniting into groups. Since the former determine the latter more than the latter determine the former, social psychology should precede rather than follow sociology proper in the order of studies.

---

*Edward Alsworth Ross, *Social Psychology: An Outline and Source Book* (New York: Macmillan, 1908), pp. 1–9, 76–81.

[1] The present treatise is, therefore, by no means the same as *psychological sociology*, for it omits the psychology of groups. The writer doubts whether it is practicable or wise to treat the psychological side of sociology quite apart from the morphological side.

PLANES PRODUCED BY A COMMON ENVIRONMENT
OR EXPERIENCE ARE NOT SOCIAL

Social psychology pays no attention to the non-psychic parallelisms among human beings (an epidemic of disease or the prevalence of chills and fever among the early settlers of river-bottom lands), or to the psychic parallelisms that result therefrom (melancholia or belief in eternal punishment). It neglects the uniformities among people that are produced by the direct action of a common physical environment (superstitiousness of sailors, gayety of open-air peoples, suggestibility of dwellers on monotonous plains, independent spirit of mountaineers), or by subjection to similar conditions of life (dissipatedness of tramp printers, recklessness of cowboys, preciseness of elderly school teachers, suspiciousness of farmers).

RACE TRAITS ARE NOT SOCIAL PLANES

Social psychology ignores uniformities arising directly or indirectly out of race endowment—negro volubility, gypsy nomadism, Malay vindictiveness, Singhalese treachery, Magyar passion for music, Slavic mysticism, Teutonic venturesomeness, American restlessness. How far such common characters are really racial in origin and how far merely social is a matter yet to be settled. Probably they are much less congenital than we love to imagine. "Race" is the cheap explanation tyros offer for any collective trait that they are too stupid or too lazy to trace to its origin in the physical environment, the social environment, or historical conditions.

SOCIAL PLANES ARISE FROM HUMAN INTERACTIONS

Social psychology deals only with uniformities due to *social* causes, *i.e.*, to *mental contacts* or *mental interactions*. In each case we must ask, "Are these human beings aligned by their common instincts and temperament, their common geographical situation, their identical conditions of life, or by their *interpsychology*, *i.e.*, the influences they have received from one another or from a common human source?" The fact that a mental agreement extends through society bringing into a common plane great numbers of men does not make it *social*. It is *social* only in so far as it arises out of the interplay of minds.

SOCIAL PSYCHOLOGY SHEDS LIGHT ON SOCIETY
AND ON THE INDIVIDUAL

Social psychology seeks to enlarge our knowledge of *society* by explaining how so many planes in feeling, belief, or purpose have established themselves among men and supplied a basis for their groupings, their coöperations, and their conflicts. But for the processes which weave into innumerable men certain ground patterns of ideas, beliefs, and preferences, great societies could not endure. No communities could last save those held together by social pleasure or the necessity for coöperation. National characteristics would not arise, and strife would be the rule outside of the group of men subject to the same area of characterization.

It seeks to enlarge our knowledge of the *individual* by ascertaining how much of his mental content and choice is derived from his social surroundings. Each of us loves to think himself unique, self-made, moving in a path all his own. To be sure, he finds his feet in worn paths, but he imagines he follows the path because it is the right one, not because it is trodden. Thus Cooley[2] observes: "The more thoroughly American a man is, the less he can perceive Americanism. He will embody it; all he does, says, or writes will be full of it; but he can never truly see it, simply because he has no exterior point of view from which to look at it." Now, by demonstrating everywhere in our lives the unsuspected presence of social factors, social psychology spurs us to push on and build up a genuine individuality, to become a voice and not an echo, a person and not a parrot. The realization of how pitiful is the contribution we have made to what we are, how few of our ideas are our own, how rarely we have thought out a belief for ourselves, how little our feelings arise naturally out of our situation, how poorly our choices express the real cravings of our nature, first mortifies, then arouses, us to break out of our prison of custom and conventionality and live an open-air life close to reality. Only by emancipation from the spell of numbers and age and social eminence and personality can ciphers become integers.

DIVISIONS OF SOCIAL PSYCHOLOGY

Social psychology falls into two very unequal divisions, viz., *Social Ascendency* and *Individual Ascendency*, the determination of the one by the many and the determination of the many by the one; the moulding of the ordinary person by his social environment and the moulding of the social environment by the extraordinary person. Thus the knightly pattern, the ideal of romantic love, the Westminster Catechism, and the belief in public education are at once achievements of superior persons, and elements in the social environment of innumerable ordinary persons.

For example, we may distinguish three principal sources of the feelings on slavery extant in this country in 1860.

HOW PLANES OF SENTIMENT REGARDING SLAVERY FORMED

1. *Observation or Experience of Slave Holding.* —In the South slavery was profitable, and the economic interests of that section became bound up with it. In the North it was unprofitable, and hence men could feel disinterestedly about it.

2. *Imbibing from the Social Environment.* —In the South belief in the rightfulness of slavery became first a creed and then a tradition under which the young grew up. During the seventy years from 1790 to 1860 there was a marked increase of antipathy to the negro and an extension of the color line. By 1835 pro-slavery sentiment had become so militant that abolitionism was no longer allowed to show itself openly. The generation reared in this close atmosphere could not but be biassed. Southern opinion became first

---

[2]"Human Nature and the Social Order," 36.

homogeneous, then imperious, finally intolerant. Southern feeling about slavery reached the pitch of fanaticism. Even the "poor whites" became pro-slavery. In the North antislavery sentiment became predominant, but not intolerant. In each section there formed a psychic vortex, more and more powerful, which sucked in the neutral and indifferent and imparted to them its own motion.

3. *The Initiative of the Élite.*—In the South the public men, great planters, and commercial magnates moulded sectional opinion in support of the "peculiar institution." In the North poets, divines, orators, philosophers, and statesmen built up the antislavery sentiment. Garrison, Phillips, Parker, Lovejoy, Stowe, Beecher, Lowell, Thoreau, and Whittier proclaimed the mandates of the voice within the heart.

Of these three factors the first is not social at all, the second exemplifies *social ascendency*, and the third exemplifies *individual ascendency*.

FACTORS IN THE FORMATION OF RELIGIOUS PLANES

Again, to drive the distinction home, let us consider the factors that determine the boundary line between Catholicism and Protestantism in Europe.

1. *The Affinity between the Confessions and the People.*—Says Taylor:[3]—

"The dolichocephalic Teutonic race is Protestant, the brachycephalic Celto-Slavic race is either Roman Catholic or Greek Orthodox. In the first, individualism, wilfulness, self-reliance, independence, are strongly developed; the second is submissive to authority and conservative in instincts. To the Teutonic races Latin Christianity was never congenial, and they have now converted it into something very different from what it was at first, or from what it became in the hands of Latin and Greek doctors. The Teutonic peoples are averse to sacerdotalism, and have shaken off priestly guidance and developed individualism. Protestantism was a revolt against a religion imposed by the South upon the North, but which had never been congenial to the Northern mind. The German princes, who were of purer Teutonic blood than their subjects, were the leaders of the ecclesiastical revolt. Scandinavia is more purely Teutonic than Germany, and Scandinavia is Protestant to the backbone. The Lowland Scotch, who are more purely Teutonic than the English, have given the freest development to the genius of Protestantism. Those Scotch clans which have clung to the old faith have the smallest admixture of Teutonic blood. Ulster, the most Teutonic province of Ireland, is the most firmly Protestant. The case of the Belgians and the Dutch is very striking. The line of religious division became the line of political separation, and is conterminous with the two racial provinces. The mean cephalic index of the Dutch is 75.3, which is nearly that of the Swedes and the North Germans; the mean index of the Belgians is 79, which is that of the Parisians. The Burgundian cantons of Switzerland, which possess the largest proportion of Teutonic blood, are Protestant, while the brachycephalic cantons in the East and South are the stronghold of Catholicism. South Germany, which is brachycephalic, is Catholic; North Germany, which is dolichocephalic, is Protestant. Hanover, which is Protestant, has a considerably lower index than Cologne, which is Catholic. The Thirty Years' War was a war of race as well as of religion, and the peace of Westphalia drew the line of religious demarcation with tolerable precision along the ethnic frontier.

[3] "The Origin of the Aryans," 247–249.

"Wherever the Teutonic blood is purest—in North Germany, Sweden, Norway, Iceland, Ulster, the Orkneys, the Lothians, Yorkshire, East Anglia—Protestantism found easy entrance, and has retained its hold, often in some exaggerated form. In Bohemia, France, Belgium, Alsace, it has been trodden out. In Galway and Kerry it has no footing. The Welsh and the Cornishmen, who became Protestants by political accident, have transformed Protestantism into an emotional religion, which has inner affinities with the emotional faith of Ireland and Italy. Even now Protestantism gains no converts in the South of Europe, or Catholicism in the North. Roman Catholicism, or the cognate creed of the Greek and Russian Orthodox churches, is dominant in all those lands where the brachycephalic race prevails; Protestantism is confined to the dolichocephalic Teutonic region."

2. *The Initiative of Religious Leaders.*—The work of Huss, Luther, Knox, Calvin, was, of course, a decisive factor in the formative years of Protestantism. It is less to-day, seeing that the teachings of the earlier leaders have struck root and become a tradition. Nevertheless, even now, the frontier between the confessions is disturbed by the shifting of a Newman from one side to the other.

3. *The Authority of Numbers and Tradition.*—Only the very independent mind turns Catholic in Scandinavia, where all but one in a thousand are Lutheran, or Protestant in Portugal, where all but one in ten thousand are Catholic. In religion, moreover, parental upbringing is well-nigh decisive. Save among migrants, few converts are made by one side from the other. Every man denies that his faith is inherited or thrust upon him by circumstances. On the contrary, he imagines that it is a matter of intelligent free choice. But this is an illusion. The recognized ascendency of remote historical factors in determining the religious preferences of peoples emphasizes how non-rational and unfree are the religious adhesions of men. The Irish are devotedly and stubbornly Catholic because their aforetime oppressors were Protestants. Not present causes, but Smithfield, the Armada, Knox, and Claverhouse, make England so Protestant, Scotland so Presbyterian. Long-forgotten struggles with non-Christians made Spain so bigoted as she is to-day, and Russia so Orthodox.

IMITATION VERSUS AFFINITY AS ESTABLISHER OF PLANES AMONG MEN

The second and third of these determinative factors are social, but not the first. It is evident, then, that the great rival to Imitation as the key to social uniformities is Affinity. Thus it has been maintained that there is an inner sympathy between agriculture and orthodoxy, between commerce and heresy, between machine industry and scepticism, between artists and socialism.

The affinities or suitabilities that govern choices present themselves more clearly in races than in peoples, in peoples than in communities, in communities than in individuals. Thus great numbers of individuals are Catholic from some form of imitation, yet the brachycephalic race seems to be Catholic from affinity. Innumerable persons wear tweeds and cheviots on account of fashion, yet the ultimate reason for the vogue of these stuffs is their suitability to certain damp chill climates. Despite the mob mind in them, the Crusades display a good deal of rationality. They were expeditions for the conquest of powerful talismans. There is probably an *affinity* between parliamentary institutions and the English-speaking peoples on their present plane of culture. The frequent illworking of such institutions in southern Europe and South America suggests that among the Latins they persist by *imitation*.

★ ★ ★

LAWS OF MASS PHENOMENA

Laws of Crazes

The laws of crazes may be formulated as follows:—

1. *The Craze Takes Time to Develop to Its Height.*—The panic of 1893 began in April and reached its height in August, but socio-psychic phenomena began to manifest themselves only in 1894 in the form of the great sympathetic railway strike, labor riots, and the departure for the national capital of ten bodies of penniless unemployed "commonwealers" to petition Congress for work. The susceptibility of the public continued through 1896, and was responsible for the strong emotional currents in the presidential campaign of that year.

2. *The More Extensive Its Ravages, the Stronger the Type of Intellect That Falls a Prey to It.*—In the acute stages of a boom or a revival, even the educated, experienced, and hard-headed succumb. Perhaps no better instance can be cited than the progress of a Messianic craze among the Jews. In 1666 a Jew named Sabbathai Zevi declared himself publicly as the long-expected Messiah. A maniacal ecstasy took possession of the Jewish mind. Men, women, and children fell into fits of hysterics. Business men left their occupations, workmen their trades, and devoted themselves to prayer and penitence. The synagogues resounded with sighs, cries, sobs for days and nights together. All the rabbis who opposed the mania had to flee for their lives. The fame of Sabbathai spread throughout the world. In Poland, in Germany, in Holland, and in England, the course of business was interrupted on the Exchange by the gravest Jews breaking off to discuss this wonderful event. In Amsterdam the Jews marched through the streets, carrying with them rolls of the Torah, singing, leaping, and dancing, as if possessed. Scenes still more turbulent and wild occurred in Hamburg, Venice, Leghorn, Avignon, and many other cities. Learned men began to give in their adhesion. Everywhere prophets and prophetesses appeared, thus realizing the Jewish belief in the inspired nature of Messianic times. Men and women, boys and girls, in hysterical convulsions screamed praises to the new Messiah. At last, from all sides rich men came to Sabbathai, putting their wealth at his disposal. Many sold all they possessed and set out for Palestine. Traffic in the greatest commercial centres came to a complete standstill; most of the Jewish merchants and bankers liquidated their affairs. The belief in the divine mission of Sabbathai was made into a religious dogma of equal rank with that of the unity of God.[4]

3. *The Greater Its Height, the More Absurd the Propositions That Will Be Believed or the Actions That Will Be Done.*—At the zenith of the South Sea craze companies formed "to make deal boards out of sawdust," "for extracting silver from lead," "for a wheel of perpetual motion," "for furnishing funerals to any part of Great Britain," could

[4] Sidis, "The Psychology of Suggestion," 327–329.

sell stock. Finally one bold speculator started "a company for carrying on an undertaking of great advantage, but nobody to know what it is!"

4. *The Higher the Craze, the Sharper the Reaction from It.*—The prostration of a "busted boom" town is so extreme that its unboomed rivals forge ahead of it. The reaction from a purely emotional religious revival often leaves the cause of real religion worse off than it was at first. This perhaps is why experienced churches like the Roman Catholic have no use for revivals.

5. *One Craze Is Frequently Succeeded by Another Exciting Emotions of a Different Character.*—Says Jones:[5] "It is interesting to note that the emotions which have been generated by speculative excitement and intensified by panic depressions have been frequently transferred to religious subjects and have, in the United States at certain times, given rise to remarkable revivals of religion following close upon the heels of panics." "A contemporary account of the extraordinary revival movement of 1857 says: 'It was in October of this year (1857) that Mr. Lamphier, a missionary of the Dutch Reformed Church, thought, in his own heart, that an hour of daily prayer would bring consolation to afflicted business men.' In a few weeks those holding the meetings were astonished to find the crowds growing too large for the buildings. The Methodist Church on John Street and the Dutch Reformed Church on Fulton Street were opened daily. Next, Burton's Theatre was hired, and throughout the winter noonday prayer-meetings were held at numerous places in the city." "Even the firemen and policemen held their prayer-meetings, so that we may feel perfectly assured of the truth of what the writer says when he adds, 'It is doubtful whether under heaven was seen such a sight as went on in the city of New York in the winter and spring of the year 1857–1858.' 'From New York as a centre, the mysterious influence spread abroad till it penetrated all New England in the East, southward as far as Virginia, and even beyond, westward to Buffalo, Cincinnati, Chicago, St. Louis.' "

6. *A Dynamic Society Is More Craze-Ridden Than One Moving Along the Ruts of Custom.*—In a dynamic society so many readjustments are necessary, such far-reaching transformations are experienced in half a lifetime, that the past is discredited. One forms a habit of breaking habits. Ancestral wisdom, the teachings of social experience are refuted and discarded at so many points that they lose their steadying power. The result is that instead of aping their forefathers, people ape the multitude.

It is a delusion to suppose that one who has broken the yoke of custom is emancipated. The lanes of custom are narrow, the hedge-rows are high, and view to right or left there is none. But there is as much freedom and self-direction in him who trudges along this lane as in the "emancipated" person, who finds himself in the open country free to pick a course of his own, but who, nevertheless, stampedes aimlessly with the herd. A dynamic society may, therefore, foster individuality no more than a static society. But it *does* progress, and that, perhaps, ought to reconcile us to the mental epidemics that afflict us.

7. *Ethnic or Mental Homogeneity Is Favorable to the Craze.*—The remarks of Giddings regarding like-mindedness and the crowd apply equally well here. Caste lines break

---

[5] "Economic Crises," 209, 210.

the sweep of the craze. The English are proof against mob mind chiefly because they stand on such different levels. Americans are on a prairie. The English are on terraces. The gentleman, the shopkeeper, or the clerk looks with disdain upon an agitation spreading among workingmen, and instead of feeling drawn by the rush of numbers, is, in fact, repelled. Caste makes a society immune to craze, even if the remedy is worse than the disease.

THEORY OF THE FAD

The *fad* originates in the surprise or interest excited by novelty. Roller skating, blue glass, the planchette, a forty days' fast, tiddledy-winks, faith healing, the "13-14-15" puzzle, baseball, telepathy, or the sexual novel attract those restless folk who are always running hither and thither after some new thing. This creates a swirl which rapidly sucks into its vortex the soft-headed and weak-minded, and at last, grown bigger, involves even the saner kind. As no department of life is safe from the invasion of novelty, we have all kinds of fads: philosophic fads, like pessimism or anarchism; literary fads, like the Impressionists or the Decadents; religious fads, like spiritualism or theosophy; hygienic fads, like water-cure or breakfast foods; medical fads, like lymph or tuberculin; personal fads, like pet lizards or face enamel. And of these orders of fads each has a *clientèle* of its own.

FADDISM OR PROGRESS

In many cases we can explain vogue entirely in terms of novelty fascination, and mass suggestion. But, even when the new thing can make its way by sheer merit, it does not escape becoming a fad. It still will have its penumbral ring of rapt imitators. So there is something of the fad even in bicycling, motoring, massage, antisepsis, and physical culture. Indeed, it is sometimes hard to distinguish faddism from the enthusiastic welcome and prompt acceptance accorded to a real improvement. For the undiscerning the only touchstone is time. Here, as elsewhere, "persistence in consciousness" is the test of reality. The mere novelty, soon ceasing to be novel, bores people, and must yield to a fresh sensation; a genuine improvement, on the other hand, meets a real need and therefore lasts.

WHY FADS FLOURISH NOWADAYS

Unlike the craze, the fad does not spread in a medium especially prepared for it by excitement. It cannot rely on the heightened suggestibility of people. Its conquests, therefore, imply something above mere volume of suggestion. They imply prestige. The fad owes half its power over minds to the prestige that in this age attaches to the new.

— · — · — · — · — · — · — · — · — · — · — · —

CHARLES HORTON COOLEY

*Primary Groups**
and
Looking-Glass Self (The Social Self)†

PRIMARY GROUPS

By primary groups I mean those characterized by intimate face-to-face association and coöperation. They are primary in several senses, but chiefly in that they are fundamental in forming the social nature and ideals of the individual. The result of intimate association, psychologically, is a certain fusion of individualities in a common whole, so that one's very self, for many purposes at least, is the common life and purpose of the group. Perhaps the simplest way of describing this wholeness is by saying that it is a "we"; it involves the sort of sympathy and mutual identification for which "we" is the natural expression. One lives in the feeling of the whole and finds the chief aims of his will in that feeling.

It is not to be supposed that the unity of the primary group is one of mere harmony and love. It is always a differentiated and usually a competitive unity, admitting of self-assertion and various appropriative passions; but these passions are socialized by sympathy, and come, or tend to come, under the discipline of a common spirit. The individual will be ambitious, but the chief object of his ambition will be some desired place in the thought of the others, and he will feel allegiance to common standards of service and fair play. So the boy will dispute with his fellows a place on the team, but above such disputes will place the common glory of his class and school.

The most important spheres of this intimate association and coöperation—though by no means the only ones—are the family, the play-group of children, and the neighborhood or community group of elders. These are practically universal, belonging to all times and all stages of development; and are accordingly a chief basis of what is universal in human nature and human ideals. The best comparative studies of the family, such as those of Westermarck[1] or Howard,[2] show it to us as not only a universal institution, but as more alike the world over than the exaggeration of exceptional customs by an earlier school had led us to suppose. Nor can any one doubt the general prevalence of play-groups among children or of informal assemblies of various kinds among their elders. Such association is clearly the nursery of human nature in the world about us, and there is no apparent reason to suppose that the case has anywhere or at any time been essentially different.

---

*Charles Horton Cooley, *Social Organization* (New York: Charles Scribner's Sons, 1909), pp. 23–31.

†Charles Horton Cooley, *Human Nature and the Social Order* (New York: Charles Scribner's Sons, 1902), pp. 147–153, 164–169.

[1] The History of Human Marriage.

[2] A History of Matrimonial Institutions.

As regards play, I might, were it not a matter of common observation, multiply illustrations of the universality and spontaneity of the group discussion and coöperation to which it gives rise. The general fact is that children, especially boys after about their twelfth year, live in fellowships in which their sympathy, ambition and honor are engaged even more, often, than they are in the family. Most of us can recall examples of the endurance by boys of injustice and even cruelty, rather than appeal from their fellows to parents or teachers—as, for instance, in the hazing so prevalent at schools, and so difficult, for this very reason, to repress. And how elaborate the discussion, how cogent the public opinion, how hot the ambitions in these fellowships.

Nor is this facility of juvenile association, as is sometimes supposed a trait peculiar to English and American boys; since experience among our immigrant population seems to show that the offspring of the more restrictive civilizations of the continent of Europe form self-governing play-groups with almost equal readiness. Thus Miss Jane Addams, after pointing out that the "gang" is almost universal, speaks of the interminable discussion which every detail of the gang's activity receives, remarking that "in these social folk-motes, so to speak, the young citizen learns to act upon his own determination."[3]

Of the neighborhood group it may be said, in general, that from the time men formed permanent settlements upon the land, down, at least, to the rise of modern industrial cities, it has played a main part in the primary, heart-to-heart life of the people. Among our Teutonic forefathers the village community was apparently the chief sphere of sympathy and mutual aid for the commons all through the "dark" and middle ages, and for many purposes it remains so in rural districts at the present day. In some countries we still find it with all its ancient vitality, notably in Russia, where the mir, or self-governing village group, is the main theatre of life, along with the family, for perhaps fifty millions of peasants.

In our own life the intimacy of the neighborhood has been broken up by the growth of an intricate mesh of wider contacts which leaves us strangers to people who live in the same house. And even in the country the same principle is at work, though less obviously, diminishing our economic and spiritual community with our neighbors. How far this change is a healthy development, and how far a disease, is perhaps still uncertain.

Besides these almost universal kinds of primary association, there are many others whose form depends upon the particular state of civilization; the only essential thing, as I have said, being a certain intimacy and fusion of personalities. In our own society, being little bound by place, people easily form clubs, fraternal societies and the like, based on congeniality, which may give rise to real intimacy. Many such relations are formed at school and college, and among men and women brought together in the first instance by their occupations—as workmen in the same trade, or the like. Where there is a little common interest and activity, kindness grows like weeds by the roadside.

But the fact that the family and neighborhood groups are ascendant in the open and plastic time of childhood makes them even now incomparably more influential than all the rest.

Primary groups are primary in the sense that they give the individual his earliest and completest experience of social unity, and also in the sense that they do not change in the same degree as more elaborate relations, but form a comparatively permanent source out

[3] Newer Ideals of Peace, 177.

of which the latter are ever springing. Of course they are not independent of the larger society, but to some extent reflect its spirit; as the German family and the German school bear somewhat distinctly the print of German militarism. But this, after all, is like the tide setting back into creeks, and does not commonly go very far. Among the German, and still more among the Russian, peasantry are found habits of free coöperation and discussion almost uninfluenced by the character of the state; and it is a familiar and well-supported view that the village commune, self-governing as regards local affairs and habituated to discussion, is a very widespread institution in settled communities, and the continuator of a similar autonomy previously existing in the clan. "It is man who makes monarchies and establishes republics, but the commune seems to come directly from the hand of God."[4]

In our own cities the crowded tenements and the general economic and social confusion have sorely wounded the family and the neighborhood, but it is remarkable, in view of these conditions, what vitality they show; and there is nothing upon which the conscience of the time is more determined than upon restoring them to health.

These groups, then, are springs of life, not only for the individual but for social institutions. They are only in part moulded by special traditions, and, in larger degree, express a universal nature. The religion or government of other civilizations may seem alien to us, but the children or the family group wear the common life, and with them we can always make ourselves at home.

By human nature, I suppose, we may understand those sentiments and impulses that are human in being superior to those of lower animals, and also in the sense that they belong to mankind at large, and not to any particular race or time. It means, particularly, sympathy and the innumerable sentiments into which sympathy enters, such as love, resentment, ambition, vanity, hero-worship, and the feeling of social right and wrong.[5]

Human nature in this sense is justly regarded as a comparatively permanent element in society. Always and everywhere men seek honor and dread ridicule, defer to public opinion, cherish their goods and their children, and admire courage, generosity, and success. It is always safe to assume that people are and have been human.

It is true, no doubt, that there are differences of race capacity, so great that a large part of mankind are possibly incapable of any high kind of social organization. But these differences, like those among individuals of the same race, are subtle, depending upon some obscure intellectual deficiency, some want of vigor,, or slackness of moral fibre, and do not involve unlikeness in the generic impulses of human nature. In these all races are very much alike. The more insight one gets into the life of savages, even those that are reckoned the lowest, the more human, the more like ourselves, they appear. Take for instance the natives of Central Australia, as described by Spencer and Gillen,[6] tribes having no definite government or worship and scarcely able to count to five. They are generous to one another, emulous of virtue as they understand it, kind to their children

---

[4] De Tocqueville, Democracy in America, vol. i, chap. 5.
[5] These matters are expounded at some length in the writer's Human Nature and the Social Order.
[6] The Native Tribes of Central Australia. Compare also Darwin's views and examples given in chap. 7 of his Descent of Man.

LOOKING-GLASS SELF (THE SOCIAL SELF)

he social self is simply any idea, or system of ideas, drawn from the communicative
1at the mind cherishes as its own. Self-feeling has its chief scope *within* the general
)t outside of it, the special endeavor or tendency of which it is the emotional aspect
3 its principal field of exercise in a world of personal forces, reflected in the mind
-orld of personal impressions.

5 connected with the thought of other persons it is always a consciousness of the
ir or differentiated aspect of one's life, because that is the aspect that has to be
ed by purpose and endeavor, and its more aggressive forms tend to attach them-
to whatever one finds to be at once congenial to one's own tendencies and at
e with those of others with whom one is in mental contact. It is here that they are
eeded to serve their function of stimulating characteristic activity, of fostering
ersonal variations which the general plan of life seems to require. Heaven, says
eare, doth divide

e state of man in divers functions,
ting endeavor in continual motion,

feeling is one of the means by which this diversity is achieved.

:eably to this view we find that the aggressive self manifests itself most conspicu-
an appropriativeness of objects of common desire, corresponding to the individ-
d of power over such objects to secure his own peculiar development, and to the
)f opposition from others who also need them. And this extends from material
-o lay hold, in the same spirit, of the attentions and affections of other people, of
of plans and ambitions, including the noblest special purposes the mind can
, and indeed of any conceivable idea which may come to seem a part of one's life
·ed of assertion against someone else. The attempt to limit the word self and its
·s to the lower aims of personality is quite arbitrary; at variance with common
xpressed by the emphatic use of "I" in connection with the sense of duty and
1 motives, and unphilosophical as ignoring the function of the self as the organ
zed endeavor of higher as well as lower kinds.

the "I" of common speech has a meaning which includes some sort of reference
)ersons is involved in the very fact that the word and the ideas it stands for are
1a of language and the communicative life. It is doubtful whether it is possible
1guage at all without thinking more or less distinctly of someone else, and
:he things to which we give names and which have a large place in reflective
·e almost always those which are impressed upon us by our contact with other
1ere there is no communication there can be no nomenclature and no devel-
3ht. What we call "me," "mine," or "myself" is, then, not something separate
eneral life, but the most interesting part of it, a part whose interest arises from
·ct that it is both general and individual. That is, we care for it just because it is
of the mind that is living and striving in the common life, trying to impress
the minds of others. "I" is a militant social tendency, working to hold and
place in the general current of tendencies. So far as it can it waxes, as all life
ink of it as apart from society is a palpable absurdity of which no one could
10 really *saw* it as a fact of life.

and to the aged, and by no means harsh to women. Their faces as s
graphs are wholly human and many of them attractive.

And when we come to a comparison between different stages in
the same race, between ourselves, for instances, and the Teutonic
Caesar, the difference is neither in human nature nor in capacity, b
the range and complexity of relations, in the diverse expression of
essentially much the same.

There is no better proof of this generic likeness of human natur
joy with which the modern man makes himself at home in literatu
remote and varied phases of life—in Homer, in the Nibelung tales,
tures, in the legends of the American Indians, in stories of fronti
sailors, of criminals and tramps, and so on. The more penetrating
life is studied the more an essential likeness to ourselves is revealed

To return to primary groups: the view here maintained is th
something existing separately in the individual, but a *group-natu
society*, a relatively simple and general condition of the social min
on the one hand, than the mere instinct that is born in us—though
something less, on the other, than the more elaborate develop
ments that makes up institutions. It is the nature which is dev
those simple, face-to-face groups that are somewhat alike in al
family, the playground, and the neighborhood. In the essential s
found the basis, in experience, for similar ideas and sentiment
these, everywhere, human nature comes into existence. Man d
cannot acquire it except through fellowship, and it decays in iso

If this view does not recommend itself to commonsense I
tion will be of much avail. It simply means the application at
society and individuals are inseparable phases of a common w
find an individual fact we may look for a social fact to go w
nature in persons there must be something universal in associat

What else can human nature be than a trait of prim
attribute of the separate individual—supposing there were any
characteristics, such as affection, ambition, vanity, and re
apart from society. If it belongs, then, to man in associati
association is required to develop it? Evidently nothing
phases of society are transient and diverse, while human n
and universal. In short the family and neighborhood life
nothing more is.

Here as everywhere in the study of society we must lear
wholes, rather than in artificial separation. We must see
family and local groups as immediate facts, not as combin
perhaps we shall do this best by recalling our own experi
sympathetic observation. What, in our life, is the family
know of the we-feeling? Thought of this kind may help us
that primary group-nature of which everything social is the

★　★　★

life,
life,
findi
by a

pecul
sustai
selves
varian
most
those
Shakes

Th
Se
and sel
Ag
ously i
ual's ne
danger
objects
all sort
entertai
and in
derivativ
sense as
other hi
of specia
Tha
to other
phenome
to use l
certainly
thought
people.
oped tho
from the
the very
that phase
itself upo
enlarge its
does. To t
be guilty w

Der Mensch erkennt sich nur im Menschen, nur
Das Leben lehret jedem was er sei.[7]

If a thing has no relation to others of which one is conscious he is unlikely to think of it at all, and if he does think of it he cannot, it seems to me, regard it as emphatically *his*. The appropriative sense is always the shadow, as it were, of the common life, and when we have it we have a sense of the latter in connection with it. Thus, if we think of a secluded part of the woods as "ours," it is because we think, also, that others do not go there. As regards the body I doubt if we have a vivid my-feeling about any part of it which is not thought of, however vaguely, as having some actual or possible reference to someone else. Intense self-consciousness regarding it arises along with instincts or experiences which connect it with the thought of others. Internal organs, like the liver, are not thought of as peculiarly ours unless we are trying to communicate something regarding them, as, for instance, when they are giving us trouble and we are trying to get sympathy.

"I," then, is not all of the mind, but a peculiarly central, vigorous, and well-knit portion of it, not separate from the rest but gradually merging into it, and yet having a certain practical distinctness, so that a man generally shows clearly enough by his language and behavior what his "I" is as distinguished from thoughts he does not appropriate. It may be thought of, as already suggested, under the analogy of a central colored area on a lighted wall. It might also, and perhaps more justly, be compared to the nucleus of a living cell, not altogether separate from the surrounding matter, out of which indeed it is formed, but more active and definitely organized.

The reference to other persons involved in the sense of self may be distinct and particular, as when a boy is ashamed to have his mother catch him at something she has forbidden, or it may be vague and general, as when one is ashamed to do something which only his conscience, expressing his sense of social responsibility, detects and disapproves; but it is always there. There is no sense of "I," as in pride or shame, without its correlative sense of you, or he, or they. Even the miser gloating over his hidden gold can feel the "mine" only as he is aware of the world of men over whom he has secret power; and the case is very similar with all kinds of hid treasure. Many painters, sculptors, and writers have loved to withhold their work from the world, fondling it in seclusion until they were quite done with it; but the delight in this, as in all secrets, depends upon a sense of the value of what is concealed.

In a very large and interesting class of cases the social reference takes the form of a somewhat definite imagination of how one's self—that is any idea he appropriates—appears in a particular mind, and the kind of self-feeling one has is determined by the attitude toward this attributed to that other mind. A social self of this sort might be called the reflected or looking-glass self:

Each to each a looking-glass
Reflects the other that doth pass.

As we see our face, figure, and dress in the glass, and are interested in them because they are ours, and pleased or otherwise with them according as they do or do not answer to what we should like them to be; so in imagination we perceive in another's mind some

---

[7]"Only in man does man know himself; life alone teaches each one what he is."—Goethe, *Tasso*, act 2, sc. 3.

thought of our appearance, manners, aims, deeds, character, friends, and so on, and are variously affected by it.

A self-idea of this sort seems to have three principal elements: the imagination of our appearance to the other person; the imagination of his judgment of that appearance, and some sort of self-feeling, such as pride or mortification. The comparison with a looking-glass hardly suggests the second element, the imagined judgment, which is quite essential. The thing that moves us to pride or shame is not the mere mechanical reflection of ourselves, but an imputed sentiment, the imagined effect of this reflection upon another's mind. This is evident from the fact that the character and weight of that other, in whose mind we see ourselves, makes all the difference with our feeling. We are ashamed to seem evasive in the presence of a straightforward man, cowardly in the presence of a brave one, gross in the eyes of a refined one, and so on. We always imagine, and in imagining share, the judgments of the other mind. A man will boast to one person of an action—say some sharp transaction in trade—which he would be ashamed to own to another.

It should be evident that the ideas that are associated with self-feeling and form the intellectual content of the self cannot be covered by any simple description, as by saying that the body has such a part in it, friends such a part, plans so much, etc., but will vary indefinitely with particular temperaments and environments. The tendency of the self, like every aspect of personality, is expressive of far-reaching hereditary and social factors, and is not to be understood or predicted except in connection with the general life. Although special, it is in no way separate—speciality and separateness are not only different but contradictory, since the former implies connection with a whole. The object of self-feeling is affected by the general course of history, by the particular development of nations, classes, and professions, and other conditions of this sort.

★ ★ ★

The process by which self-feeling of the looking-glass sort develops in children may be followed without much difficulty. Studying the movements of others as closely as they do they soon see a connection between their own acts and changes in those movements; that is, they perceive their own influence or power over persons. The child appropriates the visible actions of his parent or nurse, over which he finds he has some control, in quite the same way as he appropriates one of his own members or a plaything, and he will try to do things with this new possession, just as he will with his hand or his rattle. A girl six months old will attempt in the most evident and deliberate manner to attract attention to herself, to set going by her actions some of those movements of other persons that she has appropriated. She has tasted the joy of being a cause, of exerting social power, and wishes more of it. She will tug at her mother's skirts, wriggle, gurgle, stretch out her arms, etc., all the time watching for the hoped-for effect. These performances often give the child, even at this age, an appearance of what is called affectation, that is she seems to be unduly preoccupied with what other people think of her. Affectation, at any age, exists when the passion to influence others seems to overbalance the established character and give it an obvious twist or pose. It is instructive to find that even Darwin was, in his childhood, capable of departing from truth for the sake of making an impression. "For instance," he says in his autobiography, "I once gathered much valuable fruit from my father's trees and hid it in the shrubbery, and then ran in breathless haste to spread the news that I had discovered a hoard of stolen fruit."[8]

The young performer soon learns to be different things to different people, showing that he begins to apprehend personality and to foresee its operation. If the mother or nurse is more tender than just she will almost certainly be "worked" by systematic weeping. It is a matter of common observation that children often behave worse with their mother than with other and less sympathetic people. Of the new persons that a child sees it is evident that some make a strong impression and awaken a desire to interest and please them, while others are indifferent or repugnant. Sometimes the reason can be perceived or guessed, sometimes not; but the fact of selective interest, admiration, prestige, is obvious before the end of the second year. By that time a child already cares much for the reflection of himself upon one personality and little for that upon another. Moreover, he soon claims intimate and tractable persons as *mine*, classes them among his other possessions, and maintains his ownership against all comers. M., at three years of age, vigorously resented R.'s claim upon their mother. The latter was "*my* mamma," whenever the point was raised.

Strong joy and grief depend upon the treatment this rudimentary social self receives. In the case of M. I noticed as early as the fourth month a "hurt" way of crying which seemed to indicate a sense of personal slight. It was quite different from the cry of pain or that of anger, but seemed about the same as the cry of fright. The slightest tone of reproof would produce it. On the other hand, if people took notice and laughed and encouraged, she was hilarious. At about fifteen months old she had become "a perfect little actress," seeming to live largely in imaginations of her effect upon other people. She constantly and obviously laid traps for attention, and looked abashed or wept at any signs of disapproval or indifference. At times it would seem as if she could not get over these repulses, but would cry long in a grieved way, refusing to be comforted. If she hit upon any little trick that made people laugh she would be sure to repeat it, laughing loudly and affectedly in imitation. She had quite a repertory of these small performances, which she would display to a sympathetic audience, or even try upon strangers. I have seen her at sixteen months, when R. refused to give her the scissors, sit down and make believe cry, putting up her under lip and snuffling, meanwhile looking up now and then to see what effect she was producing.

In such phenomena we have plainly enough, it seems to me, the germ of personal ambition of every sort. Imagination co-operating with instinctive self-feeling has already created a social "I," and this has become a principal object of interest and endeavor.

Progress from this point is chiefly in the way of a greater definiteness, fulness, and inwardness in the imagination of the other's state of mind. A little child thinks of and tries to elicit certain visible or audible phenomena, and does not go back of them; but what a grown-up person desires to produce in others is an internal, invisible condition which his own richer experience enables him to imagine, and of which expression is only the sign. Even adults, however, make no separation between what other people think and the visible expression of that thought. They imagine the whole thing at once, and their

---

[8] Life and Letters of Charles Darwin, by F. Darwin, p. 27.

idea differs from that of a child chiefly in the comparative richness and complexity of the elements that accompany and interpret the visible or audible sign. There is also a progress from the naïve to the subtle in socially self-assertive action. A child obviously and simply, at first, does things for effect. Later there is an endeavor to suppress the appearance of doing so; affection, indifference, contempt, etc., are simulated to hide the real wish to affect the self-image. It is perceived that an obvious seeking after good opinion is weak and disagreeable.

I doubt whether there are any regular stages in the development of social self-feeling and expression common to the majority of children. The sentiments of self develop by imperceptible graduations out of the crude appropriative instinct of new-born babes, and their manifestations vary indefinitely in different cases. Many children show "self-consciousness" conspicuously from the first half year; others have little appearance of it at any age. Still others pass through periods of affectation whose length and time of occurrence would probably be found to be exceedingly various. In childhood, as at all times of life, absorption in some idea other than that of the social self tends to drive "self-consciousness" out.

— · — · — · — · — · — · — · — · — · —

GEORGE HERBERT MEAD

*The Social Self**

Recognizing that the self can not appear in consciousness as an "I," that it is always an object, *i.e.*, a "me," I wish to suggest an answer to the question, What is involved in the self being an object? The first answer may be that an object involves a subject. Stated in other words, that a "me" is inconceivable without an "I." And to this reply must be made that such an "I" is a presupposition, but never a presentation of conscious experience, for the moment it is presented it has passed into the objective case, presuming, if you like, an "I" that observes—but an "I" that can disclose himself only by ceasing to be the subject for whom the object "me" exists. It is, of course, not the Hegelism of a self that becomes another to himself in which I am interested, but the nature of the self as revealed by introspection and subject to our factual analysis. This analysis does reveal, then, in a memory process an attitude of observing oneself in which both the observer and the observed appear. To be concrete, one remembers asking himself how he could undertake to do this, that, or the other, chiding himself for his shortcomings or pluming himself upon his achievements. Thus, in the redintegrated self of the moment passed, one finds both a subject and

*George H. Mead, "The Social Self," *The Journal of Philosophy, Psychology and Scientific Methods* 10 (1913): 374–380.

an object, but it is a subject that is now an object of observation, and has the same nature as the object self whom we present as in intercourse with those about us. In quite the same fashion we remember the questions, admonitions, and approvals addressed to our fellows. But the subject attitude which we instinctively take can be presented only as something experienced—as we can be conscious of our acts only through the sensory processes set up after the act has begun.

The contents of this presented subject, who thus has become an object in being presented, but which still distinguish him as the subject of the passed experience from the "me" whom he addressed, are those images which initiated the conversation and the motor sensations which accompany the expression, plus the organic sensations and the response of the whole system to the activity initiated. In a word, just those contents which go to make up the self which is distinguished from the others whom he addresses. The self appearing as "I" is the memory image of the self who acted toward himself and is the same self who acts toward other selves.

On the other hand, the stuff that goes to make up the "me" whom the "I" addresses and whom he observes, is the experience which is induced by this action of the "I." If the "I" speaks, the "me" hears. If the "I" strikes, the "me" feels the blow. Here again the "me" consciousness is of the same character as that which arises from the action of the other upon him. That is, it is only as the individual finds himself acting with reference to himself as he acts towards others, that he becomes a subject to himself rather than an object, and only as he is affected by his own social conduct in the manner in which he is affected by that of others, that he becomes an object to his own social conduct.

The differences in our memory presentations of the "I" and the "me" are those of the memory images of the initiated social conduct and those of the sensory responses thereto.

It is needless, in view of the analysis of Baldwin, of Royce and of Cooley and many others, to do more than indicate that these reactions arise earlier in our social conduct with others than in introspective self-consciousness, *i.e.*, that the infant consciously calls the attention of others before he calls his own attention by affecting himself and that he is consciously affected by others before he is conscious of being affected by himself.

The "I" of introspection is the self which enters into social relations with other selves. It is not the "I" that is implied in the fact that one presents himself as a "me." And the "me" of introspection is the same "me" that is the object of the social conduct of others. One presents himself as acting toward others—in this presentation he is presented in indirect discourse as the subject of the action and is still an object,—and the subject of this presentation can never appear immediately in conscious experience. It is the same self who is presented as observing himself, and he affects himself just in so far and only in so far as he can address himself by the means of social stimulation which affect others. The "me" whom he addresses is the "me," therefore, that is similarly affected by the social conduct of those about him.

This statement of the introspective situation, however, seems to overlook a more or less constant feature of our consciousness, and that is that running current of awareness of what we do which is distinguishable from the consciousness of the field of stimulation, whether that field be without or within. It is this "awareness" which has led many to assume that it is the nature of the self to be conscious both of subject and of object—to be subject of action toward an object world and at the same time to be directly conscious of this subject as subject,—"Thinking its non-existence along with whatever else it thinks." Now, as Professor James pointed out, this consciousness is more logically conceived of as consciousness—the thinker being an implication rather than a content, while the "me" is but a bit of object content within the stream of consciousness. However, this logical statement does not do justice to the findings of consciousness. Besides the actual stimulations and responses and the memory images of these, within which lie perforce the organic sensations and responses which make up the "me," there accompanies a large part of our conscious experience, indeed all that we call self-conscious, an inner response to what we may be doing, saying, or thinking. At the back of our heads we are a large part of the time more or less clearly conscious of our own replies to the remarks made to others, of innervations which would lead to attitudes and gestures answering our gestures and attitudes towards others.

The observer who accompanies all our self-conscious conduct is then not the actual "I" who is responsible for the conduct in *propria persona*—he is rather the response which one makes to his own conduct. The confusion of this response of ours, following upon our social stimulations of others with the implied subject of our action, is the psychological ground for the assumption that the self can be directly conscious of itself as acting and acted upon. The actual situation is this: The self acts with reference to others and is immediately conscious of the objects about it. In memory it also redintegrates the self acting as well as the others acted upon. But besides these contents, the action with reference to the others calls out responses in the individual himself—there is then another "me" criticizing, approving, and suggesting, and consciously planning, *i.e.*, the reflective self.

It is not to all our conduct toward the objective world that we thus respond. Where we are intensely preoccupied with the objective world, this accompanying awareness disappears. We have to recall the experience to become aware that we have been involved as selves, to produce the self-consciousness which is a constituent part of a large part of our experience. As I have indicated elsewhere, the mechanism for this reply to our own social stimulation of others follows as a natural result from the fact that the very sounds, gestures, especially vocal gestures, which man makes in addressing others, call out or tend to call out responses from himself. He can not hear himself speak without assuming in a measure the attitude which he would have assumed if he had been addressed in the same words by others.

The self which consciously stands over against other selves thus becomes an object, an other to himself, through the very fact that he hears himself talk, and replies. The mechanism of introspection is therefore given in the social attitude which man necessarily assumes toward himself, and the mechanism of thought, in so far as thought uses symbols which are used in social intercourse, is but an inner conversation.

Now it is just this combination of the remembered self which acts and exists over against other selves with the inner response to his action which is essential to the self-conscious ego—the self in the full meaning of the term—although neither phase of self-consciousness, in so far as it appears as an object of our experience, is a subject.

It is also to be noted that this response to the social conduct of the self may be in the rôle of another—we present his arguments in imagination and do it with his intonations and gestures and even perhaps with his facial expression. In this way we play the rôles of all our group; indeed, it is only in so far as we do this that they become part of our social environment—to be aware of another self as a self implies that we have played his rôle or that of another with whose type we identify him for purposes of intercourse. The inner response to our reaction to others is therefore as varied as is our social environment. Not that we assume the rôles of others toward ourselves because we are subject to a mere imitative instinct, but because in responding to ourselves we are in the nature of the case taking the attitude of another than the self that is directly acting, and into this reaction there naturally flows the memory images of the responses of those about us, the memory images of the responses of others which were in answer to like actions. Thus the child can think about his conduct as good or bad only as he reacts to his own acts in the remembered words of his parents. Until this process has been developed into the abstract process of thought, self-consciousness remains dramatic, and the self which is a fusion of the remembered actor and this accompanying chorus is somewhat loosely organized and very clearly social. Later the inner stage changes into the forum and workshop of thought. The features and intonations of the *dramatis personae* fade out and the emphasis falls upon the meaning of the inner speech, the imagery becomes merely the barely necessary cues. But the mechanism remains social, and at any moment the process may become personal.

It is fair to say that the modern western world has lately done much of its thinking in the from of the novel, while earlier the drama was a more effective but equally social mechanism of self-consciousness. And, in passing, I may refer to that need of filling out the bare spokesman of abstract thought, which even the most abstruse thinker feels, in seeking his audience. The import of this for religious self-consciousness is obvious.

There is one further implication of this nature of the self to which I wish to call attention. It is the manner of its reconstruction. I wish especially to refer to it, because the point is of importance in the psychology of ethics.

As a mere organization of habit the self is not self-conscious. It is this self which we refer to as character. When, however, an essential problem appears, there is some disintegration in this organization, and different tendencies appear in reflective thought as different voices in conflict with each other. In a sense the old self has disintegrated, and out of the moral process a new self arises. The specific question I wish to ask is whether the new self appears together with the new object or end. There is of course a reciprocal relation between the self and its object, the one implies the other and the interests and evaluations of the self answer exactly to the content and values of the object. On the other hand, the consciousness of the new object, its values and meaning, seems to come earlier to consciousness than the new self that answers to the new object.

The man who has come to realize a new human value is more immediately aware of the new object in his conduct than of himself and his manner of reaction to it. This is due to the fact to which reference has already been made, that direct attention goes first to the object. When the self becomes an object, it appears in memory, and the attitude which it implies has already been taken. In fact, to distract attention from the object to the self implies just that lack of objectivity which we criticize not only in the moral agent, but in the scientist.

Assuming as I do the essentially social character of the ethical end, we find in moral reflection a conflict in which certain values find a spokesman in the old self or a dominant part of the old self, while other values answering to other tendencies and impulses arise in opposition and find other spokesmen to present their cases. To leave the field to the values represented by the old self is exactly what we term selfishness. The justification for the term is found in the habitual character of conduct with reference to these values. Attention is not claimed by the object and shifts to the subjective field where the affective responses are identified with the old self. The result is that we state the other conflicting ends in subjective terms of other selves and the moral problem seems to take on the form of the sacrifice either of the self or of the others.

Where, however, the problem is objectively considered, although the conflict is a social one, it should not resolve itself into a struggle between selves, but into such a reconstruction of the situation that different and enlarged and more adequate personalities may emerge. Attention should be centered on the objective social field.

In the reflective analysis, the old self should enter upon the same terms with the selves whose rôles are assumed, and the test of the reconstruction is found in the fact that all the personal interests are adequately recognized in a new social situation. The new self that answers to this new situation can appear in consciousness only after this new situation has been realized and accepted. The new self can not enter into the field as the determining factor because he is consciously present only after the new end has been formulated and accepted. The old self may enter only as an element over against the other personal interests involved. If he is the dominant factor it must be in defiance of the other selves whose interests are at stake. As the old self he is defined by his conflict with the others that assert themselves in his reflective analysis.

Solution is reached by the construction of a new world harmonizing the conflicting interests into which enters the new self.

The process is in its logic identical with the abandonment of the old theory with which the scientist has identified himself, his refusal to grant this old attitude any further weight than may be given to the other conflicting observations and hypotheses. Only when a successful hypothesis, which overcomes the conflicts, has been formulated and accepted, may the scientist again identify himself with this hypothesis as his own, and maintain it *contra mundum.* He may not state the scientific problem and solution in terms of his old personality. He may name his new hypothesis after himself and realize his enlarged scientific personality in its triumph.

The fundamental difference between the scientific and moral solution of a problem lies in the fact that the moral problem deals with concrete personal interests, in which the whole self is reconstructed in its relation to the other selves whose relations are essential to its personality.

The growth of the self arises out of a partial disintegration,—the appearance of the different interests in the forum of reflection, the reconstruction of the social world, and the consequent appearance of the new self that answers to the new object.

— · — · — · — · — · — · — · — · — · — · —

NORMAN TRIPLETT

*First Experiment in Social Psychology: Pacemaking and Competition**

DESCRIPTION OF APPARATUS

The apparatus for this study consisted of two fishing reels whose cranks turned in circles of one and three-fourths inches diameter. These were arranged on a Y shaped frame work clamped to the top of a heavy table, as shown in the cut. The sides of this frame work were spread sufficiently far apart to permit of two persons turning side by side. Bands of twisted silk cord ran over the well lacquered axes of the reels and were supported at C and D, two meters distant, by two small pulleys. The records were taken from the course A D. The other course B C being used merely for pacing or competition purposes. The wheel on the side from which the records were taken communicated the movement made to a recorder, the stylus of which traced a curve on the drum of a kymograph. The direction of this curve corresponded to the rate of turning, as the greater the speed the shorter and straighter the resulting line.

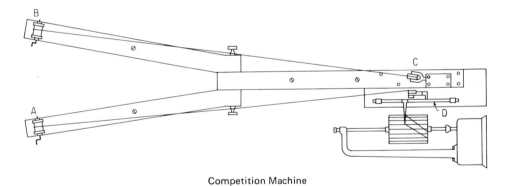

Competition Machine

METHOD OF CONDUCTING THE EXPERIMENT

A subject taking the experiment was required to practice turning the reel until he had become accustomed to the machine. After a short period of rest the different trials were made with five-minute intervals between to obviate the possible effects of fatigue.

A trial consisted in turning the reel at the highest rate of speed until a small flag sewed to the silk band had made four circuits of the four-meter course. The time of the trial was taken by means of a stop-watch. The direction of the curves made on the drum likewise furnished graphic indications of the difference in time made between trials.

*Norman Triplett, "The Dynamogenic Factors in Pacemaking and Competition," *American Journal of Psychology* 9 (1897): 507–533. This selection excerpted from pp. 518–527, 532–533.

LIMITS OF ERROR

Frequent trials of the machinery showed very small errors. In each regular trial the flag travelled 16 meters. For ten test trials the average number of turns of the reel necessary to send it over this course was found to be 149.87, with a mean variation of .15, showing that the silk did not slip to any appreciable extent. If 40 seconds be taken as the average time of a trial (which is not far wrong), .15 of a turn will be made in .04 second.

Care was also exercised to have the kymograph maintain, so far as possible, a uniform rate of turning. When fully wound up it would run for nearly three hours. The actual running time in taking the six trials of a subject was about 4 minutes, or 40 seconds per trial. In testing, the drum was rotated during 4 minutes. The time necessary to repeat this amount of rotation was found, by trials, to be 4 minutes and 3 seconds, thus showing a retardation in each trial of about one-eightieth of the former trial as shown on the drum. The direct time of trials was taken with a stop-watch. It is from records thus taken that the tables given are composed. The drum cruves, however, are important as giving a graphic representation of whatever changes occurred during the progress of the trial. The stylus, responding immediately to every change in rate of turning, gives clearly: indications of the force of competition, of the effects of adverse stimulation, fatigue, and other phenomena. The tendency of the retardation of the drum would be to diminish all these effects by one-eightieth—an amount not appreciable to the eye.

STATEMENT OF RESULTS

In the course of the work the records of nearly 225 persons of all ages were taken. However, all the tables given below, and all statements made, unless otherwise specified, are based on the records of 40 children taken in the following manner: After the usual preliminaries of practice, six trials were made by each of 20 subjects in this order: first a trial alone, followed by a trial in competition, then another alone, and thus alternating through the six efforts, giving three trials alone and three in competition. Six trials were taken by 20 other children of about the same age, the order of trials in this case being the first trial alone, second alone, third a competition trial, fourth alone, fifth a competition, and sixth alone.

By this scheme, a trial of either sort, after the first one, by either of the two groups, always corresponds to a different trial by the opposite group. Further, when the subjects of the two groups come to their fourth and sixth trials, an equal amount of practice has been gained by an equal number of trials of the same kind. This fact should be remembered in any observation of the time made in trials by any group.

During the taking of the records, and afterwards in working them over, it was seen that all cases would fall into two classes:

First. Those stimulated—

1. to make faster time in competition trials,
2. in such a way as to inhibit motion.

Second. The small number who seemed little affected by the race.

The three tables which follow are made up from the records of the 40 subjects mentioned. The classification was in general determined by the time record as taken by the watch.

The first table gives the records of 20 subjects who, on the whole, were stimulated positively. The second table contains 10 records of subjects who were overstimulated. The third table shows the time of 10 subjects who give slight evidence of being stimulated.

The probable error used in the tables is that for a single observation:

$$r = .6745 - \sqrt{\frac{\Sigma v2}{n - 1}}$$

Its magnitude is large from the nature of the case. To ascertain how large this should properly be, the individual differences of the subjects of Group A in Table I were eliminated in the following manner: The average of the six trials made by each subject was taken as most fairly representing him. With this as a basis the six trials were reduced to percentages—thus doing away with peculiarities due to age and disposition. By this means the probable errors of this group for the six trials in order were 2.57, 1.43, 1.81, 2.24, 1.11, 1.55. A similar reduction should be made in the probable error of all the tables.

In the tables, A represents a trial alone, C a trial in competition.

TABLE I. SUBJECTS STIMULATED POSITIVELY

Group A

	Age	A	C	A	C	A	C
Violet F.	10	54.4	42.6	45.2	41.	42.	46.
Anna P.	9	67.	57	55.4	50.4	49.	44.8
Willie H.	12	37.8	38.8	43.	39.	37.2	33.4
Bessie V.	11	46.2	41.	39.	30.2	33.6	32.4
Howard C.	11	42.	36.4	39.	41.	37.8	34.
Mary M.	11	48.	44.8	52.	44.6	43.8	40.
Lois P.	11	53.	45.6	44.	40.	40.6	35.8
Inez K.	13	37.	35.	35.8	34.	34.	32.6
Harvey L.	9	49.	42.6	39.6	37.6	36.	35.
Lora F.	11	40.4	35.	33.	35.	30.2	29.
Average	11	47.48	41.88	42.6	39.28	38.42	36.3
P. E.		6.18	4.45	4.68	3.83	3.74	3.74
Gains			5.6	.72	3.32	.86	2.12

Group B

	Age	A	A	C	A	C	A
Stephen M.	13	51.2	50.	43.	41.8	39.8	41.2*
Mary W.	13	56.	53.	45.8	49.4	45.	43.*
Bertha A.	10	56.2	49.	48.	46.8	41.4	44.4
Clara L.	8	52.	44.	46.	45.6	44.	45.2
Helen M.	10	45.	45.6	35.8	46.2	40.	40.
Gracie W.	12	56.6	50.	42.8	39.	40.2	41.4
Dona R.	15	34.	37.2	36.	41.4	37.	32.8
Pearl C.	13	43.	43.	40.	40.6	33.8	35.
Clyde G.	13	36.	35.	32.4	33.	31.	35.
Lucile W.	10	52.	50.	43.	44.	38.2	40.2
Average	11.7	48.2	45.68	41.2	42.78	39.	39.82
P. E.		5.6	4.	3.42	3.17	2.89	2.84
Gains			2.52	4.48	1.58	3.78	.82

*Left-handed.

TABLE II. SUBJECTS STIMULATED ADVERSELY

Group A

	Age	A	C	A	C	A	C
Jack R.	9	44.2	44.	41.8	48.	44.2	41.
Helen F.	9	44.	51.	43.8	44.	43.	41.2
Emma P.	11	38.4	42.	37.	39.6	36.6	32.
Warner J.	11	41.6	43.6	43.4	43.	40.	38.
Genevieve M.	12	36.	36.	32.6	32.8	31.2	34.8
Average	10.4	40.84	43.32	39.72	41.48	39.	37.4
P. E.		2.41	3.57	3.25	3.85	3.55	2.52

Group B

	Age	A	A	C	A	C	A
Hazel M.	11	38.	35.8	38.2	37.2	35.	42.
George B.	12	39.2	36.	37.6	34.2	36.	33.8
Mary B.	11	50.	46.	43.4	42.	48.	36.8
Carlisle B.	14	37.	35.4	35.	33.4	36.4	31.4
Eddie H.	11	31.2	29.2	27.6	27.	26.8	28.8
Average	11.8	39.08	36.48	36.36	34.76	34.4	34.56
P. E.		4.61	4.07	3.89	3.71	5.33	3.45

TABLE III. SUBJECTS LITTLE AFFECTED
BY COMPETITION

Group A

	Age	A	C	A	C	A	C
Albert P.	13	29.	28.	27.	29.	27.	28.6
Milfred V.	17	36.4	29.	29.4	30.2	30.2	32.2
Harry V.	12	32.	32.	32.6	32.6	32.6	31.6
Robt. H.	12	31.4	31.4	32.2	35.4	35.	32.4
John T.	11	30.2	30.8	32.8	30.6	32.8	31.8
Average	13	31.8	30.24	30.8	31.56	31.5	31.3
P. E.		1.9	1.13	1.71	1.7	2.06	1.05

Group B

	Age	A	A	C	A	C	A
Lela T.	10	45.	37.4	36.8	36.	37.2	38.
Lura L.	11	42.	39.	38.	37.	37.	38.
Mollie A.	13	38.	30.	28.	30.	30.2	29.6
Anna F.	11	35.	31.8	32.4	30.	32.	30.4
Ora R.	14	37.2	30.	29.	27.8	28.4	26.8
Average	11.8	39.44	33.64	32.84	32.16	32.96	32.16
P. E.		3.11	2.88	3.03	2.75	2.69	3.71

The 20 subjects given in Group A and Group B, of Table I, in nearly all cases make marked reductions in the competition trials. The averages show large gains in these trials and small gains or even losses for the succeeding trials alone. The second trial for Group A is a competition, for Group B a trial alone. The gain between the first and second trials of the first group is 5.6 seconds, between the first and second trials of the second group, 2.52 seconds. The latter represents the practice effect—always greatest in the first trials, the former the element of competition plus the practice. The third trial in Group A—a trial alone—is .72 seconds slower than the preceding race trial. The third trial in Group B—a competition—is 4.48 seconds faster than the preceding trial alone. The fourth trials in these two groups are on an equality, as regards practice, from an equal number of trials of the same kind. In the first case the gain over the preceding trial is 3.32 seconds. In the latter there is a loss of 1.58 seconds from the time of the preceding competition trial. In like manner there is an equality of conditions in regard to the sixth trial of these groups, and again the effect of competition plainly appears, the competition trial gaining 2.12 seconds, and the trial alone losing .82 seconds with respect to the preceding trial. These are decided differences. Curve No. 1 in Chart II is a graphical representation of them.

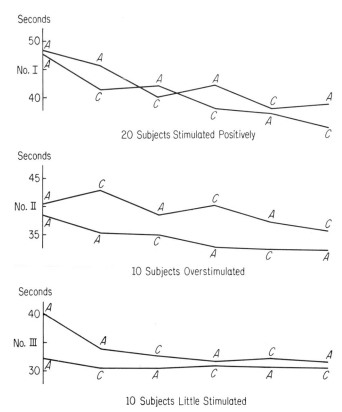

Chart II. Solid line represents Group *A*; dotted line represents Group *B*.

The 10 subjects whose records are given in Table II are of interest. With them stimulation brought a loss of control. In one or more of the competition trials of each subject in this group the time is very much slower than that made in the preceding trial alone. Most frequently this is true of the first trial in competition, but with some was characteristic of every race. In all, 14 of the 25 races run by this group were equal or slower than the preceding trial alone. This seems to be brought about in large measure by the mental attitude of the subject. An intense desire to win, for instance, often resulting in over-stimulation. Accompanying phenomena were labored breathing, flushed faces and a stiffening or contraction of the muscles of the arm. A number of young children of from 5 to 9 years, not included in our group of 40, exhibited the phenomena most strikingly, the rigidity of the arm preventing free movement and in some cases resulting in an almost total inhibition of movement. The effort to continue turning in these cases was by a swaying of the whole body.

This seems a most interesting fact and confirmatory of the probable order of development of the muscles as given by Dr. Hall and others. In the case of those sufficiently developed to have the fast forearm movement, fatigue or overstimulation seemed to bring a recurrence to the whole arm and shoulder movement of early childhood, and if the fatigue or excitement was sufficiently intense, to the whole body movement, while younger children easily fell into the swaying movement when affected by either of the causes named.

It reminds one of the way in which fatigue of a small muscle used in ergographic work, will cause the subject to attempt to draw on his larger muscles, or, of the man who moves to the city and acquires the upright carriage and springing step of the city-bred man, who, when greatly fatigued, insensibly falls into the old "clodhopper" gait. This tendency to revert to earlier movements and also old manners of speech, as Höpfner has shown in his "Fatigue of School Children," is common, when, for any reason, the centers of control are interfered with. It may be said, therefore, that in the work under consideration the chief difference between this group and the large group in Table I, was a difference in control; the stimulation inhibiting the proper function of the motor centers in the one case, and reinforcing it in the other. This, at least, seemed apparent from the characteristics exhibited by the two classes. Observation of the subjects of this class under trial, and careful scrutiny of their graphic records, show how decided gains were sometimes lost by the subject "going to pieces" at the critical point of the race, not being able to endure the nervous strain. Yet there exists no sharp line of division between subjects stimulated to make faster time and those affected in the opposite way. In some instances the nervous excitement acted adversely in every race trial, while in others, a gain in control, enabled the subject to make a material reduction in the last competition. A. B., one of three adults affected adversely, is an athletic young man, a fine tennis and hand-ball player, and known to be stimulated in contests of these kinds. It was noticed that in his competition trials time was lost because of his attempt to take advantage of the larger muscles of the arm and shoulder. After many trials and injunctions to avoid the movement he gained sufficient control to enable him to reduce the time in the competitions.

A. V., an adult of nervous organization, went half through his race with a great gain over his trial alone, but seeing his antagonist pushing his closely, broke down and lost the most of the gain made in the first half. The time of the trial alone was 38.6 seconds, that of the competition was 37.2 seconds. A comparison of the time in which the halves of the trials were made was computed in the following way: On the ordinate of the graph is measured the distance the stylus travels across the drum during 150 turns of the reel—the number in a trial. The distance on the abscissa between the ordinates running through the ends of the curve of any trial gives the time of the trial.

Parallel abscissas were drawn at the extremities of the curves, and a third one-half way between them. Half of the turns made in a trial were thus on each side of this middle line, and the times in which these turns were made were proportional to the segments of this line made by the curve intersecting it. By this means it was found that A. V. made the first 75 turns in his competition trial in 15 seconds, the second half in 22.2 seconds. By the same means, each half of the preceding trial alone was 19.3 seconds—an exception to the rule that the last half is slower because of fatigue.

Other curves when worked out in this way gave similar results. The time record, therefore, it must be seen, is not always a true index to the amount of stimulation present. Had the trials consisted of but half as many turns the effect of competition as it appears in the tables would have been shown much more constantly. Table II would have been a smaller group if indeed any necessity existed for retaining it.

A comparison of the time made by the different groups shows that the subjects of Table I are much slower than those of Table II, and that a still greater difference exists between this group and the subjects found in Table III. It may be said that they are slower because of greater sluggishness of disposition, and that the reductions made are largely a result of the subjects warming up. This, indeed, may be a part of the cause for it, but as the larger reductions coincide with the competition trials this cannot be held to completely account for it. A glance over the individual records discovers some facts which furnish a plausible partial explanation, when taken in connection with the following fact. The age at which children acquire control of the wrist movements, a large factor in turning the reel with speed, was found to be about 11 years in general, although a few of 9 and 10 years had this power. Now, of the 20 subjects composing Table I, 7 are 10 years of age or younger, while two others, age 13, are left-handed and being compelled to use the right hand are slow in consequence. So, here are 9 subjects, a number nearly equal to the group in Table II or Table III, who had a reason for being slow. Were these omitted from the count, the time of the initial trial would be found not to vary materially from that of Table II.

Besides the lack of muscular development of the younger subjects mentioned above, many of the subjects of Table I seemed not to have proper ideals of speed. The desire to beat, if it did nothing else, brought them to a sense of what was possible for them. The arousal of their competitive instincts and the idea of a faster movement, perhaps, in the contestant, induced greater concentration of energy.

The subjects in Table III, are a small group who seemed very little affected by competition. They made very fast time, but they are older than the average; their muscular control was good, and they had the forearm movements. Practice gains while somewhat apparent at first in some cases, are, as shown by curve No. 3 of the chart, on the whole, less in amount. Their drum records show fewer fluctuations and irregularities, and less pronounced fatigue curves at the end.

There seems to be a striking analogy between these subjects and those racing men who are fast without a pace, but can do little or no better in a paced or competition race.

★ ★ ★

EFFECT OF A HIGHER RATE ON COUNTING

An experiment on vocalization was made wherein a higher rate was suggested to the subject.

Ten subjects took the work described below on six successive days. Each was required to count aloud from 1 to 20 and repeat, as rapidly as articulation permitted, for 5 seconds. Three trials were made. The operator now counted at a faster rate and asked the subject to follow that rate. Three trials of this kind were made. This may be called Programme A.

Programme B differed from this merely in the one particular that the operator did no counting, but the three preliminary trials alone were followed instead by three similar trials alone—the intervals between trials, however, remaining the same.

Five subjects began with Programme A and five with Programme B, alternating each day, so that in the course of the six days each person had three experiences with each programme. The average sum counted by each subject during the series of trials is given below. Dividing by nine will give the average number counted in a single trial of that kind.

	Programme A			Programme B		
Cases	No. Alone	After a Higher Rate is Given	Gain	No. Alone.	Alone, no Rate Given	Gain
10	288.4	307.6	19.2	287.	288.5	1.5

The difference between the averages of the first two columns, 19.2, is the average gain of the ten subjects after they have had given them the idea of a faster rate of counting. Under this programme each individual makes a gain, under the other, where no higher rate is given, seven make smaller gains, three lose, and the average gain is but 1.5.

The principle of ideomotor action has wide application in human life. In the cases cited the observance of motion in another became a stimulus to greater effort. It may, however, have the opposite effect. A correspondence of rhythm of movement seems necessary to make it of aid. Two boys jumping together, or one following immediately at the sight of the other's jump, will not cover the distance possible in jumping alone, because the swaying of the body, and swinging of the arms, not being synchronous or rhythmic become a distraction. So one soon becomes fatigued when walking with a person out of step.

CONCLUDING STATEMENT

From the above facts regarding the laboratory races we infer that the bodily presence of another contestant participating simultaneously in the race serves to liberate latent energy not ordinarily available. This inference is further justified by the difference in time between the paced competition races and the paced races against time, amounting to an average of 5.15 seconds per mile up to 25 miles. The factors of shelter from the wind, encouragement, brain worry, hypnotic suggestion, and automatic movement, are common to both, while the competitors participate simultaneously in person only in the first.

In the next place the sight of the movements of the pacemakers or leading competitors, and the idea of higher speed, furnished by this or some other means, are probably in themselves dynamogenic factors of some consequence.

2 · SOCIAL PSYCHOLOGICAL BEHAVIOR OF ANIMALS

H. HEDIGER

*Social Dominance**

THE PREDATOR-PREY RELATIONSHIP

The relation of animal to animal is of fundamental importance for solving the problem of keeping wild animals; especially as man himself often plays the part of predator, in so far as he may be of danger to other animals, even to the largest and to those most capable of self-defence. Man is the universal enemy of nearly all animals in the free state, and as this is so we should not speak of the predator-prey, but of the enemy-prey relationship. The enemy may thus be either man or a beast of prey. The animal runs away from its enemy, and from man too, in whom it sees a dangerous enemy in the form of a superior beast of prey. Man is, as it were, the focus of the animal's escape reaction.

The escape reaction is the animal's normal response to an enemy's approach, and all behaviour mechanism, including crouching down, is aimed at avoiding the enemy. The author has shown in detail elsewhere (1934), (1937), that in the presence of an enemy, an animal or bird does not simply run or fly away; the escape reaction is subject to definite laws, quantitatively and qualitatively. These facts, indispensable for understanding the following explanation, may be summed up like this: on suddenly encountering an enemy, the animal shows a characteristic escape reaction, specific for sex, age, enemy, and surroundings, as soon as the enemy approaches within a definite distance (the flight distance). The escape reaction may perhaps have the characteristics of an 'Appetenz relationship' in Lorenz's sense, for M. Holzapfel ((1940) 278) thinks it restores the animal to its relative state of rest, disturbed by the enemy. This state of rest can only be restored when enemy and victim are once more at a distance greater than the animal's specific flight distance. The presence of an enemy within that distance produces a condition of violent disturbance.

In flight, the animal is urged by the impulse to escape from its enemy. If it is

*From *Wild Animals in Captivity* by H. Hediger, Dover Publications, Inc., New York, 1964, pp. 19–26. Reprinted through permission of the publisher.

followed and gradually overtaken by the enemy, the animal's flight reaction suddenly changes when the enemy comes within the animal's defence distance. The attack resulting from this change, always with the character of self defence (emergency), is called the defence reaction, and is characteristic for each species. Finally, it may be that owing to the presence of an enemy the animal wants to escape, but circumstances may prevent it; for instance, it may find itself cornered, or feel that it is. In such a situation it shows (again specifically) critical reaction the moment its enemy reaches the critical distance. This critical reaction consists of an attack, with emergency characteristics. Flight, defence, and critical distances are specific, within certain limits, and may be accurately measured, often within inches.

By far the chief pre-occupation of wild animals at liberty is finding safety i.e. perpetual safety from enemies, and avoiding enemies. The be-all and end-all of its existence is flight. Hunger and love occupy only a secondary place, since the satisfaction of both physical and sexual wants can be postponed while flight from the approach of a dangerous enemy cannot. In freedom, an animal subordinates everything to flight; that is the prime duty of an individual, for its own preservation, and for that of the race.

The relationship between prey and predator is governed by certain laws in two respects:

1. In the characteristic behaviour of the prey towards its enemy (the predator) and
2. In the behaviour of the predator towards its prey.

The existence of these laws has been mentioned elsewhere (H. Hediger ((1941) 38). Here it will only be necessary to emphasize that feeding, just like flight, is controlled by certain strictly observed rules. This is true of carnivores and herbivores, and does not simply consist in aimlessly capturing and devouring prey or swallowing at random masses of greenstuff. The intake of food in carnivores, herbivores and omnivores (flesh eaters, plant eaters and animals of mixed diet) depends on quality, quantity and time, and often also on space. It is connected with definite localities and territories (space-time pattern).

As regards quality of food, R. Hesse ((1924) 15) distinguishes between euryphagous animals i.e. those that eat many different foods, or even anything edible, and stenophagous animals i.e. those that have a specialized diet. Generally speaking, we tend to think that a wild animal's food is more restricted than it actually is. In other words, most animals are much more euryphagous than we suppose. Thus among the carnivores proper, purely flesh eaters are rare; so are purely plant or even grass eaters among ungulates, or purely seed eaters among birds. Only a few examples need be quoted. According to W. Schoenichen ((1938) 38), the fox, apart from his own already highly varied meat diet, eats fish and crabs, worms, great green grasshoppers, and other insects, besides fruit and berries. On the other hand, F. F. Darling ((1937) 7) observed in the field that red deer ate frogs, thus becoming temporarily carnivorous. Even animals that look least like rodents turn vegetarian in exceptional cases. C. R. Carpenter ((1934) 37) recorded the plants eaten by free roaming howler monkeys (*Alouatta palliata*) between January and May 1932. He had each plant identified. In all there were fifty six different species belonging to twenty nine genera! Moreover this list was far from complete. A. Jacobi ((1931) 222) mentions twenty two different species of flowering plants chosen by Scandinavian reindeer for their diet, although they have always been regarded as exclusively lichen-feeders.

A. Leopold ((1939) 254) is right in talking of the tremendous variety of foods eaten by most game species. Game eat a greater variety of species than humans do, the lack of refrigerators to the contrary notwithstanding. The author quotes a record of 1,659 investigations of stomach contents, according to which Bobwhite quails ate 927 different kinds of food. In Pennsylvania, deer were observed to browse on 113 shrubs, rabbits (cottontails) on seventy one *etc.* Th. Hubback (1939) quotes a detailed list of the food plants of the Sumatra rhinoceros, and H. Grote ((1943) 13) mentions the varied diet of the capercailzie. A. Leopold ((1939) 259) distinguishes between the following four classes among free wild animals:

Preferred food or delicacies
Staple foods
Emergency foods, and
Roughage.

True monophagous animals, eating only one type of food are, contrary to belief, extraordinarily rare. Even specialized fish or egg eaters have a far wider range in their choice of food than would be supposed from the rigid classification found in textbooks. Among flesh and plant eaters, monotony of diet in the everyday meaning of the term is only to be found in books and zoological gardens. Too strong a warning cannot be given against over schematized classification of food, based on tooth structure and theoretically coordinated diet.

It is scarcely necessary to add that food consumption is also determined quantitatively; fundamentally, the danger of overfeeding is very remote in the natural state. The quantity of food taken at a meal is directly related to whether the animal can be classified as a continuous or an occasional feeder. Continuous feeders take relatively small amounts of food; occasional feeders on the other hand *e.g.* snakes, take large amounts at a time. Permanent feeders in the strictest sense of the word, with the possible exception of filter feeders *e.g.* shellfish and parasites, probably do not exist, since as a rule feeding activity is definitely regulated. Its rhythm of activity and repose causes an animal to take its meals during the day, in the night, or at twilight. Time of day is intrinsically less important here than suitable light intensity. Animals that shun the light are forced to feed in the dark just as much as a diurnal bird of prey, for example, is compelled to seek its food only when the light is sufficient for its purpose. Feeding may also depend on internal rhythms: in the case of most snakes it is interrupted by the various phases of skincasting; in the case of mammals, by hibernation, rutting *etc* in the case of birds (penguins) by moult. Only one requisite for seeking or eating food is usually necessary. The animal must be put in the food situation, to borrow a phrase from the Umweltbiologists.

Internal changes are usually the cause of this stimulus, though in the case of some animals *e.g.* the European salmon, it can also be induced externally. By dangling a tempting bait in front of it, a salmon can be persuaded to snap at it, even when it is not able to swallow or digest it. The feeding of a ruminant presents a special case, divided so to speak, into a temporary and a final phase, both resulting in situations completely different in time and place. Rapid snatching of food on exposed grassland is followed by a leisurely chewing of the cud in the comparative quiet of the resting ground. In chewing the cud, the number of movements made in masticating each mass of food sent up from the paunch into the mouth is specific *i.e.* characteristic for each separate species; it may be thirty in certain Cervidae (red deer), or in some Bovidae (species of cattle) over seventy. Likewise the rhythmic side-to-side movement of the lower jaw during rumination is often characteristic of each species. Owing to anisognathia (unequal width of upper and lower jaws) only half the lower jaw can come into contact with the corresponding half of the upper jaw during simple chewing. Whilst some species like the camels regularly alternate between both sides of the lower jaws (pattern—left, right, l, r, l, r, l, r), others like most antelopes chew with the left half of the lower jaw for a time, and then change to the right half (pattern l, l, l, l,—r, r, r, r). The way in which food is offered is of great importance. Bats will not take any prey that clings to a flat support; lizards ignore motionless prey. Not all ungulates are ground-feeders; giraffes and moose, for instance, find their food at a certain height above ground level; many birds cannot take hanging food, and so on.

BIOLOGICAL RANK

In the section on the mosaic overlapping territories the many different ways that species living in freedom are bound to be interconnected were pointed out. One of the most important kinds of connection is obviously the enemy-prey relationship. In addition to the above, one other important type of relationship must be mentioned here, that of biological rank. It has been more fully outlined elsewhere (H. Hediger (1940)). Here it will simply be distinguished from the enemy-prey relationship, from which it differs fundamentally. Biological rank means a hierarchy, based upon definite rules, among those species and genera which closely resemble each other in their physical make-up (*e.g.* ruminants, monkeys, cats, and bears), with areas and biotopes overlapping. To some extent it implies a state of biological competition. Generally, these competitors try to avoid each other; the biologically inferior species as a rule gets out of the way of its superior, to avoid a fight. When competitors do come face to face, the superior has the advantage in every respect over the inferior, especially in obtaining food, in freedom of movement, in choice of resting and sleeping places *etc.* The following hierarchies may be used for illustration:

ibex—chamois—roe deer
or mountain eagle—raven-jackdaw
or grizzly bear—American black bear
or gorilla—chimpanzee

etc. The freedom of the subordinate species is in every way greatly restricted by this relationship; it must always yield to the superior and give precedence to it. Usually it is clear from the outset which species is the superior, and no fighting, real or pretence, is necessary to prove it. On the other hand, there are cases among predatory animals *e.g.* walrus-seal, in which it is difficult to distinguish this from an enemy-prey relationship; in certain circumstances the walrus overpowers and devours its biologically inferior relative, if the latter allows itself to be captured. The seal is not the normal prey of the walrus, and is only taken in exceptional circumstances.

SOCIAL RANK

Just as the species as a whole can form part of a strict biological hierarchy, a single individual can take its place in a social hierarchy among the animals with which it lives. Only in rare cases does a society of related animals form either an amorphous (unorganized) group, or a band of individuals equal among themselves. Far oftener a regular order of precedence is established, of linear or complex type. There is a comprehensive literature on this. The premier place (α-position), which often involves all kinds of advantages for the animal concerned, is occasionally linked with a particular sex in a single species. The second place is called the β-position, the third, γ-position and so on; the lowest individual in the social hierarchy is the ω-individual. The premier place among most monkeys, the American bison, wild horses, guanacos, pheasants, pigeons *etc* is always occupied by a male. Among African elephants, kiangs, chamois, ibex, red deer, sparrows *etc* on the other hand, always by a female. Further, the role of leader and of guide in individual species (*e.g.* the chamois and capuchin monkeys) may fall to one and the same animal, or (as in the moose) may be taken by two individuals. In a chamois herd on the move the α-female invariably leads; the α-elk never goes first but lets the so-called secondary stags, socially inferior to him, do so. Among the elephants, furthermore, male individuals ranking high socially act as a rearguard to the moving herd. In many animals specific marching order is observed. The criterion for position on the social ladder is not as a rule physical strength, but usually certain psychological characteristics. This factor is seen in the organization of a shoal of fish, and is of considerable significance in the animal-man relationship.

The status of the individual in the social order is of great importance for its whole existence. A definite ceremonial is assigned to each grade in intercourse with its fellows; any infringement of this ceremonial means rebuke or fighting. Recently R. Schenkel (1947) has given a vivid description of the wolf. Field workers have repeatedly had to emphasize that the popular conception of 'golden freedom' is purely a product of the human imagination, and is certainly not a biological fact. Neither the fish in its shoal nor the monkey in its troop is free as an individual. C. R. Carpenter significantly remarks ((1942) 181) that the monkey or ape in its natural group in the tropical forest has its freedom of movement strictly limited by the structure of its group. The behavior-ceremonial is waived only in the case of very young animals, not yet socially important; these may be permitted almost any liberties towards the adults, but as they grow older they often suffer really harsh treatment. F. Goethe ((1937) 42) observed that immature herring gulls suffered when in the company of their elders. He remarks that these young gulls show unmistakable complexes in the presence of elder members of their species, so hard has been the school in which they have learned how to behave. He has often watched young gulls take fright and fly off when a nearby old gull moved just to preen itself, with no thought at all for the immature gulls. According to A. Pratt ((1937) 23), mother koalas when necessary give their own growing cubs cuffs on the posterior with their monkey-like hands. According to J. Beninde ((1937) 200), the red-deer calf's obedience is exacted if need be by hard and energetic kicks from the forelegs. Socially high ranking stags in male herds usually drive lesser rankers before them, as a safety measure so to speak. In so doing, they occasionally use their antlers if the weaker stags move on too slowly (*ibid* 203). The vigour with which rutting stags fight for their social position (and at the same time for the conquest of a territory and of the females included in it) is too familiar to mention. The stag is simply the popular example of similar fights of social significance among antelopes, elephants, primates and carnivores.

Socially conditioned fighting can also become violent among poikilothermous (cold-blooded) vertebrates; here it clearly shows the aggravating effects of confined space. Thus R. Mertens ((1940) 192) found continental lizards not so socially pugnacious as insular types, living together in more crowded conditions. Greater living density, where the animals have less room to spread out, increases social quarrels to the extent of open anti-social behaviour. This fact, through its connection with confinement of space, is of great importance for life in captivity. Every reptile lover knows from experience that it is quite impossible with most of the *Anolis* species to keep two or more healthy males in a terrarium, without the lizards fighting and wounding each other more or less severely (*ibid* 189). Elsewhere Mertens states that the intolerance of lizards, obviously under the influence of confined space on islands, yet in complete freedom, is striking, and often develops into cannibalism. This anti-social effect of confinement, with increased pugnacity, has also been mentioned by F. F. Darling ((1937) 35) in his comparison of red deer living in freedom and in parks. He comes to the conclusion that overcrowding, or confined space, leads to anti-social behaviour.

MATING PATTERN AND REPRODUCTION CEREMONIAL

Among our earliest knowledge of animal sociology is the fact that animals show the most varied types of mating, from promiscuity to lifelong monogamy. Far less attention has been paid to the fact that mating or pairing is normally associated with a definite ceremonial, often so strict that it cannot take place if the appropriate ceremonial is in any way disturbed. The ceremonial sometimes consists of a series of complicated symbolic actions, which may require special objects, indispensable to their performance. Thus, as a necessary adjunct for mating, certain terns (*Sterna*) require a fish, with which the female is symbolically fed by the male at one phase of the complicated ceremonial (N. Tinbergen (1939) 224). Detailed accounts of the extremely complex pairing ceremonial of *Anatinae* (surface ducks) are to be found in K. Lorenz's excellent investigations (1940), (1941).

The physiological idea of mating (coition to order), familiar through the keeping of animals for breeding purposes, should certainly not be applied to the pairing and mating of free wild animals. Even in closely related species the ceremonial may differ widely, as O. Antonius (1937) has shown for various Equidae (members of the horse family). Finally, personal sympathies and antipathies often play a decisive role among wild animals. A meeting between a mature male and female of the same species, mammal or fish, does not invariably lead to pairing or mating. Unlike the case of domestic animals, the rutting period of wild animals is mostly confined to definite seasons.

In three consecutive years F. M. Chapman ((1939) 78) observed the onset of heat in a free coati (*Nasua*). In 1935, the period began on 29 January, in 1936 on the 27th, and in 1937 again on the 27th. The period of heat came to an end as punctually in 1935 on 11 February, in 1936 on the 10th, and 1937 on the 18th. Among wild animals the foundation of a family, or the preparation for it, is often regularly dependent on a fixed ceremonial (display), a fixed time (rut), and often on a fixed place (mating ground) as well. Sexual behaviour is closely linked with the space-time pattern.

REFERENCES

Antonius, O. 1937. Über Herdenbildung und Paarungseigentümlichkeiten der Einhufer. *Z. Tierpsychol.* Vol 1, No 3

Beninde, J. 1937. *Zur Naturgeschichte des Rothirsches.* Leipzig

Carpenter, C. R. 1942. Societies of Monkeys and Apes. *Biological Symposia* Vol 8

Chapman, F. M. 1939. *La vie animale sous les tropiques.* Paris

Darling, F. F. 1937. *A Herd of Red Deer.* London

Goethe, F. 1937. Beobachtungen und Untersuchungen zur Biologie der Silbermöwe. *J. Ornithol.* Vol 85, No 1

Grote, H. 1943. Beiträge zur Biologie von Auer- und Birkhuhn *Z. Jagdkde.* Vol 5, p 7–40

Hediger, H. 1934. Beitrag zur Herpetologie und Zoogeographic Neu Britanniens. *Zool. Jb.* Vol 65

―――― 1937. Die Bedeutung der Flucht im Leben des Tieres und in der Beurteilung tierischen Verhaltens im Experiment. *Naturwiss.* Vol 25, No 12

―――― 1940. Zum Begriff der biologischen Rangordnung. *Rev. suisse Zool.* Vol 47, No 3

―――― 1941. Biologische Gesetzmässigkeiten im Verhalten von Wirbeltieren. *Mitt. naturf. Ges. Bern*

Hesse, R. 1924. *Tiergeographie auf ökologischer Grundlage.* Jena

Holzapfel, M. 1940. Triebbedingte Ruhezustände als Ziel von Appetenz-Handlungen. *Naturwiss.* Vol 28, No 18

Hubback, T. 1939. The Asiatic Two-Horned Rhinoceros. *J. Mammalogy* Vol 20

Leopold, A. 1939. *Game Management.* New York and London

Lorenz, K. 1940. Durch Domestikation verursachte Störungen arteigenen Verhaltens. *Z. angew. Psychol. Charakterk.* Vol 59, No 1/2

―――― 1941. Bewegungsstudien an Anatinen. *J. Ornithol.* Vol 89

Mertens, R. 1940. *Aus dem Tierleben der Tropen* Frankfurt a/Main

Pratt, A. 1937. *The Call of the Koala.* Melbourne

Schenkel, R. 1947. Ausdrucksstudien an Wölfen. *Behavior* Vol 1, p 81–129

Schoenichen, W. 1938. *Taschenbuch der in Deutschland geschützten Tiere.* Berlin

Tinbergen, N. 1939. On the Analysis of Social Organisation among Vertebrates, with special Reference to Birds. *Amer. Midl. Nat.* Vol 21, No 1

―― · ― · ― · ― · ― · ― · ― · ― · ― · ― · ― · ― · ―

V. C. WYNNE-EDWARDS

Homeostatic Theory of Social Organization *

A century ago, indeed, in the worst days of the North Pacific fur-seal fishery, things got so bad that vessels had to mount cannon to defend themselves and international

*V. C. Wynne-Edwards, *Animal Dispersion in Relation to Social Behavior* (New York: Hafner; Edinburgh & London: Oliver & Boyd, 1962), pp. 7–14. Reprinted by permission of Oliver and Boyd Ltd. and the author.

incidents and bloodshed occurred; this was finally prevented and the present extremely successful scientific management made possible, by the North Pacific Sealing Convention of 1911—perhaps the first international treaty of the kind.

There are in fact five lessons to be learnt from this phenomenon of overfishing, the importance of which it would be difficult to exaggerate. The first is that *overfishing reduces both the yield per unit effort and the total yield*; in some circumstances, if sufficiently severe, it can damage the stock beyond recovery and even lead to its extermination. This actually happened in the 19th Century through the commercial exploitation in North America of the passenger pigeon (*Ectopistes migratorius*)—'the most impressive species of bird that man has ever known' (Schorger, 1955, p. viii;). . . . Secondly, the size of the optimum catch is not self-evident, and can be determined and adjusted only in the light of experience. Thirdly, the participants must all come to a common agreement or convention to limit their catch, preferably *while the stock is still at or near its maximum abundance and productivity*, and must forego any immediate personal advantage in favour of the long-term benefit of the community as a whole. Fourthly, argument about who shall participate and how much he shall take ought always to be transferred to some higher court, so that direct destructive and wasteful competition is entirely eliminated from the catching of the actual fish. Fifthly, no profitable fishery is immune from over-exploitation; the consequences are certain to follow wherever the optimum rate of cropping is persistently exceeded. Exactly the same is true of any other kind of profitable, renewable, living resource, whether of game, fur-bearers, or—if nutrients are not returned to the soil, or plants are killed or regeneration impaired—even if of natural vegetation.

The importance of these inferences lies, of course, in the fact that there is no difference in principle between man exploiting fish or whales and any other predator exploiting any other prey. All predators face the same aspects of exactly the same problem. It is impossible to escape the conclusion, therefore, that *something must, in fact, constantly restrain them, while in the midst of plenty, from over-exploiting their prey.* Somehow or other 'free enterprise' or unchecked competition for food must be successfully averted, otherwise 'overfishing' would be impossible to escape: this could only result in lasting detriment to the predators and the risk, if they persisted in it, that the prey might be exterminated altogether.

That some such restraint often exists in nature is most easily comprehended, perhaps, in a situation where a population of animals has to depend for a period on a standing crop, which must be made to last out until the season comes round for its renewal or until alternative foods become available. Many small northern birds, for instance, are provisioned ahead for four or five months in the winter by the standing crop of seeds of a few species of trees or herbs, or by a finite stock of overwintering insects. It would be fatal to allow birds to crowd in freely in autumn up to the maximum number that could for the moment be supported by the superabundance of food, without regard to later consequences. The optimum population-density, on the contrary, would generally be one that could be carried right through till the spring on the same stock of food, supposing the birds were winter-resident species such as tits (*Parus*), robins (*Erithacus*) or woodpeckers (*Pici*). To achieve this optimum it would clearly be necessary to put a limit on the population-density *from the beginning*, while the resource was still untapped.

The need for restraint in the midst of plenty, as it turns out, must apply to all animals whose numbers are ultimately limited by food whether they are predators in the ordinary sense of the word or not. It is commonly the only way in which plenty can be conserved and maintained. It applies in general as forcibly to herbivores as to carnivores. Ruminants, for instance, are notoriously capable of impairing fertility by long-continued overgrazing; as is well known, this has resulted, in the brief span of history, in reducing large tracts of primeval forest and natural grassland in the Near and Middle East and other ancient centres of pastoral civilisation almost to the bare stones. The habitat generally contains only a finite total quantity of those nutrient elements, such as nitrogen, phosphorus, potassium and calcium, on the repeated circulation of which the continuity of life depends. One of them usually sets a limit to primary productivity. It seems probable, in closed communities at any rate, that selection will favour an optimal balance in the rate of circulation and in the proportion of the total that is held at any given moment by (i) the animal biomass, (ii) the plant biomass, and (iii) the remainder of the system. The hoarding of precious nutrients within the animal biomass, which is likely to be accentuated by over-population, may, especially if it is followed by emigration on a large scale, seriously prejudice the continued productivity of the system as a whole.

Where we can still find nature undisturbed by human interference, whether under some stable climax of vegetation or proceeding through a natural succession, there is generally no indication whatever that the habitat is run down or destructively overtaxed. On the contrary the whole trend of ecological evolution seems to be in the very opposite direction, leading towards the highest state of productivity that can possibly be built up within the limitations set by the inorganic environment. Judging by appearances, chronic over-exploitation and mass poverty intrude themselves on a mutually-balanced and thriving natural world only as a kind of adventitious disease, almost certain to be swiftly suppressed by natural selection. It is easy to appreciate that if each species maintains an optimum population-density on its own account, not only will it be providing the most favourable conditions for its own survival, but it will automatically offer the best possible living to species higher up the chain that depend on it in turn for food.

Such *prima facie* argument leads to the conclusion that it must be highly advantageous to survival, and thus strongly favoured by selection, for animal species (1) to control their own population-densities, and (2) to keep them as near as possible to the optimum level for each habitat they occupy.

Regarding the first of these conditions, the general hypothesis of self-limitation of animal numbers has been growing rapidly in favour among animal ecologists in recent years (*e.g.*, Kalela, 1954; A. J. Nicholson, 1954; Errington, 1956; Wynne-Edwards, 1955; Andrewartha, 1959); so far as it goes the evidence given already in the introductory section of course confirms it. To build up and preserve a favourable balance between population-density and available resources, it would be necessary for the animals to evolve a control system in many respects analogous to the physiological systems that regulate the internal environment of the body and adjust it to meet changing needs. Such systems are said to be homeostatic or self-balancing, and it will be convenient for us to use the same word. Physiological homeostasis has in general been slowly perfected in the course of evolution, and it is thus the highest animals that tend to be most independent of environmental influences, as far as the inward machinery of the body is concerned.

Population homeostasis, it may be inferred, would involve adaptations no less complex, and it might therefore be expected that these would similarly tend to reach the greatest efficiency and perfection in the highest groups.

We are going to discover in the concluding chapters of the book that such homeostatic adaptations exist in astonishing profusion and diversity, above all in the two great phyla of arthropods and vertebrates. There we shall find machinery for regulating the reproductive output or recruitment rate of the population in a dozen different ways—by varying the quota of breeders, the number of eggs, the resorption of embryos, survival of the newborn and so on; for accelerating or retarding growth-rate and maturity; for limiting the density of colonisation or settlement of the habitat; for ejecting surplus members of the population, and even for encompassing their deaths in some cases in order to retrieve the correct balance between population-density and resources. Not all types of adaptation have been developed in every group, though examples of parallel evolution are abundant and extraordinarily interesting. Indeed this newest manifestation of homeostasis in the processes of life seems unlikely to remain long in doubt.

THE EXISTENCE OF NATURAL CONVENTIONS

At this point, however, we must leave the subject of homeostasis temporarily in order to consider the second conclusion of our *prima facie* argument, namely that it would be advantageous to be able to keep the population-density at or near the optimum level. We are still concerned with those species of animals—knowing them to be in the great majority—whose numbers are ultimately limited by the resource of food.

It should first be recognised that, unless they are on the verge of extinction, all animals and plants have a great latent power of increase. Physiological provision is made, even in the slowest breeders, for the production of offspring in excess of what is needed merely to sustain the population. In order to prevent a geometrical progression of increase, therefore, some kind of brake must be applied; and if this is to allow the increase to proceed freely when the population-density is low and economic conditions permit it, but to prevent density going any higher once a particular limiting threshold has been reached, then the application of the brake requires to be 'density-dependent'. That is to say, that when the density is low, multiplication will be relatively unhindered, but as it mounts towards a ceiling the checks on increase will become progressively more severe, until population losses through death and emigration catch up with the gains from reproduction and immigration, and the increase is brought to a halt.

When an experimental population is set up in some kind of a confined universe with a finite but regularly renewed supply of food, whether the population consists of *Drosophila*, flour-beetles, *Daphnia*, *Lebistes* (guppies) or mice—to name some of the commonest experimental animals—this is exactly what happens. . . . The experiments can be replicated time and again, and if the universe is made the same, the population will reach the same predictable ceiling of numbers each time within a narrow margin of error. It will be a matter of special remark when the experiments come to be described that the ceiling is never imposed by starvation, except perhaps indirectly in mice where the mothers often run out of milk at high population-densities, with profound effects on the production of recruits. On the contrary, the ceiling is normally imposed, and the level indefinitely maintained, while the members of the population are in good health—sometimes actually fat—and leading normal lives. Guppies, for instance, still breed and viviparously produce young, but after the ceiling is reached and there are no vacancies in the population, the young are gobbled up by their elders within a few minutes of their birth. . . .

It is not necessary here to go into the subject of external density-dependent checks on population—caused by agents such as predators, parasites and pathogens that are likely to take a mounting percentage of lives as population-density rises and economic conditions become more severe. . . . It will suffice for the present to say that these external checks, while they may sometimes be extremely effective in preventing population-density from rising, are on the whole hopelessly undependable and fickle in their incidence, and not nearly as perfectly density-dependent as has often been imagined. They would in most cases be incapable of serving to impose the ceilings found in nature; what is more, experiment generally shows that they are unnecessary, and that many if not all the higher animals can limit their population-densities by intrinsic means. Most important of all, we shall find that self-limiting homeostatic methods of density-regulation are in practically universal operation not only in experiments, but under 'wild' conditions also.

Towards the fringe of its range of existence and population-density of any particular species of animal is often overwhelmingly dictated by the physical conditions of the environment—heat, cold, drought, shelter and the like—and by such biotic factors as the presence of better-adapted competitors or the absence of requisite vegetational cover; and it is frequently one of these factors that precludes any further geographical extension of its range. If we ignore the fringe, however, and confine our attention to the more typical part of the range, dispersion in the great majority of animals reflects the productivity of the habitat in terms of food, in just the same way as we saw in the special case of Jespersen's correlation between pelagic birds and plankton. That this is so is nowhere in serious dispute; and if we take care to exclude minority of species where the food correlation is weak or absent, we can repeat once more that food is generally the ultimate factor determining population-density, and the one that predominates far above others.

We have already the strongest reasons for concluding, however, that population-density must at all costs be prevented from rising to the level where food shortage begins to take a toll of the numbers—an effect that would not be felt until long after the optimum density had been exceeded. It would be bound to result in chronic over-exploitation and a spiral of diminishing returns. Food may be the *ultimate* factor, but it cannot be invoked as the *proximate* agent in chopping the numbers, without disastrous consequences. By analogy with human experience we should therefore look to see whether there is not some natural counterpart of the limitation-agreements that provide man with his only known remedy against overfishing—some kind of density-dependent convention, it would have to be, based on the quantity of food available but 'artificially' preventing the intensity of exploitation from rising above the optimum level. Such a convention, if it existed, would have not only to be closely linked with the food situation, and highly (or better still perfectly) density-dependent in its operation, but, thirdly, also capable of eliminating the direct contest in hunting which has proved so destructive and extravagant in human experience.

It does not take more than a moment to see that such a convention could operate extremely effectively through the well-known territorial system adopted by many kinds of birds in preparation for the breeding season. Instead of limiting the number of expeditions and fixing the total annual catch like the International Whaling Commission, conventional behaviour in this case limits the number of territories occupied in the food-gathering area. Birds will not, of course, submit to being overcrowded beyond a certain density, nor to the reduction of their territories below a basic minimum size, so that territorial behaviour is perfectly capable of imposing a ceiling on population-density (as C. B. Moffat realised in 1903). In its action it is completely density-dependent, allowing the habitat to fill amid mounting rivalry up to a conventional maximum density, after which any further intrusion is fiercely repelled. Where territories retain this simple primitive character as feeding areas, and where enough information is available, the evidence indicates that minimum territory size is inversely related to the productivity of the habitat: in other words, it is closely linked with the presumptive food-supply. Finally, our last condition is completely met, in that the contest among the participants is all for the possession of territory, and once they have established their claim to the ground they can do the actual food-getting in perfect peace and freedom, entirely without interference from rivals.

The substitution of a parcel of ground as the object of competition in place of the actual food it contains, so that each individual or family unit has a separate holding of the resource to exploit, is the simplest and most direct kind of limiting convention it is possible to have. It is the commonest form of tenure in human agriculture. It provides an effective proximate buffer to limit the population-density at a safe level (which is obviously somewhere near the optimum though we can only guess in animals how nearly perfection is attained); and it results in spreading the population evenly over the habitat, without clumping them in groups as we find in many alternative types of dispersion.

Much space is devoted in later chapters to studying the almost endless diversity of density-limiting conventions, and only the briefest indication of their range can be given here. What must first be appreciated is their artificial or slightly unreal quality. The food-territory just considered is concrete enough—it is the very place where food is found and gathered. But some birds have territories in which they nest but do not feed; and some have only token territories which are the nest-sites they possess and defend in a breeding colony. These, as we shall see later, perform exactly the same function, because the number of acceptable nest-sites in the colony is 'artifically' limited by the birds' traditional behaviour. In a rookery, for instance, the fullest membership of the community, conferring the right to breed belongs only to those pairs that can secure a nest-site, construct and defend a nest. Supernumerary' unauthorised' nests are constantly pillaged, and there are almost always in consequence a good many non-breeding adults present. These latter, however, may be accepted members of the rookery population, all of whom have the free right to all the resources of the communal territory of the rookery. . . . Communal feeding-territories have been closely studied also in a few other birds, such as the Australian 'magpie' *Gymnorhina tibicen* (Dr. Robert Carrick, orally), and in *Crotophaga ani* and *Guira guira* in Cuba and Argentina respectively (Davis, 1940a and b); but it will appear later that the phenomenon is evidently a general one, applying, not in the breeding season alone, to many birds that flock and to gregarious mammals at any time. In solitary mammals such as foxes the home-ranges of individuals freely overlap; but each *bona fide* resident must have the established use of a traditional earth or den in order to be tolerated and allowed the freedom of the local resources; and so it goes on. . . .

In most cases the personal status of the individual with respect to his rivals assumes a great importance; and in fact conventional contests frequently come to be completely divorced from tangible rewards of property, and are concerned solely with personal rank and dominance. All who carry sufficient status can then take whatever resources they require without further question or dispute. We shall find that, although widespread and common, these abstract goals of conventional competition are especially characteristic of gregarious species.

The subject is evidently a complex one, that will require much amplification. Enough introduction has perhaps been given, however, to reveal that conventional competition really exists, and to suggest the forms the prizes or goals can take and the way they can be made to serve as dummies or substitutes for the ultimate goal that should never be disputed in the open—the bread of life itself.

1.4. SOCIAL ORGANISATION

In any homeostatic system there are necessarily two component processes. One is the means of bringing about whatever changes are required to restore the balance when it is disturbed, or to find a new balance when this becomes necessary through changes in conditions external to the system. It has already been briefly indicated in the previous section that populations (among the higher animals at any rate) do have the necessary powers to adjust their own population-densities. The other essential component of homeostasis is an input of information, acting as an indicator of the state of balance or imbalance of the system, that can evoke the appropriate corrective response. A stimulus is required that will check and reverse the trend of the system when the balance sways in one direction, in order to bring it back into equilibrium. A device of this kind is familiar to electronic engineers in the design of stable electrical systems, and is described by them as negative feed-back.

In the balance that we are considering here it is postulated that population-density is constantly adjusted to match the optimum level of exploitation of available food-resources; and as food-supply 'futures' change with the changing seasons the population-density must be adjusted to match—in so far as this is possible in existing circumstances. What is needed is the way of feed-back, therefore, is something that will measure or reflect the demand for food, assessing the number of mouths to be fed in terms of present and prospective supplies; to use another analogy, it has to undertake the instrumentation, and to respond to population-density and economic conditions in the same general way as a thermometer is used in a thermostatic system.

Free contest between rivals for any commodity will readily provide such an indicator. The keener the demand the higher the price in mettle and effort required to obtain the reward: the tension created is thus ideally density-dependent. One of our guiding first principles, however, is that undisguised contest for food inevitably leads in the end to over-exploitation, so that a conventional goal for competition has to be evolved in its stead; and it is precisely in this—surprising though it may appear at first sight—that social organisation and the primitive seeds of all social behaviour have their origin. This is a discovery (if it can be so described) of the greatest importance to the theory.

Any open contest must of course bring the rivals into some kind of association with one another; and we are going to find that, if the rewards sought are conventional rewards, then the association of contestants automatically constitutes a society. Putting the situation the other way round, a society can be defined for our purposes as *an organisation capable of providing conventional competition*: this, at least, appears to be its original, most primitive function, which indeed survives more or less thinly veiled even in the civilised societies of man. The social organisation is originally set up, therefore, to provide the feed-back for the homeostatic machine.

REFERENCES

Andrewartha, H. G. Self-regulatory mechanisms in animal populations. *Aust. J. Sci.*, 22: 200–5.

Kalela, O. 1954. Über den Revierbesitz bei Vögeln und Säugetiersen als population-sökologischer Faktor. *Ann. zool. Soc. 'Vanamo'*, 16, no. 2: 48 pp.

Moffat, C. B. 1903. The spring rivalry of birds: some views on the limit to multiplication. *Irish Naturalist*, 12: 152–66.

Schorger, A. W. 1955. *The passenger pigeon, its natural history and extinction.* Madison, Wis.

Wynne-Edwards, V. C. 1955. Low reproductive rates in birds, especially sea-birds, *Acta XI Congr. Int. Orn., Basel:* 540–7.

— ꞏ — ꞏ — ꞏ — ꞏ — ꞏ — ꞏ — ꞏ — ꞏ — ꞏ — ꞏ —

3 · ATTITUDE MEASUREMENT

L. L. THURSTONE

*Similar Attributes or Similar Reactions Scale for Attitude Testing**

It is the purpose of this paper to describe a new psycho-physical method for measuring the psychological or functional similarity of attributes. Its development was motivated primarily for the solution of a particular problem in the measurement of social attitudes and it is in terms of this problem that the new psychophysical method will be described.

Let each of a group of N individuals be labeled as to the presence or absence of each of n attributes. This means that we are dealing with N persons and that each of these persons declares the presence or absence in him of each of the n attributes. It does not matter for our present purposes whether the declarations are made by these people for themselves or by others for them. In our particular problem we are dealing with a list of n statements of opinion and each person has the option of endorsing or rejecting each of the n opinions. The statement of an opinion is here regarded as a description of an attribute and the subject merely indicates whether he possesses the attribute. A similar analysis might be made for a series of traits which are supposed to describe people along an extroversion-introversion continuum, an ascendance-submission continuum, and so on. Our primary interest is here in the attitude continuum.

We postulate, for verification, an attitude continuum for the n opinions. Let them describe different attitudes toward the church for purposes of illustration. Some of the opinions reflect attitudes very favorable and loyal to the church; others are neutral or slightly favorable, while still others are slightly or strongly antagonistic to the church. We want an objective procedure for ascertaining whether any particular set of opinions really behaves as a continuum when the endorsements are analyzed.

Let us consider first a pair of opinions, one of which is clearly favorable to the church and the other as clearly antagonistic.

*L. L. Thurstone, "Theory of Attitude Measurement," *Psychological Review* 36 (1929): 222–241.

1. I feel the church services give me inspiration and help to live up to my best during the following week.
2. I think the church seeks to impose a lot of worn-out dogmas and medieval superstitions.

Now, on a common sense basis, we should expect to find that of the people who endorse opinion 1 relatively few will endorse opinion 2. Similarly, those who endorse 2 will only seldom endorse 1. The following pair of opinions would probably behave differently.

1. I feel the church services give me inspiration and help to live up to my best during the following week.
3. I believe the church is the greatest influence for good government and right living.

If we consider the group of people who endorse 1 we should expect a rather high proportion also endorsing 3 because the two statements are both favorable to the church. The attitudes represented by these two statements may be expected to co-exist in the same person while 1 and 2 are more or less mutually exclusive.

These facts suggest the possibility of measuring the psychological similarity of opinions in terms of the endorsements. For the two opinions we shall have the three following facts:

$n_{(1)}$ = the total number of individuals in the group N who endorse opinion No. 1.

$n_{(2)}$ = the total number of individuals in the group N who endorse opinion No. 2.

$n_{(12)}$ = the total number of individuals in the group N who endorse both 1 and 2.

Other things being equal, a relatively high value for $n_{(12)}$ means that the two statements are similar. A relatively low value for $n_{(12)}$ means that the two opinions are more or less mutually exclusive.

We shall avoid mere correlational procedures since it is possible in this case to do better than merely to correlate the attributes. When a problem is so involved that no rational formulation is available, then some quantification is still possible by the calculation of coefficients of correlation or contingency and the like. But such statistical procedures constitute an acknowledgment of failure to rationalize the problem and to establish the functions that underlie the data. We want to measure the separation between the two opinions on the attitude continuum and we want to test the validity of the assumed continuum by means of its internal consistency. This can not be done if we had merely a set of correlational coefficients unless we could also know the functional relation between the correlation coefficient and the attitude separation which it signifies. Such a function requires the rationalization of the problem and this might as well be done, if possible, directly without using the correlational coefficients as intermediaries.

Before summarizing these endorsement counts into an index of similarity we shall introduce another attribute of the statement, namely, its reliability. Suppose that there are $N_{(1)}$ individuals in the experimental population whose attitudes toward the church are such that they really should endorse statement 1 if they were conscientious and accurate and if the statement of opinion were a perfect statement of the attitude that it is intended to reflect. Now suppose that as a result of imperfections, obscurities, or irrelevancies in the statement, and inaccuracy or carelessness of the subjects, there are only $n_{(1)}$ endorsements of this statement. Then the reliability of the opinion would be defined by the ratio

$$p_1 = \frac{n_{(1)}}{N_{(1)}}. \tag{1}$$

The notation p_1 means the probability that the statement will be endorsed by a subject who would endorse it if he were accurate and if the statement were a perfect expression of the attitude it is intended to convey. The question naturally arises as to how to ascertain the value of N_1 which could be obtained directly only if the statement were perfect and the subjects absolutely accurate.

We shall consider three methods of determining approximately the reliability of each statement.

1. Let the whole list of opinions be presented twice in random order. If there are fifty opinions in the experimental list there would be one hundred opinions to be read to the subjects, each opinion being repeated once. Let the endorsement counts for opinion 1 be as follows.

n_1 = total number of subjects who endorse the first presentation of No. 1.
n_1' = total number of subjects who endorse the second presentation of No. 1.
n_{12} = total number of subjects who endorse both presentations of No. 1.

The proportion of those who checked 1 who also checked 2 is

$$p_1 = \frac{n_{12}}{n_1}. \tag{2}$$

and we shall assume that this proportion is the same as the proportion of those whose attitudes are of opinion 1 who actually checked that opinion. In other words,

$$p_1 = \frac{n_1}{N_1}. \tag{1}$$

Similarly for the second presentation of the same opinion we have

$$p_1 = \frac{n_{12}}{n_1'} = \frac{n_1'}{N_1}. \tag{3}$$

But we can not expect the experimental values of n_1 and n_1' to be exactly the same so we shall use them both for determining the value of p_1 by the product of (2) and (3) so that

$$p_1^2 = \frac{n_{12}^2}{n_1 n_1'}$$

and hence

$$p_1 = \frac{n_{12}}{\sqrt{n_1 n_1'}} \qquad \text{(reliability of an opinion).} \tag{4}$$

2. A second procedure which should give at least roughly comparable results is as follows. Let the entire list of opinions be sorted into any convenient number of groups by the method of equal appearing intervals. The statements may then be placed in rank order from those that are most antagonistic to the church to those that are most favorable. The detailed procedure for this scaling has been described elsewhere.[1] Then any two adjacent opinions will reflect practically the same attitude especially if the list is as long as 40 or 50 opinions or more over the whole available range of the attitude continuum.

Let any two adjacent opinions in this rank order series be numbered 1 and 2 respectively. The total number of individuals in the experimental population whose attitudes are represented approximately by the adjacent opinions 1 and 2 may be designated N_{12}. If both of the statements were perfect and if the subjects were absolutely accurate, then we should expect to find n_{12} to be very nearly equal to N_{12}, which is the full number of subjects whose attitudes are that of opinions 1 and 2. Strictly speaking, we are combining here two factors of reliability into one, namely the reliability of each opinion and the mean conscientiousness of the subjects. The reliability of the statement is the probability that a subject will endorse it if the subject's attitude is that of the opinion. It is a function of such characteristics of the statement as obscurity, subtlety or indirectness of its meaning, or actual ambiguity in its meaning. The realiability of the subject is the probability that he will endorse the opinions that he really should endorse in order truly to represent his attitude. This reliability is a function of such factors as the conscientiousness of the subject and the experimental arrangement. If the subject is asked to read several hundred statements of opinion he will not read them so carefully as if he is asked to read only a dozen. But we have combined these factors of reliability into a single index, the probability that the statement will be endorsed by the people who should endorse it. If this type of analysis should prove to be fruitful there will no doubt be further investigations in which these factors of reliability are analyzed separately and explicitly.

Since there are N_{12} individuals who should check opinion 1 and since the actual number who checked this opinion is only n_1 the probability that this statement will be endorsed by those who should endorse it

$$p_1 = \frac{n_1}{N_{12}} \tag{5}$$

and, similarly,

$$p_2 = \frac{n_2}{N_{12}}. \tag{6}$$

These two probabilities are assumed to be practically uncorrelated so that

$$n_{12} = N_{12}p_1p_2 = \frac{n_1 n_2}{N_{12}} \tag{7}$$

---

[1] For distinction here made between opinion and attitude see Thurstone, L. L., 'Attitudes Can Be Measured,' *Amer. J. Sociol.*, 1928, 33, 529–554. In this paper is described the construction of an attitude scale by the method of equal appearing intervals.

or

$$N_{12} = \frac{n_1 n_2}{n_{12}} \tag{8}$$

and hence

$$p_1 = \frac{n_{12}}{n_2} \tag{9}$$

and

$$p_2 = \frac{n_{12}}{n_1}. \tag{10}$$

The assumption that the two probabilities of endorsement are uncorrelated is probably incorrect because the subject who is conscientious in reading one of these opinions will of course be likely to be conscientious also in reading the second opinion and consequently the probability that the two opinions will both be endorsed is not, strictly speaking, the product of the two separate reliabilities. The approximation is perhaps sufficient for our purposes and it may be hoped that it introduces no violent error.

The above procedure enables us to estimate the reliabilities of the opinions in terms of known data but this particular method requires that the opinions in the experimental list be first sorted into a rank order series by the method of equal appearing intervals or into a simple rank order series.

3. A third procedure is really identical with the second above except that instead of obtaining adjacent opinions by submitting the entire series of opinions to a large group for sorting, the experimenter selects adjacent statements by inspection. This is certainly not a safe procedure and it should be discouraged. A modification that could be acceptable is to select pairs of opinions that are paraphrased forms of the same statement, and then apply the logic of the second procedure above. It is by no means certain that these three methods of determining the reliability of a statement will give similar values. It might very well happen that the first procedure described above gives a measure of reliability in terms of factors more restricted than those which enter into the second and third procedures. If such is the case the first procedure gives values that are too high while the second and third procedures may give values more appropriate to our purposes.

We now have the following statistical facts about the two opinions whose separation on the attitude continuum is to be ascertained.

n_1 = total number of individuals who endorsed opinion No. 1.
n_2 = total number of individuals who endorsed opinion No. 2.
n_{12} = total number of individuals who endorsed both opinions.
p_1 = reliability of opinion No. 1.
p_2 = reliability of opinion No. 2.

Let one of the opinions have its scale value at S_1 on the attitude continuum of Figure 1. Let there be N_1 persons in the experimental group who should endorse it if they were absolutely accurate and if the statement of opinion were a perfect representation of the attitude it is intended to convey. The actual number of subjects who really do

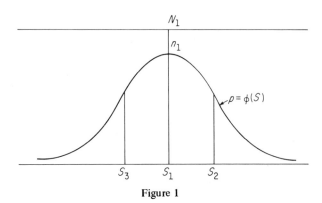

Figure 1

check this opinion is

$$n_1 = N_1 p_1, \tag{11}$$

in which p_1 is the reliability of the statement.

Now consider another statement whose scale value is at S_2 on the attitude continuum. Since there is a difference $(S_2 - S_1)$ between the attitudes of these two statements we should not expect all of the n_1 subjects to endorse this second statement. If it were perfect in reliability, then the number of subjects in the group n_1 who also endorse statement 2 will be

$$n_1 \phi = N_1 p_1 \phi, \tag{12}$$

where ϕ is some value less than unity. Now, it is reasonable to assume that if the two statements are far apart on the scale, then the proportion ϕ of the group n_1 who also endorse the distant statement 2 will be small. This is represented in Figure 1 by the fact that ϕ is a maximum when the separation $(S_2 - S_1)$ is small while it approaches zero as this separation becomes large. We shall assume that this function is symmetrical about the axis at S_1 so that

$$p_{1(k)} = \phi(S_k - S_1)^2, \tag{13}$$

in which $p_{1(k)}$ is the proportion of those who endorse statement 1 who also endorse statement k while S_k is the scale value of statement k. Our assumption is that $p_{1(k)}$ is a function of the separation $(S_k - S_1)$ but that it is independent of the sign of the separation which is an arbitrary matter.

We must also take into consideration the fact that statement 2 is probably imperfect as well as statement 1. Let its reliability be p_2 and we shall then say that the number of those who check statement 1 who also check statement 2 is

$$n_{12} = n_1 \phi p_2 = N_1 p_1 p_2 \phi. \tag{14}$$

The number of those who checked No. 1 who also checked No. 2 is of course the same as the number of those who checked No. 2 and who also checked No. 1. Hence, we may write, by analogy,

$$n_{12} = N_2 p_1 p_2 \phi \tag{15}$$

or

$$n_{12} = n_1 p_2 \phi,$$
$$n_{12} = n_2 p_1 \phi, \tag{16}$$

and hence

$$n_{12}^2 = p_1 p_2 n_1 n_2 \phi^2 \tag{17}$$

or

$$\phi = \frac{n_{12}}{\sqrt{p_1 p_2 n_1 n_2}}. \tag{18}$$

This is the coefficient of similarity of two statements of opinion. When this value is relatively high, the two statements belong close together on the scale but when ϕ is small they are far apart.

This formula may be used to determine the reliabilities p_1 and p_2 if the two statements are known to have practically the same scale value. This fact may be known either because of the fact that they are statements of the same idea, one being a paraphrase of the other, or by being scaled by the method of equal appearing intervals, previously described. Since the coefficient ϕ deviates from unity supposedly only on account of the scale separations, it is in this case unity, the two statements having practically the same scale value. Then

$$1 = \frac{n_{12}}{\sqrt{p_1 p_2 n_1 n_2}}. \tag{19}$$

But

$$N_1 = N_2,$$

since both of these symbols represent the same quantity, namely the number of people in the total group who should endorse both statements at the same scale value if both statements were perfect. Hence

$$N_1 = N_2 = \frac{n_1}{p_1} = \frac{n_2}{p_2} \tag{20}$$

or

$$n_1 p_2 = p_1 n_2 \tag{21}$$

and

$$p_2 = \frac{p_1 n_2}{n_1}. \tag{22}$$

Substituting (22) in (19) we have

$$1 = \frac{n_{12}}{\sqrt{p_1 p_2 n_1 n_2}} = \frac{n_{12}}{p_1 n_2}, \tag{23}$$

and hence

$$p_1 = \frac{n_{12}}{n_2} \qquad \text{(for identical or adjacent opinions)}, \tag{24}$$

and, by analogy,

$$p_2 = \frac{n_{12}}{n_1} \qquad \text{(for identical or adjacent opinions)}. \tag{25}$$

Our next problem concerns the exact formulation of the function

$$\phi_{1k} = f(S_k - S_1).$$

We shall try first the assumption that it is Gaussian so that

$$\phi_{12} = \frac{1}{\sqrt{2\pi} \cdot \sigma} e^{\frac{-(s_1 - s_2)^2}{2\sigma^2}} \tag{26}$$

This means that if a man has endorsed any particular perfect statement No. 1, the probability that he will also endorse another perfect statement No. 2, distant from No. 1 by the scale separation $|S_1 - S_2|$, is assumed to be a Gaussian function of the scale separation. This assumption can be tested empirically by the internal consistency of the scale, but the function can also be studied directly without this assumption by methods that will be left for separate publication. We shall assume for the present experiment that this ϕ-function has a maximum value of unity when the scale separation is zero.

We shall test the index of similarity on a set of ten statements of opinions selected at random from different parts of an attitude scale of 45 such statements. The random set of ten statements is less unwieldy to handle for illustrative purposes than the whole list of 45 in the church scale because the index involves a comparison of each statement with every other statement in the whole list. There will be therefore $10 \cdot 9 \cdot \frac{1}{2} = 45$ comparisons for a set of 10 statements while there would be $45 \cdot 44 \cdot \frac{1}{2} = 990$ comparisons necessary to handle the whole table of 45 statements.

The ten statements were selected so as to represent several degrees of attitude toward the church, including favorable, unfavorable, and indifferent opinions. Each statement is identified by a code number as follows:

2. I feel the church services give me inspiration and help to live up to my best during the following week.
4. I find the services of the church both restful and inspiring.
6. I believe in what the church teaches but with mental reservations.
11. I believe church membership is almost essential to living life at its best.
15. Sometimes I feel that the church and religion are necessary and sometimes I doubt it.
32. I believe in sincerity and goodness without any church ceremonies.
34. I think the organized church is an enemy of science and truth.
35. I believe the church is losing ground as education advances.
41. I think the church seeks to impose a lot of worn-out dogmas and medieval superstitions.
43. I like the ceremonies of my church but do not miss them much when I stay away.

TABLE 1. NUMBER OF DOUBLE ENDORSEMENTS FOR ALL
PAIRS OF OPINIONS

	11	*2*	*4*	*6*	*43*	*15*	*32*	*35*	*41*	*34*
11	*454*	334	349	209	60	66	64	85	19	15
2	334	*573*	492	263	72	85	81	88	23	15
4	349	492	*696*	354	127	163	148	152	26	28
6	209	263	354	*620*	152	221	220	225	67	54
43	60	72	127	152	*265*	122	116	116	46	33
15	66	85	163	221	122	*407*	207	214	72	67
32	64	81	148	220	116	207	*546*	315	142	136
35	85	88	152	225	116	214	315	*548*	165	166
41	19	23	26	67	46	72	142	165	*224*	123
34	15	15	28	54	33	67	136	166	123	*219*
p	.57	.72	.80	.57	.31	.43	.63	.61	.60	.71

In Table 1 we have all the necessary raw data. There are three types of fact here recorded: (1) The total number of individuals who endorsed each of the ten statements. These are found in the diagonal of the table. For example, there were 696 individuals who endorsed statement 4 in the total group of about 1,500 persons who filled in the complete attitude scale. (2) The total number of individuals who endorsed any particular statement and any other particular statement. These data are found in the body of the table. For example, there were 263 individuals who endorsed both statements 6 and 2. (3) The reliability of each of the ten statements. These are found in the last row of the table. They were determined by the second method described above which was applied to each of the statements in the whole scale of forty-five opinions. For example, the reliability of statement 32 is .63 which means that it was endorsed by 63 per cent of the estimated number of people who should have endorsed it if the statement had been perfect and if the subjects had been perfect in their reading and endorsing.

TABLE 2. THE ϕ-COEFFICIENTS OF SIMILARITY FOR ALL
PAIRS OF OPINIONS

	11	*2*	*4*	*6*	*43*	*15*	*32*	*35*	*41*	*34*
11	1.00	1.02	.92	.69	.41	.31	.21	.29	.10	.07
2	1.02	1.00	1.03	.69	.39	.32	.22	.24	.10	.06
4	.92	1.03	1.00	.80	.59	.52	.34	.35	.10	.10
6	.69	.69	.80	1.00	.89	.89	.63	.65	.31	.23
43	.41	.39	.59	.89	1.00	1.02	.69	.70	.44	.29
15	.31	.32	.52	.89	1.02	1.00	.85	.89	.47	.41
32	.21	.22	.34	.63	.69	.85	1.00	.93	.66	.59
35	.29	.24	.35	.65	.70	.89	.93	1.00	.78	.73
41	.10	.10	.10	.31	.44	.47	.66	.78	1.00	.85
34	.07	.06	.10	.23	.29	.41	.59	.73	.85	1.00

In Table 2 we have listed the ϕ-values for all the comparisons. This is done by equation 18. The following is an example of the calculation of the ϕ-coefficient for the two statements 4 and 32 with data from Table 1.

$$\phi_{4.32} = \frac{148}{\sqrt{.80 \times .63 \times 696 \times 546}} = .34.$$

It is seen that the table is symmetrical. The entries along the diagonal are necessarily unity because there is of course no scale separation between a statement and itself. We shall now use these ϕ-values to measure the scale separation between all pairs of statements. This is done by entering an ordinary probability table with the values of ϕ in order to ascertain the deviation from the mean in terms of the standard deviation of the assumed Gaussian function. Each of these deviations will be regarded tentatively as the scale separation between the two statements concerned. When the value of ϕ is small we shall therefore assign a rather large separation to the two statements. When the value of ϕ is high, near unity, we shall assign a rather small scale separation to the statements. It is more convenient for this problem to use a probability table in which the maximum ordinate is unity than to use a table in which the total area is unity so that the maximum ordinate is .4. It is also more convenient to use a probability table which is entered with the ordinate to ascertain the deviation rather than to use a table which is entered with deviations or proportions to ascertain the ordinates. The latter kind of probability table requires interpolation for this problem. The separation between statements 43 and 6 may be taken as an example. The ϕ-coefficient for these two statements is .89 as shown in Table 2. With this ordinate of the probability curve, the deviation is $.48\sigma$ as recorded in Table 3.

TABLE 3. EXPERIMENTAL SCALE SEPARATIONS BETWEEN ALL PAIRS OF OPINIONS

$(S_{top} - S_{side})$

	11	2	4	6	43	15	32	35	41	34
11	.00	.00	-.41	-.86	-1.34	-1.53	-1.77	-1.57	...	...
2	.00	.00	.00	-.86	-1.37	-1.51	-1.74	-1.69	...	...
4	.41	.00	.00	-.67	-1.03	-1.14	-1.47	-1.45	...	...
6	.86	.86	.67	.00	- .48	- .48	- .96	- .93	-1.53	-1.71
43	1.34	1.37	1.03	.48	.00	.00	- .86	- .84	-1.28	-1.57
15	1.53	1.51	1.14	.48	.00	.00	- .57	- .48	-1.23	-1.34
32	1.77	1.74	1.47	.96	.86	.57	.00	- .38	- .91	-1.03
35	1.57	1.69	1.45	.93	.84	.48	.38	.00	- .70	- .79
41	...	...	...	1.53	1.28	1.23	.91	.70	.00	- .57
34	...	...	...	1.71	1.57	1.34	1.03	.79	.57	.00

The sign of the deviation is determined by the end of the scale which is arbitrarily called positive. In the present case the origin was arbitrarily placed at the opinion least favorable to the church namely statement 34. Therefore the statements favorable to the church are arbitrarily called positive with regard to the statements that are unfavorable to the church. It is entirely immaterial for scaling purposes which ends of the sequence of opinions are designated as positive and negative.

The signs in Table 3 are recorded so as to show $(S_{top} - S_{side})$. For example, the scale separation $(S_{43} - S_6)$ is found at the intersection of 43 at the top with 6 at the side. It is $-.48\sigma$. Similarly the separation $(S_6 - S_{43})$ is found at the intersection of 6 at the top with 43 at the side. It is $+.48\sigma$. The two halves of the table are symmetrical about the diagonal of zero entries. The ten statements were arranged in Table 1 in order of scale values determined by the method of equal appearing intervals.[2] All separations as large as $2.\sigma$ or larger were ignored in Table 3 because when the separations become as large as that

[2] A monograph 'The Measurement of Attitude Toward the Church' by Thurstone and Chave, not yet published. This monograph describes the construction and use of a scale of 45 opinions about the church and the distributions of attitude in several large groups.

their reliabilities become too low to be acceptable. It is entirely arbitrary at what limit we shall drop the separations. They might be extended indefinitely if the observations were weighted but that is too awkward. In these tables we have recorded separations only as large as 2.σ. There may also be some uncertainty as to how far the Gaussian curve can be used for the function $\sigma = f(s)$ and this is another reason for not using scale separations larger than about 2.σ.

We are now ready to determine the average scale separation between successive statements in the present list of ten. It is done as follows:

Let S_1 and S_2 be the scale values of any two statements whose separation is to be measured. Then

$$x_{12} = S_1 - S_2 \tag{27}$$

is a direct measurement of this separation which is obtained by the index of similarity ϕ_{12}. This index is in turn a function of the raw data $n_1, n_2, n_{12}, p_1, p_2$ so that

$$\phi_{12} = \frac{n_{12}}{\sqrt{n_1 n_2 p_1 p_2}} = \frac{1}{\sqrt{2\pi}\sigma} e^{\frac{-(s_1-s_2)^2}{2\sigma^2}} = \frac{1}{\sqrt{2\pi}\sigma} e^{\frac{-x_{12}^2}{2\sigma^2}}. \tag{28}$$

But we also have many indirect measurements of x_{12} which may be shown as follows.

Let S_k be the scale value of any other statement except 1 and 2. Then

$$S_1 - S_k = x_{1k},$$
$$S_2 - S_k = x_{2k},$$

so that

$$S_1 - S_2 = x_{1k} - x_{2k}, \tag{29}$$

and hence

$$S_1 - S_2 = \frac{1}{n}(\Sigma x_{1k} - \Sigma x_{2k}). \tag{30}$$

This equation is more accurate then (27) because it makes use of all the data in Table 1 while equation (27) makes use of only one of the σ-coefficients. Applying equation (30) to the data of Table 3 where n is in each of the nine successive comparisons the number of paired values, we obtain the successive scale separations shown in Table 4. We set the origin arbitrarily at statement 34 so that the final scale values from this origin are as shown in Table 4. For example, the final scale separation between opinions 4 and 6 is obtained by equation 30. There are eight paired values for these two opinions in Table 3. The numerical values are as follows:

$$\Sigma x_{4k} = +5.35, \quad n = 8,$$
$$\Sigma x_{6k} = +0.46, \quad S_4 - S_6 = +0.6113.$$

Note that the sum Σx_{6k} takes a different value when equation 30 is used to determine the scale separation between opinions 6 and 43 because there are then available ten paired values instead of eight for the interval 4 to 6.

TABLE 4

34	0.0000
	.2757
41	.2757
	.5629
35	.8386
	.0800
32	.9186
	.4010
15	1.3196
	.1370
43	1.4566
	.3370
6	1.7936
	.6113
4	2.4049
	.2275
2	2.6324
	.0388
11	2.6712

We now want to test the internal consistency of our calculations. On the basis of the final scale values of Table 4 we may construct a table of calculated scale separations. This has been done in Table 5. For example, the scale values of statements 43 and 35 are 1.46 and .84 respectively. Consequently the calculated scale separation $(S_{43} - S_{35})$ is +0.62 as recorded in Table 5, and the separation $(S_{35} - S_{43})$ is the same distance with sign reversed, namely −0.62, also recorded in the same table. The separations of Table 5 are based entirely on the ten scale values of Table 4.

TABLE 5. CALCULATED SCALE SEPARATIONS OF ALL PAIRS OF OPINIONS $(S_{top} - S_{side})$

	11	2	4	6	43	15	32	35	41	34	Σ
11	.00	−.04	−.27	−.88	−1.21	−1.35	−1.75	−1.83	− 2.40	− 2.67	−12.40
2	.04	.00	−.23	−.84	−1.18	−1.31	−1.71	−1.79	− 2.36	− 2.63	−12.01
4	.27	.23	.00	−.61	− .95	−1.09	−1.49	−1.57	− 2.13	− 2.40	− 9.74
6	.88	.84	.61	.00	− .34	− .47	− .88	− .96	− 1.52	− 1.79	− 3.63
43	1.21	1.18	.95	.34	.00	− .14	− .54	− .62	− 1.18	− 1.46	− .26
15	1.35	1.31	1.09	.47	.14	.00	− .40	− .48	− 1.04	− 1.32	1.12
32	1.75	1.71	1.49	.88	.54	.40	.00	− .08	− .64	− .92	5.13
35	1.83	1.79	1.57	.96	.62	.48	.08	.00	− .56	− .84	5.93
41	2.40	2.36	2.13	1.52	1.18	1.04	.64	.56	.00	− .28	11.55
34	2.67	2.63	2.40	1.79	1.46	1.32	.92	.84	.28	.00	14.31
Σ	12.40	12.01	9.74	3.63	.26	−1.12	−5.13	−5.93	−11.55	−14.31	0.00

Now we want to know how closely these calculated scale separations of Table 5, based on the ten scale values, agree with the 45 experimentally independent scale separations of Table 3. The discrepancies between Tables 3 and 5 are listed individually in Table 6. The descrepancies between the experimental and the calculated scale separations in Table 6 vary between zero and .32σ with a mean discrepancy of only .106σ. This mean discrepancy is only about 1–25 or 4 per cent of the range of the scale values, 2.67σ, for the ten statements. Another set of ten statements, also selected at random from the entire list, has been subjected to the same analysis with comparable results.

TABLE 6. DISCREPANCIES BETWEEN EXPERIMENTAL AND CALCULATED SCALE SEPARATIONS

	11	2	4	6	43	15	32	35	41	34	Σ
11	.00	.04	-.14	.02	-.13	-.18	-.02	.26	–	–	-.15
2	-.04	.00	.23	-.02	-.19	-.20	-.03	.10	–	–	-.15
4	.14	-.23	.00	-.06	-.08	-.05	.02	.12	–	–	-.14
6	-.02	.02	.06	.00	-.14	-.01	-.08	.03	-.01	.08	-.07
43	.13	.19	.08	.14	.00	.14	-.32	-.22	-.10	-.11	-.07
15	.18	.20	.05	.01	-.14	.00	.17	.00	-.19	-.02	-.08
32	.02	.03	-.02	.08	.32	.17	.00	-.30	-.27	-.11	-.08
35	-.26	-.10	-.12	-.03	.22	.00	.30	.00	-.14	.05	-.08
41	–	–	–	.01	.10	.19	.27	.14	.00	-.29	.42
34	–	–	–	-.08	.11	.02	.11	-.05	.29	.00	.40
Σ	.15	.15	.14	.07	.07	.08	.08	.08	-.42	-.40	0.00

$$\text{Average discrepancy} = \frac{\Sigma |x_o - x_c|}{N} = \frac{9.34}{88} = 0.106$$

The question might be raised why we have not used correlational coefficients instead of the ϕ-coefficient here described. Dissimilarity can of course be indicated merely by a correlational index or by contingency methods. Such indices do not constitute measurement except by a generous interpretation of the word measurement. We have attempted truly to measure degree of functional dissimilarity of two attributes or reactions. In order to satisfy what seems to be a fundamental requirement of measurement it is reasonable to expect that if the difference between two entities a and b is, let us say, plus five units, and if the difference between two entities b and c is, let us say, plus three units, then the difference between the two entities a and c should be the sum of these two differences, namely, plus eight units, if all three quantities really measure the same attribute.

This simple requirement is not satisfied by correlational coefficients. It the correlation between a and b is .80 and that of b and c is .40 it does not follow that the correlation between a and c is some additive function of these coefficients. We have postulated a continuum, the attitude scale, and we want to measure separations between points on this continuum so that our measurements are internally consistent; so that $(a - b) + (b - c) = (a - c)$ but such consistency is not found by correlational procedures.

Let it be desired to measure the areas of a lot of circles. Let the diameter of each circle be used as an index of area. It is now possible to arrange the circles in rank order according to area by means of the diameter-index. It is also possible to say of two circles that they must have the same areas because their diameters are equal, but these diameter measurements are hardly to be called measurements of areas. Equal increments of the diameter-index do not correspond to equal increments of what we set out to measure, namely area. The unit of measurement of the diameter does not correspond to a constant increment of area. All of this is childishly simple but the reasoning is the same as regards correlational coefficients. They are not measures of dissimilarity. They are merely numerical indices of dissimilarity. In fact, correlation coefficients are what one resorts to in the absence of hypothesis and rational formulation. If the problem admits of rational formulation, then that function should be written and tested directly by experiment. If the problem is so complex that it defies analysis we can still correlate the variables and represent by correlation coefficients the degree of association between them. That is better than nothing, but it is not really measurement by our simple criteria. These considerations have led me to regard correlation coefficients as symbols of defeat. They constitute a challenge to try again and to outgrow the necessity for using them.

My efforts recently in psychological measurement have been to define in every case a continuum, to allocate people, tasks, and other entities to the continuum under investigation, and to check its validity by the simple criteria that have just been described. I believe that such efforts will prove more fruitful for psychological theory than merely to correlate everything with everything else under heaven.

The results of our attempt to construct an attitude continuum are shown graphically in Figure 2, in which the ten opinions are shown with their allocations to the attitude

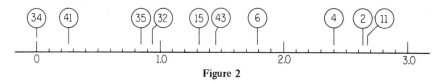

Figure 2

scale. An actual scale for measuring attitude should contain many more opinions and they should be so selected that they constitute as far as possible an evenly graduated scale. The church scale previously referred to has 45 opinions which have been selected from a list of 130 so as to constitute an evenly graduated scale. Our present purpose has been to show how the *method of similar reactions* enables us to construct such a scale from the records of endorsements. It is hoped that the method may also prove useful as an objective test for the validity of other concepts such as extroversion-introversion, ascendance-submission, and the like.

SUMMARY

We have developed a new psychophysical method for measuring the psychological dissimilarity of attributes. This method assumes that if two attributes tend to coexist in the same individual they are regarded as functionally similar while if they are more or less mutually exclusive so that they tend not to coexist in the same individual, then they are functionally dissimilar. The degree of similarity is measured in terms of the ϕ-coefficient which enables us to allocate the attributes along a single continuum, and to measure the degree of similarity by scale separations on this continuum or scale. The method may be called a *method of similar attributes* or *a method of similar reactions*.

The ϕ-coefficient enables us to ascertain whether a series of attributes really belong functionally on the same continuum. This is done by the test of internal consistency as shown in Table 6. The method has been applied to the record of endorsements of 1,500 people to ten statements of opinion about the church. It has been shown that these opinions can be allocated to a single continuum with measured scale separations. It has been the purpose of this study to make a rational formulation for the association of attributes by which the existence of continuity in a series of attributes may be experimentally established and by which their functional dissimilarities, the scale separations, may be truly measured. For these purposes correlational procedures are inadequate because correlational coefficients are not measurements.

EMORY S. BOGARDUS

*Social Distance Scale**

Social distance refers to "the grades and degrees of understanding and intimacy which characterize pre-social and social relations generally."[1] The following experiments[2] were conducted to find out just *how* and *why* these grades of understanding and intimacy vary. Two hundred and forty-eight persons, chiefly members of two graduate and upper division classes in social psychology, were asked to classify the following list of racial and language groups in three columns, putting in the first column those races toward which as races and not as individuals a friendly feeling was felt; in column two, the races toward which a feeling of neutrality was experienced; and in column three, the races whose mention aroused feelings of antipathy and dislike.

TABLE I. RACIAL GROUPS

1. Armenian	13. German	25. Norwegian
2. Bulgarian	14. Greek	26. Portuguese
3. Bohemian	15. Hindu	27. Filipino
4. Canadian	16. Hungarian	28. Polish
5. Chinese	17. Irish	29. Roumanian
6. Czecho-Slovak	18. Italian	30. Russian
7. Dane	19. Japanese	31. Servian
8. Dutch	20. Jew-German	32. Scotch
9. English	21. Jew-Russian	33. Spanish
10. French	22. Mexican	34. Syrian
11. French-Canadian	23. Mulatto	35. Swedish
12. Finn	24. Negro	36. Turk

Each person was then asked to re-copy the three columns: to rearrange column one, putting first those races toward which the greatest degree of friendliness was felt, and the others in order; to start off column two with the races toward which the nearest perfect degree of neutrality was experienced, and so on; and to rearrange column three, putting first those races toward which the greatest antipathy was experienced and then the others in order of decreasing antipathy. Each person was also asked to give the races from which both his father and mother were descended. Twenty-four races were represented, as [shown in Table II].

Many persons were not sure of their racial descent, saying that they would have to consult their parents or other relatives before they could be certain. The extensive degree of this low ebb in racial consciousness was surprising; it was offset, however, in most cases by pronounced race antipathies.

The discussion of the races toward which friendly feeling was expressed and of those to which a neutral reaction was made will be omitted here in order that full space may be given to the "antipathy column." Suffice it to say that friendly feeling was expressed in

*Emory S. Bogardus, "Social Distance and Its Origins," *Journal of Applied Sociology* 9 (1925): 216–226.
[1] Cf. R. E. Park, "The Concept of Social Distance," *Jour. of Applied Sociology*, VIII:339–44.
[2] Suggested by Dr. Park.

TABLE II. RACES OF THE 248 PARTICIPANTS

English	174	Jew-Russian	3
Scotch	120	Japanese	3
Irish	109	Hungarian	2
German	86	Mulatto	2
French	65	Negro	2
Dutch	50	Norwegian	2
Canadian	8	Russian	2
Spanish	8	Armenian	1
Swedish	8	Bulgarian	1
Dane	4	French-	
Chinese	6	Canadian	1
Italian	4	Filippino	1
Jew-German	4		

general toward the races to which the 248 judges themselves belonged, and that the "neutral feeling" column was composed of races concerning which ignorance was expressed. "I don't know anything about them" was a common answer.

The races toward which the greatest or prime antipathy was felt were tabulated and are given in Table III.

TABLE III. RACES AGAINST WHICH THE GREATEST ANTIPATHY WAS EXPRESSED

Turk	119	Servian	3	French	2
Negro	79	Russian	8	Roumanian	2
Mulatto	75	Czecho-Slovak	8	Spanish	2
Japanese	61	Syrian	6	Swedish	2
Hindu	44	Bulgarian	6	Canadian	0
Jew-German	42	Filipino	5	Dane	0
Mexican	41	Italian	5	Dutch	0
Jew-Russian	41	Bohemian	4	French-	
German	38	Finn	4	Canadian	0
Chinese	30	Polish	3	Norwegian	0
Greek	19	Irish	3	Scotch	0
Armenian	17	Portuguese	3		
Hungarian	11	English	2		

Table III gives interesting results, but it does not explain the reasons for any of the antipathetic attitudes that were expressed. In order to penetrate explanations and causes each of the 248 persons was asked to select the race for which he felt the greatest antipathy and describe in detail the circumstances as nearly as he could recall them under which this dislike originated and developed. Not his opinions but his experiences direct and indirect were requested. It was asked that these be written out as fully and freely as possible and with special attention to all important details that occurred.

This personal experience data proved to be as enlivening and interesting as the more formal data were colorless except as one was tempted to "read into" them reactions of his own. The personal experience description of the origins and development of racial antipathy fell into certain classifications.

I. The first and largest grouping of materials was composed of *traditions and accepted opinion*. It is clear after reading the data that hearsay evidence coming from both one's personal friends and from relative strangers in one's own "universe of discourse" who possess prestige in one's own eyes are widely influential in creating social distance. In the case of nearly every one of the 119 persons who placed the Turks at the head of their antipathy columns tradition and accepted opinion were the main, if not the only, factor operating. This second-hand evidence came chiefly from one's elders, parents, preachers, returned missionaries telling of massacres of Armenians by the Turks, newspaper articles of a similar character, motion pictures showing Turks as "villains," and from Armenian eye-witnesses of Turkish cruelties. Many of the 119 persons said that they had never seen a Turk, much less did they know even one.

The person who relies heavily on second-hand and hear-say racial reports usually gives evidence of having entered *imaginatively* into them so often and so thoroughly that they seem to have become his own personal experiences. Three large chances for error enter into these handed-down traditions and opinions, namely: (1) the possibility of erroneous observations in the first place; (2) the likelihood of errors creeping into the repeating of these statements; and (3) the probability of entering into them imaginatively from the standpoint of one's own peculiar biases and experiences rather than from the viewpoint of the persons about whom they center. It is factors such as these which rule hearsay evidence out of civil and criminal courts; and yet, in studying the origins of race antipathy it appears that handed-down traditions and opinions greatly predominate.

1. All my store of unpleasant reactions against the Turks is not based on any personal knowledge of them. I do not even know a representative of this people; never glimpsed a Turk in gentle or in savage mood, never, except in imagination. But I have much second-hand knowledge. I have derived it from the lurid headlines of newspapers, from magazine articles on revelations of pseudo-political intrigue, from the stories dealing with the exotic life behind the mysterious veil and barred window. In church I have heard of Turkish atrocities to helpless missionaries. I have heard of the Turkish aversion to our culture and ideals talked of at dinner, at club meetings, and on the street. Nowadays I hear of the young Turk, with his intellectual veneer but who is the same unspeakable old Turk underneath.

2. When I was a young child my father one night at the dinner table spoke of some of the cruel practices of the Turks, which made a deep impression on me and perhaps started my aversion to the race. Another thing is a picture in a book of my father's, in which a Turk is selecting a woman for his harem. Father's prejudiced attitude of explanation together with the picture made a lasting impression on me. In studying geography in school I learned of the Turks' attitudes toward woman and this caused me to hate the race. In history classes in high school I studied the Crusades and the Turks' cruelty impressed me. Later I have read of the terrible massacres the Turks have committed. Parent, teacher, and reading are the main sources of my hatred of the Turk.

3. I have never before really stopped and thought out the reasons why I dislike the Turks and when I do I really don't know any logical reasons why I dislike them. When I was a child I always heard so much about the cruelty of the Turks and the horrible tortures and persecutions they inflicted upon the Christians. Hence, I have always pictured a Turk as a vile, greasy-looking individual with a long curved knife in his mouth.

4. The dislike that creeps over me when I think of the Turks is not the product of any intimate association with any of them, but is rather the result of

propaganda sponsored by the various molders of public opinion, such as the press and the church. This propaganda has been directed against the extreme cruelty, the debased morality, and the religion in whose name the acts of cruelty and immorality have been perpetrated. I cannot divorce the Turk from the slaughter of Armenians, neither from the despoiling of innocent girls and women. When I was about seven years old I saw some moving pictures of the Turks. The Turks seemed to have no morals or anything that I could admire; they were uncouth and murderous animals instead of men. I believe that there is some good, however, in the Turk. But I am so immersed in the pictures of his cruelty that I feel unpleasant when I think of him.

II. Unpleasant racial sense impressions *personally experienced* in the early years of life are many. Sometimes *fear* is aroused; again, *disgust*. In either case there is a sensory image that is often described as "horrifying." The fact that these images were experienced in childhood gives them a more or less permanent character. Illustrations of the experiences arousing *fear* are given in Cases 5–10.

5. We lived in a town in the middle west. My father was having some improvements made about our residence and hired a negro to do the work. This negro was an old darky of perhaps fifty odd years. He lived alone, in a little shack on the outskirts of the town. We children always called him "nigger Martin" and our older brothers and sisters used to use this name when they wanted anything done. "Nigger Martin will get you if you aren't good" meant more than the words to us. The negro Martin was digging a large ditch near our house. Of course child fashion we were there and observed everything that went on. After awhile it became tiresome to us so we thought we'd have some fun. As he threw up shovel-full after shovel-full of dirt we picked up pieces of dirt and threw at him. He became angry (I don't blame him) and told us that if ever he caught us we'd "catch it." We ran and did not bother him again. The next day he came and continued the work. We came to watch, and without the slightest warning he grabbed me into the ditch. I was so frightened and I cried and screamed while the others went to tell father. When he came and "saved" me I was a most happy but frightened girl. The name "nigger" of any sort always frightened me from that day on. That incident and all our training about the negro has naturally made me dislike and fear them.

6. My father used to rent land to the Japanese to raise strawberries on. One evening long past bed time we heard loud cries issuing from the quarters where the Japanese were living. Father rushed over and found that a Japanese from a neighboring farm had tried to kill one of the Japanese at our place with a hoe. The latter seized an iron rod and had laid out the former. My father was never able to find out the real cause. As I was very young I was much frightened at the noise. I was also afraid that my Daddy might be killed in the mix-up. Many nights after that I would jump from my sleep believing that the Japanese were attacking me. My prejudice against them dated from that night and I have never been able to overcome that distrust.

7. One afternoon I started from our hotel for a walk and I became lost. Until then the white robes and wrapped heads of the Turkish shop keepers had thrilled me. But when I discovered that I was "cut off" from the rest of the world—my world at least—I saw only very black eyes and sneering smiles. I asked my way and was greeted with a stream of broken English and wild gestures. As I hurried up the little street I seemed to be followed and surrounded by Turks. Even the recent Sheik vogue has not reconciled me to Turkish people.

8. My first encounter with the Negro was in Louisville, Kentucky, where I went to dinner at a hotel and happened to look into the kitchen where a colored

man was preparing the food. At the sight of this black face, offset with those terrible white whites of the eye, I was unable to eat my dinner, and so I left the table and went to my room.

9. When I was small we lived next to a farm cultivated by a Turk, and as we rode past his house he would throw rocks at us and make lots of noise. His face had a look of cruelty, and as I remember it now I can imagine his doing some of the things I read that they do in Turkey.

10. When I was about eight years old I went for a hike in the hills and on returning I had to pass through some Chinese vegetable gardens where a Chinese was seemingly picking strawberries. When I came along he jumped out and grabbed me, but I started running with him running close after me. He yelled something at me in Chinese. Finally I reached home, but ever after that I have been much afraid of Chinamen.

III. The illustrations of *disgust* as a type of sensory impressions leading to race antipathy are numerous. Frequently disgust and fear, as in Case 15, are aroused together. In Case 14 the emotion of disgust has been thought about until it has become almost a definitely organized sentiment.

11. I don't like them (Germans) because two-thirds of them are square-headed, pig-headed—and fat too. They try to domineer and cow their wives. I don't like their voices—thick and guttural—nor their avoidupois.

12. I spent several weeks at a summer resort in Michigan where there were many wealthy Jews, who made a great display of their wealth, wore a great amount of flashy jewelry and expensive clothes and yet they were most penurious when paying for board, lodging, or souvenirs. These experiences gave me the impression that Jews are greedy, miserly, selfish, egotistical, fond of display, because the individuals I came in contact with had these characteristics.

13. When I was five my parents brought me to California and I entered a school where I was forced to meet Armenians continually. In high school one-fourth to one-third were Armenians. No one desired to sit in class beside a repulsive-looking, vile-smelling, and yet insolent Armenian. Continual feuds kept the school in a seething tumult. To one who liked good old Anglo-Saxon names, the *varous* of the Armenian *ian* was repulsive. It is almost tragic to see a beautiful old home, now ill-kept and swarming with a truly Rooseveltian family of Armenians. During the time I lived in Fresno I saw nothing in the Armenian to make him endurable. Industry and the ability to out-Jew a Greek are his only useful characteristics. As I saw him, he is filthy, stingy, insolent, forward, and unattractive physically, mentally, and morally. Oppressed in Eurasia, the Armenian swells with unnatural expansion when, here in America, the oppression is no longer felt.

14. "Let the Chinese be damned of body and soul" has been the by-word of the English toward my innocent people for more than half a century. Although one of the oldest and outstanding Christian nations of the world, she has poisoned the body and mind of a generation of Chinese through the opium traffic. She is continuing this treachery with greater effort. This is unthinkable; that a God-fearing, out-and-out Christian nation is peddling a drug of that nature in this day and age. I cannot tolerate hypocrisy in any individual; then should I tolerate a nation as such? Decent society outlaws dope peddlers; therefore decent civilization in like manner should outlaw nations as such.

15. When I was about twelve years old I went to Mexico with my father. It was about the time the United States was having trouble with Mexico (1916). Some Mexican soldiers were passing by; my father was looking in another direction; one of the Mexican men standing near tried to grab me. Probably he

wanted ransom. He was so disgusting. He was such a coward and sneak and ever afterward I disliked all Mexicans. It seems to me that they will do almost anything when your back is turned.

IV. Unpleasant race impressions *experienced* in *adulthood* are also common. As a rule these anti-racial attitudes represent a generalization of experiences with one or a few individuals of the given race. Although there may be a recognition that the given experiences have been related to the less socially developed members of the race in question or from non-typical individuals the aversion is likely to spread to the whole race. Again, *fear* and *disgust* prevail.

16. I have spent about all my life along the Mexican border; in Mexico, Arizona and Sonora, and also California and Baja California. While working with a Mexican you have to watch him, that is, if you have anything he is liable to want. At one time a Mexican worked for us several months. He was friendly and a conscientious worker. When the work was over the Mexican left with no feeling on either side. The next night he came back and stole my best saddle. I got the saddle back but it did not increase my love for a Mexican. Five Mexicans came into a border store and shot three of my schoolmates. One of my near relatives spent six months in a Mexican prison. He was never given a trial and was finally released without one. Three Mexicans murdered one of our neighbors and beat up his wife and children so badly that it was three days before any of them could tell the story. These Mexicans were never caught but two others were hanged for the crime. Three of my father's cousins were killed by Mexicans; one of my uncles was killed and another maimed for life by Mexicans. One of my schoolmates helped tear down a Mexican flag; he was caught at four o'clock in the afternoon and by seven o'clock had been sentenced to face the firing squad the next morning at five. His father went alone and unarmed and by swearing a lot took his son from the Mexican jail.

17. I once had a job where I was asked to work beside a Negro at the same bench. His attitude of arrogance and superiority soon turned me against him. His low morality was evidenced by the stories and experiences he told. This gave me the impression that all Negroes are bad.

18. When I first came to college I met a number of Filippino men students. I was as cordial to them as I was to any of the other foreign students, but the Filippino men made advances and assumed a certain familiarity which I resented and disliked. They, more than any other foreign group, seemed to be so ambitious of becoming intimate friends with American girls. Several of my friends have had similar experiences with this group.

19. I took a check from a well-known Hindu, while working in a department store, and upon calling the bank found that there were no funds to meet it. When the manager investigated he found that the Hindu had five accounts, and that he would transfer his money from one to another every two months and write checks on the account just closed. I have found that many Hindus have instructed the banks not to cash any checks drawn on them that are not signed in both Latin script and in their own hieroglyphics, and sometimes require that a check bear the thumb-print of its writer.

Case 20. My boss is a Russian Jew, and not a bad man to work for at times, except that he always expects too much of a person. Outside of being my boss he is a good fellow and I hold nothing against him. But there are hundreds of Jews in the neighborhood, and he is one of the few I can say this about. I actually hate to see the majority of them come into the store. They expect you to wait on them first and let the others wait. No matter what you do for them they are never satisfied. They enter the store with a sarcastic expression on their faces that makes you want to throw them out. They usually get excited and become very insulting. I have actually known American ladies to walk out of the store when the boss gets excited, and needless to say, men walk out in order to prevent a fight.

In asking for data the writer specifically requested that "experiences" only be described and generalization and denunciation be avoided; the latter procedure, however, crept into nearly all the papers; it averaged half the space in nearly fifty per cent of all the papers and was the only characteristic of a few, especially of those whose antipathetic feeling was pronounced. Later personal interviews with representative individuals showed that this practice was due not to a desire to dodge the issue, but to a widespread habit of generalizing first and then belatedly of examining actual experiences and of analyzing these.

Moreover, this generalization habit was usually on the basis, first of tradition and opinion, and second, of experiences with a few individuals from the lower levels of a "despised race," or with a few better class individuals showing their worst natures to their "enemies"—something not necessarily peculiar to any race. Sometimes a single sensory image engendering fear or disgust or both, and experienced in childhood, is the basis of a generalization against a whole race. While there are definite feeling bases of an inherited nature that lead naturally to race antipathies, unscientific generalizations upon a few personal outstanding adverse experiences or upon many adverse traditions is an outstanding datum.

— · — · — · — · — · — · — · — · — · — · — · — · —

RENSIS LIKERT

*Likert Technique for Attitude Measurement**

Attempts to measure the traits of character and personality are nearly as old as techniques for the measurement of intellectual capacity, yet it can scarcely be claimed that they have achieved a similar success. Part, at least, of the difficulty has lain in the statistical difficulties which are encountered when everyday aspects of social behavior, ordinarily handled as qualitative affairs, are treated from the mathematical point of view. The present study, although part of a larger investigation undertaken in 1929 by Gardner Murphy, aims primarily at the solution of a technical problem which has arisen in relation to the quantitative aspects of the study of social attitudes.

The history and present status of research upon personality traits in general, and social attitudes in particular, have been so thoroughly surveyed by Murphy (21,

*Rensis Likert, "A Technique for the Measurement of Attitudes," *Archives of Psychology* 140 (1932): 1–55 (whole). Excerpted from pp. 5–6, 12–15, 21–26, 33–35, 44–55.

pp. 381–386, and 22, pp. 558–690), Bain (4), Vetter (41), Katz and Allport (16), Watson (43), and others, that no useful purpose would be served in attempting such a study here.

Nevertheless, among the hundreds of efforts to measure social attitudes during the last few years, the careful procedures developed by Thurstone (34, 38) have naturally and rightly received special attention. These are characterized by a special endeavor to equalize the step-intervals from one attitude to the next in the attitude scale, using the familiar methods of psychophysics for such determinations. The Thurstone methods have been shown to yield a satisfactory reliability, and, in terms of correlations between scores and case histories as evaluated by judges, a satisfactory validity (29).

Many obvious affinities appear between the present study and those of Thurstone, yet in a sense the present report constitutes a radical departure from the concepts which Thurstone has published, as, for example, in the use of judges.

A number of statistical assumptions are made in the application of his attitude scales,–e.g., that the scale values of the statements are independent of the attitude distribution of the readers who sort the statements (38, p. 92),–assumptions which, as Thurstone points out, have not been verified. The method is, moreover, exceedingly laborious. It seems legitimate to inquire whether it actually does its work better than the simpler scales which may be employed, and in the same breath to ask also whether it is not possible to construct equally reliable scales without making unnecessary statistical assumptions. Since so much is being published about attitude measurement, it seems worth while to raise these questions and to report on some results relative to the problem. It is feared that some will mistakenly interpret this article as an "attack" on Thurstone's methods. I therefore wish to emphasize in the strongest terms that I am simply endeavoring to call attention to certain problems of method, and that I am very far from convinced that the present data close the question.

The method by which the questionnaire was constructed was as follows. Having determined to study intensively the matter of international, inter-racial and economic attitudes, and, to a minor degree, political and religious attitudes, among large numbers of college students at typical American universities, a survey was made of the questionnaires already administered by other psychologists for these purposes. Among those which proved especially helpful were those of G. B. Neumann (23), C. W. Hunter (15) and R. W. George (9). In addition, about two hundred newspapers and magazines were rapidly surveyed during the autumn of 1929, declarations of opinion being culled for consideration, special emphasis being given to the more dogmatic types of opinion frequently found in editorials. A small number of questions were included from books, addresses and pamphlets, and a number were made up by the experimenters. Wherever it was possible to use questionnaire material which had previously been extensively tried out, and where, in a sense, "norms" were available, we preferred to use the questions exactly as they stood. In a few cases, it was necessary to abbreviate and simplify the questions in order to make sure that only one issue was involved and that ambiguity was avoided. In those instances in which we made up our own questions, we sought to emphasize simplicity, clarity, and brevity.

Without exception, the questions were presented in such a form as to permit a "judgment of value" rather than a "judgment of fact." Phrases such as "The United

States should," or "We ought to," or "No man should be allowed" constantly reappeared. In a few instances it may seem on first inspection that a question has to do with a question of fact, but closer analysis will reveal the highly arbitrary character of such "facts." Perhaps the least desirable of all the questions used was the following: "Is war at present a biological necessity?" Such a question appears to many minds to be categorically a factual one; for example, from a neo-Malthusian point of view it may be regarded as capable only of an affirmative answer. The term "necessity," however, refers here more to the student's attitudes toward various wants than to any of those types of necessity which are discussed by physicists or logicians. This is not offered in defense of the use of this particular item, which is regarded as one which should have been omitted; this explanation is offered only to make clear that at least in the great majority of cases and, we hope, in all, the inquiry has to do with the wants, desires, conative dispositions of the subjects, not with their opinions regarding matters of fact.

One further generalization may be offered regarding the plan underlying the choices of questions. Since value judgments are required, it was conceived that every issue might be presented in such a way as to allow the subject to take sides as between two clearly opposed alternatives. Furthermore each issue was so drawn that two conflicting groups of persons were either named or implied, and the subject allowed to affiliate himself with one or with the other group. In the struggle of the Negro, for example, to attain economic, political, or social equality, where the white man resists such equality, the subject has an opportunity either to take or to refuse to take the Negro standpoint. In the case of the conflict of relatively unfavored economic groups against those who enjoy special opportunities, and in the case of weaker nations which demand greater territorial or economic expansion than is at present permitted them, the same opportunity to ally oneself with one or the other of two opposing factions is involved. Again, it is not asserted that we have in all cases succeeded in framing an ideal "conflict issue." We would urge, however, that the great majority of conflict issues covered in our survey are empirically important issues, in which students at American universities actually do have opportunity to take sides and with regard to which the great majority have heard repeated discussions; secondly, that the results constitute in themselves an empirical check on the degree of success with which a tendency to take the side of a given group does enter into our questions in such a way as to be empirically measured. High specificity would have meant, among other things, that we had certainly failed in finding any general pro-Negro, anti-Japanese, etc. attitudes, and would have led to statistical difficulties of various sorts in handling incoherent masses of unrelated material. The clear-cut generality of certain attitudes, such as pro-Negro, internationalism, etc., shows that it is precisely in the field of *affiliation with or against* certain social groups that the most definite results are obtained.

Through collaboration with instructors, the attitudes tests were given to undergraduates (chiefly male) in nine universities and colleges extending from Illinois to Connecticut and from Ohio and Pennsylvania to Virginia. (The names of the institutions cannot appropriately be printed here, only the Columbia College data, Group D, being identified.) The total number of individuals participating was somewhat above 2000 but the data here intensively analyzed were derived from only 650 persons. The attitudes test, called a SURVEY OF OPINIONS, was first given in the late fall of 1929 (to all groups except Group C and Group F which were given the test in 1931) and, by arrangement with instructors, a retest given 30 days later. Some items from the first test and many new items were included in this second test. The first test required on the average about 40 minutes and the retest a slightly longer time.

The kind of questionnaire material to be reported here falls into four main classes. In the first, questions were to be answered by a Yes, a question mark, or a No, as for example, "Do you favor the early entrance of the United States into the League of Nations?" YES ? NO. Next came a series of multiple-choice questions in which one of five possible answers was to be selected, for example: "Using the term 'armaments' to mean equipment devised for war rather than for police purposes, our policy should be to favor: (a) absolute and immediate disarmament of all nations, (b) rapid and drastic reduction of the armaments of all nations, (c) slow but steady reduction of all armaments, (d) maintenance for a long time of approximately the present military and naval strength of all the powers, (e) our free military and naval expansion unembarrassed by agreements with other nations." Third, there was a series of propositions to be responded to by the words (a) *strongly approve*, (b) *approve*, (c) *undecided*, (d) *disapprove*, (e) *strongly disapprove*, for example: "All men who have the opportunity should enlist in the Citizens Military Training Camps." Fourth, a series of abbreviated newspaper narratives about social conflicts, terminating in a sentence describing the *outcome* of this conflict, the student being asked to indicate his response to this outcome, for example: "A group of Japanese truck-farmers in Southern California, through their industry and lower standards of living, are able to undersell their American competitors. The American farmers insist that IT IS THE DUTY OF ALL WHITE PEOPLE TO PURCHASE ONLY FROM WHITE FARMERS." This last form of question makes use of the same set of five responses mentioned above, *strongly approve*, *approve*, *undecided*, *disapprove*, and *strongly disapprove*.

★ ★ ★

IV. RESULTS

1. The Signa Method of Scoring

In order to compare one type of statement with another such as the "multiple choice" with the "strongly approve," it was necessary to devise some technique whereby they might be made comparable. In attempting to work out such a technique, it was noticed that a great number of the five-point statements, i.e. the "multiple choice" or "strongly approve" statements (in each case the subject being offered five alternatives from which to choose), yielded a distribution resembling a normal distribution.

Table I shows some typical distributions obtained with the five-point statements. These percentages are based on a sample of 100 cases, all male, from one university. Of the two distributions which were quite skewed, number 7 of the Negro scale, was the more skewed. The other was number 6 of the Negro scale. It is interesting to note that if a group of Southern students are included in the distributions they become less skewed. Thus, for statement number 7 of the Negro scale the percentages for 100 male students from a college in Virginia are, respectively, 4, 3, 17, 18 and 58. Statements number 5 and 6 of the Imperialism scale are illustrative of a slight bi-modality which was found in a few of the "strongly approve" type of statements.

TABLE I. PERCENTAGE OF INDIVIDUALS CHECKING THE DIFFERENT ALTERNATIVES. COMPUTED FROM A SAMPLE OF 100 CASES, ALL MALE, FROM A SINGLE UNIVERSITY

Scale	Statement Number	MULTIPLE CHOICE STATEMENTS *Alternatives*				
		a	*b*	*c*	*d*	*e*
Negro	7	1	1	3	8	87
Negro	8	29	42	26	3	0
Imperialism	3	11	43	27	15	4

Scale	Statement Number	STRONGLY APPROVE STATEMENTS *Alternatives*				
		Strongly Approve	*Approve*	*Un-decided*	*Dis-approve*	*Strongly Disapprove*
International-ism	16	13	43	21	13	10
Negro	9	3	17	14	44	22
Imperialism	5	32	52	10	5	1
Negro	10	24	49	17	7	3
Imperialism	6	10	27	17	35	11

On the basis of this experimental evidence and upon the results of others (8, pp. 542–548, 28, pp. 71–91), it seems justifiable for experimental purposes to assume that attitudes are distributed fairly normally and to use this assumption as the basis for combining the different statements. The possible dangers inherent in this assumption are fully realized. This assumption is made simply as part of an experimental approach to attitude measurement. It is a step which it is hoped subsequent work in this field will either make unnecessary or prove justifiable. Perhaps this assumption is not correct; its correctness or incorrectness can best be determined by further experiment.

The percentage of individuals that checked a given position on a particular statement was converted into sigma values. This was done for each of the five-point statements which in our opinion had to do with internationalism. Table 22 of Thorndike's tables (30) greatly facilitated this calculation. These tables assume that one hundred per cent of the cases fall between –3 and +3 sigma. The values given in the table are the average sigma values of intervals represented by the stated percentages, the origin considered to be at the mean. The sigma deviations were always taken from the mean and the positive value was assigned to the end which seemed to favor internationalism, the negative being assigned to the end which favored nationalism. To avoid using negative values the arbitrary zero may be placed at –3 sigma rather than at the mean. These signs were designated in an arbitrary fashion and then verified objectively (see pages 48–52). The sigma values were computed from percentages obtained from a sample of 100 cases, all male, selected from one particular university. Table II shows the percentage of individuals checking each of the different alternatives and the corresponding sigma values for statement number sixteen of the Internationalism scale.

The statements selected were checked for internal consistency or "clustering," by finding the reliability, using odd statements vs. even statements. The fourteen five-point statements used yielded moderately high reliabilities when tried on three different groups with between 30 and 35 subjects in each group. Two of these groups were from the same

TABLE II. DATA FOR STATEMENT NUMBER 16 OF THE
INTERNATIONALISM SCALE

Alternative	Strongly Approve	Approve	Un- decided	Dis- approve	Strongly Disapprove
Percentage checking	13%	43	21	13	10
Corresponding sigma value	−1.63	−.43	+.43	+.99	+1.76
Corresponding 1 to 5 value	1	2	3	4	5

university, the third was from another university in an entirely different geographical area. These results indicate a "cluster" or attitude variable which we are justified in treating as a unit, so far as these three groups are concerned. The reliabilities obtained for these groups are given in Table III. These results and the following considerations seem to justify the statement that the sigma scoring technique is the most satisfactory now available for attitude measurement. It not only seems to avoid many of the shortcomings of existing methods of attitude measurement, but at the same time retains most of the advantages present in methods now used.

TABLE III. RELIABILITY COEFFICIENTS—SIGMA
SCORING METHOD—FOURTEEN STATEMENTS
DEALING WITH INTERNATIONALISM
Odds vs. Evens (7 items vs. 7 items)

Group	N	Raw	Corrected
A	30	.76	.86
B	32	.79	.88
F	33	.75	.86

In the first place, the sigma scoring method meets the requirement stated by Thurstone (38, p. 56):

Ideally, the scale should perhaps be constructed by means of the voting only. It may be possible to formulate the problem so that the scale values of the statements may be extracted from the records of actual voting. If that should be possible, then the present procedure of establishing the scale-values by sorting will be suspended.

Further, it avoids the difficulties encountered when using a judging group to construct the scale. A number of these difficulties have been pointed our by Rice (27). The following quotation deals with one of the major shortcomings of any technique employing a judging group (27, pp. 190–191):

The difficulties of building scales similar to Thurstone's and of applying them to the measurement of the attitudes of social groups, become increasingly difficult once we leave the classroom, the discussion club and the other small, comparatively infrequent and highly selected groups that enjoy having experiments tried upon them. Such groups already have developed ways of making their attitudes articulate. It is the more numerous work-a-day groupings of society, which are inaccessible to his controlled measurements, about whose attitudes the social scientist is in the most need of information. Students may be required, good natured academicians may be cajoled, and sundry needy persons may be paid to sort cards containing propositions into eleven piles. But it is difficult to imagine securing comparable judgments, or satisfactory measurements in the final application, from bricklayers, business men, Italian-Americans, nuns, stevedores, or seamstresses. And, unless the scale itself is based upon equal-seeming differences to a random sample of the group which is to be measured, its validity—the degree to which it measures that which it purports to measure—becomes open to question.

Another decided advantage of the sigma technique is that it yields reliabilities as high as those obtained by other techniques, with fewer items. This is possible because it uses an approach to the problem somewhat different from that conventionally used. Previously attempts have been made to find the scale value of each particular statement along a continuum; a person's score being then determined by the scale value of the statements that he accepts. In this study, however, each statement becomes a scale in itself and a person's reaction to each statement is given a score. These scores are then combined by using a median or a mean. Eggan's study reported by Thurstone (35) lends further evidence to support the method presented here.

In contemplating this method of measuring attitudes it is well to realize that the stronger the generic set toward one extreme or the other extreme of an attitude continuum, the more it influences the specific reactions. When the generic set is not strong then the specific items themselves largely determine the reaction. In the latter case, however, the reaction is seldom very intense but rather mildly pro or con. That is, the individual's reactions, so far as that particular attitude is concerned, do not deviate widely from the average.

The sigma technique also yields scores the units of which are equal throughout the entire range. Likewise, the same kinds of measures can be obtained with it as are obtained with other techniques now in existence (38). Thus it is possible to obtain the most typical measure of an individual's attitude and also the range or dispersion of his attitude.

Needless to say the construction of an attitude scale by the sigma method is much easier than by using a judging group to place the statements in piles from which the scales values must be calculated.

Among the excellent characteristics of Thurstone's method of attitude construction (38) are the objective checks which he has devised for ambiguity and irrelevance. Similar objective checks can be applied to the sigma technique, if desired. The application of these objective checks are fully discussed [in the appendix].

It is interesting to note that the scores on the international statements using the sigma technique correlate +.67 with the Thurstone-Droba War scale (6) (data from Group F). When corrected for attenuation, this becomes +.77. This relationship is present even though the statements on the whole are quite dissimilar.

2. The Simpler Method of Scoring

Although the sigma technique seemed to be quite satisfactory for the intended use, it was decided to try a simpler technique to see if it gave results comparable with the sigma technique. If it did, the simpler method would save considerable work in a general survey type of study of this kind. The simpler technique involved the assigning of values of from

1 to 5 to each of the five different positions on the five-point statements. The ONE end was always assigned to the negative end of the sigma scale, and the FIVE end to the positive end of the sigma scale. (See Table II.)

After assigning in this manner the numerical values to the possible responses, the score for each individual was determined by finding the average of the numerical values of the positions that he checked. Actually, since the number of statements was the same for all individuals, the sum of the numerical scores rather than the mean was used. The reliability of odds vs. evens for this method yielded essentially the same values as those obtained with the sigma method of scoring. The scores obtained by this method and the sigma method correlated almost perfectly as will be seen in Table IV.

TABLE IV. COEFFICIENTS OF CORRELATION BETWEEN SCORES OBTAINED BY THE SIGMA METHOD, THE 1-5 METHOD, AND THE 1-7 METHOD

Group	N	International (15 Statements)			Negro (10 Statements)
		σ vs. 1-5	1-5 vs. 1-7	σ vs. 1-7	σ vs. 1-5
A	30	.991	.990		.987
B	32	.995	.993		.992
F	33	.995	.990	.997	

The same results were obtained when the values of 1, 3, 4, 5, and 7 were assigned to the different positions corresponding respectively to 1, 2, 3, 4 and 5. In the former case, it will be noted that the extremes were given slightly greater weight. This method likewise correlated very highly with the sigma method and with the 1 to 5 method as shown in Table IV.

These results seem to justify the use of the simpler methods of scoring since they yield almost identical results with the sigma method and similarly do not involve any of the errors likely to be present in any technique in which experts, judges, or raters are used.

5. Comparison of the Simpler Method with the Thurstone Method of Scoring

Two groups, C and F, were given the Thurstone-Droba War scale (6) as well as the SURVEY OF OPINIONS. Table VIII shows the reliability coefficients obtained for the Thurstone scale and for the Internationalism scale, derived from the SURVEY OF OPINIONS, for these two groups. The reliability coefficients of the Thurstone test, obtained by correlating Form A against Form B, was respectively .78 and .74 for the two groups. The reliability for the two forms combined, as determined by the Spearman-Brown formula, becomes .88 and .85, respectively. The same reliability is obtained by the present Internationalism scale with 24 items as is obtained by combining both forms of the Thurstone-Droba scale with a total of 44 items. Thus using the method here described, a measure of a person's attitude as reliable as that obtained by the Thurstone method is secured by asking him to react to one-half as many items. The coefficients of correlation between the Internationalism scale and the Thurstone-Droba scale are also given in Table VIII.

TABLE VIII. COMPARISON OF THE THURSTONE-DROBA WAR SCALE AND THE INTERNATIONALISM SCALE

Group	N	Reliability Coefficients Thurstone-Droba Scale		Reliability Coefficients of Internationalism Scale	Internationalism Scale vs. Thurstone-Droba Scale	
		Form A vs. B 22 Items vs. 22	Corrected A & B 44 Items	24 Items	Raw	Corrected For Attenuation
C	54	.78	.88	.88	.71	.81
F	32	.74	.85	.88	.65	.75

In view of the fact that the method presented here when compared with the Thurstone method gave evidence of yielding the same reliability with fewer items, or higher reliabilities with the same number of items, it was decided to try the 1 to 5 method of scoring upon the Thurstone-Droba War scale to see how it would compare with Thurstone's method of scoring. Using Group C each individual was asked to indicate whether he strongly agreed, agreed, was undecided, disagreed, or strongly disagreed with each statement in the Thurstone-Droba War scale, Forms A and B.

Four statements in each form were not used in the scoring because it was found virtually impossible to determine whether to assign a value of 1 or 5 to the "strongly agree" alternative. An illustration of such a statement is number 5 in Form A: "Compulsory military training in all countries should be reduced but not eliminated." It is impossible to tell whether a person is agreeing or disagreeing with the "reduction" aspect of this statement or the "not eliminated" aspect. A person who strongly opposes compulsory military training would disagree or strongly disagree with the "*not eliminated*" aspect, whereas a person who favors compulsory military training would disagree or strongly disagree with the "*reduction*" aspect of the statement. Obviously for the 1 to 5 method of scoring the statement is double-barreled and of little value because it does not differentiate persons in terms of their attitudes. Persons at either extreme of the attitude continuum can readily check the same alternative.

Another illustration of a statement that could not be used is number 17 of Form B: "Wars often right tremendous wrongs." This might be treated as a statement concerning fact, and could well be agreed with or disagreed with by a person regardless of his attitude. The other statements that were not used follow:

Form A, statements number 8, 10 and 17.
Form B, statements number 5, 10 and 20.

The criterion of internal consistency, discussed on pages 50–52 was used as an objective check to see (1) whether the numerical values were properly assigned and (2) whether each statement differentiated the extremes in the manner expected.

The results expected were obtained and are shown in Table IX. The 1 to 5 method of scoring with fewer items used on each form yielded as high a reliability coefficient for *one* form as the Thurstone method did for the *two* forms combined. The most plausible explanation for this higher reliability obtained by the 1 to 5 method has already been suggested on page 24.

TABLE IX. COMPARISON OF THE THURSTONE AND THE 1 TO 5 METHOD OF SCORING THE THURSTONE-DROBA WAR SCALE DATA FROM GROUP "C" (*N* = 54)

	Form A vs. B	
	Raw	*Corrected*
Thurstone-Droba scale scored 1-5 method (18 questions only used in each form instead of 22)	(18 vs. 18)	(36 items)
	.88	.94
Regular Thurstone scoring	(22 vs. 22)	(44 items)
	.78	.88

COEFFICIENT OF CORRELATION BETWEEN THE TWO METHODS

	Raw	*Corrected for Attenuation*
Thurstone scale (44 items) vs. 1-5 scoring of Thurstone scale (36 items)	.83	.92

The two methods of scoring correlate quite highly, namely .83, which when corrected for attenuation becomes .92. It is possible that if the same statements had been used in both methods, rather than four less in each form on the 1 to 5 scoring, a still higher coefficient of correlation between the two methods would have been obtained.

APPENDIX

THE METHOD OF CONSTRUCTING AN ATTITUDE SCALE

I. The Selection of Statements

Each statement should be of such a nature that persons with different points of view, so far as the particular attitude is concerned, will respond to it differentially. Any statement to which persons with markedly different attitudes can respond in the same way is, of course, unsatisfactory.

The results obtained in constructing the present scales demonstrate the value of the following criteria. These criteria were kept in mind in collecting the statements for the original Survey of Opinions.

1. It is essential that all statements be expressions of *desired behavior* and not statements of *fact*. Two persons with decidedly different attitudes may, nevertheless, agree on questions of fact. Consequently, their reaction to a statement of fact is no indication of their attitudes. For example, a person strongly pro-Japanese and a person strongly pro-Chinese might both agree with the following statements:

> The League of Nations has failed in preventing Japan's military occupation of Manchuria.

or

> Japan has been trying to create in Manchuria a monopoly of trade, equivalent to closing the "open-door" to the trade of other countries.

To agree with them or believe them true is in no way a measure of attitude.

Rice (27, p. 184) has clearly stated the importance of recognizing this criterion when in discussing the Thurstone technique he says:

> What is the possibility that the acceptance or rejection by a subject of a statement upon the completed scale may represent a rational judgment concerning the truth or falsity of the statement made? It would seem to exist. If so, the validity of the statement as an index of attitude is destroyed or impaired.

In dealing with expressions of desired behavior rather than expressions of fact the statement measures the present attitude of the subject and not some past attitude. The importance of dealing with present rather than past attitudes has been emphasized by Thurstone (38) and Murphy (22, p. 615). A very convenient way of stating a proposition so that it does involve desired behavior is by using the term *should*. The use of *should* is well illustrated in the "strongly approve" type of statements shown on pages 15–20.

2. The second criterion is the necessity of stating each proposition in *clear, concise, straight-forward statements*. Each statement should be in the simplest possible vocabulary. No statement should involve double negatives or other wording which will make it involved and confusing. Double-barreled statements are most confusing and should always be broken in two. Often an individual wishes to react favorably to one part and unfavorably to the other and when the parts are together he is at a loss to know how to react. Thus in the following illustration a person might well approve one part and disapprove another part:

> In order to preserve peace, the Unites States should abolish tariffs, enter the League of Nations, and maintain the largest army and navy in the world.

To ask for a single response to this statement makes it meaningless to the subject. This statement should be divided into at least three separate statements.

The simplicity of the vocabulary will, of course, vary with the group upon whom the scale is intended to be used, but it is a desirable precaution to state each proposition in such a way that persons of less understanding than any member of the group for which the test is being constructed will understand and be able to respond to the statements. Above all, regardless of the simplicity or complexity of vocabulary or the naïveté or sophistication of the group, each statement *must avoid every kind of ambiguity*.

3. In general it would seem desirable to have each statement so worded that the modal reaction to it is approximately in the middle of the possible responses.

4. To avoid any space error or any tendency to a stereotyped response it seems desirable to have the different statements so worded that about one-half of them have one end of the attitude continuum corresponding to the *left* or *upper* part of the reaction alternatives and the other half have the same end of the attitude continuum corresponding to the *right* or *lower* part of the reaction alternatives. For example, about one-half the statements in the Internationalism scale have the international extreme corresponding with "Strongly approve" while the other half has it corresponding with "Strongly disapprove." These two kinds of statements ought to be distributed throughout the attitude test in a chance or haphazard manner.

5. If multiple choice statements are used, the different alternatives should involve *only a single attitude variable* and not several.

II. Constructing the Scale

It is usually desirable to prepare and select more statements than are likely to be finally used, because after trying the statements upon a group, some may be found to be quite unsatisfactory for the intended purpose. For this reason after selecting a good number of statements they should be given to the group or a part of the group whose attitudes we wish to measure. The sample used should be sufficiently large for statistical purposes.

For purposes of tabulation and scoring, a numerical value must be assigned to each of the possible alternatives. If five alternatives have been used, it is necessary to assign values of from one to five with the three assigned to the undecided position on each statement. The ONE end is assigned to one extreme of the attitude continuum and the FIVE to the other; this should be done consistently for each of the statements which it is expected will be included in the scale. Thus if we arbitrarily consider the "favorable to the Negro" extreme FIVE and "unfavorable to the Negro" extreme ONE, the alternative responses to the following statements would be assigned the values shown:

Numerical Value	"How far in our educational system (aside from trade education) should the most intelligent negroes be allowed to go?
1	(a) Grade school.
2	(b) Junior high school.
3	(c) High school.
4	(d) College.
5	(e) Graduate and professional schools."

"In a community where the negroes outnumber the whites, a negro who is insolent to a white man should be:

5	(a) excused or ignored.
4	(b) reprimanded.
3	(c) fined and jailed.
2	(d) not only fined and jailed, but also given corporal punishment (whipping, etc.).
1	(e) lynched."

"All negroes belong in one class and should be treated in about the same way."

	STRONGLY APPROVE	APPROVE	UNDECIDED	DISAPPROVE	STRONGLY DISAPPROVE
Value	(1)	(2)	(3)	(4)	(5)

"Where there is segregation, the negro section should have the same equipment in paving, water, and electric light facilities as are found in the white districts."

	STRONGLY APPROVE	APPROVE	UNDECIDED	DISAPPROVE	STRONGLY DISAPPROVE
Value	(5)	(4)	(3)	(2)	(1)

Some may object to the designation made, saying that the terms "favorable" and "unfavorable" are ambiguous or that the favorable attitude is just opposite to that here considered favorable. Thus, if one wishes to call favorable to the Negro the following responses to the statements shown on pages 18-19, no serious objections will be raised providing that he is consistent in his designations; to do so, however, does seem to be less reasonable and not in accord with common usage.

So far as the measurement of the attitude is concerned, it is quite immaterial what the extremes of the attitude continuum are called; the important fact is that persons do

Statement Number	Response
1	Yes
2	Yes
3	No
4	No
5	No
6	(e)
7	(a)
8	(e)
9	Strongly approve
10	Strongly approve
11	Strongly disapprove
12	Strongly disapprove
13	Strongly approve
14	Strongly disapprove
15	Strongly approve

differ quantitatively in their attitudes, some being more toward one extreme, some more toward the other. Thus, as Thurstone has pointed out in the use of his scales, it makes no difference whether the zero extreme is assigned to "appreciation of" the church or "depreciation of" the church, the attitude can be measured in either case and the person's reaction to the church expressed.

The split-half reliability should be found by correlating the sum of the odd statements for each individual against the sum of the even statements. Since each statement is answered by each individual, calculations can be reduced by using the sum rather than the average.

An objective check ought then to be applied to see (1) if the numerical values are properly assigned and (2) whether the statements are "differentiating." One possible check is item analysis which calls for calculating the correlation coefficient of each statement with the battery. If a negative correlation coefficient is obtained, it indicates that the numerical values are not properly assigned and that the ONE and FIVE ends should be reversed. If a zero or very low correlation coefficient is obtained, it indicates that the statement fails to measure that which the rest of the statements measure. Such statements will be called undifferentiating. Thurstone (38) refers to them as irrelevant or ambiguous. By "undifferentiating" we merely mean that the statement does not measure what the battery measures and hence to include it contributes nothing to the scale. A statement which is undifferentiating for a scale measuring one attitude continuum may be quite satisfactory for a scale measuring another attitude continuum. The following are some of the reasons why a statement may prove undifferentiating:

1. The statement may involve a different issue from the one involved in the rest of the statements, that is, it involves a different attitude continuum.

2. The statement may be responded to in the same way by practically the entire group. For example, the response to the following statement was practically the same upon the part of all students—some two thousand—to whom it was given: "Should the United States repeal the Japanese Exclusion Act?"

3. The statement may be so expressed that it is misunderstood by members of the group. This may be due to its being poorly stated, phrased in unfamiliar words, or worded in the form of a double-barreled statement.

4. It may be a statement concerning fact which individuals who fall at different points on the attitude continuum will be equally liable to accept or reject.

It is, of course, desirable in constructing an attitude scale that the experimenter exercise every precaution in the selecting of statements so as to avoid those that are undifferentiating. However, item analysis can be used as an objective check to determine whether the members of a group react differentially to the statement in the same manner that they react differentially to the battery; that is, item analysis indicates whether those persons who fall toward one end of the attitude continuum on the battery do so on the particular statement and vice versa. Thus item analysis reveals the satisfactoriness of any statement so far as its inclusion in a given attitude scale is concerned.

No matter for what *a priori* reasons the experimenter may consider a statement to belong in a scale, if the statement, when tried on a group, does not measure what the rest of the statements measure, there is no justification for keeping that statement in the battery. After all, we are interested in measuring the attitudes of the members of the group, not those of the experimenter.

There is no reason to expect that the logical analysis of the person who selects the statements will necessarily be supported by the group. Quite often, because of a lack of understanding of the cultural background of the group, the experimenter may find that the statements do not form the clusters or hierarchies that he expected. It is as important psychologically to know what these clusters are as it is to be able to measure them.

The degree of inclusion, i.e. the size of the correlation coefficient between the item and the battery, required for a particular statement will no doubt be a function of the purpose for which the attitudes are being measured. If a general survey type of study is being undertaken the degree of inclusion required will be less than when a more specialized aspect of attitudes is being studied. A similar relationship is to be noted in the measurement of intelligence.

The only difficulty in using item analysis is that the calculation of the necessary coefficients of correlation is quite laborious. The criterion of internal consistency was tried and the results obtained were found to be comparable with the results from item analysis. Table X Shows a comparison of the results obtained from item analysis and the criterion of internal consistency. It will be noted that the relation between the order of excellence for the different statements as determined by item analysis and the criterion of internal consistency as expressed by rho is +.91. Since the criterion of internal consistency is much easier to use then item analysis and yet yields essentially the same results, its use is suggested.

In using the criterion of internal consistency the reactions of the group that constitute one extreme in the particular attitude being measured are compared with the reactions of the group that constitute the other extreme. In practice approximately ten per cent from each extreme was used. Table XI shows the criterion of internal consistency applied to the Internationalism scale for Group D. This criterion acts as an objective check upon the correct assigning of numerical values in that if the numerical values are reversed on a particular statement the extreme high group will score low on that statement and the extreme low group will score high, i.e. we will obtain a negative difference between the two extreme groups on that question. Furthermore, if a statement is undif-

TABLE X. COMPARISON OF THE RESULTS OBTAINED FROM THE APPLICATION OF THE CRITERION OF INTERNAL CONSISTENCY AND ITEM ANALYSIS TO THE NEGRO SCALE FOR GROUPS "A" AND "B" COMBINED—($N = 62$)

Column 1	Column 2	Column 3	Column 4	Column 5
1	.69	1.7	2	5
2	.64	1.5	6	6
3	.51	1.7	10	11
4	.18	0.4	14	14
5	.62	1.3	7	8
6	.40	0.7	11	13
7	.12	0.1	15	15
8	.39	1.1	12	10
9	.26	0.9	13	12
10	.65	2.7	5	1
11	.60	1.2	8	9
12	.54	1.4	9	7
13	.67	2.3	4	2
14	.74	2.0	1	3
15	.68	1.6	3	4

rho (Column 4 vs. Column 5) = +.91

Column 1—Statement numbers.
Column 2—Coefficient of correlation between the score on the individual statement and the average score on all fifteen statements.
Column 3—Difference between the average score of the highest 9 individuals and the lowest 9 individuals.
Column 4—Order of excellence as determined by item analysis based upon the coefficients of correlation shown in Column 2.
Column 5—Order of excellence as determined by the criterion of internal consistency based upon the differences shown in Column 3.

ferentiating it will not differentiate or discriminate the two extreme groups, i.e. the high group will not score appreciably higher than the low group upon that statement.

Finally, on the basis of the results obtained from item analysis or the criterion of internal consistency and having due regard for all the factors concerned, one should select the most differentiating statements for the final form or forms of the attitude test. If, through this selection of the more differentiating statements, statements concerning a particular aspect of the attitude being measured are eliminated, then, obviously, the final scale can only be said to measure the attitude continuum represented by the remaining statements. For example, if it is found by the use of these objective checks that statements concerning the economic status of the Negro involve an attitude continuum other than that of statements having to do with the social equality of the Negro, the former should not be mixed with the latter. On the contrary, two attitude scales should be constructed. If, on the other hand, these two groups of statements are found to involve the same attitude continuum, they can be combined into a single scale. As previously stated, the degree of inclusion required or desired will generally be a function of the purpose for which the attitude scales are being used.

A sufficient number of statements should be used in each form to obtain the desired reliability. In preparing the final form or forms, it would be desirable to apply the fourth criterion stated under "The Selection of Statements."

Because a series of statements form a unit or cluster when used with one group of

TABLE XI. CRITERION OF INTERNAL CONSISTENCY APPLIED TO THE INTERNATIONALISM SCALE FOR GROUP "D"—(N = 100)

STATEMENT NUMBERS

HIGH GROUP

Indiv. No.	Score	Three-Point Statements												Five-Point Statements												
		1	2	3	4	5	6	7	8	9	10	11	12	13	14	15	16	17	18	19	20	21	22	23	24
85	103	4	4	4	4	4	4	4	4	4	4	4	4	5	5	5	5	5	5	5	5	5	5	5	5
65	104	4	4	3	4	4	4	4	4	4	4	4	4	5	5	5	5	5	5	5	5	5	5	5	4
13	102	4	4	4	4	4	4	4	4	4	4	4	4	5	5	3	5	5	5	5	5	5	3	3	5
10	101	4	4	4	4	4	4	4	4	4	4	4	4	4	3	3	4	5	5	5	5	5	4	5	5
71	101	2	4	4	4	4	4	2	4	4	4	4	4	5	3	4	5	5	5	3	5	5	5	5	5
98	100	4	4	4	4	4	4	4	4	4	4	4	4	4	3	5	4	5	5	4	4	5	5	3	4
27	98	4	2	4	4	4	4	4	4	4	4	4	4	4	5	3	5	5	5	3	5	5	5	5	5
60	98	4	4	4	4	4	4	2	4	2	4	4	4	5	5	3	5	5	5	3	4	5	4	5	5
64	98	4	4	4	4	4	4	4	4	2	4	4	4	4	3	4	3	5	5	5	5	5	4	5	4
Sum of 9-high		34	34	35	36	36	36	32	36	32	36	36	36	42	37	35	40	45	45	40	44	45	35	41	42
Sum of 9-low		18	20	20	28	24	29	21	20	22	21	34	23	21	24	22	15	31	22	15	22	24	17	14	22
D		16	14	15	8	12	7	11	16	10	15	2	13	21	13	13	25	14	23	25	22	21	18	27	20
D/9		1.8	1.6	1.7	.9	1.3	.8	1.2	1.8	1.1	1.7	.22	1.4	2.3	1.4	1.4	2.8	1.6	2.6	2.8	2.4	2.3	2.0	3.0	2.2
Order		1.5	5	3.5	10	7	11	8	1.5	9	3.5	12	6	6.5	11.5	11.5	2.5	10	4	2.5	5	6.5	9	1	8

(3-point statements and 5-point statements treated separately)

LOW GROUP

Indiv. No.	Score	1	2	3	4	5	6	7	8	9	10	11	12	13	14	15	16	17	18	19	20	21	22	23	24
17	49	2	2	2	2	2	2	4	4	2	2	2	2	1	2	1	1	2	2	1	2	4	2	2	2
77	54	2	2	2	2	2	2	2	2	2	2	4	2	2	3	3	1	4	2	1	2	2	2	1	2
22	60	2	2	2	2	4	4	2	2	3	3	4	2	4	3	1	3	4	2	2	2	4	2	1	2
35	61	2	2	2	2	3	3	2	2	2	2	4	4	2	2	3	1	3	2	3	1	3	2	2	2
53	62	2	2	2	4	2	2	2	2	4	4	4	3	2	3	2	2	2	3	1	3	1	1	1	2
69	62	2	2	4	2	2	4	2	2	2	2	4	2	2	3	3	2	4	1	1	4	5	2	1	1
94	63	2	2	2	4	2	4	2	2	4	2	2	4	2	2	3	2	4	4	2	3	2	2	2	2
21	64	2	2	2	4	2	4	3	2	2	2	4	2	2	3	3	1	4	4	2	2	1	2	3	4
88	64	2	4	2	4	2	2	2	2	2	2	4	4	4	3	3	1	4	4	2	2	1	2	3	3
Sum of 9-low		18	20	20	28	24	29	21	20	22	21	34	23	21	24	22	15	31	22	15	22	24	17	14	22

subjects which justifies combining the reactions to the different statements into a single score, it does not follow that they will constitute a unit on all other groups of persons with the same or different cultural backgrounds. For example, an examination of the statements in the Imperialism scale will reveal that it contains statements having to do with imperialism both in China and Latin America, and while it is true that these statements form a sufficient cluster to justify their being treated as a unit with the groups used, still with other groups of persons with markedly different attitudes toward China or Latin America it is probably that this single scale would have to be divided into two or more scales.

The ease and simplicity with which attitude scales can be checked for split-half reliability and internal consistency would seem to make it desirable to determine the reliability and examine the internal consistency of each attitude scale for each group upon which it is used. It is certainly reasonable to suppose that just as an intelligence test which has been standardized upon one cultural group is not applicable to another so an attitude scale which has been constructed for one cultural group will hardly be applicable in its existing form to other cultural groups.

BIBLIOGRAPHY

1. Allport, F. H. and Hartman, D. A. The measurement and motivation of atypical opinion in a certain group. Am Pol. Sci. Rev., 1925, *19*, 735–760.
2. Allport, G. W. The composition of political attitudes. Amer. J. Sociol., 1929, *35*, 220–238.
3. Allport, G. W. and Vernon, P. E. The field of personality. Psychol. Bull., 1930, *27*, 677–730.
4. Bain, R. Theory and measurement of attitudes and opinion. Psychol. Bull., 1930, *27*, 357–379.
5. Chave, E. J. and Thurstone, L. L. The measurement of social attitudes, Attitude Toward God, Scale No. 22. Chicago. Univ. of Chicago Press. 1931.
6. Droba, D. D. The measurement of social attitudes. Attitude Toward War. Chicago. Univ. of Chicago Press. 1930.
7. Filter, R. O. An experimental study of character traits. J. Appl. Psychol., 1921, *5*, 297–317.
8. Folsom, J. K. Social psychology. New York. Harpers. 1931.
9. George, R. W. A comparison of Pressey X-O scores with liberal-conservative attitudes. Master's essay in Columbia Univ. Libr. 1925.
10. Hartmann, G. W. Precision and accuracy. Arch. Psychol. 1928, No. 100.
11. Hartshorne, H. and May, M. A. Studies in deceit. New York. Macmillan. 1928.
12. Hartshorne, H., May, M. A. and Maller, J. B. Studies in service and self-control. New York. Macmillan, 1929.
13. Hartshorne, H., May, M. A. and Shuttleworth, F. K. Studies in the organization of character. New York. Macmillan. 1930.
14. Hinckley, E. D. A scale for measuring attitude toward the negro. Chicago. Univ. of Chicago Press. 1930.
15. Hunter, C. W. A comparative study of the relationship existing between the white race and the negro race in the State of North Carolina and in the City of New York. Master's essay in Columbia Univ. Libr. 1927.

16. Katz, D., Allport, F. H. and Jenness, M. B. Students' attitudes; a report of the Syracuse University Reaction Study. Syracuse. Craftsman Press. 1931.

17. Kulp, D. H., II, and Davidson, H. B. Can Neumann's "Attitude Indicator" be used as a test? Teach. Coll. Rec., 1931, *32*, 332–337.

18. Maller, J. B. Character and personality tests. New York. Teach. Coll. 1932.

19. Mathews, C. O. The effect of the order of printed response words on an interest questionnaire, J. Educ. Psychol., 1929, *20*, 128–134.

20. Moore, H. T. Innate factors in radicalism and conservatism. J. Abn. and Soc. Psychol., 1925, *20*, 234–244.

21. Murphy, G. An historical intoduction to modern psychology. New York. Harcourt, Brace and Company. 1929.

22. Murphy, G. and Murphy, L. B. Experimental social psychology. New York. Harper. 1931.

23. Neumann, G. B. A study of international attitudes of high school students. Teach. Coll. Contrib. Educ. 1927. No. 239.

24. Newcomb, T. M. The consistency of certain extrovert-introvert behavior patterns in 51 problem boys. Teach. Coll. Contrib. Educ. 1929. No. 382.

25. Porter, E. Student opinion on war. Doctoral dissertation in Univ. of Chicago Libr. 1926.

26. Rice, S. A. Report, Inst. of methods of rural sociol. research. U. S. Dept. of Agriculture. 1930. 11–20.

27. Rice, S. A. Statistical studies of social attitudes and public opinion. In Rice, S. A. (Ed.), Statistics in social studies, pp. 171–192. Philadelphia. Univ. of Pennsylvania Press. 1930.

28. Rice, S. A. Quantitative methods in politics. New York. Knopf. 1928.

29. Stouffer, S. A. An experimental comparison of statistical and case history methods of attitude research. Doctoral dissertation in Univ. of Chicago Libr. 1930.

30. Thorndike, E. L. An introduction to the theory of mental and social measurements. Second Edition. New York. Teach. Coll. 1913.

31. Thurstone, L. L. A law of comparative judgment. Psychol. Rev., 1927, *34*, 273–286.

32. ———— . An experimental study of nationality preferences. J. Gen. Psychol., 1928, *1*, 405–425.

33. ———— . A scale for measuring attitude toward the movies, J. Educ. Res., 1930, *22*, 89–94.

34. ———— . Attitudes can be measured. Amer. J. Sociol., 1928, *33*, 529–554.

35. ———— . Commentary. In Rice, S. A. (Ed.), Statistics in social attitudes, pp. 192–196. Philadelphia. Univ. of Pennsylvania Press.

36. ———— . The measurement of opinion. J. Abn. and Soc. Psychol., 1928, *22*, 415–430.

37. ———— . Theory of attitude measurement. Psychol. Rev., 1929, *36*, 222–241.

38. ———— . and Chave, E. J. The measurement of attitude. Chicago. Univ. of Chicago Press. 1929.

39. Trow, W. C. The psychology of confidence. Arch. Psychol., 1923, No. 67.

40. ———— . Trait consistency and speed of decision. School and Soc. 1925, *21*, 538–542.

41. Vetter, G. B. The measurement of social and political attitudes and the related personality factors. J. Abn. and Soc. Psychol., 1930. *25*, 149–189.

42. Wang, C. K. A. and Thurstone, L. L. The measurement of social attitudes. Scale

No. 21, Forms A, B. Attitude toward birth control. Chicago. Univ. of Chicago Press. 1930.

43. Watson, G. Measures of character and personality. Psychol. Bull., 1932, *29*, 147–176.

— · — · — · — · — · — · — · — · — · — · —

LOUIS GUTTMAN

*Cumulative Scaling Method in Attitude Measurement**

I. INTRODUCTION

During the course of the war a new approach to the problem of scaling attitudes and public opinion, called *scalogram* analysis, was developed by the writer to aid in the study of the morale and related aspects of the United States Army. This approach has wide ramifications not only for attitude and opinion research, but for many other fields like market research, mental testing, and elsewhere where it is desired to quantify qualitative data. Not much has yet been published[1] on this approach during the five years it has been used by the Army, so that it has not been readily available to other research workers.

The work of the Research Branch of the Army Service Forces, done under the scientific leadership of Professor Samuel A. Stouffer, will be described in several volumes now being completed. One of these volumes contains a rather comprehensive treatise on the theory and practice of scalogram analysis as carried out by the Research Branch.

The purpose of the present paper is to describe another technique for scalogram analysis which can be used immediately by research workers. Justification for the technique follows from the general theory and evidence to be published in the forthcoming volumes on the Research Branch. We shall call it the *Cornell technique* for scalogram analysis to distinguish it from several alternative devices, since it was developed first for teaching purposes at Cornell. It is hoped that the reader may be able to master the technique from this present description. For a fuller exposition of the theory and a discussion of the problems of reliability, validity, and the like, he is referred to the forthcoming books on the work of the Research Branch.

The Scalogram Analysis Approach.—The Cornell technique is a procedure for testing the hypothesis that a universe of qualitative data is a scale for a given population of people, using the scalogram approach. It may also be used to test the hypothesis that the

*Louis Guttman, "The Cornell Technique for Scale and Intensity Analysis," *Educational and Psychological Measurement* 7 (1947): 247–279.

[1]The basic concepts are available in Louis Guttman, "A Basis for Scaling Qualitative Data," *American Sociological Review*, IX (1944), 139–150.

data form a quasi-scale. Of the several techniques now available for scalogram analysis,[2] the one to be described here seems to be among the simplest and most convenient for general use. It requires no special equipment and involves only very simple clerical procedures which can readily be carried out by persons unskilled in statistics.

The various techniques just referred to all do the same job since they follow the same scalogram theory; they differ only in how the work is arranged. The initial steps are common to all. First, the universe of content to be studied is defined. In an attitude or opinion study, this means deciding on the general content of the questions to be asked. Second, the population of people is defined. In an attitude or opinion survey, this means that the class of people to be interviewed is delimited.

Next come two kinds of sampling problems. One kind is the ordinary problem of random sampling of people, and the other is the sampling of items. For these two sampling problems, it is helpful to distinguish between the pre-test stage of a study and the final survey. Many fewer people can be used in a pre-test than must be used in the final survey, but fewer items can be used in the final survey than must be used in the pre-test.

In the pre-test for a survey, about 100 persons will usually constitute an adequate sample of the population to test the hypothesis of scalability. If the hypothesis is accepted, the items can then be used in the final study of the usual 3,000 or so people to obtain reliable proportions at each scale rank.

The other sampling problem is at quite a different nature; it consists of sampling the universe of content. In an attitude or opinion survey, this is done by constructing some questions which contain the required general content. In a pre-test, about a dozen questions usually can constitute an adequate sampling of the content. Since questions are constructed by the research workers, they do not fall into any standard random sampling scheme, and standard random sampling theory does not apply here. Instead, it is shown by the theory of scale analysis that *almost any* sample of about a dozen questions from the universe is adequate to test the hypothesis that the universe is scalable, provided the range of content desired is covered by the questions. If the hypothesis is accepted that the universe is scalable, then fewer questions can be used in the final study if fewer ranks are actually needed for the purposes of the final research.

Having defined the universe of content and the population of people, and having drawn a sample from each, the fifth step is to observe each person in the sample on each item or question in the sample. In an attitude or opinion survey where a questionnaire is used, this involves having the people indicate their answers to each question of the questionnaire.

---

[2] The first technique employed laborious least squares computations. See Louis Guttman, "The Quantification of a Class of Attributes: A Theory and Method of Scale Construction" in P. Horst *et al.*, *The Prediction of Personal Adjustment*, Social Science Research Council, 1941, pp. 319–348. The standard procedure used by the Research Branch involves the use of scalogram boards especially invented for this purpose by the writer; these boards are simple to build and to operate, and a description of them will be in the forthcoming publication. A tabulation technique has been devised by another member of the Research Branch; see Ward H. Goodenough, "A Technique for Scale Analysis," *Educational and Psychological Measurement*, IV (1944), 179–190. The Cornell technique was devised by the writer at first for teaching purposes, and has proved to be very useful for general research purposes. A brief statement of the procedure as carried out on IBM equipment has already been noted in E. William Noland, "Worker Attitude and Industrial Absenteeism: A Statistical Approach," *American Sociological Review*, X (1945), 503–510.

The Hypothesis of Scalability. —The problem now is to test the hypothesis, on the basis of the pre-test sample data, that the entire universe of items forms a scale for the entire population of people. Let us review what this hypothesis implies in order to see what the technique of analysis is trying to do.

The universe is said to be scalable for the population if it is possible to rank the people from high to low in such a fashion that from a person's rank alone we can reproduce his response to each of the items in a simple fashion.[3] It is understood that a perfect scale is not to be expected in practice. Data have been considered sufficiently scalable if they are about 90 percent reproducible, and if certain other conditions (to be explained later) are satisfied. For clarity, though, let us consider first a hypothetical perfect scale.

Suppose that a question from the universe is asked of a population concerning a certain political issue and that the responses are as follows:

Agree	60%
Undecided	10
Disagree	30
	100%

If "Agree" means a more favorable opinion that "Undecided," if "Undecided" is more favorable than "Disagree," and if the universe is perfectly scalable, then the following must be true. The highest 60 per cent of the people must be those who said "Agree"; the next highest 10 per cent must be those who said "Undecided"; and the lowest 30 per cent must be those who "Disagree." If another question from this scalable universe is asked and the responses are 20 per cent "Yes" and 80 per cent "No," and if "Yes" means a more favorable attitude than "No," then the top 20 per cent of the people must be those who said "Yes" and the bottom 80 per cent must be those who said "No." From the rank of a person, we can now deduce what his response must be to each of these two questions. Any person in the top 20 per cent of the population must have said "Agree" to the first question and "Yes" to the second question. Any person lower than the top 20 per cent but not lower than the top 60 per cent said "Agree" to the first question and "No" to the second question. Any person below the top 60 per cent but not below the top 70 per cent said "Undecided" to the first question and "No" to the second, and the rest of the people, the bottom 30 per cent, said "Disagree" to the first question and "No" to the second.

The various techniques for scalogram analysis are devices to find the rank order for the people which will best reproduce their responses to each of the items in this fashion. If the universe were a perfect scale, all of the techniques would involve little work and there would not be much to choose between them. It is the presence of imperfect reproducibility that raises the problem of technique.

The Cornell technique works by successive approximations. Usually just two approximations suffice to reject or accept the hypothesis of scalability. A first trial rank order for the people is established by a simple scoring scheme. For illustrative purposes, let us work out an actual case in detail. This illustration is not to be taken as a model of perfect research, but rather only to provide an example of the steps to be followed.

---

[3] For a basic discussion of the theory of scales, see Louis Guttman, "A Basis for Scaling Qualitative Data," *ibid.*

An Example of the Cornell Technique.—It was desired to find out if the students in a certain class in race relations had a scalable attitude toward one of their textbooks, *A Nation of Nations*, by Louis Adamic. A questionnaire with seven questions was made out and administered to the class of 50 students. Both the number of questions and the number of students were smaller than those ordinarily used in a pre-test; they were used here only because these smaller numbers permit displaying the full data.

The seven questions were as follows:

A Nation of Nations
Questions

1. *A Nation of Nations* does a good job of analyzing the ethnic groups in this country.

Strongly agree	Agree	Undecided
_____ 4	_____ 3	2

Disagree	Strongly disagree
_____ 1	_____ 0

2. On the whole, *A Nation of Nations* is not as good as most college textbooks.

Strongly agree	Agree	Undecided
_____ 0	_____ 1	2

Disagree	Strongly disagree
_____ 3	_____ 4

3. Adamic organizes and presents his material very well.

Strongly agree	Agree	Undecided
_____ 4	_____ 3	2

Disagree	Strongly disagree
_____ 1	_____ 0

4. As a sociological treatise, Adamic's book does not rate very high.

Strongly agree	Agree	Undecided
_____ 0	_____ 1	2

Disagree	Strongly disagree
_____ 3	_____ 4

5. Adamic does not discuss any one group in sufficient detail so that a student can obtain a real insight into problems of ethnic group relations in this country.

Strongly agree	Agree	Undecided
_____ 0	_____ 1	2

Disagree	Strongly disagree
_____ 3	_____ 4

6. By providing a panorama of various groups, *A Nation of Nations* lets the student get a good perspective on ethnic group relations in this country.

Strongly agree	Agree	Undecided
_____ 4	_____ 3	2

Disagree	Strongly disagree
_____ 1	_____ 0

7. *A Nation of Nations* is good enough to be kept as a textbook for this course.

Strongly agree	Agree	Undecided
_____ 4	_____ 3	2

Disagree	Strongly disagree
_____ 1	_____ 0

II. CONTENT SCALE ANALYSIS

We now describe, step by step, how the analysis of the responses is carried out by the Cornell technique:

1. Weights for the first trial are assigned to each category of each question, using the successive integers beginning with zero. In this example, since each set of answers has five categories, the weights range from 0 to 4. In each question, the higher weights are assigned to the categories judged to express a more favorable attitude. This judging of ranks of categories is not to be regarded as final; the consequent analysis will either verify the judging or determine how to revise it.

2. A total score is obtained for each person by adding up the weights of the categories he falls into. In our example, since the maximum weight for each person is four, and the total number of questions is seven, the total scores can range from zero to 28.

3. The questionnaires are shuffled into rank order according to the total scores. In our example, we have arranged them from high to low.

4. A table is prepared, like Table 1 below, with one column for each category of each question and one row for each person. Since each of our questions has five categories, and since there are seven questions, we have 35 columns in our table. There are 50 students, so we have 50 rows. The first five columns are for the five categories of the first question, the second five columns for the five categories of the second question, etc.

5. The response of each person to each question is indicated on the table by placing an X in his row in the column for each category into which he falls. In our example, we have labeled the columns according to the questions and the weights of the categories. The first person is the one with the highest score, which is 28. He had checked the response weighted 4 in each of the questions, so he has seven X's in his row, each under the respective columns for the categories with weight 4. There were two persons with a score of 25. The arrangement of people with the same score is arbitrary. Of the two persons in our example with a score of 25, the one placed first had a response of 4 to the first two questions, a response of 3 to the third question, of 4 to the fourth question, of 3 to the fifth and sixth questions, and of 4 to the seventh question. Similarly, the X's in Table 1 indicate the response of each of the remaining persons to each question. Every person answers every question[4] so that there are seven X's in each row. *Table 1 gives a complete record of all the data obtained by the survey with respect to the area.*

6. At the bottom of Table 1 are the frequencies of response for each category. Category 4 of question 1 had nine people in it, whereas category 3 of the same question had 27 people, etc. The sum of the frequencies of the five categories in each question is always the total number of people in the sample, which in this case is 50.

7. Now we come to the test for scalability. If the universe is a scale and if the order in which we have placed the people is the scale rank order, then the pattern of X's in Table 1 must be of a particularly simple kind. Let us consider the first question in the Table. If response 4 is higher than response 3, and if 3 is higher than 2, and if 2 is higher than 1 (response) happens to have no frequency in this case), then the nine people in

---

[4] If people sometimes fail to respond to a question, then another category is added entitled "No Answer," which is weighted and treated like any other category for that question. In the present example, there were no "No Answers."

TABLE 1. A NATION OF NATIONS
(First Trial: Content)

Score	1					2					3					4					5					6					7				
	4	3	2	1	0	4	3	2	1	0	4	3	2	1	0	4	3	2	1	0	4	3	2	1	0	4	3	2	1	0	4	3	2	1	0
28	x	x				x	x				x					x	x				x					x					x				
25	x	x				x	x					x				x						x				x	x				x				
25	x					x					x							x				x				x		x			x				
24	x					x	x				x						x				x		x			x					x				
23	x	x				x	x				x					x		x			x	x				x	x				x	x			
23		x				x					x	x				x						x						x							
23	x					x	x				x					x			x		x					x	x				x	x			
22	x	x					x					x					x		x													x			
21		x					x					x					x				x	x				x	x					x			
21	x						x					x					x					x				x	x				x	x			
21		x					x					x						x				x					x				x	x			
21	x											x									x						x					x			
21				x															x					x		x									
20		x				x	x					x						x			x	x				x	x					x			
20	x	x				x						x					x					x				x	x				x				
20						x					x					x	x							x		x					x	x			
19		x				x					x								x			x				x					x				
19	x	x					x		x								x				x							x				x			
18	x	x				x	x				x	x		x		x	x				x	x					x				x	x			
18	x	x				x	x					x	x			x	x					x	x				x				x	x			
18		x				x	x						x			x			x			x			x		x				x	x			

17		x					x					x							x					x			x						x			
17		x				x						x							x					x				x					x			
16		x					x						x						x					x			x						x			
16		x							x				x						x			x					x						x			
16		x							x			x					x								x		x						x			
16		x					x					x						x						x			x								x	
15		x					x					x					x							x					x						x	
15			x						x			x								x		x					x						x			
15		x					x				x							x							x				x					x		
14				x			x							x				x						x			x						x			
14		x					x					x							x					x					x					x		
13				x						x		x							x					x		x						x				
13		x							x			x					x							x					x						x	
12				x			x							x				x						x				x						x		
12		x					x							x				x						x					x						x	
11		x							x				x							x				x				x						x		
11			x						x				x					x					x						x						x	
10				x					x			x								x				x			x								x	
9		x								x		x								x				x				x								x
8				x					x			x								x				x					x						x	
7		x								x				x						x				x				x								x
7				x					x			x								x					x				x						x	
7				x					x					x					x					x					x						x	
6				x					x					x						x				x					x						x	
5				x					x					x					x						x				x							x
5				x						x			x							x					x				x						x	
4				x						x		x								x					x					x						x
Freq.	9	27	2	12	0	8	24	0	13	5	10	25	8	7	0	3	7	16	14	10	3	14	5	21	7	9	21	7	12	1	11	19	5	11	4

category 4 should be the top nine people. Actually, six of them are the top six and the other three scatter farther down the column. Similarly, the twenty-seven people in category 3 should be below the first nine people and should go down to the thirty-sixth person (36 = 9 + 27). Again, this is not perfectly true for our data. A similar examination for the other items shows that there is a substantial error of reproducibility in their present form. The approximate number of errors need not be counted at this stage, since it is evidently more than 15 per cent of all the 350 responses (350 = 7 × 50, the number of questions times the number of people) in Table 1.

8. It has seldom been found that an item with four or five categories will be sufficiently reproducible if the categories are regarded as distinct. One reason for this is the verbal habits of people. Some people may say "Strongly Agree" where others may say "Agree," whereas they have essentially the same position on the basic continuum but differ on an extraneous factor of verbal habits. By combining categories, minor extraneous variables of this kind can be minimized. By examining the overlapping of the X's within the columns of each question, it can be determined how best to combine the categories so as to minimize the error of reproducibility for the combinations. In question 2, for example, categories 4 and 3 seem to intertwine, so they are combined. Similarly, in the same question, categories 1 and 0 seem to intertwine, so they are combined. In question 4, on the other hand, we combine categories 3, 2, and 1, leaving categories 4 and 0 separate. The way to combine categories is determined for each question separately. The combinations decided upon for this example on the basis of Table 1 are given in Table 2.

TABLE 2. COMBINATIONS OF CATEGORIES

Question	Combinations
1	(4) (3) (2,1,0)
2	(4,3) (2,1,0)
3	(4,3,2) (1,0)
4	(4) (3,2,1) (0)
5	(4,3,2) (1,0)
6	(4,3) (2,1,0)
7	(4) (3) (2,1,0)

If it is desired to keep many scale types, then as little combination as possible should be done. However, if not many scale types are desired, the categories may be combined as far as one wishes even though this may not raise producibility. There is no harm in combining categories that could otherwise remain distinct with respect to scale error; all that is lost by such a combination is one scale type. On the other hand, categories may *require* combination in order to reduce error; they should be combined in the manner indicated by Table 1 and not arbitrarily.

9. A second trial rank order for the people can now be established on the basis of the combined categories. This is done by reassigning weights. Since the first question now has three categories (that is, three combinations), these are assigned the weights 0, 1, and 2. Question 2 now has two categories. These could be assigned the weights 0 and 1. In the present example the weights 0 and 2 are used instead, since keeping the range of weights relatively constant from item to item often helps to establish a better ranking for the people when there is error of reproducibility present.[5]

[5]In a perfect scale, *any* set of weights, provided they have the proper rank order for the categories, will yield a perfect rank ordering for the people.

10. Each person is now given a new score which represents his second trial rank order. This is done by re-scoring his questionnaire according to the new weights. This re-scoring is easily done from Table 1. Using a strip of paper which is as wide as the Table, the new weights for the old categories can be written directly on the edge of the strip. Placing the strip across the row for a person, the weights are added according to where the X's lie. For our example, the strip would have for its first five columns the weights 2, 1, 0, 0, 0, weight 2 being placed in the column which was the old category 4, the weight 1 in the column which was the old category 3, and the 0's being in the old columns 2, 1, and 0 which are now combined. For question 2, the strip would have for the five columns the weights 2, 2, 0, 0, 0. Similarly, the new weights for the other questions can be written down to be used over the old columns of Table 1. The person who was formerly first on Table 1, with a score of 28, now has a score of $2 + 2 + 2 + 2 + 2 + 2 + 2 = 14$. The second person in Table 1 also gets a score of 14. The third person in Table 1 now gets a score of $2 + 2 + 2 + 1 + 2 + 2 + 2 = 13$; and so on for each person.

11. The people are now shifted into the rank order of their new scores, and Table 3 is prepared from the combined data just as Table 1 was prepared from the original data. Question 1 now has three columns, question 2 has two columns, etc. The data of Table 1 are modified to fit Table 3 according to the combinations indicated in Table 2. The columns of Table 3 now refer to the combined categories, and the scores of Table 3 are the second trial scores just obtained in the preceding step.

12. The error of reproducibility in Table 3 seems much smaller than in Table 1, and we shall now count up the actual errors. This is done by establishing *cutting points* in the rank order of the people which separate them according to the categories in which they would fall if the scale were perfect. For question 1, which has three categories, we need two cutting points. The first seems to fall between the last person with score 12 and the first person with score 11. All people above this cutting point should be in category 2, and all people below should not be in category 2. Since there is one person in category 2 below this point, we have one error for category 2. A second cutting point is needed to separate category 1 from category 0; since these two categories overlap somewhat, its exact location is not essential since moving it slightly up or down will not change the amount of error. It should be placed so as to minimize the error, but this may be done in several adjacent ways. One way is to place the cutting point between the second and third persons with score 4. Below this point we find three errors in category 1, and above this, we find five errors in category 0. The total number of errors in question 1 is $1 + 3 + 5 = 9$. Since there are 50 responses to question 1, this means 18 per cent. This error could be reduced, of course, by combining the last two columns and leaving question 1 as a dichotomy. Then there would be only the one error in the first column. Such a further dichotomization need not be done if there is relatively little error in the other questions so that the error over all questions is not much more than 10 per cent.

Question 2 has two categories in the second trial, and the cutting point which will minimize the error is between the last two scores 6, which makes two errors in the first column and four errors in the second column of question 2. Similarly, question 3 has a cutting point between the last score 2 and the first score 1, leaving three errors in its second column. Question 4 gets two cutting points, questions 5 and 6 one cutting point, and question 7 two cutting points. The total number of errors in the whole of Table 3 is 40, which is 11 per cent of all the responses. We can, therefore, conclude in view of the

TABLE 3. A NATION OF NATIONS
(Second Trial: Content)

Score	1			2		3		4			5		6		7		
	2	1	0	2	0	2	0	2	1	0	2	0	2	0	2	1	0
14	x			x		x		x			x		x		x		
14	x			x		x		x			x		x		x		
13	x			x		x			x		x		x		x		
13	x			x		x			x		x		x		x		
13	x			x		x			x		x		x		x		
13	x			x		x			x		x		x		x		
12	x			x		x				x	x		x		x		
12	x			x		x		x			x			x	x		
11		x		x		x			x		x		x			x	
11		x		x		x			x		x		x			x	
11		x		x		x			x		x		x			x	
11			x	x		x			x		x		x		x		
11		x		x		x			x		x		x			x	
11		x		x		x			x		x		x			x	
11		x		x		x			x		x		x			x	
11		x		x		x			x		x		x			x	
10		x		x		x			x			x	x		x		
10		x		x		x			x		x		x				x
10		x		x		x			x			x	x		x		
9	x				x	x			x		x		x				x
9		x		x		x			x			x	x			x	
9		x		x		x			x			x	x			x	
9		x		x		x			x			x	x			x	
9		x		x		x			x			x	x			x	
9		x			x	x			x		x		x			x	
8		x		x		x			x			x	x				x
7		x		x		x				x		x	x				x
7		x			x	x			x			x	x			x	
7			x		x	x			x		x		x				x
6		x		x		x			x			x		x			x
6		x		x		x			x			x		x			x
6		x		x		x			x			x		x			x
6			x	x		x				x		x	x				x
6			x		x	x			x		x			x		x	
5			x	x		x			x			x		x			x
4			x	x		x				x		x		x			x
4		x			x	x			x			x		x			x
4			x		x	x				x		x	x				x
3			x		x	x			x			x		x			x
3		x			x	x				x		x		x			x
3			x		x	x				x		x		x		x	
3			x		x	x			x			x		x			x
2			x		x	x				x		x		x			x
2			x	x			x			x		x		x			x
2			x		x		x		x			x		x		x	
2		x			x		x		x			x		x			x
1		x			x		x			x		x		x			x
1			x		x		x		x			x		x			x
1			x		x		x			x		x		x		x	
0			x		x		x			x		x		x			x
Freq.	9	27	14	32	18	43	7	3	37	10	22	28	30	20	11	19	20

fact that much of the error occurs in question 1 and could be eliminated by combining two categories in that question, that this area is scalable. From a person's rank order, we can reproduce his response to each question *in terms of combined categories* with 89 per cent accuracy (or better, if we combine the last two columns of question 1).

13. The per cent reproducibility alone is not sufficient to lead to the conclusion that the universe of content is scalable. The frequency of responses to each separate item must also be taken into account for a very simple reason. Reproducibility can be artificially high simply because one category in each item has a very high frequency. It can be proved that the reproducibility of an item can never be less than the largest frequency of its categories, regardless of whether the area is scalable or not. For example, question 3 in Table 3 has quite an extreme kind of distribution. Forty-three students are in one category, and seven in the other. Under no circumstances, then, could there be more than seven errors made on this item, regardless of whether or not a scale pattern existed. Or again, question 4 in Table 3 has thirty-seven cases in its modal category and thirteen cases in the other two categories. Under no circumstances, then, could item 4 have more than thirteen errors. Clearly, the more evenly the frequencies are distributed over the categories of a given item, the harder it is for reproducibility to be spuriously high. Questions 5 and 6 in Table 3 each have high reproducibility, each having five errors; these are not artificially high because question 5 has only twenty-eight cases in its more frequent category and question 6 has thirty cases for its modal frequency. The maximum possible error for question 5 is twenty-two, and for question 6 it is twenty. The scale pattern represents quite a substantial reduction from this maximum error. An empirical rule for judging the spuriousness of scale reproducibility has been adopted to be the following: no category should have more error in it than non-error. Thus, the category with weight 2 in question 1 (Table 3) has eight non-errors and one error; category with weight 1 in this same question has twenty-four non-errors and three errors; category 0 has nine non-errors and five errors. Thus question 1 fits this rule. Question 3 comes periously near to not fitting the rule. While the first column of question 3 (in Table 3) has no error, the second column has three errors compared to four non-errors. Similarly, the first column of question 4 has one error compared to two non-errors. It is because evenly distributed questions like 5 and 6 have little error and because the errors in the other questions, like in 3 and 4, are not too widely displaced from where they ought to be, that we consider this area to be scalable.

In constructing a sample of items to be used in a test for scalability, at least some of the items should be constructed, if at all possible, to obtain a uniform distribution of frequencies. Such items afford a good test of scalability. However, items with non-uniform frequencies are also needed in order to get differentiated scale types, so both kinds of items must be used. The more categories that are retained in an item, the sharper is the test for scalability, because error—if it really should be there—has a better possibility to appear when there are more categories.

III. INTENSITY ANALYSIS

Separating "Favorable" from "Unfavorable" People.—Since the expression of opinion about the textbook, *A Nation of Nations*, is sufficiently scalable, it is meaningful to say that one student likes the book better than another. There is a meaningful rank ordering of the students according to their opinion of the book. This ordering is expressed by the scale scores assigned in the second trial. A student with a higher score than another says the same or better things about the book (within scale error).

There is a further question that is of interest to the research worker. Given that the individuals can be ranked according to their degree of favorableness, is there a cutting point in this rank order such that we can say that all people to the right of the point are "favorable" and all people to the left are "unfavorable"? One person may be more favorable than another, yet both may be favorable. Obtaining just a rank order does not distinguish between being favorable and being unfavorable; it merely reflects being *more* favorable and *less* favorable and does not tell if a point is reached beyond which being *less* favorable actually means being "unfavorable."

An objective answer to this problem is provided by the use of the *intensity function.*

The theory of intensity analysis will be explained in detail in the forthcoming publication on the work of the Research Branch. For our purposes, all we need to know is that it provides a solution to the traditional problem of question "bias." No matter how questions are worded or "loaded," use of the intensity function will yield the same proportion of the group as favorable and unfavorable. The intensity function provides an invariant zero point for attitudes and opinions.

There are several techniques for obtaining intensity in a questionnaire, as will be discussed in the volumes to be published on the work of the Research Branch. We shall discuss only two here, as carried out by the Cornell technique. These are very simple indeed to perform. The first is the *fold-over* technique, and the second is the *two-part* technique. The fold-over technique is theoretically less justifiable than the two-part technique. However, it does have some practical advantages in some cases.

The Fold-Over Technique.—The fold-over technique consists simply of re-scoring the content questions in order to obtain an intensity score. This is easily done for the form of question used to study opinions about *A Nation of Nations.* The following weights are assigned to the check list of answers: "Strongly agree" and "Strongly disagree" receive a weight of 2; "Agree" and "Disagree" receive a weight of 1; and "Undecided" receives a weight of 0.[6] Thus the apparently more intense responses receive higher weights, and the apparently less intense responses receive lower weights, regardless of whether the responses appear to be "favorable" or "unfavorable."

Weighting the responses in this way means that in order to obtain an intensity score, we are in fact combining opposite ends of the check list, so that there are but three (combined) intensity categories per question. Intensity, as obtained in this fashion, is not in general scalable. Instead, it forms what is called a quasi-scale. In a quasi-scale, there is no perfect relationship between a person's response to each question and his score on all the questions; instead, there is a gradient. The higher a person's score, the more *likely* he is to give a high response to each item, but there is not the high certainty that exists in the case of a scale. This can be seen in our example of Adamic's textbook. Arranging the data into a scalogram according to total intensity score, we obtain the configuration shown in Table 4. Each question now has three categories which represent the three

---

[6] These weights can be written on a strip of paper to be put over Table 1 and added up there to obtain an intensity score for each person.

TABLE 4. A NATION OF NATIONS
(Intensity)

Score	1			2			3			4			5			6			7		
	2	1	0	2	1	0	2	1	0	2	1	0	2	1	0	2	1	0	2	1	0
14	x			x			x			x			x			x			x		
12		x		x				x		x			x			x			x		
11		x		x			x				x			x		x			x		
11	x			x				x		x				x			x		x		
11	x					x	x				x			x		x			x		
11	x			x			x					x		x		x			x		
10		x		x				x			x			x		x			x		
10	x					x	x					x		x		x			x		
10	x					x	x				x			x			x		x		
9	x					x	x			x					x			x	x		
9		x		x					x	x			x				x			x	
9		x			x			x			x		x				x			x	
9		x		x				x			x		x				x				x
9		x		x				x			x			x		x					x
9		x			x		x			x			x				x				x
9		x		x				x		x				x				x	x		
9		x		x				x		x				x				x	x		
8		x				x	x			x				x		x					x
8		x		x			x			x				x		x					x
8		x		x			x				x		x				x				x
8		x		x			x			x				x		x					x
8		x		x			x					x	x			x					x
8		x		x			x					x		x		x			x		
7		x		x			x				x			x		x					x
7	x			x			x				x				x	x					x
7	x			x					x			x	x					x	x		
7		x		x			x				x		x			x					x
7		x		x			x				x		x					x			x
7		x			x		x				x		x			x					x
7		x		x			x				x		x			x					x
7			x	x			x			x			x			x					x
7		x		x			x				x		x			x					x
7		x			x		x				x		x			x					x
7		x		x			x					x	x			x					x
7		x			x		x				x		x			x					x
7		x		x			x					x	x			x						x
6		x		x			x					x	x			x						x
6		x		x					x	x			x			x					x
6		x		x					x	x			x			x					x
6		x		x			x					x			x	x					x
6		x		x				x				x		x		x					x
6		x		x				x				x	x			x					x
6		x		x				x				x	x			x					x
6		x		x					x		x		x			x					x
6		x		x				x			x		x			x						x
6		x		x				x				x	x			x					x
5		x		x					x	x			x					x			x
4		x		x					x			x			x	x					x
4		x		x			x					x	x					x			x
3			x	x					x			x			x	x					x
Freq.	9	39	2	13	37	0	10	32	8	13	21	16	10	35	5	10	33	7	15	30	5

intensity steps. There is a density gradient of responses. There are no clear-cut streaks in the category columns but, instead, gradually tapering densities that blend from one category into the next. Combining categories still will not yield a scalable pattern.

According to the basic theory of intensity analysis, intensity should be a perfectly scalable variable. The equations of scale analysis show that there is a second component in every scale of content which is a U- or J-shaped function of the scale scores. This component has been identified as the intensity function of the content scale. What we are trying to do is to obtain this intensity by direct empirical methods. The fact that our observed intensity is not perfectly scalable shows that it is not the pure intrinsic intensity we are seeking. No perfect way has yet been found for obtaining intensity; but satisfactory results are obtainable even with imperfect intensity techniques. Instead of a perfect intensity function, we will get one that can have considerable error in its relationship to the content scale scores.

Plotting Intensity Against Content.—The empirical intensity function is obtained by plotting the intensity scores just obtained against the content scores obtained from the previous section from the second content trial. The scattergram is shown in Table 5. The frequency in boldface in each column of Table 5 corresponds to the position of the

TABLE 5. A NATION OF NATIONS
(Scattergram of Intensity and Content)

Intensity	Content (Second Trial)							Total
	0–2	3–5	6–8	9–10	11	12–13	14	
14							1	1
13								0
12	1							1
11				1		2	1	4
10					1	2		3
9	4	1	1		1	1		8
8	2	1	1	2				6
7	1	1	4	2	4	1		13
6		1	3	4	2			10
5		1						1
4		1			1			2
3		1						1
Total	8	7	9	9	9	6	2	50

median intensity for the respective columns. If the pure intrinsic intensity were being measured by our technique, there would be no scatter about these medians at all, but intensity would be a perfect U- or J-shaped function of the content scores. Despite the presence of error, however, the approximate shape of the true intensity function is clear from the shape of the curve along which the columnar medians lie. The curve descends from the right, or the more favorable content scores, reaches its low point at the next to the last interval to the left (contents scores 3–5), and then rises again at the last interval to the left. The content scores 3–5, then, must be the approximate interval which contains the zero-point of the attitude. Students to the left of this interval can be said to have *negative* attitudes and students to the right can be said to have *positive* attitudes toward the textbook. Students in the 3–5 interval cannot be divided into positives and negatives without the aid of additional questions which will help to differentiate more precisely between their ranks.

On the basis of Table 5, we can conclude, then, that about 8 students did not like the textbook, 35 students did like the textbook, while 7 students were in between these. This division of the students into those with favorable and those with unfavorable attitudes does not depend upon the particular way we worded our questions. The same intensity curve, with the same proportion to the right and to the left of the zero-point, would have been obtained if we had used other questions or other wordings, provided only that these other questions were scalable with the present questions. Proof of this invariant property of the intensity function is given in the forthcoming volumes on the Research Branch's work.

Need for Larger Sample of People.—An important caution must be sounded here. The example we are working with must be regarded as a highly fortunate one in one sense for the purposes of this exposition. It is rare indeed to find as low error as we have in the intensity function so that the intensity curve and zero-point show out quite clearly on the basis of our small sample of 50 cases. In general this will be far from the case. To perform an intensity analysis safely, when there is a substantial error present—which is the usual case—ordinarily from one to three thousand cases are needed to obtain stable medians. To perform the scalogram analysis, it is also safer to use more than 50 cases. A hundred cases is a desirable minimum to use in the pre-test, as well as a dozen or so items instead of seven as we have used in our illustrative example. If the pre-test has established that the universe of items is scalable, the final study should be done on the usual number of cases used in opinion surveys if reliable results with respect to intensity are to be obtained. The hypothesis of scalability can be tested in a pre-test on relatively few people because of its specialized character. However, *proportions* of the population at any given rank or on one side of the zero-point are subject to ordinary sampling error; larger samples of people must be used for reliable results with respect to them.

Drawbacks to the Fold-Over Technique.—The fold-over technique for intensity has two theoretical drawbacks to it, as well as some practical ones. First, the intensity scores obtained thereby are not experimentally independent of the content scores because exactly the same answers are used for both of the scores. This may give rise to some spuriousness in the relationship between the two. Second, it assumes that "Strongly agree" and "Strongly disagree" are approximately equal in intensity and opposite in direction, and similarly for "Agree" and "Disagree," while it is assumed that "Undecided" approximately straddles the zero-point. These assumptions need not be true at all. In fact, the occasional falsity of these assumptions is one contribution to error in the obtained intensity scores.

If the assumptions were true, life would be much easier for research workers. It would not be necessary to ask a series of questions in order to obtain a zero interval because the "Undecided" category for any question would provide such an interval. But, unfortunately, it is clear that in a series of questions on the same issue, the people who are "Undecided" on one question can all be "Agreed" on another question. It is just because we cannot interpret the bias of a question by looking at its content that such a technique like that of the intensity function is needed.

While the fold-over technique does have these two theoretical drawbacks, it does seem to average out the errors involved in violating the above assumptions and to provide a proper U- or J-shaped curve in many cases.

A practical disadvantage to the fold-over technique has been found in the case of

man-in-the-street interviews, where people would avoid the "strongly" categories almost
completely, so that not much differentiation in intensity could be obtained. In such a
case, a two-part technique is necessary. An advantage of the fold-over over the two-part
technique is that it takes less space and time in administering questionnaires. The two-
part technique will be illustrated in the next example.

IV. ANOTHER EXAMPLE OF CONTENT AND INTENSITY ANALYSIS

A Universe Is Not Necessarily a Scale.—A set of items constructed from a single
universe of content is not necessarily scalable. The notion of universe of content and the
notion of scalability are quite distinct. If a universe of content is not scalable, it can
sometimes be broken down into sub-universes, some of which may be scalable separately.
If a universe is not scalable for a given population of people, then it is not meaningful to
assign a single rank order to the people with respect to the total content. Indeed, if
arbitrary scores were assigned to non-scalable data, intensity analysis should find that
there was no U- or J-shaped intensity function and no invariant zero-point for dividing
the population into positives and negatives.

An example of such a non-scalable case is the one next to be given. It will also
illustrate the two-part intensity technique. The content for this second example concerns
another textbook used in the same course as the first. The 50 students in the class were
asked the following questions about *Black Metropolis* (by Drake and Cayton):

Black Metropolis

Questions

1. (a) On the whole, as textbooks go, how good do you think *Black Metropolis* is?
   (Check one answer)

Very good	Good	Fairly good
—— 5	—— 4	—— 3

Passable	Not very good	Terrible
—— 2	—— 1	—— 0

   (b) How strongly do you feel about this? (Check one answer)

Very strongly	Pretty strongly
—— 3	—— 3

Somewhat strongly	Not strongly at all
—— 1	—— 0

2. (a) In your opinion, does *Black Metropolis* present a good sociological analysis of
   the Negro community in Chicago?

   An excellent analysis
   —— 5

   A very good analysis
   —— 4

   A pretty good analysis
   —— 3

   It has only a few good points
   —— 2

Not a very good analysis

——   1

A pretty bad analysis

——   0

(b) How strongly do you feel about this?

Very strongly		Pretty strongly
—— 3	——	2

Somewhat strongly		Not strongly at all
—— 1	——	0

3. (a) To what extent does the book afford the student a real insight into the problems of race relations in Chicago?

Not much at all

——   0

A somewhat limited insight

——   1

Fairly good insight		A good insight
—— 2	——	3

A very good insight		An excellent insight
—— 4	——	5

(b) How strongly do you feel about this?

Very strongly		Pretty strongly
—— 3	——	2

Somewhat strongly		Not strongly at all
—— 1	——	0

4. (a) In general, how well does the book organize and present its material?

Very poorly		Not very well
—— 0	——	1

Fairly well		Quite well		Very well
—— 2	——	3	——	4

(b) How strongly do you feel about this?

Very strongly		Pretty strongly
—— 3	——	2

Somewhat strongly		Not strongly at all
—— 1	——	0

5. (a) Some parts of *Black Metropolis* emphasize statistical data and other parts quote personal interviews a great deal. Do you believe that the authors have succeeded in blending these data properly, or have they failed?

Succeeded very well

——   4

Succeeded pretty well

——   3

Succeeded at least more than they have failed

——   2

Pretty much failed		Definitely failed
—— 1	——	0

TABLE 6. BLACK METROPOLIS
(First Trial: Content)

Score	1						2						3						4					5					6					7				
	5	4	3	2	1	0	5	4	3	2	1	0	5	4	3	2	1	0	4	3	2	1	0	4	3	2	1	0	4	3	2	1	0	4	3	2	1	0
30	x						x						x						x					x					x					x				
29		x						x						x						x					x					x					x			
28	x						x						x						x					x					x					x				
28	x						x						x						x					x					x					x				
28	x							x						x						x					x					x					x				
27		x							x				x						x					x					x					x				
27	x								x				x						x					x						x					x			
27	x						x							x						x					x					x					x				
27	x													x					x					x						x					x			
26	x													x					x						x						x					x		
26	x						x							x						x					x					x					x				
26		x						x						x						x				x							x					x		
26	x							x						x					x						x					x					x				
26	x							x						x						x				x						x					x				
25	x							x						x					x						x				x					x				
25		x					x						x							x					x						x				x			
25	x								x				x						x					x						x						x		
25	x							x						x					x						x						x				x			
24	x						x							x						x					x					x					x				
24	x							x					x						x					x						x					x			
24	x						x							x						x					x						x					x			
24	x							x					x							x				x						x					x				

24			x				x						x							x					x						x				x			
24	x							x						x						x						x					x			x				
23		x						x						x						x					x							x		x				
23		x					x							x						x					x							x			x			
23	x							x							x				x							x					x				x			
23		x						x							x					x					x						x			x				
23	x							x							x					x					x							x		x				
22		x							x					x						x				x								x			x			
22			x					x					x							x				x								x				x		
22		x						x								x				x					x					x					x			
22	x							x							x						x				x							x		x				
21			x				x							x								x		x								x			x			
21		x						x					x							x						x							x		x			
21		x							x						x						x				x					x					x			
21		x						x							x						x			x								x			x			
20			x						x						x				x						x						x					x		
20			x					x								x					x				x					x					x			
19			x						x					x								x		x								x			x			
19			x				x									x					x				x							x			x			
19		x						x						x								x			x								x		x			
18			x					x									x		x						x							x				x		
16				x				x						x							x					x						x					x	
16				x					x						x						x						x			x						x		
14					x			x						x									x				x			x							x	
14			x						x							x						x				x						x				x		
13			x						x								x					x				x						x				x		
Freq.	18	19	10	2	1	0	12	26	12	0	0	0	12	22	10	4	2	0	14	21	9	5	1	16	26	6	2	0	2	19	12	15	2	20	22	6	2	0

(b) How strongly do you feel about this?

    Very strongly   Pretty strongly

——   3 ——   2

    Somewhat strongly   Not strongly at all

——   1 ——   0

6. (a) Some students complain that the textbook often makes fuzzy statements, so that it is not clear what position it takes or what it is driving at. To what extent do you agree with this complaint?

    Completely agree

——   0

    Agree for the most part   Undecided

——   1 ——   2

    Disagree   Completely disagree

——   3 ——   4

(b) How strongly do you feel about this?

    Very strongly   Pretty strongly

——   3 ——   2

    Somewhat strongly   Not strongly at all

——   1 ——   0

7. (a) Do you think *Black Metropolis* is good enough to be kept as a textbook for this course?

    Definitely yes   Yes   Undecided

——   4 ——   3 ——   2

    No   Definitely not

——   1 ——   0

(b) How strongly do you feel about this?

    Very strongly   Pretty strongly

——   3 ——   2

    Somewhat strongly   Not strongly at all

——   1 ——   0

Each question is in two parts. The first part is to study content, and the second part is to study intensity. Notice that the number of categories in the content parts are not uniform from question to question. It is not essential for a scalogram analysis that there be any uniform format for the questions. In the same series of items, some can be trichotomies, some can have six categories, and some can have two categories, etc. Nor is the wording of the categories of special importance. Short phrases or long phrases, etc., can be used. Five and six categories were used in the present example because it was suspected in advance that the students would give apparently favorable answers to all questions put to them, so the apparently favorable responses were made more numerous in the check list of answers in order to help obtain differentiation in rankings.

The Cornell technique was used to analyze the content parts of the seven questions on *Black Metropolis*. The first trial weights are those indicated with the questions, and the first trial scalogram is shown in Table 6. All of the items were found to have so much error that they required dichotomization. The combinations of categories used and the results of the second trial are shown in Table 7. There is still too much error in Table 7.

TABLE 7. BLACK METROPOLIS
(Second Trial: Content)

Score	1		2		3		4		5		6		7	
	1	*0*	*1*	*0*	*1*	*0*	*1*	*0*	*1*	*0*	*1*	*0*	*1*	*0*
7	x		x		x		x		x		x		x	
7	x		x		x		x		x		x		x	
7	x		x		x		x		x		x		x	
7	x		x		x		x		x		x		x	
7	x		x		x		x		x		x		x	
7	x		x		x		x		x		x		x	
7	x		x		x		x		x		x		x	
7	x		x		x		x		x		x		x	
7	x		x		x		x		x		x		x	
7	x		x		x		x		x		x		x	
7	x		x		x		x		x		x		x	
7	x		x		x		x		x		x		x	
7	x		x		x		x		x		x		x	
7	x		x		x		x		x		x		x	
7	x		x		x		x		x		x		x	
6	x		x		x		x			x	x		x	
6		x	x		x		x		x		x		x	
6	x			x	x		x		x		x		x	
6	x			x	x		x		x		x		x	
6	x			x	x		x		x		x		x	
6	x		x		x		x		x			x	x	
6	x		x			x	x		x		x		x	
6	x		x		x			x	x		x		x	
6	x			x	x		x		x		x		x	
6	x		x		x			x	x		x		x	
6	x		x		x		x		x			x	x	
6	x		x		x		x		x			x	x	
6	x		x			x	x		x		x		x	
6	x		x			x	x		x		x		x	
5	x			x		x	x		x		x		x	
5	x		x			x	x			x	x		x	
5	x		x			x	x		x			x	x	
5	x			x	x		x		x			x	x	
5	x		x		x		x			x		x	x	
5	x		x		x			x	x			x	x	
4		x	x		x		x			x	x			x
4		x	x		x		x			x	x			x
4		x	x		x			x	x		x			x
4	x		x		x			x	x			x		x
4	x		x			x		x	x			x	x	
4	x			x		x	x			x	x		x	
3		x		x		x		x	x		x		x	
3		x	x			x		x	x			x	x	
3		x	x			x		x	x			x	x	
3		x	x		x			x	x			x		x
3		x	x			x		x	x			x	x	
2		x		x		x		x	x			x	x	
1		x		x		x		x	x			x		x
0		x		x		x		x		x		x		x
0		x		x		x		x		x		x		x
Combination	(5,4)	(3, 2,1,0)	(5,4)	(3, 2,1,0)	(5,4)	(3, 2,1,0)	(4,3)	(2, 1,0)	(4,3)	(2, 1,0)	(4,3,2)	(1,0)	(4,3)	(2, 1,0)
Frequency	37	13	38	12	34	16	35	15	42	8	33	17	42	8

TABLE 8. BLACK METROPOLIS
(Intensity)

Score	1				2				3				4				5				6				7			
	3	2	1	0	3	2	1	0	3	2	1	0	3	2	1	0	3	2	1	0	3	2	1	0	3	2	1	0
21	x				x				x				x				x				x				x			
20		x			x				x				x				x				x				x			
20		x			x				x				x				x				x				x			
20					x				x				x				x					x			x			
19	x				x				x				x				x				x				x			
18	x				x				x					x			x					x			x			
18	x					x			x					x			x					x			x			
18		x				x			x					x				x				x			x			
17	x				x				x				x				x				x					x		
17		x			x				x				x				x					x				x		
17					x					x			x					x			x					x		
17	x				x				x				x				x				x						x	
17						x				x			x					x						x		x		
16	x								x				x				x					x			x			
16	x				x				x				x				x				x				x			
16					x					x			x					x				x				x		
16		x			x					x			x				x						x					x
16			x		x					x							x					x				x		
15		x			x				x				x					x			x				x			
15		x			x				x				x					x				x				x		
15		x			x				x					x				x				x		x				
15		x			x				x					x			x					x						x

4	21	17	6	16	18	10	1	9	25	15	2	10	25	13

1	7	23	19	4	3	23	20

2	8	9

Freq.

15
14
14
14
14
13
13
13
13
13
12
12
11
11
11
11
11
10
10
9
3
0

Several of the questions have more error than non-error. We therefore judge the total content not to be scalable, since no further trials can be made when all items are dichotomous.

Therefore, we cannot speak of degrees of "favorableness" of opinion about *Black Metropolis* for this class of students. We cannot say that one student likes the book better than another student. He may like it better in one of the aspects and not better in another. There is apparently not a single ranking possible in the total content studied by the questionnaire. If the study were to be carried further, what would be done would be to try to break the content down into sub-areas, make up a dozen or so questions for each of the sub-areas, administer the sub-areas to the class, and analyze each separately by scalogram analysis. Such a further study was not made for this present example.

The Two-Part Intensity Technique.—Since the total content is not scalable, it is hardly worthwhile to study intensity. However, in order to see how the two-part technique operates, let us go through with it anyhow. Each part (b) of the 7 questions on *Black Metropolis* was weighted according to the weights indicated in the list of questions above, and trial intensity scores were obtained thereby. Intensity again seems to be a quasi-scale. Obtaining a quasi-scale, however, has no bearing on the scalability of the *content.* The scalogram for the trial intensity is shown in Table 8. Plotting the trial intensity scores against the second trial content scores yields the scattergram in Table 9. Again, the frequencies in boldface in each column indicate the median position for intensity for the respective columns.

As stated previously, fifty cases are far from sufficient to obtain stable column medians when there is a substantial intensity error present, which seems to be the case

TABLE 9. BLACK METROPOLIS
(Scattergram of Intensity and Content)

Intensity	Content (Second Trial)								Total
	0	1	2	3	4	5	6	7	
21							1		1
20							1	2	3
19						1			1
18					1		1	1	3
17					2	1	1	1	5
16							1	4	5
15				1	2		1	2	6
14	1			1		1	1	1	5
13				1		2	1	2	6
12		1	1				1		3
11				1	1	1	2	1	6
10				1			2		3
9	1								1
3							1		1
0								1	1
Total	2	1	1	5	6	6	14	15	50

here. However, we have strong reason to believe that the absence of a U- or J-shaped curve of medians in Table 9 is not merely due to sampling error, but rather to the fundamental lack of scalability of the content.

An Intensity Curve from a Final Survey.—To give the reader a picture of what final results will look like in practice in a complete study, we present some data from a study by the Research Branch. Ten questions were asked of a cross-section of 1800 enlisted men with respect to the expression of job satisfaction in the Army. The content was found to be scalable. Intensity was obtained by the two-part technique. The relationship between intensity and content is shown in Table 10. The frequencies in boldface in the

TABLE 10. AN EXAMPLE OF THE INTENSITY FUNCTION: JOB SATISFACTION IN THE ARMY

Intensity Score	Content Score											Total
	0	*1*	*2*	*3*	*4*	*5*	*6*	*7*	*8*	*9*	*10*	
8	23	46	27	33	22	19	24	42	25	23	24	308
7	7	24	31	26	33	31	22	40	21	15	5	255
6	1	7	29	17	30	24	35	42	15	11	..	211
5	6	14	14	29	20	34	27	34	19	10	..	197
4	2	3	15	17	32	33	36	36	10	1	..	185
3	..	1	17	19	22	29	33	25	11	1	..	158
2	1	4	9	19	25	34	31	32	1	4	1	161
1	..	2	2	12	35	39	38	30	8	..	1	167
0	..	3	7	12	29	43	33	26	3	1	..	157
Total	40	104	151	184	248	286	279	307	103	66	31	1,799

columns show the median intensity for the respective columns. Content score 5 seems to be approximately the zero interval. Men to the right of this score can be said to have *positive* job satisfaction, and men to the left to have *negative* job satisfaction.

In conclusion, it should be pointed out that the intensity curve provides not only an objective zero-point, but also a picture of the relative strength with which an attitude or opinion is held. Differing shaped curves, when plotted on the percentile metric, show differing degrees of sharpness in the division of attitudes or opinions. Illustrations of this will be given in future publications.[7]

[7] See Guttman, Louis and Suchinyh. "Intensity and a Zero Point for Attitude Analysis," *American Sociological Review*, XII (1947), 57–67.

— · — · — · — · — · — · — · — · — · —

CHARLES E. OSGOOD
GEORGE J. SUCI
PERCY H. TANNENBAUM

*Semantic Differential Technique**

One of the significant by-products of our work in experimental semantics, we believe, has been a new approach and rationale for attitude measurement. It has been feasible to identify "attitude" as one of the major dimensions of meaning-in-general and thus to extend the measurement procedures of the semantic differential to an important area of social psychology. In working in this area with the differential we have also found evidence for a general principle governing some aspects of cognitive processes—a *principle of congruity*. Although the operation of this principle is not necessarily limited to the attitudinal dimension of the meaning space, we first encountered it in connection with research on attitude measurement and will therefore introduce it in this context.

ATTITUDE MEASUREMENT

A Definition of Attitude

Despite a plethora of definitions of "attitude" in contemporary social science, some consensus and agreement is evident, particularly with respect to the major properties that attitudes are assumed to possess. Most authorities are agreed that attitudes are learned and implicit—they are inferred states of the organism that are presumably acquired in much the same manner that other such internal learned activity is acquired. Further, they are predispositions to respond, but are distinguished from other such states of readiness in that they predispose toward an *evaluative* response. Thus, attitudes are referred to as "tendencies of approach or avoidance," or as "favorable or unfavorable," and so on. This notion is related to another shared view—that attitudes can be ascribed to some basic bipolar continuum with a neutral or zero reference point, implying that they have both direction and intensity and providing a basis for the quantitative indexing of attitudes. Or, to use a somewhat different nomenclature, attitudes are implicit processes having reciprocally antagonistic properties and varying in intensity.

This characterization of attitude as a learned implicit process which is potentially bipolar, varies in its intensity, and mediates evaluative behavior, suggests that attitude is part—to some authorities, the paramount part—of the internal mediational activity that operates between most stimulus and response patterns. This identification of attitude with anticipatory mediating activity has been made most explicit by Doob (1947), who, casting attitude within the framework of Hullian behavior theory, identified it with the "pure stimulus act" as a mediating mechanism.

*Charles E. Osgood, George J. Suci, and Percy H. Tannenbaum, *The Measurement of Meaning* (Urbana, Ill.: University of Illinois Press, 1957), pp. 189–199. Reprinted by permission.

Still lacking, however, is an identification and localization of attitude per se within this general system of mediational activity. Our work in semantic measurement appears to suggest such an identification: If attitude is, indeed, some portion of the internal mediational activity, it is, by inference from our theoretical model, part of the semantic structure of an individual, and may be correspondingly indexed. The factor analyses of meaning may then provide a basis for extracting this attitudinal component of meaning.

In all of the factor analyses we have done to date . . . a factor readily identifiable as evaluative in nature has invariably appeared; usually it has been the dominant factor, that accounting for the largest proportion of the total variance. Despite different concepts and different criteria for selecting scales, high and restricted loadings on this factor were consistently obtained for scales like *good-bad*, *fair-unfair*, and *valuable-worthless*, while scales which were intuitively non-evaluative in nature, like *fast-slow*, *stable-changeable*, and *heavy-light*, usually had small or negligible loadings on this factor. It seems reasonable to identify attitude, as it is ordinarily conceived in both lay and scientific language, with the evaluative dimension of the total semantic space, as this is isolated in the factorization of meaningful judgments.

In terms of the operations of measurement with the semantic differential, we have defined the *meaning* of a concept as its allocation to a point in the multidimensional semantic space. We then define *attitude* toward a concept as the projection of this point onto the evaluative dimension of that space. Obviously every point in semantic space has an evaluative component (even though the component may be of zero magnitude, when the evaluative judgments are neutral), and, therefore, every concept must involve an attitudinal component as part of its total meaning. This does not imply that the evaluative or attitudinal dimension is necessarily stable in orientation with respect to other dimensions of the space; as we found . . . depending upon the concept or set of concepts being judged, "purely" evaluative scales, like *good-bad*, may rotate so as to correspond in alignment with the potency factor, the sensory adiency factor, and so on. In other words, the kind of evaluation may shift with the frame of reference determined by the concepts (e.g., political, aesthetic, and so on).

Measurement Procedure with the Semantic Differential

Following the definition and rationale above, to index attitude we would use sets of scales which have high loadings on the evaluative factor across concepts generally and negligible loadings on other factors, as determined from our various factor analytic studies. Thus, scales like *good-bad*, *optimistic-pessimistic*, and *positive-negative* should be used rather than scales like *kind-cruel*, *strong-weak*, or *beautiful-ugly* because the latter would prove less generally evaluative as the concept being judged is varied. However, since the concept-by-concept factoring work on which the present rationale is based was not done at the time most of the attitude measurement reported here was undertaken, we have not always satisfied this ideal criterion. For purposes of scoring consistency, we have uniformly assigned the unfavorable poles of our evaluative scales (e.g., *bad*, *unfair*, *worthless*, etc.) the score "1" and the favorable poles (*good*, *fair*, *valuable*) the score "7"—this regardless of the presentation of the scales to subjects in the graphic differential, where they should be randomized in direction. We then merely sum over all evaluative ratings to obtain the attitude "score." A more refined method would be to weight each scale in terms of its evaluative factor loading for the concepts being judged, but this would be extremely laborious and, if the scales are "purely" evaluative as defined above, would probably add little to the precision of the instrument. It should also be noted that in practice we usually include a considerable number of scales representing other factors—this is done both to obscure somewhat the purpose of the measurement and to provide additional information on the meaning of the concept as a whole, aside from the attitude toward it.

The major properties of attitude that any measurement technique is expected to index are readily accommodated by this procedure. *Direction* of attitude, favorable or unfavorable, is simply indicated by the selection of polar terms by the subject; if the score falls more toward the favorable poles, then the attitude is taken to be favorable, and vice versa. A score that falls at the origin, defined by "4" on the scales, is taken as an index of neutrality of attitude. *Intensity* of attitude is indexed by how far out along the evaluative dimension from the origin the score lies, i.e., the polarization of the attitude score. Although on a single scale there are only three levels of intensity, "slightly," "quite," and "extremely" in either direction, summing over several evaluative scales yields finer degrees of intensity. If six scales are used, for example, we have a range of possible scores from six (most unfavorable), through 24 (exactly neutral), to 42 (most favorable), there being 18 degrees of intensity of attitude score in each direction. On the basis of earlier work (see Katz, 1944; Cantril, 1946) it is assumed that a neutral rating is one of least intensity in terms of attitude. *Unidimensionality* of the attitude scale is provided automatically in the factor analytic procedures from which the scales are selected. If the scales used are selected on the basis that they all have high and pure loadings on the same factor—ideally maintaining this consistency across various factor analyses—unidimensionality must obtain. In other words, factor analysis is itself a method for testing the dimensionality of the items or scales entering into a test.

Evaluation of the Differential as a Measure of Attitude

1. *Reliability.* Test-retest reliability data have been obtained by Tannenbaum (1953). Each of six concepts (labor leaders, the Chicago Tribune, Senator Robert Taft, legalized gambling, abstract art, and accelerated college programs) was judged against six evaluative scales (*good-bad*, *fair-unfair*, *valuable-worthless*, *tasty-distasteful*, *clean-dirty*, and *pleasant-unpleasant*) by 135 subjects on two occasions separated by five weeks. Attitude scores were computed by summing over the six scales, after realignment according to a constant evaluative direction. The test-retest coefficients ranged from .87 to .93, with a mean *r* (computed by *z*-transformation) of .91. Additional reliability data, which confirm this, were obtained in another study and are given in Table 31.

2. *Validity.* The evaluative dimension of the semantic differential displays reasonable face-validity as a measure of attitude. For example, Suci (1952) was able to differentiate between high and low ethnocentrics, as determined independently from the E-scale of the Authoritarian Personality studies, on the basis of their ratings of various ethnic concepts on the evaluative scales of the differential. Similarly, evaluative scale ratings were found to discriminate in expected ways between shades of political preference, by Suci in his study of voting behavior (see pp. 104–24) and by Tannenbaum and Kerrick in their pictorial political symbolism study (see pp. 296–99). However, unlike the measurement of

TABLE 31. VALIDITY AND RELIABILITY COEF-
FICIENTS FOR SEMANTIC DIFFERENTIAL
ATTITUDE SCORES (s) AND THURSTONE
SCALE SCORES (t)

	(1)	(2)	(3)	(4)
Attitude Object	$r_{s_1 t_1}$ *	$r_{s_1 t_2}$	$r_{t_1 t_2}$	$t_{s_1 s_2}$
The Church	.74	.76	.81	.83
Capital Punishment	.81	.77	.78	.91
The Negro	.82	.81	.87	.87

*The subscripts 1 and 2 refer to the first and second testing, respectively.

meaning in general, in the case of attitude we have other, independently devised measuring instruments which have been used and against which the present technique can be evaluated. We report two such comparisons, the first with Thurstone scales and the second with a Guttman-type scale.

(a) *Comparison with Thurstone scales.* Each of three concepts (the Negro, the church, and capital punishment) was rated against a series of scales, including five purely evaluative ones (*fair-unfair, valuable-worthless, pleasant-unpleasant, clean-dirty,* and *good-bad*). In addition, subjects indicated their attitudes on Thurstone scales specifically designed to scale these attitude objects—the standard scale for the Church, Form B of the Negro scale, and Form A of the Capital Punishment scale (see Thurstone, 1931). Subjects were divided into two groups for testing purposes: one group (N = 23) was given the semantic differential form first, followed approximately one hour later by the Thurstone tests, and the other group (N = 27) had the reverse order. Two weeks after this initial session, the subjects again took both tests, except that this time their respective orders were reversed. The latter session was run to obtain reliability information on both types of attitude measuring instruments. Columns (1) and (2) of Table 31 present the product-moment correlations between the semantic differential (s) and Thurstone (t) scale scores for each of the three objects of judgment, on the initial test session ($r_{s_1 t_1}$) and on the second test session ($r_{s_2 t_2}$); columns (3) and (4) present the test-retest reliability coefficients for the Thurstone scales ($r_{t_1 t_2}$), and for the evaluative scores on the differential ($r_{s_1 s_2}$), again for each of the three concepts judged. It may be seen that the reliabilities of the two instruments are both high and equivalent. The correlation between the semantic differential scores and the corresponding Thurstone scores is significantly greater than chance (p < .01) in each case, and in no case is the across-techniques correlation significantly lower than the reliability coefficient for the Thurstone test. The differences in the between-techniques correlations from first to second testing sessions are well within chance limits. It is apparent, then, that whatever the Thurstone scales measure, the evaluative factor of the semantic differential measures just about as well. Indeed, when the six validity coefficients are corrected for attenuation, each is raised to the order of .90 or better.

(b) *Comparison with a Guttman scale.* Recently, an opportunity to test the validity of the evaluative factor of the differential as a measure of attitude against a scale of the Guttman type arose. A 14-item Guttman-type scale (reproducibility coefficient: .92) had been developed, at the expense of some time and labor, to assess the attitudes of farmers toward the agricultural practice of crop rotation. At approximately the same time, the semantic differential was being used in connection with a series of television programs dealing with agricultural practices, and one of the concepts included was Crop Rotation. Although these studies were conducted independently, 28 subjects were found who had been exposed to both testing instruments. The Guttman scale had been administered first in all cases and the time between the two tests varied considerably, from only three days to almost four weeks. With attitude scores on the differential obtained by summing over the three evaluative scales used (*good-bad*, *fair-unfair*, and *valuable-worthless*), the rank order correlation between the two instruments was highly significant (rho = .78; p <.01). Again we may say that the Guttman scale and the evaluative scales of the differential are measuring the same thing to a considerable degree.

The findings of both of these studies support the notion that the evaluative factor of the semantic differential is an index of attitude. It is, moreover, a method of attitude assessment that is relatively easy to administer and easy to score. Although it does not tap much of the *content* of an attitude in the denotative sense (e.g., the specific reactions which people having various attitudes might make, the specific statements that they might accept), it does seem to provide an index to the location of the attitude object along a general evaluative continuum. That the semantic differential *in toto* may provide a richer picture of the meaning of the attitude object than just the evaluative dimension is a point to which we return momentarily.

The Question of Generalized Attitude Scales

It is apparent that the semantic differential may be used as a generalized attitude scale. Using exactly the *same* set of evaluative scales, we have seen that correlation between our scores and those obtained with specific Thurstone scales are *equally* high for such diverse attitude objects as War, Negro, and Capital Punishment. If we were careful to select as our evaluative scales those which maintain high and pure loading on the evaluative factor regardless of the concept class being judged, it is probable that such high correlations with standard attitude-measuring instruments would be obtained regularly. The question, however, is whether the use of generalized attitude scales is justified and valuable.

Attitude scales of the generalized type were introduced some two decades ago by Remmers and his associates (see Remmers, 1934; Remmers and Silance, 1934) in an attempt to overcome the laborious work involved in developing scales by the Thurstone equal-appearing-interval technique. The same basic procedure was followed, but instead of having statements referring to single attitude objects, they were couched in terminology designed to be applicable to a variety of objects. A number of such "master" scales were developed, each applicable to a particular class of objects—e.g., a scale for attitude toward any social institution, toward any proposed social action, and so forth. Most of these master scales were fairly reliable (median coefficient, .70) and, on the whole they compared favorably with specific Thurstone scales.

These Remmers scales were criticized on many grounds and from many quarters, however: that generalized statements cannot apply with equivalent meaning to different attitude objects (see Krech and Crutchfield, 1948; Clark, 1953), that generality is achieved with a loss of detailed information about the structure of the attitude (see

Campbell, 1953), that subjects are responding to the abstracted symbol and not in terms of the content of the issue as such (see Newcomb, 1941), and so on. All of these arguments, in one way or another, aim at the question of validity, as does McNemar's (1946) scathing criticism based on lack of correlation in some cases with Thurstone scales; for example, Dunlap and Kroll (1939) found that a generalized scale correlated only .28 with specific Droba scale for attitudes toward war. On the other hand, Campbell (1953) reported that in four of five direct comparisons, the correlations between Remmers and Thurstone scales were as high as the reliability coefficients of the latter themselves.

At any rate, such generalized scales have fallen into disuse. Nevertheless, they have some very definite values which warrant their further development. For one thing, they are *economical*—if their validity can be assumed in new situations, they make unnecessary the development and standardization of specific scales for every attitude object, saving money, time, and effort. For another thing, they are *available at the proverbial moment's notice*—Remmers (1954) cites the case where the master scale for attitude toward any proposed social action was applied immediately following President Roosevelt's announcement of the proposed enlargement of the Supreme Court. But unquestionably, the major scientific value of generalized attitude scales is the matter of *comparability*: When a subject has one attitude score on a Thurstone scale for war and another score on a Thurstone scale for capital punishment, we can conclude only in a most tenuous manner, if at all, that he is less favorably disposed toward one than the other. When exactly the same yardstick is used to measure both attitudes however—again assuming that the generality of the instrument is valid—such direct comparison becomes much more tenable. In later portions of this book, particularly in experiments testing the congruity hypothesis, several examples will be given of studies which would be impossible without the use of generalized, standard measuring instruments, in this case the semantic differential.

When used as a measure of attitude, the semantic differential carries even further the logic used by Remmers in developing his generalized scales. Rather than having different "master" scales for different classes of attitude objects, exactly the same set of evaluative dimensions would be used for all objects of judgment. Rather than using "statements" of any sort with which the subject must agree or disagree, scales defined by pure, abstracted linguistic evaluators would be used. These are at present *ideal* conditions, because we have not as yet done the systematic research necessary to select such scales. From our available factorial data on single concepts we need to select those scales which maintain a high loading on the evaluative factor, regardless of its orientation for judgments of particular concepts; then we need to test the generality of these scales by comparing them with a battery of varied, specific attitude-measuring instruments, demonstrating (a) that these scales maintain high intercorrelation among themselves across the objects being evaluated and (b) that the summation scores derived from them jointly display high and roughly equal correlations with the various specific attitude-measuring instruments used as criteria. The evidence we have collected so far indicates that this will be a likely conclusion.

Such an instrument, if developed, will still face many of the criticisms aimed at Remmers' scales. Krech and Crutchfield's argument that generalized scales cannot apply with equivalent meaning to varieties of specific objects or concepts would be met by the procedures of developing our evaluative matrix—i.e., by the demonstration that the scales selected do maintain their high and pure evaluative loading despite the nature of the concept being judged. Campbell's argument that generality is achieved at the cost of losing richer information about the structure of the attitude does not seem to us to be a criticism of an instrument *as a measure of attitude*, assumed to be a unidimensional attribute. Other methods can be used to get at the more detailed structure of a concept's meaning; indeed, the semantic differential as a whole (e.g., the profile of the object against the *n*-dimensional differential) is designed to get at just such information, as we suggest in the next section. Finally, there is Newcomb's criticism that in using such scales, subjects react in terms of symbols and not in terms of issue content—he cited the case where people who rate symbols like Fascism very unfavorably may actually agree with many of the beliefs of Fascists. This is not as much a criticism of generalized attitude scales as it is of *the phrasing of the concept* judged; these subjects did have unfavorable attitudes toward the concept Fascism and simultaneously favorable attitudes toward statements of authoritarian policies—if subjects are illogical and inconsistent, this is not a fault of the measuring instrument. In fact, comparison of the evaluative locations of concepts like Fascist and Senator McCarthy, or even a phrase like Centralization of Power in the Hands of a Strong Leader, would reveal just such logical inconsistencies. One of the advantages of the semantic differential in this regard is its flexibility with respect to the nature of the concept judged—ordinary nouns, phrases, pictures, cartoons, and even sonar signals have been used at one time or another.

Meaning vs. Attitude in the Prediction of Behavior

One of the most common criticisms of attitude scales of all types is that they do not allow us to predict actual behavior in real-life situations. Like most such arguments, this one is overdrawn. Most proponents of attitude measurement have agreed that attitude scores indicate only a *disposition* toward certain *classes* of behaviors, broadly defined, and that what overt response actually occurs in a real-life situation depends also upon the context provided by that situation. We may say, for example, that a person with an extremely unfavorable attitude toward Negro may be expected to make some negatively evaluating overt response to an object of this attitude if he is in a situation in which he does not anticipate punishment from others about him. As Doob (1947) has put it, "overt behavior can seldom be predicted from knowledge of attitude alone." But there is more involved here than this: It can also be said that the attitudinal disposition itself accounts for only part of the intervening state which mediates between situations and behaviors, albeit perhaps the dominant part. The *meaning* of Negro to the individual subject is richer by far than what is revealed by his attitude score. Within the framework of the theoretical model underlying our own research, attitude is one—but only one—of the dimensions of meaning, and hence provides only part of the information necessary for prediction.

By combining judgments derived from scales representing other dimensions with those derived from the evaluative factor alone, additional information can be obtained and prediction presumably improved. Two people may have identical *attitudes* toward a concept (as determined by allocation to the evaluative dimension alone), and yet have quite different meanings of the concept (as determined by the profiles as wholes). Consider, for example, one of Tannenbaum's observations in the Thurstone comparison study reported above: One subject rated The Negro as *unfavorable*, *strong*, and *active*; another subject rated The Negro as equally *unfavorable*, but also as *weak* and *passive*. Although no behavioral criteria were available in this study, it seems likely that the former subject would behave differently in a real-life situation (e.g., with fear and avoidance) than the latter. While it is true that different attitudes imply different behaviors toward the objects signified, at least in some contexts, it is not true that the same attitude automatically implies the same behaviors.

A recent pilot study by Tannenbaum demonstrates how increasing the dimensionality of judgment utilized within the differential can increase predictability. This does not, unfortunately, involve direct, overt bevavior toward the objects of attitude, but it does approach closer to that real-life situation. Subjects (N = 40) were asked to judge three nationality concepts—Germans, Chinese, and Hindus—against a series of semantic differential scales representative of the three major factors of meaning repeatedly obtained in factor analysis. In addition, these subjects also rated each of the nationalities on a modified Bogardus Social Distance Scale. Separate factor scores were computed for each subject on each concept, and correlation coefficients were then computed both between these scores (e.g., evaluation/potency, potency/activity, etc.) and between them and the Bogardus ratings—as might be expected—multiple correlation analysis showed that the predictability of the social distance ratings was significantly enhanced by addition of information from the other factors. On the concept Germans, for example, evaluative scores correlated only .22 with the Bogardus scale, yet combining all three yielded a multiple correlation of .78. The increases in predictability for the other two concepts were not so great—from .62 to .80 for Chinese and from .59 to .72 for Hindus—but support the same conclusion.

— · — · — · — · — · — · — · — · —

HADLEY CANTRIL

*Self-Anchoring Striving Scale**

The solution was to invent what I call the Self-Anchoring Striving Scale, a direct outgrowth of the transactional point of view, described in the last chapter.[1] This scale seems to provide a simple, widely applicable, and adaptable technique for tapping the unique reality world of an individual and learning what it has in common with that of others.

A person is asked to define on the basis of *his own* assumptions, perceptions, goals, and values the two extremes or anchoring points of the spectrum on which some scale

*Hadley Cantril, *The Pattern of Human Concerns* (New Brunswick, N. J.: Rutgers University Press, 1965), pp. 22-27. Reprinted by permission.

measurement is desired—for example, he may be asked to define the "top" and "bottom," the "good" and "bad," the "best" and the "worst." This self-defined continuum is then used as our measuring device.

While the Self-Anchoring Striving Scale technique can be used on a wide variety of problems, it was utilized in this study as a means of discovering the spectrum of values a person is preoccupied or concerned with and by means of which he evaluates his own life. He describes as the top anchoring point his wishes and hopes as he personally conceives them and the realization of which would constitute for him the best possible life. At the other extreme, he describes the worries and fears, the preoccupations and frustrations, embodied in his conception of the worst possible life he could imagine. Then, utilizing a nonverbal ladder device (see Figure III-1), symbolic of "the ladder of life," he is asked

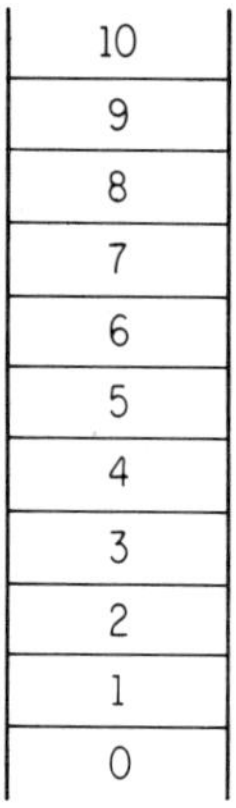

10
9
8
7
6
5
4
3
2
1
0

Figure III-1. Ladder device.

where he thinks he stands on the ladder today, with the top being the best life *as he has defined it*, the bottom the worst life *as he has defined it*. He is also asked where he thinks he stood in the past and where he thinks he will stand in the future. He is then asked similar questions about the best and worst possible situations he can imagine for his country so his aspirations and fears on the national level can be learned. Again, the ladder is used to find out where he thinks his country stands today, where it stood in the past, and where it will stand in the future.

The actual questions, together with the parenthetical instructions to interviewers, are given below:

1. (A) All of us want certain things out of life. When you think about what really matters in your own life, what are your wishes and hopes for the future? In other words, if you imagine your future in the *best* possible light, what would your life look like then, if you are to be happy? Take your time in answering; such things aren't easy to put into words.

   PERMISSIBLE PROBES: What are your hopes for the future? What would your life have to be like for you to be completely happy? What is missing for you to be happy? (Use also, if necessary, the words "dreams" and "desires."]

   OBLIGATORY PROBE: Anything else?

(B) Now taking the other side of the picture, what are your fears and worries about the future? In other words, if you imagine your future in the *worst* possible light, what would your life look like then? Again, take your time in answering.

    PERMISSIBLE PROBE: What would make you unhappy? [Stress the words "fears" and "worries."]

    OBLIGATORY PROBE: Anything else?

    Here is a picture of a ladder. Suppose we say that the top of the ladder (POINTING) represents the best possible life for you and the bottom (POINTING) represents the worst possible life for you.

(C) Where on the ladder (MOVING FINGER RAPIDLY UP AND DOWN LADDER) do you feel you personally stand at the *present* time? Step number _____

(D) Where on the ladder would you say you stood *five years ago*? Step number

_____

(E) And where do you think you will be on the ladder *five years from now*? Step number _____

2. (A) Now, what are your wishes and hopes for the future of our country? If you picture the future of (name of country) in the *best* possible light, how would things look, let us say, ten years from now?

    OBLIGATORY PROBE: Anything else?

  (B) And what, about your fears and worries for the future of our country? If you picture the future of (name of country) in the *worst* possible light, how would things look about ten years from now?

    OBLIGATORY PROBE: Anything else?

  (C) Now, looking at the ladder again, suppose your greatest hopes for (name of country) are at the top (POINTING); your worst fears at the bottom (POINTING). Where would you put (name of country) on the ladder (MOVING FINGER RAPIDLY UP AND DOWN LADDER) *at the present time*? Step number

_____

  (D) Where did (name of country) stand *five years ago*? Step number _____

  (E) Just as your best guess, where do you think (name of country) will be on the ladder *five years from now*? Step number _____

A number of questions were then asked to give details about the individual's background: age, occupation, religion, education, whether or not he owned his own land or was an agricultural worker, marital status, political preference, economic status, and the like. These items, of course, had to be varied in different cultures according to what was and was not relevant, what was and was not possible to obtain, such as political preference in certain countries.

It will be noticed that on the questions dealing with personal aspirations and fears, when a person was asked to imagine his future in the best and worst possible lights, the question was left open without any specification of what was meant by the future; whereas when asked about the future with respect to the nation, the question included the phrase "How would things look, let us say, ten years from now?" But in both the personal and national questions when the ladder ratings were obtained, people estimated where they felt they, or the nation, stood five years before or would stand five years from then. The reason for this was that in careful pretesting it was found unwise and artificial to structure the personal future, but if the future of the nation was left indeterminate, people were bewildered. People could imagine the future of their country as they might like to see it or as they might fear it a decade from the time they were questioned. But when it came to the actual task of making a rating on the ladder, the ten-year interval both for personal and national seemed too far away to be predictable, and so the five-year interval was used.

Interviewers were instructed to take verbatim reports as much as possible. All interviewers were, of course, natives of the country, or, where it was important, of the region of the country in which they interviewed.

In order to organize the study in each country, explain the rationale of the method, and do what training was necessary—in some instances, such as Yugoslavia, where no such survey work had been done before one had to start from scratch—either Lloyd Free or I visited the country, worked out arrangements with the best organization that could be found to do the work, and spent considerable time going over all the details with those who were to cooperate with us.

Some skeptics may continue to say that when people are asked the sort of questions used in this study, they cannot be expected to give honest answers: people will falsify, idealize to their own advantage and glorification, talk in terms of high-sounding abstractions or the like. All of the evidence belies this: the protocols obtained appeared throughout to be plausible, honest, and sincere. Others may say that the survey instrument itself is a crude or slipshod device which taps only superficialities and off-the-cuff reactions. But the instrument of the social survey, like a violin, can be used skillfully or clumsily.

It should be emphasized over and over again that the ratings people assign either themselves or the nation are entirely subjective: hence a rating of, say, 6 given by one person by no means indicates the same thing as a 6 given by another person. This obvious point is mentioned here because experience has shown that some people misunderstand the whole rationale of this technique by assuming that the scale is like an intelligence test where a given rating has a precise and presumably somewhat universal connotation. As will be seen later on in the text, an American who gives himself a rating of 6 for the present may be projecting a standard of living for himself that will include "enough money to own a boat and send my four children to private preparatory school"; the wife of a Havana worker who gives herself the same rating will say that her aspiration is "to have enough food and clothes so we don't have to beg for things"; an Indian sweeper who also rates his present standing on the ladder at 6 will say among other things that "the main thing I want is to have the government give me woolen clothes to wear in the wintertime." Similarly, of course, the shifts in the ladder ratings from past to present and present to future are equally subjective. All ratings are anchored within an individual's own reality world.

It should also be made clear that no claims are made that the Self-Anchoring Striving Scale gets at "everything" it is important to know about an individual. A person is not going to talk about his sexual frustrations, about some misdemeanor or petty theft that may preoccupy him, about many things that are highly personal or socially unacceptable. Furthermore, and most important as noted throughout the later discussion, individuals do not mention aspects of life they take for granted—thus, for example, American college students tend not to mention a high standard of living, which they assume they will have, but on the other hand will talk about the place in society they want to attain or how they measure up to their own standards. Despite such limitations—which would be severe if one were, say, a clinical psychologist—*for the level of accounting* that affords insight into the problems I have set for myself, the Self-Anchoring Striving Scale has proved an enormously rich and useful device. Furthermore, results obtained by this method will, I believe, be meaningful through a long span of time and thus have greater permanence than results based on questions more affected by circumstances and changes of the context within which they are asked.

One of the problems that had to be overcome was translating the original questions from English into the various languages used. In some cases this was by no means an easy task, and considerable time was spent with experts to be sure the translation contained the precise nuances wanted. One of the methods often utilized in this translation process was to have someone who knew the native language, as a native, for example, an Arab, and who also was completely fluent in English translate our questions into Arabic. Then someone whose native language was English but who had a perfect command of Arabic would translate the Arabic back into English so a comparison could be made with the original question and, through discussion and further comparisons, difficulties could be ironed out.

Translations from English had to be made into the following twenty-six other languages which we list here alphabetically: Arabic, Bengali, Cebuano, German, Gujarati, Hausa, Hebrew, Hindi, Ibo, Ilocano, Ilongo, Malayalam, Marathi, Oriya, Polish, Portuguese, Serbo-Croatian, Slovenian, Spanish, Tagalog, Tamil, Telugu, Urdu, Waray, Yiddish, and Yoruba.

THE CODING SCHEME

In order to obtain quantitative comparisons between different individuals, groups, people, and cultures, a coding scheme for a content analysis of all material was developed on an empirical basis. In order to get some preliminary feel of the wide variety of comments that I knew would have to be accommodated in such a study; I made a trip around the world, stopping in many countries, and having our questionnaire translated and administered to as many different kinds of people as could be conveniently found. In this way about 3,000 interviews were made entirely on a preliminary basis and without any special regard to careful sampling. These were all translated into English so that I could go over them and, with Lloyd Free, work out our coding scheme. The original code went through several revisions. The code used in classifying the material reported in this book contains 145 different items (34 concerning personal aspirations, 33 for personal fears, 42 for national aspirations, and 36 for national fears). We left in the code all items that received at least 5 percent mention in any country. While these 145 items cover the vast majority of subjects mentioned by people, special categories were added from time to time to take care of unusual preoccupations that loomed uniquely important in particular cultures—for example, the problem of reunification in West Germany, or the problem of the "cheapening of Israel culture" as a national fear in Israel. The complete code used is given in Appendix A.

In dealing with *personal* aspirations and fears, the code moves outward in terms of wider horizons of awareness and concern: from items having to do with self or family (for example, "emotional stability and maturity," "decent standard of living for self or family," "happy family life"); to items involving other people, the community, or the nation ("freedom" "economic stability in general," "equal opportunities irrespective of race or color"); to items dealing with international or world affairs ("peace," "better world").

In the case of *national* aspirations and fears, comments are coded under the following major headings: Political (for example, "honest government," "national unity"); Economic ("improved or decent standard of living in general, greater national prosperity," "employment, jobs for everyone"); Social ("social justice," "eliminate discrimination and prejudice based on race or color"); International Relations, Cold War, Peace ("disarmament, control or banning of nuclear weapons," "maintenance of neutrality"); and Independent Status, and Importance of the Nation ("maintain or attain the position of a world power," "national independence").

Since the coding was of the utmost importance for the validity of our research, either Mr. Free or I usually made a second trip to each country at the time coding was undertaken to explain the coding system and go over a sample of questionnaires that had been translated into English with the individuals who were to work on the coding scheme. It very quickly proved inadvisable, as well as a most expensive and almost insuperable job, to have all questionnaires translated into English for coding by us: it was much better to have the coding done locally or in a neighboring country by highly intelligent and highly trained people so that nuances of meaning in the native language would not be lost. After a week or two of intensive work with the coders, a reliability of around 95 percent between coders with each other or coders with us could be achieved.

In order to make the data more manageable for overall national and personal comparisons, a number of specific code items were later combined into "general categories," which give a broader overview and make it possible to have meaningful comparisons without being swamped with details.

— · — · — · — · — · — · — · — · — · — · — · — · —

J. L. MORENO

*Sociometry**

*J. L. Moreno, *Who Shall Survive? Foundations of Sociometry, Group Psychotherapy and Socio-drama* (Beacon, N. Y.: Beacon House, 1953), pp. 48–57. Reprinted by permission of the publisher and the author.

Sociometry aspires to be a science within its own right. It is the indispensable prologue for all the social sciences. Without giving up the vision of totality by an inch, it has retreated from the maximum to the minimum, to the social atoms and molecules. It can therefore be called a sociology of the microscopic dynamic events, regardless of the size of the social group to which it is applied, small or large. The result of sociometric development has been that the investigation of the smallest social aggregates has become more interesting than that of the large ones. For the future development of sociometry it may be desirable to separate it as a special discipline and to consider it as a microscopic and microdynamic science underlying all social sciences. It has several subdivisions like microsociology, microanthropology, microeconomics, microsociatry, microecology. It is not merely a slogan indicating a special type of research, a single method or a number of techniques. Its present stage of development is still embryonic and scattered but there can be no question as to the potentialities of the new science. For the future progress of the social sciences it is of the greatest importance that a science of sociometry is set up and delineated, and its relation to other social sciences defined. Its range and boundaries, its operations and objectives are already more sharply visible than the same references in sociology or anthropology. It does not supplant and it must not overlap with anthropology or economics, for instance, but their findings on the overt, macroscopic level may receive a new interpretation from the point of view of sociometric research.

The old definitions of sociology: "Science of Society" and "Science of Social Phenomena" did not need any further specification until *the development of social microscopy and the discovery of the sociometric matrix suggested the division between macroscopic and microscopic social disciplines.* Before this there did not exist any dynamic, material reason to digress from Comte's opinion that sociology is a unitary science of society.

The logico-methodological argument of Georg Simmel and Leopold von Wiese in favor of separating sociology from other social science specialties as, for instance, historical sociology and social philosophy, was a necessary step to clear the way through the jungle of disciplines. But these divisions occurred, metaphorically speaking, on the floors above; the basement underneath remained untouched by them. This time a division of the social sciences became urgent in the *vertical* dimension. For every macroscopic social discipline a microscopic social discipline could be envisioned, microsociology, versus macrosociology, microanthropology versus macroanthropology, microeconomics versus macroeconomics, microecology versus macroecology, etc. The final arbiter for such drastic division is the productivity it has for research. In other sciences division proved fruitful for the advancement of knowledge as between anatomy and histology or physics and chemistry. By putting together all the microscopic social sciences into one block the focus of the social investigator will be more sharpened in the choice of hypotheses and experimental design and in giving these areas the systematic attention they deserve.

The old definition of sociology should, therefore, give place to another which is more in accord with what sociologists actually deal with—*the science of the macroscopic systems of human society, their description and measurement.*

The resistance in some quarters against sociometric theory and terminology is largely due to its claim of representing a new science; but it did this because it could not see how the new outlook and the new discoveries could be incorporated into the old framework of concepts of the social sciences without undue sacrifice of clarity and order. When, out of new empirical and experimental evidence new concept dynamically arises, it is against the spirit of science to force it into an outworn and limited framework of classification and interpretation, out of reverence for tradition. What is relevant to new concept goes also for new terminology; with new concept and new evidence appropriate terms logically arise. The recommendation of academic sociologists to adapt new constructs to old terms and phrases as "social process," "social statics," "social dynamics," etc., is not easily accomplished. Properly coined terms in a new discipline help the advance of knowledge and stir up the imagination of the investigator. The matter is entirely different when a new term and meaning, for instance, "actor" is used for an old term and meaning as "organism"; or a new term and meaning "act" is used for an old term and meaning "behavior"; then the change is unwarranted.

Such behavior is not new in the history of science; it reminds one of the period when chemistry was emerging as a new discipline. The "operations" which characterized the new science of chemistry were rapidly accepted but antiquated interpretations, as the phlogiston theory, were preferred. Similarly, one of the difficulties in the development of sociometry has been the rapid assimilation of its techniques, operations and methods, and the parallel ignorance of and resistance against its theories. This has proven to be unfortunate, not only for the formulation of significant hypothesis, but also for the further refinement of the techniques themselves. One could follow with amusement how rapidly sociometric techniques such as the sociogram, the sociometric test, small group analysis, role playing, psychodrama and sociodrama were taken for granted as techniques, but their theoretical background, the concepts of the actor in situ, the alter or auxiliary ego, spontaneity, creativity, tele, warming up, social atom, psychosocial networks of communication, sociodynamic effect, etc., were taken lightly, ignored or smuggled into literature without reference to the source. This would not be so serious if these hypotheses would have developed independently from sociometric techniques, but as it is they developed and they were imposed by empirical evidence; they have been the result of rigorous thinking in working through the material gathered. This circumstance is unfortunate for yet another reason. The new system of theories and concepts do not only give important clues for significant hypotheses, they are also important prerequisites for the proper use of the techniques and for the setting up of productive experiments.

Sociometry is to a large extent a classificatory science, and generalizations can be made on the basis of such classifications. Geography and geology are examples of other classificatory sciences. Their counterpart within sociometry is psychological or sociometric geography. Some day a psychological geography of our planetary human population will be drawn without any reference to outside criteria. In fact, as soon as the whole field can be tackled as a unit, the cause-effect relation as well as any other relation may be visible; then there will not be any criterion left outside of it and the experimental method will not be necessary for proof.

Sociometry deals with the mathematical study of psychological properties of populations, the experimental technique of and the results obtained by application of quantitative methods. This is undertaken through methods which inquire into the evolution and organization of groups and the position of individuals within them. One of its special concerns is to ascertain the quantity and expansion of the psychological currents as they pervade populations.

My first definition of sociometry was, in accordance with its etymology, from the Latin and Greek, but the emphasis was laid not only on the second half of the term, i.e., on "metrum," meaning measure, but also on the first half, *i.e.*, on "socius," meaning companion. The old dichotomy, qualitative versus quantitative is resolved, within the sociometric method, in a new way. The qualitative aspect of social structure is not destroyed or forgotten, it is integrated into the quantitative operations, it acts from within. The two aspects of structure are treated in combination and as a unit. Both principles, it seemed to me, had been neglected, but the "socius" aspect had been omitted from deeper analysis far more than the "metrum" aspect. The "companion," even as a problem, was unrecognized. The measurement of interpersonal relations as well as the experimental production of social interaction have never been seriously tackled. What remains of a society to be investigated if the individuals themselves and the relationships between them are considered in a fragmentary or wholesale fashion? Or, to put it in a positive way, the individuals themselves and the interrelations between them must be treated as the nuclear structure of every social situation.

The phrase sociometry has a linguistic relatedness in construction to other, traditional scientific terms: biology, biometry; psychology, psychometry; sociology, sociometry. From the point of view of systematics it is preparatory to topical fields as sociology, anthropology, social psychology, social psychiatry. It is concerned with the "socius" and "metric" problems common to *all* social fields. It has developed three departments of research: (a) dynamic, or revolutionary sociometry, engaged in problems of social change; (b) diagnostic sociometry, engaged in social classification; and (c) mathematical sociometry.

Sociometry starts practically as soon as we are in a position to study social structure as a whole and its parts at the same time. This was impossible as long as the problem of the individual was still a main concern, as with an individual's relation and adjustment to the group. Once the full social structure could be seen as a totality it could be studied in its minute detail. We thus became able to describe sociometric facts (descriptive sociometry) and to consider the function of specific structures, the effect of some parts upon others (dynamic sociometry).

Viewing the social structure of a certain community as a whole, related to a certain locality, with a certain physical geography, a township filled with homes, schools, workshops, the interrelations between their inhabitants in these situations, we arrive at the concept of the sociometric geography of a community. Viewing the detailed structure of a community we see the concrete position of every individual in it, also, a nucleus of relations around every individual which is "thicker" around some individuals, "thinner" around others. This nucleus of relations is the small social structure in a community, a *social atom*. From the point of view of a descriptive sociometry, *the social atom is a fact, not a concept*, just as in anatomy the blood vessel system, for instance, is first of all a descriptive fact. It attained conceptual significance as soon as the study of the development of social atoms suggested that they have an important function in the formation of human society.

Whereas certain parts of these social atoms seem to remain buried between the individuals participating, certain parts link themselves with parts of other social atoms and these with parts of other social atoms again, forming complex chains of interrelations which are called, in terms of descriptive sociometry, *sociometric networks*. The older and wider the network spreads the less significant seems to be the individual contribution toward it. From the point of view of dynamic sociometry these networks have the function of shaping social tradition and public opinion.

It is different and more difficult, however, to describe the process which attracts individuals to one another or which repels them, that flow of feeling of which the social atom and the networks are apparently composed. This process may be conceived as *tele*. Tele is two-way empathy, like a telephone it has two ends. We are used to the notion that feelings emerge within the individual organism and that they become attached more strongly or more weakly to persons or things in the immediate environment. We have been in the habit of thinking not only that these totalities of feelings spring up from the individual organism exclusively, from one of its parts or from the organism as a whole, but that these physical and mental states after having emerged reside forever within this organism. The feeling relation to a person or an object has been called attachment or fixation but these attachments or fixations were considered purely as individual projections. This was in accord with the materialistic concept of the individual organism, with its unity, and, we can perhaps say, with its microcosmic independence.

The hypothesis that feelings, emotions or ideas can "leave" or "enter" the organism appeared inconsistent with this concept. The claims of parapsychology were easily discarded as unfounded by scientific evidence. The claims of collectivistic folk unity of a people appeared romantic and mystical. This resistance against any attempt to break the sacred unity of the individual has one of its roots in the idea that feelings, emotions, ideas must reside in some structure within which they can emerge or vanish, and within which they can function or disappear. If these feelings, emotions and ideas "leave" the organism, where then can they reside?

When we found that social atoms and networks have a persistent structure and they develop in a certain order we had extra individual structures—and probably there are many more to be discovered—in which this flow can reside. These may be conceived as two-way or multiple-way structures. One-way or projected feelings do not make sense sociometrically. They require the complementation of "retrojected" feelings, at least, potentially. This has been studied particularly through *sociometric perception tests*. One part does not exist without the other. It is a continuum. We must assume at present, until further knowledge forces us to modify and refine this concept, that some real process in one's life situation is sensitive and corresponds to some real process in another person's life situation and that there are numerous degrees, positive, negative and neutral, of these interpersonal sensitivities. The tele between any two individuals may be potential. It may never become active unless these individuals are brought into proximity or unless their feelings and ideas meet at a distance through some channel, for instance, the networks. These distance or tele effects have been found to be complex sociometric structures produced by a long chain of individuals each with a different degree of sensitivity for the same tele, ranging from total indifference to a maximum response.

A social atom is thus composed of numerous tele structures; social atoms are again parts of still a larger pattern, the sociometric networks which bind or separate large groups of individuals due to their tele relationships. Sociometric networks are parts of a still larger unit, the sociometric geography of a community. A community is again part of the largest configuration, the sociometric totality of human society itself.

SOCIOMETRY IN RELATION TO OTHER
SOCIAL SCIENCES

Sociometry cuts through all social sciences as it deals with social phenomena at a deep level where they merge or more precisely before they "e"merge into "psychological," "sociological," "anthropological," or "economic" phenomena. This should by no means indicate that these departments do not attain usefulness and meaning on the macroscopic level of their emergence on which the differences between them become articulate and distinct.

Sociometry and Psychology

The sociometrist takes the position that as long as we as experimenters draw from every individual the responses and materials needed, we are inclined—because of our nearness to the individual—to conceive the tele as flowing out of him towards other individuals and objects. This is certainly correct on the individual-psychological level, in the preparatory phase of sociometric exploration. But as soon as we transfer these responses to the sociometric level and study them not singly but in their interrelations, important methodological reasons suggest that we conceive this flowing feeling, the tele, as an inter-personal or more accurately and broadly speaking, "as a sociometric structure."

Sociometry and Sociology

The sociometric experiment does not base its discoveries upon the interview or "questionnaire" method (a frequent misunderstanding); it is an action method, an action practice. The sociometric researcher assumes the position of the "status nascendi" in research; he is interiorating the experimental method, a participating actor. He insists on sticking to the material inquiry and does not permit himself to step out into the logical part unless he can safely do so. He tries to measure what can be measured, to validate what can be validated, but he disdains measurement and validation for their own sakes.

According to Sociometry, social systems are attraction-repulsion-neutrality systems. Human preferential systems cannot be examined adequately by the old methods of fact-finding objectively as statistical methods and observational methods, but the methods themselves and the instruments derived from them have to undergo a process of subjectification in order to return to the researcher endowed with a more profound objectivity, having gained a grasp of the social processes on the depth level.

This new sociometric objectivity owes a great deal to sociomicroscopic studies. By sociomicroscopic configurations we do not mean only the informal small groups, but the dynamic social units of which they are comprised, the pattern variants of social atoms, the clustering of social atoms into larger associations invisible to the eye of the human observer (social molecules), psychosocial networks, the clustering of numerous such networks into more comprehensive formations; finally the study of dyads, triangles, quadrangles, pentagons, and chains of persons. We assumed that the study of these primary atomic structures of human relations is the preliminary and indispensable groundwork to most macrosociological investigations.

Sociometry and Anthropology

The real data of a sociometric anthropology have died with the people after a cultural system has perished. If the cultural system is still in existence, a sociometric method should be applied to it in order to tap the actual dynamic processes operating within it. A sociometrically oriented anthropologist studying the family system of a culture would utilize two guiding hypotheses: (1) the existence of "informal" group structures surrounding the official family setting like a social aura; (2) the existence of "sub"-family forms of social organizations, forms of association including various individuals and structural relations but which may have never crystallized.

The micro-anthropologist may arrive at the generalization that there is a *universal sociometric matrix* with many varieties of structures underlying all known and potential family associations, an interweaving and crossing of numerous sociatomic and cultural-atomic processes, but not necessarily identical with the family of one type or another as a social group.

An interesting example of the sociometric approach to anthropology may be illustrated in the following example. Let us examine two different family cultural structures: (1) In an Islamic culture, a harem, consisting of twelve individuals of a single family unit, and (2) in our American setting a comparable group of twelve individuals organized into six family units of two. The Islamic group's official role structure may be identified as the male head of the household, six wives and five servants (eunuchs), comprising one household. The American group's official role structure may be identified as six husband-wife relationships comprising six families. The official institutional structures which exist externally within these two cultural systems are profoundly different from a structural point of view, due to the different dynamics of harem polygamy as compared to American monogamy. Each institutional setting imposes entirely different roles upon the individual members of the two different systems. Each system exhibits to the casual observer a considerable degree of stability and conformity to the official societal roles.

The application of sociometric techniques to the two different household systems revealed the following: in the harem sociogram the male household head is the center of all the female attractions. In the American sociogram one male is the center of all feminine attraction similar to the male household head of the harem.

Is is demonstrated that two diametrically opposed institutional structures, which externally present two entirely different "official" patterns may produce identically similar "sociometric" structures. This points out the sociometric-matrix which a microscopically oriented anthropology would reveal to the investigator.

Sociometry turned the attention of the Psychologist, Sociologist and the Anthropologist away from marginal primitive social systems to the present societies in which *they* are participant actors as well as observers. The responsible domain of social science requires expansion to include the immediate and practical structuring and guidance of present day human society on all its levels from the physical up to the societal plane. This job may have to begin by cleaning up our research shelves and laboratories, and concentrating all our efforts upon a few strategically selected points. The weakest spot in the armor of present day society and culture is its ignorance of its own social structure, especially of the small local structures in which people actually spend their lives. The time has come for sociometry to move from the closed into the "open" community. By means of practical, direct and immediate demonstrations of the usefulness of the sociometric methods faith in science can be regained and cemented. By such means can science be "saved" and put to full use. With the cooperation of "all" the people we should be able to create a social order worthy of the highest aspirations of our times. This is the meaning of revolutionary, dynamic sociometry.

— . — . — . — . — . — . — . — . — . —

4 · ATTITUDE CHANGE

ROBERT P. ABELSON
MILTON J. ROSENBERG

Balance Model in Attitude Change*

When Euler taught logic to the Princess by drawing the overlapping circles and circles within circles, he was also illustrating the well-known fact that human beings have to learn the principles of formal logic. They do not, it is generally agreed, always or even often think logically. So, if behavioral scientists are to study and understand the processes of ordinary, everyday thinking, they must develop new approaches, including the recognition that thinking is colored by emotional attitudes. By using a system based on a definition of cognitive elements and the relations between them, a psychological mathematical model has been constructed for use in the rigorous experimental analysis of attitudinal cognition.

Several lines of theoretical and research interest have gradually been converging upon the study of "cognitive structure," especially in the area of social attitudes. Attitudes, by the definitions of Smith, Bruner and White (18), Peak (14), Rosenberg (17), Green (7) and many others, involve both affective and cognitive components. These components interact intimately with one another, so that cognitions about attitudinal objects are not felt to be meaningfully analyzable without consideration of affective forces. Theorists are reluctant even to consider cognitive units of an attitude apart from other cognitive units, preferring to treat cognition as "structured" into meaningful wholes (13, 19). Krech and Crutchfield (12, p. 152) define attitude globally as "an enduring organization of motivational, emotional, perceptual and cognitive processes with respect to some aspect of the individual's world." They state (p. 108) "Each of our perceptions does not lead 'a life of its own' but is embedded in an organization of other perceptions—the whole making up a specific cognitive structure." Smith, Bruner, and White (18, p. 286), in discussing attitude measurement, caution, "Recent advances in the theory and technique of attitude measurement . . . have yet to take this complexity [of opinions] into account. Characteristically, they have conceived of attitudes as a matter of pro-ness and con-ness. . . . We would

*Reprinted from "Symbolic Psycho-logic: A Model of Attitudinal Cognition," *Behavioral Science*, Vol. 3, No. 1 (1958), pp. 1-13, by permission of James G. Miller, M. D., Ph. D., Editor.

question whether it is reasonable to expect them to generate the dimensions required for an adequate description of opinion. [An adequate description] comes rather from intensive explorations. . . ." Asch (2) is another author who has employed a holistic concept of attitude structure. He seeks to explain certain attitude change phenomena in terms of the "restructuring" of the attitudinal object (3). Rokeach (16) treats structure as an individual difference variable of cognitive style, defining one extreme, dogmatism, as "a relatively closed cognitive organization of beliefs and disbeliefs about reality . . . which . . . provides a framework for patterns of intolerance and qualified tolerance toward others."

This Gestalt emphasis, motivated by the desire to construct an accurate model of the phenomenal organization of attitudes, has underscored the difficulties inherent in attempts to deal analytically with a set of cognitive units or elements. Nevertheless, if psychologists are to talk about "cognitive structure," they must do something about it; there must be a correspondence between theory and some sort of research operation. At least two important recent theoretical developments, Festinger's (6) "dissonance theory," and Heider's (10) "theory of cognitive balance," deal conceptually with the effects of organizing forces and affective forces upon cognitive elements. Both theories are concerned with changes in cognitive structure. Festinger's theory deals mainly with inconsistencies between belief and action, and attempts to specify certain circumstances under which there will be more or less change in belief as an outgrowth of cognitive "dissonance," due to such inconsistencies. The research operations which are used to test Festinger's theory are not addressed to the details of cognitive structure, but rather to single-response predictions derivative from the theory. Heider's theory is addressed to structural details of cognition, but there has been no research operation available to investigate these details with particular attitude contents. On the other hand, the recently proposed methodological devices of Rosenberg (17) and Abelson (1) are not completely anchored in a general theory of attitudes. A fresh approach to the measurement of cognitive structure is clearly called for.

This paper proposes one such approach. We have drawn some inspiration from Cartwright and Harary's (5) objective system for the examination of "structural balance," from Heider's (10) ideas on cognitive balance, and are also intellectually indebted to Zajonc (20), who has suggested clever procedural devices in eliciting cognitive material. Otherwise, the system to be proposed is our own, albeit with a strong historical tether. The paper is divided into two parts: the "Psychological Model" and the "Mathematical System."

THE PSYCHOLOGICAL MODEL

Cognitive Elements

Human thought, for all its complexity and nuance, must involve some cognitive representation of "things," concrete and abstract. These things or concepts are the *elements* of our system. Though it does not seem absolutely necessary, we shall for convenience assume that individuals can attach some sort of verbal labels to the elements of their thinking. We will refer, then, to cognitive elements by verbal labels.

We may distinguish three broad classes of elements: Actors, Means (Actions, Instrumentalities), and Ends (Outcomes, Values). These classes are not completely exhaustive nor mutually exclusive. We propose this classification merely to suggest the variety of possible cognitive elements. To exemplify each class, consider the illustrative issue: "Having an honor system at Yale." The following elements were among those frequently elicited from Yale students in a pilot study.

Actors: myself, the Faculty, the Administration, the Student Body, a certain minority of students, the honest student. . . .
Means: the honor system, other honor systems, the present examination system, cheating, reporting those who cheat, social pressure from other students. . . .
Ends: the feeling of being trusted, mature moral standards, loyalty to friends, the University's reputation, having well-run examinations. . . .

Note that all elements are expressed here substantively to reflect their "thing-like" character.

Cognitive Relations

Of all the conceivable relations between cognitive elements, we choose to consider only four: *positive, negative, null,* and *ambivalent.* These will be denoted p, n, o, and a. (See also "Mathematical System"). We again conveniently assume that cognitive materials of a relational sort can be verbally labeled. Some typical examples of relations between elements follow:

		positive (p)	*negative (n)*	*null (o)*
Actor vs.	Actor	likes; supports	dislikes; fights	is indifferent to
	Means	uses; advocates	opposes; undermines	is not responsible for
	End	possesses; aims for	inhibits; aims against	is indifferent to
Means vs.	Actor	helps; promotes	hinders; insults	does not affect
	Means	is equivalent to	is alternative to; counteracts	is unrelated to
	End	brings about	prevents	does not lead to
End vs.	Actor	serves; is vital to	is inimical to	does not interest
	Means	justifies	obviates	cannot ensue from
	End	is consistent with	is incompatible with	is unconnected to

Ambivalent relations *(a)* are defined as conjunctions of positive and negative relations; they are psychologically secondary or "derived," and have been omitted from the above list.

Note that relations are expressed here as verbs.

Certain omissions from the above scheme may occur to the reader. Relations like "is next in line to," "is north of," etc. are certainly not included. Other phrases which imply relationship without specifying its sign, e.g., "depends upon," "is connected with," etc., are difficult to classify. Furthermore, notions of time sense, moral imperative, and conditionality or probability, e.g., "might have acted upon," "probably will help," "ought to seek," etc. are not dealt with explicitly. Time sense and conditionality are beyond the scope of the present treatment. We deal here only with cognitions of the psychological present and temporarily set aside the past, conditional past, future, and conditional future. As for the other exceptions to the scheme, note that their phrasing tends to be affectless. Dispassionate descriptions of, say, the mating habits of flamingoes or the operation of a nuclear reactor or the economic situation in Viet Nam would probably contain many relations impossible to classify. But such descriptions are reportorial, not attitudinal. When cognition is invested with affect, when the Actors, Means, and Ends are responded to emotionally, then the relations become classifiable in terms of the present system. Our intent is to be able to code all relations occurring in attitudinal cognitions into these four broad categories.

Cognitive Units or Sentences

Cognitive units are built out of pairs of elements, connected by a relation. That is, the basic "sentences" of attitudinal cognition are of the form

$$ArB$$

where A and B are elements and r is a relation. Many sentences which at first seem more complicated than the simple ArB unit may be reduced to such a unit by broadening the definition of an element. For example, consider the sentence,

"Nasser (A) insists on (p) all Suez tolls (B) belonging to (p) Egypt (C)." (Here p denotes a positive relation.) This sentence, symbolically, is $Ap(BpC)$. But regard (BpC as a new element D, the broader conception "all Suez tolls belonging to Egypt." Then we have simple ApD.

In this way, we reduce our catalogue of basic sentences to four:

$$ApB$$
$$AnB$$
$$AoB$$
$$AaB$$

The Conceptual Arena. The Structure Matrix

For the convenience of both theory and operation, we conceive of an attitude as being defined over a certain delimited though perhaps large *conceptual arena*. We restrict attention, in other words, to those elements which are (phenomenally) relevant to the given issue or attitude object.

Operationally, what one can do is this. Following Zajonc (20), we ask the subject to list all the words or short phrases that come to mind as he mulls over a given topic, such as "Having an Honor System at Yale" or "The State Department Ban on Reporters Going to Red China." Subjects will typically write several phrases in rapid-fire order, then pause, give one or two more, and finally stop. These words or phrases are not always "noun-like," but by simple instructions to the subject, they can be reworded satisfactorily and be treated subsequently as the cognitive elements. This procedure yields the conceptual arena idiosyncratic to each subject.[1]

After the arena is defined, the relations between pairs of elements may be mapped. We conceptualize a matrix setting forth the relations between each element and every

---

[1] For some experimental purposes, it is more convenient to define a common conceptual arena for a group of subjects. Some topics yield low overlap between subjects, but other topics possess sufficient overlap so that it is worthwhile to construct a group arena encompassing the most generally salient elements.

other. This matrix we denote the *structure matrix*, R (see the "Mathematical System"). As an illustration of a structure matrix, consider the following:

STRUCTURE MATRIX; TOPIC: HAVING AN HONOR SYSTEM AT YALE

	1. Ego	2. Honest Student	3. Report Cheater	4. Feel Trust	5. Cheat by Few	6. Honor System
Ego (the subject himself)	p	p	n	p	n	o
The honest student	p	p	n	p	o	p
Reporting cheaters	n	n	p	o	n	p
Feeling trusted	p	p	o	p	o	p
Cheating by a few	n	o	n	o	p	n
An honor system	o	p	p	p	n	p

The entries in this matrix were elicited by instructing a subject to fill the *middles* of sentences linking his elements (the six listed). He wrote these "open-middled" sentences:

The honest student *feels very reluctant about* reporting cheaters.
The honest student *possesses* the feeling of being trusted.
The honor system *is fine for* the honest student.
The honor system *promotes* the feeling of being trusted.
Cheating by a few *is cut down by* reporting cheaters.
The honor system *is harmed by* cheating by a few.
The honor system *involves* reporting cheaters.

The verb forms in these sentences were coded[2] into the relations p and n shown in the matrix. In addition, the subject himself was asked whether he felt favorable, neutral, or unfavorable toward each element. His responses are shown in the first row (column) of the matrix.

All relations between elements and themselves are taken to be positive. Also, relations are considered to be symmetric; i.e., if $A r B$, then $B r A$. Our preliminary work does not suggest a pressing need to revise these assumptions.

The structure matrix is our basic description of attitudinal cognition. One may wish to superimpose further refinements upon the structure such as the intensity of different relations, the confidence with which they are held, time perspective, and so on. In this paper, we answer only the simplest question, "In what way can the structure matrix be used to characterize the fundamental structural varieties of attitudinal cognition, apart from specific content?"

Thinking. Psycho-Logic

Individual cognitive units may originate in various ways—through exposure to written information, through social pressure, emotional need, thinking, etc. Once originated, these units may be manipulated in thought.

We propose a set of rules by which an individual imputes or discovers new symbolic sentences by combining two old sentences with an element in common. We hypothesize that *these rules apply only when the individual thinks about the topic,* or "rehearses the arguments" (11, p. 129).

---

[2]In order to circumvent the coding problem, one may require the subject to choose his verb forms from a precoded list. This version is presently being attempted. Full details of the entire procedure will be set forth elsewhere.

Rule 1. A*p*B and B*p*C implies A*p*C.

Rule 2. A*p*B and B*n*C implies A*n*C.

Rule 3. A*n*B and B*n*C implies A*p*C.

Rule 4. A*o*B and B*r*C implies nothing about the relation between A and C, irrespective of *r*.

Rule 5. If A*p*C and A*n*C are both implied, or if one is held initially and the other implied, then A*a*C. This is the definition of the ambivalent relation.

Rule 6. A*a*C and C*p*D implies A*a*D.

Rule 7. A*a*C and C*n*D implies A*a*D.

Rule 8. A*a*C and C*a*D implies A*a*D.

Each rule above has several equivalent forms not listed, arising from the symmetry assumption A*r*B = B*r*A.

Though we have given formal status to these rules,[3] note that the verbal corollaries are not necessarily logical at all. Exemplify Rule 3 by the sentences:

> India (A) opposes (*n*) U.S. Far Eastern policy (B)
> U.S. Far Eastern policy (B) is directed against (*n*) Communism (C).
> *Therefore*, India (A) is in favor of (*p*) Communism (C).

Such "reasoning" would mortify a logician, yet it can be found in much this form inside of millions of heads. Thus we speak of the formal system as *psycho-logic* rather than as *logic*.

We assume that thinking about a topic *must be motivated before it will occur*. Some possible motivating conditions[4] would be these:

1. Pressure to reach a decision on the topic.

2. Socially derived needs to appear informed on the topic, to converse well about it, to win over other, etc. Anticipation of the relevant social situations would motivate thinking.

3. Relevance of the topic to needs, conflicts, and persisting preoccupations. Activation of such processes would generate pressure to think.

4. A general "cognitive style" of the individual such that thinking per se is satisfying. For such individuals, mere mention of the topic might motivate thinking.

Suppose that a given individual is motivated to think about a given topic. He already possesses certain relevant cognitive units. Using psycho-logic, he imputes new units. These new units may or may not be compatible with his existing units. Referring back to the India-China example, if the individual had originally thought, "India (A) resists the influence of (*n*) Communism (C)," then he would be confronted with the coexistence of A*p*C and A*n*C. By Rule 5, this is expressed A*a*C, the ambivalent relation, which might translate back into words thus:

> The relationship between India (A) and Red China (C) is very confusing (*a*).

---

[3] The entire set of rules may be organized into one with the aid of Tables 1 and 2 of The "Mathematical System." Letting R denote the structure matrix, derived or imputed sentences may be found from the matrix multiplication of R by itself. The powers R^2, R^3, etc. yield imputations which are successively more removed from the original sentences.

[4] The potency of these various motivating conditions could be subjected to empirical test, using before and after measures of cognitive structure and experimental manipulation of motivating conditions in-between. One such experiment has in fact been carried out by Zajonc (20), using a different theoretical context. See his discussion of "cognitive tuning."

On the other hand, had he originally held ApC, then the imputed sentence ApC would reinforce rather than contradict his original view.

Balance and Imbalance

Certain structure matrices are characterized by the interesting property that no amount of thinking (i.e., imputing of new relations according to the rules above) leads the individual into any inconsistency (i.e., ambivalent relation). The cognitive structures represented by such matrices are said to be *balanced*. When the structure matrix is such that one or more ambivalent relations will be discovered in thinking, the structure is said to be *imbalanced*. (Our statement of the mathematical condition for cognitive balance is given in the "Mathematical System.") In common-sense terms, a balanced cognitive structure represents a "black and white" attitude. The individual views some elements as good and the other elements as bad. All relations among "good elements" are positive (or null), all relations among "bad elements" are positive (or null), and all relations between good and bad elements are negative (or null).

Redressing Imbalance

Heider (10), Festinger (6), Osgood and Tannenbaum (14), and others have postulated that individuals strive to reduce or redress cognitive imbalance, or "dissonance." This is probably especially true for attitudinal cognitions. It is important to note, however, that potential imbalance will remain undiscovered by an individual unless he is motivated to think about the topic and in fact does so. Assuming these necessary preconditions, suppose that an individual does come upon a cognitive inconsistency in his attitude. What can he do about it? Three things:

1. Change one or more of the relations.
2. Redefine, "differentiate," or "isolate" one or more elements.
3. Stop thinking.

A simple example will illustrate the first two methods. The third method is self-explanatory. Take the three elements, E, C, G: Ego (a Yale student), Having Co-eds at Yale, and Getting Good Grades. The subject might tell us,

"I'm for having co-eds at Yale." (EpC)

"I want good grades." (EpG)

"Having co-eds at Yale would undoubtedly interfere with getting good grades." (CnG)

This attitudinal cognition

$$
R = \begin{array}{c c c c} & E & C & G \\ E & p & p & p \\ C & p & p & n \\ G & p & n & p \end{array}
$$

is imbalanced. Never having been forced to take a consistent stand on the issue, however, our subject may readily tolerate (or even be unaware of) this imbalance. Now suppose that the issue is hotly debated and our subject thinks. The imbalance becomes apparent and he seeks a balance-producing resolution.

Method 1. He alters any one of the three relations, by abandoning the desire for good grades, by opposing the admission of co-eds, or by rationalizing to the effect that "Co-eds do not really interfere with getting good grades (in fact, they enhance the chances, etc.)"

Method 2. (The following is one of various possibilities.) He differentiates the concept "Getting good grades" into "Getting A's" and "Getting C's" and then reasons that while co-eds may interfere with getting A's, they don't interfere with getting C's, and what he really wants is not to get A's but to get C's.

It is assumed that under sufficient pressure to continue thinking, the individual will try Methods 1 and 2, presumably seeking a relatively effortless means to achieve balance. If these attempts fail, because certain relations are resistant to change and certain elements are difficult to redefine, the individual may resort to Method 3 which is to stop thinking. If, however, strong pressures, internal or external, do not permit him to stop thinking, he will re-examine the topic, seeking a more complex utilization of either or both of the first two methods. And so on. With extremely strong pressure to continue thinking, some cognitive units will in all probability ultimately yield to one attack or another.[5] With weak pressure and a structure that is highly resistant to change, the individual will most likely stop thinking, and his attitudinal structure will revert to its state before he started thinking.

In other words, we envision an extensive hierarchy of cognitive solutions to the problem of reducing imbalance. Experimental prediction of outcome is extremely difficult under these circumstances, and represents a considerable challenge. The next section presents a crude preliminary step toward meeting the challenge.

Experimental Prediction of Cognitive Changes

Our present machinery is not refined enough to permit predictions with respect to Method 2 above, "redefining the elements." It would appear feasible, however, to restrict experimentally the availability of this alternative (the arguments of Asch [3] to the contrary) and focus upon Method 1.

The question we pose for ourselves is this: "Given an imbalanced structure[6] with highly stably defined elements, can we predict which particular set of relations in the whole conceptual arena will be changed in order to achieve balance?"

The mathematical system presented later in detail is helpful in providing what we hope will be an approximate answer. In that system, the *complexity of imbalance* of a structure is defined as the *minimum number of changes of relations necessary to achieve balance.*[7] The system also implies a way of identifying which particular changes consti-

---

[5]So-called "conversion experiences" may be representative of the extreme case: very extensive cognitive changes are characteristic of this phenomenon.

[6]One may provoke imbalance experimentally by strong persuasive communication aimed at a given cognitive unit. We are presently launching an experiment of this type.

[7]Cartwright and Harary (5) have proposed a different index for degree of structural imbalance. The present index is simpler to compute, and has also the appealing feature that it refers to the dynamic property of change in structure. Harary, in a personal communication, has indicated that he has recently and independently hit upon an index equivalent to the present one. He calls it the "line index of balance." A "line" in his terminology is a relation in our terminology. His "line index of balance" is the minimal number of lines (relations) whose negation yields balance. He points out that negation in the sense of changed sign and negation in the sense of deletion or elimination are equivalent insofar as balancing is concerned. Where we say "change of relation," this may be taken to mean change from p to either n or o, and change from n to either p or o.

tute the minimum set, or, when there are alternative minimal sets, identifies all of them. In addition, the "next to minimal" sets of changes can be identified, and so on.

Working under the highly tentative heuristic assumption that all relations are equally resistant to change, the least effortful balancing operation on an imbalanced structure is the one that requires the fewest changed relations. A predicted set of changes can easily be generated under this assumption.

The steps involved in the analysis are:

1. Write down the structure matrix.

2. Find the row (column) with the largest plurality of n's over p's, exclusive of the p in the main diagonal of the matrix. Change all n's to p's and p's to n's, in both the row and the corresponding column (leaving the diagonal entry p unchanged). Ignore the o entries.

3. Repeat the previous step on a new row (column).

4. Continue the change operations on selected rows and columns until the number of n's in the matrix cannot be further reduced.[8]

This irreducible minimum number defines the complexity of imbalance. Duplication due to symmetry is avoided by counting n's on one side of the diagonal only. The entries where the n's appear identify the minimal set. If the minimum number can be attained in more than one way, the sets so identified are alternative "solutions." If the minimum number is zero, then the structure is balanced. The entire procedure is based upon Theorem 13 of the "Mathematical System."

The method will now be illustrated with the Yale student's structure on "Having an honor system at Yale," presented in an earlier section.

His structure matrix was:

	1. Ego	2. Honest student	3. Report cheater	4. Feel trust	5. Cheat by few	6. Honor system
1. Ego	p	p	n	p	n	o
2. The honest student	p	p	n	p	o	p
3. Reporting cheaters	n	n	p	o	n	p
4. Feeling trusted	p	p	o	p	o	p
5. Cheating by a few	n	o	n	o	p	n
6. An honor system	o	p	p	p	n	p

Row 5 contains three n's and one p. We then carry out the change operation on Row 5 and Column 5, carrying p into n (except in the diagonal) and n into p. The result is:

	1.	2.	3.	4.	5.	6.
1.	p	p	n	p	p	o
2.	p	p	n	p	o	p
3.	n	n	p	o	p	p
4.	p	p	o	p	o	p
5.	p	o	p	o	p	p
6.	o	p	p	p	p	p

[8]A certain amount of trial-and-error may be required before reaching a final decision. This decision is not automatic; the change operation is sometimes useful on a row and column with a plurality of p's over n's—a temporary *increase* in the number of n's can lead to an ultimate further reduction in the minimum number of n's.

Both remaining *n*'s lie in Row 3. Three *p*'s also lie in this row, but one of them is the unchanging diagonal element, so that essentially it is two *n*'s versus two *p*'s. The change operation on Row 3 and Column 3 would yield

	1.	2.	3.	4.	5.	6.
1.	p	p	p	p	p	o
2.	p	p	p	p	o	p
3.	p	p	p	o	n	n
4.	p	p	o	p	o	p
5.	p	o	n	o	p	p
6.	o	p	n	p	p	p

The number of *n*'s here is also two. It is evident that the number of *n*'s cannot be further reduced by the change operation. It is also evident upon further inspection that no other set of change operations will yield as few as two *n*'s. Thus the structure matrix is of complexity *two* and there are two alternate minimal solutions to the balancing problem.

The first solution tells us that had the subject's initial relations between elements 3 and 1, and 3 and 2 not been as they were, there would not have been any imbalance. In other words, achieving balance requires changing the relations between elements 3 and 1, and elements 3 and 2. Looking back at his original structure matrix, this means that were he to *favor* reporting cheaters, or at least not be opposed, and also regard honest students as favoring or not opposing reporting cheaters, his structure would be balanced. The "good elements" would be balanced. The "good elements" would be *Ego*, *The honest student*, *Reporting cheaters*, *Feeling trusted*, and *The honor system*, while *Cheating by a few* would be a "bad element." In short, "We honest students would all feel trusted in an honor system. A few cheaters might violate the system, but they should be reported."

The second solution tells us that the subject must change the relations between elements 3 and 5, and elements 3 and 6 to achieve balance. In other words, were he to view *Reporting cheaters* as not identified with the honor system, and as in any case ineffective in cutting down *Cheating by a few* his structure would be balanced. *Ego*, *The honest student*, *Feeling trusted*, and *The honor system* would be "good elements," and *Reporting cheaters* and *Cheating by a few*, "bad elements." A hypothetical quote would read, "We honest students would all feel trusted in an honor system. A few cheaters might violate the system, but I wouldn't feel right about reporting them and it probably wouldn't work anyway. There are a few lousy guys who will always try to foul things up."

We make no claim that this subject would necessarily make one or the other of these changes in striving for a balanced structure. We only claim that if the strengths of all relations are equal, the above changes would be preferred for their simplicity.

We are now working on various means for empirical measurement of the strength of relations. Incorporation of the strength variable in the model will represent an important refinement.

THE MATHEMATICAL SYSTEM

The mathematical system is designed specifically for dealing analytically with the structure of attitudinal cognitions. There is some exercise of invention in suiting definitions and devices to the problem at hand; otherwise, the system is a self-contained axiomatic treatment of a standard mathematical nature. Many of the results parallel those of Harary (8, 9) although his mathematical treatment differs from the present one.

Consider a set E of four "relations": p, n, o, and a (the positive, negative, null, and ambivalent relations of the Psychological Model) with the following properties under the fundamental operations of addition and multiplication:

[1] $r + 0 = r$
[2] $r + r = r$ for all $r \in$ E
[3] $r + a = a$
[4] $p + n = a$
[5] $r \cdot p = r$
[6] $r \cdot 0 = 0$ for all $r \in$ E
[7] $r \cdot a = a$ for $r = p, n,$ or a
[8] $n \cdot n = p$

Each operation is taken to be commutative, so that

[9] $r_1 + r_2 = r_2 + r_1$
[10] $r_1 \cdot r_2 = r_2 \cdot r_1$ for all $r_1, r_2 \in$ E

These fundamental definitions may readily be scanned in the following addition and multiplication tables:

TABLE 1. ADDITION TABLE FOR
RELATIONS

+	p	n	o	a
p	p	a	p	a
n	a	n	n	a
o	p	n	o	a
a	a	a	a	a

TABLE 2. MULTIPLICATION TABLE FOR
RELATIONS

	p	n	o	a
p	p	n	o	a
n	n	p	o	a
o	o	o	o	o
a	a	a	o	a

It will be noted that the inverse operations, subtraction and division, are not uniquely defined for all pairs of elements. For example, the equation

$$p + x = p$$

cannot be uniquely solved for x. A similar situation holds for the equations

$$a \cdot x = a$$
and $$o \cdot x = o.$$

However, the associative and distributive properties of multiplication and addition hold in this system.

[11] $(r_1 + r_2) + r_3 = r_1 + (r_2 + r_3)$

[12] $(r_1 \cdot r_2) \cdot r_3 = r_1 \cdot (r_2 \cdot r_3)$ $\Big\}$ for all $r_1, r_2, r_3 \in E$

[13] $r_1 \cdot (r_2 + r_3) = r_1 \cdot r_2 + r_1 \cdot r_3$

Now consider an $N \times N$ matrix R with elements $r_{ij} (i = 1, 2, \cdots N; j = 1, 2 \cdots N)$ such that:

[R1] all $r_{ij} = p, n,$ or o

[R2] $r_{ii} = p$ for all i

[R3] $r_{ij} = r_{ji}$ for all i and j.

These stipulations define a *structure matrix*. Denote the class of all $N \times N$ structure matrices R by $\mathfrak{R}^{(N)}$, or when the context clearly refers to any arbitrary fixed N, simply $\mathfrak{R}$.

Define the pseudo-determinant[9] $\dagger R \dagger$ of a matrix R as

[14]
$$\dagger R \dagger = \sum_{\text{all } \phi} \prod_{i=1}^{N} r_{i\phi_i}$$

where ϕ is a permutation on the integers $i = 1, 2, \cdots N$, and ϕ_i is the integer into which i is carried by the permutation. The rules of addition and multiplication are as given previously. Otherwise, this idiosyncratic definition corresponds to the usual definition of a determinant (4) except that no algebraic signs are attached to the individual products involved in the summation. They are all positive, so to speak. The prefix "pseudo-" is intended to warn of this distinction from an ordinary determinant.

The pseudo-determinant provides the basis for an interesting partition of the class $\mathfrak{R}$ of all structure matrices. Note that specification [R2] for R-matrices requires all elements on the main diagonal to be p. Thus the term in $\dagger R \dagger$ corresponding to all $\phi_i = i$ must be the product $(p \cdot p \cdots p) = p$, regardless of the nature of the off-diagonal elements of a given R. Given that at least one term in the summation in [14] equals p, it readily follows from Table 1 and condition [11] that

[15] $\dagger R \dagger = p$ or a, for all $R \subset \mathfrak{R}$

The former is true if and only if *no* term in the summation [14] equals n.

Definition. If $\dagger R \dagger = p$, then R is said to be *balanced*. If $\dagger R \dagger = a$, then R is said to be *imbalanced*.

The definition in these terms is completely equivalent to the definition of balance in the psychological model and to the definition of "structural balance" given by Cartwright and Harary (5). Proof of this equivalence is straightforward but space-consuming and will be omitted here. The heart of the matter is the equivalence between permutations in the pseudodeterminant and "cycles" of cognitive elements.

Definition. $\mathfrak{R}_0$ is the class of all balanced R-matrices. $\mathfrak{R}_a$ is the class of all imbalanced R-matrices. Clearly the union $\mathfrak{R}_0 \cup \mathfrak{R}_a = \mathfrak{R}$.

[9]Often referred to as the "permanent."

A further partition of the class $\mathcal{R}_a$ is possible, giving rise to an index of the complexity or degree of imbalance in any given imbalanced R.

To accomplish this, it is convenient to define a class $\mathfrak{T}$ of square *transformation matrices* T with elements t_{ij} such that:

[T1]   All t_{ij} = the element s ("sameness") or the element c ("change")

[T2] $t_{ii} = s$ for all i.

[T3] $t_{ij} = t_{ji}$ for all i and j.

The specifications [T1-3] are parallel to the specifications [R1-3], and indeed, the elements s and c will be defined in such a way as to parallel the elements p and n.

Multiplication is the main operation in which the elements s and c enter, as follows:

[16] $s \cdot s = s$

[17] $s \cdot c = c \cdot s = c$

[18] $c \cdot c = s$

[19] $s \cdot r = r$,   for $r = p, n$, or o.

[20] $c \cdot p = n$

[21] $c \cdot n = p$

[22] $c \cdot o = o$

The elements s and c may readily be understood as representing "sameness" and "change" respectively. A transformation matrix T embodies a set of changes which may be applied to a structure matrix R, in a way to be described later.

The operation of addition is also defined on c and s. It is commutative and associative.

[23] $c + c = c$

[24] $s + s = s$

[25] $c + s = a$

[26] $a + c = a$

[27] $a + s = a$

The addition of c or s to p, n, or o is not defined.

The pseudo-determinant of T is defined as it was for R in equation [14].

[28]
$$\dagger T \dagger = \sum_{\text{all } \phi} \prod_{i=i}^{N} t_{i\phi_i}$$

There are only two possibilities for the value of $\dagger T \dagger$, just as there were for $\dagger R \dagger$ by equation [15].

[29] $\dagger T \dagger = s$ or a,   for all $T \subset \mathfrak{T}$

The former is true if and only if *all* terms in the summation [28] equal s.

Definition. If $\dagger T \dagger = s$, then T is said to be *passive*. If $\dagger T \dagger = a$, then T is said to be *active*.

Denote by $\mathfrak{T}_0$ the class of all passive T-matrices and by $\mathfrak{T}_a$ the class of all active T-matrices. Clearly the union

$$\mathfrak{T}_0 \quad \mathfrak{T}_a = \mathfrak{T}$$

Theorem 1 (The "Interchange Condition"). A matrix T is passive if and only if, for all h, i, j, k,

$$t_{hj}t_{ik} = t_{hk}t_{ij}$$

Proof. To prove sufficiency, we use the definition [28]. Consider the term

$$\prod_{i=1}^{N} t_{i\phi i}$$

in the summation, corresponding to some permutation ϕ. If no interchange of a pair of column subscripts alters the value of a product, then it must follow that no permutation of N column subscripts alters the product. In particular, the permutation ϕ^{-1} would not. But ϕ^{-1} carries $\prod_{i=1}^{N} t_{i\phi i}$ into $\prod_{i=1}^{N} t_{ii}$, which equals s by [T2]. Therefore $\prod_{i=1}^{N} t_{i\phi i}$ necessarily equals s. This being true for all terms in the summation, thus $\dagger T \dagger = s$, and T is passive.

To prove that any violation of the "interchange condition" $t_{hj}t_{ik} = t_{hk}t_{ij}$ necessarily implies T nonpassive, suppose that at least one set h, i, j, k were found with $t_{hj}t_{ik} = c \cdot t_{hk}t_{ij}$. (Every case of violation of the interchange condition must be expressable in this way, since elements of T can only equal s or c). Now consider any term Π_1 of [28] in which $t_{hj}t_{ik}$ appears. Let the product of the remaining elements in the term be denoted Π_0, that is, $\Pi_1 = t_{hj}t_{ik}\Pi_0$. By definition of the pseudo-determinant, the product Π_0 also appears in another term, namely $\Pi_2 = t_{hk}t_{ij}\Pi_0$. Whatever the value of Π_0, it follows that $\Pi_1 = c \cdot \Pi_2$, whence $\dagger T \dagger = a$, since not all terms in [28] equal s.

Theorem 2. The interchange condition of Theorem 1 is satisfied if and only if, for each pair h and i of rows in T, either

[i] $t_{hj} = c \cdot t_{ij}$ for all j, or

[ii] $t_{hj} = s \cdot t_{ij}$ for all j.

Rows satisfying [i] we shall call *antagonistic*, and satisfying [ii], *compatible*.

Proof. Any columns j and k of two antagonistic rows, h and i, would by [i] display

$$t_{hj} = ct_{tj}$$
$$t_{hk} = ct_{ik}$$

Whence

$$t_{hj}(ct_{ik}) = t_{hk}(ct_{ij}),$$

or

$$c(t_{hj}t_{ik}) = c(t_{hk}t_{ij}).$$

Thus

$$t_{hj}t_{ik} = t_{hk}t_{ij},$$

the interchange condition. A similar derivation holds for compatible rows, with s appearing wherever c does above.

For the proof of necessity, note that a pair of rows which is neither antagonistic nor compatible will violate the interchange condition, since then some j and k will exist for which

$$t_{hj} = c t_{ij}$$

$$t_{hk} = s t_{ik}$$

and

$$t_{hj} t_{ik} = c t_{hk} t_{ij}.$$

Corollary 1. A T-matrix is passive if and only if every pair of rows is either antagonistic or compatible.

Corollary 2. A T-matrix is passive if and only if its rows can be partitioned into two sub-sets, α and $\overline{\alpha}$, such that all pairs of rows in α are compatible, all pairs in $\overline{\alpha}$ are compatible, and all pairs with one member in each subset are antagonistic.

Next we proceed to define a special operation of one T-matrix on another.

Definition. The *application* $TU = W$, where $T, U \subset \mathfrak{T}$ are matrices of the same order (N), is defined simply by

$$w_{ij} = t_{ij} u_{ij} \qquad \text{for all } i, j.$$

The definition immediately implies $W \subset \mathfrak{T}$, since the conditions $[T1\text{-}3]$ must be satisfied by the elements w_{ij} of W. In other words,

Theorem 3. The class $\mathfrak{T}^{(N)}$ is closed under the operation of application.

The following theorems may be proved with dispatch.

Theorem 4. Application is commutative.

$$TU = UT, \text{ with } T, U \subset \mathfrak{T}^{(N)}$$

Theorem 5. Application is associative.

$$(TU)V = T(UV), \text{ with } T, U, V \subset \mathfrak{T}^{(N)}$$

Definition. The *identity transformation* $S \subset \mathfrak{T}$ is given by the matrix with all $t_{ij} = s$. (Note that $S \subset \mathfrak{T}_0$; that is, the identity transformation is a passive transformation). Clearly $ST = T$ for all $T \subset \mathfrak{T}$, by virtue of [16] and [17].

Theorem 6. Every $T \subset \mathfrak{T}$ is self-inverse, i.e.,

$$T \cdot T = S$$

This follows immediately from the definition of application and rules [16] and [18].

Theorem 7. The class $\mathfrak{T}_0^{(N)}$ is closed under application.

Proof. If $T \subset \mathfrak{T}_0^{(N)}$, then by Theorem 1

$$t_{hj}t_{ik} = t_{hk}t_{ij} \qquad \text{for all } h, i, j, k.$$

If $U \subset \mathfrak{T}_0^{(N)}$, then

$$u_{hj}u_{ik} = u_{hk}u_{ij} \qquad \text{for all } h, i, j, k.$$

Then for $W = TU$, we will have for all h, i, j, k

$$
\begin{aligned}
w_{hj}w_{ik} &= (t_{hj}u_{hj})(t_{ik}u_{ik}) \\
&= (t_{hj}t_{ik})(u_{hj}u_{ik}) \\
&= (t_{hk}t_{ij})(u_{hk}u_{ij}) \\
&= (t_{hk}u_{hk})(t_{ij}u_{ij}) \\
&= w_{hk}w_{ij},
\end{aligned}
$$

and thus $W \subset \mathfrak{T}_0^{(N)}$.

Definition. Let $_iT^*$, the "allegiance transform on i," denote the T-matrix with
  (i) $t_{ij} = t_{ji} = c$ for a given i and all $j \neq i$.
  (ii) all other elements $= s$.
  By Corollary 1 of Theorem 2, $_iT^* \subset \mathfrak{T}_0$, since the above definition implies that row i is antagonistic to all other rows, while any two rows $g \neq i$ and $h \neq i$ are compatible. From this and Theorem 7, we infer

Theorem 8. An application of the form

$$U = \prod_{i \epsilon \alpha} {_iT^*},$$

where α is any subset of the integers 1 to N, implies $U \subset \mathfrak{T}_0$.

Corollary 1. All $U \subset \mathfrak{T}_0$ formed as above must satisfy Corollary 2 of Theorem 2. The subset α above and the subset α of the previous Corollary are in fact one and the same. This may be shown by a straightforward albeit clumsy tracing through of the elements u_{hk} of U for the separate cases $(h, k \epsilon \alpha), (h, k \epsilon \overline{\alpha}), (h \epsilon \alpha, k \epsilon \overline{\alpha}), (h \epsilon \overline{\alpha}, k \epsilon \alpha)$.
  Now, since specification of various partitions α generates an exhaustive catalogue of passive T-matrices by Corollary 2 of Theorem 2, and since a passive T-matrix with any given partition α may in fact be constructed by successive application on matrices of the form T^*, we have the important

Theorem 9. All passive T-matrices can be constructed by applications of the form

$$\prod_{i \epsilon \alpha} {_iT^*}$$

Rewording this, we may say that the *set of allegiance transforms $_iT^*$ is a "basis" for the class* $\mathfrak{T}_0$.

  Returning to the analysis of R-matrices, we establish the

Definition. The application $TR = Q$, where $T \subset \mathfrak{T}^{(N)}, R \subset \mathfrak{R}^{(N)}$ is given by

$$q_{ij} = t_{ij} \cdot r_{ij} \qquad \text{for all } i, j$$

This directly implies $Q \subset \mathfrak{R}^{(N)}$, by the rules $[R1\text{-}3]$ and $[19\text{-}22]$.

The application of a transformation matrix thus carries one structure matrix into another. This is an important tool, since it enables the analysis of R-matrices to proceed in terms of analysis of their transforms, which is often simpler.

Theorem 10. $(TU)R = T(UR)$, with $T, U \subset \mathfrak{T}^{(N)}$ and $R \subset \mathfrak{R}^{(N)}$

Proof follows immediately from the above definition.

Let us examine what happens when a passive T is applied to a balanced R.

Theorem 11. A transformation $T \subset \mathfrak{T}_0$ applied to an $R \subset \mathfrak{R}_0$ yields some $Q \subset \mathfrak{R}_0$. That is, *passive transforms of balanced R-matrices are balanced.* (Recall from the psychological model that balanced R-matrices represent "black and white" attitudes. A passive transform will change one or more elements from "black" to "white," or "white" to "black," but leave the state of balance undisturbed.)

Proof. The pseudo-determinant of Q is

$$Q = \sum_{\text{all } \phi} \prod_{i=1}^{N} q_{i\phi_i}$$

$$= \sum_{\text{all } \phi} \prod_{i=1}^{N} (t_{i\phi_i} \cdot r_{i\phi_i})$$

$$= \sum_{\text{all } \phi} \left\{ \prod_{i=1}^{N} t_{i\phi_i} \right\} \left\{ \prod_{i=1}^{N} r_{i\phi_i} \right\},$$

since all t and r elements commute. But the former product is s for all ϕ when $T \subset \mathfrak{I}_0$, and the latter product is p for some ϕ and possibly o for others, though it is never n when $R \subset \mathfrak{R}_0$ (see the remarks following conditions $[29]$ and $[15]$).

Therefore,

$$\dagger Q \dagger = p, \qquad \text{and } Q \subset \mathfrak{R}_0.$$

Next, consider the case of imbalanced R-matrices. Given some $R \subset \mathfrak{R}_a$, it is always possible to find at least one $X \subset \mathfrak{T}$ such that $XR = Q \subset \mathfrak{R}_0$. In particular, one could choose $X \subset \mathfrak{T}$ with the property that $x_{ij} = c$ wherever $r_{ij} = n$, and s otherwise. Then all entries in Q would be either p or o and clearly $\dagger Q \dagger = p$, ergo $Q \subset \mathfrak{R}_0$. Now consider applications of the form $(WX)R$, with $W \subset \mathfrak{T}_0$ (and thus $WX = V \subset \mathfrak{T}$, by Theorem 3).

$$(WX)R = W(XR) = WQ = \text{some } Q' \subset \mathfrak{R}_0,$$

using Theorems 10 and 11. The construction WX enables the formation of many transforms carrying a given imbalanced R into a balanced one, once the special transform X is established. The various transforms $V = WX$ differ from each other in the number of c-entries they contain, suggesting a

Definition. The *complexity* of an imbalanced R-matrix is the integer m, determined as follows:

[i] Construct $X \subset \mathfrak{X}$ with $x_{ij} = c$ wherever $r_{ij} = n$ and s otherwise.

[ii] Form all possible applications $V = WX$, with $W \subset \mathfrak{X}_0$

[iii] Count the number of c-entries in each V, dividing by two to avoid duplication due to symmetry.

[iv] Denote by m the *minimum* count thus determined.

The complexity of imbalance, then, is the *minimum number of changes necessary to produce balance*.

Denote the class of all $R \subset \mathfrak{R}_a$ with complexity m by $\mathfrak{R}_m$. This provides the partition, promised earlier, of the class $\mathfrak{R}_a$ into $\mathfrak{R}_1, \mathfrak{R}_2, \mathfrak{R}_3$, etc.

Theorem 12. A transformation $T \subset \mathfrak{X}_0$ applied to an $R \subset \mathfrak{R}_m$ yields some $P \subset \mathfrak{R}_m$. That is, *complexity of imbalance is invariant under a passive transformation*.

Proof. The complexity of R, denoted say m_1, is defined on the class of matrices WX, where $W \subset \mathfrak{X}_0$ and X is such that $XR = Q \subset \mathfrak{R}_0$.

Now consider the complexity m_2 of the transform $P = TR$. We establish an analogue Y of the previous X by choosing $Y = XT$. Then,

$$YP = (XT)(TR) = XSR = XR = Q \subset \mathfrak{R}_0.$$

Thus m_2 is defined on the class of matrices WY, with $W \subset \mathfrak{X}_0$. But $WY = WXT = (WT)X$.

Now we have m_1 defined on WX, and m_2 defined on $(WT)X$. But since the only requirement on W is that it be a member of the class $\mathfrak{X}_0$, and since by Theorem 7 the application (WT) must be a member of $\mathfrak{X}_0$ inasmuch as $T \subset \mathfrak{X}_0$, it follows that the class of (WT) is identical to the class of W. (They both correspond to $\mathfrak{X}_0$.) Therefore the class of all WX is identical to the class of all $(WT)X$, and $m_1 = m_2$.

Theorem 13. Complexity of imbalance is invariant under all "allegiance" transformations of the form

$$\prod_{i \in \alpha} {}_i T^*.$$

This follows immediately from Theorems 9 and 12.

The operational simplifying procedure recommended in the psychological model for determining complexity of imbalance is a consequence of this theorem. "Changes of allegiance" do not alter the complexity of imbalance, so that one may reverse p's and n's in any successive set of rows and columns until the complexity of imbalance is apparent.

Many other theorems may be derived from this system. However, limitations of space make it imperative to conclude here.

We state one final result, without proof.

Theorem 14. The maximum complexity possible for an $N \times N$ R-matrix is

$$m_{\max}.\,(N) = \frac{N^2 - 2N + \delta}{4}\,\delta = \begin{cases} 1 \text{ if } n \text{ odd} \\ 0 \text{ if } n \text{ even} \end{cases}$$

REFERENCES

1. Abelson, R. P. A technique and a model for multi-dimensional attitude scaling. *Publ. opin. Quart.*, 1954, 18, 405–418.
2. Asch, S. E. *Social psychology*. New York: Prentice-Hall, 1952.
3. Asch, S. E., Block, H., & Hertzman, M. Studies in the principles of judgments and attitudes: I. Two basic principles of judgment. *J. Psychol.*, 1938, 5, 219–251.
4. Birkhoff, G., & MacLane, S. *A survey of modern algebra*. New York: Macmillan, 1947.
5. Cartwright, D., & Harary, F. Structural balance: a generalization of Heider's theory. *Psychol. Rev.*, 1956, 63, 277–293.
6. Festinger, L. *Theory of cognitive dissonance*. Evanston: Row Peterson, 1957.
7. Green, B. F. Attitude measurement. In G. Lindzey (Ed.) *Handbook of social psychology*. Cambridge: Addison-Wesley, 1954.
8. Harary, F. On the notion of balance of a signed graph. *Mich. math. J.*, 1953–54, 2, 143–146.
9. Harary, F. A line index for structural balance. (In process of publication.)
10. Heider, F. Attitudes and cognitive organization. *J. Psychol.*, 1946, 21, 107–112.
11. Hovland, C. I., Janis, I. L., Kelley, H. H. *Communication and persuasion*. New Haven: Yale Univ. Press, 1953.
12. Krech, D., & Crutchfield, R. *Theory and problems of social psychology*. New York: McGraw-Hill, 1948.
13. Lewin, K. *Field theory in social science*. New York: Harper, 1951.
14. Osgood, C. E., & Tannenbaum, P. H. The principle of congruity in the prediction of attitude change. *Psychol. Rev.*, 1955, 62, 42–55.
15. Peak, H. Attitude and motivation. In M. Jones (Ed.) *Nebraska symposium on motivation*, 1955. Lincoln: Univ. of Nebraska Press, 1955.
16. Rokeach, M. The nature and meaning of dogmatism. *Psychol. Rev.*, 1954, 61, 194–204.
17. Rosenberg, M. Cognitive structure and attitudinal affect. *J. abnorm. soc. Psychol.*, 1956, 53, 367–372.
18. Smith, M. B., Bruner, J. S., & White, R. W. *Opinions and personality*. New York: Wiley, 1956.
19. Tolman, E. C. *Purposive behavior in animals and men*. New York: Century, 1932.
20. Zajonc, R. B. Structure of cognitive field. Unpublished doctoral dissertation, Univ. of Michigan, 1954.

CARL I. HOVLAND
IRVING L. JANIS
HAROLD H. KELLEY

*Persuasion and Attitude Change**

The effectiveness of a communication is commonly assumed to depend to a considerable extent upon who delivers it. Governmental agencies take great pains to have their statements presented to Congress by the most acceptable advocates. Backyard gossips liberally sprinkle the names of respectable sources throughout their rumors. The debater, the author of scientific articles, and the news columnist all bolster their contentions with quotations from figures with prestige.

Approval of a statement by highly respected persons or organizations may have much the same positive effect as if they originate it. The organizer of a publicity campaign acquires a list of important persons who, by allowing their names to be displayed on the letterheads of the campaign literature, tacitly approve the campaign's objectives. The impact of a message probably depends also upon the particular publication or channel through which it is transmitted. The credibility of an advertisement seems to be related to some extent to the reputation of the particular magazine in which it appears ([27] p. 660).

The examples above suggest the importance of persons, groups, or media which can be subsumed under the general category of "sources." Differences in effectiveness may sometimes depend upon whether the source is perceived as a speaker who originates the message, an endorser who is cited in the message, or the channel through which the message is transmitted. However, the same basic factors and principles probably underlie the operation of each of the many types of sources, so an analysis of the psychological processes mediating the reactions to one kind of source may be expected to be applicable to other types. In this chapter we shall deal primarily with situations in which the effects are attributable to a single clear-cut source, which is usually an individual speaker who communicates directly to the audience and gives his own views on an issue. We shall refer to this kind of source as a "communicator."

In terms of the analysis of opinion change presented in the preceding chapter, a communicator can affect the change process in a variety of ways. For example, if he is a striking personality and an effective speaker who holds the attention of an audience, he can increase the likelihood of attentive consideration of the new opinion. If he is personally admired or a member of a high status group, his words may raise the incentive value of the advocated opinion by suggesting that approval, from himself or from the group, will follow its adoption. When acceptance is sought by using arguments in support of the advocated view, the perceived expertness and trustworthiness of the communicator may determine the credence given them.

We shall assume that these various effects of the communicator are mediated by attitudes toward him which are held by members of the audience. Any of a number of different attitudes may underlie the influence exerted by a given communicator. Some may have to do with feelings of affection and admiration and stem in part from desires to be like him. Others may involve awe and fear of the communicator, based on perceptions of his power to reward or punish according to one's adherence to his recommendations or demands. Still other important attitudes are those of trust and confidence. These are related to perceptions of the communicator's credibility, including beliefs about his knowledge, intelligence, and sincerity.

These and other attitudes which affect communicator influence are learned by each individual in a variety of influence situations. Through his experiences of accepting and rejecting social influences, the individual acquires expectations about the validity of various sources of information and learns that following the suggestions of certain persons is highly rewarding whereas accepting what certain others recommend is less so. The products of this learning, which constitute a complex set of attitudes toward various persons as sources of influence, generalize to a wide variety of other persons, groups, and agencies and thereby affect the individual's reactions to communications which he perceives to emanate from them.

If the conditions of learning these attitudes are variable (as they almost inevitably are), the communicator characteristics relevant to the amount of influence exerted cannot be expected to fall into neat categories; they are probably specific as to time and cultural setting. For example, the specific attributes of persons who are viewed as powerful or credible can be expected to differ from culture to culture. There is also likely to be some degree of variability within a given culture, particularly as different subject matters are considered. However certain kinds of attitudes, such as those related to affection, the communicator's power, and his credibility, are probably important in all societies. Moreover, the general principles concerning the antecedents and consequences of such attitudes may be expected to have a high degree of generality, at least within our own culture.

The limited area chosen for investigation in our research program concerns the factors related to *credibility* of the source. Analysis of this area in the present chapter will focus on two problems. How do differences in the credibility of the communicator affect 1) the way in which the content and presentation are perceived and evaluated? 2) the degree to which attitudes and beliefs are modified? In analyzing the findings bearing on these questions, we shall briefly consider possible psychological processes underlying the observed effects and the changes that occur with the passage of time.

BACKGROUND

An individual's tendency to accept a conclusion advocated by a given communicator will depend in part upon how well informed and intelligent he believes the communicator to be. However, a recipient may believe that a communicator is capable of transmitting valid statements, but still be inclined to reject the communication if he suspects the communicator is motivated to make nonvalid assertions. It seems necessary, therefore, to make a distinction between 1) the extent to which a communicator is perceived to be a source of valid assertions (his "expertness") and 2) the degree of confidence in the communicator's intent to communicate the assertions he considers most valid (his "trustworthiness"). In any given case, the weight given a communicator's assertions by his audience will depend upon both of these factors, and this resultant value can be referred to as the "credibility" of the communicator. In this section we shall review some of the background material bearing upon the two components of credibility: expertness and trustworthiness.

A variety of characteristics of the communicator may evoke attitudes related to expertness. For example, the age of a communicator may sometimes be regarded as an indication of the extent of his experience. A position of leadership in a group may be taken as an indication of ability to predict social reactions. In certain matters persons similar to the recipient of influence may be considered more expert than persons different from him. An individual is likely to feel that persons with status, values, interests, and needs similar to his own see things as he does and judge them from the same point of view. Because of this, their assertions about matters of which the individual is ignorant but where he feels the viewpoint makes a difference (e.g., about the satisfaction of a given job or the attractiveness of some personality) will tend to carry special credibility. Hence the research on the factors of age, leadership, and similarity of social background may involve the expertness factor to some extent.[1]

[1] That older persons tend to be more influential than younger ones is suggested by a variety of investigations. Some of the relevant findings come from research aimed at identifying the persons within a community from whom advice is sought [31, 38]. Such characteristics as education, income, and participation in local organizations do not differentiate those frequently sought for advice and those little sought. However, there is some tendency for persons to seek advice from those somewhat older than themselves.

Several studies involve simultaneous variations in the ages of recipients and communicator. Duncker [14] found young children more likely to be influenced by the food preference of an older child than vice versa. Berenda [5] found a similar relation in a length-judging situation where a single child was exposed to the unanimous and wrong answers of eight classmates. The younger children were influenced more than the older ones. However, her evidence on age is complicated by changes in the social relationships with increased age and by age differences in ability to make the necessary judgments in the absence of social influence. Both Duncker and Berenda find that adults had surprisingly little influence in these situations. We take this to indicate the operation of other important factors which are unrelated or inversely related to the age difference between influencer and recipient (e.g., desire to retain the approval of other members of one's peer group, similarity of influencer to recipient in status and interests). Age appears as an important variable in a number of other studies of influence but usually as a characteristic of the recipients rather than of the communicator.

As a special case of the expertness factor, leaders of groups might be expected to be more influential in matters pertaining to the group norms than rank-and-file members. Recent research by Chowdhry and Newcomb [11] indicates that leaders are superior to other group members in their ability to estimate the consensus of opinion within the group on matters related to the common interests and goals. (That this is not true for all intragroup issues is indicated by Hites and Campbell [17] who find no superiority for leaders.) Such superiority could form the basis for acquiring confidence in leaders' assertions about how various events will be received by the members or about future decisions of the group. Relatively little existing evidence is directly pertinent to this generalization. Other studies demonstrate the influence of opinions attributed to national leaders and the heads of churches and political parties [9, 26, 36], but it is likely that subjects in these studies possess not only attitudes of trust toward these persons but attitudes of affection and respect.

In their analysis of the special properties of direct face-to-face influence, Lazarsfeld, Berelson, and Gaudet suggest that one of the advantages of personal contacts may be that the individual tends to encounter persons similar to himself ([25] p. 155). Redl [33] discusses the importance of similarity as a factor in the infectious spread of influence among the members of a face-to-face group, a phenomenon frequently observed among delinquent adolescents and referred to as "behavioral contagion."

Few systematic investigations have been made of the effects of variations in expertness on opinion change, but suggestive results come from a number of studies. Typical findings are those of Bowden, Caldwell, and West [7], concerning attitudes toward various solutions of the economic problem of an appropriate monetary standard for the United States. Using subjects from a broad age range, they determined the amount of agreement with statements when attributed to men in different professions (e.g., lawyers, engineers, educators). The statements were approved most frequently when attributed to educators and businessmen, and least frequently when attributed to ministers. A study by Kulp [24] provides evidence that for graduate students in education the social and political opinions of professional educators and social scientists are somewhat more influential than the opinions of lay citizens. While other factors may have been involved, it seems likely that the results of these studies are partly attributable to differences in perceived expertness of the various sources.

With respect to the second component of credibility, there have been numerous speculations about the characteristics of communicators which evoke attitudes of trust or distrust and about the consequences of these attitudes for acceptance of communications. One of the most general hypotheses is that when a person is perceived as having a definite *intention* to persuade others, the likelihood is increased that he will be perceived as having something to gain and, hence, as less worthy of trust. As Lazarsfeld, Berelson, and Gaudet ([25] pp. 152-153) have pointed out, casual and nonpurposive conversations probably derive part of their effectiveness from the fact that the recipient of a remark does not have the critical and defensive mental set that he typically carries into situations where he knows others are out to influence him. Remarks such as those overheard in subways and other crowded public places would be especially effective in this respect because under such circumstances it is quite apparent that the speaker has no intention to persuade the bystanders. This phenomenon seems to be exploited in some of the techniques currently used in commercial advertising.

A specific set of cues as to the motives or intentions of the communicator has to do with symbols of his social role. Persons in some occupations and offices (e.g., radio announcers, publicity agents, salesmen) are known to be under special pressures to communicate certain things and not others. For other roles, for example that of the newspaper reporter, the pressures may be perceived to operate in the direction of giving all the facts as accurately as he can ascertain them. That publicity men assume greater credibility will be accorded news stories as compared with advertisements is manifested by their repeated attempts to obtain publicity for their clients in the news columns ([13] pp. 323-324).

When several persons are in similar conflicts between their "undesirable" impulses and internalized social prohibitions, the act of one of them, whether it be in the direction of expressing the impulses or in reaffirming conformity to the prohibitions, serves to evoke the same act in the others. In short, the conflict resolution found by one person is imitated by others who have similar conflicts. This is, perhaps, a specific instance of the more general tendency when confronted with a problem to imitate the solutions found by others in the same dilemma. Perhaps the term "expert" should be broadened to include persons who have found adequate solutions to the problem an individual faces, even though in other respects they may be no more experienced than he and may be very much like him. This may account for some of the instances noted by Duncker [14] and Berenda [5] where peers or slightly older children were found to be more influential than adults.

Suggestive evidence on the importance of the communicator's being considered sincere rather than "just another salesman" is provided by Merton's analysis of Kate Smith's war bond selling campaign during which she broadcast continuously for eighteen hours [*30*]. It appears that one of the main reasons for her phenomenal success was the high degree of sincerity attributed to her by the audience: ". . . *she really means* anything she ever says" (p. 83). Even though she appeared frequently on commercially sponsored programs and engaged in much the same promotional activities as other radio stars, the public felt that in carrying out the bond drive she was interested only in the national welfare and did not care about the personal publicity she would obtain. One of the most interesting suggestions of Merton's analysis is that the marathon effort itself may have contributed to her reputation as a sincere, unselfish person. Even among the persons who regularly listened to her programs (as well as among nonlisteners), more of those who heard the marathon were convinced of her selflessness in promoting the bonds than of those who failed to hear it. "Above all," Merton says, "*the presumed stress and strain of the eighteen-hour series of broadcasts served to validate Smith's sincerity*" (p. 90).

The possible effects on opinion change of attitudes of trust or distrust toward communicators are suggested by some correlational data from Hovland, Lumsdaine, and Sheffield ([*18*] pp. 100–103). The basic data involve audience reactions to the War Department's orientation films. The pertinent attitudes were not specifically directed toward the communicator but consisted rather of general judgments as to the purposes for which the film was being presented. After viewing "The Battle of Britain" the soldiers were asked this open-ended question: "What did you think was the reason for showing this movie to you and the other men?" On the basis of their answers, the men were classified as to whether they considered the film's purpose to be "propagandistic" (in the sense of having a manipulative intent) or "informational." A comparison of the two groups in terms of the opinion changes produced by the film revealed it to be less effective with men who judged its intent to be manipulative than with men considering it informational. This correlation may merely indicate a general attitude toward the content of the film which is reflected in both opinion change and judgments of the film. But another possible interpretation is that there exists a tendency to reject communications which are perceived as being manipulative in intent.

The material just considered suggests that attitudes related to the expertness and trustworthiness of a communicator may affect his influence. Evidence from systematic research can contribute much to determining the conditions under which this phenomenon occurs and, in addition, can answer questions as to the specific processes involved. In the next section we shall consider the available evidence from the point of view of the two following problems:

First, do variations in the characteristics of a communicator with respect to expertness and trustworthiness affect recipients' evaluations of his presentation and of the arguments and appeals he uses? This problem becomes particularly important when a communication is constructed so as to derive much of its effectiveness from persuasive arguments and motivating appeals. Sometimes a communication presents only a conclusion, without supporting argumentation, and its acceptance appears to be increased merely by attributing it to a prestigeful or respected source. A large proportion of past experimental investigations of communicator effects—the studies of "prestige suggestion"

—have concentrated upon this particular phenomenon [2, 24, 26, 36]. Presumably, the observed effects are mediated by an increased incentive value of the recommended opinion brought about through implicit promises of approval from the communicator or the group he represents, or through implicit assurances, by virtue of the authoritativeness of the source, that the opinion has adequate justification in fact and logic. But when a communication includes explicit supporting evidence and arguments, the question arises as to whether they are judged to be any more relevant, sound, or logical when presented by a highly credible source than by a less credible one. In brief, to what extent is the effectiveness of the supporting argumentation dependent upon attitudes toward the communicator?

Second, how do variations in the communicator characteristics related to expertness and trustworthiness affect the amount of opinion change produced by a communication? This, of course, is the crucial problem for persuasive communications. It is necessary to investigate opinion change independently of the kinds of changes specified above. As we shall see, the characteristics of the communicator may affect evaluations of the presentation without necessarily affecting the degree to which the conclusion is accepted.

RESEARCH EVIDENCE

As noted earlier, it has been suggested that perceptions of the communicator's intentions to persuade his audience may affect judgments of his credibility. A study by Ewing [15] deals with a special aspect of this problem—the degree of agreement between a communicator's announced intentions and the audience's initial bias. The results suggest that this variable affects the amount of opinion change produced and that this effect may be mediated by different evaluations of the presentation. Two groups of subjects were given the same communication which, as compared with the subjects' initial opinions, was unfavorable toward Henry Ford. In the introduction and throughout his presentation the propagandist made explicit statements about his intention: in one group he claimed that his purpose was to make people feel more favorable toward Ford and in the other group to make them feel less favorable.

The results on opinion change, presented in Figure 1, show that more change in the direction of the communication was produced in the first group where the intent of the propagandist was represented as being in agreement with the subjects' initial bias.

In general, Ewing's results support the hypothesis that when a communication comes from an unknown or ambiguous source, acceptance will be increased if, at the beginning, the communicator explicitly claims that his own position is in accord with that held by the audience. His results suggest that this effect occurs even when the communication advocates a view directly opposed to the audience's initial opinions. This outcome would not be expected, of course, when the content of the communication obviously and repeatedly belies the communicator's statement of his intent.

Ewing presents further analysis of his data which suggests that this result may be influenced by how favorably the recipients react to the communication in terms of its bias, logic, etc. Apparently these evaluations depend not only upon the content but upon the amount of conflict between the initial bias of the recipient and the avowed intention of the communicator. If a communicator presents material in support of a conclusion

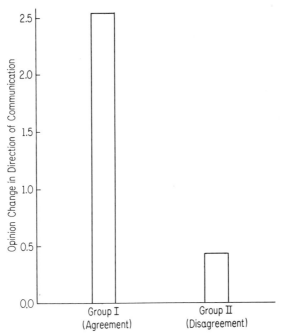

Figure 1. Degree of opinion change as related to agreement or disagreement between communicator's avowed intention and audience's initial opinions. Data from Ewing [15].

somewhat different from his avowed position, this may sometimes be taken to indicate great objectivity in his thinking and form the basis for confidence in his arguments.

An experimental variation in source credibility through the use of communicators differing in trustworthiness was produced in the study by Hovland and Weiss [20] of retention effects (cf. pp. 254-256). The general procedure consisted of presenting an identical communication to two groups, in one case from a source of high credibility and in the other from one of low credibility. Opinion questionnaires were administered before, immediately after, and a month after the communication. Four different topics were selected, each presented to some subjects by a source of high credibility and to other subjects by one of low credibility. Affirmative and negative versions of each topic were employed.

Each of the subjects (college students in an advanced undergraduate course) received a booklet containing one article on each of the four topics with the name of the source given at the end of each article.

The four topics and the sources used in the experiment were as follows:

	High Credibility Source	*Low Credibility Source*
A. *Antihistamine Drugs:* Should the antihistamine drugs continue to be sold without a doctor's prescription?	*New England Journal of Biology and Medicine*	Magazine A (A mass circulation monthly pictorial magazine)

	High Credibility Source	Low Credibility Source
B. *Atomic Submarines:* Can a practicable atomic-powered submarine be built at the present time?	Robert J. Oppenheimer	*Pravda*
C. *The Steel Shortage:* Is the steel industry to blame for the current shortage of steel?	*Bulletin of National Resources Planning Board*	Writer A (An antilabor, anti-New Deal, "rightist" newspaper columnist)
D. *The Future of Movie Theaters:* As a result of TV, will there be a decrease in the number of movie theaters in operation by 1955?	*Fortune* magazine	Writer B (A woman movie-gossip columnist)

A questionnaire administered before the communication obtained judgments from the subjects as to the trustworthiness of a long list of sources, including the specific ones used. An analysis of these judgments revealed very definitely that the sources used with the communications differed greatly in their credibility. The four high credibility sources were judged to be trustworthy by 81 to 95 per cent of the subjects; the low credibility sources were judged trustworthy by 1 to 21 per cent.

Evaluations of presentation. The differences in initial attitudes toward the sources definitely affected audience evaluations of the presentation, which were obtained immediately after exposure to the communication. The data summarizing audience evaluations of the four presentations are given in Table 1. Even though the communications being judged were identical as to content, it can be seen that the presentations were considered to be "less fair" and the conclusions to be "less justified" when the source was of low rather than of high credibility. Although responses to these questions may have involved reactions to the entire communication situation rather than just evaluations of the arguments and conclusions per se, they do indicate that judgments of content characteristics,

TABLE 1. EFFECTS OF HIGH AND LOW CREDIBILITY SOURCES ON EVALUATIONS OF FAIRNESS AND JUSTIFIABILITY OF IDENTICAL COMMUNICATIONS

A. Per cent considering author "fair" in his presentation

Topic	High Credibility Source N*	Per Cent	Low Credibility Source N	Per Cent
Antihistamines	31	64.5	27	59.3
Atomic Submarines	25	96.0	36	69.4
Steel Shortage	37	24.3	26	19.2
Future of Movies	29	93.1	33	63.7
Mean		65.6		54.9

B. Per cent considering author's conclusion "justified" by the facts

Topic	High Credibility Source N*	Per Cent	Low Credibility Source N	Per Cent
Antihistamines	31	67.7	27	51.8
Atomic Submarines	25	80.0	36	44.4
Steel Shortage	37	32.4	26	26.9
Future of Movies	29	58.6	33	42.4
Mean		58.2		41.8

*N = number of cases used.
From Hovland and Weiss [20]

such as how well the facts in a given communication justify the conclusion, are significantly affected by variations in the source.

Opinion change. Opinion change in the direction advocated by the communication occurred significantly more often when it originated from a high credibility source than when from a low one. Table 2 presents the results on opinion change shown immediately

TABLE 2. NET CHANGES OF OPINION IN DIRECTION OF COMMUNICATION FOR SOURCES CLASSIFIED BY EXPERIMENTERS AS OF HIGH OR LOW CREDIBILITY*

	Net percentage of cases in which subjects changed opinion in direction of communication			
Topic	*High Credibility Sources*		*Low Credibility Sources*	
	N	*Per Cent*	*N*	*Per Cent*
Antihistamines	31	22.6	30	13.3
Atomic Submarines	25	36.0	36	0.0
Steel Shortage	35	22.9	26	−3.8
Future of Movies	31	12.9	30	16.7
Mean		23.0		6.6
Difference			16.4	
p			<.01	

*Net changes = positive changes *minus* negative changes. Cf. [18] pp. 302–305 for a discussion of the use of this measure.

From Hovland and Weiss [20]

after the communication. The expected difference is obtained on three of the four topics, the exception being the one having to do with the future of movie theaters.

When data were obtained on opinion changes shown four weeks after having read the articles, the differential effectiveness of sources with high and low credibility had disappeared; there were no significant differences between them. This resulted from decreased acceptance of the point of view advocated by the high credibility sources and increased acceptance of the position of the low credibility sources. The former result could be attributed to forgetting of the content, decreased awareness of the communicator's credibility, or both. The increase in opinion change shown by the low credibility group, however, suggests that the negative effects of the "untrustworthy" source wore off and permitted the arguments presented in the communication to produce a delayed positive effect. According to this explanation, the effect of the source is maximal at the time of the communication but decreases with the passage of time more rapidly than the effects of the content. This is one of the mechanisms that can account for an increased adherence to the communicator's conclusion after a lapse of time.

This explanation suggests that in the present experiment there was relatively independent retention of the source and content, with the sustained effects apparently determined primarily by retention of the content. The phenomenon would be expected to occur when the communication contains not only the source's opinion but supporting evidence and arguments. This expectation is based upon the assumption that these supporting aspects of the communication can be evaluated on their own merits and without regard to the source. They will not initially evoke evaluative responses involving the source to the degree that the purely "opinion" aspects of the message will. Subsequently they will more frequently occur without accompanying responses which label the source and bring it to mind.

Under other conditions, however, one may expect the source and the content to be closely associated in memory. For example, when the communication presents a message that only one or a few persons could have originated, retention of the content will tend to be accompanied by retention of the source. If a person hears a radio talk by a cabinet member about policy decisions made in the President's Cabinet, he is likely to recall the source when he recalls the assertion. On the other hand, if the assertion could have emanated from a variety of sources, retention of the two will tend to be independent.

The preceding hypotheses may be specific cases of a more general proposition: the stronger the perceptual response to the source during initial exposure to the communication, the more likely it is that the source will be evoked when, on subsequent occasions, any aspect of the communication situation is present. Strong responses to a communicator would presumably occur when the communication situation highlights his uniqueness as a source or when the situation forces the audience to consider his characteristics in evaluating the assertion. Other factors may operate in the same manner; e.g., when the communicator's manner of speaking elicits a strong emotional response to him, the audience will be especially likely to remember who presented the message. A systematic exploration of these factors awaits further investigation.

Another study involving variations in source credibility was conducted by Kelman and Hovland [23]. During regular class periods students taking senior work in a summer high school were requested to listen to a recording of an educational radio program ostensibly to judge its educational value. In the course of this program a guest speaker was introduced who proceeded to give a talk favoring extreme leniency in the treatment of juvenile delinquents. Three different versions of the introduction to the speaker were used. In a *positive* version he was identified as a judge in a juvenile court—a highly trained, well-informed, and experienced authority on criminology and delinquency; sincere, honest, and with the public interest at heart. In a *neutral* version he was identified as a member of the studio audience, chosen at random. No information about him was given.[2] In a *negative* version he was also presented as selected from the studio audience, but it came out in the introductory interview that he had been a delinquent as a youth and was currently involved in some shady transactions, being out on bail after arrest on a charge of dope peddling. During the interview he openly expressed low regard for the law and great disrespect for his parents, even though they had provided well for him. Many of

[2]A difficult problem is raised in this investigation by the attempt to establish a "neutral" source to serve as a base line from which to measure positive and negative effects. Kelman and Hovland recognize that the source they define as "neutral" may not be completely neutral, but there seems to be no way of telling whether he is or not. Presumably, a neutral source is one that would *not* modify the effectiveness of a communication from what it would be purely on the merits of the arguments and material contained therein. It is difficult to conceive of an operation to provide an indication of the effectiveness of a communication purely on its own merits since all of our methods for presenting communications necessarily involve some kind of source. Perhaps the closest we ever approach neutrality is when an experimenter, representing himself to be completely unbiased in the matter, presents a set of arguments "which have been suggested" by vague and indefinite persons. Under these circumstances, where the source of a message is ambiguous, if the arguments are contrary to strong initial biases the resultant change may consist of a negative labeling of the source and hostile attitudes toward it. These attitudes, however, would be outcomes of the communication and not attitudes pertaining to the neutrality of the source as initially presented.

his statements showed that he was self-centered and that his favoring leniency was motivated by self-interest.

The basic opinion data were obtained by an adaption of the Wang-Thurstone scale on attitudes toward the treatment of criminals. The scale was administered immediately after the communication and three weeks later. Before the communication, a special set of attitude items bearing on the same issue had been used to insure the comparability of the ten classes involved in the experiment.

Evaluations of presentation. Audience reactions to the presentation were obtained directly after the communication. The results are summarized in Table 3. With identical

TABLE 3. AUDIENCE EVALUATIONS OF THE SAME TALK ON JUVENILE DELINQUENCY WHEN DELIVERED BY POSITIVE, NEUTRAL, AND NEGATIVE COMMUNICATORS

Judgment	Nature of the Source		
	Positive *N = 110*	*Neutral* *N - 60*	*Negative* *N = 102*
Percent judging him as giving a "completely fair" or "fair" presentation . . .	73%	63%	29%
	For positive vs. negative, p < .001		

From Kelman and Hovland [23]

content, audience judgments concerning the fairness of the presentation were much more favorable when it was given by the positive communicator than by the negative one. The judgments for the neutral communicator were intermediate but more similar to those for the positive one.

Opinion change. The opinion results closely parallel the evaluations of the presentation. In Table 4 it can be seen that the group hearing the communication from the

TABLE 4. IMMEDIATE EFFECTS OF DIFFERENT COMMUNICATORS ON OPINION SCORES*

Group	*N*	*Mean †*
Positive communicator	97	46.7
Neutral communicator	56	45.7
Negative communicator	91	42.8

*A high score represents the position of leniency advocated in the communication.
^{†t}pos.-neg. = 4.11 $p < .001$
^{t}pos.-neutr. = 0.79 $p = .21$
^{t}neutr.-neg. = 2.36 $p < .01$
From Kelman and Hovland [23]

positive source favored more lenient treatment (as indicated by a higher score) than those hearing it from the negative source. The fact that the opinion scores produced by the neutral source are more similar to those of the positive source, taken in conjunction with the pattern of evaluations described above, suggests that attitudes toward fairness and trustworthiness played a greater role on this issue than did attitudes related to expertness.

Three weeks after the communication, an alternative form of the attitude scale was administered. The differences among the experimental groups were no longer present. As in the case of the experiment by Hovland and Weiss, there had been a decrease in acceptance of the communication for those having had the positive communicator and a slight increase for those having had the negative communicator. . . .

A study by Hovland and Mandell [19] concerns primarily the variable of trustworthiness. A communication on the topic "Devaluation of Currency" was given to college students in introductory psychology classes. On the basis of a general discussion of the American monetary system and the description of some historical examples, the communication led up to a conclusion favoring the devaluation of our currency, which for some subjects was stated explicitly and for others was not. (For a discussion of conclusion drawing cf. pp. 100–105.) An introduction was used which elicited either 1) suspicion of the communicator's motives or 2) belief in his impartiality. For subjects in the suspicion variation, the speaker was introduced as the head of a large importing firm. Since it was explicitly stated in the communication that importers would profit from devaluation, it was expected that this introduction would give the audience the impression that the speaker had something to gain by having his conclusion accepted. In the second (nonsuspicion) variation, the communicator was introduced as an economist from a leading American university.

The subjects were asked to give their opinions on the issue before and after the speech. At the latter time they were also asked to give their reactions to the program and speaker.

Evaluations of presentation. The results of two of the questions on evaluations of the presentation are shown in Table 5. They indicate that the suspicion-arousing introduction was successful in leading the audience to view the "motivated" speaker as having done a poorer job and as having been less "fair and honest" in his presentation than the "impartial" communicator. This is true despite the fact that the content and conclusion of the

TABLE 5. EVALUATIONS OF IDENTICAL COMMUNICATIONS WHEN PRESENTED BY SUSPECT AND NONSUSPECT COMMUNICATORS

A. Question: "Do you think this radio program did a good or a poor job of giving the facts on devaluation of currency?"

	Nonsuspect Communicator (N = 113)		Suspect Communicator (N = 122)
Per cent of subjects answering "A very good job"	41.1		21.1
Difference		20.0	
p		<.001	

B. Question: "Do you feel that the speaker was fair and honest about America's devaluating its currency or did the facts seem too one-sided?"

	Nonsuspect Communicator (N = 113)		Suspect Communicator (N = 122)
Per cent of subjects saying communicator gave a "fair and honest" picture	52.7		36.7
Difference		16.0	
p		<.01	

From Hovland and Mandell [19]

speech were identical for the two. Thus it appears that cues as to the communicator's motives influenced judgments of his presentation and content.

Opinion change. The results indicate that the communication produced no greater net change in opinions when emanating from the nonsuspect communicator than when from the suspect one ($p = .23$ using a one-tailed test [22]). Thus, even though the experimental variation produced large differences in the subjects' evaluations of the two presentations, the subsequent differences in opinion change are quite small. This finding highlights the necessity of assessing various communicators in terms of their effectiveness in producing changes in opinion rather than relying merely on audience evaluation of the presentation of the content. In this experiment, sizable variations in judgments of the impartiality of the presentation made little difference in the amount of opinion change produced. Further research is needed to determine the conditions under which this outcome will occur in contrast to that obtained in the preceding experiments.

In summary, the research evidence indicates that the reactions to a communication are significantly affected by cues as to the communicator's intentions, expertness, and trustworthiness. The very same presentation tends to be judged more favorably when made by a communicator of high credibility than by one of low credibility. Furthermore, in the case of two of the three studies on credibility, the immediate acceptance of the recommended opinion was greater when presented by a highly credible communicator.

From the results, it is not possible to disentangle the effects of the two main components of credibility—trustworthiness and expertness—but it appears that both are important variables. In the Hovland and Mandell study where the suspect source differed from the nonsuspect one primarily in characteristics relevant to trustworthiness (motives, intentions), a marked effect occurred on judgments of the fairness of the presentation, but there was little effect on amount of opinion change. The small effect on opinions may be attributable to a special combination of factors such that the content of the speech and the qualifications of the speaker were more important than his personal motives. On the other hand, in the Kelman and Hovland investigation, it appears that variations in attitudes related to fairness and trustworthiness were responsible for the sizable differences in amount of opinion change.

It may be noted in passing that even with untrustworthy sources the over-all effect was usually in the direction favored by the communication. The negative communicator tended merely to produce *less* positive change than the positive source. Presumably, the arguments contained in the communications produced large enough positive effects to counteract negative effects due to the communicator. Negative or boomerang effects might be expected where no arguments are contained in a communication delivered by a negative source or when the audience members anticipate that his conclusions will consistently be in opposition to their best interests.

REFERENCES

1. Allport, G. W., and Postman, L. *The psychology of rumor.* New York, Holt, 1947.
2. Asch, S. E. Studies in the principles of judgments and attitudes: II. Determination of judgments by group and ego standards. *J. Soc. Psychol.*, 1940, *12*, 433–465.
3. Asch, S. E. The doctrine of suggestion, prestige and imitation in social psychology. *Psychol. Rev.*, 1948, *55*, 250–276.

4. Asch, S. E. *Social psychology*. New York, Prentice-Hall, 1952.
5. Berenda, Ruth W. *The influence of the group on the judgments of children*. New York, Columbia Univ., King's Crown Press, 1950.
6. Birch, H. G. The effect of socially disapproved labeling upon a well-structured attitude. *J. Abnorm. Soc. Psychol.*, 1945, *40*, 301–310.
7. Bowden, A. O., Caldwell, F. F., and West, G. A. A study in prestige. *Am. J. Sociol.*, 1934, *40*, 193–204.
8. Brown, J. S. The generalization of approach responses as a function of stimulus intensity and strength of motivation. *J. Comp. Psychol.*, 1942, *33*, 209–226.
9. Burtt, H. E., and Falkenburg, D. R., Jr. The influence of majority and expert opinion on religious attitudes. *J. Soc. Psychol.*, 1941, *14*, 269–278.
10. Cantril, H. *The psychology of social movements*. New York, John Wiley, 1941.
11. Chowdhry, Kalma, and Newcomb, T. M. The relative abilities of leaders and non-leaders to estimate opinions of their own groups. *J. Abnorm. Soc. Psychol.*, 1952, *47*, 51–57.
12. Coffin, T. E. Some conditions of suggestion and suggestibility. *Psychol. Monogr.*, 1941, *53*, No. 4.
13. Doob, L. W. *Public opinion and propaganda*. New York, Holt, 1948.
14. Duncker, K. Experimental modification of children's food preferences through social suggestion. *J. Abnorm. Soc. Psychol.*, 1938, *33*, 489–507.
15. Ewing, T. N. A study of certain factors involved in changes of opinion. *J. Soc. Psychol.*, 1942, *16*, 63–88.
16. Heider, F. Attitudes and cognitive organization. *J. Psychol.*, 1946, *21*, 107–112.
17. Hites, R. W., and Campbell, D. T. A test of the ability of fraternity leaders to estimate group opinion. *J. Soc. Psychol.*, 1950, *32*, 95–100.
18. Hovland, C. I., Lumsdaine, A. A., and Sheffield, F. D. *Experiments on mass communication*. Princeton Univ. Press, 1949.
19. Hovland, C. I., and Mandell, W. An experimental comparison of conclusion-drawing by the communicator and by the audience. *J. Abnorm. Soc. Psychol.*, 1952, *47*, 581–588.
20. Hovland, C. I., and Weiss, W. The influence of source credibility on communication effectiveness. *Publ. Opin. Quart.*, 1951, *15*, 635–650.
21. Hull, C. L. *Principles of behavior*. New York, Appleton-Century, 1943.
22. Jones, L. V. Tests of hypotheses: one-sided vs. two-sided alternatives. *Psychol. Bull.*, 1952, *49*, 43–46.
23. Kelman, H. C., and Hovland, C. I. "Reinstatement" of the communicator in delayed measurement of opinion change. *J. Abnorm. Soc. Psychol.*, 1953, *48*, 327–335.
24. Kulp, D. H., II. Prestige, as measured by single-experience changes and their permanency. *J. Educ. Res.*, 1934, *27*, 663–672.
25. Lazarsfeld, P. F., Berelson, B., and Gaudet, Hazel. *The people's choice; how the voter makes up his mind in a presidential campaign*. New York, Duell, Sloan & Pearce, 1944.
26. Lewis, Helen B. Studies in the principles of judgments and attitudes: IV. The operation of "prestige suggestion." *J. Soc. Psychol.*, 1941, *14*, 229–256.
27. Lucas, D. B., and Britt, S. H. *Advertising psychology and research*. New York, McGraw-Hill, 1950.
28. Luchins, A. S. On agreement with another's judgments. *J. Abnorm. Soc. Psychol.*, 1944, *39*, 97–111.

29. Luchins, A. S. Social influences on perception of complex drawings. *J. Soc. Psychol.*, 1945, *21*, 257–273.
30. Merton, R. K. *Mass persuasion; the social psychology of a war bond drive.* New York, Harper, 1946.
31. Merton, R. K. Patterns of influence: A study of interpersonal influence and of communications behavior in a local community. In P. F. Lazarsfeld and F. N. Stanton, eds., *Communications research, 1948–1949.* New York, Harper, 1949. Pp. 180–219.
32. Murphy, G., Murphy, Lois B., and Newcomb, T. M. *Experimental social psychology* (rev. ed.). New York, Harper, 1937.
33. Redl, F. Group emotion and leadership. *Psychiatry*, 1942, *5*, 573–596.
34. Rosenbaum, G. Temporal gradients of response strength with two levels of motivation. *J. Exp. Psychol.*, 1951, *41*, 261–267.
35. Rosenbaum, G. Stimulus generalization as a function of level of experimentally induced anxiety. *J. Exp. Psychol.*, 1953, *45*, 35–43.
36. Saadi, M., and Farnsworth, P. R. The degrees of acceptance of dogmatic statements and preferences for their supposed makers. *J. Abnorm. Soc. Psychol.*, 1934, *29*, 143–150.
37. Sherif, M., and Cantril, H. *The psychology of ego-involvements.* New York, John Wiley, 1947.
38. Stewart, F. A. A sociometric study of influence in Southtown. *Sociometry*, 1947, *10*, 11–31.

— · — · — · — · — · — · — · — · — · —

MUZAFER SHERIF

*Psychology of Social Norms (Attitudes)**

The experiment reported in this paper was carried out in the conviction that we need not leave the main field of experimental psychology (as many psychologists do today) to find concepts adequate for the psychology of attitudes. In the work of the Wurzburg psychologists, we find important experimental beginnings. Here it was found that that aspect of the stimulus field is especially observed which the subject is set to observe. Unfortunately the implications of this experimental work and subsequent investigations which it inspired have not been made an integral part of social psychology.

Taking the stimulus side of the problem into consideration, it will be safe to say this: indefinite, unstructured fields of stimulation are especially useful in getting positive results in experiments dealing with the influence of suggestion and kindred social influence.

*Muzafer Sherif, "An Experimental Approach to the Study of Attitudes," *Sociometry* 1 (1937): 90–98. Reprinted by permission.

In such cases the stimulus field more easily yields itself to organization in different ways. In this paper our aim is to show how an indefinite stimulus field can be organized or determined by one kind of social influence.

In our opinion autokinetic movement is a very convenient phenomenon which can be utilized to investigate in the laboratory various kinds of social influence. Experimentally it is easy to produce autokinetic movements. In a completely dark room a single point of light which is fixed at some distance from us and which is physically stationary cannot be localized at a fixed point in space. It moves, and may move in any direction, because there are no other visible points or objects in relation to which it can be localized.

The present experiment is an extension of the results of the previous experiments with the autokinetic movement. It will suffice in this paper to give the main findings of the previous experiments. The technique and procedure are described elsewhere (1, 2). For our present purposes the main findings may be summarized in a few sentences:

When an individual perceives autokinetic movement which lacks an objective standard of comparison, and is asked during repeated stimulation to report in terms of the extent of movement, he subjectively establishes a range of extent and a point (a standard or norm) within that range which is peculiar to himself, differing from the range and point (standard or norm) established by other individuals.

When individuals face the same unstable, unstructured situation as members of a group *for the first time*, a range and a norm (standard) within that range are established which are peculiar to the group. When a member of the group faces the same situation subsequently *alone*, after once the range and norm of his group have been established, he perceives the situation in terms of the range and norm that he brings from the group situation.

The ranges and norms established in the above cases are not prescribed arbitrarily by the experimenter or by any other agent. They are formed in the course of the experimental period and may vary from individual to individual, or from group to group, within certain limits.

Our concern being the study of social influence, we may go further and put the question: can we experimentally make the subject adopt a prescribed range and norm directed by specific social influences?

Different kinds of social influences may be experimentally utilized to define certain prescribed ranges and norms. Among many possible ones we took the following: (a) The influence of group situations on the individual as a member of the group. We have already mentioned the main conclusion of this previous work. (b) The influence of the direct suggestion of the experimenter in raising or lowering the reported extents of movement. (c) The influence of a fellow member with prestige (cooperating with the experimenter) on another ("naive") member of the group. (d) The influence of one naive member on the judgments of another. In this last case there is no prestige effect, because the subjects have not met each other prior to the experiment.

We shall say only a few words about the experiments under (b). If the subject is distributing his judgments, say, about three inches, without any socially introduced influence, the remark of the experimenter, "you are underestimating the distances" tends to raise the point round which the judgments are distributed to about five or six inches.

The following experiment under (c) shows how the autokinetic phenomenon can be utilized as a sensitive index of the prestige effect of one person on another:

Here we report verbatim the account of an experiment with prestige:

"Miss X and I (Assistant in Psychology, Columbia University) were subjects for Dr. Sherif. I was well acquainted with the experiment but Miss X knew nothing whatsoever about it. Since she was a close friend of mine, and I carried some prestige with her, Dr. Sherif suggested that it would be interesting to see if we could predetermine her judgments. It was agreed beforehand that I was to give no judgments until she has set her own standard. After a few stimulations it was quite clear that her judgments were going to vary around five inches. At the next appropriate stimulation, I made a judgment of twelve inches. Miss X's next judgment was eight inches. I varied my judgments around twelve inches and she did the same. Then I changed my judgment to three inches, suggesting to Dr. Sherif that he had changed it. She gradually came down to my standard, but not without some apparent resistance. When it was clear that she had accepted this new standard, Dr. Sherif suggested that I make no more judgments lest I might influence hers. He then informed her on a subsequent stimulation that she was underestimating the distance which the point moved. Immediately her judgments were made larger and she established a new standard. However, she was a little uneasy with it all, and before the experiment had progressed much farther, whispered to me 'Get me out of here,'

"When we were again in my office, I told her that the point had not moved at all during the experiment. She seemed quite disturbed about it, and was very much embarrassed to know that we had been deceiving her. Noting her perturbation, I turned the conversation to other matters. However, several times during our conversation she came back to the subject, saying, 'I don't like that man' (referring to Dr. Sherif) and similar statements indicating her displeasure with the experience. It was not until some weeks later when she was again in my office that I discovered the full extent of her aversion. I asked her to serve as a subject for me in an experiment and immediately she exclaimed, 'Not down in *that* room,' pointing to Dr. Sherif's experimental room."

The experiment which will be given presently deals with the influence of a fellow member in the adoption of a prescribed norm. There were seven groups in this experiment, each group consisting of two members. In every group one subject cooperated with the experimenter, i. e., deliberately distributed his judgments within the range and around the norm assigned to his by the experimenter beforehand. The other subject was unaware of this predetermination. The degree of this "naive" subject's conformity to the norm and range of the cooperating subject may be taken as the index of the social influence. In all the groups the subject who was cooperating with the experimenter was the same person. This was done in order to keep the influencing member constant in all groups.

The range and norm prescribed for every group were different. For the first group, the prescribed range was 1-3 inches, 2 inches being the prescribed norm. For the second group, the prescribed range was 2-4, and 3 inches the norm, and so on to the eighth group for which the range and norm were 7-9 and 8 respectively. It will be observed that the prescribed range was rather narrow; consequently in the course of the experimental period the cooperating subject gave no judgments which deviated from the norm by more than one inch in either direction.

In the first experimental session, both subjects (the cooperating and the "naive") took part. After each exposure of the point of light for two seconds, the subjects spoke their judgments aloud one at a time and the experimenter recorded these on separate sheets of different colored pads. In order not to stress the factor of primacy, the cooperating subject was instructed to let the other subject utter his judgment first, at least half of the time. The social influence in our previous experiments with the autokinetic effect was found to be not so much a function of this and that separate judgments as of the temporal sequence of judgments. Fifty judgments were taken from each subject.

In the second session only the naive subject was present, so that we might see how much of the prescribed range and norm he carried from the first group session. In this individual session also, fifty judgments were taken. As the norm formation in the auto-kinetic effect is a fragile and, in a sense, artificial formation, such an arbitrary prescrip-tion may break down easily beyond a certain number of judgments. Our whole point is that the autokinetic effect can be utilized to show a general psychological tendency and not to reveal the concrete properties of norm-formation in actual life situations.

In the presentation of results we give the prescribed range and norm, and the number of judgments of the "naive" subject falling within the prescribed range, and his norms (as represented by the median of the distribution of his judgments) in the first (group) and second (individual) sessions. The means and medians of the distributions of the judgments given by the cooperating subject in the group sessions are not exactly identical with the prescribed norms, though the modes and ranges are the same. We did not think it neces-sary for him to memorize a perfectly normal distribution. Our aim is chiefly to show a fundamental psychological tendency related to norm-formation.

GROUP 1

Prescribed	Experimentally obtained (from "naive" S)	
	Session I (in group)	Session II (alone)
Range 1-3 inches	1-5	1-4
Norm 2	3.36	2.62
No. of the 50 judgments falling within the prescribed range	41	47

At the end of the second (individual) session the subject was asked to answer in writing four questions related to the problem. The answers to two of the questions further verify our former results. We shall therefore confine ourselves to the introspec-tions given to the other two questions which are important for our present paper. These questions were: (1) What was the distance that the light most frequently moved? (this was formulated to find our whether the subjects became conscious of the norm formed in the course of the experiment); (2) Were you influenced by the judgments of the other person who was present during the first session? (this question was formulated in order to find out whether the subjects were conscious of the fact that they were being influenced by the cooperating subject).

The introspections of the subject in Group 1 are important for any theory of sugges-tion and norm formation:

1. "Most frequent distance was 2 inches. Seemed to be more consistently 2 inches second day than on first day.

2. "Yes, they were despite my efforts to be impartial. Probably many of my judg-ments were inordinately large because of small distances given by other subject. I thing this was an attempt at avoiding suggestion and in so doing going to the other extreme. I do not think I was influenced by first day's judgments on the second day. I tried to be

impartial in my judgments the first day. I felt resentment toward the other subject the first day because of the successive equal judgments by him. I tried to be objective toward this feeling: that is to banish the thought. But I feel that this resentment caused my judgments to differ from his by a greater amount than they would have if the judgments had been kept separate; that is if I had not heard his judgments. The second day I felt more independence in my judgments and I believe that these judgments were therefore more accurate."

GROUP 2

Prescribed	Experimentally obtained (from "naive" S)	
	Session I *(in group)*	*Session II* *(alone)*
Range 2-4 inches	1-10	1-5
Norm 3 inches	4.25	3.77
No. of the 50 judgments falling within the prescribed range	30	43

The introspections to the two questions were:
1. "Three or four inches were the most frequent estimates.
2. "No, I was not influenced by the other person. This I believe was because I stated my estimates first for the most part."

GROUP 3

Prescribed	Experimentally obtained (from "naive" S)	
	Session I *(in group)*	*Session II* *(alone)*
Range 3-5	2-8	3-6
Norm 4	4.61	4.57
No. of the 50 judgments falling within the prescribed range	43	49

The introspections follow:
1. "(a) 4 inches yesterday.
   "(b) 5 inches today.
2. "Yes, My first judgments are much higher than those following. In a way I scaled them down to ranges nearer to his. The majority of times I gave my judgments first. The same distance seemed shorter after a few trials. My judgments were influenced by yesterday's. I measured them by the same scale both days."

GROUP 4

Prescribed	Experimentally obtained (from "naive" S)	
	Session I *(in group)*	*Session II* *(alone)*
Range 4-6	3-6	3-6
Norm 5	5.20	5.21
No. of the 50 judgments falling within the prescribed range	47	46

The introspections:
1. "5 inches.
2. "For the first three or four times. After that, no."

GROUP 5

Prescribed	Experimentally obtained (from "naive" S)	
	Session I (in group)	Session II (alone)
Range 5-7	3-7	3-7
Norm 6	5.50	5.42
No. of the 50 judgments falling within the prescribed range	34	35

The introspections:

    1. "Five inches both days.

    2. "No. I was not influenced by the presence of another person. But I sincerely believe that my partner was exaggerating the distance when he made his estimate. I say this because it seemed to me that he hesitated several seconds after I gave my estimate ... "

GROUP 6

Prescribed	Experimentally obtained (from "naive" S)	
	Session I (in group)	Session II (alone)
Range 6-8	3-8	4-8
Norm 7	5.94	6.18
No. of the 50 judgments falling within the prescribed range	24	27

The introspections:

    1. "7 most frequent, 5 next frequent.

    2. "No, I was not influenced."

GROUP 7

Prescribed	Experimentally obtained (from "naive" S)	
	Session I (in group)	Session II (alone)
Range 7-9	4-12	6-9
Norm 8	7.40	7.83
No. of the 50 judgments falling within the prescribed range	17	40

The introspections:

    1. "The most frequent distance was about 8 inches. The next most frequent was about 7 inches.

    2. "I think it did make a difference when somebody else was with me. When I gave my judgment first, there was no difference, of course, but when he was with me I sometimes, though not all the time, modified my judgment when it was very far from his, and when I thought that I might easily have been mistaken. Of course, this did not occur frequently, but I cannot deny that it happened sometimes."

GENERAL CONCLUSION

From these results we may conclude that the subjects may be influenced to perceive an indefinite stimulus field in terms of an experimentally introduced norm. The degree of the influence may be different in different subjects. It may be great as is the case of the subject of group 4. It may not be so striking as is the case of the subject of group 5. It may be negligible as is the case with the subject of group 6. Even in this last mentioned case, an influence on the norm (not in the range) is evident.

The introspections reveal that the subjects become conscious of the norm which develops in the course of the experiment. However, they need not be conscious of the fact that they are being influenced toward that norm by the other member of the group. (See introspections of the subjects in groups 1, 2 and 4.) In connection with this point, it is interesting to note that in some cases, the *conformity* to the prescribed range and norm when the *influencing* person is no longer present (Session II) is closer than the *conformity* produced by his actual presence. (See the results of groups 2, 3, 6, 7.)

It seems to us that the psychological process embodied in these facts may be basic to the daily phenomena of suggestion, especially to the role of suggestion in the formation of attitudes. It is not a rare occurrence in everyday life to react negatively or hesitatingly to suggestion on some topic raised by an acquaintance while in his presence, but to respond positively after leaving him (perhaps there is a disinclination to accept suggestions readily unless there is some strong prestige or pressing demand; to appear easily yielding is not so pleasant for an "ego").

Attitudes, whatever else they may be, imply *characteristic modes of readiness in reacting* to definite objects, situations and persons. Our experiment has demonstrated in a simple way how a *characteristic* kind of readiness may be experimentally obtained in relation to an indefinite stimulus field. Perhaps this may constitute a step in the direction of the truly psychological investigation of attitudes.

REFERENCES

1. Sherif, M.—A study of some social factors in perception. *Arch. Psychol.*, No. 187, 1935.
2. _____ *The Psychology of Social Norms*, New York: Harper's, 1936, chapter VI, pp. 89–112.

— · — · — · — · — · — · — · — · —

IRVING SARNOFF

*Psychoanalytic Theory of Social Attitudes**

Psychoanalytic theory describes the mechanisms of ego defense which serve to protect the individual against external and internal threat. Many attitudes are

*Irving Sarnoff, "Psychoanalytic Theory and Social Attitudes," *Public Opinion Quarterly* 24 (1960): 251–279. Reprinted by permission of the author and the publisher.

acquired and maintained in the service of such mechanisms. Where people cannot escape from threatening forces from without, they will often incorporate the hostile forces and identify with the aggressor, as in the case of some members of a minority group taking on the prejudices of the majority toward them. Or people will maintain old attitudes by denying and distorting the reality of existing dangers. Threatening internal impulses may be repressed and projected onto others, or sometimes may lead to the appearance of attitudes directly opposed to the repressed wishes.

For more than three decades following Freud's lectures at Clark University in 1909, psychoanalytic theory enjoyed little respectability in the precincts of American psychology. Nevertheless, a few hardy empiricists began gradually to provide the scientific groundwork for a *rapprochement*; and, by the middle of World War II, a sufficient body of data was on hand to warrant an extensive review of objective investigations of psychoanalytic concepts.[1]

In the field of attitude research, the impact of psychoanalytic theory was not felt until quite recently. Indeed, the major impetus behind this impact may be attributed, in all probability, to a single book, *The Authoritarian Personality*, which appeared only ten years ago.[2] Since that time, however, psychoanalytic concepts have been increasingly and fruitfully utilized in studies which have sought to illuminate the motivational determinants of attitude formation and change.[3]

CONCEPTUAL FRAMEWORK

Because of the growing interest in psychoanalytic theory among students of social attitudes, it may be useful to spell out a conceptual framework by means of which several basic tenets of psychoanalytic thought may be systematically applied in research on attitudinal phenomena. The concepts of *motive, conflict, ego defense*, and *attitude* will serve as points of anchorage for this presentation; and an attempt will be made to show how the cement of psychoanalytic ideas may be used to interrelate these broad concepts in approaching the investigation of particular social attitudes.

Motive

Let us begin with a formal definition, after which each of its constituent assumptions will be discussed. *A motive is an internally operative, tension-producing stimulus which provokes the individual to act in such a way as to reduce the tension generated by it and which is capable of being consciously experienced.*

[1] R. R. Sears, *A Survey of Objective Studies of Psychoanalytic Concepts*, New York, Social Science Research Council, 1943.
[2] T. W. Adorno, E. Frenkel-Brunswik, D. J. Levinson, and R. N. Sanford, *The Authoritarian Personality*, New York, Harper, 1950.
[3] Cf. A. R. Cohen, "Experimental Effects of Ego-defense Preference on Interpersonal Relations," *Journal of Abnormal Social Psychology*, Vol. 52, 1956, pp. 19–27; D. Katz, C. McClintock, and I. Sarnoff, "The Measurement of Ego Defense as Related to Attitude Change," *Journal of Personality*, Vol. 25, 1957, pp. 465–474; I. Sarnoff, "Identification with the Aggressor: Some Personality Correlates of Anti-Semitism among Jews," *Journal of Personality*, Vol. 21, 1951, pp. 199–218; I. Sarnoff and S. M. Corwin, "Castration Anxiety and the Fear of Death," *Journal of Personality*, Vol. 27, 1959, pp. 374–385; I. Sarnoff, "Reaction Formation and Cynicism," *Journal of Personality*, Vol. 28, 1960, pp. 129–143.

1. *A motive is an internally operative, tension-producing stimulus.* All living organisms are "open" systems which both receive and emit stimuli. Consequently, although only a stimulus which is registering within our bodies can be regarded as the basis of a motive, the initial energic source of any internally operative stimulus may be conceived as emanating largely from external objects or largely as a by-product of our intrinsic physiological processes.

2. *A motive provokes the individual to act in such a way as to reduce the tension generated by it.* For as long as we live, our bodies are destined to contain a multitude of internal, tension-producing stimuli. Hence, we may be described as living in an endless state of motivation. Indeed, as Freud so brilliantly called to our attention, the tensions generated by our motives continue to press for reduction even while we are asleep; and in our dreams we may slyly seek to gratify wishes which we might vehemently repudiate during our waking hours.[4] In a word, our motives necessitate the performance of actions which might reduce the tensions they produce. Conversely, all the actions which we do undertake may be regarded as efforts to reduce the tensions generated by our motives.

Although all our observable actions may be conceived as functioning to siphon off tension, different acts seem clearly to be predicated on different internally operative stimuli. The responses which ensure the greatest reduction of the tension generated by one motive may be completely ineffective in lessening the tension produced by another source of stimulation: scratching may soothe an itching back, but only eating can fill an empty stomach. Accordingly, it is necessary to evaluate responses in terms of their ability to reduce the tensions associated with qualitatively different stimuli.

3. *A motive is capable of being consciously experienced.* Motives, of course, are never accessible to direct observation; they are always inferred from samples of the individual's overt behavior. A person's harsh voice, florid face, and clenched fists lead us to conclude that he is angry.

But the content of our private world of consciousness is replete with thoughts, images, and sensations which may well be token motivational states whose existence cannot always be inferred from observations of overt movements alone. Thus both naive introspection and a vast body of clinical experience suggest the reasonable assumption, to be followed here, that motives provoke *covert* tension-reducing responses as well as *overt* ones.

Conflict

Whenever two or more motives are activated at the same time, their coalescence produces a state of conflict. Stated somewhat differently, conflict emerges from the fact that the individual is required simultaneously to reduce the tensions generated by all the motives which are operative at any point in time; and since different motives require different responses if their special tensions are to be reduced, the individual cannot respond to any one of the motives without necessarily postponing the reduction of tension generated by all of the other motives.

If there were no way to resolve conflict among his motives, the individual's behavior would become diffuse and incoherent. He could hardly begin to reduce the tension of a

[4] S. Freud, *A General Introduction to Psychoanalysis*, New York, Permabooks, 1958.

single motive without being immediately pressed into action on behalf of his other motives. Indeed, he might well become the passive victim of his own opposing desires and be condemned, thereby, to endless and futile vacillation. One need only think of Hamlet's plight to gain an appreciation of the debilitating effects of motivational conflict which is permitted, for too long a time, to go unresolved. On the other hand, one could not make decisions at all, properly speaking, unless one were able consciously to entertain alternative inclinations and their likely consequences. In any event, it would appear that, however much conflict he is able consciously to contain, the individual must develop a repertoire of techniques for keeping his inevitably chronic state of conflict from reducing him to helpless incoherence.

To sustain a sequence of responses necessary to reduce the tension which accompanies a conflict among motives, the individual is obliged (1) to establish the relative priority of his responses to each of the motives involved in the conflict, and (2) to defer his responses to all the other motives at the time he is responding to a given motive in the established hierarchy.

The position of a motive in a hierarchy is determined by the intensity of the tension which it generates. The more tension generated by a particular motive, the higher will its position be in the hierarchy, i.e. the sooner will the individual respond to it as compared to the other motives with which it is in conflict.

Insofar as the motives which comprise a conflict differ in intensity, they present the individual with no difficulty in establishing a hierarchy among them. However, simultaneously acting motives are often of equal intensity. Nevertheless, if he is to act at all, i.e. to make responses aimed at reducing the tension which accompanies his motivational conflict, he must, eventually, give priority to one or the other of these equally intense motives.

While the imposition of a hierarchy upon conflicting motives is an essential step in the resolution of conflict, it does not *ipso facto* provide a mechanism for deferring responses to all the other motives in the hierarchy at the time when the individual is responding to each of the motives in its hierarchical order. But it is apparent that such a deferment is mandatory if the individual is to succeed in making the number and kind of responses necessary to reduce the tension of one motive before he begins to respond to those motives which, although lower in the hierarchical order, are, nevertheless, simultaneously operative.

If a motive has come to be associated with the arousal of intolerable fear, its deferment is, as we shall presently see, effected by means of one of the ego defenses. However, if a motive is consciously acceptable to the individual, he can undertake either or both of the following responses in deferring the reduction of its tension: (1) He may simply withhold his overt motor response to it, while at the same time remaining conscious of its presence. Such a response would be termed *inhibition*. (2) He may temporarily obliterate the *perception* of all motives except the one to which he is responding overtly at any given time. A response of this sort would be termed *suppression*. *The aim of suppression is merely to postpone the necessity for reducing the tension generated by simultaneously acting motives.* To put it another way, suppression facilitates the orderly reduction of conflicting motives in accordance with their position in the individual's motivational hierarchy. Typically, a person who is attempting to suppress a motive is aware of his efforts to focus attention or concentrate on a limited range of thoughts, fantasies, or external objects which are associated with the attempt to reduce the tension of one motive in preference to other motives. Typically, too, the suppressed motive can be readily recalled by the individual if he makes a deliberate attempt to do so.

Generally speaking, the intensity of a motive is a function of the extent to which its reduction determines the survival of the organism. In the case of socialized human beings, however, motives concerned with the perpetuation of the self-concept generate a degree of tension which may be equal to, if not greater than, any of his motives which are related to his biological survival. And while motives pertinent to one's self-concept may be learned initially in the process of reducing the tension of survival-linked motives, they often seem to take precedence over the latter in the individual's response repertoire. Thus, as a cursory glance at military history reveals, men will often knowingly give up their lives in the process of reducing the tension of motives induced by a challenge to their self-concepts.

Ego Defense

According to Freud, the growing child is caught in a struggle between his innate, physiologically based motives and the demands of his environment. On the one hand, the child is inclined immediately to reduce any tension which is generated by his motives, and to make whatever tension-reducing response is innately required by the special properties of the motive. On the other hand, adults who rear the child tend (1) to punish the child for responding immediately, and in the innately required manner, to some of his motives, and (2) to reward the making of new, culturally valued responses to those motives. Since the child must adapt to his environment if he is to survive, he is obliged to learn how to reduce the tension of his motives in a socially prescribed manner. In the course of this learning, the child develops a configuration of perceptual and motor skills which helps him to *maximize the reduction of the tension of his motives within the scope of the constraints of his environment.* Freud has called this configuration the *ego.*

It follows, from the circumstances which promoted its development, that the chief perceptual function of the ego is to maintain a state of consciousness in which the individual can correctly assess the properties of both his motives and his external environment. For unless the individual can accurately perceive his motives, he cannot reduce the tensions which they generate. Similarly, unless the person can accurately perceive the constraints of his environment, he cannot make those responses which maximize the reduction of his tension and, at the same time, minimize jeopardy to himself.

Just as the threat of danger provides a major impetus to the origin of the ego, so do threatening events exert the greatest strain on the ego's perceptual function. For these threatening events—parental punishment, for example—induce the motive of fear. Actually, there is only one type of response which is sufficient to reduce the tension of the fear motive: separation of the individual from the feared object. However, the young child, owing to his relative helplessness, is often unable to separate himself from the threatening object in a manner which will reduce the tension of his fear motive. Under these conditions, the perceptual function of the ego may fail, if the stimuli of the fear motive become too intense for conscious containment. Indeed, if too much fear is aroused, the individual may lose consciousness altogether. In fainting or losing consciousness completely, the individual necessarily fails to perceive his other motives, in addition to his fear motive.

To preclude such a catastrophic state of helplessness, the individual attempts to defend his ego. That is, he tends to respond to intolerable fear in such a way as to minimize its incapacitating effect upon the ego's perceptual function. In short, the individual responds by eliminating from conscious awareness (1) the fear motive when it exceeds his threshold of tolerance for fear, and (2) any other motive associated with the evocation of a threatening event which has, in the past, aroused excessive fear. These are the previously mentioned covert responses to which Freud applied the name *ego defense*, since their aim is to preserve the functioning of the ego.

Owing to the vicissitudes of their life histories, individuals differ in the strength of their egos. Accordingly, people differ in their degree of tolerance of fear. Some individuals have strong egos and can consciously contain intense fear for extended periods of time; other individuals, by contrast, have weak egos and can only briefly tolerate the conscious perception of their fear motive. In any case, because all children are confronted with a variety of threatening events at a time when their egos are still weak, all people will have developed a repertoire of ego defenses by the time they reach adulthood. Since it is possible to prevent the conscious perception of a motive by making a number of kinds of ego-defensive response, people will differ in the type of ego defense they employ against the same motives. In contrast to the operation of *suppression*, people are not aware of the expenditure of any effort in the functioning of their ego defenses. Moreover, motives which have been eliminated from consciousness by an ego defense are not readily amenable to recall, even after lengthy and deliberate efforts to remember them.

While all of the ego defenses function to eliminate the perception of consciously unacceptable motives, only two of them—*denial* and *identification with the aggressor*—bring about such an elimination by distorting the perception of objects in the *external* environment. That is, denial and identification with the aggressor aim at obliterating the individual's perception of those aspects of his environment which, he has learned, are capable of arousing intolerable fear. Thus, by not perceiving or by failing fully to acknowledge threatening aspects of his world, the individual can prevent those aspects from exerting the fear-arousing effects they would otherwise have.

Apart from denial and identification with the aggressor, the ego defenses described by Freud aim directly at eliminating the perception of an internal stimulus, i.e., the unacceptable motive *per se. Repression* is the most basic of these kinds of defense, the one whose effects stimulate the development of all the remaining ego defenses. Briefly, this development may be sketched in the following manner: Let us say that a young child is stimulated by an autoerotic sexual motive. To reduce the tension generated by that motive, the child responds by manipulating his genitals. Let us suppose, now, that the child's parents have a severely disapproving attitude toward any overt expression of the sexual motive. Eventually, they discover the child's sexual activity and punish him for it. Moreover, they threaten him with even worse punishment if he should persist in such activities in the future. Indeed, they imply by their punishment that they disapprove of the very existence of the sexual motive itself, as well as any behavior aimed at reducing the tension it generates.

The parental responses to the child's sexual behavior have aroused his intense fear. Yet he cannot respond to his feared parents in a manner which is adequate to reduce his fear. On the one hand, he is too weak to impose his will on his parents and, hence, force them to accept both his sexual motive and response to it. On the other hand, he is too dependent upon the parents for the reduction of tensions generated by his survival-linked motives to flee from them: he needs their love, protection, and nurture. Since his survival-linked motive (fear) is more intense than his sexual motive, it takes precedence over the latter in the child's motivational hierarchy. Accordingly, the child attempts to alter his behavior in such a way as to prevent the occurrence of parental threat and the fear motive which that threat aroused. The most obvious thing he can do, first of all, is to inhibit his sexual behavior, to refrain from responding overtly to his consciously perceived sexual motive. However, since the tension generated by the sexual motive is very great, the child finds it impossible entirely to refrain from responding overtly to it. Moreover, since the device of suppression can, at best, only temporarily obscure the perception of the sexual motive, it cannot permit the child to engage in the undistracted reduction of his non-sexual motives. Finally, since the child's parents had, by implication, punished not only the child's overt responses to the sexual motive but also his *possession* of the motive *per se*, the child's very perception of his sexual motive causes him to anticipate punishment. In view of all of these factors, the child finds it increasingly difficult to reconcile his sexual motive with the maintenance of his personal safety. Ultimately, the child is driven to the point at which the only way of ensuring his safety is to attempt *permanently* to eliminate his now dangerous sexual motive from conscious perception. By *repressing* his sexual motive, the child brings about an inner transformation which permits him to remain in harmonious contact with his parents and, at the same time, frees him of the necessity of responding overtly to the tension generated by his sexual motive. For, after the act of repression has been accomplished, the sexual motive has, insofar as the child's awareness is concerned, ceased to exist for him. And since he no longer perceives himself as *having* a sexual motive, he need no longer overtly respond to it in a way which has elicited parental punishment and evoked his intolerable fear.

If the response of *repression* had actually abolished the sexual motive rather than merely obliterating the individual's conscious perception of it, the conflict previously created by the simultaneous activation of the sexual and fear motives would have been permanently resolved. However, the sexual motive persists, albeit unconsciously, and so does the necessity to reduce the tension generated by it. If the child were to perceive his sexual motive in its original form, he would, of course, be faced with the temptation of responding to it overtly and, hence, exposing himself again to the parental punishment and fear he had striven, through the use of repression, to preclude. Thus, the child is required to make additional responses to bolster the effects of the original act of repression.

One of the things the child can do to support the defense of repression is to make the same sort of responses to the motive as were involved in its initial repression—in short, to re-repress the motive, so to speak. However, the child may also make a number of qualitatively different responses in order to keep from perceiving motives which have already been repressed, but which continue to intrude on his consciousness. For example, the child may employ the ego defense of *projection*, a response which involves the attribution to others of motives which he cannot consciously accept as his own.

Ego defenses and anxiety. The concept of anxiety was troublesome to Freud and, in the course of his theorizing, he felt obliged to change his original ideas about it. Initially,

Freud saw anxiety as the by-product of repressed libido; as an unpleasant emotion which was stimulated by the protracted failure to reduce the tension of the sexual motive. Subsequently, Freud tended to classify anxiety under the ego defenses. In this latter view, Freud regarded anxiety (in contrast to fear, or what he sometimes termed "objective anxiety") as a danger signal, a stimulus which heralded the incipient emergence into consciousness of a repressed motive.[5] *Under this formulation, anxiety represents an anticipation of the fear which the individual would experience if he should attempt overtly to reduce the tension of the repressed motive and if such an overt response were to elicit the same kind of punishing reactions from others that led the individual to repress the motive in the first place.*

But while anxiety may well be a warning signal which functions in the interest of the ego defenses, it is also a very powerful motive in its own right. That is, unlike the entirely imperceptible functioning of the various ego defenses, anxiety is experienced as a noxious affect. Indeed, since the anxiety motive, by nature of its historical development, is linked to fear, its tension-producing qualities are as intense as those of the fear motive. Here, when anxiety is aroused, it exerts, like fear, the greatest priority in the individual's hierarchy of motives. But whereas the individual can reduce the tension of his fear by separating himself from an obvious external threat, he is unable, typically, to find an external provocation for his anxiety. If anything, he may feel that something is clearly "wrong" with him, since his anxiety emerges in situations which, he knows, others may face calmly. Because the source of anxiety inheres in the possible perception of one's consciously unacceptable motives, the only effective way of reducing the level of anxiety is through the use of one of the individual's ego defenses. Thus, just as the imminent emergence into awareness of a repressed motive triggers off anxiety, so does the ego-defensive obliteration of the perception of those motives tend to reduce the tension of the anxiety motive.

Because its interpersonal origins and emotional overtones are similar to anxiety, the motive of guilt has sometimes been viewed as a species of anxiety;[6] and, indeed, the history of guilt may be traced to parental disapproval and punishment. Developmentally, however, anxiety appears before guilt, because its evocation is related to the formation of the ego and the individual's earliest efforts at survival and adaptation. Guilt, on the other hand, must await the development of a later psychological structure, the superego, which encompassess all the moral scruples which have been imposed upon the child by those who rear him. Once these scruples have been internalized, they can no longer be ignored with impunity. On the contrary, actual or even contemplated violation of one's moral scruples tends to arouse guilt and its attendant need for punishment.

Owing to its unpleasant subjective qualities as well as its distasteful behavioral implications (i.e., the necessity to seek punishment as expiation), guilt is a motive whose conscious perception the individual may find intolerable. Consequently, individuals may be inclined to employ various ego-defensive mechanisms in an attempt to keep guilt below the threshold of conscious awareness. It should be noted that while both guilt and anxiety may be evoked by the same stimulus, such as a lewd photograph, it is possible to reduce the tension of the guilt motive by engaging in some form of overtly self-punishing

[5] S. Freud, *Inhibitions, Symptoms, and Anxiety*, London, Hogarth, 1949.
[6] O. Fenichel, *The Psychoanalytic Theory of Neurosis*, New York, Norton, 1945.

response. The reduction of anxiety, however, can be accomplished only through the functioning of one of the ego defenses.

Ego defenses and symptoms. Although the ego defenses eliminate the perception of threatening motives, they do not thereby reduce the tension generated by those motives. On the contrary, to reduce the tension of a motive it is necessary to make *overt* responses, the quality of which is determined by the special properties of the motive in question. But in the case of an unconscious motive, the individual's anxiety would be aroused if he were to respond to the motive's special qualities with the same kind of overt responses which elicited the punishment that led to the original ego-defensive purging of the motive from consciousness. Hence, the individual must develop a new repertoire of overt responses which function to reduce the tension of his unconscious motives. In Freudian parlance, these newly learned responses are called *symptoms.*

A symptom is, therefore, an overt, tension-reducing response whose relationship to an unconscious motive is not perceived by the individual. In respect to their tension-reducing qualities, symptoms may be placed into two categories: those which are maximally reductive of tension and those which are only partially reductive of tension. Examples of both type of symptom may best be illustrated in connection with the overt expression of the same consciously unacceptable motive. Suppose two parents harbor a great deal of unconscious hatred toward their children. Parent A, exhibiting the first type of symptom, gives direct and open vent to his aggression—not only by continually disparaging her child, but also by whipping him at the slightest provocation. However, since she cannot consciously accept her aggressive motive, Parent A is obliged consciously to divest her destructive actions of aggressive *intent* and, instead, to see in her hostility the fulfillment of an altruistic motive such as the desire to elevate the child's moral stature.

The second type of symptom, shown in the case of Parent B, only partially reduces the tension of an unconscious motive because it involves a greater compromise with those motives which oppose the overt expression of the unconscious motive in question. Thus, for Parent B, a direct and open display of hostility toward her child would stir too much guilt. However, by being sufficiently overprotective, Parent B can succeed, albeit deviously, in expressing a good deal of her underlying aggression. For instance, Parent B may become so concerned with the safety and welfare of her child that she crushes his self-confidence and deprives him of pleasures readily accessible to children of other parents. In exercising this stifling "care" of her child, Parent B, unlike Parent A, is not being obviously and directly punitive or disparaging.

Attitude

The definition of attitude used here is one about which a certain amount of agreement exists among contemporary psychologists: *a disposition to react favorably or unfavorably to a class of objects.* This disposition may, of course, be inferred from a variety of observable responses made by the individual when he is confronted by a member of the class of objects toward which he has an attitude: facial expressions, postures, locomotions, sounds of voice, and verbalizations. An individual need not be aware of his attitude or of the behavior on the basis of which his attitude is inferred by others. However, insofar as psychologists have employed self-rating verbal scales as their operational measures of attitudes, they have been dealing with attitudes of which the individual—at least after filling out a questionnaire about his attitudes—is aware. In addition, verbalized attitudes of this sort tend to be couched in a set of cognitions about the attitudinal objects—articulated ideas and perceptions within which the favorable or unfavorable dispositions toward a given class of objects are imbedded.

Since attitudes are inferred from overt responses, and since overt responses are made in order to reduce the tension generated by motives, we may assume that attitudes are developed in the process of making tension-reducing responses to various classes of objects. In short, *an individual's attitude toward a class of objects is determined by the particular role those objects have come to play in facilitating responses which reduce the tension of particular motives and which resolve particular conflicts among motives.*

It should be noted, in line with the preceding discussion of ego defense, that the tension generated by a given motive may be reduced by a number of quite different overt responses. It follows, therefore, that quite divergent attitudes held by different individuals toward the same class of objects may merely reflect different ways in which those individuals have learned to reduce the tension generated by the same motive. Conversely, identical attitudes may mediate the reduction of quite different motives, just as the same overt response of smiling may be used to reduce the tension generated by the motives of love, anxiety, or even hatred.

In view of the various relationships which may obtain between attitudes and motives, it should be apparent that no attitude is, in itself, an entirely reliable indicator of the motive whose tension it is helping to reduce. But if this is true, how are we to go about making the kind of educated guess about the relationship between particular attitudes and particular motives which will permit us to conduct systematic research on the motivational bases of attitudes? Briefly, the pursuit of any answer to this question would follow these steps: (1) One examines carefully the behavior from which the attitude is inferred. (2) Having closely observed the overt responses which are taken to reflect the individual's attitude, one postulates all the motives whose tension might plausibly be reduced by those responses. (3) One then makes an *independent* assessment of the manner in which the individual tends to reduce the various motives which have been postulated. By independent assessment is meant an observation of the individual's responses to the motives in question under conditions which do not involve a response to the particular attitudinal object under consideration. (4) If the independent assessment of the individual's mode of tension reduction leads one to believe that he is aware of the relationship between his behavior and the motives which have been postulated, one tends to conclude that he is also aware of the tension-reducing function of the responses from which his particular attitude was originally inferred. If, on the other hand, the above assessment suggests that the individual cannot consciously accept the motive whose tension is, presumably, being reduced by some of the overt responses of which he is aware, we assume that the behavioral measure of his attitude may also be regarded as a symptom. Moreover, the particulars of this independent assessment of the relationship between the individual's overt responses and his motives requires us, as we shall see, to postulate which mechanisms of ego defense mediate the individual's overt response to his consciously unacceptable motives.

DISCREPANCIES AND CONGRUITIES IN THE RELATIONSHIPS
BETWEEN ATTITUDES AND MOTIVES

An individual's attitude may appear to be either consonant with or discrepant from the motive whose tension it is functioning to reduce. Thus, at the extreme of congruence, the attitude merely anticipates those overt responses which directly and maximally reduce the tension of a motive of which the individual is consciously aware. On the other hand, at the extreme of discrepancy, the attitude indicates the operation of covert ego-defensive responses which—in the interests of anxiety reduction—not only preclude direct and maximal reduction of the tension generated by an individual's repressed motives but which aim, in fact, to obscure his perception of their very existence.

Attitudes and Consciously Acceptable Motives

In reducing the tension of a motive, the individual develops a repertory of responses to it. If the motive is one he can consciously accept, the individual's overt responses to it will maximally reduce the tension generated by that motive. To maximally reduce tension, the individual's overt (observable) response must (1) directly mirror the special properties of the motive, and (2) persist for a length of time proportional to the intensity of the motive. In addition, *the individual will be cognizant of his motive as well as its functional relationship to his overt tension-reducing responses*. Finally, the individual will experience no anxiety as a result of his awareness, nor will he be obliged to expend a portion of his available energy in making ego-defensive responses.

Given the above conditions, the individual will orient himself toward objects in his environment in such a way as maximally to reduce the tension of his motive. In terms of his acceptable motives, the objects in the individual's environment fall into two classes: (1) those to which he must have access and toward which he must make a specific overt response if the tension of a given motive is to be maximally reduced, and (2) those which facilitate or thwart the possibility of making the specific overt response necessary to reduce the tension of a motive. Frequently, these facilitating or thwarting objects either lead to or block the individual's access to those objects to which he must respond in a specific way if the tension of his motives are to be maximally reduced.

Because attitudes are dispositions to respond favorably or unfavorably to objects, they should, *in the case of consciously acceptable motives*, be determined by the role which objects play in the maximal reduction of tension generated by the individual's motives. Thus, if an individual's motive is known to be acceptable to him, it should be possible to predict a variety of his attitudes toward objects in his environment. Let us suppose that Individual X has acquired an achievement motive. In order to reduce the tension generated by that motive, he is obliged to make quite specific responses under quite specific conditions. If Individual X fully accepts his achievement motive, we would expect him to have a favorable attitude toward those conditions of work which permit him to make the response upon which the criteria of achievement can be imposed; those concrete objects, such as prizes, medals, and certificates, which connote the fact of achievement; and those persons who provide the opportunity to make responses which reduce the tension of the achievement motive. On the other hand, Individual X ought to have unfavorable attitudes toward those conditions of work which preclude or limit the possibility of making responses upon which the criteria of achievement can be imposed; those concrete objects, such as low pay, which connote the failure to achieve; those persons who create or threaten to create obstacles in the pursuit of achievement criteria.

In order further to illustrate the relationship between attitude and motive when the motive is consciously acceptable to the individual, let us consider two more of Individual X's motives: aggression and fear. The aggressive motive is often provoked by objects which thwart the individual in his attempts at motive satisfaction. Once it is induced, the aggressive motive can be maximally reduced only by making hostile or combative responses to those objects which provoked it. And since attitudes anticipate responses, it follows that the individual will develop an unfavorable attitude toward those objects to which he must respond with hostile acts in order to reduce maximally the tension of his aggressive motive.

Paradoxically enough, but in accordance with the formulation presented here, people will tend to develop favorable attitudes toward those objects which facilitate the maximal reduction of their aggressive motive. Thus, if someone in Individual X's office were to help him in bringing about the downfall or embarrassment of one of X's hated rivals, X would tend to have a favorable attitude toward his accomplice. It is conceivable that the reduction in prejudice which many white troops in integrated combat units appeared to experience in regard to their attitude toward Negroes[7] can be attributed to the fact that they were in a position to observe Negroes in the process of reducing a strong motive which they shared with them—hatred of the enemy.

Quite frequently, the objects which provoke aggression also provoke the fear motive. Thus, both fear and aggression are likely to be aroused when the individual is confronted with an object which directly threatens his survival. If the individual is able to accept his fear consciously, he attempts to make overt responses which will maximally reduce its tension. Accordingly, he will respond by attempting to separate himself from the feared object; the unfavorableness of his attitude toward the threatening object ought to be influenced by his distance from it, i.e., its capacity to harm him. The closer the object gets to him, the greater his fear of it and, hence, the more unfavorable his attitude toward it. As the threatening object loses its capacity to harm, the individual should grow less fearful of it and develop a more favorable attitude toward it. Similarly, the individual ought to develop favorable or unfavorable attitudes toward other objects which he perceives either to thwart or facilitate the making of those responses to the threatening object which will maximally reduce the fear induced by that object.

Even if all the motives which comprise a particular motivational conflict are consciously acceptable to him, the individual obviously cannot respond in any way which will provide simultaneous and maximal reduction of the tensions of all his motives. In order to obtain a maximal reduction in tension for any one of his consciously acceptable motives, the individual must keep his responses to the other motives in abeyance. The two kinds of response which permit the postponement of maximal tension-reducing responses to consciously acceptable motives—inhibition and suppression—have already been discussed. It only remains to be pointed out, therefore, that attitudes may be

[7]S. A. Stouffer et al., The American Soldier, Vol. I, Princeton, N. J., Princeton University Press, 1949.

formed in the process of facilitating the effect of these postponing responses as well as in the eventual process of reducing the tensions of the consciously acceptable motives *per se*. Considered from the standpoint of inhibition, for example, an individual's disposition to respond favorably or unfavorably to an object may be determined by the extent to which a given disposition is required if the individual is to avoid making an overt, tension-reducing response to the inhibited motive. Such phenomena as hypocrisy, duplicity, and other types of interpersonal deception may involve just such a discrepancy between an individual's behavior (from which his attitude is inferred) and his conscious and inhibited motive.

Another example of attitudes which are formed in order to facilitate either inhibition or suppression can be found in Katz and Schank's classical observation of discrepancies between publicly and privately expressed attitudes.[8] From the standpoint of the preceding discussion, one's publicly and privately expressed attitudes are equally "real" or "valid." For they both facilitate the making of responses to motives. However, it is likely that the publicly expressed attitudes more often reflect the facilitation of inhibiting or suppressing responses to motives. Thus, if the attitude implied tension-reducing responses which the respondent believes might evoke unwanted disapproval, the respondent may wish to inhibit such responses when they are open to public scrutiny. One way of preventing the overt emergence of potentially punishable responses is to make them with less force or, still better, to make qualitatively different sorts of response which are not commonly associated with the inhibited motive. In private, however, when the individual feels free from potential punishment, he can permit the overt expression of those responses which maximally reduce the motive he had inhibited or suppressed in public. Consequently, his attitude should change as he changes from a motive-inhibiting response to a motive-reducing response.

Attitudes and Consciously Unacceptable Motives

From the standpoint of his consciously unacceptable motives, the individual's attitudes toward objects are determined by their function in facilitating (1) covert ego-defensive responses aimed at precluding the perception of consciously unacceptable motives and (2) overt symptomatic responses which permit the individual to reduce the tension produced by his consciously unacceptable motives.

Because the reduction of the tension of a consciously unacceptable motive is mediated by ego-defensive responses, the relationship between an attitude and a consciously unacceptable motive is considerably more complicated than the relationship between an attitude and a consciously acceptable motive. And knowledge of any given attitude *per se* is an insufficient basis for inferring the particular consciously unacceptable motive to which it is functionally related, or, indeed, for inferring that it is related to a consciously unacceptable motive rather than a consciously acceptable one. Thus, for example, Individual A may *deliberately* behave in such a way that his prejudiced neighbors are led to infer that he shares their anti-Negro attitudes. Approving of Individual A's anti-Negro attitude, his neighbors patronize his store—thus bringing about the maximal reduction of a consciously acceptable motive which is highly placed in Individual A's motivational

[8]D. Katz and R. L. Schank, *Social Psychology*, New York, Wiley, 1938.

hierarchy—the motive to make money. On the other hand, the same anti-Negro attitude may, for Individual B, facilitate the making of ego-defensive responses which function to preclude his awareness of the fact that he possesses an aggressive motive. Thus, if the motive of aggression is consciously unacceptable to Individual B, he may use the ego defense of projection in order to attribute it to Negroes.

Because the individual's consciously unacceptable motives cannot be reliably predicted solely on the basis of his manifest attitudes, a precise determination of the functional relationship between an attitude and a consciously unacceptable motive involves a postulation of which *combination* of consciously unacceptable motive and ego defense might plausibly account for the *particular* overt responses from which the attitude is inferred. After conceptualizing this most plausible combination of ego defense and consciously unacceptable motive, one must proceed *empirically* to demonstrate the relationship between that combination and the attitude it is presumed to support. In general, such attempted empirical demonstrations have, in the past, employed correlational methods. Thus, as exemplified by the extremely influential research report, *The Authoritarian Personality*,[9] responses to attitude scales are correlated with responses to personality scales, projective tests, or interviews. The particular measures of personality are coded in terms of the motivational and ego-defensive categories required by the investigator's guiding hypotheses. The resulting correlations between the attitudinal and personality measures provide the evidence on the basis of which the hypotheses are evaluated.

The other method of testing hypotheses concerning the functional relationships between attitudes and consciously unacceptable motives is, of course, experimental. While the logical advantages of an experimental over a correlational approach are quite apparent, so are the difficulties of contriving adequate experimental manipulations for, and controls over, the complex variables involved. These difficulties may, perhaps, account for the fact that relatively few experiments have been conducted in this area. In any case, an experimental test of the functional relationship between an attitude and a consciously unacceptable motive would require, depending on the particular prediction, either the manipulation of the ego defenses which presumably function to obliterate the perception of the consciously unacceptable motive whose functional relationship to the attitude has been postulated, or the arousal of the motive against whose conscious perception the individual is supposed to be defending himself by use of a particular mechanism of ego defense. If manipulation or arousal produce the predicted changes in those responses toward objects from which the attitude in question is inferred, the experiment is held to have supported the original hypothesis.

It may be useful now to give examples of the process of logical inference by means of which conceptual links may be built between particular attitudes, on the one hand, and particular ego-defensive and symptomatic responses to consciously unacceptable motives, on the other. For the making of such conceptual links is not merely an exercise in logical reasoning. On the contrary, it would appear that systematic empirical research in this area is feasible only if one can first adequately conceptualize the relationships among attitudes and consciously unacceptable motives.

[9] Adorno *et al., op cit.*

Attitudes Which Facilitate the Perceptual Obliteration of Threatening External Stimuli

As previously stated in the section on ego defense, a threatening external stimulus is one which is capable of arousing a motive which the individual cannot consciously contain. According to Freud, the individual can preclude such an arousal by using two mechanisms of defense—denial and identification with the aggressor—which in different ways serve to obliterate those aspects of external stimuli which are threatening to him.

Attitudes which facilitate the ego defense of denial. The defense of denial is inferred from the individual's failure to perceive, or to acknowledge the perception of, a stimulus which impinges on his sensorium and which is presumed to have threatening implications for him. More commonly, perhaps, denial is inferred by a failure or reluctance to acknowledge the magnitude of the threat inherent in a stimulus which the individual does, in fact, perceive as a threatening one. Although no empirical research has yet demonstrated the relationship between the defense of denial and the formation of any particular attitude, a number of examples, some taken from attitude research, illustrate how attitudes facilitate the responses involved in denial.

Concerning the reluctance to acknowledge the perception of an occurrence which has threatening implications for the individual, an example is the commonplace reaction to the news of the death of a relative or close friend. Frequently, such news evokes the response: "Oh, no!" Here we see an almost reflexive rejection of the threat contained in the fact of death. Similarly in so far as death is concerned, young children often refuse to accept the fact that their favorite pet has died. Hence, long after the animal has been interred, the child may continue to behave as if it were still alive. Thus, the child may persist in calling out the dead pet's name and addressing it as if the pet, rather than empty space, stood beside him.

Quite analogous behavior is exhibited by adults who assert, in the face of impending doom, "It can't happen to me." Variations are reported in Allport, Bruner, and Jandorf's study of victims of Nazi terror.[10] In spite of clear indications that Nazi persecution of Jews was spreading throughout Germany, it was apparently possible for some Jews, in the still relatively unaffected areas, to feel that they would somehow be spared or by-passed by the Nazis; that although the Nazi persecution had already reached out to strike down people they knew personally in other cities, it would leave them unscathed.

It is possible that the use of the defense of denial contributes to one of the curious attitudinal phenomena reported in recent years. That fear-inducing appeals sometimes effect a resistance to attitude change[11] may be partly accounted for by the fact that some people begin to fail to perceive or refuse to acknowledge their perception of the threatening communications. Indeed, the fact that some people reacted to the fear-inducing communication by changing their attitudes in a direction opposite to that intended by the appeal may indicate both that they have a low threshold for the tolerance

[10] G. W. Allport, J. S. Bruner, and E. M. Jandorf, "Personality under Social Catastrophe: Ninety Life-histories of the Nazi Revolution," in C. Kluckhohn *et al.*, editors, *Personality in Nature, Society, and Culture*, New York, Knopf, 1953. pp. 436–455.

[11] I. L. Janis, and S. Feshbach, "Effects of Fear-arousing Communications," *Journal of Abnormal Social Psychology*, Vol. 48, 1953, pp. 78–92.

of fear *and* that they tend to make use of denial, rather than some other mechanism of ego defense, in preventing a threatening stimulus from exceeding their tolerance for the conscious perception of the fear motive.

A similarly curious failure to be moved in the direction suggested by a fear appeal is represented by the fact that cigarette smokers often do not stop smoking despite their knowledge of a strong correlation between lung cancer and smoking. Instead, the reaction of some smokers to this evidence is paradoxical, to say the least: they begin smoking even more than they did before. Unless one postulated a suicidal motive whose tension is being reduced by the increase in smoking, a possible explanation would appear, once again, to involve the mechanism of denial. Thus, by increasing their amount of smoking, some smokers may be attempting to deny its threatening aspects. Another way of denying the threat involved in smoking is for an individual to smoke as much as he did previously, but to perceive a decrease in the number of cigarettes he smokes. This particular form of denial is often used by obese people who undertake a diet. They may eat less than they did before at each of the three regular meals, but they may also nibble so persistently at food throughout the day that they make up the difference. Yet their nibbling may be imperceptible to them.

As has been suggested in these examples of denial of smoking and eating behavior, the threatening stimulus against which the individual uses the defense need not always be entirely separate from himself. On the contrary, one's own behavior or one's own body may contain threatening aspects which the individual wishes to deny. For example, certain clinical cases dramatically underscore the extent to which a person may go in denying those aspects of his anatomy which have come to have threatening implications for him. Thus, lesbians and homosexuals sometimes undertake to alter their appearance to look as much as possible like members of the opposite sex.

Attitudes which facilitate the ego defense of identification with the aggressor. Identification with the aggressor is inferred when an individual adopts the behavior and attitudes of a person who threatens to arouse his intolerable fear. In doing so the individual ceases to perceive the aggressor as being so separate from and at such odds with himself. In short, as he comes to share the aggressor's characteristics, the individual becomes less capable of perceiving a difference (between himself and the aggressor) which might lead the aggressor to threaten him.

The operation of the mechanism of identification with the aggressor was implicit in the example of the boy who was obliged to repress his autoerotic sexual motive. Indeed, the conditions under which that repression occurred are very conducive to the use of identification with the aggressor. For, it may be recalled, the child was at the mercy of aggressors, his parents, who not only had the capacity to arouse his intolerable fear but were, in fact, strenuously arousing it. Moreover, the child could neither flee from the omnipresent threat nor overcome it by counterforce. He was obliged somehow to change himself in order to reduce the threat to his existence. Accordingly, it may now be said that, before repressing his sexual motive, the child would have been expected, theoretically, to identify with his parents' sexual attitudes. That is, having first perceived and adopted his parents' disapproving attitudes towards his sexual motive, he then repressed his *internal* perception of that motive.

It should be noted that identification with the aggressor, like the other mechanisms of ego defense, functions unconsciously and automatically. That is, the individual is not aware of the fact that he is adopting a particular behavior or attitude in order to minimize his perception of the threatening implications of another person's behavior toward him. This lack of awareness is not true, of course, in the case of conscious emulation or hero worshipping—conditions in which an individual *deliberately* attempts to practice and learn the behavior of someone whom he *likes or admires.*

Other examples of the use of this particular mechanism of defense are not difficult to find: a pupil involuntarily mimicking the grimaces of a menacing teacher;[12] a child forcing another child to submit to an "examination" after he has himself been disquieted by a genuine medical examination;[13] prisoners turning on their fellow inmates with the same cruelty with which they themselves have been treated by their guards.[14] Indeed, Freud postulated that this mechanism of defense was to be found at the heart of the process by means of which all of us develop an enduring conscience: parents, however kindly they treat their children, are inevitably obliged to exercise some form of coercive discipline and, hence, evoke the child's tendency to resort to the defense of identification.

Insofar as ethnic minorities are exposed to disparagement by majority group members, they are placed in an interpersonal context which is likely to encourage the use of identification with the aggressor. Accordingly, the prejudices which members of a social minority develop toward their own group may be viewed as possible reflection of such a process.

With this reasoning in mind, the phenomenon of Jewish anti-Semitism has been studied in an effort to test several hypotheses derived from the concept of identification with the aggressor.[15] In the study an attempt was made to predict personality differences between Jews who have tended to internalize the anti-Semitic attitudes emanating from majority-group bigots and Jews who have been relatively resistant to the internalization of such hostile attitudes. Specifically, it was found that subjects classified as High in anti-Semitism differed from those in the Low category in the following predicted ways: (1) The Highs had more negative attitudes and fewer positive attitudes toward themselves and their parents; (2) The Highs tended more frequently to be passive in the face of interpersonal hostility and were less prone to retaliate actively against aggressors.

Since the results of this study were derived from a small and relatively homogeneous population of male college students, they preclude generalization to all members of the Jewish group. However, the results of the study do lend empirical support to some aspects of the Freudian theory of indentification with the aggressor.

Attitudes Which Facilitate the Perceptual Obliteration of Threatening Internal Stimuli

While denial and identification with the aggressor function to eliminate the perception of external stimuli which threaten to arouse consciously unacceptable motives, other defenses of the individual help him to eliminate the perception of internal stimuli which

[12] A. Freud, *The Ego and the Mechanisms of Defense*, New York, International Universities Press, 1948.

[13] A. Balint, *The Psychoanalysis of the Nursery*, London, Routledge, 1953.

[14] B. Bettelheim, "Individual and Mass Behavior in Extreme Situations," *Journal of Abnormal Social Psychology*, Vol. 38, 1943, pp. 417–452.

[15] Sarnoff, "Identification with the Aggressor."

are associated with the consciously unacceptable motive *per se*. Three of the chief defenses against the perception of threatening internal stimuli are repression, projection, and reaction formation.

Attitudes which facilitate the ego defense of repression. Repression is inferred when the individual cannot voluntarily recall a motive of which he had once been consciously aware, or a sensation or cognition, associated with a motive, of which he had once been consciously aware.

Freud conceived repression to be the most fundamental defense against the perception of threatening internal stimuli. Although repression has been utilized as an explanatory intervening variable, its *unique* relationship to a particular social attitude has not been clearly demonstrated. For example, in conceptualizing the so-called authoritarian personality, Adorno *et al.* invoke at least three other ego defenses in addition to repression.[16] Thus, the authoritarian individual is seen as one who, first of all, represses his aggressive motive toward his parents. He then uses the following ego defenses in attempting to cope with the tension of his consciously unacceptable aggression: (1) Reaction formation, by means of which he develops a consciously favorable attitude toward his parents; (2) projection, by means of which he attributes his consciously unacceptable hostility to others; (3) displacement, by means of which he reroutes toward persons who are weaker than himself whatever aggression is still consciously acceptable to him. Having conceptualized these various ego-defensive contributions to the development of authoritarian attitudes, the investigators attempted to combine their measurement in an over-all personality index. Of course, it may well be true that all these mechanisms do contribute to the complex set of responses from which the authoritarian attitude is inferred. However, it is equally true that the *particular* functional relationship of repression to particular aspects of the authoritarian attitude cannot be properly evaluated by the kind of global approach employed by the California investigations.

Because these authoritarian attitudes comprise a variety of social prejudices, as well as a number of economic, political, and interpersonal attitudes, it would still appear necessary to study systematically the effect of repression on the formation of *all* these attitudes and the particular effects upon them of the other mechanisms of defense which are presumed to be related to them.

It should be noted that it appears to be very difficult to arrange a satisfactory operational test of the relationship between the repression of a particular motive and the formation of an attitude which functions to facilitate the repression of that motive. From an experimental viewpoint, hypnosis might be a feasible way of solving the methodological problem. For example, the ingenious hypnotic manipulations used by Erickson would appear to indicate that via post-hypnotic suggestion it is possible to induce the repression of a motive of which the subject was clearly aware prior to the hypnotic state.[17] By attempting to re-arouse that motive in the post-hypnotic condition, the experimenter can observe the emergence of the behavior which the individual uses to maintain repression and from which repression-facilitating attitudes may be inferred. For example, the subject whose repressed motive is being stirred may become restive and develop a keen interest in

---

[16] *Op. cit.*

[17] M. H. Erickson, "Experimental Demonstrations of the Psychopathology of Everyday Life," in S. Tomkins, editor, *Contemporary Psychopathology*, Cambridge, Mass., Harvard University Press, 1944, pp. 517–528.

some activity by which he would hope to divert his attention, as well as the experimenter's, from the consciously unacceptable motive. Under these circumstances, the subject may suddenly develop a disposition to respond to objects which facilitate repressive responses to his incipient but consciously unacceptable motive.

Attitudes which facilitate the ego defense of projection. Several allusions have already been made to the mechanism of projection. By attributing his own consciously unacceptable motives to others, the individual is able to avoid perceiving them as belonging to him. Thus, projection permits the individual to be preoccupied with the perception of other people's motives rather than his own.

Owing to their content, prevailing social prejudices would appear to be especially attractive to persons who use projection as a way of precluding the perception of their consciously unacceptable motives. Social prejudices involve the ascription of undesirable traits and characteristics to various groups. In our own culture, these undesirable characteristics often include behavior which overtly reduces the tensions of the motives of sex and aggression. With our tradition of Judeo-Christian morality, we tend to disapprove of the sexual and aggressive motives. People who have been punished for attempting to reduce the tension of their own sexual and aggressive motives will be inclined to repress these motives. If, following such repression, they *also* use the mechanism of projection to preclude the conscious emergence of the tensions which their unconscious motives continue to induce, they will tend to attribute their sexual and aggressive motives to others. Thus, they should be inclined to accept prevailing prejudices which depict given groups as possessing the culturally disapproved sexual and aggressive motives.

In a similar way, other culturally disapproved behavior may be functionally related to motives which the individual cannot consciously accept. Thus, greediness and slovenliness may be indirectly associated with the reduction of motives stimulated by repressed oral and anal libido, respectively; individuals who tend to project those motives in an effort to remain consciously unaware of them may readily accept social prejudices which characterize various groups as being grasping and unclean.

Although the previously mentioned California studies did not sort out the differential contributions of the various types of ethnic prejudice to the facilitation of the mechanism of projection, the content of the prejudices which were investigated would appear to have a special attraction for those subjects who tended to project their sexual and aggressive motives onto others. Indeed, it begins to appear that—*insofar as consciously unacceptable motives do form the basis of an individual's disposition to agree with prevailing anti-minority stereotypes*—projection plays a larger role than any of the other mechanisms of ego defense. Thus, in planning a series of experimental studies on the motivational bases of attitude change, Sarnoff and Katz first thought it reasonable to use a composite measure of several ego defenses in order to categorize subjects on a general dimension of ego defensiveness.[18] It was predicted that the level of a subject's ego defensiveness would determine the extent and the direction of change in his attitude toward Negroes upon his being exposed to two kinds of communication: (1) those which provide insight into the psychodynamic relationship between anti-Negro attitudes and ego defensiveness, and (2) those which provide accurate information about Negroes.

[18] I. Sarnoff and D. Katz, "The Motivational Bases of Attitude Change," *Journal of Abnormal Social Psychology*, Vol. 49, 1954, pp. 115–124.

Although subjects with various amounts of ego defensiveness did show some of the predicted differential changes in their attitude toward Negroes,[19] a close examination of the indices which comprised the ego-defensiveness measure suggested that projection was the only mechanism which actually contributed to the predictive power of the composite ego-defensiveness score. This *ex post facto* finding stimulated a follow-up experiment which provided evidence that the measure of projection, when separately employed, could predict attitude change, while the measure of the other ego defenses failed to yield reliable predictions.[20]

Attitudes which facilitate the ego defense of reaction formation. The defense of *reaction formation* is inferred when an individual makes overt responses which are directly contrary to those required for the maximal reduction of the tension generated by a consciously unacceptable motive. By behaving in this way the individual expends the energy, the *counter-cathexis* in Freudian terminology, necessary to keep the motive repressed, and maintains a perception of himself as being responsive to motives which are as dissimilar as possible to those which he does, in fact, possess.

The particular flavor of reaction formation may, perhaps, best be imparted by comparing its behavioral effects to that of another ego defense against the same consciously unacceptable motive. Let us suppose that two individuals use different mechanisms of ego defense against the same consciously unacceptable aggressive motive. If individual A uses projection, he tends to attribute his own consciously unacceptable aggressive motive to other persons. Hence, he would be inclined to see others as being driven by aggressive motives. Individual B, however, has learned to use the defense of reaction formation rather than projection as a way of supporting his original repression of the aggressive motive. Consequently, B might develop a repertory of outgoing and affectionate behavior toward others. Indeed, he might be inclined to forgive quickly and turn the "other cheek," even if unfairly treated by others. Finally, in order to facilitate his use of reaction formation, he might readily accept idealistic views of mankind and enthusiastically propound attitudes which favor peace, brotherhood, and tolerance among men. Although this behavior might, in another person, reflect genuine and consciously acceptable motives of affection and generosity, for the person using reaction formation against aggression it represents a variety of ways of precluding his own awareness of a motive which is consciously unacceptable to him.

Recently, the author undertook an experiment to evaluate a hypothesis, derived from the foregoing reasoning, about the dynamics of reaction formation.[21] In this experiment the social attitude of cynicism was viewed as facilitating the use of the defense of reaction formation against a consciously unacceptable motive of affection for others. From the definition, it may be deduced that an individual who uses reaction formation as a defense against the perception of his own unconscious affection ought to behave coolly, if not with blatant hostility, toward others. By accepting skeptical and uncomplimentary views of human nature, the individual can more readily respond to others with the

---

[19]D. Katz, I. Sarnoff, and C. McClintock, "Ego-defense and Attitude Change," *Human Relations,* Vol. 9, 1956, pp. 27-45.
[20]Katz *et al.* "The Measurement of Ego Defense as Related to Attitude Change."
[21]Sarnoff, "Reaction Formation and Cynicism."

coolness and hostility required by his reaction formation against affection. Hence, the acceptance of a cynical attitude toward mankind may help the individual to remain unaware that he actually harbors affectionate feelings toward others.

From this theoretical analysis, it follows that one would expect empirically to obtain a positive correlation between a measure of reaction formation against affection and a measure of cynicism. Such a correlation ought not necessarily to be very pronounced, since all cynics are not the victims of reaction formation. Any given individual may have learned cynicism through experience or may be quick to endorse cynical comments out of conformity to some perceived norm. But although there may not be a very close correspondence between the habitual strength of an individual's reaction formation against affectionate feelings and his general level of cynicism, the individual's level of cynicism ought, at least temporarily, to reflect the effects of reaction formation against unconscious affectionate feelings toward others, *under conditions which arouse those unconscious feelings*. For when confronted by stimuli which evoke his affectionate feelings, the person who has a strong reaction formation against such feelings should become anxious. In order to reduce his anxiety (which is itself unpleasant) and to preclude the danger which the anxiety connotes, the individual has to expend a fresh charge of energy against his newly aroused unconscious motive. If the individual uses reaction formation as a defense against his unconscious affection, his fresh expenditure of energy ought to be reflected by a rise in the intensity of his level of consciously felt cynicism. Finally, assuming that an intense arousal of affection evokes more anxiety among individuals with a strong reaction formation against affection than among those whose reaction formation against affection is weak, the former individuals should become relatively more cynical than the latter as the intensity of the affection-arousing stimulus increases.

The methodology of this experiment, therefore, was designed to test the specific hypothesis that persons who are high in reaction formation against affection (HRF) would become more cynical after the arousal of their affectionate feelings toward others than persons who are low in reaction formation against affection (LRF).

Eighty-one male undergraduates were randomly assigned to one of the two experimental conditions in a "before-after" design which permitted the manipulation of two levels of affectionate feelings toward others. Before being placed in the experimental conditions, the subjects filled out booklets containing a scale of cynicism (CS) and a measure of reaction formation (RF). High arousal of affection (HA) was induced by a "live" dramatic presentation of an altered excerpt from William Saroyan's play, *Hello Out There*. Low arousal of affection (LA) was induced by a tape recording of the same excerpt. Following the experimental manipulations, the subjects filled out the original CS questionnaire and several other measures including checks on their perceptions of the affection-arousing stimuli.

The results showed that both HRF and LRF subjects tended to move in a less cynical direction after being exposed to both the HA and LA conditions. However, the HRF subjects were more resistant to such a change in attitude, and the difference between HRF and LRF subjects in mean CS shift scores under the HA condition was statistically significant at the .03 level, on the basis of a one-failed test. No statistically reliable difference between HRF and LRF subjects in the mean CS shift scores was obtained under the LA condition. Also in line with initial theoretical expectations was the finding of a low but statistically significant positive correlation between the pre-experimental measure of cynicism and the measure of reaction formation.

Although the results of the experimental manipulations produced effects consonant with theoretical expectations, they were equivocal in some respects. Additional analyses with the aid of an interrun control group, however, were sufficient to rule out the most likely alternative explanations of the original results. Consequently, this experiment is interpreted as having provided some empirical support for the psychoanalytic concept of reaction formation.

Attitudes Which Facilitate Overt Symptomatic Responses to the Tensions of Consciously Unacceptable Motives

It is often impossible for the individual to use denial effectively to avoid the perception of those of his overt responses from which he might infer the existence of a consciously unacceptable motive. Thus, for example, many of the individual's tension-reducing responses are made to other persons; and even if an individual were not inclined to perceive the behavior involved in the reduction of tension of his consciously unacceptable motives, the persons affected by the behavior not only frequently perceive it but also call it to the individual's conscious attention. Moreover, since repressed motives continue endlessly to generate tension, the individual is obliged to reduce their tensions in a manner which will permit him both to perceive the overt behavior which does, in fact, reduce the tensions of his repressed motives and to remain unaware of the relationship between the perceived behavior and the repressed motives whose tensions it is reducing.

The individual has two ways of accomplishing this dual objective, both of which we have alluded to in our previous discussion of symptoms. The first technique is to make direct and maximally reductive responses to the consciously unacceptable motive, but, having perceived those responses, to misinterpret their true motivational intent. The second technique is to make overt responses which indirectly and partially reduce the special tensions of the consciously unacceptable motive, but, having perceived these responses, to misinterpret their motivational intent. Both these techniques involve the use of an ego defense, *rationalization*, which permits the individual to misinterpret the motivational aim of those perceived aspects of his behavior which reduce the tension of a consciously unacceptable motive.

Attitudes which serve to facilitate the rationalization of behavior which is maximally reductive of a consciously unacceptable motive. As may be concluded from the foregoing material, rationalization is inferred whenever the individual interprets his behavior in the light of his consciously acceptable motives, although it is, in fact, reductive of his consciously unacceptable motives. Since rationalization permits an individual to have his cake and eat it too, it is a widely used mechanism of ego defense. Its use in our own culture appears to be especially encouraged by our emphasis on logic and reason, on the one hand, and religious values, on the other. Thus, in our society one can hardly pass a day without being obliged to offer a rational or morally acceptable reason for some aspect of one's behavior.

A few commonplace examples will illustrate the manner in which attitudes may facilitate the mechanism of rationalization. Perhaps the most disarming instance of rationalization occurs when an individual interprets his patently destructive behavior in the light of an altruistic rather than an aggressive motive. Indeed, it is ironical to note that some of modern man's greatest atrocities against his fellow men have been committed in the name of the Christian God of love and forgiveness. Thus, the leaders of the Inquisition tortured, and even put to death, those persons who, from the standpoint of the Inquisition, did not have the proper attitude toward Christianity. Similarly, in every modern war between nations, Christian clergymen have frequently invoked the name of God as they rallied to the patriotic support of their countries.[22] By seeing God on their side, the clergymen could interpret hostile actions toward the enemy country as the expression of God's will.

Of course, consciously unacceptable aggression is not the only motive whose maximally reductive responses are widely rationalized. As was indicated previously in the discussion of projection, our society also tends strongly to disapprove of the sexual motive. Consequently, behavior which is obviously related to the reduction of sexual tensions may be rationalized as an expression of motives other than the sexual one. Extreme examples of this sort of rationalization may sometimes be seen among persons who serve on censorship boards—agencies, often self-appointed, which presume to protect the moral virtue of the public in general or that of some particular social group. Such persons may seek to justify their constant contact with pornography as expressing their altruistic concern for the tender hearts and minds of the youth of the nation; or, once again, they may see themselves as instruments of God's will, helping to guard His flock from sin and Satan.

To support such rationalizations, a censor may be inclined to accept the following sorts of attitude: (1) that man is essentially a creature of unbridled impulse; (2) that social life and, indeed, civilization itself would be destroyed if people were not taught to check their licentious inclinations; (3) that it is criminal to shirk active participation in work which contributes to the moral elevation of mankind.

Attitudes which facilitate the rationalization of partially reductive responses to consciously unacceptable motives. It has already been shown how attitudes may facilitate the rationalization of maximally reductive overt responses to a consciously unacceptable motive. But insofar as partially reductive symptoms are perceived by the individual, they must also be rationalized. There are, for example, individuals who feel compelled to wash their hands so frequently that their skin gets raw and chafed. This compulsive symptom may indirectly reduce the guilt which is aroused by an unconscious masturbatory motive. Of course, the individual does not realize the symbolic function of his hand-washing compulsion. Nevertheless, he perceives his behavior, and is often obliged to "explain" it to himself as well as others. For example, he may frequently have to leave the company of others in order to fulfill the dictates of his compulsion. And since he does not wish to interpret, or have others interpret, his hand washing as an indication of mental derangement, he seeks to find a suitable rationale for it. Thus, he may seek to justify it as an appropriate precaution in a world rife with germs and filth. Accordingly, he may develop very positive attitudes toward public health agencies and measures, principles of sanitation, new drugs, disinfectants, and pesticides. Conversely, he may develop very unfavorable attitudes toward dirt, old-fashioned plumbing, and hotels which do not provide a sink in the bedroom.

[22] J. F. Brown, *Psychology and the Social Order*, New York, McGraw-Hill, 1936.

In regard to the rationalization of a more subtle symptom, we may again cite the illustration of an overprotective mother whose solicitude actually produces destructive rather than constructive effects upon her child's welfare. Such a mother may facilitate the justification of her excessive solicitude by forming attitudes which, in general, emphasize the dangers a child may encounter in the process of interacting with his environment. Thus, in regard to the child's potential playmates, the mother may eagerly accept any prevailing psychological or philosophical doctrine which portrays children (not her own, of course) as being little animals who are driven by uncontrollable aggressive urges. On the other hand, she may be violently opposed to child-rearing ideologies which advocate parental permissiveness and emphasize the essential role which the child's own misadventures may play in building his ego.

SUMMARY

In an effort to implement the systematic application of psychoanalytic theory to empirical research on social attitudes, this paper has shown how various facets of psychoanalytic thought may be used to interrelate the concepts of motive, conflict, ego defense, and attitude. After defining and discussing each of these four broad concepts, the presentation focused upon the particular manner in which specific attitudes may contribute to the reduction of tension generated by specific motives. Accordingly, the functional relationships between attitudes and both consciously acceptable and consciously unacceptable motives were explored in detail. Finally, since it was held that the expression of an unconscious motive is always mediated by one of the ego defenses, examples were given of the ways in which social attitudes may facilitate the operation of the following ego defenses: denial, identification with aggressor, repression, projection, reaction formation, and rationalization.

— · — · — · — · — · — · — · — · — · — · — · — · —

WILLIAM GRIFFITT
DONN BYRNE

*Attitude Similarity and Attraction**

An essential step in the development of normal science is the acquisition of a paradigm characterized by a body of corroborated procedures, operations, measuring devices, empirical laws, and a theoretical superstructure. This paper de-

*William Griffitt and Donn Byrne, "Procedures in the Paradigmatic Study of Attitude Similarity and Attraction," *Representative Research in Social Psychology* 1 (1970): 33–48. Reprinted by permission.

scribes a paradigm for the study of interpersonal attraction. The general procedures and findings are summarized in order to place in context some of the
methodological issues raised by this research. Data are presented to indicate
stability of the stimulus variables and subjects' attitudes over the time interval
between attitude measurement and experimental confrontation with a stranger.
A theoretical model in which the evaluation of any given stimulus object is a
positive linear function of the proportion of positively reinforcing stimuli associated with it is described.

Kuhn (1962) has emphasized that an essential step in the development of what he
terms "normal science" is the acquisition of a paradigm. A scientific paradigm is characterized by a specific body of research consisting of procedures, operations, measuring
devices, empirical laws, and a theoretical superstructure—all accepted by a group of
scientists. Within any given research areas, then, acquisition of a paradigm involves explicit agreement about procedures, and so on, at least among a small group of individuals
interested in the same phenomena. Such agreement makes it possible to accumulate
knowledge through attempts to increase the precision, reliability, and scope with which
the facts are known and through continual formulation and modification of theoretical
propositions put forward to account for the data.

Throughout the past seventy or eighty years, the study of attitude similarity and
attraction has been characterized by the use of diverse methodologies, operations, measuring devices, and theoretical orientations (Byrne, 1969). The resulting potpourri of data
clearly resembles a pre-paradigm period of research that Kuhn defines as " . . . a condition
in which all members practice science but in which their gross product scarcely resembles
science at all" (1962, p. 100). That is, cumulative scientific progress is not possible when
investigators interested in a single phenomenon not only utilize different procedures and
operations, but even become enamored with "methodological creativity" to the extent
that a single investigator seldom employs consistent procedures across experiments.

The procedures, operations, measures, and general body of research findings described here represent one attempt at achieving paradigmatic research within the area of
attitude similarity and attraction. The basic assumptions of this particular mini-paradigm
have been summarized previously (Byrne, 1969, p. 48):

> First, a meaningful increase in knowledge is possible only if the same operations
> or empirically determined equivalents of those operations serve as connecting
> links across experiments. Second, theoretical constructs refer to the experimen-
> tal variables and their extensions and derivatives rather than to the "real-life"
> variables from which these operational constructs originated. Third, as a matter
> of individual inclination, the initial theoretical model is broadly based on be-
> havior theory and utilizes a stimulus-response language system. It is hoped that
> the seeming banality of the first two statements will be mitigated by the knowl-
> edge that such assumptions are not universally shared.

GENERAL PROCEDURES AND FINDINGS

The basic procedure used in much of the initial work in this line of research involves
a variant of an approach first utilized by Smith (1957). Individually, or in small groups,
subjects are told that they are taking part in a study of interpersonal judgment in which
they will be given certain information about another individual and then asked to make
several judgments concerning him. Prior to exposure to the stranger's attitudes, subjects

are administered an attitude scale designed to assess their opinions on a variety of issues. The information about the stranger provided during the experimental session is the stranger's responses to the same attitude issues.

Before going into detail about methodological considerations, we will attempt a brief summary of a number of studies that have been conducted within this paradigm. Byrne and Nelson (1965) demonstrated that there is a positive linear relationship between the *proportion* of the total group of attitudes on which the stranger and the subject are in agreement and the subject's attraction toward that stranger. This functional relationship between similarity and attraction has consistently been supported (Byrne, 1969). With respect to procedural equivalences, it has been demonstrated that the linear relationship is maintained when attitudinal information is presented on tape recordings, in sound color movies (Byrne & Clore, 1966), and through face-to-face interactions (Byrne & Griffitt, 1966b). Further stimulus extensions to nonattitudinal similarity-dissimilarity, such as defense mechanisms (Byrne & Griffitt, 1969; Bryne, Griffitt & Stefaniak, 1967), self concept (Griffitt, 1966, 1969), and intellectual ability (London, 1967), demonstrate the generality of the similarity-attraction relationship across stimulus variables. It should be noted that in these investigations of the effects of stimulus variation, an empirical link across experiments has been maintained through the consistent inclusion of the same response measure to assess attraction. This practice does not imply that the Interpersonal Judgment Scale (IJS) that we have used constitutes the only conceivable way to measure attraction or even necessarily the best way; consistency of measurement is stressed for the seemingly obvious reason that it is the only way to obtain meaningful results across experiments.

The similarity-attraction function has been found to be quite consistent across a wide variety of samples beyond the familiar college subject population. The relationship holds among children at least down through the fourth grade level (Byrne & Griffitt, 1966a), among poorly educated individuals of lower socioeconomic status such as members of the Job Corps Training Program, and among older individuals including surgical patients at a medical school hospital, alcoholics, and schizophrenics (Byrne, Griffitt, Hudgins, & Reeves, in press). In cross-cultural research, the similarity-attraction effect has also been found among Japanese, Indian, and Mexican students in studies paralleling those with American samples (Byrne, Gouaux, Griffitt, Lamberth, Murakawa, Prasad, Prasad, & Ramirez, in preparation).

In research designed to extend the generality of the response measure, the IJS is used *along with* an additional measure or measures. Other behavioral indices that yield results equivalent to the IJS include a social distance scale (Schwartz, 1966), voting preference (Byrne, Bond, & Diamond, in press), and a wooden judgment apparatus in which tokens are inserted to indicate feelings (Byrne, Lamberth, Palmer, & London, in press). Other measures of attraction currently under investigation include nonverbal behavioral acts, such as seating preferences (Baskett & Byrne, 1969; Clore, 1969) and visual contact (Efran, 1969).

METHODOLOGICAL QUESTIONS

Before moving to a discussion of the theoretical interpretation of the attraction findings, we will describe examples of the way in which research within a paradigm inevitably leads to increased concentration on methodology. Interest in and concern with analysis of procedures are, of course, restricted almost entirely to those working within a given paradigm. Though such concern is essential to disentangle empirical complexities and to permit progress, reports of methodological studies are unlikely to be publishable in the ordinary journals of a busy pre-paradigmatic field. Those with editing responsibilities in social psychological journals often express the idea that articles are acceptable if they contain material that is "newsworthy," "surprising," "novel," or "counterintuitive." These journalistic criteria often lead to keen titles and lively reading matter, but they offer scant encouragement to efforts at methodological evaluation and improvement.

THE ATTITUDE SCALE

The attitude scales used have varied in number of topics ranging from four (Byrne, Clore, & Worchel, 1966) to 56 (Byrne, London, & Griffitt, 1968). Individuals are asked to indicate their opinions on such topics as belief in God, political parties, gardening, and a variety of other issues. Responses are made on simple scales with the following format:

7. Belief in God (check one)

_____ I strongly believe that there is a God.
_____ I believe that there is a God.
_____ I feel that perhaps there is a God.
_____ I feel that perhaps there is no God.
_____ I strongly believe that there is no God.

THE ATTRACTION MEASURE

The measure of attraction consists of simple rating scales that ask two of the most frequently used questions in sociometric research. Each subject is asked to indicate whether he feels that he would like or dislike the stranger and whether he believes he would enjoy or dislike working with the stranger. These two items are:

5. Personal Feelings (check one)

_____ I feel that I would probably like this person very much.
_____ I feel that I would probably like this person.
_____ I feel that I would probably like this person to a slight degree.
_____ I feel that I would probably neither particularly like nor particularly dislike this person.
_____ I feel that I would probably dislike this person to a slight degree.
_____ I feel that I would probably dislike this person.
_____ I feel that I would probably dislike this person very much.

6. Working Together in an Experiment (check one)

_____ I believe that I would very much dislike working with this person in an experiment.
_____ I believe that I would dislike working with this person in an experiment.
_____ I believe that I would dislike working with this person in an experiment to a slight degree.
_____ I believe that I would neither particularly dislike nor particularly enjoy working with this person in an experiment.

———— I believe that I would enjoy working with this person in an experiment to a slight degree.

———— I believe that I would enjoy working with this person in an experiment.

———— I believe that I would very much enjoy working with this person in an experiment.

Each of these two variables is measured on a seven-point scale, scored from one to seven, and then summed to constitute the measure of attraction which ranges from two (most negative) to 14 (most positive). Conceptualized as a two-item response measure, the attraction score has been found to have a split-half reliability of .85 (Byrne & Nelson, 1965).

The attraction measures are the last two items in the six-item IJS (Byrne, 1966, pp. 41–43) in order to disguise to some degree the major purpose of the experiment and to lend credence to the instructions concerning interpersonal judgment. The first four items, which follow the format of the attraction items, call for evaluations of the stranger's intelligence, knowledge of current events, morality, and adjustment.

DIFFERENTIAL ITEM IMPACT

With the use of multiple attitude items which vary with respect to content or topic, an immediate question is whether or not items with different content have differential "impact" on the subjects. Topic variables such as importance and interest become relevant concerns within this context. A pool of 56 topics has been scaled with respect to importance (Byrne & Nelson, 1964) and interest (Clore & Baldridge, 1968). The latter investigators reported that importance and interest ratings are highly correlated ($r = .80$) and are to a large extent interchangeable. The conditions under which topic impact variables may be expected to exert effects on attraction responses to agreement-disagreement have been summarized by Byrne, London, and Griffitt (1968) and Clore and Baldridge (1968). Specifically, if a stranger expresses opinions on items heterogeneous in importance and if the similarity level is at an intermediate point between .00 and 1.00, then items of differential importance affect attraction differentially.

THE SIMULATION METHOD

Two approaches have been used to determine the response of the simulated stranger; each has certain inherent advantages and disadvantages.

With the *unique stranger technique*, the bogus attitude responses are prepared in advance by the experimenter according to a prearranged schedule of proportion of agreements dictated by the experimental design. The specific items chosen to be similar or dissimilar to those of the subject are randomly selected for each subject within each agreement condition.[1] The variation of stimuli within each cell results in control via randomization of both the content of the items on which similarity occurs and the order of presentation of similar and dissimilar items.

[1] When studying the effects of differential topic importance or interest, selection of specific topics for agreement-disagreement is systematic.

As shown earlier, each item consists of a six-point scale with three points representing varying strengths of opinion in one direction (for example, pro-integration) and three points representing varying strengths of opinion in the other direction (for example, anti-integration). Using the "constant discrepancy" simulation method, similarity is defined as a response that is one scale point away from the subject's response but on the same side of the neutral point as the subject's response. A dissimilar response is defined as one that is three scale points discrepant from the subject's response on the opposite side of the neutral point. The use of this constant discrepancy pattern as shown in Table 1

TABLE 1. CONSTANT DISCREPANCY SIMULATION PATTERN

Subject's Response	Response of Simulated Stranger	
	Similar	Dissimilar
1	2	4
2	1 or 3	5
3	2	6
4	5	1
5	4 or 6	2
6	5	3

eliminates discrepancy differences among similar items *and* dissimilar items and insures that the total discrepancy will be the same for each subject within each similarity condition. That is, with the constant discrepancy method, proportion of similar attitudes and discrepancy are totally dependent stimulus dimensions ($r = 1.00$).

Why all of this concern with a seemingly minute aspect of the stimulus? Whenever investigators are involved in predicting a specific response, any variable influencing that response becomes a focus of interest. The discrepancy effect was first demonstrated by Nelson (1965), and it has been shown that attraction responses are jointly and independently affected by discrepancy and by proportion of similarity (Byrne, Clore, & Griffitt, 1967).

The second simulation method, the *standard stranger technique*, is useful under certain circumstances. As opposed to the unique stranger technique where each subject receives a tailormade bogus stranger, each standard stranger subject receives one of two established patterns of responses from a stranger. One simulation Pattern (A) is selected through the use of a table of random numbers, and a second pattern (B) is prepared as a mirror-image of the first. Half of the subjects then receive the A pattern and half the B pattern of responses. Here, proportion of similar attitudes and discrepancy are determined for each subject *after* he has participated in the experiment, and are dependent on the chance relationships between the randomly selected responses of A or B which he recieved and his own responses to the attitude scale. With a reasonably large N the distribution of similarity values will be aproximately normal with a mean similarity proportion of .50 and a mean discrepancy per item score of about 1.75.

The unique stranger design enables the experimenter to control precisely the similarity conditions to which individual subjects are assigned. It also enables him to utilize simulation methods allowing for agreement-disagreement on specific combinations of items and, in general, to maintain considerable control over additional stimulus variables in which he might be interested. The primary disadvantage of this method is that at least two sessions (pretesting and experiment) are required, and they must be separated by a time interval of sufficient length to prepare the stranger's responses for each subject.

Use of the standard technique allows the entire experiment to be conducted in a single session. Each subject first responds to the attitude questionnaire and then receives the bogus responses prepared in advance according to the standard A or B pattern. The essential disadvantage of this technique is that the experiment has little control over the number of subjects falling in specific similarity proportion conditions or the similarity condition in which any specific subject falls. In addition, no control is possible over item discrepancy scores which will vary across subjects within proportion conditions. With a standard stranger design, correlations between similarity proportions and item discrepancy scores have been found to vary from -.45 to -.93.

THE UNIQUE STRANGER TECHNIQUE AND STABILITY OVER TIME

There is a potential problem with the unique stranger technique that could distort the findings of such research. When the subject's attitudes are measured at Time I and the stranger's attitudes are presented at Time II, any attitude change on the part of the subject results in differences between subject-stranger similarity as defined by the experimenter and as experienced by the subject. Thus, within our paradigm, it is important to know the test-retest reliability of the attitude scale items and (a related question) the test-retest reliability of the stimulus dimensions manipulated in the experiment.

Item reliability has been investigated by Nelson (1965) and by the present authors. The two studies employed different, but overlapping, twelve-item attitude scales as well as two-week time intervals. Subjects in the Nelson study were 40 undergraduate students in the freshman English course at the University of Texas; in the present study 36 Texas undergraduates in the introductory psychology course served as subjects. The reliability coefficients are shown in Table 2. It is evident that responses to these issues are reasonably stable over the two-week interval, so one may assume with considerable confidence that the subjects' opinions at the time of the experiment are substantially the same as at pretesting. It is also clear that some topics (for example, community bomb shelters, welfare legislation, and dating in high school) tend to fluctuate over time more than others (for instance, fraternities and sororities, money, and war). Therefore, error variance in measuring attraction should be reduced when the experimenter employs the more stable type of attitude item.

A second aspect of the stability question has to do with possible changes in the values of the similarity proportions and item discrepancy scores because of changes in the subject. The item stability coefficients shown in Table 2 suggest that substantial changes should not be expected, but less indirect evidence is needed as well.

Based on an experiment using the 12 topics indicated in Table 2 with 36 subjects, test-retest data were obtained with respect to proportion and discrepancy. Two weeks after pretesting, subjects were again asked to fill out the 12-item attitude scale and to examine the simulated responses of an anonymous stranger. Similarity proportions and discrepancy scores were calculated on the basis of both pretest and retest attitudinal responses of the subjects. The test-retest coefficients were found to be .85 (proportion) and .88 (discrepancy) across the two-week interval. The pretest and retest mean values for

TABLE 2. TWO-WEEK TEST-RETEST RELIABILITIES OF ATTITUDE ITEMS

Topic	Reliability Coefficient	
	Present Study	Nelson (1965)
Classical music	.85	
Community bomb shelters		.74
Dating in high school		.55
Drinking		.91
Foreign language requirement		.85
Fraternities and sororities	.92	.88
Grading system	.80	
Integration	.86	
Men's vs. women's adjustment to stress		.89
Money	.93	
Political parties	.80	.81
Preparedness for war	.80	.71
Religion	.78	
Smoking		.87
Strict discipline of children	.86	.73
Tipping		.73
Undergraduate marriages	.89	
War	.95	
Welfare legislation	.82	.69

these two variables are shown in Table 3. The reliabilities of the stimulus conditions would seem to be of sufficient magnitude to alleviate strong concerns over the use of this technique. Further, the stimulus-response relationships using the usual stimulus values

TABLE 3. MEAN PRETEST AND RETEST VALUES OF PROPORTION AND DISCREPANCY VARIABLES

	Pretest	Retest
Proportion of similar attitudes	.49	.49
Discrepancy per item	1.69	1.70

(established on the basis of the pretest) did not differ from those calculated on the basis of the retest. For similarity-attraction, the correlations were .37 and .39; for discrepancy-attraction, the correlations were −.39 and −.45.

Although slight differences between techniques have been detected in the slope and Y-intercept of the similarity-attraction function (Byrne, 1969), the shape and essential features of the function are not affected by different simulation techniques, and should be based simply on the demands of the experimental design.

METHODOLOGY AND THE PARADIGM

The procedures and operations outlined here have been extensively utilized in the research described earlier in an attempt to bring research on attitude similarity and attraction into the framework of a paradigmatic science. The consequence of such methodological consistency is, not surprisingly, empirical consistency. Research findings become cumulative and comparable across experiments. Increased precision, reliability, and scope is obtained. One's goal in science is nether surprise nor novelty, though such a statement is apparently "counterintuitive" to many social psychologists. If, however, surprises or novel findings do occur (Byrne, Lamberth, Palmer, & London, in press), the experimenter may be relatively confident that the anomaly is not a function of gratuitous methodological variations. Kuhn (1962, p. 52) points out:

> Without the special apparatus that is constructed mainly for anticipated functions, the results that lead ultimately to novelty could not occur. And even when the apparatus exists, novelty ordinarily emerges only for the man who, knowing *with precision* what he should expect, is able to recognize that something has gone wrong. Anomaly appears only against the background provided by the paradigm.

THEORETICAL FRAMEWORK

As suggested at the beginning of this article, the authors favor a theoretical model based on behavior theory utilizing a stimulus-response language system. More specifically, following a conditioning paradigm, it has been proposed (Clore & Byrne, in press) that the evaluation of any given stimulus object is a positive linear function of the proportion of positively reinforcing stimuli that have been associated with it. Stimuli with positive and negative reinforcement properties are hypothesized to act as unconditioned stimuli which, respectively, evoke positive and negative implicit affective responses. Any discriminable stimulus, including a person, associated with such unconditioned stimuli becomes a conditioned stimulus capable of eliciting the implicit affective responses. The affective responses, in turn, mediate overt evaluative responses, such as verbal assessments, preferences, and approach-avoidance behaviors.

With respect to the relationship between similarity and attraction, the fit between model and data has been demonstrated in four distinct ways. First, it has been shown that agreeing and disagreeing attitude statements act, respectively, as positive and negative reinforcers in learning situations (Byrne, Griffitt, & Clore, 1968; Byrne, Young, & Griffitt, 1966; Golightly & Byrne, 1964; Lamberth & Gay, 1969; Reitz, Douey, & Mason, 1968). Second, agreeing and disagreeing attitude statements have been shown to evoke positive and negative evaluations of feelings (Clore & Byrne, in press). Third, when previously neutral strangers are presented in association with agreeing or disagreeing statements, the strangers are subsequently and appropriately evaluated, either positively or negatively (Clore & Byrne, in press; Sachs, 1969). Fourth, when nonattitudinal reinforcements are associated with another person, the effect on attraction parallels that found with attitudes (Golightly, 1965; Griffitt, 1968; Griffitt & Guay, in press; Hughes, 1969; Kaplan & Olczak, 1969; McDonald, 1962).

With all stimulus elements that influence attraction (personality trait-descriptions, race, behavioral preferences, physical attractiveness, attitudes, economic status, evaluative statements) conceptualized as constituting positive and negative units of information of varying weights, it has been helpful to extend the model to account for any stimulus-attraction relationship. Once coefficients have been weighted for different stimulus elements, it is possible to predict attraction responses as a linear function of the weighted proportion of positive stimuli on the basis of the formula:

$$Y = m \left[\frac{\Sigma(P \times M)}{\Sigma(P \times M) + \Sigma(N \times M)} \right] + k$$

in which Y is the attraction response, P and N are positive and negative stimulus elements, M is a weighting coefficient, and m and k are empirically derived constants (Byrne, 1969; Byrne & Rhamey, 1965).

OVERVIEW

The purpose of the present report has been to outline a program of research on the determinants of interpersonal attraction. The overall strategy has been to isolate and analyze a lawful relationship in a simple and controllable experimental paradigm and to gradually increase the complexity of its stimulus and response components through a series of systematic extensions of its original boundary conditions. This may be seen as a process ranging from narrow and artificial laboratory experimentation on one extreme to broad application in a complex real life setting on the other. Applications to date have included such diverse possibilities as computer dating (Lindgren & Byrne, in press), including cooperative hehavior in interpersonal bargaining (Tornatzky & Geiwitz, 1968), persuasion (Corrozi & Rosnow, 1968), and learning in the classroom (Lott, 1969). It is obviously assumed that the most fruitful approach to such generality and complexity is best achieved by the progression from simplicity to complexity.

Often, pressured by the very real demands of society, social psychologists are tempted to provide immediate solutions to highly complex real life problems without the necessary conceptual or factual foundation valid application requires. Such solutions often prove to be verbal chimeras. With respect to the research endeavor described here, we contend that one must thoroughly understand the determinants of attraction as measured by, for example, two seven-point rating scales before expecting to understand the determinants of love and hate as encountered in the real world. The present emphasis on methodological and conceptual consistency and on gradual progression from narrow simplicity to broad complexity within a unified research paradigm is proposed not only as a program of basic research in social psychology but also as the most utilitarian approach to the potential solution of the myriad problems of interpersonal relationships.

REFERENCES

Baskett, G. G., & Byrne, D. Seating choice as a function of attitudinal similarity-dissimilarity. Paper presented at meetings of the Southwestern Psychological Association, Austin, April, 1969.

Byrne, D. *An introduction to personality: A research approach*. Englewood Cliffs, New Jersey: Prentice-Hall, 1966.

Byrne, D. Attitudes and attraction. In L. Berkowitz (Ed.), *Advances in experimental social psychology*. Vol. 4. New York: Academic Press, 1969. Pp. 35–89.

Byrne, D., Bond, M. H., & Diamond, M. J. Response to political candidates as a function of attitude similarity-dissimilarity. *Human Relations*, in press.

Byrne, D., & Clore, G. L., Jr. Predicting interpersonal attraction toward strangers presented in three different stimulus modes. *Psychonomic Science*, 1966, *4*, 239–240.

Byrne, D., Clore, G. L., & Griffitt, W. Response discrepancy versus attitude similarity-dissimilarity as determinants of attraction. *Psychonomic Science*, 1967, *7*, 397–398.

Byrne, D., Clore, G. L., Jr., & Worchel, P. The effect of economic similarity-dissimilarity on interpersonal attraction. *Journal of Personality and Social Psychology*, 1966, *4*, 220–224.

Byrne, D., Gouaux, C., Griffitt, W., Lamberth, J., Murakawa, N., Prasad, M. B., Prasad, S. A., & Ramirez, M. The twain meets in the similarity-attraction relationship. In preparation.

Byrne, D., & Griffitt, W. A developmental investigation of the law of attraction. *Journal of Personality and Social Psychology*, 1966, *4*, 699–702. (a)

Byrne, D., & Griffitt, W. Similarity versus liking: A clarification. *Psychonomic Science*, 1966, *6*, 295–296. (b)

Byrne, D., & Griffitt, W. Similarity and awareness of similarity of personality characteristics as determinants of attraction. *Journal of Experimental Research in Personality*, 1969, *3*, 179–186.

Byrne, D., Griffitt, W., & Clore, G. L., Jr. Attitudinal reinforcement effects as a function of stimulus homogeneity-heterogeneity. *Journal of Verbal Learning and Verbal Behavior*, 1968, *7*, 962–964.

Byrne, D., Griffitt, W., Hudgins, W., & Reeves, K. Attitude similarity-dissimilarity and attraction: Generality beyond the college sophomore. *Journal of Social Psychology*, in press.

Byrne, D., Griffitt, W., & Stefaniak, D. Attraction and similarity of personality characteristics. *Journal of Personality and Social Psychology*. 1967, *5*, 82–90.

Byrne, D., Lamberth, J., Palmer, J., & London, O. Sequential effects as a function of explicit and implicit interpolated attraction responses. *Journal of Personality and Social Psychology*, in press.

Byrne, D., London, O., & Griffitt, W. The effect of topic importance and attitude similarity-dissimilarity on attraction in an intrastranger design. *Psychonomic Science*, 1968, *11*, 303–304.

Byrne, D., & Nelson, D. Attraction as a function of attitude similarity-dissimilarity: The effect of topic importance. *Psychonomic Science*, 1964, *1*, 93–94.

Byrne, D., & Nelson, D. Attraction as a linear function of proportion of positive reinforcement. *Journal of Personality and Social Psychology*, 1965, *1*, 659–663.

Byrne, D., & Rhamey, R. Magnitude of positive and negative reinforcements as a determinant of attraction. *Journal of Personality and Social Psychology*, 1965, *2*, 884–889.

Byrne, D., Young, R. K., & Griffitt, W. The reinforcement properties of attitude statements. *Journal of Experimental Research in Personality*, 1966, *1*, 226–276.

Clore, G. L. Attraction and interpersonal behavior. Paper presented at meetings of the Southwestern Psychological Association, Austin, April, 1969.

Clore, G. L., & Baldridge, B. Interpersonal attraction: the role of agreement and topic interest. *Journal of Personality and Social Psychology*, 1968, *9*, 340–346.

Clore, G. L., & Byrne, D. The process of personality interaction. In R. B. Cattell (Ed.), *Handbook of modern personality theory*. Chicago: Aldine, in press.

Corrozi, J. F., & Rosnow, R. L. Consonant and dissonant communications as positive and negative reinforcements in opinion change. *Journal of Personality and Social Psychology*, 1968, *8*, 27–30.

Efran, M. G. Visual interaction and interpersonal attraction. Unpublished doctoral dissertation, University of Texas, 1969.

Golightly, C. C. The reinforcement properties of attitude similarity-dissimilarity. Unpublished doctoral dissertation, University of Texas, 1965.

Golightly, C., & Byrne, D. Attitude statements as positive and negative reinforcements. *Science*, 1964, *146*, 798–799.

Griffitt, W. B. Interpersonal attraction as a function of self-concept and personality similarity-dissimilarity. *Journal of Personality and Social Psychology*, 1966, *4*, 581–584.

Griffitt, W. B. Attraction toward a stranger as a function of direct and associated reinforcement. *Psychonomic Science*, 1968, *11*, 147–148.

Griffitt, W. B. Personality similarity and self-concept as determinants of interpersonal attraction. *Journal of Social Psychology*, 1969, *78*, 137–146.

Griffitt, W., & Guay, P. "Object" evaluation and conditioned affect. *Journal of Experimental Research in Personality*, in press.

Hughes, R. L. "Object" evaluation: a reinterpretation of affect conditioning in the reinforcement model of attraction. Unpublished master's thesis, University of Texas, 1969.

Kaplan, M. F., & Olczak, P. V. Attitude similarity and direct reinforcement as determinants of attraction. Unpublished manuscript, 1969.

Kuhn, T. S. *The structure of scientific revolutions.* Chicago: University of Chicago Press, 1962.

Lamberth, J., & Gay, R. A. Differential reward magnitude using a performance task and attitudinal stimuli. Paper presented at meetings of the Western Psychological Association, Vancouver, June, 1969.

Lindgren, H. C., & Byrne, D. *Psychology: an introduction to a behavioral science.* (3rd ed.) New York: Wiley, in press.

London, O. H. Interpersonal attraction and abilities: social desirability or similarity to self? Unpublished master's thesis, University of Texas, 1967.

Lott, A. J. Some indirect measures of interpersonal attraction. Paper presented at meetings of the Southwestern Psychological Association, Austin, April, 1969.

McDonald, R. D. The effect of reward-punishment and affiliation need on interpersonal attraction. Unpublished doctoral dissertation, University of Texas, 1962.

Nelson, D. A. The effect of differential magnitude of reinforcement on interpersonal attraction. Unpublished doctoral dissertation. University of Texas, 1965.

Reitz, W. E., Douey, J., & Mason, G. Role of homogeneity and centrality of attitude domain on reinforcing properties of attitude statements. *Journal of Experimental Research in Personality*, 1968, *3*, 120–125.

Sachs, D. H. Differential conditioning of evaluative responses to neutral stimuli through association with attitude statements. Paper presented at meetings of the Southwestern Psychological Association, Austin, April, 1969.

Schwartz, M. S. Prediction of individual differences in the arousal of the effectance motive and in interpersonal attraction toward a stranger identified with the arousal of the effectance motive. Unpublished doctoral dissertation, University of Texas, 1966.

Smith, A. J. Similarity of values and its relation to acceptance and projection of similarity. *Journal of Psychology*, 1957, *43*, 251–260.

Tornatzky, L., & Geiwitz, P. J. The effects of threat and attraction on interpersonal bargaining. *Psychonomic Science*, 1968, *13*, 125–126.

5 · COGNITIVE CONSISTENCY THEORIES OF ATTITUDE CHANGE

FRITZ HEIDER

Balance Theory in Attitude Change*

Attitudes towards persons and causal unit formations influence each other. An attitude towards an event can alter the attitude towards the person who caused the event, and, if the attitudes towards a person and an event are similar, the event is easily ascribed to the person. A balanced configuration exists if the attitudes towards the parts of a causal unit are similar (1).

It is tempting to generalize from this statement and to omit the restriction to causal unit formation. Do units in general interact with attitudes in a similar way?

In trying out this hypothesis we shall understand by attitude the positive or negative relationship of a person p to another person o, or to an impersonal entity x which may be a situation, an event, an idea, or a thing, etc. Examples are: to like, to love, to esteem, to value, and their opposites. A positive relation of this kind will be written L, a negative one $\sim L$. Thus, pLo means p likes, loves, or values o, or, expressed differently, o is positive for p.

The relation "unit" will be written U. Examples are: similarity, proximity, causality, membership, possession, or belonging. pUx can mean, for instance, p owns x, or p made x; $p \sim Ux$ means p does not own x, etc. Other relations which, in many ways, seem to function like units are: p is familiar with, used to, or knows well o or x, and p is in situation x. In lumping together all these relations we are, of course, aware of the dissimilarities between them. Only in a first approximation can they be treated as belonging to one class.

The hypothesis may be stated in greater detail thus: (a) A balanced state exists if an entity has the same dynamic character in all possible respects. (e.g., if p admires and at

*Fritz Heider, "Attitudes and Cognitive Organization," *The Journal of Psychology* 21 (1946): 107–112. Reprinted by permission of the publisher and the author.

the same time likes o); in other words, if pLo or $p \sim Lo$ is true for all meanings of L. (We may anticipate here that the analogous statement for pLo does not seem to hold in a general way.) (b) A balanced state exists if all parts of a unit have the same dynamic character (i.e., if all are positive, or all are negative), and if entities with different dynamic character are segregated from each other. If no balanced state exists, then forces towards this state will arise. Either the dynamic characters will change, or the unit relations will be changed through action or through cognitive reorganization. If a change is not possible, the state of imbalance will produce tension.

The first part of the hypothesis refers to influence of dynamic relations or attitudes on each other. Since the different dynamic relations are not included in each other logically ("p likes o" does not imply "p admires o"), the same o or x can be positive in one respect and negative in another. An example in point is the conflict between duty and inclination. A tendency exists to make the different dynamic relations agree with each other by means of cognitive restructuring (excuses or rationalizations). Another example would be the tendency to admire loved persons and to love admired persons.

More numerous are the possibilities to which the second part of the hypothesis refers. They can be grouped according to the entities making up the configurations: (a) person and non-person (p, x); (b) two persons (p, o); (c) two persons and a non-person (p, o, x); (d) three persons (p, o, q). Many of the examples seem to substantiate the hypothesis. Examples which do not fit may eventually lead to greater insight into the nature of the dynamic characters and of the unit relations. All examples refer to p's life space. This is true even of oLp which therefore means: p thinks that o likes or admires p.

(a) p *and* x. Since the own person (p) is usually positive, a balanced state will exist if p likes what he is united with in any way, or if he dislikes the x he is segregated from. The cases $(pLx) + (pUx)$ and $(p \sim Lx) + (p \sim Ux)$ are balanced. Examples: p likes the things he made; p wants to own the things he likes; p values what he is accustomed to.

(b) p *and* o. Analogously, the two balanced states for p and o will be: $(pLo) + (pUo)$ and $(p \sim Lo) + (p \sim Uo)$. Examples: p likes his children, people similar to him; p is uneasy if he has to live with people he does not like; p tends to imitate admired persons; p likes to think that loved persons are similar to him.

pUo is a symmetrical relation, i.e., pUo implies oUp. That they belong to a unit is true for p and o in the same way, though their roles in the unit may be different (for instance, if U is a causal unit). However, pLo is non-symmetrical since it does not imply oLp. It is in line with the general hypothesis to assume that a balanced state exists if pLo and oLp (or $p \sim Lo$ and $o \sim Lp$) are true at the same time. Attraction or repulsion between p and o are then two-way affairs; the relation is in symmetrical harmony. pLo is a non-symmetrical relation logically, but psychologically it tends to become symmetrical. Examples: p wants to be loved by an admired o; p dislikes people who despise him. oLp is similar to pLo in its relation to pUo. Examples: p likes to meet people who, he is told, admire him.

(c) p, o, *and* x. The combinations become more numerous with three entities making up the configurations. Only a few possibilities can be mentioned. We shall always give the balanced state in symbols before stating the examples which refer to it.

$(pLo) + (pLx) + (oUx)$. Both o and x are positive and parts of a unit. Examples: p admires clothes of loved o; p wants to benefit his friend o; p likes to think that his friend benefits him. A seeming exception is the case of envy. If o owns x (oUx) and p likes x (pLx), $p \sim Lo$ may often follow. This exception can be derived from the fact that ownership is a one-many relation. A person can own many things but each thing can, ordinarily, be owned only by one person. Therefore "o owns x" excludes "p owns x," or oUx implies $p \sim Ux$. Since pLx may tend toward pUx, conflict is introduced.

Implications between unit relations often lead to conflict. Lewin's three cases of inner conflict rest on implications. Approach to a positive valence may imply withdrawal from another positive valence. Withdrawal from a negative valence may imply approach to another negative valence. Finally, approach to a positive valence may imply approach to a negative valence if both are located in the same region. Analogously, one can talk of three cases of outer conflict between persons. pUx may imply $o \sim Ux$ (for instance, if U means ownership), and if both want x, conflict (competition) will arise. In the same way conflict appears if p and o want to get away from x but only one of them can do so (if $p \sim Ux$ implies oUx, and vice versa). Lastly, it may happen that p likes x and o hates it, but p and o have to move together (pUx implies oUx, e.g., in marriage). They either can both have x, or both not have it.

Trying out variations of the triad (pLo) + (pLx) + (oUx), we find that (pLo) + (pLx) + (oLx) also represents a balanced case. Examples: p likes what his friend o likes; p likes people with same attitudes. This case is not covered by the hypothesis unless we treat L as equivalent to U. Actually, in many cases the effects of L and U in these configurations seem to be the same. Furthermore, this case shows the psychological transitivity of the L relation. A relation R is transitive if aRb and bRc imply aRc. Thus, p tends to like x if pLo and oLx hold. As in the case of the symmetry of the pLo relation, we again have to stress the difference between logical and psychological aspect. Logically, L is not transitive but there exists a psychological tendency to make it transitive when implications between U relations do not interfere with transitivity. The relation U, too, seems to be in this sense psychologically transitive. (pUo) + (oUx) can lead to pUx: p feels responsible for what people belonging to him do.

Taking into account these considerations, we can reformulate the hypothesis: (a) In the case of two entities, a balanced state exists if the relation between them is positive (or negative) in all respects, i.e., in regard to all meanings of L and U. (b) In the case of three entities, a balanced state exists if all three possible relations are positive in all respects.

The question arises whether, with a triad, one can make any generalizations about balanced cases with negative relations. For instance, (pLo) + ($o \sim Ux$) + ($p \sim Lx$) is balanced. Examples: p likes o because o got rid of something p dislikes. In this case two entities, p and o, are related positively to each other, while both are related negatively to the third entity x. This holds generally: the triad of relations is in balance, if two relations are negative and one positive. This statement can be derived from the assumption that L and U are, in a balanced configuration, exchangeable, symmetrical, and transitive. L and U can then be treated as formally analogous to an identity relation. The "balanced" cases with three terms are for this relation: $a = b, b = c, a = c; a = b, b \neq c, a \neq c;$ $a \neq b, b \neq c, a \neq c$. By substituting L or U for the identity sign one obtains the balanced cases for these relations, though the case with three negative relations does not seem to constitute a good psychological balance, since it is too indetermined.

Therefore, the second part of the hypothesis must be stated as follows: (c) In the case of the three entities, a balanced state exists if all three relations are positive in all respects, or if two are negative and one positive.

$(pLo) + (oLx) + (pUx)$. Examples: p likes o because o admired p's action; p wants his friend o to like p's productions; p wants to do what his friends admire.

$(pUo) + (pLx) + (oLx)$. Examples: p wants his son to like what he likes; p likes x because his son likes it.

(d) p, o, and q. Among the many possible cases we shall only consider one. $(pLo) + (oLq) + (pLq)$. Examples: p wants his two friends to like each other. This example shows, as the parallel case with x instead of q, the psychological transitivity of the L relation.

However, the transitivity of the L relation is here restricted by implications between unit relations when L represents a one-one love relation. p does not want his girl friend o to fall in love with his boy friend q because oLq in this case implies $o \sim Lp$, which conflicts with pLo. Jealousy, as well as envy and competition, is derived from implications between unit relations.

After this discussion of the different possibilities there are several more points worth mentioning which refer to examples of different groups. One is the problem of self evaluation. High self regard of p can be expressed by pLp, low self regard by $p \sim Lp$ (though the two p's in these expressions are not strictly equivalent). All of the examples so far considered presupposed pLp. However, one also has to take into account the possibility of $p \sim Lp$. As to be expected, it plays a rôle contrary to that of pLp. Examples: if p has low self regard he might reject a positive x as too good for him; if p has guilt feelings he will think he ought to be punished; if his friend admires his product he will think it only politeness. A negative action attributed to himself will produce $p \sim Lp$, etc.

The equivalence of the L and U relations seems to be limited by the fact that often the U relation is weaker than the L relation. One can assume, that pLx brings about pUx (p wants to have a thing he likes) more often than pUx produces pLx (p gets to like a thing which belongs to him). Again $(pLo) + (oLx)$ usually will lead to pLx (transitivity), but $(pUo) + (oUx)$ will not do so if there holds at the same time $p \sim Lo$.

We saw that one can derive forces towards actions, or goals, from the configurations. It can also happen, that the choice of means to a goal is determined by these patterns. If p wants to produce oLx, and he knows that oLp holds, he can do so by demonstrating to o the relation pLx, because $(oLp) + (pLx)$ will lead to oLx. If p wants to bring about oLp, and he knows that oLx holds, he can produce pUx, for instance, he will perform an act o approves of.

An examination of the discussed examples suggests the conclusion that a good deal of inter-personal behavior and social perception is determined—or at least co-determined—by simple cognitive configurations. This fact also throws light on the problem of the understanding of behavior. Students of this problem often mentioned the aspect of rationality which enters into it. Max Weber and others pointed out one kind of rationality in behavior, namely, the rationality of the means-end relation. Choosing the appropriate means to gain an end makes for a "good," a "rational" action, and we can understand it. In Lewin's concept of hodological space this kind of rationality is elaborated. However, understandable human behavior often is not of this sort, but is based on the simple configurations of U and L relations. Since they determine both behavior and perception we can understand social behavior of this kind.

REFERENCE

1. Heider, F. Social perception and phenomenal causality. *Psychol. Rev.*, 1944, 51, 358–374.

— · — · — · — · — · — · — · — · — · — · — · — · —

THEODORE M. NEWCOMB

Communicative Acts:
*The A-B-X System (The Acquaintance Process)**

This paper points toward the possibility that many of those phenomena of social behavior which have been somewhat loosely assembled under the label of "interaction" can be more adequately studied as communicative acts. It further points to the possibility that, just as the observable forms of certain solids are macroscopic outcomes of molecular structure, so certain observable group properties are predetermined by the conditions and consequences of communicative acts.

The initial assumption is that communication among humans performs the essential function of enabling two or more individuals to maintain simultaneous orientation toward one another as communicators *and* toward objects of communication. After presenting a rationale for this assumption, we shall attempt to show that a set of propositions derived from or consistent with it seems to be supported by empirical findings.

CO-ORIENTATION AND THE A-B-X SYSTEM

Every communicative act is viewed as a transmission of information, consisting of discriminative stimuli, from a source to a recipient.[1] For present purposes it is assumed that the discriminative stimuli have a discriminable object as referent. Thus in the simplest possible communicative act one person (A) transmits information to another person (B) about something (X). Such an act is symbolized here as AtoBreX.

The term "orientation" is used as equivalent to "attitude" in its more inclusive sense of referring to both cathectic and cognitive tendencies. The phrase "simultaneous orienta-

---

*Theodore M. Newcomb, "An approach to the Study of Communicative Acts," *Psychological Review* 60 (1953): 393–404. Copyright 1953 by the American Psychological Association, and reproduced by permission.

[1] This statement is adapted from G. A. Miller's definition: " 'information' is used to refer to *the occurrence of one out of a set of alternative discriminative stimuli*. A discriminative stimulus is a stimulus that is arbitrarily, symbolically, associated with some thing (or state, or event, or property) and that enables the stimulated organism to discriminate this thing from others" (9, p. 41).

tion" (hereinafter abbreviated to "co-orientation") itself represents an assumption; namely, that A's orientation toward B and toward X are interdependent. A-B-X is therefore regarded as constituting a system. That is, certain definable relationships between A and B, between A and X, and between B and X are all viewed as interdependent. For some purposes the system may be regarded as a phenomenal one within the life space of A or B, for other purposes as an "objective" system including all of the possible relationships as inferred from observations of A's and B's behavior. It is presumed that a given state of the system exists when a given instance of AtoBreX occurs, and that as a result of this occurrence the system undergoes some change (even though the change be regarded as only a reinforcement of the pre-existing state).

The minimal components of the A-B-X system, as schematically illustrated in Figure 1, are as follows:

1. A's orientation toward X, including both attitude toward X as an object to be approached or avoided (characterized by sign and intensity) and cognitive attributes (beliefs and cognitive structuring).

2. A's orientations toward B, in exactly the same sense. (For purposes of avoiding confusing terms, we shall speak of positive and negative *attraction* toward A or B as persons and of favorable and unfavorable attitudes toward X.)

3. B's orientation toward X.

4. B's orientation toward A.

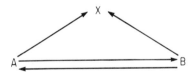

Figure 1. Schematic illustration of the minimal A-B-X system.

In order to examine the possible relationships of similarity and difference between A and B, we shall make use of simple dichotomies in regard to these four relationships. That is, with respect to a given X at a given time, A and B will be regarded as cathectically alike (++ or − −) or different (+ − or − +) in attitude and in attraction; and as cognitively alike or different. We shall also make use of simple dichotomies of degree—i.e., more alike, less alike. We shall refer to lateral similarities of A's and B's orientations to X as *symmetrical* relationships.

This very simple system is designed to fit two-person communication. In the following discussion these additional limitations will be imposed, for simplicity's sake: (a) communicative acts will be treated as verbal ones, in face-to-face situations; (b) initiation of the communicative act is considered to be intentional (i.e., such acts are excluded as those which the actor assumes to be unobserved); (c) it is assumed that the "message" is received—i.e., that the communicative act is attended to by an intended recipient, though not necessarily with any particular degree of accuracy; and (d) A and B are assumed to be group members, characterized by continued association.

The assumption that co-orientation is essential to human life is based upon two considerations of complementary nature. First, the orientation of any A toward any B (assuming that they are capable of verbal communication) is rarely, if ever, made in an environmental vacuum. Even in what seems the maximally "pure" case of two lovers oblivious to all but each other, both singly and both jointly are dependent upon a common environment; and their continued attachment is notoriously contingent upon the discovery or development of common interests beyond themselves. It is not certain that even their most person-oriented communications (e.g., "I love you") are devoid of environmental reference. The more intense one person's concern for another the more sensitive he is likely to be to the other's orientations to objects in the environment.

Second, the orientation of any A capable of verbal communication about almost any conceivable X is rarely, if ever, made in a social vacuum. There are few if any objects so private that one's orientations toward them are uninfluenced by others' orientations. This is particularly true with regard to what has been termed "social reality" (3); i.e., the less the possibility of testing one's assumptions by observing the physical consequences of those assumptions, the greater the reliance upon social confirmation as the test of what is true and valid. And even when assumptions can be put to the direct test (e.g., the child can find out for himself about the stove which he has been told is hot), social reality is often accepted as the quicker or the safer test. As various linguists have pointed out, moreover, a good deal of social reality is built into the very language with which we communicate about things. Under the conditions of continued association which we are assuming, A and B as they communicate about X are dependent upon each other, not only because the other's eyes and ears provide an additional source of information about X, but also because the other's judgment provides a testing ground for social reality. And to be dependent upon the other, in so far as such dependence influences behavior, is to be oriented toward him.

In short, it is an almost constant human necessity to orient oneself toward objects in the environment and also toward other persons oriented toward those same objects. To the degree that A's orientation either toward X or toward B is contingent upon B's orientation toward X, A is motivated to influence and/or to inform himself about B's orientation toward X. Communication is the most common and usually the most effective means by which he does so.

SYMMETRY OF ORIENTATION

Much of the remainder of this paper will deal with the relationships between A's and B's orientations toward X, within the postulated A-B-X system. The implications of this model are: (a) that while at any given moment the system may be conceived of as being "at rest," it is characterized not by the absence but by the balance of forces; and (b) that a change in any part of the system (any of the four relationships portrayed in Figure 1) may lead to changes in any of the others. We shall also make the assumption (not inherent in the model) that certain forces impinging upon the system are relatively strong and persistent, and that thus there are "strains" toward preferred states of equilibrium.

This assumption, related to the initial one concerning the co-orientation function of communication, is as follows. To the degree that A's orientation toward X is contingent upon B's orientation toward X, A's co-orientation will be facilitated by similarity of his own and B's orientation toward X. The first advantage of symmetry—particularly of cognitive symmetry—is that of ready calculability of the other's behavior; the more similar

A's and B's cognitive orientations, the less the necessity for either of them to "translate" X in terms of the other's orientations, the less the likelihood of failure or error in such "translations," and thus the less difficult and/or the less erroneous the co-orientation of either. Second, there is the advantage of validation of one's own orientation toward X; the more similar A's and B's orientations, either cognitive or cathectic (particularly in the many areas where validation is heavily dependent upon "social reality"), the more confident each of them can be of his own cognitive and evaluative orientations. Co-orientation is of course possible with little or no symmetry, but the facilitative value of symmetry for co-orientation is considerable.

If these advantages are commonly experienced as such, communicative acts resulting in increased symmetry are likely to be rewarded, and symmetry is likely to acquire secondary reward value. This is the basis of our assumption of a persistent "strain toward symmetry," under the conditions noted.

These assumptions may now be brought together in terms of the following inclusive postulate: *The stronger the forces toward A's co-orientation in respect to B and X, (a) the greater A's strain toward symmetry with B in respect to X; and (b) the greater the likelihood of increased symmetry as a consequence of one or more communicative acts.* The latter part of the postulate assumes the possibility of modified orientations toward X on the part of both A and B, who over a period of time exchange roles as transmitters and receivers of information.

Several testable propositions are derivable from this postulate. First, if the likelihood of instigation to and achievement of symmetry varies as a function of forces toward co-orientation, the latter varies, presumably, with valence of the objects of co-orientation—i.e., of intensity of attitude toward X and of attraction toward B. That is, under conditions such that orientation toward either B or X also demands orientation toward the other, the greater the valence of B or of X the greater the induced force toward co-orientation, and thus the greater the likelihood of both instigation toward and achievement of symmetry.

Such research findings as are known to the writer are in support of these predictions. Experimental results reported by Festinger and Thibaut (5), by Schachter (12), and by Back (1) indicate that attempts to influence another toward one's own point of view vary as a function of attraction. In the second of these studies it is shown that communications within a cohesive group are directed most frequently toward those perceived as deviates, up to a point where the deviate is sociometrically rejected (i.e., attraction decreases or becomes negative), beyond which point communication to them becomes less frequent. It is also shown in this study that frequency of influence-attempting communication varies with degree of interest in the topic of group discussion.

Some of these same studies, and some others, present data concerning symmetry as a consequence of communication. Thus Festinger and Thibaut, varying "pressure toward uniformity" and "perception of homogeneous group composition," found actual change toward uniformity following a discussion to be a function of both these variables, but some change toward uniformity took place in every group, under all conditions. Back found that subjects who started with different interpretations of the same material and who were given an opportunity to discuss the matter were influenced by each other as a direct function of attraction.

Findings from two community studies may also be cited, as consistent with these laboratory studies. Newcomb (10), in a replicated study of friendship choices as related to political attitudes in a small college community, found on both occasions that students at each extreme of the attitude continuum tended to have as friends those like themselves in attitude. Festinger, Schachter, and Back (4), in their study of a housing project, found a correlation of +.72 between a measure of attraction and a measure of "conformity in attitude." No direct observations of communication are made in these two studies; the relevance of their findings for the present point depends upon the assumption that frequency of communication is a function of attraction. This assumption is clearly justified in these two particular investigations, since in both communities there was complete freedom of association. As noted below, this assumption is not justified in all situations.

Other testable propositions derivable from the general postulate have to do with A's judgments of existing symmetry between himself and B with respect to X. Such judgments (to which the writer has for some time applied the term "perceived consensus") are represented by the symbol B-X, within A's phenomenal A-B-X system. Such a judgment, under given conditions of demand for co-orientation with respect to a given B and a given X, is a major determinant of the likelihood of a given AtoBreX, since strain toward symmetry is influenced by perception of existing symmetry. Such a judgment, moreover, is either confirmed or modified by whatever response B makes to AtoBreX. The continuity of an A-B-X system thus depends upon perceived consensus, which may be viewed either as an independent or as a dependent variable.

According to the previous proposition, the likelihood of increased symmetry (objectively observed) as a consequence of communicative acts increases with attraction and with intensity of attitude. The likelihood of perceived symmetry presumably increases with the same variables. Judgments of symmetry, like other judgments, are influenced both by "reality" and by "autistic" factors, both of which tend, as a function of attraction and intensity of attitude, to increase the likelihood of perceived consensus. Frequency of communication with B about X is the most important of the "reality" factors, and this, as we have seen, tends to vary with valence toward B and toward X. As for the "autistic" factors, the greater the positive attraction toward B and the more intense the attitude toward X, the greater the likelihood of cognitive distortion toward symmetry. Hypothetically, then, perceived symmetry with regard to X varies as a function of intensity of attitude toward X and of attraction toward B.

A considerable number of research studies, published and unpublished, are known to the writer in which subjects' own attitudes are related to their estimates of majority or modal position of specified groups. Only a minority of the studies systematically relate these judgments to attraction, and still fewer to intensity of attitude. Among this minority, however, the writer knows of no exceptions to the above proposition. The most striking of the known findings were obtained from students in several university classes in April of 1951, in a questionnaire dealing with the very recent dismissal of General MacArthur by President Truman:

	pro-Truman Ss who . . .	anti-Truman Ss who . . .
attribute to "most of my closest friends"		
pro-Truman attitudes	48	2
anti-Truman attitudes	0	34
neither	4	4
attribute to "most uninformed people"		
pro-Truman attitudes	6	13
anti-Truman attitudes	32	14
neither	14	13

If we assume that "closest friends" are more attractive to university students than "uninformed people," these data provide support for the attraction hypothesis. Comparisons of those whose own attitudes are more and less intense also provide support, though less strikingly, for the hypothesis concerning attitude intensity.

Perceived symmetry, viewed as an independent variable, is obviously a determinant of instigation to symmetry-directed communication. Festinger (3), with specific reference to groups characterized by "pressures toward uniformity," hypothesizes that "pressure on members to communicate to others in the group concerning item x increases monotonically with increase in the perceived discrepancy in opinion concerning item x among members of the group," as well as with "relevance of item x to the functioning of the group," and with "cohesiveness of the group." And, with reference to the choice of recipient for communications, "The force to communicate about item x to a particular member of the group will increase as the discrepancy in opinion between that member and the communicator increases [and] will decrease to the extent that he is perceived as not a member of the group or to the extent that he is not wanted as a member of the group" (3, p. 8). Support for all of these hypotheses is to be found in one or more of his and his associates' studies. They are consistent with the following proposition: the likelihood of a symmetry-directed AtoBreX varies as a multiple function of perceived discrepancy (i.e., inversely with perceived symmetry), with valence toward B and with valence toward X.

Common sense and selected observations from everyday behavior may also be adduced in support of these propositions. For example, A observes that an attractive B differs with him on an important issue and seeks symmetry by trying to persuade B to his own point of view; or A seeks to reassure himself that B does not disagree with him; or A gives information to B about X or asks B for information about X. From all these acts we may infer perception of asymmetry and direction of communication toward symmetry. Selected observations concerning symmetry as a consequence of communication are equally plentiful; there is, in fact, no social phenomenon which can be more commonly observed than the tendency for freely communicating persons to resemble one another in orientation toward objects of common concern. The very nature of the communicative act as a transmission of information would, on a priori grounds alone, lead to the prediction of increased symmetry, since following the communication both A and B possess the information which was only A's before. B will not necessarily accept or believe all information transmitted by A, of course, but the likelihood of his doing so presumably varies not only with attraction toward A but also with intensity of attitude toward X, since in the long run the more important X is to him the more likely it is that he will avoid communicating with B about X if he cannot believe him. Thus the propositions have a considerable degree of face validity.

But everyday observation also provides instances to the contrary. Not all communications are directed toward symmetry, nor is symmetry an inevitable consequence of communication, even when attraction is strong and attitudes are intense. A devoted husband may refrain from discussing important business matters with his wife, or two close friends may "agree to disagree" in silence about matters of importance to both. People who are attracted toward one another often continue to communicate about subjects on which they continue to disagree—and this is particularly apt to happen with regard to attitudes which are intense, contrary to our theoretical prediction.

In sum, the available research findings and a considerable body of everyday observation support our predictions that instigation toward, perception of, and actual achievement of symmetry vary with intensity of attitude toward X and attraction toward B. The readiness with which exceptions can be adduced, however, indicates that these are not the only variables involved. The propositions, at best, rest upon the assumption of *ceteris paribus*; they cannot account for the fact that the probabilities of A's instigation to communicate about a given X are not the same for all potential B's of equal attraction for him, nor the fact that his instigation to communicate to a given B are not the same for all X's of equal valence to him. We shall therefore attempt to derive certain further propositions from our basic assumption that both instigation to and achievement of symmetry vary with strength of forces toward co-orientation in the given situation.

DYNAMICS OF CO-ORIENTATION

The foregoing propositions represent only a slight extrapolation of Heider's general principle (6) of "balanced states" in the absence of which "unit relations will be changed through action or through cognitive reorganization." In a later paper devoted specifically to the implications of Heider's hypotheses for interrelationships among attitudes toward a person and toward his acts, Horowitz *et al.* (8) note the following possible resolutions to states of imbalance: (a) the sign-valence of the act is changed to agree with that of the actor, (b) the reverse of this; and (c) the act is cognitively divorced from the actor; in addition, of course, the disharmony may be tolerated.

Orientations as attributed by A to B are here considered as equivalent to acts so attributed, in Heider's sense, and symmetry is taken as a special case of balance. Assume, for example, the following asymmetry in A's phenomenal system: +A:X, +A:B, -B:X, +B:A (i.e., A has positive attitude toward X, positive attraction toward B, perceives B's attitude toward X as negative, and B's attraction toward A as positive). Any of the following attempts at "resolution," analogous to those mentioned by Heider, are possible: (a) - A:X; (b) - A:B; or (c) cognitive dissociation. These can occur in the absence of any communication with B. Attempts at harmony (symmetry) may also be made via communications directed toward +B:X. And, if such attempts fail, the three alternatives mentioned as possible without communication are still available. Finally, there is the possibility of compromise, following communication (e.g., agreement on some midpoint), and the possibility of "agreeing to disagree."

Such acts of resolution are made necessary, according to the present theory, by the situational demands of co-orientation on the one hand and by the psychological strain toward symmetry on the other. But symmetry is only a facilitating condition for coorientation, not a necessary one. While (as maintained in the preceding propositions) the probabilities of symmetry vary, *ceteris paribus*, with demand for co-orientation, the theory does not demand that a symmetry-directed AtoBreX occur in every instance of strong demand for co-orientation. On the contrary, the theory demands that it occur only if, as, and when co-orientation is facilitated thereby. We must therefore inquire more closely into the nature of the forces toward co-orientation as related to possible forces against symmetry.

One kind of situational variable has to do with the nature of the forces which result in association between A and B. Of particular importance are constrained (enforced) vs.

voluntary association, and association based upon broad as contrasted with narrow common interests. The range of X's with regard to which there is demand for co-orientation is presumably influenced by such forces. The relevant generalization seems to be as follows: *The less the attraction between A and B, the more nearly strain toward symmetry is limited to those particular X's co-orientation toward which is required by the conditions of association.* This would mean, for example, that as attraction between two spouses decreases, strain toward symmetry would increasingly narrow to such X's as are required by personal comfort and conformity with external propriety; similarly, the range of X's with regard to which there is strain toward symmetry is greater for two friendly than for two hostile members of a chess club.

The problem of constraint has already been noted. In some of the studies cited above it was assumed that frequency of communication varies with attraction, but this is not necessarily true under conditions of forced association. Two recent theoretical treatises deal with this problem.

Homans, one of whose group variables is "frequency of interaction" (though not communication, specifically), includes the following among his other propositions: "If the frequency of interaction between two or more persons increases, the degree of their liking for one another will increase, and vice versa"; and "The more frequently persons interact with one another, the more alike in some respects both their activities and their sentiments tend to become" (7, p. 120). (The latter proposition, which closely resembles the one here under consideration, apparently takes a much less important place in Homans' system than the former.) Almost immediately, however, the latter proposition is qualified by the statement, "It is only when people interact as social equals and their jobs are not sharply differentiated that our hypothesis comes fully into its own." In nearly every chapter, moreover, Homans (whose propositions are drawn *post hoc* from various community, industrial, and ethnological studies) points to the limitations which are imposed by constraining forces—particularly those of rank and hierarchy—upon the relations among attraction, similarity of attitude, and communication.

Blake manages to incorporate these considerations in a more rigorous proposition. Noting that hostility cannot be considered as the simple psychological opposite of positive attraction, he proposes to substitute a curvilinear for Homans' linear hypothesis: " . . . when pressures operate to keep members of a group together, the stresses that drive toward interaction will be stronger in *both* positive and negative feeling states than in neutral ones" (2). This proposition seems consistent with the present argument to the effect that demands for co-orientation are likely to vary with the nature and degree of constraints upon association; hence communicative acts, together with their consequences, will also vary with such constraints.

Another situational variable deals with the fact that, under conditions of prescribed role differentiation, symmetry may take the form of "complementarity" (cf. 11) rather than sameness. For example, both a man and his small son may (following a certain amount of communication of a certain nature) subscribe to the *same norms* which prescribe *differentiated behavior* for a man and boy with respect to a whiskey and soda. If the father drinks in the son's presence, there are demands upon both of them for co-orientation; but there is strain toward symmetry only with respect to "the code," and not with respect to personal orientation toward the whiskey and soda. The code becomes the X with regard to which there is strain toward symmetry. In more general terms, *under conditions of differentiation of A's and B's role prescriptions with regard to X, the greater the demand for co-orientation the greater the likelihood of strain toward symmetry with respect to the role system* (rather than with respect to X itself).

A third situational variable has to do with the possibility that symmetry may be threatening. Particularly under circumstances of shame, guilt, or fear of punishment there are apt to be strong forces against a symmetry-directed AtoBreX, even though—in fact, especially when—attitude toward X (the guilty act) and attraction toward B (a person from whom it is to be concealed) are strong. Under these conditions it is the demand for co-orientation which creates the problem; if A could utterly divorce X (his own act) from B, he would not feel guilty. Forces toward symmetry, however, are opposed by counterforces. Demand for co-orientation induces strain toward symmetry, but does not necessarily lead to a symmetry-directed AtoBreX.

A theoretically analogous situation may result from the omnipresent fact of multiple membership groups. That is, strains toward symmetry with B_1 in regard to X may be outweighed by strains toward symmetry with B_2, whose orientations toward X are viewed as contradictory with those of B_1. This is often the case when, for example, two good friends "agree to disagree" about something of importance to both. Thus in one study (14) it was found that those members least influenced by reported information concerning their own group norms were those most attracted to groups whose norms were perceived as highly divergent from those of the group in question.

Communicative acts, like others, are thus subject to inhibition. Such "resolutions" as "agreement to disagree," however, represent relatively stressful states of equilibrium. It is therefore to be expected, in ways analogous to those noted by Lewin in his discussion of the quasi-stationary equilibrium, that A-B-X systems characterized by such stress will be particularly susceptible to change. Such change need not necessarily occur in the particular region of the system characterized by maximal strain.

The dynamics of such a system are by no means limited to those of strains toward symmetry, but must include changes resulting from acceptance of existing asymmetry. The possible range of dynamic changes is illustrated in Figure 2. (In this figure,

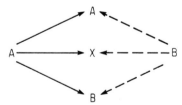

Figure 2. Schematic illustration of A's phenomenal A-B-X system.

the A and B at either side represent persons as communicators; the A and B in the center represent the same persons as objects of co-orientation. The broken lines represent A's judgments of B's orientations.) Given perceived asymmetry with regard to X, and demand for co-orientation toward B and X, the possibilities for A are such that he can:

1. achieve, or attempt to achieve, symmetry with regard to X

    (a) by influencing B toward own orientation,

    (b) by changing own orientation toward B's,

    (c) by cognitively distorting B's orientation;

2. introduce changes in other parts of the system

    (a) modify his attraction toward B,

    (b) modify his judgment of own attraction for B,

    (c) modify evaluation of (attraction toward) himself (A),

    (d) modify his judgment of B's evaluation of himself (B);

3. tolerate the asymmetry, without change.

As suggested by this listing of possible "solutions," the perception of asymmetry, under conditions of demand for co-orientation, confronts A with a problem which he can attempt to solve behaviorally (i.e., by communicative acts) and/or cognitively (i.e., by changing either his own orientations or his perception of B's orientations). Whatever his chosen "solution," it has some effect upon A's phenomenal A-B-X system—either to reinforce it or to modify it. As a result of repeatedly facing and "solving" problems of co-orientation with regard to a given B and a given X a relatively stable equilibrium is established. If A is free either to continue or not to continue his association with B, one or the other of two eventual outcomes is likely: (a) he achieves an equilibrium character-ized by relatively great attraction toward B and by relatively high perceived symmetry, and the association is continued; or (b) he achieves an equilibrium characterized by relatively little attraction toward B and by relatively low perceived symmetry, and the association is discontinued. This "either-or" assumption under conditions of low con-straint presupposes a circular relationship between attraction and the perception of symmetry. The present theory demands this assumption of circularity, and empirical evidence (under conditions of relative freedom from constraint) seems to support it.

Under conditions of little or no freedom to discontinue association, no such circular-ity is assumed. The conditions which dictate continued association also dictate the re-quirements for co-orientation, which are independent of attraction. The empirical data suggest that the degree to which attraction is independent of symmetry varies with the degree of *perceived* (rather than the degree of objectively observed) constraint.

GROUP PROPERTIES

It follows from the preceding assumptions and propositions that there should be predictable relationships between certain properties of any group and variables having to do with communicative behavior within that group. A group's structural properties, for example, viewed as independent variables, may create problems and may provide solu-tions to other problems of communication. Viewed the other way around, many proper-ties of a group are outcomes of its communicative practices. Evidence from many sources points to distinctive properties of groups which are precisely those which the foregoing considerations would lead us to expect, either as conditions for or as consequences of a given kind and frequency of communicative acts.

Three kinds of properties are briefly noted. Each of them is hypothetically related (either as dependent or as independent variable) to the probabilities of the occurrence of a given kind of communicative act.

1. *Homogeneity of orientation* toward certain objects. All descriptive accounts of interacting groups note this property, in one way or another and by one label or another. As applied to behavior, it does not necessarily refer to similarity of action on the part of all group members, but only of demand or expectation; e.g., all expect each to take his own differentiated role. In order to account for the observed facts it is necessary to make the assumptions (not previously made in this paper) that information may be transmitted in nonverbal ways, and with or without intention to do so—e.g., a person's behavior with regard to a given object informs observers about his orientation to it.

If communication is thus broadly defined, then the degrees of homogeneity of orientation of a given group with respect to specified objects are presumably related to communication variables with respect to those objects. It is not hypothesized that homogeneity is an invariable function of any single index of communication (frequency, for example), but rather that it varies in accordance with the dynamics of A-B-X systems. While there are often extra-group determinants of homogeneity of orientation, it seems reasonable to view this very important group property as an outcome of the conditions and consequences of communicative acts.

2. *Homogeneity of perceived consensus* (i.e., homogeneity of judgments of homogeneity of orientation). This property, though not often specifically mentioned in the literature on groups, is usually implicitly assumed. Most communication presupposes a considerable degree of perceived as well as objective homogeneity of orientation. The very fact of using language or gesture presupposes the assumption of consensus among communicants as to the information transmitted by the use of symbols.

Homogeneity of orientation and of perceived consensus does not, in spite of implicit assumptions to the contrary, have an invariant relationship; judgments of homogeneity may be of any degree of accuracy. If, as in the village reported by Schanck (13), each of many dissenters from a supposed norm believes himself the only dissenter, this state of pluralistic ignorance is an important group property, and is plausibly described by the author as an outcome of certain practices of communication. Any degree of homogeneity of perceived consensus, representing any degree of accuracy, is hypothetically an outcome of previous communicative acts and a determinant of future ones.

3. *Attraction among members.* Relationships of positive attraction of some degree invariably characterize continuing groups under conditions of minimal constraint, and are commonly found even under conditions of considerable constraint. This is so commonly the case that Homans (7) ventures the almost unqualified hypothesis that "liking" increases with frequency of interaction, and vice versa. Viewed in the light of the hypothetical dynamics of A-B-X systems, Homans' proposition would be amended to the effect that interpersonal attraction varies with the degree to which the demands of co-orientation are met by communicative acts.

These are not, of course, the only group properties of significance, nor are these properties outcomes exclusively of intragroup communication. (Some properties of almost any group, particularly at early stages of its history, derive largely from individual characteristics which its members bring to it.) It appears to be the case, nevertheless, that the hypothetical conditions and consequences of communicative acts are not limited to groups of two, and that some of the important properties of observed groups are consistent with the hypothetical dynamics of A-B-X systems.

SUMMARY

Communicative acts, like other molar behaviors, may be viewed as outcomes of changes in organism-environment relationships, actual and/or anticipated. Communicative acts are distinctive in that they may be aroused by and may result in changes anywhere within the system of relations between two or more communicators and the objects of their communication. It seems likely that the dynamics of such a system are such that from an adequate understanding of its properties at a given moment there can be predicted both the likelihood of occurrence of a given act of communication and the nature of changes in those properties which will result from that act.

Some of the most significant of group properties are those which, hypothetically, vary with intragroup communicative acts. It should therefore be rewarding to discover whether support for the present hypotheses, as apparently provided by the scattered evidence now available, can be confirmed in more systematic ways. If so, there are promising possibilities of investigating the phenomena of social interaction by viewing them as events within communication systems.

REFERENCES

1. Back, K. The exertion of influence through social communication. *J. abnorm. soc. Psychol.*, 1951, *46*, 9-23.
2. Blake, R. R. The interaction-feeling hypothesis applied to psychotherapy groups. *Sociometry*, in press.
3. Festinger, L. Informal social communication. In L. Festinger, K. Back, S. Schachter, H. H. Kelley, and J. Thibaut, *Theory and experiment in social communication.* Ann Arbor: Institute for Social Research, Univer. of Michigan, 1950.
4. Festinger, L., Schachter, S., & Back, K. *Social pressures in informal groups.* New York: Harper, 1950.
5. Festinger, L., & Thibaut, J. Interpersonal communications in small groups. *J. abnorm. soc. Psychol.*, 1951, *46*, 92-99.
6. Heider, F. Attitudes and cognitive organization. *J. Psychol.*, 1946, *21*, 107-112.
7. Homans, G. C. *The human group.* New York: Harcourt Brace, 1950.
8. Horowitz, M. W., Lyons, J., & Perlmutter, H. V. Induction of forces in discussion groups. *Hum. Relat.*, 1951, *4*, 57-76.
9. Miller, G. A. *Language and communication.* New York: McGraw Hill, 1951.
10. Newcomb, T. M. *Personality and social change.* New York: Dryden, 1943.
11. Parsons, T., & Shils, E. A. (Eds.) *Toward a general theory of action.* Cambridge: Harvard Univer. Press, 1951.
12. Schachter, S. Deviation, rejection and communication. *J. abnorm. soc. Psychol.*, 1951, *46*, 190-207.
13. Schanck, R. L. A study of a community and its groups and institutions conceived of as behaviors of individuals. *Psychol. Monogr.*, 1932, *43*, No. 2 (Whole No. 195).
14. White, M. S. Attitude change as related to perceived group consensus. Unpublished doctoral dissertation, Univer. of Michigan, 1953.

— . — . — . — . — . — . — . — . — . —

LEON FESTINGER

*Theory of Cognitive Dissonance**

The basic background of the theory consists of the notion that the human organism tries to establish internal harmony, consistency, or congruity among his opinions, attitudes, knowledge, and values. That is, there is a drive toward consonance among cognitions. In order to deal with this notion in a somewhat more precise manner, I have imagined cognition to be decomposable into elements or, at least, clusters of elements. The following theoretical statements have been made about the relations among these cognitive elements:

1. Pairs of elements can exist in irrelevant, consonant, or dissonant relations.

2. Two cognitive elements are in an irrelevant relation if they have nothing to do with one another.

3. Two cognitive elements are in a dissonant relation if, considering these two alone, the obverse of one element follows from the other.

4. Two cognitive elements are in a consonant relation if, considering these two alone, one element follows from the other.

Starting from these definitions, a number of situations have been denoted as implying the existence of cognitive dissonance.

1. Dissonance almost always exists after a decision has been made between two or more alternatives. The cognitive elements corresponding to positive characteristics of the rejected alternatives, and those corresponding to negative characteristics of the chosen alternative, are *dissonant* with the knowledge of the action that has been taken. Those cognitive elements corresponding to positive characteristics of the chosen alternative and negative characteristics of the rejected alternative are *consonant* with the cognitive elements corresponding to the action which has been taken.

2. Dissonance almost always exists after an attempt has been made, by offering rewards or threatening punishment, to elicit overt behavior that is at variance with private opinion. If the overt behavior is successfully elicited, the person's private opinion is dissonant with his knowledge concerning his behavior; his knowledge of the reward obtained or of the punishment avoided is consonant with his knowledge concerning his behavior. If the overt behavior is not successfully elicited, then his private opinion is consonant with his knowledge of what he has done, but the knowledge of the reward not obtained or of the punishment to be suffered is dissonant with his knowledge of what he has done.

3. Forced or accidental exposure to new information may create cognitive elements that are dissonant with existing cognition.

4. The open expression of disagreement in a group leads to the existence of cognitive

*Reprinted from *A Theory of Cognitive Dissonance* by Leon Festinger with the permission of the publishers, Stanford University Press, pp. 260–266. Copyright © 1957 by Leon Festinger.

dissonance in the members. The knowledge that some other person, generally like oneself, holds one opinion is dissonant with holding a contrary opinion.

5. Identical dissonance in a large number of people may be created when an event occurs which is so compelling as to produce a uniform reaction in everyone. For example, an event may occur which unequivocally invalidates some widely held belief.

Thus far, dissonance and consonance have been defined as "all or none" relations— that is, if two elements are relevant to one another, the relation between them is either dissonant or consonant. Two hypotheses have been advanced concerning the magnitude of dissonance or consonance.

1. The magnitude of the dissonance or consonance which exists between two cognitive elements will be a direct function of the importance of these two elements.

2. The total magnitude of dissonance which exists between two clusters of cognitive elements is a function of the weighted proportion of all the relevant relations between the two clusters which are dissonant, each dissonant or consonant relation being weighted according to the importance of the elements involved in that relation.

Starting with these hypotheses about the magnitude of dissonance, a number of operational implications seem clear.

1. The magnitude of postdecision dissonance is an increasing function of the general importance of the decision and of the relative attractiveness of the unchosen alternatives.

2. The magnitude of postdecision dissonance *decreases* as the number of cognitive elements corresponding identically to characteristics of chosen and unchosen alternatives *increases*.

3. The magnitude of the dissonance resulting from an attempt to elicit forced compliance is greatest if the promised reward or threatened punishment is either *just sufficient* to elicit the overt behavior or is *just barely not sufficient* to elicit it.

4. If forced compliance is elicited, the magnitude of the dissonance *decreases* as the magnitude of the reward or punishment *increases*.

5. If forced compliance fails to be elicited, the magnitude of the dissonance *increases* as the magnitude of the reward or punishment *decreases*.

6. The magnitude of the dissonance introduced by the expression of disagreement by others *decreases* as the number of existing cognitive elements consonant with the opinion *increases*. These latter elements may correspond either to objective, nonsocial items of information or to the knowledge that some other people hold the same opinion.

7. The magnitude of the dissonance introduced by disagreement from others *increases* with *increase* in the importance of the opinion to the person, in the relevance of the opinion to those voicing disagreement, and in the attractiveness of those voicing disagreement.

8. The greater the difference between the opinion of the person and the opinion of the one voicing disagreement, and, hence, the greater the number of elements which are dissonant between the cognitive clusters corresponding to the two opinions, the greater will be the magnitude of dissonance.

One now comes to the point of stating the central hypotheses of the theory, namely:

1. The presence of dissonance gives rise to pressures to reduce that dissonance.

2. The strength of the pressure to reduce dissonance is a function of the magnitude of the existing dissonance.

These hypotheses lead, naturally, to a consideration of the ways in which dissonance may be reduced. There are three major ways in which this may be done.

1. By changing one or more of the elements involved in dissonant relations.
2. By adding new cognitive elements that are consonant with already existing cognition.
3. By decreasing the importance of the elements involved in the dissonant relations.

Applying these considerations to actual situations leads to the following:

1. Postdecision dissonance may be reduced by increasing the attractiveness of the chosen alternative, decreasing the attractiveness of the unchosen alternatives, or both.
2. Postdecision dissonance may be reduced by perceiving some characteristics of the chosen and unchosen alternatives as identical.
3. Postdecision dissonance may be reduced by decreasing the importance of various aspects of the decision.
4. If forced compliance has been elicited, the dissonance may be reduced by changing private opinion to bring it into line with the overt behavior or by magnifying the amount of reward or punishment involved.
5. If forced compliance fails to be elicited, dissonance may be reduced by intensifying the original private opinion or by minimizing the reward or punishment involved.
6. The presence of dissonance leads to seeking new information which will provide cognition consonant with existing cognitive elements and to avoiding those sources of new information which would be likely to increase the existing dissonance.
7. When some of the cognitive elements involved in a dissonance are cognitions about one's own behavior, the dissonance can be reduced by changing the behavior, thus directly changing the cognitive elements.
8. Forced or accidental exposure to new information which tends to increase dissonance will frequently result in misinterpretation and misperception of the new information by the person thus exposed in an effort to avoid a dissonance increase.
9. Dissonance introduced by disagreement expressed by other persons may be reduced by changing one's own opinion, by influencing the others to change their opinion, and by rejecting those who disagree.
10. The existence of dissonance will lead to seeking out others who already agree with a cognition that one wants to establish or maintain and will also lead to the initiation of communication and influence processes in an effort to obtain more social support.
11. Influence exerted on a person will be more effective in producing opinion change to the extent that the indicated change of opinion reduces dissonance for that person.
12. In situations where many persons who associate with one another all suffer from the identical dissonance, dissonance reduction by obtaining social support is very easy to accomplish.

To conclude this brief summary of the theory, there are a few things to be stated concerning the effectiveness of efforts directed toward dissonance reduction.

1. The effectiveness of efforts to reduce dissonance will depend upon the resistance to change of the cognitive elements involved in the dissonance and on the availability of information which will provide, or of other persons who will supply, new cognitive elements which will be consonant with existing cognition.

2. The major sources of resistance to change for a cognitive element are the responsiveness of such cognitive elements to "reality" and the extent to which an element exists in consonant relations with many other elements.

3. The maximum dissonance which can exist between two elements is equal to the resistance to change of the less resistant of the two elements. If the dissonance exceeds this magnitude, the less resistant cognitive element will be changed, thus reducing the dissonance.

— · — · — · — · — · — · — · — · — · — · — · —

CHARLES E. OSGOOD
GEORGE J. SUCI
PERCY H. TANNENBAUM

*Congruity Principle**

So far in this book we have been dealing essentially with a descriptive analysis of the dimensionality of the meaning space and the development of techniques for allocating concepts to this space. But cognitive events such as are involved in meaning formation and change do not transpire in isolation from one another; human learning and thinking, the acquisition and modification of the significance of signs, involve continuous interactions among cognitive events. In this section we turn our attention to analysis of the manner in which meanings interact and are thereby changed. In the course of our work on the nature and measurement of meaning we have gradually formulated a very general principle of cognitive interaction, which we call *the principle of congruity*. Although we first discussed it in connection with the prediction of attitude change (see Osgood and Tannenbaum, 1955), and therefore include it in the present chapter, we think it is broader than this in implication, and therefore try to give it in as general form as we can at this time.

NATURE OF THE CONGRUITY PRINCIPLE

.... Any sign presented in isolation elicits its characteristic mediation process, this total process being made up of some number of bipolar reaction components which are

*Charles E. Osgood, George J. Suci, and Percy H. Tannenbaum, *The Measurement of Meaning* (Urbana, Ill.: University of Illinois Press, 1957), pp. 199–216.

elicited at various intensities. The total representational process is assumed to be coordinate with a point in the semantic measurement space, this point projecting onto the several dimensions of the space in correspondence with the kinds and intensities of the reaction components elicited. Thus, two signs having different meanings, such as ATHLETE and LAZY, must elicit different mediation processes, produce different profiles against the semantic differential, and thus be associated with different points in the semantic space. But what happens when two (or more) signs are presented simultaneously, e.g., when the subject sees the phrase LAZY ATHLETE? Common sense tells us that some interaction takes place—certainly a *lazy* athlete is much less active, perhaps less potent, and probably less valuable than he would be otherwise. If interactions of this sort are lawful, and we can get some understanding of the laws, then it should be possible to predict the results of word combination like this and related phenomena.

Since the various dimensions of the semantic space are assumed to be independent, we may deal with a single dimension for simplicity in analysis and then generalize the argument to all dimensions. Also, for the sake of simplicity, we shall treat only the minimum case of interaction between two signs, again assuming that the formulation can be generalized to any number of interacting signs. The general congruity principle may be stated as follows: *Whenever two signs are related by an assertion, the mediating reaction characteristic of each shifts toward congruence with that characteristic of the other, the magnitude of the shift being inversely proportional to intensities of the interacting reactions.* This "shift," obviously, may be in intensity, direction, or both. Thus, if sign A elicits an intensely favorable evaluative component and sign B only a slightly unfavorable evaluative component, the compromise will be such that the reaction to A will be only slightly modified, but that to B relatively more modified. For this principle to acquire some usefulness, it is necessary to be explicit about what is meant by "assertion" and by "congruence."

Assertion as a Condition for Cognitive Interaction. Individuals have varied meanings for a near infinity of signs, yet there is no interaction among them, and no consequent meaning change, except when they are brought into the peculiar evaluative relation to one another that we shall call an *assertion.* As anthropologists well know, members of a culture may entertain logically incompatible attitudes toward objects in their culture (e.g., ancestor worship and fear of the spirits of the dead; Christian and business ethics, etc.), as long as these ideas are not brought into direct relation. But an assertion is more than simple contiguity in time and/or space (although these factors are presumably also necessary). Take for example, the following utterance: "Tom has the reputation of being an angel; Sam, on the other hand, is a devil." Although SAM and ANGEL are more contiguous as signs, the linguistic structure is such that TOM and ANGEL are associated as signs—i.e., they are related by an assertion, and will interact. Nor is this a phenomenon solely of language structure. If we see Tom standing in a crowd on a station platform, waving and smiling at the distant figure of a girl on the departing train, although Tom is closer physically to other people in the crowd, there is an assertion implicit in "waving and smiling at" which relates TOM and GIRL-ON-TRAIN. Just as the copula in the basic English sentence (A *is* B) relates subject and object and is a condition for cognitive interaction, so does the *action* of objects and people with respect to each other serve to relate them and set up pressures toward congruity. A news photo of Mrs. Roosevelt smiling and shaking hands with a little colored boy is just as effective in setting up the conditions for attitude change as would be a policy statement on her part.

Now such assertions, or coupling actions, may be either *associative* or *dissociative*, which corresponds to the basic distinction in all languages between affirmation and negation. The basic form in English for *association* is the paradigm /A *is* B/, e.g., LAZY ATHLETE equals /ATHLETE *is* LAZY/, but there are innumerable variations on this theme—A *is an instance of* B, A *loves* B, A *helps* B, A *goes with* B, A *shakes hands with* B, and so on, whether occurring as perceptual events or language signs, are assertions which associate the included objects of judgment. The basic form in English for *dissociation* is the paradigm /A *is not* B/, and again there are innumerable variations—A *is not an instance of* B, A *hates* B, A *hinders* B, A *avoids* B, A *strikes* B, and so on, are assertions which dissociate the included objects of judgment.

The forms that assertions may take, as we have seen, are highly variable: *simple linguistic qualification* (lazy athlete / or walks gracefully); *simple perceptual contiguity* (e.g., an advertisement showing a pretty girl with her hand possessively on the hood of a new automobile); *statements of classification* ("Tom is an ex-con," "Mr. Frank Smith is a Democrat," "Cigarettes contain nicotine") where to the extent that there is difference in meaning between number and class some pressure toward congruity is assumed to exist; *source-object assertions* ("University president bans research on krebiozen," "Communists dislike strong labor unions," and Mrs. Roosevelt shaking hands with the little colored boy); and of course, more complex statements which may include several overlapping assertions (e.g., "The fun-loving people of New Orleans love their colorful Mardi Gras," where we have /people of New Orleans *are* fun-loving/, /Mardi Gras *is* colorful/ and /people of New Orleans (as modified) *love* Mardi Gras (as modified)/). In terms of our theory, the signs included in messages embodying such assertions are in constant interaction and are constantly being modified in meaning by the principle of congruity— in the last example, the strait-laced Puritan, who takes a very dim view of fun-loving will arrive at a much less favorable evaluation of both the people of New Orleans and Mardi Gras.

We realize that these examples do not provide a precise definition of "assertion." Although we are able to distinguish situations involving assertions (and hence dynamic interaction among sign-processes) from situations not involving assertions on an intuitive basis, so far we have not been able to make explicit the criteria on which we operate.

The Direction and Location of Congruence. If we were unable to state the direction and location' of congruence in cognitive interactions, our principle would be of little value. By taking into account the nature of the assertion, whether associative (+) or dissociative (−), and the original, pre-interaction locations or the meanings of the signs being related (as measured by some such instrument as the semantic differential), however, we can make specific statements about congruence and hence make predictions about change in attitude or meaning. The general statement is as follows: *Whenever two signs are related by an assertion, they are congruent to the extent that their mediating reactions are equally intense, either in the same* (compatible) *direction of excitation in the case of associative assertions or in opposite* (reciprocally antagonistic) *directions in the case of dissociative assertions.* It should be kept in mind that we are referring to a single dimension or component of the cognitive system taken at a time here, and that "intensity" or reaction of a component is assumed to be coordinate with "polarization" (extremeness) of judgment in the measurement space. We state the principle in mediation theory terms principally in the interest of generality.

Let us first take an example where both signs are equally intense in the same, compatible direction: EISENHOWER *is in favor of* FREEDOM OF THE PRESS. Assuming that on the evaluative factor, at least, EISENHOWER and FREEDOM OF THE PRESS are equally favorable, the assertion is already perfectly congruent and no pressure toward meaning change is expected. A similar situation for typical members of our culture would exist for the statement HITLER *was in favor of* MASS EXTERMINA-TION, except for the unfavorable locations of both signs. But what about the statement EISENHOWER *stifles* FREEDOM OF THE PRESS (or the equivalent, HITLER *favored* FREEDOM OF THE PRESS)—assuming the subject is completely credulous? Here we have equally favorable signs *dissociated*, and the point of congruity for each would be an equally intense, but reciprocally antagonistic reaction (e.g., a strongly unfavorable reaction to either EISENHOWER or to FREEDOM OF THE PRESS); since the signs are equally polarized, the result should be a cancellation to zero evaluation of both. A similar situation exists when oppositely evaluated signs are related by an *associative* assertion, and the subject is credulous, e.g., HITLER *favored* FREEDOM OF THE PRESS. The case in which a highly favored source is against a highly disfavored object is again perfectly congruent, e.g., EISENHOWER *condemns* MASS EXTERMINATION. We expect sources we like to sponsor ideas we favor and denounce ideas we are against, and vice versa.

Now let us suppose that one of the signs included in an assertion is *neutral* on the dimension being dealt with—EISENHOWER *is cordial to* the MINISTER FROM SIAM. Here we must ask what reaction to the unknown or neutral item *would be* congruent. Since EISENHOWER is highly positive and since we have an associative assertion, a perfectly congruous state of affairs would exist *if* MINISTER FROM SIAM were also highly favorable in meaning. Following our principles, (a) the congruent position for EISENHOWER is neutrality and the congruent position for MINISTER FROM SIAM is extreme favor, and (b) the shift toward congruence is inversely proportional to the existing intensities of the reaction to the signs; therefore, all of the shift in meaning is concentrated upon the MINISTER FROM SIAM, who becomes highly favored. Similar situations and resolutions apply to all cases where one member is neutral, e.g., EISEN-HOWER *strikes out at* the JASON JONES POLICY, COMMUNISTS *welcome* ABRIGOTO *with open arms*, PROFESSOR SO-AND-SO *favors* PREMARITAL SEXUAL RELATIONS, etc. The familiar "I am against sin" technique, of course, is another case in point, where the unknown political aspirant strives to raise his own evaluation by assertions dissociating himself from various unsavory persons and policies.

COORDINATION WITH MEASUREMENT OPERATIONS

To handle cases that are not polar in nature and to make quantitative prediction and analysis possible, it is now necessary to coordinate the congruity principle with the operations of measurement by the semantic differential. Knowing the direction of the assertion, either associative or dissociative, we need to determine the projections or locations of the two signs *in isolation* in order to predict what the effects of their interaction will be in combination—on as many dimensions as we wish to predict. Since intensity of a reaction component is coordinate with *polarization* on a factor of the differential, we may assign to each sign included in an assertion a value p representing its factor score on a given dimension, expressed as a deviation from the neutral point. For the evaluative factor we arbitrarily assign + to the favorable direction and – to the unfavorable direction. Thus p has a range from –3 to +3. Utilizing our principle, we may now define the *location of congruence*, p_c, for each sign as follows:

for associative assertions, $\quad p_{o1} = p_2$ and,
$$p_{o2} = p_1;$$

for dissociative assertions, $\quad p_{o1} = -p_2$ and,
$$p_{o2} = -p_1,$$

where the subscripts refer to signs 1 and 2 respectively. Figure 16 provides some graphic illustrations. In example (1) we have a positive assertion relating two equally favorable signs (the nature of the assertion, associative or dissociative, is indicated by the + or – sign on the bar connecting the concepts); in this case the positions of perfect congruity already exist. In all other cases the existing locations are not those of maximum congruity, and the latter position is indicated by a dashed circle for each concept (in this figure, in anticipation of the following experimental report on the prediction of attitude change, one sign in each assertion is called S for *source* and the other C for *concept*). Note that in keeping with the principle, the position of congruity is always that equal in degree of polarization to the other sign, in either the same (associative) or opposite (dissociative) directions.

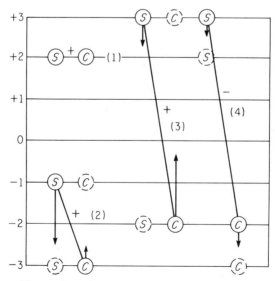

Figure 16. Graphic examples of four situations in which a source (S) makes an assertion (+ or –) about a concept (C). Positions of maximum congruity are indicated by broken circles; predicted changes in attitude are indicated by arrows.

The total amount of "pressure of incongruity" existing in the cognitive system for any given assertion is always equal to the difference (expressed in scale units) between the existing location of each concept and its location of maximal congruity. That is, symbolizing this "pressure" by P,

$$P_1 = p_{o1} - p_1 \text{ and,}$$
$$P_2 = p_{o2} - p_2.$$

And therefore, substituting from the equations given earlier,

for associative assertions, $\quad P_1 = p_2 - p_1 \text{ and,}$
$$P_2 = p_1 - p_2;$$

for dissociative assertions, $\quad P_1 = -p_2 - p_1 \text{ and,}$
$$P_2 = -p_1 - p_2$$

the resulting signs of these equations giving the direction of P, either yielding shift in a favorable direction $(+)$ or in an unfavorable direction $(-)$ in the case of the evaluative factor. For example (2) in Figure 16, the pressures toward congruity are -2 and $+2$ respectively for the source and concept. Inspection of the other examples indicates that the magnitudes of pressure on the signs included in the same assertion are always equal, although they may be different in direction (i.e., $|P_1| = |P_2|$).

It will be recalled, however, that this total "pressure" toward congruity is not distributed equally among the signs included in an assertion. Rather, the principle states that the shift in reaction toward congruity is *inversely* proportional to the original intensities of the reactions to the signs—the more polarized one sign relative to the other, the less change it undergoes. Letting the symbol C stand for *change*, the following equations take into account this inverse proportionality and predict the amount and direction of the shift to be expected from each sign when they are related in an assertion:

$$C_1 = \frac{|p_2|}{|p_1| + |p_2|} P_1 \text{ and,}$$

$$C_2 = \frac{|p_1|}{|p_1| + |p_2|} P_2,$$

where the polarizations of the signs are taken at their absolute values regardless of sign and hence the sign of the equation as a whole (i.e., the direction of change predicted) depends upon the sign of P—the change is always in the direction of increased congruity. The solid arrows in Figure 16 represent the magnitudes and directions of change to be expected in each of the cases given; note that in every case the less polarized member is shifted more than the more polarized member. (The arrows for case (3) do not meet at a common point as they should according to this equation in an associative assertion. This is because the magnitudes of change have been corrected for the *incredulity* inherent in this situation; see Osgood and Tannenbaum, 1955.) When we are dealing with associative assertions only, in which the resolution of congruity is necessarily to a single, common point along the dimension, and when we are interested in the point of resolution rather than the amount of change, the following formula may be used:

$$p_R = \frac{|p_1|}{|p_1| + |p_2|} p_1 + \frac{|p_2|}{|p_1| + |p_2|} p_2$$

where p_R is the degree of polarization, in one direction or the other, of the point of resolution. In a study on the effects of word mixture, for example (cf. p. 278), we use this formula to predict the meanings of word combinations like LAZY ATHLETE from the measured meanings of the components.

CONGRUITY AND LEARNING

The congruity principle as stated above strictly applies only to that *momentary* situation in which the decoding of two signs of different meanings is simultaneous. At this point, the theory says, the interaction is such that the meaning of each sign is completely shifted to the point of mutual congruence. Such a situation is closely approached in the word-mixture case where an adjective modifies a noun, in the perceptual situation where one object is perceived in immediate assertive contiguity with another. As the relation diverges from this perfect simultaneity among mediation process, the magnitude of the congruity effect presumably decreases—perhaps as a negatively accelerated function of the time interval, in common with other similar relations—but the effects should still be proportionate to those predicted at simultaneity. In other words, we would expect the effect of one sign upon another to decrease as the time interval between them increases, e.g., as the time between perceiving LAZY and perceiving ATHLETE increases. We have no evidence on this in relation to congruity per se, but Howes and Osgood (1954) have demonstrated what is certainly a correlated effect of time interval upon associations made to combinations of signs.

Even though the effect of synchronous presentation of two signs like LAZY and ATHLETE may be such as to shift them completely toward a point of mutual congruity, it is certain that this effect is not permanent—word meanings would be as fluid as quicksilver if this were the case! After each such cognitive interaction, we assume that the meanings of the related signs tend to "bounce" back to their original locus—the representational process elicited in isolation is again much as it was before. However, this does not mean that repeated cognitive interactions have no effect which persists; like the bough that is repeatedly bent in a particular direction, the mediation process characteristic of a sign will gradually change toward congruence with the other signs with which it is associated. This is the basis, we suspect, for *semantic change* in languages over time, and even in the short run we can note such effects—FIFTH AMENDMENT has become a somewhat unfavorable term, even to college students we have studied, presumably as a result of persistent and pernicious associative relation with COMMUNIST.

It is clear that we are dealing here with *learning*—the modification in mediation processes as a result of "experience" in cognitive interaction. The underlying notion is much like that of ordinary conditioning, in fact may easily incorporate conditioning. We have a situation in which the reaction elicited by a stimulus (sign) is different from what it was previously, due to congruity effects; if this new reaction is repeatedly elicited by this sign, because it appears persistently in interaction with the same other signs, then this new reaction will gradually supersede the original reaction produced in isolation. Let us now phrase this as a *congruity-learning principle*: *Each time two signs are related in an assertion, the intensity of the mediating reaction characteristic of each in isolation is shifted toward that characteristic of each in interaction, by a constant fraction of the difference in intensity.* Since the difference in intensity (or location along the dimension) decreases with each "trial," this means that the reactions characteristic of both signs must approach a point of common intensity (of the same or antagonistic reactions), which is the point of congruity, according to a negatively accelerated function. In other words, this generates a typical learning curve, for which the terminal point or asymptote is predictable from the initial locations of the signs. Again, it is assumed that this principle operates identically but independently along all dimensions of the cognitive system and that it can be generalized to any number of interacting signs. It should be reiterated, however, that all this is by way of tentative theorizing, still to be verified by experimental investigation.

CONGRUITY AND THE PREDICTION OF ATTITUDE CHANGE

Perhaps the most typical situation in which one expects to find changes in attitude is that in which some *source* makes some evaluative statement about some object or *concept* in a message that is received and decoded by a receiver. If we consider the source as one sign, the concept evaluated as another sign, and the evaluative statement as an assertion which relates them, then we have the necessary conditions for operation of the congruity principle. Although the theoretical model presented above does not pretend to take into account all of the variables that influence attitude change, it does cover those which are most significant with respect to both the direction (favorable or unfavorable) and the *relative* magnitude of change to be expected in any given situation. These variables are the existing attitude of the subject toward the source, the existing attitude toward the concept, and the nature of the assertion relating them. The predictions generated by the theory apply to attitude changes toward both sources and the concepts they evaluate.

Tannenbaum (1953) devised an experimental situation in which these predictions could be directly tested. On the basis of a pretest, three source-concept pairs were selected which met the following criteria: (a) approximately equal numbers of subjects holding favorable, neutral, and unfavorable original attitudes toward them; (b) lack of correlation between attitude toward the source and toward the concept making up each pair. The three source-concept pairs thus selected were LABOR LEADERS with LEGAL-IZED GAMBLING, CHICAGO *Tribune* with ABSTRACT ART, and SENATOR ROB-ERT TAFT with ACCELERATED COLLEGE PROGRAMS. One of the standard attitude-change testing designs was used in the experiment proper: A group of 405 college students was given a *before-test*, in which the six experimental concepts, along with four "filler" concepts, were judged against a form of the semantic differential including six highly and purely evaluative scales. Five weeks later the same subjects were given very realistic news articles and editorials to read (made up like clippings from actual news-papers); both in the headlines and in the body of these short articles assertions relating source and concept were given several times, associative assertions being made in the story for each source-concept pair given to one-half of the subjects and dissociative assertions being made for the same source-concept pair for the other half of the subjects. Immediately after reading the three news items, subjects were given the *after-test*, again judging the same sources and concepts against the same semantic differential. Original attitude scores, ranging from six (most unfavorable) to 42 (most favorable), toward each source and concept were determined from the *before-test* results; subjects distributed into nine cells on each story; source +, concept +, source +, concept 0; source +, concept −; source 0, concept +; etc.

Before reporting the results of this experiment, let us consider the nature of the situation theoretically and the way in which predictions were generated. Since measurement of the meanings of the signs is made in isolation and after the assertions relating them have been presented and removed, it is apparent that we are dealing with the persisting aftereffects of congruity, e.g., with a learning situation rather than a momentary interaction situation such as occurs in judging the meaning of LAZY ATHLETE. However, since the exact number of assertions relating source with concept varied in the news items, and since we do not know the constants of the congruity-learning function in any case, we cannot predict the exact magnitude of the effect on attitude change—except that it will be something less than the maximum. We can, however, predict the *relative* magnitude of attitude change for subjects falling in the various cells above. Knowing the original scale locations for source and concept (e.g., +2, −1) and the nature of the assertion presented (associative or dissociative), we can apply the formulae for C given

TABLE 32. PREDICTED (UPPER VALUES IN CELLS) AND OBTAINED (LOWER VALUES IN CELLS) CHANGES IN ATTITUDE

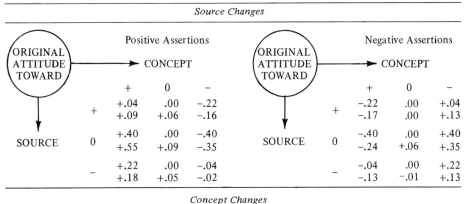

Source Changes

ORIGINAL ATTITUDE TOWARD → CONCEPT	Positive Assertions				ORIGINAL ATTITUDE TOWARD → CONCEPT	Negative Assertions		
		+	0	−		+	0	−
SOURCE	+	+.04 / +.09	.00 / +.06	−.22 / −.16		+.22...		
	+	+.04 +.09	.00 +.06	−.22 −.16	+	−.22 −.17	.00 .00	+.04 +.13
	0	+.40 +.55	.00 +.09	−.40 −.35	0	−.40 −.24	.00 +.06	+.40 +.35
	−	+.22 +.18	.00 +.05	−.04 −.02	−	−.04 −.13	.00 −.01	+.22 +.13

Concept Changes

ORIGINAL ATTITUDE TOWARD → CONCEPT	Positive Assertions				ORIGINAL ATTITUDE TOWARD → CONCEPT	Negative Assertions		
		+	0	−		+	0	−
SOURCE	+	+.04 +.18	+.40 +.91	+.22 +.39	+	−.22 −.33	−.40 −.67	−.04 −.14
	0	.00 +.14	.00 +.29	.00 +.18	0	.00 −.27	.00 −.29	.00 −.13
	−	−.22 −.09	−.40 −.18	−.04 −.04	−	+.04 +.07	+.40 +.08	+.22 +.06

above to both source and concept to predict the amount of attitude change that would be expected under simultaneous conditions. Then to take into account the fact that this is a learning situation, we may take some constant fraction of C—we used 1/5 arbitrarily to approximate the observed values—as the predicted attitude change in the experiment. The direction and order of magnitude of the predictions are not affected by this procedure.

On each of three stories under each of the two assertion conditions, it was possible to assign 15 subjects to each of the nine cells mentioned above as representing a different combination of original source-concept attitudes. The average expected C and average obtained C (*after-test* score minus *before-test* score) was computed for each cell. These predicted and obtained attitude-change scores, expressed in seven-step scale values, are presented in Table 32.[1] (The article by Osgood and Tannenbaum, 1955, previously referred to gives tables from which values of C for all possible combinations of original scale values can be read.) The first thing to note is that in every case where a direction of attitude change is predicted (e.g., cases where something other than zero is predicted), the sign of the obtained change corresponds to that predicted—there are 24 such cases in the table. To get at the success with which the principle predicts the relative magnitude of effect, we may correlate predicted and obtained changes; correlation over this table is .91.[2]

For the results of this experiment, then, the principle of congruity yields reasonably accurate predictions. Methodologically it should be emphasized that it is the use of the semantic differential *as a generalized attitude scale* that makes it possible to test this principle. In all cases of cognitive interaction, two or more signs are involved; only to the extent that we are able to measure them in common, comparable units can we test the implications of the congruity principle quantitatively.

★ ★ ★

SOME LIMITING AND PARAMETRIC CONDITIONS OF CONGRUITY

Both in the experiment just reported and in several to be covered later we have been made aware of a number of factors which affect operation of the principle of congruity—it seldom operates in a pure, uncomplicated fashion, as might be expected from the complexity of human cognitive processes. Here we shall indicate our awareness of at least some of these factors, as reference points for further research for the most part. In some cases we have a little data to contribute.

1. *Contiguity of signs in assertions.* Whether measurement is made of compromises at the time of assertion (e.g., the LAZY ATHLETE case) or of the signs in isolation following assertion (e.g., congruity-learning effects), the degree of contiguity in both time and space should affect the magnitude of congruity effect predicted. In the latter case it should appear in the fractional constant by which the meaning of the sign is shifted on each trial, but this in turn presumably depends upon the shift produced at the moment of assertion. We expect to be able to show that, for example, as the modifier LAZY is displaced from the nominal object ATHLETE in syntactical constructions of various

---

[1] As corrected for incredulity, see Osgood and Tannenbaum, 1955.
[2] As corrected for an assertion constant, see Osgood and Tannenbaum, 1955.

types, the effect upon the meaning of ATHLETE will diminish according to some lawful function.

2. *Intensity of assertion.* By operating on the copula of English statements or on the kind of assertive action in perceptual situations, the intensity of either associative or dissociative assertions can be modified. In language, for example, it seems intuitively true that A *gives 100 per cent support to* B is a stronger assertion than A *is cordial to* B, and that therefore the congruity effect should be greater in the former case. We have done no experiments on this, but they should be relatively straightforward.

3. *Credulity of assertions.* The congruity hypothesis in its pure form as presented above assumes complete credulity of assertions on the part of subjects. Presented with the statement, EISENHOWER *is an exponent of* COMMUNISM, it assumes the typical American receiver will "believe" this assertion and be affected accordingly. But this is not the way human receivers handle grossly incongruous messages: one typical way of "getting out of the field" cognitively is to *discredit the given or implied source* of the assertion as a whole—"This is a trick by some subversive columnist designed to deceive us," "This is obviously part of an experiment on us by some crazy professor," etc. Another type of resolution, allowing the subject to retain his existing frame of reference, is to *rationalize* the assertain—this is a typical American reaction to Russian "peace overtures" ("Look out, it's a trick to get us to relax our defenses"), and vice versa, no doubt. Another reaction to highly incongruent assertions is blank bewilderment and failure to comprehend what was said; and this may, of course, be accompanied by adjustive "mis-cognition" in which the subject swears the statement said EISENHOWER *is an opponent of* COMMUNISM.

In a very rough and preliminary attempt to make adjustments for incredulity, we have simply subtracted from incongruous assertions (+ favors –, + against +, – favors +, and – against –) a value which increases according to a negatively accelerated function with the degree of such incongruity. In other words, we assumed on intuitive grounds that an extremely incongruous assertion like EISENHOWER (+3) *sponsors* COMMUNISM (–3) is disproportionately much less credulous than a mildly incongruous assertion like EISENHOWER (+3) *praises* BULGARIA (–1). The arbitrary function used for making such corrections is given in Osgood and Tannenbaum (1955). Actually, it should be possible to ascertain the incredulity function independently of attitude change and thus determine the relationship empirically. A proposed experiment might take the following form: Subjects are presented with a large number of assertions and are told that some are "fake" and some are "valid" (e.g., come from acceptable sources); we would predict that the frequency of "fake" judgments would be some increasing function of the previously measured incongruity of the signs related in the assertions. The shape of this function would be our main interest here.

4. *Relevance of the assertion.* Quite apart from the purely evaluative locations of the signs, it appears that the *relevance* of the signs related to each other influences the magnitude of the congruity effect. Even though the sources in the following assertions may be equally favorable in general evaluation—DR. X *attacks* U.S. PUBLIC HEALTH SERVICE *on polio program* VS. AIR PILOT Y *attacks* U.S. PUBLIC HEAlTH SERVICE *on polio program*—it certainly seems likely that the congruity effect will be greater in the former than in the latter case. It is possible that "relevance" here is akin to the sharing of

characteristic attributes (or frame of reference) in the sense developed by Suci and described earlier (see pp. 116–20); this relation, however, has not been investigated.

The data from one experiment bearing directly on this question of relevancy in relation to the amount of attitude change are available.[3] On the basis of a pre-test, four relevant source-concept pairs were selected—HENRY WALLACE with PROTECTIVE FARM TARIFFS; MUSEUM OF MODERN ART with ABSTRACT ART; U.S. DEPARTMENT OF AGRICULTURE with FLEXIBLE PRICE SUPPORTS, and JOHN FOSTER DULLES with RECOGNITION OF RED CHINA. All subjects (undergraduates) indicated their attitudes toward these objects on six evaluative scales of the semantic differential, both before and after exposure to the appropriate material. There were two groups of 40 subjects each. One group was exposed to two stories in which the sources were relevant to the concepts (e.g., WALLACE with PROTECTIVE TARIFFS, and DULLES with RED CHINA), and two stories where the source-concept association was "non-relevant" (e.g., MUSEUM with FLEXIBLE PRICE SUPPORTS, and U.S. DEPARTMENT OF AGRICULTURE with ABSTRACT ART.) The second group also had two relevant and two non-relevant situations, but the reverse of those as in the first group.

As indicated in Table 33, the principle of congruity was able to predict much more efficiently (over-all $p < .01$) under relevant conditions than non-relevant ones. Only with the concept RECOGNITION OF RED CHINA were the non-relevant predictions significantly greater than the relevant ones. It is of interest to note too, that even under non-relevant conditions, congruity predicted significantly better than chance.

TABLE 33. PER CENT OF TOTAL ATTITUDE SHIFT BY INDIVIDUAL SUBJECTS PREDICTED BY PRINCIPLE OF CONGRUITY*

Sources	Per Cent as Predicted in Relevant Situation	Per Cent as Predicted in Non-relevant Situation	P_{diff}
U.S. Department of Agriculture	79	67	.05
Museum of Modern Art	90	92	NS
Henry Wallace	81	56	.01
John Foster Dulles	82	73	NS
Combined Sources	83	71	.01
Concepts			
FLEXIBLE PRICE SUPPORTS	99	87	.01
PROTECTIVE TARIFFS	98	86	.01
ABSTRACT ART	87	63	.01
RED CHINA	85	97	.01
COMBINED CONCEPTS	92	82	.01

*All figures are rounded to the nearest per cent.

5. *Meaning of the copula or action itself as a variable.* In many cases the linguistic copula or the assertive action itself has meaning apart from its associative or dissociative function. Take for example the linguistic assertion JONES *lied about* SMITH or the behavioral situation in which A *saves the life of* B. Not only do we have a dissociative relation between JONES and SMITH and an associative one between A and B indicated,

[3]This study was conducted by Dr. Jean S. Kerrick at the University of California in 1955.

but we also have the implied assertions that JONES *is* A LIAR and A *is* A LIFESAVER. By the congruity principle, then, we should expect attitude toward JONES to be less favorable and attitude toward A to be more favorable, quite apart from their relations with the third members of the assertions. What we are saying is that all lexical (meaningful) members in assertions, whether they occur as subjects, copulas, or objects, participate in cognitive congruity interactions. Although we have done no direct experiments on this, these notions have been utilized fruitfully in a new method of content analysis (see Osgood, Saporta, and Nunnally, 1956). Also, the effect of the copula of assertions upon congruity predictions was noted by Osgood and Tannenbaum (1955) in the attitude-change study reported above, and had to be taken into account. In this case—where a source makes an assertion about a concept (SENATOR TAFT *sponsors* ACCELERATED COLLEGE PROGRAMS)—it seemed likely that the concept would absorb more of the copula effect (e.g., being sponsored vs. being denounced) than the source. In any event, analysis showed that in every case but one where direct comparisons were possible, concepts showed greater magnitudes of attitude change than did sources (17/18 cases).

SUMMARY

The congruity principle appears to be a very general process operating whenever cognitive events interact. These interactions are such that the representational processes characteristic of related signs are modified toward congruity with each other, degree of modification being inversely proportional to the original intensities of the processes in isolation. The effects of such interactions persist and accumulate as do other learning phenomena, resulting in changes in the meanings of the signs when measured in isolation. So far our experiments have dealt mainly with congruity phenomena as they occur in language behavior, in the attitude area, in word meanings, and in the aesthetics area. But it seems likely to us that congruity will also apply to overt behavioral situations, e.g., to changes in the like-dislike structure of interacting groups (sociometry and group dynamics) and to the interactions between individuals and objects in their environment. Using notions very much like these, Festinger (in a forthcoming book) has done many experiments in this behavioral area. Newcomb (1953) has also utilized similar notions in his theoretical analysis of interpersonal communication. The earliest expression of ideas dealing with "congruity" in human thinking, at least in contemporary psychology, may be found in a paper by Heider (1946).

REFERENCES

Campbell, D. T. (1953). Generalized attitude scales. In O. K. Buros (ed.), *The fourth mental measurements yearbook.* Highland Park, N. J.: Gryphen Press, pp. 90–91.
Cantril, H. (1946). The intensity of an attitude. *J. abnorm. soc. Psychol., 41*, 129–36.
Clark, E. K. (1953). Generalized attitude scales. In O. K. Buros (ed.), *The fourth mental measurements yearbook.* Highland Park, N. J.: Gryphen Press, pp. 91–92.
Doob, L. W. (1947). The behavior of attitudes. *Psychol. Rev., 54*, 135–56.
Dunlap, J. W., and A. Kroll. (1939). Observations on the methodology of attitude scales. *J. soc. Psychol., 10*, 475–87.
Heider, F. (1946). Attitudes and cognitive organization. *J. Psychol., 21*, 107–12.

Katz, D. (1944). The measurement of intensity. In H. Cantril (ed.), *Gauging public opinion.* Princeton: Princeton University Press, pp. 51–65.

Krech, D., and R. S. Crutchfield. (1948). *Theory and problems in social psychology.* New York: McGraw-Hill.

McNemar, Q. (1946). Opinion-attitude methodology. *Psychol. Bull., 43,* 289–374.

Newcomb, T. M. (1953). An approach to the study of communicative acts. *Psychol. Rev., 60,* 393–404.

Osgood, C. E., and Zella Luria, S. Saporta, and J. C. Nunnally. (1956). *Evaluative assertion analysis.* Urbana: Inst. of Communications Research, University of Illinois. (Mimeographed.)

_____, and P. H. Tannenbaum. (1955). The principle of congruity in the prediction of attitude change. *Psychol. Rev., 62,* 42–55.

Remmers, H. H. (1934). Studies in attitudes. *Bull. Purdue Univ. Stud. Higher Educ., 35,* No. 4.

_____, and Ella B. Silance. (1934). Generalized attitude scales, *J. soc. Psychol., 5,* 298–312.

Suci, G. J. (1952). A multidimensional analysis of social attitudes with special reference to ethnocentrism. Unpublished doctor's dissertation, University of Illinois.

Tannenbaum, P. H. (1953). Attitudes toward source and concept as factors in attitude change through communications. Unpublished doctor's dissertation, University of Illinois.

6 · DYADIC RELATIONSHIPS

JOHN W. THIBAUT
HAROLD H. KELLEY

Social Psychology of Groups: Dyadic Interaction*

Our conceptualization of the dyad, a two-person relationship, begins with an analysis of interaction and of its consequences for the two individuals concerned. The major analytic technique used throughout the book is a matrix formed by taking account of all the behaviors the two individuals might enact together. Each cell in this matrix represents one of the possible parts of the interaction between the two and summarizes the consequences for each person of that possible event. Although consequences can be analyzed and measured in many ways, we have found it desirable to distinguish positive components (*rewards*) from negative components (*costs*). The many factors affecting the rewards and costs associated with each portion of the matrix are described and note is taken of certain sequential effects that are not handled systematically in the present scheme.

The actual course of interaction between two individuals is viewed as only partially predictable from the matrix. Initial interactions in a forming relationship are viewed as explorations which sample only a few of the many possibilities. Interaction is continued only if the experienced consequences are found to meet the standards of acceptability that both individuals develop by virtue of their experience with other relationships. Several such standards that an individual may apply are indentified, and these are related to such phenomena as attraction, dependence, and status. These concepts then set the stage for the more intensive analysis carried forward in subsequent chapters.

To clarify the ways in which the matrix of outcomes may be used in the prediction of behavior, we conclude the chapter by discussing in some detail the conditions under which it may be so used and anticipating briefly some of the further applications of the matrix to problems developed later in the book.

*John W. Thibaut and Harold H. Kelley, *The Social Psychology of Groups* (New York: John Wiley & Sons, 1959), pp. 10–29.

2.1 ANALYSIS OF INTERACTION

The essence of any interpersonal relationship is *interaction*. Two individuals may be said to have formed a relationship when on repeated occasions they are observed to interact. By interaction it is meant that they emit behavior in each other's presence, they create products for each other, or they communicate with each other. In every case we would identify as an instance of interaction there is at least the possibility that the actions of each person affect the other.

There are many things that an individual can do in interaction with another person. It might be said that each person has a vast repertoire of possible behaviors, any one of which he might produce in an interaction. There are many different ways of describing and analyzing the items in this repertoire. For example, a boy and girl are observed in their first conversation. The observer may list the specific bodily movements and verbal statements each makes; or he may simply describe the general "progress" that each makes with the other—what each attempts to accomplish in the interaction and the extent to which this is achieved. Although the exact choice depends somewhat upon the problem considered, for most purposes we have chosen to employ a unit of analysis that is intermediate between these extremes. In the example we would note that the boy first tells about his recent activities on the football field. He then, perhaps with considerable embarrassment and in a back-handed way, compliments the girl on her appearance. He finally helps her with an algebra problem. The girl's behavior would be described in similar terms.

Our unit for the analysis of behavior is referred to as the *behavior sequence* or *set*. Each unit to be identified consists of a number of specific motor and verbal acts that exhibit some degree of sequential organization directed toward the attainment of some immediate goal or end state. Typically, a sequence of this sort consists of some responses that are mainly instrumental in moving the person toward the final state. Other responses —perceptual, interpretive, consummatory in nature—can usually be identified as affording appreciation or enjoyment of the goal state. If enough observations were at hand, the elements of a given sequence could be identified on the basis of certain statistical regularities: the elements would be found to occur together repeatedly and to be performed in certain sequential arrangements. Transitions from one sequence to another would be observed as points at which serial dependency is low, actions at the end of a sequence providing relatively little basis for predicting what actions will follow.

The organization apparent in behavior sequences suggests that the person maintains a more or less constant orientation or intention throughout the sequence. We refer to this aspect of the behavior sequence as *set*, although loosely we use set and behavior sequence interchangeably. When a behavior sequence is observed, we may say that the individual has assumed a certain set. The probabilities of occurrence of the instrumental and appreciative behaviors comprising the sequence are heightened when the appropriate set is aroused. However, a set may be aroused without the corresponding behavior sequence being enacted. Thus the concept of set is useful in considering situations in which there is a tendency to produce a given sequence but in which this tendency does not, for various reasons, result in overt performance of the sequence. In this case we may still deduce the existence of a set if certain other manifestations (evidence of conflict or tension) are present. The specific set or sets aroused at any given time depend upon instigations, both from within the person (e.g., need or drive states) and from outside (incentives, problem situations or tasks confronting him, experimental instructions), and the reinforcement previously associated with enactment of the set. The stability- of a set depends upon the temporal persistence of the stimuli that serve to instigate it.

Each person's repertoire of behaviors consists of all possible sets he may enact (or behavior sequences may perform) and all possible combinations of these sets. Any portion of the stream of interaction between two persons can be described in terms of the items they *actually produce* from their respective repertoires.

2.1.1 The Consequences of Interaction

When the interactions of a number of persons are observed, it usually becomes quite apparent that interaction is a highly selective matter, both with respect to who interacts with whom and with respect to what any pair of persons interacts about. Not all possible pairs of individuals are observed to enter into interaction, and any given pair enacts only certain of the many behaviors they are capable of. Although there are several different ways of accounting for this selectivity, we assume that in part it indicates that different interactions in different relationships have different consequences for the individual. Some relationships are more satisfactory than others, and the same is true of some interactions within a given relationship. The selectivity observed in interaction reflects the tendency for more satisfactory interactions to recur and for less satisfactory ones to disappear.

The consequences of interaction can be described in many different terms, but we have found it useful to distinguish only between the rewards a person receives and the costs he incurs.

By rewards, we refer to the pleasures, satisfactions, and gratifications the person enjoys. The provision of a means whereby a drive is reduced or a need fulfilled constitutes a reward. We assume that the amount of reward provided by any such experience can be measured and that the reward values of different modalities of gratification are reducible to a single psychological scale.

By costs, we refer to any factors that operate to inhibit or deter the performance of a sequence of behavior. The greater the deterrence to performing a given act—the greater the inhibition the individual has to overcome—the greater the cost of the act. Thus cost is high when great physical or mental effort is required, When embarrassment or anxiety accompany the action, or when there are conflicting forces or competing response tendencies of any sort. Costs derived from these different factors are also assumed to be measurable on a common psychological scale, and costs of different sorts, to be additive in their effect.

The consequences or *outcomes* for an individual participant of any interaction or series of interactions can be stated, then, in terms of the rewards received and the costs incurred, these values depending upon the behavioral items which the two persons produce in the course of their interaction. For some purposes it is desirable to treat rewards and costs separately; for other purposes it is assumed that they can be combined into a single scale of "goodness" of outcome, with states of high reward and low cost being given high-scale values and states of low reward and high cost, low-scale values. Admittedly, such a scaling operation would be a very ambitious enterprise and would present a number of technical difficulties. However, the present interest is in the theoretical consequences of such an operation (real or imaginary) rather than in its technical properties or even its feasibility.

2.1.2 The Matrix of Possible Interactions and Outcomes

All portions of the interaction between two persons, A and B, can be represented by the matrix shown in Table 2-1. Along the horizontal axis of this matrix are placed all the items in A's behavior repertoire and along the vertical axis, the items in B's repertoire.

TABLE 2-1. MATRIX OF POSSIBLE INTERACTIONS AND OUTCOMES

A's repertoire

	a_1	a_2	...	a_n	a_1a_2	a_1a_3	...	$a_1a_2...a_n$
b_1	r_A,c_A / r_B,c_B	etc.	...					
b_2	etc.							
⋮	⋮							
b_n								
b_1b_2								
b_1b_3								
⋮								
$b_1b_2...b_n$								

B's repertoire

The cells of the matrix represent all possible events that may occur in the interaction between A and B, since at each moment the interaction may be described in terms of the items (consisting of one or more sets) that each one is *enacting*. (This assumes that each person is always in some set, even if only in a passive set in which he merely makes the responses necessary to observe, interpret, or appreciate what the other person is doing.) Although Table 2-1 presents the matrix in its most general form, for many purposes a much simpler matrix will provide an adequate description of the possibilities. This will be true, for example, when an experimenter restricts his subjects to a limited number of responses or when an observer partitions his subjects' behavioral repertoires into a small number of mutually exclusive and exhaustive classes.

Entered in each cell of the matrix are the outcomes, in terms of rewards gained and costs incurred, to each person of that particular portion of the interaction. If rewards and costs are combined into a single scale of goodness of outcome, the matrix can be simplified as in Table 2-2.

TABLE 2-2. MATRIX OF POSSIBLE OUTCOMES, SCALED ACCORDING TO OVER-ALL GOODNESS OF OUTCOMES

A's repertoire

	a_1	a_2	$\cdots$	
b_1	6 / 2	1 / 0	$\cdots$	
b_2	1 / 4	2 / 5	$\cdots$	
$\vdots$	$\vdots$	$\vdots$		

B's repertoire

2.2 EXOGENOUS DETERMINANTS OF REWARDS AND COSTS

The reward and cost values entered in the matrix in Table 2-1 depend in the first place upon factors that are more or less external *to the relationship*. Each individual carries his values, needs, skills, tools, and predispositions to anxiety with him as he moves among the various relationships in which he participates. Hence we refer to them as *exogenous* factors.

The magnitude of rewards to be gained by the two members from the various elements will depend upon their individual needs and values and the congruency of the behaviors or behavioral products with these needs and values. Each person's rewards may be derived (1) directly from his own behavior and/or (2) from the other's behavior. The former consist of rewards the individual could produce for himself if he were alone. Any rewards he receives that depend in any way upon the other individual, even if only upon the presence of the other, will be considered as depending upon the other's behavior. For example, A obtains satisfaction from doing things for B. We can interpret this to mean that B can produce rewards for A (probably at very low cost) by simply assuming a passive set in which he receives A's contributions, and perhaps, acknowledges receipt in some way.

In what might be characterized as a true trading relationship all of each person's rewards are derived from the other's efforts. More typical, perhaps, is the case in which each one's rewards depend in part upon his own behaviors and in part upon the other's behaviors.

When A produces an item from his repertoire, his costs depend on his skills and on the availability to him of efficient tools or instruments as well as on the degree to which anxiety or discomfort is associated with producing the various elements. Where A's actions are concerned, B's costs depend on the degree to which any of A's behaviors are punishing to him, whether by arousing anxiety or embarrassment or by causing physical harm.

2.3 ENDOGENOUS DETERMINANTS OF REWARDS AND COSTS

The second class of determinants of rewards and costs includes those intrinsic to the interaction itself, referred to as *endogenous* factors. The central point is that the specific values associated with a given item in A's repertoire depend upon the particular item in B's repertoire with which, in the course of the interaction, it is paired.

As noted in the discussion of sets, the performance of a set requires making a series of responses, some of which are primarily instrumental in nature and others, primarily consummatory. Even the enjoyment of one person's performance by another requires that the latter make some responses of an attentive and consummatory type. For all responses of which a person is capable there are other responses that are more or less incompatible with them. By incompatibility is meant that these responses tend to interfere with the performance of one another. The performance of one response serves as a distraction or disturbance to the performance of the other.

One consequence of this interference is to raise the costs required to produce one or both responses. In the extreme case one or both responses may be completely inhibited by the other. There is also the likelihood that under conditions of interference one or both responses will be performed less well (i.e., less strongly, less rapidly, or less accurately). In this regard, however, there is the possibility that, for simple, easy-to-perform, overlearned, highly integrated responses, interference may not affect or may even improve the quality of performance.

Response interference may exist, of course, whenever a person is enacting two or more sets at the same time. If A produces the item a_1a_3 from his repertoire and if set a_1 includes responses incompatible with those in a_3, then the total costs involved are likely to be greater than if he had on one occasion enacted a_1 and on another, a_3. Furthermore, the total rewards might very well have been greater in the latter case. The reward and cost values associated with the item a_1a_3 in A's repertoire will reflect any such interference effects that may exist.

Interference may also be created by a set which, though partially aroused, is not overtly enacted. For example, A may by producing set a_1 at the same time that there are weak instigations to set a_3. The latter behavior sequence may not be enacted but response *tendencies* may be aroused which interfere with the optimal production of a_1. The partial arousal of sets is important in interaction because, as noted earlier, the behaviors of other persons often act as instigators of sets. So interaction affords many opportunities for response interference to arise.

Consider the implications of response interference for the effects of interaction upon rewards and costs. Assume that A produces set a_1 from his repertoire. The cost of producing the responses subsumed under this set will be minimal (where the minimum depends on such relatively stable exogenous factors as his tools and skills) only if no tendencies to make incompatible responses exist at the same time. If while A is performing a_1, B is also enacting set b_2 and this action partially arouses set a_3 in A, a set which is incompatible with a_1, then A's costs of producing a_1 are likely to be heightened and the quality of his behavior to be decreased. If the reward value of a_1, either to A himself or to B, depends upon the quality of A's performance, this will also suffer.

If b_2 interferes with a_1, then a_1 is likely also to interfere with b_2. (Here we assume that interference is frequently a symmetrical relation.) One consequence of this interference is that A's enjoyment of b_2 may be attenuated by virtue of its being presented while he is in set a_1. His costs of making the necessary consummatory responses are likely to be raised. He will have to work harder to "receive" and "process" the content of b_2. His rewards may also be reduced because of his not being able to give the necessary attention or consideration to B's performance of b_2. The same situation may, of course, be considered from the point of view of B's costs and rewards.

In general, response interference raises the cost of making responses, whether these are the instrumental responses essential to the enactment of a set or the attentive, interpretive, and appreciative responses essential to its consummation. Interference may also operate to lower rewards by producing a deterioration in the quality of responses made. This deterioration of quality may not occur, however, for activities that are well learned and performed more or less automatically. In the presence of an incompatible set such responses may even be enacted with greater intensity, frequency, or accuracy than usual, which might be expected to result in the availability of more or better rewards and, possibly, in an intensification of the pleasures derived from appreciating or consuming them.

The foregoing statements about the effects on reward-cost outcomes of the simultaneous arousal of incompatible sets may be represented in the simplified form of Table 2-3. This table shows the outcomes to A when we consider a simple situation in which

TABLE 2-3. POSSIBLE OUTCOMES TO *A*
WHERE EACH MEMBER'S REPERTOIRE
HAS ONLY TWO SETS

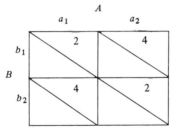

each member has only two sets in his repertoire. Note that the hypothetical numbers entered in the table have been arranged to show a statistical interaction effect, that is, the size of A's outcome depends on the particular combination of one of his own sets with one of B's sets. The patterning of outcomes to A might conceivably have occurred in the following way:

If b_1 partially arouses some responses (or set) incompatible with a_1 and if b_2 is similarly incompatible with a_2, then interference either in B's production of the behavior or in A's attending to, interpreting, or consuming the rewards would reduce A's outcomes, in this case from 4 units to 2 units.

This example is merely illustrative and should be taken only to suggest a way in which a statistical interaction of outcomes may be derived from the effects of interference or facilitation.

2.3.1 Sequential Effects

Another type of endogenous determinant of rewards and costs in the dyad has to do with the time-patterning of the various items of a repertoire. The rewards and costs derived from the enactment of an item in a repertoire will be affected by the prior items enacted. More specifically, as the same behaviors are repeated over and over, the reward value of each unit of behavior may decrease over time. This is the commonly observed tendency of a need state to *satiate*. A parallel effect would be expected on the cost side. As the same behavior is repeated, the production of the behavior will become gradually more costly as *fatigue* sets in.

Because of these two effects of immediate repetition, the successive arousal of the same set would require increasingly strong instigations to overcome fatigue, and at the same time the recipient of the behavior would become less and less likely, as satiation develops, to instigate the producer to repeat his behavior. Hence the likelihood of immediate re-arousal of a set usually will be less than the likelihood of initial arousal of that set. As a direct consequence, in order to keep rewards up and costs down, both members of a dyad are likely to shift, over time, from one item to another in their repertoires with very little immediate repetition of the same items.

Although there will be a tendency to avoid such situations, sometimes there will be overridingly strong instigations from the task requirements or from outside the dyad to repeat the same sets. Relationships in which such instigations are chronic or in which repertoires include too few alternatives to permit nonrepetition will either be dissolved or become intermittent.

Although these sequential effects are undoubtedly important, we will disregard them in entering numbers in the reward-cost matrices. This does not imply any disparagement of the significance of such sequential effects but only that they must be studied by means other than those of such reward-cost matrices as are described here. Nor does this mean that the numbers entered to describe reward-cost outcomes are totally free from satiation and fatigue effects. The psychologically scaled rewards and costs of individual items of a repertoire would be expected to include any experienced fatigue (as cost increase) or satiation (as reward decrease), insofar as these effects occur within a single item. However, satiation and fatigue will not be reflected in a matrix as an accumulation over a sequence of identical or similar items. The numbers entered in a matrix represent instead the maximum rewards and minimum costs on the assumption that there is no transfer of satiation or fatigue from item to item.

2.4 THE ACTUAL COURSE OF INTERACTION

The matrix formed by A's and B's behavioral repertoires taken jointly defines all the different things they might possibly do in interaction with each other. The reward-cost values in the matrix represent the outcomes each person would experience for each of the manifold interaction possibilities. In a sense, the facts summarized in this matrix set the limits within which their actual interaction must occur. The actual course of their interaction cannot, however, be predicted merely from a knowledge of this matrix. Whether or not interaction will be begun, what course it will actually take, and what reward-cost positions each individual will actually achieve—these all depend upon a number of factors only some of which are related to the matrix of possible outcomes.

Interaction may begin for quite different reasons. One or both persons may know something about the other and, on the basis of this information, may anticipate that interaction would yield good outcomes. This would result in a deliberate decision to seek out the other person and interact with him. Under other circumstances the two persons may be thrown together by the operation of factors beyond their control. Their jobs may bring them together, common friends may introduce them, or residence in the same neighborhood may result in a chance meeting. In these instances interaction is begun in response to the immediate situation without any necessary anticipation of the possible consequences by either participant.

Whether or not interaction continues, once begun, depends upon similar considerations. If good outcomes are experienced in initial contacts or if these contacts lead the persons to anticipate good outcomes in the future, the interaction is likely to be repeated; and, of course, the external influences of work, friends, and neighborhood may continue to make interaction necessary.

According to the view expressed above, the early exploratory interactions are very important in determining the further fate of the potential relationship. The interaction occurring during this period may be conceived as a sampling process in which the pair of individuals, by virtue of the items each selects from his behavioral repertoire, experience a sample of the possible interactions and outcomes represented by their joint matrix. The sampling analogy suggests a number of generalizations. For example, the greater the proportion of good outcomes in the matrix, the more likely they are to be experienced during early contacts. Similarly, the larger the sample drawn (that is, the more different interactions in the first encounter), the greater the likelihood the two individuals will experience the better of the outcomes potentially available to them. Of course, the interactions sampled are unlikely to be representative of the entire universe of possibilities. The situation in which first contact occurs may favor the arousal of certain sets to the exclusion of others. For example, only certain kinds of behaviors are appropriate when two men meet in the course of their work. There are general cultural mores which deal with the correct things to do and say when first introduced to another person. Even in the absence of external instigations to certain sets, the individual may draw selectively from his behavioral repertoire. In new relationships in which the ultimate payoff is uncertain individuals are unlikely to produce items of high cost to themselves. For example, A may completely avoid mentioning a certain esoteric interest if this has evoked contempt in other relationships. If this happens to be an interest B shares and enjoys discussing, one of the best outcomes potentially available in the A-B relationship may be completely overlooked.

Whatever the nature of the early exchanges between A and B, they will voluntarily continue their association only if the experienced outcomes (or inferred but as yet unexperienced outcomes) are found to be adequate. This raises the problem, to which we next turn, of the criteria against which experienced or anticipated outcomes are evaluated.

2.5 EVALUATION OF OUTCOMES: COMPARISON LEVELS

In evaluating the adequacy of the sampled and anticipated outcomes of a relationship, the members of a dyad will have need for some kind of standard or criterion of the acceptability of outcomes. At least two important kinds of standard for such an evaluation can be identified. To try to make the distinction between these two standards as intuitively clear as possible, we may begin by saying that the first of these, called the *comparison level* (or CL), is the standard against which the member evaluates the "attractiveness" of the relationship or how satisfactory it is. The second, called the *comparison level for alternatives* (or CL_{alt}), is the standard the member uses in deciding whether to remain in or to leave the relationship. The two standards are distinguished in recognition of the fact that circumstances may require a person to remain in a relationship that he regards as unsatisfactory. Although these standards are described and illustrated in some detail in Chapters 6, 7, and 10, a bit of elaboration is probably called for.

CL is a standard by which the person evaluates the rewards and costs of a given relationship in terms of what he feels he "deserves." Relationships the outcomes of which fall above CL would be relatively "satisfying" and attractive to the member; those entailing outcomes that fall below CL would be relatively "unsatisfying" and unattractive. The location of CL on the person's scale of outcomes will be influenced by all of the outcomes known to the member, either by direct experience or symbolically. It may be taken to be some modal or average value of all known outcomes, each outcome weighted by its "salience," or strength of instigation, which depends, for example, upon the recency of experiencing the outcome and the occurrence of stimuli which serve as reminders of the outcome. Because these factors are likely to be absent or weak in the case of relationships and interactions that are unattainable, the latter will ordinarily have little weight in determining the location of CL.

CL_{alt} can be defined informally as the lowest level of outcomes a member will accept in the light of available alternative opportunities. It follows from this definition that as soon as outcomes drop below CL_{alt} the member will leave the relationship. The height of the CL_{alt} will depend mainly on the quality of the best of the member's available alternatives, that is, the reward-cost positions experienced or believed to exist in the most satisfactory of the other available relationships.

As in the case of CL, the outcomes that determine the location of CL_{alt} will be weighted by their *salience* (how strongly they are instigated). Unlikely outcomes in the alternative relationship will usually have little weight in fixing the location of CL_{alt} because, again, the salience of such outcomes will ordinarily be rather low.

The alternative relationships with which the present one is compared in evolving the CL_{alt} may include other dyads, more complex relationships, or even the alternative of joining no group, of working or being alone. From this last alternative it appears that a member's CL_{alt} will usually be heightened to the degree that he is independently able to produce rewards for himself at competitive costs. More precisely, the CL_{alt} will be heightened by any favorable reward-cost positions that a member can regularly attain by virtue of his ability to carry self-produced rewards with him from relationship to relationship. Since such rewards are portable, the attractiveness of all alternatives is increased by an amount equal to these rewards.

From the foregoing comments it is plain that if a relationship is to form and survive positions above CL_{alt} must exist and positions below CL_{alt} must be eliminated from the relationship. What may not be quite so obvious is that the CL_{alt} may also eliminate some of the best positions in the reward-cost space. Specifically, A's good outcomes will be eliminated from the relationship if these outcomes are attainable only when B's costs of producing them are so high that B's corresponding outcomes are below his CL_{alt}. An increasing proportion of A's best outcomes can be attained in the relationship (1) the lower is B's CL_{alt} and (2) the greater the degree to which the goodness of A's and B's outcomes are positively associated; that is, both have high rewards and/or low costs in some cells of the matrix (Table 2-1) and low rewards and/or high costs in other cells. These two conditions mean that a given dyad can make possible the attainment of better reward and cost values than are available in other relationships only if, to some degree, each member's behavior in the dyad contributes to the other's rewards without a corresponding excessive increase in his own costs. In short, a prerequisite for the existence of the dyad is a dependence of the rewards of each upon the other's behavior, that is, a condition of interdependence.

To summarize the main points developed so far, the formation of a relationship depends largely upon

(1) the matrix of the possible outcomes of interaction;

(2) the process of exploring or sampling the possibilities; and *ultimately*

(3) whether or not the *jointly* experienced outcomes are above each member's CL_{alt}.

2.5.1 Attraction and Dependence in the Dyad

We have asserted that whether or not an individual attains (or at least expects to attain) reward-cost positions above his CL_{alt} determines whether or not he will remain in a given dyadic relationship. It is but a small step to the further assumption that the degree to which his attained positions exceed his CL_{alt} determines how greatly he depends on the dyad for favorable outcomes. Accordingly, the numbers entered in the cells of the simplified matrix of possible outcomes (Table 2-2) will usually be scaled from CL_{alt} as the zero point. The entries in such a matrix indicate the degree to which each person is dependent upon the dyad, and the pattern of entries shows the manner in which the two persons are interdependent.

However, the individual may be greatly dependent on the dyad without its being "attractive" to him to a commensurate degree—without his being satisfied with the relationship. In other words, a member's dependency on the group (hence, as we will see in Chapter 7, its power over him) is not necessarily highly correlated with his attraction to the group, his "morale" or satisfaction from belonging to it.

It is to afford a way of dealing with this possible discrepancy between dependency and attraction that CL_{alt} is distinguished from CL, where, to repeat, the former's relevance is to dependency and the latter's relevance is to attraction. In any viable relationship the individual's outcomes will be located above his CL_{alt}; but his CL may have several different positions in relation to his outcomes and CL_{alt}. First, it may be below both. In this case the individual may be expected to be highly satisfied with the relationship. It affords him outcomes superior to his CL, and at the same time he is provided with only slightly less favorable outcomes in his available alternative relationships. The relationship may be highly attractive without his necessarily being greatly dependent on it.

Second, his CL may be below his outcomes but above his CL_{alt}. In this instance he will find the relationship satisfactory, but his dependence upon it will exceed his attraction to it.

Finally, there is the very important class of *nonvoluntary* relationships in which the CL exceeds the individual's outcomes (and, of course, his CL_{alt}). Any relationship has a nonvoluntary component to the degree that salient outcomes, unavailable in the relationship, are superior to those that exist in the relationship. In this respect, relationships will vary only in degree. However, we rather arbitrarily define a nonvoluntary relationship as one in which the individual's outcomes in the relationship fall below his CL. Here he would be expected to be dissatisfied with the relationship. In extreme cases, as in prisons and concentration camps, the outcomes in the relationship may be so poor that hardly any still poorer alternatives are available. This type of relationship is described in Chapter 10.

A person's attraction to a dyad depends upon his evaluation of his outcomes in relation to his CL, where the CL reflects the entire population of outcomes known to the person. An important subclass of such outcomes is that which includes the outcomes perceived to be attained by one's partner in the relationship; hence one's own outcomes may come to be evaluated in relation to a standard based on such perceived outcomes. A consideration of these evaluations permits us to introduce the concept of *status*, further discussion of which is deferred to Chapter 12.

2.6 THE NATURE AND UTILITY OF THE OUTCOME MATRIX

As used here, the matrix is a device for representing the joint outcomes from social interaction accruing to the members of a dyad. In subsequent chapters we attempt to extend the application of the matrix in two ways: (1) to aid in assessing the viability of a group, the satisfactions and patterns of interdependence of its members, and the processes through which the members influence and control one another, and (2) to permit an analysis of behavior in groups larger than the dyad. In view of its pervasive utilization in the remainder of the book, it seems advisable to be as clear as possible about its nature and functions.

The matrix closely resembles the payoff matrices used in game theory (Luce and Raiffa, 1957). Our matrix would describe a non-zero-sum game, inasmuch as A does not necessarily achieve his payoffs at B's expense or vice versa. However, in important ways our assumptions about this matrix differ from game theoretic assumptions. First, we do not assume that the values in the matrix are fixed, even over short time spans. Because of satiation and fatigue, if the combination of actions represented by a particular cell is repeated, on successive occasions the reward values are likely to decline and the costs to increase. One important consequence is that interaction is not ordinarily the mere repetition of one combination of best items. Interaction is not usually a game in which there is a single best or *dominant* solution. Rather, it often consists of successive movements from one cell of the matrix to another.

Second, we do not assume that the persons begin the game with complete knowledge of the entire matrix and the payoffs contained therein. These facts are discovered through a process of exploration, partly trial and error in nature and partly governed by prediction, extrapolation, etc. The reward-cost matrix is the matrix of *objectively* available outcomes. However, for some purposes we shall assume that the matrix describes the *subjective* understandings and anticipations of the possible interactions and outcomes, however inadequately these may represent the actual universe of possibilities.

The use of the matrix in this book may also be compared with that of Deutsch (1957) in his investigations of interpersonal trust. There are many different sources of the rewards and costs that we summarize in each cell. For example, in an experimental situation the experimenter might award points or dollars in a way that depends on the joint decisions of the two subjects. But the subjects might also gain satisfaction from other sources, as, for example, from helping each other or from competing with each other. We assume that *all* of the outcomes to the individual resulting from a given joint action are indicated by his payoff numbers in the various cells. In contrast, Deutsch has followed the convention of using the matrix to represent only the payoffs delivered formally by the experimenter. Other sources of variations in rewards are introduced by experimental instructions (e.g., giving the subjects a cooperative versus a competitive "orientation"), but these are treated outside the game matrix. The matrices seem, for Deutsch, to be largely a means of depicting the formal structure of experimental situations. His theoretical orientation is not primarily a game theoretic one but consists instead of a logical and phenomenological analysis of various interpersonal constructs. We raise this point of comparison not as an adequate characterization of Deutsch's approach but to emphasize the fact that our analysis always assumes that *all of the relevant variations in costs and rewards are represented by the matrix values.*

Since matrices of the type proposed here have not been widely used in social psychology, it is perhaps not too serious a digression to consider the possible utility of this device, particularly in the prediction of behavior. The reward-cost matrix, as we have previously said, is an "objective" statement of the possible outcomes, given the behavior repertoires of the two persons. This matrix is only a description of the *consequences* of behaviors and strictly speaking cannot be used to predict the behaviors themselves. Only under certain conditions does it seem possible to predict behavior from such a matrix.

Consider the use of A's outcomes to predict his behavior. Suppose that B enacts a given behavior and further suppose that the reward-cost matrix is such that the outcomes to A vary, depending upon what he does in turn. Suppose we actually observe A's behavior in a large number of such instances and then place in each cell of the matrix, alongside the reward-cost values, the proportion of the observed instances (given each of B's several behaviors) in which A manifests each of his behaviors. We refer to these proportions as *probabilities* of each of A's behaviors, understanding each one to indicate the likelihood that A will perform a certain act, given the fact that B has performed a certain one.

If there are no major discrepancies between these probabilities and the corresponding reward-cost values, then the reward-cost values could be used to predict behavior. If there are major discrepancies, the values cannot be so used and merely indicate consequences of behavior.

In this book we limit ourselves to the use of reward-cost matrices on the grounds that in ordinary social relationships the two sets of values ultimately tend to correspond fairly well. We will now attempt to defend this view. In order to do so, we must comment briefly upon the determinants of behavior and their contributions to discrepancies between the consequences of an act and the probability that it will occur. We have chosen to use a very simple behavior theory which we believe to be largely compatible with more sophisticated models and precise enough for present purposes. We assume that the probability of any one of A's behaviors being elicited is a function of two factors: (1) the strength of instigation to it (from either external or internal stimuli) and (2) previously experienced reinforcement resulting from it. Probability of occurrence reflects both of these factors, whereas the objective reward-cost matrix reflects only the reinforcement consequent on the act.

We can, then, identify two classes of situations in which there may be discrepancies between the probability of elicitation and the outcome:

(1) When responses are so dependably under the control of a stimulus that they can be elicited even when the consequences are unfavorable.

(2) When the objective reinforcements have not yet been experienced.

The first class of situations includes a variety of behaviors which depend for their elicitation mainly upon strong instigation or which are so "ready" to be elicited that little instigation is necessary. One such class would be reflexive behavior, such as elimination responses in the infant and startle responses. Another class would include the highly overlearned habits or routines that occur dependably whenever appropriate cues set them off. Routines would include those learned through special training and drill and social-role practice. Phenomenally, these are the instances in which a person acts without taking account of consequences. (For example, soldiers, firemen, and policemen are trained to react automatically in danger situations without regard to reward-cost outcomes.) Time pressure or urgency of action may be viewed as heightening the effects of instigations. This is illustrated by the children's game "Simon says." The readiness to behave imitatively, probably even initially a powerful factor, is established by practice trials during which imitation is appropriate. Then, under the necessity of acting quickly, children imitate the action of the leader even when it constitutes an error (presumably a negative outcome for the child).

The second class of situations includes those in which the contingencies between specific behaviors and particular objective reinforcements have not been experienced enough to have been learned. These would consist often of situations that are objectively novel, whether recognized as such or not. Phenomenally, the person does not yet have sufficient information about the objective consequences to take account of them accurately, even though, being under no strong instigations or time pressure, he may have time to do so. Time pressure and powerful instigations may act not only to prevent the use of information about consequences (as indicated earlier) but may also prevent the acquisition of accurate and adequate information in the first place. A person's exploration and sampling of the matrix may be severely limited and biased by these factors. The processes of acquiring information about the matrix of consequences are a major concern in discussing the formation and development of social relationships.

Under other conditions there is high correspondence between the probability of behavior elicitation and the reward-cost outcomes. This is true when (1) instigations are in line with outcomes *or* (2) when instigations are weak and outcomes are known in advance.

Is it defensible to believe that, as we have already asserted, situations of noncorrespondence tend over time to generate the conditions for correspondence, hence enabling a matrix of outcomes to form the basis for a useful theory of interaction? We think so for the reasons that follow.

A person does learn the consequences of his actions if given the opportunity (time, exposure) and if he has the talents. Moreover, when a person enters a relationship in which there are powerful instigations to behaviors with unfavorable consequences, some sort of change is very probable: either he leaves, or the instigations are somehow eliminated or made more appropriate. If they come from inappropriate habits he has carried into the relationship, he may relearn more suitable ones. If the instigations are provided by others' behavior, they may change their behavioral output in order to insure survival of the relationship (assuming it matters to them). The socialization of reflexive and other kinds of "primitive" behavior consists largely of selective adaptations by which the individual learns to seek favorable (or at least nonpunishing) occasions for discharging urgently instigated behavior and the social environment tends to provide accommodating occasions. (Adult Western males generally urinate in the toilets provided for them rather than in the streets.) In brief, by selectivity and relearning on the part of the individual and by a kind of accommodation to him on the part of social arrangements, there tends to develop an approximate correspondence between instigations to behaviors and the consequences of behavior. Discrepancy between instigation and outcome perhaps mainly characterizes unstable and transient relationships or the early stages of relationships that later stabilize.

For these reasons we believe there will typically be in any given relationship increasing correspondence between the antecedent determinants of behavior and the reward-cost consequences of behavior. Therefore, the reward-cost matrix becomes increasingly useful in predicting behavior as relationships become stable. It should be emphasized, however, that this does not mean that such behavior is governed by anticipations of consequences, covert calculation of the relative merits of different actions, or the deliberate attempt to maximize outcomes. Quite the contrary. Precisely because instigations do correspond increasingly well with outcomes, the individual may, with impunity, act more and more automatically (in response to habits, routines, or role prescriptions) and give less and less attention to the surveillance of his environment, the discernment of response alternatives, and the weighing of consequences. When the matrix is stable, an adaptive solution (in terms of cost minimization) is provided by routines that obviate these complex cognitive activities and automatize the procedures for gaining adequate outcomes. After sufficient experience in a stable situation (after the person has surveyed it thoroughly, rehearsed his repertoire of responses, and formed an adequate conception of the interdependency pattern), he can often formulate rules for the moment-to-moment choice of behaviors. Rules that other persons have found successful in similar relationships are frequently available to him in the form of role prescriptions taught by exhortation or example.

When following these routines, behavioral choices may provide good and even (perhaps) maximal outcomes. However, to repeat, adaptive performance need not be construed as evidence of a continuing, deliberate, purposive hedonism.

Only when these routines break down—when a changed situation begins to provide instigations to behaviors having poor outcomes—need the individual return to a consideration of consequences. At these points of discontinuity old routines may be maladaptive and no appropriate alternative routines may be available. At these critical junctures the person may become deliberate and thoughtful as to consequences—when he enters a new relationship, undertakes a new task, acquires new items in his response repertoire, or learns to make new discriminations as to the states of the external world. If he is not coerced by strong instigations, he may lengthen his time perspective and attempt to guide his behavior by an assessment of the long-term consequences. At these decision points, if the person has the ability and means of acquiring accurate information and of rehearsing his response alternatives, the matrix describing the objective consequences of each action becomes especially pertinent to the prediction of behavior.

In short; when the situation is relatively stable, behavioral routines that operate as though they have taken account of the outcome matrix tend to become adaptive solutions. When the situation changes, reflecting its change in a new outcome matrix, the new matrix will also have utility in predicting behavior if certain conditions are met.

Finally, over and above the advantages of the outcome matrix that have been noted, there is an important additional class of reasons, given our present aim, for using such a matrix rather than a matrix of probabilities. In dealing with many kinds of social events it is important not only to be able to assess the probability of various behaviors but also (and especially) to be able to describe and perchance to predict some psychological states of the person: his attraction to the group, his subjective status, his satisfaction with a social role, and the impact on him of types of power which control his fate.

— · — · — · — · — · — · — · — · — · — · — · — · — · —

J. STACY ADAMS
A. KIMBALL ROMNEY

*Operant Conditioning or Functional Theory of Authority**

An important segment of social interaction that requires systematic analysis is the behavioral control of one person over another: in other words, authority. The purpose of this paper is to analyze this type of interaction for the dyad, showing of what variables it is a function.

Authority, as defined below, is seen as a special case of verbal behavior as analyzed by Skinner (1957), and is consonant with his definition of the "mand." Thus, the analysis of authority will make fundamental use of the concept of the reciprocal reinforcement of

*J. Stacy Adams and A. Kimball Romney, "A Functional Analysis of Authority," *Psychological Review* 66 (1959): 234–251. Copyright 1959 by the American Psychological Association, and reproduced by permission.

behavior. The general aim is to carry through an analysis of the dyadic situation, and simple extensions of it, that specifies the conditions that are relevent to the occurrence of "authority behavior" and the variables of which such behavior is a function.

We begin with a definition of authority. A basic paradigm of an authority sequence will then be given and the variables of which such an authority sequence is a function will be discussed in detail. Finally, functional relationships between authority sequences will be analyzed.

DEFINITION OF AUTHORITY

We define authority as follows: Person A has authority over Person B, in a given situation, when a response of A, under the control of deprivation or aversive stimulation and specifying its own reinforcement, is reinforced by B.

This definition implies that authority is a social relation under the dual or reciprocal control of both A and B. It is social in the sense that it requires behavior on the part of both A and B and that the behavior of A constitutes a stimulus for B and vice versa. For the relation to be maintained, B's behavior must be reinforcing for A and A's behavior must be reinforcing for B. As will be discussed later, the controlling relation of A over B may be enduring or temporary, and it may extend over a large or small range of B's responses.

The relation of authority is asymmetrical in that A's initial response (such as a command, request, suggestion, etc.) specifies its own reinforcement, whereas B's does not. The reinforcement is provided by B's response, if the response reduces the state of deprivation or withdraws aversive stimuli for A. For the maintenance of the relationship B's response must be likewise reinforced by A, but the reinforcement is not specified as in the case of A.

The phrase, "in a given situation," indicates that the authority relation is not assumed to be a general one between individuals regardless of time and place. Authority is learned in specific situations, although it may later be transferred to other situations by such processes as stimulus induction. The phrase also implies the reversibility of the relation from one situation to another. This reversibility may violate the usual definition of and feeling for "authority." For example, one readily accepts the notion of a father's authority over his son, while one would balk at a statement of a child's "authority" over his father. Yet, precisely the same functional relationships may hold in both cases, as we shall demonstrate. It is, therefore, both rigorous and useful to speak of a person's having "authority" over another whenever the same relationships are found, even though this practice might do violence to everyday usage.

The clause, "under the control of deprivation or aversive stimulation," indicates that it is not sufficient to know only the topography of the response of A, but that it is also necessary to specify the controlling variables of the response of A. For example, if A says, "Water, please," in the presence of B, we must know whether the controlling variable of that response is water deprivation or some other deprivation, or whether it is aversive stimulation.

When it is said that the response of A specifies its own reinforcement, we assume that there is "communication" between A and B. Not only does the presence of B, in part, set the occasion for the response of A, but the reinforcement of A's response is contingent upon a response by B. Thus authority behavior is necessarily verbal behavior as defined by Skinner (1957), i.e., behavior the reinforcement of which is contingent upon stimulation of and response by another individual. The definitions of all other terms used in the analysis closely follow the behavioral, empirical definitions given by Verplanck (1957).

BASIC PARADIGM OF AN AUTHORITY SEQUENCE

The central idea in authority relations is that of the reciprocal control and reinforcement of behavior of two persons. Basically, the paradigm is that a response of one person, A, is reinforced by another person, B, and that, in turn, the reinforcing response of B is, itself, reinforced by A. Such an interaction will be called an *authority sequence*. An example is the situation in which Person A asks B for water and B complies by giving A water. Figure 1 gives an illustration of the process. The figure is divided into two parts, the top half representing stimuli and responses directly related to Person A, while the lower half pertains to Person B. The interaction between A and B begins at the far left of the figure with A in a state of deprivation and in the presence of a discriminative stimulus, S_d and $S_B{}^D$. These stimuli set the occasion for the response R_{A1}, "Give me water." S_d is the stimulus, presumably physiological in the example, that results from water deprivation. $S_B{}^D$ is the discriminative stimulus resulting from B's presence in A's environment. $S_B{}^D$ is a discriminative stimulus with respect to R_{A1} in this illustration by virtue of previous conditioning. The response, "Give me water," would not occur unless A were thirsty; nor would it occur unless someone were present to give A water. In some sense, R_{A1} is "appropriate" only in the presence of S_d and $S_B{}^D$, and these stimuli may therefore be viewed as "setting the occasion for" and as having control over R_{A1}. As will be seen, this control is not exclusive, however, for it is the reinforcement of R_{A1} in the presence of the two stimuli that is crucial for the demonstration of authority.

Once the verbal command, "Give me water," has been emitted, it is a stimulus to B. Specifically, it is a discriminative stimulus, $S_{A1}{}^D$, in that it sets the occasion for a

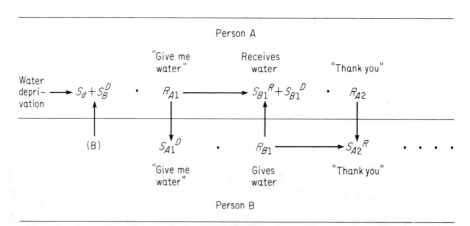

Figure 1. Authority sequence with initial response under control of deprivation.

response by B that is later reinforced. The major characteristic of R_{A1} is that it specifies how B can reinforce it. B is in fact "told" that the response, "Give me water," will be reinforced by giving water to A. When B gives water to A, his response, R_{B1}, constitutes the reinforcement, $S_{B1}{}^R$ of response R_{A1}. In addition, R_{B1} is also a discriminative stimulus, $S_{B1}{}^D$, that sets the occasion for a further response by A. The response in this example is, "Thank you," R_{A2}. In turn, R_{A2}, a generalized reinforcer, constitutes a reinforcement of R_{B1}. Although the reciprocal reinforcement of responses on that part of A and B is terminated arbitrarily in the present example, R_{A2} itself would need to be reinforced by a further response of B, perhaps the verbal response, "You're welcome," or a nod or smile. As the dots to the far right of Figure 1 suggest, the sequence is theoretically infinite, though in practice it is finite.

The use of only one discriminative stimulus ($S_B{}^D$) is greatly simplifying a situation encountered in "real life." The essence of the model is in no way affected by this simplification, however. Quite complex stimuli could be made discriminative—i.e., given "sign" status—in an experimental situation, and an authority sequence from "real life" could be replicated.

In the illustrative sequence of behavior presented, it is important to note that if the sequence is interrupted at any point, predictable consequences follow. Assume, for example, that B does not give water to A, after A has said, "Give me water." This might be because R_{A1} did not result in a discriminative stimulus for B, i.e., it had no "meaning" for B because of lack of previous learning. Or it may be that R_{A1} resulted in a discriminative stimulus that set the occasion for a response other than giving water, perhaps telling A to get his own water. Whatever the reason for not giving water to A, the consequence would be for R_{A1} to undergo some extinction. Similarly, if the sequence were interrupted by A's not emitting R_{A2}, B's response, R_{B1}, giving water, would undergo some extinction, with the result that the probability of R_{A1}'s being reinforced would be decreased. As before, the probability of A's emitting R_{A1} would then be smaller. In both instances where the sequence is interrupted, it is evident that A's authority over B is decreased, at least in this particular situation. It is interesting to note that in the first instance the decrease in A's authority is primarily "because" of a failure attributable to B. In the second instance, however, A's authority is affected "because" of his failure to reinforce B's response, R_{B1}. The use of "because" here is very loose, of course; no attribution of causality to A and B as persons is intended. Their responses are completely determined, except on their very first occurrence, by their previous reinforcement history and by antecedent stimulus conditions.

In Figure 1, A's initial response was partly under the control of deprivation. Instead it could have been under the partial control of aversive stimulation. For example, B might have been making some disturbing noise and this aversive stimulus might have set the occasion for the response, "Keep quiet!" It is also true that B's response, R_{B1}, need not necessarily be reinforced by the presentation of a positive reinforcing stimulus. It could have been reinforced by the withdrawal of an aversive stimulus or conditioned aversive stimulus. Figure 2 shows how aversive stimuli might exercise control in an authority interaction.

An aversive noise stimulus, $S_n{}^{av}$, and a discriminative stimulus, $S_B{}^D$, set the occasion for the responses R_{A1} and $R_{A1}{}^{av}$, constituted by the verbal response, "Keep quiet!" and

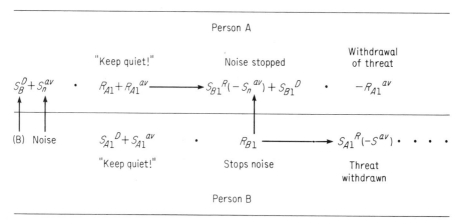

Figure 2. Authority sequence with initial response under control of aversive stimulation.

an implied threat carried by the accentuation and intonation of the verbal response. Thus B is presented with a discriminative verbal stimulus, $S_{A_1}{}^D$, and a conditioned aversive stimulus, $S_{A_1}{}^{av}$. These stimuli set the occasion for stopping the noise, indicated in the figure as R_{B_1}. This response consists of the withdrawal of the aversive noise stimulus, $S_n{}^{av}$, and constitutes a negative reinforcing stimulus for A, as well as a discriminative stimulus, $S_{B_1}{}^D$, setting the occasion for a further response. The response, in this example, is the withdrawal of implicit threat and is labelled, $-R_{A_1}{}^{av}$. This, in turn, is an appropriate negative reinforcing stimulus for B's response, R_{B_1}. As in the previous example, the sequence of behavior is stopped at this point. Thus, we have here an interesting case of escape conditioning, with an implied threat as a conditioned aversive stimulus, as well as one of avoidance conditioning with respect to the negative reinforcing stimulus inferred from the threat.

In a manner analogous to that presented earlier, interruption of the behavioral sequence has implications for the authority A has over B. If B, for example, does not stop making noise (perhaps because of the inadequate control of $S_{A_1}{}^D$ and $S_{A_1}{}^{av}$), A's response, "Keep quiet!" will undergo some extinction and A's authority over B will be weakened under the particular circumstances described. However, B's lack of compliance may of itself constitute additional aversive stimulation for A and thus set the occasion for a new response, perhaps, "If you don't stop that noise, you'll suffer the consequences," which may generate enough additional aversive stimulation for B to make him stop the noise. If this occurred, A would maintain his authority over B, though at some additional expense. A could, of course, alternatively "leave the field," in which case there would be no question of authority over B.

The sequence in Figure 2 would also be interrupted if A did not withdraw aversive stimulation after B had complied with his command. The consequence would be that R_{B_1} would have less likelihood of occurring in the future, a fact which would tend to reduce the probability of occurrence of R_{A_1} and $R_{A_1}{}^{av}$ and, therefore, would tend to reduce A's authority over B in this illustrative situation. As was pointed out before, the resulting loss of control of A over B might set the occasion for new responses by A.

In both the illustrations given thus far, certain assumptions have been made which need to be made explicit before the implications of the paradigm are further explored. Some of the assumptions concern the discriminative status of stimuli. For example, it is assumed in Figure 1 that B is a discriminative stimulus ($S_B{}^D$) setting the occasion for the response, "Give me water." But by definition a discriminative stimulus is one in the presence of which a response is reinforced and in the absence of which it is unreinforced. Since A's response, R_{A1}, is not reinforced until some time later, B cannot initially be a discriminative stimulus in the sense of setting the occasion for R_{A1}. What is assumed, then, is some previous learning, i.e., some previous temporal contiguity of response (R_{A1}) and reinforcing stimulus ($S_{B1}{}^R$) in the presence of B. The assumption is, however, only one of convenience, and what has been said applies to the free operant situation as well. If A had merely emitted spontaneously the response, "Give me water," in the presence of B (and in the context of deprivation), and if B had responded appropriately to reinforce A's response, the behavioral consequences would have been the same as previously discussed. The only difference is that B would have been a mere stimulus without discriminative properties. However, on *subsequent* occasions B would have discriminative characteristics, assuming further that A's responses had been unreinforced on some occasion when B was absent. The same line of reasoning applies to other stimuli which appear as discriminative stimuli in the figures.

Another assumption is that the reciprocal reinforcement of behavior is a finite sequence. It was stated earlier that the reciprocal reinforcement sequence in the authority relation may be theoretically infinite but that we assumed it was finite in practice. The assumption is difficult to substantiate even though everyday observation suggests that persons in an authority relation do not reinforce each other's responses ad infinitum. There are, of course, cases where reinforcement continues for considerable lengths of time, for example the endless exchange of bows that occurs when a Westerner visits a Japanese home. Nevertheless, the fact is that in our culture the interaction usually stops at approximately the point indicated in Figures 1 and 2, and that extinction is not a consequence. The reason for this may be that terminating an interaction sequence at a certain point is of itself reinforcing in that it avoids aversive consequences which would be forthcoming were the sequence not terminated. Thus, for example, in our own culture there are conventions about the termination of an interaction sequence beyond which further responding is punished by the use of conditioned aversive stimuli. As an illustration, it is commonly observed that after compliance with a request, anything beyond a "Thank you" and "You're welcome" results in raised eyebrows, a sardonic smile, or a look of impatience, which may be discriminative stimuli for stopping the interaction. When the stimuli for stopping are not known to one of the parties in the interaction (i.e., are not discriminative), responding may continue for some time, as in the bowing example above. In some situations responding beyond a given point may have the aspect of impertinence and have appropriate aversive results. Alternatively, responding beyond a certain point is unreinforced by society, and an agreed-upon sequence of reciprocal reinforcement becomes a discriminative stimulus for stopping to respond further.

CONTROLLING VARIABLES

Thus far it has been shown how an authority relation between two persons can evolve and either be maintained or be destroyed. The external events (independent variables) of which responses (dependent variables) in an authority interaction are a function will now be discussed. This will be done by grouping variables into general classes and discussing instances under class headings. The basic A–B interaction paradigm will be used throughout.

Reinforcing Stimulus Variables

Stimulus events that have the property of increasing the probability of recurrence of a preceding response are fundamental controlling variables. B's giving water to A and A's saying "Thank you" in Figure 1 are such events in that they increase the probability of A's again asking B for water when he is later water-deprived, and of B's giving A water, respectively, other variables remaining constant. In other words, certain responses such as "Give me water" have consequences which empirically increase their probability of recurrence and thus in part determine the authority A has over B.

The importance of reinforcing stimuli is more pervasive than has been suggested above, however. The discriminative character of other stimuli is dependent upon their being paired with reinforcement. Thus, for example, in Figure 1, B's presence would not constitute a discriminative stimulus for A's demanding water, unless it had been temporally contiguous with the reinforcement of A's response. Nor, in Figure 2, would A's verbal command "Keep quiet!" be a discriminative stimulus for B's stopping noisiness, unless stopping to make noise had been reinforced following the occurrence of the stimulus resulting from A's response. It can therefore be seen that a reinforcing contingency is *necessary* before a stimulus can acquire discriminative properties. This is, of course, not a *sufficient* characteristic: It is also required that the absence of a stimulus be associated with nonreinforcement before it can be a discriminative stimulus. For example, with respect to Figure 1, it would be necessary that A's response, "Give me water," be unreinforced in the absence of B.

The withholding of reinforcing stimuli following a response is the operation resulting in experimental extinction and, as an observable consequence, produces a decreased probability of response. Illustrations of this have been given previously.

The general properties and the importance of reinforcing stimuli having been pointed out, A and B as the agents or mediators of reinforcement must now be considered.

A as a reinforcer. A can act as a direct mediator of reinforcement or as a conditioned reinforcer. As a direct mediator he can both present positive reinforcers (or conditioned reinforcers) and withdraw negative reinforcers (or conditioned negative reinforcers). A father can reinforce his child for obeying a command by giving it candy. The business executive can reinforce his secretary's compliance with an order by withdrawing an implied threat, much as in the example of Figure 2. In a similar fashion the traffic policeman reinforces stopping at his gestured command by lowering his arm and, hence, removing conditioned negative reinforcers.

It is evident that, as a direct mediator of reinforcement, A can exercise considerable control over B's behavior. But it is also true that, indirectly, he exercises control over his *own* responses, for the probability of recurrence of his own responses is in part a function of the extent to which he is successful in reinforcing B's responses. Other things being equal, then, A is in some sense the master of his own authority over B. This notion is not a new one, but in the present case it has the advantage of being systematically derivable from the basic model.

A further derivation is that A's probability of successfully developing or maintaining an authority relation over B will in part be a function of the amount and variety or range of reinforcers he has available. The person who can mediate reinforcements appropriate to several states of deprivation can exercise more authority than one who can, say, provide only food (e.g., a parent versus a neighbor). The person who has access to a large range of aversive stimuli can have more authority than one who has not (e.g., a company commander versus a corporal). From a similar consideration it also follows that the greater the amount and range of reinforcers available to A, the greater the range of B's responses he can control, other variables remaining constant. Thus a parent can have wider authority than an older sister who can mete out limited punishment only and who has no money for material rewards.

As a conditioned reinforcer, either positive or negative, A may also exercise control over B's behavior, as well as indirectly over his own. Before he can act as a conditioned reinforcer, however, it is necessary that he have acted on previous occasions as a direct mediator of reinforcement, or, at least, that he be similar to someone who acted as a reinforcer. The important thing to consider is that the mere presence of A can reinforce some of B's responses, no direct reinforcement being given. For example, using the illustration of Figure 1, it is possible for A to omit saying, "Thank you," and for B's response to remain at considerable strength, provided stimulus attributes of A have become conditioned or generalized reinforcers by virtue of A's having previously, and frequently, reinforced B's responses. However, in order for the attributes of A to remain effective conditioned reinforcers (and discriminative stimuli as well), it is necessary that on occasion A mediate direct reinforcement; otherwise B's operant will undergo extinction. The same applies to A qua A as a negative conditioned reinforcer.

B as a reinforcer. The distinguishing characteristic of B as a reinforcer is that his reinforcing response has no, or only a few, degrees of freedom, as contrasted with A as a reinforcer. His reinforcing response is specified by A, by definition. To be sure, the discrete topography of his response may vary, but its net effect on A is specified. Thus, for example, B may get and bring water to A in a variety of ways, but the giving of water is the essential property of the response that will reinforce A's request and, therefore, establish or maintain the authority relation.

In a manner similar to A, B may also act as a conditioned reinforcer or negative conditioned reinforcer, in that the authority relation between the two will be maintained or strengthened. This presumes, of course, that B, or someone similar to B, will have appropriately reinforced A's behavior in the past under similar circumstances.

Generalization of A and B as conditioned reinforcers. It has been pointed out that A and B may exercise control over each other's behavior, and thus maintain or strengthen an authority relation, in their capacities as conditioned reinforcers. It is also true that conditioned reinforcement may be effected by individuals other than A and B who have physical properties similar to A and B. Thus, an officer never before encountered may act as a conditioned reinforcer of an enlisted man's compliance with an order, by virtue of the fact that he has properties similar to those of other officers who have reinforced the same response. The dimensions of similarity in this example might be the uniform and emblems of office; or the relevant dimension might be physical characteristics of verbal operants, e.g., " 'ten shun!" Similarly, the authority of policemen is partially maintained, even though never before seen personally, through stimulus induction. How often has one slowed down at the sight of an unknown policeman whose back was turned?

Deprivation and Aversive Stimulus Variables Affecting A

As stated in the definition of authority, A's initial response (order, command, request, demand, etc.) is partially under the control of deprivation or aversive stimulation, other control being exercised by discriminative stimuli (e.g., the presence of a B). This results from the fact that certain responses of the human organism are typically followed by specific consequences under certain conditions agreed upon by the social community, and that when this occurs the probability of occurrence of these responses will be a function of the deprivation or aversive stimulation paired with the reinforcing consequences. Thus the response, "Give me water," has a greater probability of occurrence under water deprivation than under satiation because other organisms are more likely to have provided water when A emitted this response and was thirsty. It should be noted that deprivation and aversive stimulation do not *necessarily* exercise control over the response. The control results from the fact that other organisms are predisposed by "societal consensus," so to speak, to respond in certain characteristic ways. This predisposition of other organisms is analogous to certain automatic consequences of the nonanimal environment. For example, picking and eating an apple is automatically reinforcing when the organism is food-deprived, though not if he is satiated. Thus, food deprivation would come to control picking and eating an apple. A similar line of reasoning applied to aversive stimulation, though in this case reinforcement consists in the withdrawal of an aversive stimulus.

The relations holding between deprivation (or aversive stimulation), response topography of A, and reinforcing response by B are stated in idealized terms. This is especially true with regard to A's response topography "specifying" its reinforcement. It is conceivable, for example, that the response, "Give me water," specified not a state of water deprivation which could be reinforced by water but rather a demand for submissiveness on the part of B, the state of deprivation being for something other than water. In such a case the content of A's response does not clearly specify the appropriate reinforcing stimulus—at least the words used do not clearly convey the state of A's deprivation. However, other aspects of the verbal response than the words may serve as appropriate discriminative stimuli for submissiveness (i.e., sheer compliance). The imperative mood of the response, for example, may serve this function. Whether it does this effectively on a particular occasion is, of course, a function of appropriate previous differential reinforcement. To put it somewhat loosely, it is a function of whether B has learned that use of the imperative mood is a "sign" for compliance regardless of the specific content of A's response.

Discriminative Stimulus Variables

In the discussion of Figures 1 and 2 the role of discriminative stimuli was made explicit. We wish to expand the discussion at this point and focus specifically on the discriminative stimuli that control A's initial response. The discriminative stimulus characteristics of responses by A and B will be omitted, as they are evident.

Two general groups of discriminative stimulus variables controlling A's initial response may be considered, stimulus characteristics of B and situational stimuli, excluding B. A general characteristic of B that may serve as a discriminative stimulus is his being an organism with the potentiality of responding. Without another person's being present, a response by A cannot be reinforced, and A cannot exercise any authority. There are, however, other relevant aspects of B. One is B as a particular individual, i.e., the stimulus characteristics of a B who has previously reinforced A's response, as opposed to a B who has not. A second is B as the incumbent in a particular role, as an office boy or corporal, for example. In this instance characteristics of B serve as discriminative stimuli for a comparatively narrow range of responses by A. In other instances characteristics of B may set the occasion for one class of responses only; for example, the elevator boy is a discriminative stimulus for the response, "Take me to the sixth," only. Thus we may think of B as having discriminative stimulus characteristics that exercise control over A's responses with different degrees of specificity. The specificity of control exercised is a function of the extent of differential reinforcement carried out in the presence of particular characteristics.

The second group of discriminative stimulus variables are situational variables. They include virtually all relevant stimuli not directly pertaining to B. Some situational variables are part of the purely physical environment. Thus, the request, "Take me to the sixth," has a low probability of being reinforced in the absence of an elevator. Similarly, "Give me water," will usually have a low probability of occurring without a source of water in the immediate environment. However, in an instance of this sort, deprivation may become so severe that it exercises almost exclusive control. The "Water, water!" of the wounded soldier on the deserted battlefield is an example. Other situational variables are of a more "social" character in that the presence of other persons, or of persons having particular types of interaction, has a controlling discriminative stimulus function. Certain kinds of commands or requests are not issued to one's wife at home in the context of a cocktail party (and would go unreinforced, if issued), though they are issued and reinforced when just family members are present. Orders may be successfully given to an employee at the office, though not at the country club.

Whether discriminative stimulus control is exercised by B proper or by situational variables, it will be achieved only after differential reinforcement. The controlling stimulus variables may, of course, be of great complexity and require considerable training. For example, an authority response, R_{A1}, will be reinforced only if Stimuli I, J, . . . , *or* N are present, *and* if Stimuli B and C are present, *and* if Stimulus R is absent. The situation is analogous to those encountered in concept formation studies (e.g., Bruner, Goodnow, & Austin, 1956). In the present instance a response is reinforced only in the presence of particular stimuli, whereas in concept formation studies a response is said to be "correct" in the presence of some stimulus combinations and "incorrect" in the presence of other combinations.

Since complex stimulus control of this type requires considerable training with differential reinforcement, it follows that in early stages of training control will be imperfect. Some variables, in the absence of others which are necessary for reinforcement, will exercise some control over a response, even though it will not be reinforced. It is also possible that during the course of differential training "irrelevant" variables would exercise some control over an authority response. This inappropriate control of stimuli results when a response is reinforced in the presence of both appropriate discriminative stimuli and irrelevant other stimuli. These stimuli then acquire some discriminative stimulus capacity. Their control is eventually weakened and abolished during further differential training.

THE FUNCTIONAL INTERRELATION OF AUTHORITY SEQUENCES

The classes of variables of which authority is a function have been specified for a two-person situation. In large groups new problems arise with respect to the arrangement of authority sequences within the group. The problems associated with relating authority sequences arise from the basic characteristics of authority and the presence of more than two persons in the total situation. This section is addressed to these problems and consists of an analysis of the ways in which authority sequences are patterned within the limitations imposed by the assumptions of authority as outlined in the preceding section.

In order for two authority sequences to be functionally related, one of the following conditions must be met: (a) authority sequence, K, or some part of it, controls authority sequence, L, or some part of it; (b) all or some part of authority sequences, K and L are under the control of a common (or similar) variable (variables); and (c) two simultaneous initial responses are made that specify incompatible reinforcement responses by B.

For purposes of exposition, these will be regarded as distinct cases of authority sequence interrelationships and will be discussed separately.

Case I: One Sequence Exercises Functional Control Over Another

There are a number of ways in which an authority sequence exercises control over a succeeding sequence, but it is important to note that an all-or-none relationship of control is not implied. The whole or any part of an authority sequence may control a succeeding sequence. This control may be either partial or complete and affect all or part of the succeeding sequence. Discussion will be limited to two basic ways in which two sequences may be functionally related.

Situation where a response in Sequence K controls a response in Sequence L. Authority sequences are frequently related by virtue of the fact that a response in the first sequence controls a response in the second. Generally speaking, with exceptions to be noted, the response by B in the first sequence is the initial response in the second sequence. For example, when a father orders his daughter to tell baby to be quiet, the response of daughter saying "quiet" to baby is B's response in the sequence father-daughter, and also the initial response in the sequence involving daughter-baby. Figure 3 gives an illustration of how the process might operate.

A's response, "Tell Johnny to be quiet," is under the control of aversive stimuli from noise being made by the baby and of B as a discriminative stimulus. B's response of going and telling baby, "Daddy says, 'be quiet,'" is under the control of the stimuli of A's initial response, i.e., of a discriminative stimulus ($S_{A_1}{}^D$) and of a conditioned aversive stimulus (S^{av}) consisting of an implied threat of punishment for noncompliance. B's response, R_{B_1}, unlike responses in the dyadic situation, does not directly reinforce A's

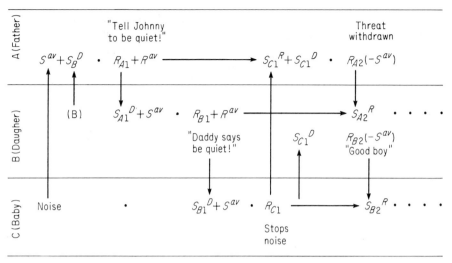

Figure 3. Response-related authority sequences.

initial response, R_{A1}. Rather, it constitutes stimuli for C to stop making noise, R_{C1}. It is C's response, R_{C1}, that reinforces the original response of A, i.e., R_{A1}. This in turn sets the occasion for A to make a response that reinforces B's response; i.e., $R_{A2}(-S^{av})$ constitutes reinforcement for R_{B1}. The form of this response might be the removal of the implied threat. In order for the behavior to be maintained, C's response, R_{C1}, must also be reinforced. In the figure this response is a discriminative stimulus for B, who makes a response something like "Good boy," R_{B2}, which reinforces the response of stopping noise, R_{C1}, by removing an aversive stimulus.

Functionally related series of this general sort take many different forms. For example, in Figure 3, it would be possible for the second response of the father, $R_{A2}(-S^{av})$, to take the form "Thank you, children" and constitute reinforcement for not only the response of the daughter, R_{B1}, but also for the response of the baby, R_{C1}. In such an event it would be unnecessary for the daughter to reinforce the baby. Another very common situation in command chains arises when, for example, the president of a company asks the vice-president for a report, and the vice-president asks a department head for the report. In this case the department head gives the report to the vice-president, who in turn gives it to the president. Here the action of the department head, C, does not directly reinforce any response by the president, but rather of the vice-president.

An inherent characteristic of situations involving a chain of command is that there is some delay in the reinforcement of A's initial response. This delay in reinforcement has implications for the readiness with which such responses are conditioned. Generally, conditioning of the response is a decreasing function of the delay between response and reinforcement. In practical situations there are techniques available to "help A across" such a time lag by presenting conditioned reinforcers during the delay period. For example, B can supply comments such as, "The report will be ready at three," "Yes, sir," "Right away, sir," "I'll attend to it immediately," and so on. Periodic "progress reports," frequent personal communications, and verbal assurances are probably manifestations of the utility of supplying some supplementary conditioned reinforcement to A where the situation involves a long delay in reinforcement. This is in accord with the findings of Perin (1943a, 1943b) and Grice (1948) on the effects of removing conditioned reinforcers upon the delay of reinforcement gradient.

Situation where a response in Sequence K is under control of Sequence L. In this situation the whole of one sequence constitutes part of the situation for a second sequence. When the second sequence can be shown to be, at least in part, under the control of the first sequence, then the two sequences are functionally related. Consideration is limited here to the situation in which no individuals who are in the first sequence are also in the second.

An authority sequence frequently controls a response in another sequence either through "imitative" mechanisms—that is to say, by serving as a discriminative stimulus—or by increasing deprivation or aversive stimulation. Consider, for example, a group of mothers and children, where the children are playing in the mud. The first mother tells her child to stop playing in the mud. The child complies and is rewarded. This authority sequence may constitute a conditioned aversive stimulus for the second mother. The aversive stimulus may be social disapproval of not following the first mother's "example." The first sequence may also be a discriminative stimulus setting the occasion for the second mother's telling her child to stop playing in the mud. If the child complies, the aversive disapproval (perhaps only implied) of the first mother is withdrawn, and the second mother's behavior is reinforced.

Case II: A Common Variable Exercises Functional Control over Two or More Sequences

Probably the simplest manner in which authority sequences are functionally related is by sharing a common controlling variable. Sequences interrelated in this way are found most commonly in large groupings of face-to-face interactions where more complex ways of arranging authority sequences becomes unwieldy. Two types may be considered: (a) where an initial response by A specifies the behavior of several people, and (b) where two or more initial responses specify a single reinforcing response on the part of one person.

Situation where an initial response specifies behavior of several individuals. The situation in which one individual, A, directs a response to a large number of individuals, B, C, . . . , N, is a common one. The authority sequences in such an event are all under the control of the variables affecting the initial response of A. For example, when a drill sergeant calls a company of soldiers to attention we have a situation where the response, "Attention!" specifies as its reinforcement the behavior of several individuals. Each pair formed by the sergeant and an individual soldier may be thought of as an authority sequence, assuming, of course, that they all come to attention and are reinforced by some behavior of the sergeant. These authority sequences are functionally related by the fact that they are all under the control of whatever variables determine the response of the sergeant, namely, calling the company to attention. The situation is illustrated in abbreviated form in Figure 4. An interesting implication of this type of authority situation is that the authority response of A is likely to remain in considerable strength and to be very resistant to extinction by virtue of the fact that the more other persons his response is addressed to, the more likelihood there is for some compliance and, hence, the more

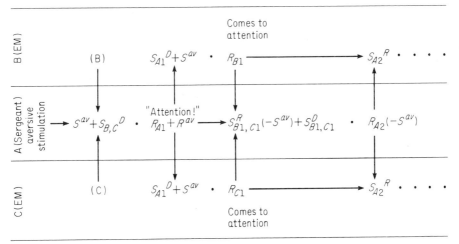

Figure 4. One-to-many authority sequences.

likely he is to get some reinforcement. In some limiting cases, of course, it is possible that the compliance of *all* Bs is the sole effective reinforcement for A. In such cases, the Bs can be treated as a single entity. It could be predicted, then, that certain military men, certain types of supervisors and foremen, teachers, housewives with large families, etc., would on the average have greater strength of authority responses in these situations than others, because there is a greater probability of their being reinforced. These are in fact persons who are often labeled "bossy."

Situations where two or more initial responses specify a single reinforcing response. Under certain circumstances to be specified below, two or more individuals may simultaneously initiate an authority sequence (give a command, request, suggest, etc.) with a third party, in which both of their responses specify the same behavior on the part of the third party as reinforcement. The example of a father and mother both saying, "Keep quiet" to their noisy child at the same time is diagrammed in Figure 5.

The sequences are here functionally related by the fact that R_{C1} is part of both sequences. Since every response in a sequence exercises some control over the sequence, these sequences are under the control of the common variables related to the common response. The sequences are also related by the fact that the aversive stimulation in partial control of R_{A1} and R_{B1} is from the same source.

This type of relation between authority sequences is subject to more restrictions than any of those previously discussed. The most important restriction is that the two initial responses by A and B must specify a response on the part of C that will reinforce both initial responses. A and B, of course, need not specify an identical response, though in practice this may often be the case. It is only necessary that the responses specified be equivalent in their effects. Figure 5 illustrates a common way in which this arises, namely, A and B are under the control of a common aversive stimulus, the noise of a child. Under other circumstances A and B could be under the control of a common deprivation. Other more complex and subtle relations are not uncommon. For example, an audience in the presence of a good performer may be under the control of common stimuli so that they

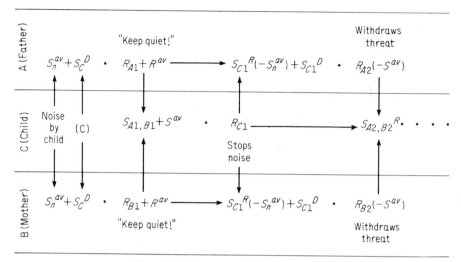

Figure 5. Many-to-one authority sequences.

all applaud and shout "Bis!" and the performer complies with an encore. Here the exact specification of the controlling variables for the audience is somewhat difficult, and there may be a variety of variables operating on different members of the audience.

Other things being equal, C is under more aversive stimulation than in the simple authority sequence by virtue of the fact that he is under multiple aversive stimulation, as shown in Figure 5 by the two implied threats symbolized by $S_{A_1}{}^{av}$ and $S_{B_1}{}^{av}$. Making the assumption that degree of control and amount of aversive stimulation (or of deprivation), up to a limit, are positively correlated, it follows that compliance will be an increasing function of aversive stimulation (or of deprivation).

Another feature to note in these types of relationships between sequences is that A and B may be viewed as a "coalition" under the control of common deprivation or aversive stimulation. When they do not act as a coalition, i.e., when they are not under common deprivation or aversive stimulation so that the initial responses specify incompatible responses on the part of C, the total relation becomes impossible to complete. That is to say, contradictory behavior may be required of C such that it is impossible for him to reinforce the responses of A and B simultaneously. We call such a situation one of *authority conflict*.

Case III: Authority Conflict

Two or more authority sequences may be functionally related in that one sequence is associated with the interruption of another or that the sequences mutually preclude the completion of each other. Specifically, sequences interfere with terminal reinforcements. In such cases there exists *authority conflict*.

Figure 6 provides an illustration. The situation is that of two bosses descending simultaneously upon their joint secretary late in the day with rush jobs. The typing jobs are of such a nature that only one can be completed. The two bosses, A and C, issue requests, R_{A_1} and R_{C_1}, with implied threats for noncompliance. These, let us assume,

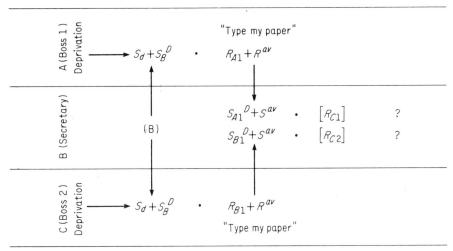

Figure 6. Authority conflict situation.

constitute discriminative stimuli plus aversive stimulation for the secretary, B. (The consequences to be discussed do not require this assumption, but it is made for the sake of reality.) Since B can comply with only one of the requests, there exist for her two incompatible (conflicting) response tendencies. These response possibilities exist for her: (a) she can comply with A's request and thus reinforce his response; (b) she can comply with C's request and thus reinforce his response; or (c) she can comply with neither request and therefore reinforce neither A's nor C's response. The consequences of the first two possibilities are analogous, while those of the third are different.

If B complies with A's request and therefore reinforces his initial response, A's response will have an increased probability of recurrence in the future under similar circumstances and C's response will tend to undergo extinction. If we now assume further that when C alone—that is, in the absence of A—makes a request of B, she complies and his behavior is reinforced, it follows that A will become a negative discriminative stimulus for C. In sum, if B reinforces C in the absence of A and does not reinforce him in the presence of A, C will "learn" to make his requests in the absence of A. In practice, this may lead to a scheduling of authority responses, as when Boss 1 directs the secretary mornings and Boss 2 directs her afternoons.

The factors which result in B's reinforcing A's behavior in preference to C's are of interest. One factor is that A may have reinforced B more frequently than had C in the past for the same or similar responses, with the result that A's response exercised greater control over B. Another possibility is that A, perhaps because of powers associated with his rank or position, could give B greater reinforcement than could C, frequency of reinforcement by A and C being equal. It might also be that, even though having reinforcing powers equal to those of C, A made greater (and "better") use of generalized reinforcers. His expression of thanks, for example, might generally be more reinforcing (it might be less perfunctory). Another factor may be that A, as opposed to C, has acquired conditioned reinforcing properties under circumstances quite different from the boss-secretary relation. Finally, if we assume a completely free operant situation and no previous learning histories, it could be that B's response to A merely has a higher operant level than the conflicting response to C.

The second case to consider is when B complies with and reinforces neither A's nor C's request. In such an instance it is clear that both A's and C's initial authority responses will undergo extinction. However, it is clearly possible for the secretary's inactivity to set the occasion for new responses on the part of A or C or both which will be reinforced. Thus, A and C might say, "Type A's paper now and C's tomorrow." Furthermore, it is possible that, if A and C, when interacting alone with B, are reinforced in their requests, they will come to make their requests only in the absence of the other. This follows from the operation of differential reinforcement and of the resultant control exercised by a negative discriminative stimulus.

What the antecedents are for nonresponse on the part of B are many and need not be enumerated. Generally, however, the situation is that both A's and C's responses and situational stimuli exercise the same degree of control over B's responses. To use a vector analogy, the vectors representing B's two response tendencies are of equal length and at 180 degrees to each other.

In the discussion of authority conflict, attention has thus far been limited to the consequences of B's responses upon the behavior of A and C. it is evident, however, that the types of conflict envisaged will have effects upon the behavior of B. One effect is that, when B reinforces the behavior of A in preference to C's and is in turn reinforced by A, her response to A will have an increased probability of recurrence, whereas any response tendency toward compliance with C's request will be weakened under similar circumstances. When B responds neither to A nor C, whatever response tendencies existed at the time will undergo extinction since they will not be reinforced. In both of these cases it is interesting to note that the conflict of responses on the part of B is self-reducing, in one case because one of the two response tendencies is weakened and in the other because both are weakened. However, the existence of conflict may have other side-effects.

If it is assumed that being in conflict results in aversive stimulation, certain consequences can be predicted. Under this assumption the secretary in the illustration will be subjected to aversive stimulation. Furthermore, this aversive stimulation will be contingent upon her responding or tending to respond to A and C. That is to say, the conflict and consequent aversive stimulation exist solely *because* of her competing responses (of course, phenomenally, B may perceive A and C as being instrumental in her conflict). It follows, then, that A and C, as well as other aspects of the total situation, will become conditioned negative reinforcers and that B will tend to *avoid* them. Making the further assumption that degree of conflict and resulting aversive stimulation are positively correlated, it also follows that the strength of B's avoidance response will increase with increasing degree of conflict. Since degree of conflict will be a function of the strength similarity of B's two incompatible response tendencies, it may be concluded that the more nearly equal the response tendencies, the greater will be the avoidance of A and C.

The preceding analysis of authority conflict has dealt exclusively with the case in which only one of two (or more) incompatible responses can be emitted by B. It can, however, also happen that one response will be emitted first and that a second will subsequently be emitted upon the completion of the first. Thus, the fictional secretary could have typed A's letter first and, upon completion of that job, could have typed C's. In such a case both A's and C's authority responses will be reinforced. However, it is evident that some delay is entailed in the reinforcement of C's responses. The consequence of this will be to weaken the effect of the reinforcement, the magnitude of the net effect being inversely proportional to the amount of delay.

SUMMARY

We have suggested the following definition of authority: A person A has authority over B, in a given situation, when a response of A, under the control of deprivation or aversive stimulation and specifying its own reinforcement, is reinforced by B. Authority, so defined, has been analyzed as a function of the following variables:

1. Reinforcing stimulus variables
   (a) A as a reinforcer
   (b) B as a reinforcer
   (c) Generalization of A and B as conditioned reinforcers
2. Deprivation and aversive stimulus variables affecting A
3. Discriminative stimulus variables.

A paradigm of an authority sequence was analyzed in terms of these variables. Series of functionally related sequences were defined as sequences under the control of one another or of common variables. Three classes of functionally related sequences were analyzed:

1. Where one sequence exercises functional control over another
2. Where a common variable exercises functional control over two or more sequences
3. Authority conflict.

The functional analysis of authority that has been presented places primary emphasis upon the reciprocal nature of authority interactions and, by so doing, suggests how authority evolves, is maintained, and may be weakened.

As the analysis suggests, it is actually improper to speak of the locus of authority, except perhaps for "shorthand" purposes. Authority is behavior and is a function of certain operationally defined variables. By adopting this functional approach, it should be possible not only to account for observations that have been made about authority, but to deduce systematically the consequences of manipulating variables in specified ways.

REFERENCES

Bruner, J. S., Goodnow, J. J., & Austin, G. A. *A study of thinking.* New York: Wiley, 1956.

Grice, G. R. The relation of secondary reinforcement to delayed reward in visual discrimination learning. *J. exp. Psychol.*, 1948, *38*, 1-16.

Perin, C. T. A quantitative investigation of the delay-of-reinforcement gradient. *J. exp. Psychol.*, 1943, *32*, 37-51. (a)

Perin, C. T. The effect of delay of reinforcement upon the differentiation of bar re-
    sponses in white rats. *J. exp. Psychol.*, 1943, *32*, 95-109. (b)
Skinner, B. F. *Verbal behavior*. New York: Appleton-Century-Crofts, 1957.
Verplanck, W. S. A glossary of some terms used in the objective science of behavior.
    Psychol. Rev., 1957, *64* (6), Part 2.

— · — · — · — · — · — · — · — · — · — · —

GEORGE CASPAR HOMANS

*Elementary Characteristics of the Human Group (Social Behavior)**

STIMULI

Let us now return to Person and Other, whom we left in the last chapter exchanging approval for help. Much of the activity each emits is at once a reward for and a stimulus to the activity of the other: when Other gives Person help he not only rewards Person but stimulates his thanks. Some of the activity has little reward-value. Such may be Person's original request for help: it may have little value for Other unless perhaps he finds the request flattering in itself. But it may still be effective as a stimulus. If in Other's past experience a request for help (the stimulus) has been the occasion on which giving help (the activity) has been followed by his getting thanks (the reward), Other is the more likely to give the help now. That is what we mean when we say that Other "expects" thanks for his help, or that he "perceives" the situation as one in which thanks may be forthcoming. Most men have gotten thanks under these conditions, but the odd man may turn up whose past experience has been different and who accordingly responds differently to the stimulus.

The power of the stimulus to elicit the behavior is no doubt greater when it has occurred in the past in conjunction with an activity that has been often rewarded, or with one that has gotten a particularly valuable reward. But since we shall speak later of the variables *frequency* and *value*, we shall say no more about them here and emphasize instead the similarity of the present stimulus to a stimulus of the past. Other is likely to give help if the present stimulus bears some resemblance to one in conjunction with which his giving help has been rewarded in the past: he may give help not only when Person asks for it but merely when Person looks helpless. The greater the similarity, the more likely he is to do so, and, by the same token, the greater the difference between the present stimulus and the past, the less likely he is to do so.

Accordingly, we offer the following as our first general proposition: (1) IF IN THE PAST THE OCCURRENCE OF A PARTICULAR STIMULUS-SITUATION HAS BEEN THE OCCASION ON WHICH A MAN'S ACTIVITY HAS BEEN REWARDED, THEN THE MORE SIMILAR THE PRESENT STIMULUS-SITUATION IS TO THE PAST ONE, THE MORE LIKELY HE IS TO EMIT THE ACTIVITY, OR SOME SIMILAR AC-TIVITY, NOW.

We must confess once more to a great inadequacy in this book. Whatever establishes the similarities and differences in question—whatever makes men discriminate between stimuli—may be exceedingly complicated. It is far more complicated for men than it is for pigeons, if only because the stimuli may be verbal. The use of language is incomparably the biggest difference between the behavior of men and that of other animals. With a man the discriminations may be the result not only of his everyday experience but also of his formal education, his reading, and the verbal arguments he may have listened to. They may be unconscious or the result of conscious reasoning. Obviously the problem of the relations between stimuli, past activities, and present ones is of the first importance, yet we shall state no further general propositions about it, and accordingly this book falls far short of being a complete psychology. Instead we shall take up particular instances of the discrimination of stimuli when it becomes necessary for us to do so. We shall be especially concerned with two cases: when the fact that a particular *person* makes a request is the decisive feature of the stimulus, and when certain patterns of stimuli—the ones men describe by saying they did not get what they deserved—release emotional behavior. We shall not otherwise be able to understand either authority or justice.

We have a reason for not going further into the discrimination of stimuli. If we are to explain why a man gives a particular activity to another the first time, we are bound to look carefully at the stimuli and at the man's past experience with the activity when other stimuli like them were present. After that, when the same kind of activity is repeated on similar occasions, we can practically take the stimuli for granted and explain changes in the activity, in quantity and value, by looking at the way it is reinforced. Most of the activities we shall consider are of this sort, as is our example, the interaction of Person and Other. We look on their behavior toward one another as a repeated exchange of help for approval, in which each activity emitted by one man is rewarded by an activity of the other, in a chain. And we turn now to propositions about the effect of reinforcement on their behavior.

VALUE AND QUANTITY

We cannot say everything at once even if everything happens that way, and therefore to make our task easier let us begin by putting on the behavior of Person and Other a restriction we shall later remove. Let us assume that, by whatever process of trial and error you please, the two have struck a tacit bargain as to the *kind* of service each will provide, and that for the time being neither will provide another kind: Other will not offer a better grade of help nor Person a warmer brand of approval. If, under this condition, an activity emitted by Person, once rewarded by an activity of Other, is not thereafter so rewarded, Person will sooner or later stop emitting the activity: if Other stops giving Person help, Person will in time stop asking for it; and if Person stops giving Other approval, Other will in time stop giving help. But we had better put the matter the other way around, and emphasize the number of times an activity *is* rewarded instead of the number of times it is not: (2) THE MORE OFTEN WITHIN A GIVEN PERIOD OF TIME A MAN'S ACTIVITY REWARDS THE ACTIVITY OF ANOTHER, THE MORE OFTEN THE OTHER WILL EMIT THE ACTIVITY. From this proposition it follows that the frequency with which Other emits activity to Person will tend to bear some proportionality to the frequency with which Person emits activity to Other; for if either allows his rate to fall off, the other, by this proposition, will eventually let his fall off too. Concretely, the more often Person thanks him, the more often Other will give him help. Just what the proportionality is we shall soon consider.

Proposition 2 refers only to the frequency of activity, but we must also consider our other variable, its value. (3) THE MORE VALUABLE TO A MAN A UNIT OF THE ACTIVITY ANOTHER GIVES HIM, THE MORE OFTEN HE WILL EMIT ACTIVITY REWARDED BY THE ACTIVITY OF THE OTHER. The more Person needs help, the more often he will ask for it and the more thanks he will give when he gets it; and the more Other needs approval the more often he will give help. From propositions 2 and 3 it follows that the frequency of *interaction* between Person and Other depends on the frequency with which each rewards the activity of the other and on the value to each of the activity he receives.

The present proposition should also answer the question of proportionality that we raised above. The number of units of activity Person emits within any limited period of time in return for a specific number of units emitted by Other we shall call the *rate of exchange* between the two activities. It is the equivalent in our nonmonetary economics of price in regular economics, for the price of a commodity in money specifies the number of units of the commodity that may be exchanged for a given number of units of another commodity. By the present proposition, the rate of exchange between approval and help should tend to equal the ratio between the value Person puts on help and the value Other puts on approval; for if Person values help relatively more than Other values approval, then he is likely to give relatively more approval than Other gives help.

But (4) THE MORE OFTEN A MAN HAS IN THE RECENT PAST RECEIVED A REWARDING ACTIVITY FROM ANOTHER, THE LESS VALUABLE ANY FURTHER UNIT OF THAT ACTIVITY BECOMES TO HIM; and therefore, by proposition 3, the less often he will emit the activity that gets him that reward: the more help Person has recently received from Other, the less, for the time being, he needs any further help and the less often he will ask for help or give thanks. Accordingly this proposition may mask the truth of proposition 2, which says that the more often Other rewards the activity of Person, the more often Person will emit the activity. For if Other rewards him often enough to begin to satiate him, his own activity will tend to fall off in frequency. This is the sort of effect we refer to when we say the propositions hold good only with "other things equal."

So far we have only considered exchange between two persons. Let us now compli-cate matters by having a Third Man enter the exchange. We are reluctant to face all the possible intricacies of a triangular relationship, nor shall we need to do so in order to explain most of the research findings reported later in this book. Let us accordingly consider only one special case. Let us assume that the Third Man is just like Person: both are equally unskilled and both set an equal value on help which they can only get from Other. This is what we shall mean when we say that Other commands a rare or scarce activity. We also assume that, in return for help, both offer the same kind of approval, and that therefore Other treats them both the same way. Both now start giving Other approval in return for his help, but his help must now be divided between the two of them. This means that at any given time each of them is apt to have received less help in the recent past than Person would have received when he was alone with Other, and that therefore, by proposition 4, any unit of help will at the given time be more valuable to each of them. But by proposition 3, the more valuable a unit of help, the more activity that is rewarded by help each of them will put out, and therefore the rate of exchange of help for approval is apt to take a turn unfavorable to both of them: each will come to give more approval for a unit of help than Person did when he was alone with Other. We may say, if we like, that Other's bargaining position has improved over what it was when he had only Person to deal with, even though no conscious bargaining need take place. Note the part played by the scarcity of help in producing this result—scarcity in the sense that Other is the only man who can supply it, and that two men now want it where only one did before. If there were any source of help alternative to Other, if Person could get from somebody else enough help to make up for the help Other now denies him, the value to him of a unit of help at any given time would not go up. In the absence of any alternative source, Person faces the problem of increasing the amount of help Other gives him; for if he leaves things as they are, he will only get half as much help as he did before. He can accomplish this result if he changes the kind of approval he gives Other so as to make it warmer and more admiring; for then a unit of approval will be more valuable to Other, and therefore, by proposition 3, Other will put out more help to get it. To both of these questions we now turn: first, to the effects produced by the presence of alternatives, and second, to the effects produced by changing the kind of activity emitted.

★ ★ ★

On Justice, we shall consider a variety of investments and their mutual relations. At the risk of gross oversimplification we shall consider only one of them here, and then only for purposes of illustration. This investment, and it is the most characteristic of investments, is a man's age. We have seen that Person asks himself whether he has received as much reward as other men, in some respect like himself, received. But one of the ways in which two men may be "like" one another is in their investments. Accordingly the more nearly one man is like another in age, the more apt he is to expect their net rewards to be equal and to display anger when his own are less. But, by the same token, to the extent that their investments are different, he may expect the other's net reward, his profit, to be greater or less than his own. If the other is older than he is himself, if the other has invested more time in living, than he may be content that the other should get a greater profit than he does himself, and he may display no anger when the other does get it. Remember that we have considered age in utter isolation from other investments. In real life there are many background characteristics of men beside their age that count, with different persons and in different cultures, as investments.

Later we shall offer evidence for a general rule of distributive justice; here we shall only state it baldly. A man in an exchange relation with another will expect that the rewards of each man be proportional to his costs—the greater the rewards, the greater the costs—and that the net rewards, or profits, of each man be proportional to his investments—the greater the investments, the greater the profit. This means that unless the investments of the two men are greatly different, each man will further expect the following condition to hold good: the more valuable to the other (and costly to himself) an activity he gives the other, the more valuable to him (and costly to the other) an activity the other gives him. Finally, when each man is being rewarded by some third party, he will expect the third party to maintain this relation between the two of them in the distribution of rewards.

Our proposition 5 then becomes: THE MORE TO A MAN'S DISADVANTAGE THE RULE OF DISTRIBUTIVE JUSTICE FAILS OF REALIZATION, THE MORE LIKELY HE IS TO DISPLAY THE EMOTIONAL BEHAVIOR WE CALL ANGER.

7 · GROUP DYNAMICS, PROCESSES, COOPERATION, CONFORMITY, AND COLLECTIVE BEHAVIOR

SOLOMON E. ASCH

Group Pressure*

I shall report the first steps of an investigation the object of which was to study some conditions that induce individuals to remain independent or to yield to group pressures when these are *contrary to fact*. The issues related to this question are important both for theory and for their human implications. Whether a group will resist or submit to given pressures may be decisive for its future. It is an equally decisive fact about a person whether he has the freedom to act according to his beliefs or whether he has failed to develop (or has lost) the possibility of independence. Current thinking has stressed the power of social conditions to induce psychological changes arbitrarily. It has taken slavish submission to group forces as the general fact and has neglected or implicitly denied the capacities of men for independence, for rising under certain conditions above group passion and prejudice. Our present task is to observe directly the interaction between individuals and groups when the paramount issue is that of remaining independent or submitting to social pressure.

A MINORITY OF ONE VS. A UNANIMOUS MAJORITY

The Experimental Procedure

To this end an experimental technique was designed as the basis for a series of studies. A group of 7 to 9 individuals, all college students, are gathered in a classroom.

*Solomon E. Asch, *Social Psychology*, ©1952, pp. 451–465. Reprinted by permission of Prentice-Hall, Inc., Englewood Cliffs, N. J.

The experimenter explains that they will be shown lines differing in length and that their task will be to match lines of equal length. The setting is that of a perceptual test. The experimenter places on the blackboard in front of the room two white cardboards on which are pasted vertical black lines. On the card at the left is a single line, the standard. The card at the right has three lines differing in length, one of which is equal to the standard line at the left. The task is to select from among the three lines the one equal in length to the standard line, as in Figure 9. The cards on which the lines appeared were

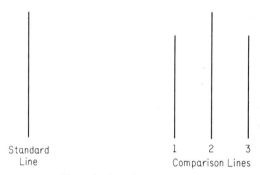

Standard   1   2   3
Line   Comparison Lines

Figure 9. Sample comparison.

$17\,^1/_2$" × 6". The lines had a standard width of $^3/_8$"; their lower ends were $2\,^1/_2$" from the lower edge of the cards. Standard lines appeared in the center of the card, while comparison lines were separated by a distance of $1^3/_4$". The numbering of the lines was done with black gum figures $^3/_4$" long, which were placed $^1/_2$" below the base of each line and directly underneath it.

The instructions to the subjects are as follows:

> This is a task which involves the discrimination of lengths of lines. You see the pair of white cards in front. On the left is a single line; on the right are three lines differing in length; they are numbered 1, 2, and 3 in order. One of the three lines at the right is equal to the standard line at the left—you will decide in each case which is the equal line. You will state your judgment in terms of the corresponding number. There will be twelve such comparisons. As the number of lines is few and the group small, I shall call upon each of you in turn to announce your judgment, which I shall record here on a prepared form. Please be as accurate as possible. Suppose we start at the right and proceed to the left.

The lines are vertical and their lower ends are at the same level. The comparison lines are numbered 1, 2, 3. Correctly matched lines are always at a distance of forty inches. In giving his judgment each subject calls out, in accordance with the instruction, the number of the comparison line ("one," "two," "three") that he judges to be equal to the standards. When all the subjects have stated their judgments, the two cards are removed and replaced by a new pair of cards with new standard and comparison lines. There are twelve sets of standard and comparison lines in all.

The differences to be discriminated are considerable; most unequal comparison lines are clearly longer or shorter than the standard. Table I shows the lengths of lines and the order in which they appeared. The comparison lines differ from the standard by varying amounts and no attempt was made to maintain a constant ratio between them. On successive trials the equal line appears in different positions, in random order. The two unequal comparison lines vary in their relation to the standard in the different trials: both are longer, or both are shorter, or one is longer and the other shorter than the standard.

TABLE I. MAJORITY RESPONSES TO STANDARD
AND COMPARISON LINES ON SUCCESSIVE TRIALS

Trials	Length of Standard Line (in inches)	Length of Comparison Lines (in inches)			Majority Error (in inches)
		1	2	3	
1*	$7\frac{1}{2}$	5	$5\frac{3}{4}$	$7\frac{1}{2}$	0
2*	5	$6\frac{1}{2}$	7	5	0
3	8	8	7	6	1
4	$3\frac{1}{2}$	$3\frac{3}{4}$	5	$3\frac{1}{2}$	$\frac{1}{4}$
5*	9	7	9	11	0
6	$6\frac{1}{2}$	$6\frac{1}{2}$	$5\frac{1}{4}$	$7\frac{1}{2}$	1
7	$5\frac{1}{2}$	$4\frac{1}{2}$	$5\frac{1}{2}$	4	1
8*	$1\frac{3}{4}$	$2\frac{3}{4}$	$3\frac{1}{4}$	$1\frac{3}{4}$	0
9	$2\frac{1}{2}$	4	$2\frac{1}{2}$	$3\frac{3}{8}$	$\frac{7}{8}$
10	$8\frac{1}{2}$	$8\frac{1}{2}$	$10\frac{1}{4}$	11	$1\frac{3}{4}$
11*	1	3	1	$2\frac{1}{4}$	0
12	$4\frac{1}{2}$	$4\frac{1}{2}$	$3\frac{1}{2}$	$5\frac{1}{2}$	1

*These designate "neutral" trials, i.e., trials to which the majority responded correctly. All other trials were "critical," i.e., the majority responded incorrectly.
Underlined figures designate the incorrect majority responses.

The experiment proceeds normally during the first two trials. The discriminations are simple; each individual monotonously calls out the same judgment. Suddenly this harmony is disturbed at the third trial. While all other subjects call the middle of the three lines equal to the standard line, a single member of the group, seated toward the end, claims the first line to be the correct one. As the experiment progresses, this incident is repeated a number of times. From time to time the same individual continues to disagree with the group. On certain other trials there is complete unanimity.

An outsider, observing the experimental situation, would, after the first few trials, begin to single out this individual as somehow different from the rest of the group and this impression would grow stronger as the experiment proceeded. After the first one or two disagreements he would note certain changes in the manner and posture of this person. He would see a look of perplexity and bewilderment come over this subject's face at the contradicting judgments of the entire group. Often he becomes more active; he fidgets in his seat and changes the position of his head to look at the lines from different angles. He may turn around and whisper to his neighbor seriously or smile sheepishly. He may suddenly stand up to look more closely at the card. At other times he may become especially quiet and immobile.

What is the reason for this peculiar behavior? The answer lies in a crucial feature of the situation that we have not yet mentioned. The subject whose reactions we have been describing is the only member of the group who is reacting to the situation as it has been described. All the others are, without his knowledge, cooperating with the experimenter by giving at certain times unanimously wrong judgments, by calling two clearly unequal lines equal. The deviations of the group estimate from the correct values are considerable, ranging from ¼″ to 1¾″. (The majority responses are underlined in Table I.) Actually the group consists of two parts: the instructed subjects, whom we shall call the *majority*, and one naive person, whom we shall call the *critical subject*, and who is in the position of a *minority of one*. The instructed majority has met with the experimenter before the experimental sessions. During discussions the aim of the experiment was fully explained and their role in the experiment was carefully rehearsed. Their instructions were to act in a natural, confident way, to give the impression that they were new to the experiment, and to present a united front in defending their judgments when necessary. The group was instructed to be friendly but firm. As far as possible, the same cooperating group met with successive critical subjects. New members of the cooperating group were often obtained from ex-critical subjects.

The critical subjects were recruited by the members of the cooperating group from among their acquaintances. They were told that an experiment in psychology was being performed for which additional subjects were required. When the naive subject arrived with his acquaintance, he found the others in the corridor or in the room, evidently waiting for the experimenter to appear. Shortly thereafter the experimenter entered and invited the group to be seated. It was also decided in advance that the critical subject was to occupy a seat near the end, usually one seat from the end. The members of the group simply took the available seats, leaving the designated seat for the critical subject. This procedure insured that the critical subject received during each trial the full impact of the majority trend before uttering his judgment. A majority of 7 to 9 seemed desirable for the purpose. Smaller groups, we feared, would lack the requisite "group volume," and larger groups are difficult to form and maintain.

1. *Responses of the cooperating group*. Altogether there were twelve judgments to be made. To seven of these the majority responded with wrong estimates. (See Table I.) The first two responses were correct in order to establish a natural starting point. All responses of the majority were unanimous. The responses of the group were recorded by the experimenter on previously prepared forms. In addition, the experimenter and his assistant made independent records of the appearance, manner, and comments of the critical subject.

2. *The group discussion*. The experiment did not come to an end with the completion of the comparisons. To bring out more clearly the reactions of the critical subject it was decided to engage him, after the exposure of the cards, in a brief, informal discussion. The experimenter opened by saying that he had noticed disagreement at certain points and asked whether there were any remarks. Although the statement was not directed at any one in particular, the critical subject usually responded. At this point the members of the group joined in. They put their questions apparently out of curiosity and interest. At first the discussion centered on how to account for the disagreement that had developed. As the critical subject began increasingly to occupy the center of the scene, he was asked to indicate who, in his opinion was right—the group or himself. He was asked whether it was likely that the entire group was in error and he alone right, how much confidence he placed in his judgments under the circumstances, and so on. The following questions were always included: "Who do you suppose was right?" If the subject replied that his judgments were correct he was asked: "Do you suppose that the entire group was wrong and that you alone were right?" How confident of your judgments are you?" "If something important depended on your answer, if this were a matter of practical consequence, how

would you act?" "What would you say to all this if you were an outsider?" The questions were asked in the order in which they are listed; any member of the group was free to raise the questions as the occasion warranted.

3. *Interview and disclosure of the experimental purpose.* At the conclusion of the discussion, which lasted approximately five minutes, the experimenter dismissed the group and asked to see the critical subject. During the interview the questions that were raised earlier were followed up, the object being to find out in greater detail the subject's reaction to the experimental situation. Toward the end of the interview the experimenter explained fully the object of the experiment and the structure of the experimental situation; this procedure was followed with all subjects. It did not seem advisable or justified to allow the subject to leave without full knowledge of what had happened. We may anticipate and say that nearly all subjects expressed interest and most were glad of the opportunity to have experienced a striking social situation from which they felt they had learned a lesson.

Finally, we may mention that in performing this experiment certain precautions must be taken for the sake of the critical individual. No subject should be allowed to leave without having the purport of the procedure fully explained. The subjects do not resent the temporary imposition practiced upon them provided they understand the purpose of the investigation. Many feel that the experiment has been an experience of some value. It brings home to them directly, and in a way that mere reading or discussions fail to do, the meaning of group opposition and the real possibility of an individual being right even if he has a unanimous public opinion against him. The critical subjects usually left with the feeling that they had witnessed a situation that touched upon a significant human problem.

This, then was the object and the design of the experiments to be described. An individual was in the midst of a group of equals all of whom were judging in public a simple perceptual relation. By means of the procedure outlined a disagreement developed between the group and one of its members. Two opposing forces acted upon the single subject: one from a clearly perceived relation and another from a compact majority. Having placed the individual in conflict with a unanimous majority we proceeded to observe its effect upon him. There was a total of 31 male critical subjects in the present experiment, which we will call Experiment 1.

Quantitative Results

How did the critical subjects respond to the unanimous opposition of the majority? Did they remain independent and repudiate the wrong trend of the group? Or did they show a tendency to yield to the majority, and if so, to what extent? We shall attempt to answer these questions first in terms of the quantitative results.

Table II contains the frequency of correct and incorrect responses in the group of 31 critical subjects. We find that two-thirds of the responses were correct and independent of the majority trend; the remaining one-third were errors identical with those of the majority. In contrast, the errors obtained in a control group of 25 subjects, who reported their judgments privately in writing, were 7.4 per cent of the total. The mean number of errors in the experimental group was 2.3; in the control group 0.5. From this we may draw two conclusions. First, the preponderance of estimates was, under the given conditions, correct and independent. Second, there occurred at the same time a pro-

TABLE II. ESTIMATES OF EXPERIMENTAL AND CONTROL GROUPS

Experiment	N	Total Number of Estimates	Correct Estimates		Pro-Majority Errors	
			F	Per Cent	F	Per Cent
I: Minority of one vs. a unanimous majority	31	217	145	66.8	72	33.2
Control	25	175	162	92.6	13	7.4

nounced movement toward the majority; their erroneous announcements contaminated one-third of the estimates of the critical subjects.

The errors were not however equally distributed among the critical subjects; indeed, there is evidence of extreme individual differences, as Table III will show. The responses

TABLE III. DISTRIBUTION OF CRITICAL ERRORS
IN EXPERIMENTAL AND CONTROL GROUPS

Number of Errors	Control Group	Experimental Group
0	14	6
1	9	7
2	2	6
3	0	4
4	0	4
5	0	1
6	0	1
7	0	2
N	25	31
Mean	0.5	2.3

of the critical group cover the entire range; there were subjects who remained completely independent, and at the other extremes were some who went with the majority without exception. One-fifth of the subjects were entirely independent; if we include those who erred only once, which may be considered within the control range, we have forty-two per cent of the group whose estimates were not appreciably affected by the experimental

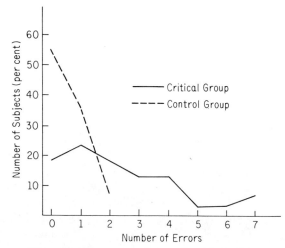

Figure 10. Frequency of errors in critical and control groups.

conditions. The range of errors in the control group was sharply curtailed, no subject erring more than twice. Figure 10 is a representation of the distribution of errors in both groups.

Finally, the errors were not equally distributed among the different critical trials, as the results of Table IV show. The frequency of errors in different trials varied from 3 to 16. In general fewest errors occurred with the shortest standard.

TABLE IV. FREQUENCY OF ERRORS ON SUCCESSIVE CRITICAL TRIALS

	Critical Trials						
	3	4	6	7	9	10	12
Experiment 1.	9	16	9	13	3	12	10
Control Experiment . .	1	10	1	1	0	0	0

In conclusion: The experimental condition significantly distorted the reported estimates. There were extreme individual differences in response to majority pressure, ranging from complete independence to complete yielding. The response to majority pressure was also a function of the physical relations between the materials compared.

Reactions to the Experimental Situation

How did the critical individuals face the situation and what was its effect upon them? Although important, the quantitative scores do not speak for themselves, since they provide no hint of the reasons for their occurrence. We shall now attempt an account of what happened, based on the observations of the subjects and of their reactions in the post-experimental interview. We shall first look more closely at the characteristics of the experimental episode and then proceed to a schematic account of the reactions they provoked in most. Finally, we will describe the outstanding individual differences observed under the same conditions.

The structure of the experimental condition. Although the critical subjects differed greatly among themselves, there were some aspects in the situation that all discerned and to which all responded.

(a) A person is in a situation in which he makes judgments about relatively simple matters of fact. At the same time he is with a group in which others, equal to himself, share in the task of making the same discriminations. All judgments are made in the clear light of day, and all are announced in public. Of particular importance is the fact that the task concerns the judgment of perceived relations that possess considerable, and at times unquestionable, certainty.

(b) As long as he is in agreement with the group, the individual is completely convinced of the accuracy of his judgments. He is confident in his own perceptions, and in this he is confirmed by the group.

(c) When the group suddenly and unexpectedly opposes the critical individual, his psychological situation alters radically. There are now two forces acting upon him. One is the force of the perceived situation itself, which because of its great clarity is decisive. The subject does not simply perceive the given relations in an abstract way; he believes in the evidence of his perceptions with all the conviction of which he is capable. The second force proceeds from the solid, unbroken opposition to the majority, which unanimously contradicts from time to time the clear state of affairs. The two forces are in diametrical opposition.

(d) A significant feature of the experimental situation is its relatively closed, self-contained character. Both the materials and the group are directly present. The contradiction is right within the psychological field; it does not seem possible to resolve it by reference to external factors, such as past experience or differences of attitude.

(e) The situation calls for action; the individual must take a stand. The necessity to declare his position publicly introduces new conditions and new forces. There is a force acting on all to report truthfully what they see; its strength varies, being a function of a number of complex conditions. There is also a force upon all subjects from the direction of the majority, which varies in quality from person to person.

Development of the dilemma. The responses to the experimental episode differed greatly from person to person. Nevertheless there were certain reactions that occurred generally. Before considering the individual differences, we shall attempt to describe, at the risk of being schematic, some of the most usual effects that the conditions aroused.

(a) *Perception of a difficulty.* No subject disregards the group judgments. Although the task calls for independent judgments, virtually no one looks upon the estimates of the group with indifference or as irrelevant. Each immediately grasps the estimates of the others in their relation to his own estimates. Further, the responses that the critical subject hears are not so many separate responses, each of which happens to coincide with the others and to diverge from his own. He notes immediately the convergence of the group responses, his divergence from them, and the contradiction between these. The situation may be represented schematically as shown in the accompanying figure.

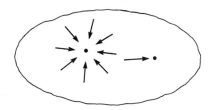

There are many other structural relations that the subject comprehends and that are the necessary conditions for the growth of a conflict. The subject knows (1) that the issue is one of fact; (2) that a correct result is possible; (3) that only one result is correct; (4) that the others and he are oriented to and reporting about the same objectively given relations; (5) that the group is in unanimous opposition at certain points with him. The group opposition has a still further property for the critical subject. It consists of the independent judgments of separate individuals and is not the produce of a joint decision. In this instance the strength of the group direction rests on the independence of the members.[1] It is on these grounds that the critical subject senses there is something wrong. Each of the points mentioned is necessary to the further development; with any of them missing the meaning of the situation would collapse.

(b) *Effort at reestablishing equilibrium.* The immediate reaction of most critical subjects is one of varying degrees of puzzlement or confusion. A few stop the proceedings at

---

[1] This statement needs to be somewhat qualified for those critical subjects who felt that members of the majority were sheepishly following the first person who happened to be wrong.

the first or second disagreement to inquire if they have understood the instructions correctly; others less bold make similar inquiries of their immediate neighbors. None are prepared for the fundamental disagreement; instead they look for a more obvious source of misunderstanding. The subjects are not yet fully in the conflict; they are in fact resisting it as a real possibility by searching for a simpler explanation. They hope that the early disagreements were episodic and that they will give way to solid unanimity. As the disagreements persist, they can no longer cling to this hope. They now believe that they are perceiving in one way, the group in another.

(c) *Localization of the difficulty in the critical subject.* Most subjects see a disturbance created, not by the majority, but by themselves. They do not call upon the majority to justify its judgments; most simply try to defend the validity of their own reactions. The subject assumes the burden of proof. He, not the majority, becomes the center of the trouble; it is he who is disrupting the consistent trend. Nearly all speak in terms of "the group contradicts what I see," not in terms of "I contradict what the group sees." In the same direction is the reluctance of many subjects to assert definitely that the majority is in error. It is noteworthy that the experimenter, too, despite full knowledge of the situation, at times perceives things in the same way, with the subject as the creator and center of disturbance.

(d) *Attempts at solution.* Once the realization has taken hold that there is a basic disagreement, the subject makes an effort to overcome the difficulty by explaining it somehow. The doubts and tensions that the disagreements engender are conditions that support the flourishing of hypotheses, all designed to bridge the inexplicable gap. Some actually help to diminish the tension. Subjects may feel that the other members of the majority are conformists, following the first subject who for some reason is inaccurate. Others may mention that some in the group are wearing glasses. Most hypotheses are, however, *ad hoc* and half-hearted. Quite frequently a subject will say that the disagreements are the result of the different positions of the observers, overlooking the inconsistency of this proposal. Still others vaguely refer to psychological illusions, or propose that the group was judging on the basis of criteria other than length. As a rule, the subjects do not take their hypotheses, which fluctuate considerably, too seriously.

Many who have heard of these experiments express surprise at the fact that few suspected the genuineness of the majority. The surprise is understandable; during the first steps of this investigation the writer himself had considerable doubts that the episode could be sustained. We may add that the effect is not the result of unusual dramatic qualities in the majority; quite tepid groups have been sufficient to produce the experimental effect. A specific factor preventing a solution is the narrowing of the subject's mental field. As soon as he becomes concerned to know why *he* is wrong and, as soon as he begins to respond to the urgencies of the situation, he becomes less free to look at it with a detached eye and to arrive at a solution that to an outsider seems relatively simple.

(e) *Centering on the object of judgment.* In their eagerness to locate the source of the difficulty the subjects now look with greater care and become more attentive and scrupulous in observing and comparing. They act to increase the clearness of their perceptions and judgments. The more the subject is out of step with the group the more anxiously does he turn to the situation itself. That one effect of group opposition is to direct the person back to the situation and to induce a heightened objectivity is a trite observation. It has, however, been neglected in psychological discussion. A particularly interesting example of this tendency is the desire expressed by a few of the more spontaneous subjects to see the lines again and to measure them. Some suddenly jump and approach the cards. It is as if these subjects were trying to eliminate the last possibility of indirectness involved in viewing the lines from a distance. A few, indeed, asserted that they would stick to their view until they were able to measure the lines. It is probable that in a less formal situation many more might have insisted on a close-up view of the cards or on the most direct test of superposition. In this behavior these subjects are showing that they are not accepting the group as the final arbiter in the matter.

(f) *Growth of self doubt.* Despite all efforts the disagreement persists. The subjects search for a principle of explanation, but they are deprived of the possibility of finding it. Nothing can be clearer or more certain than that the materials contain the relations perceived. There is something wrong, but they cannot say what it is. At this point doubt sets in for many. Some begin to fear that their senses may be deceiving them, and their consternation deepens. It is to this factor that we trace the poignancy of many reactions. Some of the most confident and independent subjects become shaken. One of these reported developing the feeling that he was either very right or very wrong. Another declared: "To me it seems I'm right, but my reason tells me I'm wrong, because I doubt that so many people could be wrong and I alone right." The responses of many others go in the same direction: "I would follow my own view, though part of my reason would tell me that I might be wrong." "From what I saw I thought I was right, but apparently I must be wrong. I began to doubt that my vision was right." "What I said appeared to me to be right, but I don't know who is right." "Now the whole class is disagreeing with me and it is possible that I may have been wrong." Some of the staunchest subjects admitted to feelings of doubt. "A little doubt came into my mind, but it was before my eyes, and I was determined to say what I saw. Even though in your mind you know you are right, you wonder why everybody else thinks differently. I was doubting myself and was puzzled."

Now differences in steadfastness between subjects emerge. Some continue firmly to defend their judgments, despite their perplexity. The following statements are representative: "I will believe that they were wrong until you show me who was right." This subject attributed the differences to his better perception. "I wouldn't believe I am wrong until I measure the lines." But others are more ready to yield to the possibility that the voice of the group is right. The following is an example: "I'd probably take that of the people here (if this were a practical situation). I'd figure my judgment was faulty. I feel puzzled . . . in all the years I've lived I haven't had any trouble like that." Still others concede even more to the majority.

Yet the subjects cannot rest in doubt. They might be relieved to find that they were wrong and the group right, provided they could understand the disagreement. But they are not permitted to resolve the difficulty in this way. No matter how shaken they may be they cannot get away from the compelling evidence of their senses. As a result the attitudes of many fluctuate rapidly during the experiment. An illustrative reaction is the following: "Probably I'm wrong . . . no, I don't mean that. If everyone saw it the other way, I guess I am wrong. But I still think I'm right." Some may suddenly begin to doubt their correctness and try to "improve" their judgment; and because they cannot succeed— the material clearly asserting its relationships—their healthy, usually taken-for-granted faith in their perceptions will suddenly reassert itself strongly. They then throw off the yoke of doubt energetically, only to have the burden of the opposition from the majority settle again on them and force them to reconsider. Lending strength to the dilemma is the sense of irreconcilability of the disagreement, the realization that two vectors that should be identical are starkly contradictory.

(g) *Longing to be in agreement with the group.* Most subjects miss the feeling of being at one with the group. In addition, there is frequent reference to the concern they feel that they might appear strange and absurd to the majority. One of the strongest subjects reported: "Despite everything there was a lurking fear that in some way I did not understand I might be wrong; fear of exposing myself as inferior in some way. It is more pleasant if one is really in agreement." Another subject asserted: "I don't deny that at times I had the feeling 'to heck with it, I'll go along with the rest.' " Or: "I felt awfully funny, everything was going against me." "I felt disturbed, puzzled, separated, like an outcast from the rest. Every time I disagreed I was beginning to wonder if I wasn't beginning to look funny."

— · — · — · — · — · — · — · — · — · —

F. J. ROETHLISBERGER
WILLIAM DICKSON

*Industrial Social Psychology: The Hawthorne Experiment**

THE WAGE INCENTIVE SYSTEM

Before describing the output situation in the Bank Wiring Observation Room, it is necessary to describe in some detail the wage incentive system under which this group worked.[1] The men were working under a system of group piecework according to which the entire department was considered a unit for purposes of payment. For each unit of equipment the department assembled and shipped out it was paid a fixed sum. The amount thus earned each week constituted the fund out of which all wages were paid. The greater the number of units completed each week by a given number of employees, the larger would be the sum to be distributed among them.

*Reprinted by permission of the publishers from Fritz J. Roethlisberger and William J. Dickson. *Management and the Worker.* Cambridge, Mass.: Harvard University Press, pp. 409–423. Copyright 1938, 1967, by the President and Fellows of Harvard College.

[1] The purpose of this description is solely to provide the reader with information on the basis of which he can understand the material to be presented in this study. Certain technical details of the payment system in operation have been omitted as being extraneous to this purpose.

The allocation of the weekly departmental earnings to the individual employees in the department was based upon their hourly rates. The hourly rates differed for individuals, depending largely upon differences in efficiency, and were guaranteed by the firm in case piece-rate earnings were insufficient to cover them. An employee's hourly rate multiplied by the number of hours he worked per week was called the daywork value of the work he accomplished. By adding together the daywork value of the work done by all the employees in the department, and subtracting the total thus obtained from the total earnings of the department, the excess of piece-rate earnings over the total daywork value was determined. This surplus divided by the total daywork value was called the "percentage." Each individual's weekly daywork earnings were then increased by this percentage and the resulting figure constituted his actual weekly wage.

Inasmuch as the employees were paid weekly and it took some time to compute the amount due each workman, the foreman estimated the number of units his department would complete in a given week one or two days before the end of the week. The pay roll organization computed earnings on the basis of these estimates. At the end of each four-week period the amount of work actually accomplished was compared with these estimates and the difference, if any, was paid to the employees along with their usual checks. The amount thus paid every four weeks was called a "monthly balance."

Under this system of payment, differences in the earnings of different operators, hours of work remaining the same, depended entirely upon differences in individual hourly rates. A uniform increase in the hourly rates of all the employees in the department, output remaining the same, would have resulted in no change in individual earnings. It would simply have lowered the "percentage" or the excess of piece-rate over daywork earnings. However, an increase in the hourly rates of a few people, output remaining the same, would have lowered the earnings of those whose rates were not changed. The only way the group as a whole could increase its earnings was by increasing total output. Partly because of this, a "bogey" was established for each job. The bogey was simply an output standard in terms of which an individual's efficiency could be measured. It was something "to shoot at" and was intended to serve in much the same way as a record does for an athlete. The closer to it the employees came, the higher their earnings would be. It will be readily seen that a raising or lowering of the bogey would in no way affect earnings except in so far as it might influence output. Raising a bogey had none of the effects of reducing a piece rate or hourly rate. This point is emphasized here because it is well to keep it in mind throughout this study.

It is apparent that under this system the earnings of any one individual were affected by the output of every other person in the group. If a person did an unusually large amount of work one week and the other operators did not increase their output proportionately, his earnings would be but slightly higher than if he had not increased his output at all. The results of his increased efforts would be spread among all the workers in the department. Conversely, if a person were unusually low in output for a time, the output of the other operators would serve to sustain his earnings at about their ordinary level.

In order to bring about a rough correspondence between output and earnings, then, adjustments in hourly rates of the operators were based largely upon individual outputs. Records were kept of each person's production for guidance in adjusting rates. These records were based upon the person's weekly average hourly output. In computing them, the individual's total weekly output was divided by standard working hours, from which time lost on account of stoppages beyond the operator's control or time spent on unfamiliar work was deducted. If such time were not deducted, the efficiency ratings of those people who for some reason were delayed would suffer in comparison with those of people who had lost little time. The time thus deducted was called a "daywork allowance" by the people in the department and was used solely for computing efficiency records.

Inasmuch as these daywork allowances will be discussed a good deal in this study, it may be well to describe them further at this time and to differentiate them from "daywork credits," with which they may be confused. The difference between a daywork allowance, as the term is used in this study, and a daywork credit is simply that the former pertains solely to the computation of efficiency records and has nothing to do with payment, whereas the latter pertains primarily to payment. This distinction can best be made clear by an illustration. Suppose one of the wiremen in the observation room spent six hours wiring, one hour soldering, and one hour cleaning solder off the workbenches. Let us assume further that the wiring and soldering jobs were on a piecework basis but that miscellaneous work like cleaning solder off the benches was on a daywork basis and was not included in the piece rate on the soldering job. Now in this case the wireman, in reporting his output for the day, would report the number of terminals he had wired, the time spent in wiring them (six hours), and then he would enter a daywork allowance claim for the two hours he had spent soldering and cleaning solder off the benches. The group chief in computing this wireman's efficiency for the day would base his computation solely on the time spent at wiring. In other words, he would divide the wireman's output by six hours instead of eight so as not to lower unduly his efficiency rating on the wiring job.

Now let us look at this same case from the standpoint of payment. Inasmuch as both the wiring job and the soldering job were on a piecework basis, the wireman, or more accurately the payment group to which the wireman belonged, would receive piecework earnings for the seven hours spent on these two jobs. In other words, no adjustment would need to be made for the hour spent at soldering. An adjustment would have to be made, however, for the hour spent at cleaning the benches. For this hour spent on daywork the wireman would be credited with his hourly rate. He would, in other words, receive a daywork credit of one hour for purposes of payment and a daywork allowance of two hours for purposes of computing his efficiency. For the most part, these daywork credits were pooled with the piecework earnings of the payment group and were distributed on a prorata basis.

It is apparent that this system, in order to function satisfactorily, required a high degree of collaboration between employee and employee and between employees and management. It demanded that each employee look constantly toward increasing or at least maintaining total output and that every other employee do the same. It demanded that each employee think not alone of his own personal interests but also of those of his fellow workmen. Thus if a person, once having achieved a high hourly rate, deliberately slowed up, he could, for a short time at least, receive in payment more than he contributed to the earnings of the group. The chief thing which would prevent him from doing this was his regard for the well-being of his co-workers and for their attitude toward him. Indeed, it could be easily understood, in fact it was expected, that the employees would group together informally to bring pressure to bear upon the slower workers.

The group chief and the section chief were also assigned an hourly rate, and they shared in the departmental earnings on the same basis as the operators. The assistant foreman and the foreman were paid on a salary basis. An allowance was made for supervision in the piece rate so that the employees in no sense "carried" the supervisors.

This, in brief, was the wage incentive plan under which the group worked. Every aspect of it was based upon some logical reason and could be defended on the grounds, first, that it should promote efficiency and, secondly, that it provided an equitable means of apportioning earnings among the employees. Both of these claims were true, however, only if the plan worked as it was supposed to and the employees acted in fact as they were presumed to act in theory. In what follows, we shall inquire to what extent these assumptions held true.

BELIEFS OF EMPLOYEES REGARDING PAYMENT SYSTEM

The Concept of a Day's Work

In interviews with the operators in the department before the study began, the investigators encountered certain beliefs which the employees seemed to hold in common. Chief among these was the concept of a day's work. This idea kept cropping up in interview after interview. Of the thirty-two men interviewed in the department before the study began, a group which included the nine wiremen later selected for the study, twenty-two discussed rates of output. Of these twenty-two, twenty said that the wiring of two equipments constituted a day's work. The other two men said they were supposed to try to make the bogey, which they correctly stated as 914 connections per hour. The following comments, quoted from interviews with members of the group under observation, are typical:

W_1: "6,600 is the bogey. You see, that's two sets. There are 3,300 connections on a set. Now on selector wiring the bogey is only 6,000, because there are only 3,000 connections on a set. In order to turn out 6,600 there, you have to wire three levels on a third set."

Int: "6,600 is your bogey then?"

W_1: "Yes, it's 6,600. You see they told us if we got out two sets a day it would be all right. That's a pretty good day's work too."

. . . . . .

W_2: "You know, some of those fellows stall around for three months before they turn out 6,000. There's no reason for that at all. I could turn out 6,000 in three weeks. I think the rest of them could if they wanted to ... I'm making around 7,000 every day.... I don't mind that [their fooling around] as long as it doesn't interfere with the work. I never fool around until I have my bogey out. That is the first thing. When I get my bogey out, then I don't mind loafing around a bit."

. . . . . .

W_3: "I turn out 6,600 regularly. That's about what is expected of us. Of course you could make out less and get by, but it's safer to turn out about 6,600."

Int: "And is 6,600 your bogey?"

W_3: "No, our bogey is higher than that. It is 914 an hour."

. . . . . .

W_4: "I think connector wiring is the better job. The boards aren't as heavy [as on selectors] and you have an extra bank. You see, the rate on connectors is around 6,600 and on selectors it's only 6,000."

. . . . . .

W_5: "I turn out 100 per cent efficiency right along. That means I turn out 6,600 a day."[2]

Int: "Is the bogey 6,600 a day?"

W_5: "No, that's not the bogey. The bogey is 7,200, I think."

. . . . . .

W_6: "Well, the bogey is pretty high. I turn out 6,600 a day right along and that is pretty good, I think, for the average."

Int: "Is that the bogey?"

W_6: "I think it is."

Int: "Then you are making 100 per cent efficiency?"

W_6: "Well, I don't know about that. I don't think I am turning out 100 per cent. You see the bogey was 914 an hour for an 8¾-hour day, so I suppose it will be about 6,600 for an 8-hour day."

. . . . . .

W_7: "6,000 a day is the rate. I guess there's another rate that's higher than that, but the bosses tell us that 6,000 is a day's work."

. . . . . .

W_8: "I make between 5,500 and 6,000. On selectors they don't have to turn out as many. I think they are supposed to turn out 6,000 a day. We have an extra bank on each set so that if we wire two sets a day we would be making 6,600 a day."

Int: "Is that the bogey?"

W_5: "Yes, I think it is."

From comments such as these it was apparent that the operators were accustomed to thinking of two equipments a day as a day's work. This was verified by the observer, who found that the operators frequently stopped wiring when they had finished their quotas even though it was not official stopping time. This concept of a day's work was of interest for two reasons. In the first place, it did not refer to the bogey or to any other standard of performance officially imposed. As compared with the day's work of which they spoke, which amounted to 6,000 or 6,600 connections depending upon the type of equipment, the bogey was considerably higher. If asked what the bogey was, some of the men could give the correct answer. Many of them, however, spoke of the day's work as being the bogey. Others said that they were supposed to turn out about two sets but they thought the bogey was higher. Still others spoke of the day's work as being the rate on the job, and the rate was held to be synonymous with bogey. Technically, the word "rate" had three quite different meanings depending on whether it referred to piece rates, hourly rates, or rates of working; yet frequently the employees made no distinction. Whatever else this confusion of terminology meant, one conclusion was certain. The bogey was not functioning as a competitive standard for this group.

[2] In order to have an efficiency of 100 per cent, a wireman would have to wire 7,312 terminals a day.

In the second place, the idea of a day's work was of interest because it was contrary to one of the basic notions of the incentive plan. Theoretically, the incentive plan was intended to obviate the problems attendant upon the determination of a day's work. The chief drawback to paying stipulated monthly, daily, or hourly wages is that there is no accurate way of determing how much work should be done for the wages received. Some criterion there must be, but if its determination were left up to the workers it is possible that they might fix upon a low standard. On the other hand, standards arbitrarily imposed by the employer might possibly be too high and entail detrimental physiological results. Where the amount of work to be done in a given time for a given wage is determined by custom, such problems may be present but they do not come to the fore. In modern industry, however, jobs are subdivided and changed so frequently that whatever influence custom might bring to bear is lost. There is no customary standard to which to appeal. One of the chief arguments to be advanced in favor of incentive plans is that under an incentive system a day's work will be determined at that point where fatigue or "pain costs" balance the worker's subjective estimate of the added monetary return. The amount of work done by different individuals should, theoretically, vary as individual capacities vary, and for any one individual variations from day to day might be expected. Under such a system, the concept of a day's work, of a specified number of units to be completed each day by every worker, has, strictly speaking, no place. In the Bank Wiring Observation Room, then, there was evidence that the wage incentive plan was not functioning entirely as it was intended to function.

The question of how two equipments came to be fixed upon as a day's work is an interesting one, but it cannot be definitely answered. Among the possible explanations, four may be mentioned. First, it might be argued that the hourly rates of the people who wired 6,000 or 6,600 terminals a day were at the maximum of the labor grade established for this kind of work. If this were so, the supervisors could not offer the men, except in unusual cases, increases in hourly rates for further increases in output, and therefore the men would tend to fix their output at that level. This explanation failed to be in any sense conclusive, however, simply because the majority of the people in the observation room had not reached the maximum of the labor grade.

Secondly, it might be argued that 6,000 or 6,600 terminals per day, or two equipments, represented the balance point between fatigue or "pain costs" of work, on the one hand, and the satisfactions to be derived from the monetary returns for that amount of work, on the other. There were, however, no evidences of fatigue among the operators in the observation room. Furthermore, some of the operators wished to turn out more work, but they were reluctant to do so in the face of the attitudes prevailing in the group. Their concept of a day's work, in other words, did not represent a personally calculated equilibrium between work and monetary return.

A third explanation is that the supervisors might have mentioned some figure as a desirable day's work when attempting to stimulate some of the slower men. They might have said, for example, "Your output is too low, you should be turning out 6,000 connections a day." The figure thus mentioned might then have become, in the operators' thinking, the standard of acceptable performance. This explanation, however, fails to explain why the supervisors should have chosen this figure instead of some other or why the operators agreed among themselves that it was wrong to exceed it. In practice the supervisors did tell some of the slower men that they should have been turning out two equipments a day, but they also told some of the other wiremen that they should have been doing more. In view of the fact that different figures were given different operators, it is difficult to understand how this explanation could account for their concept of a day's work.

Finally, it might be claimed that the wiring of two equipments was a "natural" day's work in that a wireman could complete two but not three equipments. Rather than start on a third unit he might, for the sake of tidiness and good workmanship, prefer to complete only two and start out on a new one the first thing in the morning. Although some of the operators claimed that they did get a certain satisfaction out of finishing an equipment and seeing the resulting colorful pattern of interlaced wires before them (one of them likened it to the pleasure a woman must derive from knitting), the fact is that they stopped work during the wiring of an equipment more frequently than at the end.

None of these four explanations, then, is satisfactory. There is no way of telling whether one is more plausible than the others. For this reason, the question will be dropped from further consideration. It may be well to point out, however, that one could not hold to any one of the above explanations without admitting, implicitly, that the wage incentive was not functioning as it was supposed to. For, if it were functioning as it was supposed to, the conditions assumed in these arguments would not exist.

The Day's Work as a Group Standard

As the study progressed, it became more and more apparent that the operators' conception of a day's work had a much wider significance than has thus far been implied. The interviewer, while inquiring further into this belief, found that it was related to other beliefs which the operators held quite generally. These other beliefs, which incidentally are quite common and more or less familiar to everyone, usually took the following form: "If we exceed our day's work by any appreciable amount, something will happen. The 'rate' might be cut, the 'rate' might be raised, the 'bogey' might be raised, someone might be laid off, or the supervisor might 'bawl out' the slower men." Any or all of these consequences might follow. It is difficult to produce evidence in which such apprehensions were articulated as clearly as here represented. This statement represents the summation of a variety of employees' remarks in which these fears were more or less implied. The following quotations are given to show the type of evidence upon which the above observation is based:

W_2: (After claiming that he turned out more work than anyone else in the group) "They [his co-workers] don't like to have me turn in so much, but I turn it in anyway."
(In another interview) "Right now I'm turning out over 7,000 a day, around 7,040. The rest of the fellows kick because I do that. They want me to come down. They want me to come down to around 6,600, but I don't see why I should. If I did, the supervisors would come in and ask me what causes me to drop like that. I've been turning out about that much for the last six months now and I see no reason why I should turn out less. There's no reason why I should turn out more either."

$\cdot \quad \cdot \quad \cdot \quad \cdot \quad \cdot \quad \cdot$

W_3: "No one can turn out the bogey consistently. Well, occasionally some of them do. Now since the layoff started there's been a few fellows down there who have been turning out around 7,300 a day. They've been working like hell. I think it is foolishness to do it because I don't think it will do them any good, and it is likely to do the rest of us a lot of harm."

Int: "Just how do you figure that?"

W_3: "Well, you see if they start turning out around 7,300 a day over a period of weeks and if three of them do it, then they can lay one of the men off, because three men working at that speed can do as much as four men working at the present rate."

Int: "And you think that is likely to happen?"

W_3: "Yes, I think it would. At present we are only scheduled for 40 sets ahead. In normal times we were scheduled for over 100. If they find that fewer men can do the work, they're going to lay off more of us. When things pick up they will expect us to do as much as we are now. That means they will raise the bogey on us. You see how it works?"

$\cdot$ $\cdot$ $\cdot$ $\cdot$ $\cdot$ $\cdot$

Int: "You say there is no incentive to turn out more work. If all of you did more work, wouldn't you make more money?"

W_4: "No, we wouldn't. They told us that down there one time. You know, the supervisors came around and told us that very thing, that if we would turn out more work we would make more money, but we can't see it that way. Probably what would happen is that our bogey would be raised, and then we would just be turning out more work for the same money.[3] I can't see that."

$\cdot$ $\cdot$ $\cdot$ $\cdot$ $\cdot$ $\cdot$

W_5: "There's another thing; you know the fellows give the fast workers the raspberry all the time. Work hard, try to do your best, and they don't appreciate it at all. They don't seem to figure that they are gaining any by it. It's not only the wiremen, the soldermen don't like it either. . . . The fellows who loaf along are liked better than anybody else. Some of them take pride in turning out as little work as they can and making the boss think they're turning out a whole lot. They think it's smart. I think a lot of them have the idea that if you work fast the rate will be cut. That would mean that they would have to work faster for the same money. I've never seen our rate cut yet, so I don't know whether it would happen or not. I have heard it has happened in some cases though."

$\cdot$ $\cdot$ $\cdot$ $\cdot$ $\cdot$ $\cdot$

W_6: (Talking about a relative of his who worked in the plant) "She gets in here early and goes ahead and makes up a lot of parts so that when the rest of the girls start in she's already got a whole lot stacked up. In that way she turns out a great deal of work. She's money greedy. That's what's the matter with her and they shouldn't allow that. All she does is spoil the rate for the rest of the girls."

Int: "How does she do that?"

W_6: "By turning out so much. When they see her making so much money, they cut the rate."

$\cdot$ $\cdot$ $\cdot$ $\cdot$ $\cdot$ $\cdot$

---

[3] It should be remembered that raising the bogey could not have this effect unless it resulted in lower output.

W_7: "There's one little guy down there that turns out over 7,000 a day. I think there's a couple of them. And we have to put up with it."

. . . . . .

W_8: "Some people down there have had lots more experience than others and they can't possibly turn out the rate. I know a fellow who came in there just a few months ago and he is up above average already. It won't be long before he will be turning out 7,000 or 8,000 of them."

Int: "Do you think he will?"

W_8: "Well, I think so. Some of them do it. Of course, the slower men don't like that so well."

Int: (After a discussion of a large vs. a small gang for purposes of payment) "Your earnings would probably increase as much under your present system of payment, provided that everyone increased his output proportionately."

W_8: "That would mean that somebody would be out of a job. We've only got so much work to do, you know. Now just suppose a person was doing 6,000 connections a day, say on selectors, that's two whole sets. Now suppose that instead of just loafing around when he gets through he did two more rows on another set. Well, then, when he comes to work the next morning he would have two rows to start with. Then suppose he did another whole set and two additional rows. On the third day, let's see, where would he be? On the third day he would start on the equipment that was already wired up six levels. Before long he would have an extra set done. Then where would you be? Somebody could be laid off."

Int: "Are you conscious of that when you are working? Are you consciously thinking that if you turn out over a certain amount somebody will be laid off?"

W_8: "That only stands to reason, doesn't it?"

Int: "That if you increase your output they're going to lay somebody off?"

W_8: "Yeah. Now just suppose the fellows in that room could increase their output to 7,000. I think some of them can. That would mean less work for others."

Int: "On the same basis, why do you work at all? If you turn out only 3,000 a day, you're just doing work that someone else might do."

W_8: "Yeah, but I think it should be spread around more."

Statements like these indicated that many apprehensions and fears were centered around the concept of a day's work. They suggested that the day's work might be something more than an output standard, that it might be a norm of conduct. The data obtained by the observer provided additional evidence in support of this interpretation. He found that men who persisted in exceeding the group standard of a day's work were looked upon with disfavor. This was manifested in subtle forms of sarcasm and ridicule which can best be illustrated by quoting from the observer's record:

W_6 and W_4 were kidding each other about working hard. W_6 was working very fast. W_4 was working faster than usual.

W_4: (To W_6) "Go on, you slave, work. You're enough connections ahead now to take care of Friday."

Obs: (To W_4) "Is W_6 going too fast to suit you?"

W_4: "He's nothing but a slave. A couple more rows and he'll have 8,000."

W_6: "No, I won't. I haven't got today's work out yet."

W_4: "You should have quit when you finished that set."

W_6: "I'm good for another 6,000 connections. If they'd pay me for it, I'd turn 'em out."

. . . . . .

GC$_2$ was taking the output count.

W_4: (To W_6) "How many are you going to turn in?"

W_6: "I've got to turn in 6,800."

W_4: "What's the matter—are you crazy? You work all week and turn in 6,600 for a full day, and now today you're away an hour and a quarter and you turn in more than you do the other days."

W_6: "I don't care. I'm going to finish these sets tomorrow."

W_4: "You're screwy."

W_6: "All right, I'll turn in 6,400."

W_4: "That's too much."

W_6: "That don't make any difference. I've got to do something with them."

W_4: "Well, give them to me."

W_6 did not answer.

. . . . . .

W_2: (To S_1) "Come on, get this set."

S_1: "All right." (To Obs.) "I want to introduce you to Lightning [W_2] and Cyclone [W_3]. When these two get going it's just like a whirlwind up here. Give W_2 a big chew of snuff and he just burns the solder right off the terminals."

. . . . . .

S_1: (To Obs.) "What's a guy going to do if these fellows won't quit work?"

Obs: "That's it, what?"

S_1: "Keep right on working."

Obs: "There you are. Now you've got it."

S_1: "W_2 has got 8,000 and he don't know enough to quit. Well, if he wires 8,000, I must solder 8,000. That's it, isn't it?"

Obs: "Sure."

W_6 and W_2 were the first in output and it was toward them that most of the group pressure was directed. W_6 was designated by such names as "Shrimp," "Runt," and "Slave." Sometimes he was called "Speed King," a concession to his wiring ability. W_2 was called "Phar Lap," the name of a race horse. W_1 was nicknamed "4:15 Special," meaning that he worked until quitting time. W_5 was also called "Slave" occasionally.

One of the most interesting devices by which the group attempted to control the behavior of individual members was a practice which they called "binging." This practice was noticed early in the study. The observer described it as follows:

W_7, W_8, W_9, and S_4 were engaging in a game which they called "binging." One of them walked up to another man and hit him as hard as he could on the upper arm. The one hit made no protest, and it seems that it was his privilege to "bing" the one who hit him. He was free to retaliate with one blow. One of the objects of the game is to see who can hit the hardest. But it is also used as a penalty. If one of them says something that another dislikes, the latter may walk up and say, "I'm going to bing you for that." The one who is getting binged may complain that he has been hurt and say, "That one was too hard. I'm going to get you for that one."

In the following incident binging was being used as a simple penalty:

W_9 suddenly binged W_7.

Obs: (To W_9) "Why did you do that?"

W_9: "He swore. We got an agreement so that the one who swears gets binged. W_8 was in it for five minutes, but he got binged a couple of times and then quit."

Obs: "Why don't you want W_7 to swear?"

W_9: "It's just a bad habit. There's no sense to it, and it doesn't sound good. I've been getting the habit lately and sometimes I swear when I don't want to. I never used to swear until I got next to W_8, there, and now I find myself doing it all the time."

Another time binging was advocated as a means of expressing a mutual antagonism and settling a dispute:

W_7 had his window open. W_6 walked over and opened his window wide. W_9 went over and closed W_6's window. W_6 ran over and grabbed the chain. He insisted that the window stay open. W_9 insisted that it was too drafty.

W_6: "You run your own window, I'll take care of this one."

W_9: "It's too drafty. You leave that window closed or I'll bing you."

W_6: "Go ahead, start."

W_9 glanced up to see if he could take the chain off the top of the window. W_6 held the chain tight so that W_9 couldn't loosen it. They had quite an argument.

W_6: (To W_8) "How about it? Is it too drafty over there?"

W_8: "No, it's all right."

W_6: "There you are. Now leave the window alone."

S_4: (To W_8) "What's the idea of lying?"

W_8: "I'm not."

S_4: "You're lying if you say you don't feel the draft."

W_8 did not answer.

W_7: (Tired of the argument) "Why don't you bing each other and then shut up?"

In addition to its use as a penalty and as a means of settling disputes, binging was used to regulate the output of some of the faster workers. This was one of its most significant applications and is well illustrated in the following entry:

W_8: (To W_6) "Why don't you quit work? Let's see, this is your thirty-fifth row today. What are you going to do with them all?"

W_6: "What do you care? It's to your advantage if I work, isn't it?"

W_8: "Yeah, but the way you're working you'll get stuck with them."

W_6: "Don't worry about that. I'll take care of it. You're getting paid by the sets I turn out. That's all you should worry about."

W_8: "If you don't quit work I'll bing you." W_8 struck W_6 and finally chased him around the room.

Obs: (A few minutes later) "What's the matter, W_6, won't he let you work?"

W_6: "No. I'm all through though. I've got enough done." He then went over and helped another wireman.

From observations such as these and from interviews the investigators concluded that they had come upon a set of basic attitudes. Beliefs regarding a day's work and the dangers involved in exceeding it were not confined to a few persons but were held quite generally, both by the men in the observation room and in the regular department. It was apparent that there existed a group norm in terms of which the behavior of different individuals was in some sense being regulated.

— · — · — — · — · — in — · — — · —

NEIL J. SMELSER

Value-Added Theory of Collective Behavior *

We define collective behavior as *mobilization on the basis of a belief which redefines social action.* Blumer's definition of a social movement—"[a] collective [enterprise] to establish a new order of life"—implies such a redefinition. Our conception, however, extends to elementary forms of collective behavior as well, such as the panic and the hostile outburst. Such a definition calls for clarification of such terms as "redefines" and "social action." . . .

Collective behavior must be qualified by two further defining characteristics. As the definition indicates, collective behavior is guided by various kinds of beliefs—assessments of the situation, wishes, and expectations. These beliefs differ, however, from those which guide many other types of behavior. They involve a belief in the existence of extraordinary forces—threats, conspiracies, etc.—which are at work in the universe. They also involve an assessment of the extraordinary consequences which will follow if the collective attempt to reconstitute social action is successful. The beliefs on which collective behavior is based (we shall call them *generalized beliefs*) are thus akin to magical beliefs. . . .

The third defining characteristic of collective behavior is similar to Blumer's contrast between collective and culturally prescribed behavior. Collective behavior, as we shall study it, is not institutionalized behavior. According to the degree to which it becomes institutionalized, it loses its distinctive character. It is behavior "formed or forged to meet undefined or unstructured situations."[1]

★ ★ ★

*Reprinted with permission of The Macmillan Company from *Theory of Collective Behavior* by Neil J. Smelser, pp. 8, 129–130, 168–169, 220–221, 269, 310–311, 313, 379–387. Copyright © 1963 by Neil J. Smelser.
[1] H. Blumer, "Collective Behavior," in A. M. Lee (ed.), *New Outline of the Principles of Sociology* (New York: Barnes and Noble, 1951), p. 199.

CREATION OF GENERALIZED BELIEFS

We may summarize briefly the basic themes of this complicated analysis of generalized beliefs. Essentially, all the beliefs dissected in this chapter have a kinship to one another. All are generalized attempts to reconstitute the components of social action. Their major differences stem from the particular components which each attempts to reconstitute. Hysteria and wish-fulfillment focus in different ways on facilities; hostile beliefs on mobilization; norm-oriented beliefs on norms; and value-oriented beliefs on values.

The several beliefs stand in a hierarchy of increasing complexity and inclusiveness:

Top

Value-oriented beliefs
Norm-oriented beliefs
Hostile beliefs
Wish-fulfillment beliefs
Hysterial beliefs

Bottom

This hierarchy, derived from the general relations among the components of action, reveals the components that any one belief reconstitutes. The belief in question includes all the components of the beliefs below it in the hierarchy, plus one new ingredient which gives this belief its distinctive character. Thus we identify a norm-oriented movement because of its focus on norms, but it also includes hostility, wish-fulfillment, and hysteria as elements of itself. Hostility, although containing those beliefs below it as elements, does not involve a reconstitution of either norms or values. Such are the relations among the several generalized beliefs.

The objective of this chapter has been anatomical—to analyze in theoretical terms the structure of the beliefs which accompany collective behavior of every sort. The major questions which remain are (*a*) Why does one, rather than another type of belief arise under conditions of strain? (*b*) How does each kind of belief, once having arisen, work its way into definite episodes of collective behavior?

★ ★ ★

THE PANIC

We have organized the conditions of panic into a scheme of value-added. We have listed the most indeterminate conditions first, and have proceeded to the conditions which operate with progressively greater determinacy. The first condition is structural conduciveness, which refers to the degree to which danger, communication of danger, and restricted egress can arise at all. Within the limits established by conduciveness, the next necessary condition is strain, or the presence of some danger of unknown and uncontrollable proportions. The next condition is the growth of anxiety, which is converted into hysteria by the appearance of a significant event (precipitating factor). This fixes the threat on some specific destructive agent, from which it is possible to flee in certain directions. Finally, on the basis of this hysterical belief, action is mobilized, usually under a primitive form of leadership—the "flight model"—collective flight occurs.

It is important to emphasize that this order of conditions—from indeterminate to determinate—is a logical, not a temporal order. A single event—e.g., approaching troops—may be significant in establishing the conditions of conduciveness (e.g., the belief that the avenues for escape are closing), in creating strain (e.g., the unknown strength of the approaching troops), and in precipitating the formation of a hysterical belief on the basis of which flight occurs. In this instance the analytically distinguishable necessary conditions are telescoped temporally into a single event. But unless this event is interpreted in a context of conduciveness and strain, panic cannot arise. If the approaching troops were interpreted as dangerous but as *already* having cut off access to escape completely, other reactions—resignation, apathy, desire to fight, etc.—might arise, but not panic. If the approaching troops were interpreted as neither dangerous nor cutting off escape routes, the event might precipitate curiousity or relief, but not panic.

In addition to the analytic order of determinants which eventuates in panic, we have asked also how panic may be prevented, deflected, or controlled. In doing so, we created a model of panic as a series of equilibrium states. At any given stage of the value-added process it is possible to assess the operation of those forces making for panic and those making for control. Given the balance of these forces, it is further possible to estimate the probabilities of whether the process will continue toward the panic reaction, halt in its path, take another path, or return to the state which existed before the necessary conditions began to combine. For any given panic, then, it should be possible to recapitulate the events and states leading to collective flight in terms of the general categories of conduciveness, strain, beliefs, precipitating factors, mobilization, and controls.

★ ★ ★

THE CRAZE

We shall comment on the analytic similarities and differences between the panic and boom—both of which reconstitute the Facilities Series—according to the various stages in the value-added process.

(a) Structural conduciveness. Many conditions of conduciveness are identical for the panic and the boom—the ability to commit, recommit, and withdraw resources freely. We have discussed these conditions under the concepts of maneuverability, fluidity, disposability, etc.

(b) Strain. Both the boom and panic rest on uncertainty about the current allocation of facilities, and uncertainty as how best to re-allocate these facilities. In panic, the threatening situation is defined in terms of inability to control the threat, and closing exits; hence the problem is defined in terms of *withdrawal*. In the boom, however, the situation is defined in terms of how best to overcome the threat with a supply of facilities; hence the problem of adjustment to ambiguity is defined in terms of *recommitment* of resources.

(c) Beliefs. The panic rests on a negative generalization (hysteria); the boom on a positive generalization (wish-fulfillment). The wish-fulfillment belief has a component of anxiety, whereas hysteria does not include positive wish-fulfillment as an ingredient.

(d) Precipitating factor. In both cases the precipitating factor plays the same role. It accentuates one of the prior conditions—for example it "confirms" the existence of a threat, or gives "evidence" of tremendous rewards—and in this way converts the generalized anxiety or wish into a specific hysterical or wishful belief.

(e) Mobilization. Both the panic and the boom have a real phase based on the accumulation of initial conditions and a derived stage which arises "on top of" the initial flight or plunge. The major empirical difference between the panic and the craze concerns leadership; in the panic the "flight model" tends merely to tip a balance of fear and throw the group into rout, whereas in the craze—particularly in those which cover long periods of time—the leaders actually mobilize and even manipulate the headlong rush for rewards.

(f) Social control. In theory the kinds of controls appropriate for the panic are the same as those appropriate for the boom. Empirically, however, certain differences emerge. With the possible exception of the speculative boom, "built in" controls more frequently keep the craze from getting out of hand. In panic the situation is frequently so disorganized that controls, if they are to be effective, have to be assembled "on the spot." This probably accounts for the salient role of leadership in the control of panics.

THE HOSTILE OUTBURST

We have not attempted . . . to account for the development of any single riot or related outburst. Rather we have attempted to outline the general determinants which must be present if any single outburst is to occur. We have organized these conditions into a sequence of increasing determinancy—structural conduciveness, strain, generalized beliefs, precipitating factors, and mobilization. Each of these has to be present for the next to assume the status of a determinant of a hostile outburst. Together the determinants constitute a sufficient condition for such an outburst.

In any particular outburst of hostility, the accumulation of the empirical events and situations which contain the determinants may be in any temporal order. For these events and situations to assume significance as determinants, however, they must occur in the context of—the logically prior necessary conditions. For instance, a racial incident between a Negro and a white may spark a race riot. But unless this incident occurs in the context of a structurally conducive atmosphere (i.e., an atmosphere in which people perceive violence to be a possible means of expression) and in an atmosphere of strain (i.e., an atmosphere in which people perceive the incident as symbolic of a troubled state of affairs), the incident will pass without becoming a determinant in a racial outburst.

In addition to this account of the positive determinants of hostile outbursts, we must assess the influence of several deterrents. How is the situation made less structurally conducive for hostility? How are conditions of strain alleviated? How are hostile beliefs dispelled? How can the aggrieved be prevented from communicating with one another? How can authorities head off mobilization to commit some sort of hostile act? The combination of all these factors—positive determinants and deterrents—yields a kind of equilibrium model of counteracting forces. Some forces push toward the outburst of hostility and some forces resist the influence of these forces. Depending on the relations among these forces at any given time, it is possible to estimate the future development of a potential outburst—whether it will wither away, be diverted into some other kind of behavior, be contained, or move toward an outburst of hostility.

★ ★ ★

THE NORM-ORIENTED MOVEMENT

We have outlined a model value-added process in which several determinants combine to produce a norm-oriented movement. We have illustrated each determinant by referring to a variety of movements. Empirically, of course, any given movement does not follow such a neat sequence because the several determinants continuously combine and recombine as a movement progresses, thus giving it new directions. One tactic fails, and another is taken up; the movement is infused with new energy by the occurrence of some unexpected event; an authority rebuffs a movement crudely and drives it temporarily into a violent outburst. In this chapter, we have not tried to account for the evolution of any single movement, but rather to extricate from the histories of many movements the principles which shape the development of norm-oriented movements in general.

Two final observations on the empirical unfolding of norm-oriented movements are in order. First, the events that touch off a norm-oriented movement may simultaneously give birth to other collective outbursts. The movement of a Negro family into a white neighborhood, for instance, may trigger several distinct collective outbursts: (1) panic selling by neighbors who are convinced that property values will fall drastically; (2) a hostile outburst such as stoning the house or baiting the children of the new family; (3) a norm-oriented movement such as an agitation to modify the zoning laws to prevent Negro families from moving into the neighborhood in the future. For all these outbursts the conditions of structural strain and the precipitating factor are identical. The different character of each movement is imparted by the way in which the participants of each perceive—correctly or incorrectly—the conditions of structural conduciveness and the agencies of social control. The same concrete events, then, may be experienced by subgroups in different ways, and thus stimulate a rash of related but distinct outbursts.

Second, the same kinds of strain may produce different types of outbursts over time if the conditions of structural conduciveness and the behavior of authorities change. In the 1860's and early 1870's, for instance, conditions in the eastern United States were ripe for a "boom" movement of population to the West. The passage of the Homestead Act in 1862, the encouragement to Civil War Veterans to move west, the railroads' advertising campaigns and offers of credit to migrants—all contributed to a tremendous sense of promise. These conditions, combined with the hard times which began with the financial panic of 1873, initiated a flow of migrants to the West. By the late 1870's and early 1880's, this flow had grown to a flood. Credit, speculation, and land values spiralled to extravagant heights; boom towns appeared overnight in Nebraska and Kansas.

By 1887 the speculative boom passed its peak and collapsed into a panic; for the next decade hard times settled on the whole frontier. For many who had not yet located permanently in the West, this sustained depression produced a panicky return to the East. Migration from the West between 1888 and 1892 was substantial.

★ ★ ★

THE VALUE-ORIENTED MOVEMENT

Definition. A value-oriented movement is a collective attempt to restore, protect, modify, or create values in the name of a generalized belief. Such a belief necessarily involves all the components of action; that is, it envisions a reconstitution of values, a redefinition of norms, a reorganization of the motivation of individuals, and a redefinition of situational facilities.

Our definition encompasses the phenomena designated by the labels "nativistic movement," "messianic movement," "millenarian movement," "utopian movement," "sect formation," "religious revolution," "political revolution," "nationalistic movement," "charismatic movement," and many others. Given the inclusive character of our definition and given the complexity of any value-oriented movement, we must specify at the outset the principal aspects of these movements which we will attempt to explain.

We have organized the determinants of the value-oriented movement as a value-added process. The logic is identical to the logic we used for all other kinds of collective behavior. The value-added process can be represented as a tree, which, at each point of branching, presents a number of alternative branches. The "trunk" of the tree is represented by the conditions of conduciveness, without which the value-oriented movement cannot proceed to any of the branches. In characterizing conduciveness we ask: Is the definition of the situation couched in value terms or are values differentiated from other aspects of social life? What are the possibilities of expressing grievances in the system? Is it possible for the aggrieved groups to communicate their dissatisfactions to one another? By considering such questions we set up the conditions which make a value-oriented movement possible.

These conditions of conduciveness, however, do not guarantee the appearance of a value-oriented movement. A number of other conditions must be established within the limits of conduciveness. The first of these conditions is strain. If the social structure is free from strain, even conditions of conduciveness will not create a value-oriented movement. When serious conditions of strain—the major types of which we attempted to outline—bear on the system, then behavior tends to branch toward the value-oriented movement rather than some other kind of behavior.

An important branching involves the growth of a value-oriented belief. Does there exist a set of value-oriented beliefs within which all the foci of strain can be interpreted conveniently? Does a leader appear to symbolize or formulate such a set of beliefs? If value-oriented beliefs do not crystallize, the response to strain cannot be collective, because the aggrieved groups do not share a common definition of the situation. In the absence of generalized beliefs we would expect segmented protests, but not a coordinated, collective value-oriented movement. In connection with generalized beliefs, we assessed the special role of precipitating factors, which fix the value-oriented beliefs on concrete events and situations, and thus ready the adherents for collective action.

Finally, though people widely accept a value-oriented belief, a value-oriented movement will not eventuate unless the adherents are mobilized for action. Leadership is extremely important in this stage of mobilization. Because of the character of value-oriented commitment, the possibility of internal instability and disunity of value-oriented movements is very great.

Even though all these determinants are present, it is still possible for a single value-oriented movement to branch out to one of several outcomes. This depends largely on the response of agencies of social control to the movement. Social control, considered in its broadest sense, operates throughout the development of a movement; by changing the conditions of conduciveness, by reducing strain, by discrediting opposing value-oriented beliefs, the agencies of social control may defeat or deflect a movement. In our discussion of social control, however, we concentrated on the response of agencies of social control to value-oriented movement which was already mobilized for action. According to the behavior of these agencies on three counts—flexibility, responsiveness, and effectiveness—the value-oriented movement may move in the direction of an underground conspiracy, a sect or denomination, a passive cult, or a revolutionary party.

This formulation of a movement in value-added terms has two important methodological implications:

(1) In analyzing value-oriented movements we should not search for concrete historical items—tax measures, assassinations, economic deprivations, ideologies, weak police systems, etc.—as typical determinants. Such phenomena do frequently enter the unfolding process and assume the status of determinants. No inherent quality of the phenomena themselves, however, makes them determinants. They may act as determinants in other movements, or as determinants of nothing at all. They must occur in the context of the value-added sequence as a whole if they are to assume significance as determinants of value-added movements.

(2) In considering the causes of value-oriented movements, or the role of various factors—repression, strain, ideas, or weakness and vacillation of authority—we should not represent these variables as a simple list, but must view them as an organized body of determinants, each of which comes into play only after certain patterns of the other determinants have been established. It is fruitless to seek an abstract role of some factor without considering the pattern of the outburst as a whole.

Finally, we must stress that the temporal unfolding of any given value-oriented movement does not necessarily correspond to the logical priority of determinants in the value-added process. Beliefs that are potentially revolutionary may exist temporally long before strain arises to activate these beliefs as determinants of a value-oriented movement; revolutionary organizations may lie in wait for conditions of conduciveness and strain, upon which they then capitalize. The tactics of communist groups in underdeveloped countries, for instance, are to capitalize on whatever conditions of conduciveness (e.g., repression by authorities) or strain (e.g., economic crisis) may be present. This qualification does not affect the logical status of the value-added process itself. Even though a revolutionary organization may exist well before strains arise upon which it attempts to ride to power, the same logical relations hold between strain and mobilization. Strain is a necessary condition—whether long in existence or created on the spot—for mobilization to appear as a determinant of a value-oriented movement.

SUMMARY

We presented the issues that must be confronted in any systematic attempt to account for collective behavior. We tentatively defined collective behavior, identified its major types, and specified its general determinants. . . . We outlined a conceptual framework for analyzing collective behavior. We isolated the components of social action (*viz.*, values, norms, mobilization of motivation, and facilities), explored the relations among the components, and examined the composition of each component. . . . We sketched, in terms of the components of action, the major structural strains that give rise to collective behavior. . . . We specified—again in the same terms—the general character of collective behavior. We defined it as an uninstitutionalized mobilization to reconstitute a component of social action on the basis of a generalized belief—hysterical, wish-fulfillment, hostile, norm-oriented, and value-oriented. Finally, . . . we examined the determinants of each form of collective behavior—the panic, the craze, the hostile outburst, the norm-oriented movement and the value-oriented movement. The major determinants are structural conduciveness, strain, crystallization of a generalized belief, precipitating factors, mobilization for action, and social control.

We conceive the operation of these determinants as a value-added process. Each determinant is a necessary condition for the next to operate as a determinant in an episode of collective behavior. As the necessary conditions accumulate, the explanation of the episode becomes more determinate. Together the necessary conditions constitute the sufficient condition for the episode. It should be stressed, moreover, that we view the accumulation of necessary conditions as an analytic, not a temporal process.

Because our analysis has become so detailed and our illustrations so numerous, we have perhaps on occasion obscured some of the relations among our explanatory concepts. In this final chapter we shall give an overview of these relations.

THE ISSUES THAT ARISE IN EXPLAINING COLLECTIVE BEHAVIOR

The range of relevant data to be explained is that class of phenomena known as collective behavior. The initial issue is to specify the defining characteristic of these phenomena. We chose—in contrast to many others who analyze collective behavior—to make the defining characteristic *the kind of belief under which behavior is mobilized.* Collective behavior is action based on a generalized belief, which we analyzed. . . . We also decided that though collective behavior often displays distinctive psychological states (e.g., the loss of personal identity), distinctive patterns of communication (e.g., the rumor) and distinctive patterns of mobilization (e.g., the demagogue and his following), these are not necessary defining characteristics of such behavior.

The next issue in marking out an area for study is to identify its characteristic types. The major types of collective behavior, we noted, are the panic, the craze, the hostile outburst, the norm-oriented movement, and the value-oriented movement. Having done this, we turn to the two major issues of explanation itself: the *general* determinants of collective behavior (Why does collective behavior occur at all?), and the *unique combination* of determinants for any collective episode (Why one rather than another form of collective behavior)? To these issues all our theoretical constructs are oriented.

TWO SETS OF ORGANIZING CONSTRUCTS

Our analysis of collective behavior is built on two sets of organizing constructs: the components of social action, and the value-added process. The first is a language for describing and classifying action. It is a "flow chart" for tracing the course of action, and not a direct source of explanatory hypotheses. The value-added process, on the other hand, is a means for organizing determinants into explanatory models.[2]

The two sets of organizing constructs supplement one another in the following ways:

(1) Structural conduciveness, the first stage of value-added, refers to the degree to which any structure permits a given type of collective behavior, e.g., a hostile outburst. To assess this conduciveness, we ask two questions: Do the existing structural arrangements directly encourage overt hostility? Do these arrangements prohibit other kinds of protest? In the first question we ask to what degree the existing structure "invites" people to choose overt hostility; in the second we ask to what degree the existing structure "drives" them into hostile outbursts.

If we are to discuss conduciveness in a determinate way, we must identify the possible means of reconstituting the existing structure. Here the basic components of action become relevant. They provide a basis for classifying the several avenues for reconstituting social action—viz., to redefine the situational facilities, to attack individual agents who are responsible, to reorganize norms, or to redefine the values of the system. Thus the two organizing constructs—"value-added" and the "basic components"—supplement one another. Conduciveness (a part of the value-added scheme) indicates the most general necessary condition for a collective outburst; the basic components of action indicate the major types of conduciveness.

(2) Strain refers to the impairment of the relations among parts of a system and the consequent malfunctioning of the system. In the value-added process strain is a necessary condition for any collective outburst. It can assume significance as a determinant, however, only within the scope established by the prior conditions of conduciveness. To classify the major types of strain, we again turn to the basic components of action; strain may affect facilities, organized role behavior, norms, or values.

(3) The crystallization of a generalized belief marks the attempt of persons under strain to assess their situation. They "explain" this situation by creating or assembling a generalized belief. Again, the major types of belief, and their relations to one another, are derived from the components of action.

(4) Once an episode of collective behavior has appeared, its duration and severity are determined by the response of the agencies of social control. To classify the major responses of these agencies, we turn to the components of action. We ask, for instance, what avenues of behavior—e.g., hostile expression, norm-oriented protest—these agencies attempt to close off or leave open.

GENERATING PROPOSITIONS ABOUT COLLECTIVE BEHAVIOR

In creating propositions about collective behavior we start with a master proposition and proceed, by several steps, to generate more specific propositions and to establish the conditions under which these propositions hold.

[2]Formally, the "components of action" and "value-added" have a dimension of generality-specificity in common. The components of action—values, norms, mobilization, and facilities—are organized into a hierarchy of increasing specificity. Each component can be organized into a number of increasingly specific levels. . . . The value-added process also involves a series of transitions from general to specific. The early stages (e.g., conduciveness) are conceived as general conditions, by contrast with the later stages (e.g., mobilization), which are more specific in their determination of an episode of collective behavior.

The master proposition is . . . : People under strain mobilize to reconstitute the social order in the name of a generalized belief. Stated so generally, this proposition is not very helpful in interpreting the actual data of collective outbursts. How do we make it more specific?

Initially we identify a number of different kinds of generalized belief—hysterical, wish-fulfillment, hostile, etc. Next we ask, for each belief, under what conditions people will develop such a belief and act on it? Take panic, for instance. Under what conditions of *conduciveness* do people develop and act on a hysterical belief? In reply we discuss the character of the escape situation, among other things. The condition of maximum conduciveness is limited and closing exits. Completely open or completely closed exits are not conducive to panic. By this operation we ask under what conditions of conduciveness the master proposition—specified for panic—will hold. In this way we generate increasingly more specific conditions for establishing the propositions. By introducing even more conditions—those of strain, precipitating factors, social control, etc.—we apply even more restrictions on the applicability of the proposition. Or, to put it the other way around, we successively rule out the situations in which the proposition will *not* hold. . . .

ACCEPTING OR REJECTING PROPOSITIONS ABOUT COLLECTIVE BEHAVIOR

Having introduced a number of restricting conditions on the master proposition, we arrive at statements such as the following: "Panic will occur if the appropriate conditions of conduciveness are present *and* if the appropriate conditions of strain are present *and* if a hysterical belief develops, *and* if mobilization occurs, *and* if social controls fail to operate."

How do we decide whether to accept or reject such a statement? What kinds of data do we examine? How do we handle apparently contradictory evidence, e.g., the presence of strain but no panic, conduciveness but no panic, etc.?

The ideal procedure to be followed in establishing scientific propositions is to create a laboratory situation in which all the relevant variables except one are held constant, then to manipulate this one variable systematically. In the case of the complex statement about panic, for instance, we would vary conduciveness systematically in one set of experiments, vary strain in another set, and so on, and determine whether each condition is necessary for panic. Furthermore, we could determine what combination of the conditions has to be present to produce a panic. Experimentation, however, is virtually impossible in the study of collective behavior. Ethical prohibitions prevent investigators from literally creating a panic, and practical difficulties in establishing a genuine panic in a laboratory setting are almost overwhelming.

An approximation to the laboratory situation can frequently be achieved by using statistical techniques, by which we can hold many variables constant and estimate the combined effect of several variables. As the illustrations in this volume indicate, however, existing data in the field of collective behavior seldom permit elegant statistical manipulation. In most cases our confidence in the propositions we generate must rest on another approximation to controlled experimentation. What is this approximation?

We have relied mainly on *systematic comparative illustration* from the available literature on collective behavior. This method takes two forms, positive and negative.

(a) We have attempted to identify the common characteristics of situations that produce episodes of collective behavior. For instance, we have attempted to locate an actual or perceived condition of limited and closing exits in all panic situations. (b) We have examined those situations in which a collective outburst has nearly occurred to discover which determinants were absent. In connection with riots, for instance, we studied the ways in which agencies of social control prevent the actual mobilization for attack; in this way the agencies of control prevent a determinant of a hostile outburst from operating. Sometimes we have combined these positive and negative methods of systematic comparative illustration by examining those occasions on which one form of collective behavior (e.g., a panic) turns into another (e.g., a hostile outburst). In so doing we asked which significant determinants disappear and which determinants appear, thus changing the character of the episode.

A critical issue to be posed for any proposition before it can be called a *scientific* proposition is: Can we find evidence that would lead us to reject the proposition? In connection with our analysis two types of negative evidence can be found: (a) Situations in which one or more necessary conditions (e.g., strain) are absent, but in which a collective outburst occurs. This would indicate that the condition heretofore considered necessary for the collective episode is in fact not essential. (b) Situations in which one or more necessary conditions are present but in which the collective outburst does not occur. Such situations do not, however, always constitute negative evidence. In discussing the indeterminacy of strain, we insisted that not all situations of strain need produce any particular kind of collective episode, indeed any collective episode at all. Strain, we argued, must *combine* with the other appropriate necessary conditions (conduciveness, mobilization, etc.) to be operative as a determinant. For those situations in which we find strain but no collective outburst, then, we must ask if other necessary conditions are absent. If one or more of them is absent, the presence of strain without a collective episode does not constitute negative evidence. If, however, strain *and* all the other necessary conditions are present, but no outburst occurs, this is negative evidence.

— · — · — · — · — · — · — · — · — · — · —

MORTON DEUTSCH

*Cooperation and Competition**

The concept of "co-operation" and the interrelated concept of "competition" are rarely missing in discussions of inter-personal or inter-group relations: implicitly they play

*Morton Deutsch, "A Theory of Co-operation and Competition," *Human Relations* 2 (1950): 129-152. Reprinted by permission.

a key role in the writings of many social theorists. Yet despite the obvious significance of these concepts for the understanding and control of social process,[1] there has been little in the way of explicit theorizing and virtually no experimental work with respect to the effects of co-operation and competition upon social process. The work in this area has largely been concerned with the effects of the individual's motivation to achieve under the two different conditions. None of the experimental studies has investigated the interactions between individuals, the group process that emerges as a consequence of the co-operative or competitive social situation.

The purpose of this article is to sketch out a theory of the effect of co-operation and competition upon small (face-to-face) group functioning. A subsequent article will present the results of an experimental study of such effects. Before attempting the theoretical development, the definitions and formulations of "co-operation" and "competition" made by other writers will be briefly surveyed (Section A). Immediately following this glance at the literature, the basic concepts in the theory of co-operation and competition to be offered here will be presented (Section B). The next step will be to draw some of the implications logically inherent in the basic concepts. Then, with the aid of some additional psychological assumptions, some of the psychological implications inherent in the co-operative and competitive social situations will be deduced. Hypotheses will then be developed with respect to the effects of co-operation and competition upon group process by applying these psychological implications to group situations. The last section of the paper (Section C) will develop some group concepts and show the intimate relationship between the concepts, "group" and "co-operative social situation." This intimate relationship, it will be demonstrated, provides the possibility for translating the hypotheses with respect to the effects of co-operation and competition upon group process into hypotheses about the effects of quantitative variations in group-conceptualized variables upon group process.

SECTION A

Some Existing Formulations—A Glance at the Literature

No attempt will be made to summarize the extensive writings on co-operation and competition. May and Doob (15) have done this for the literature up until 1937; only a few studies of significance have been reported since then. In addition to indicating the prominence of the concepts of competition and co-operation in social and economic theory, May and Doob have developed an elaborate theory. They distinguish between co-operation and competition in the following manner:

> Competition or co-operation is directed toward the same social end by at least two individuals. In competition, moreover, the end sought can be achieved in equal amounts by some and not by all of the individuals thus behaving; whereas in co-operation it can be achieved by all or almost all of the individuals concerned (15, p. 6).

[1] Thus Elton Mayo (see Reference 16) has written, "It is not the atomic bomb that will destroy civilization. But civilized society can destroy itself—finally, no doubt, with bombs—if it fails to understand and to control intelligently the aids and deterrents to co-operation."

Their theory primarily has to do with the conditions for, and the forms of, co-operation and competition. Their basic postulates with respect to co-operation and competition are as follows:

Postulate 5. On a social level individuals compete with one another when: (a) they are striving to achieve the same goal which is scarce; (b) they are prevented by the rules of the situation from achieving this goal in equal amounts; (c) they perform better when the goal can be achieved in unequal amounts; and (d) they have relatively few psychologically affiliative contacts with one another.

Postulate 6. On a social level individuals co-operate with one another when: (a) they are striving to achieve the same or complimentary goals that can be shared; (b) they are required by the rules of the situation to achieve this goal in nearly equal amounts; (c) they perform better when the goal can be achieved in equal amounts; and (d) they have relatively many psychological affiliative contacts with one another (15, p. 17).

Mead's survey of co-operation and competition among primitive peoples (18) accepted the following definitions:

Competition: the act of seeking or endeavoring to gain what another is endeavoring to gain at the same time.

Co-operation: the act of working together to one end (18, p. 8).

She asserts that a distinction must be made between "competition" and "rivalry." A similar distinction is made between "co-operation" and "helpfulness."

Competition is behavior oriented toward a goal in which the other competitors for the goal are secondary; rivalry is behavior oriented toward another human being, whose worsting is the primary goal.

In co-operation, the goal is shared and it is the relationship to the goal which hold the co-operating individuals together; in helpfulness, the goal is shared only through the relationship of the helpers to the individuals whose goal it actually is (18, p. 17).

Maller in his classic study of co-operation and competition among school children (14) defined a co-operative situation as one which stimulates an individual to strive with the other members of his group for a goal object which is to be shared equally among all of them. On the other hand, a competitive situation is one which stimulates the individual to strive against other individuals in his group for a goal object of which he hopes to be the sole or principal possessor.

Barnard (1) has done extensive theorizing on the nature of co-operative systems. He discusses the origin of co-operative action:

Among the most important limiting factors in the situation of each individual are his own biological limitations. The most effective method of overcoming these limitations has been that of co-operation. This requires the adoption of group, or nonpersonal purpose.

He also discusses factors that emerge from co-operation.

Co-operation is a social aspect of the total situation and social factors arise from it. These factors may be in turn the limiting factors of any situation. This arises from two considerations: (a) the processes of interaction must be discovered or invented; (b) the interaction changes the motives and interest of those participating in the co-operation.

Also considered are the persistence and survival of co-operation:

> The persistence of co-operation depends upon two conditions: (*a*) its effectiveness; and (*b*) its efficiency. Effectiveness relates to the accomplishments of the social purpose. Efficiency relates to the satisfaction of individual motives. The test of effectiveness is the accomplishment of a common purpose. The test of efficiency is the eliciting of sufficient individual wills to co-operate.
>
> The survival of co-operation, therefore, depends upon two interrelated and interdependent classes of processes: (*a*) those which relate to the system of co-operation as a whole in relation to the environment; and (*b*) those which relate to the creation or distribution of satisfactions among individuals (1, pp. 60–61).

Helen Block Lewis in two recent articles (9, 10) has presented a very stimulating viewpoint. She writes:

> A minimum requirement for co-operative behavior is not physical togetherness nor joint action, nor even synchronous, complementary behavior, but a diminution of ego-demands so that the requirements of the objective situation and of the other person may function freely. In truly co-operative work, personal needs can function only if they are relevant to the objective situation; the common objective, in other words, is more important than any personal objective. . . . Since the self is not focal, another person's activities—the co-operating person's—may be as satisfactory as your own.
>
> Competing for individual rewards, i.e., individualistic competition, on the other hand, involves a heightening of ego-demands, so that the ego-objective is more important than any common objective; i.e., the person is at the focus of consciousness, self-consciousness is at a maximum—the individual is "on the spot"—so that similar behavior may be expected from the member of the competing group and the person driven by inordinate (neurotic) ambition. Competing behavior involves seeing the objective situation as relevant to the personal need to win, or for prestige. Only personal activities, therefore, can be satisfactory (9, pp. 115–116).

This rather brief survey and a cursory glance through the works of various social theorists (5, 12, 13, 22, 24) has indicated a core of common conceptualizations running through the treatment of the co-operative and competitive social situation. Implicit in most of these conceptualizations has been the notion that the crux of the difference between co-operation and competition lies in the difference in the nature of the goal-regions in the two social situations. The conceptualization to be offered below also follows this distinction.

SECTION B

A Conceptualization of the Co-operative and Competitive Situations with a Development of Some of its Logical and Psychological Implications

1. In a *co-operative social situation* the goals for the individuals or sub-units in the situation under consideration have the following characteristic: the goal regions for each of the individuals or sub-units in the situation are defined so that a goal-region can be entered (to some degree) by any given individual or sub-unit only if all the individuals or

sub-units under consideration can also enter their respective goal-regions (to some degree). For convenience sake, the phrase "promotively interdependent goals" will be used to identify any situation in which the individuals or sub-units composing it have their goals interrelated by the characteristic defined above.[2]

2. In a *competitive social situation* the goals for the individuals or sub-units in the situation under consideration have the following characteristic: the goal-regions for each of the individuals or sub-units in the situation are defined so that if a goal-region is entered by any individual or sub-unit, (or by any given portion of the individuals or sub-units under consideration) the other individuals or sub-units will, to some degree, be unable to reach their respective goals in the social situation under consideration. For convenience sake, the phrase "contriently interdependent goals" will be used to identify any situation in which the individuals or sub-units composing it have their goals interrelated by the characteristic defined immediately above.

It should, perhaps, be noted that there are probably very few, if any, real-life situations which, according to the definitions offered above, are "purely" co-operative or competitive. Most situations of everyday life involve a complex set of goals and sub-goals. Consequently, it is possible for individuals to be promotively interdependent with respect to one goal and contriently interdependent with respect to another goal. Thus, for example, the members of a basketball team may be co-operatively interrelated with respect to winning the game, but competitively interrelated with respect to being the "star" of the team.

It is also rather common for people to be promotively interdependent with respect to sub-goals and contriently interdependent with respect to goals or vice versa.[3] For instance, advertising concerns representing different cigarette companies may be co-operatively interrelated with respect to the sub-goal of increasing the general consumption of cigarettes but competitively interrelated with respect to the goal of increasing both the relative and absolute sales of a specific brand of cigarette. Two professional tennis players with the promotively interdependent goals of earning a lot of money by putting on matches which will draw large crowds, may, under certain circumstances, be contriently interdependent with respect to winning each match.

No attempt will be made in this article to describe and analyze further the wide variety of "impure" co-operative and competitive situations which are found in everyday life. The theoretical development to be presented here will be primarily concerned with "pure" co-operative and competitive situations. However, it is believed that in many circumstances not much theoretical extrapolation is necessary to handle the more complex situations.

The conceptualizations of co-operation and competition offered in this paper, if they

---

[2] It is important to note that the definitions offered here for both the co-operative and competitive social situations are such that it is possible, from the point of view of an objective social observer (i.e.—the social scientist), for an individual to be promotively or contriently interdependent with other individuals without that individual in any sense being aware of, or psychologically affected by, this interdependence.

[3] The distinction that is being made here between "goals" and "sub-goals" is similar to the commonly made distinction between "means" and "ends." A "means" or "sub-goal" can be defined as being a psychological unit on the path to the goal and, as such, it possesses goal-like properties either as a consequence of expectations built up in the course of its previous associations with the goal or as a consequence of its currently perceived importance in obtaining the goal.

are adequate, combined with the definition of the group concept, "membership motive" (see Section C), provide an opportunity for the derivation and empirical testing of hypotheses about the effect of variations in strength of membership motive on various aspects of group functioning. This possibility is created primarily by the linkage of "co-operation" and "membership motive" through the concept "promotively interdependent goals." The empirical linkage is provided by the operational definitions of co-operation and competition that compose the experimental manipulation.

Specifically, the hypotheses relevant to group functioning must be derived from the consequences inherent in the concepts "promotively interdependent goals" and "contriently interdependent goals." In some respects the word "derivation" is being used rather loosely in this study. The "derivations," insofar as they result in hypotheses that can be empirically tested, require additional psychological assumptions. These assumptions will be stated when recognized and when feasible.

As a first step in the attempt to derive hypotheses, an attempt will be made to state the implications logically inherent in the aforementioned concepts. The second step will be to attempt to deduce psychological implications, making various psychological assumptions, from the logical implications of the concepts. The third step will be to attempt to apply these psychological implications to problems of group functioning.

Step I: The Logical Implications of the Conceptualization of the Co-operative and Competitive Social Situations

---

Promotively Interdependent Goals

If A, B, C, etc., does not obtain his goal (enter his goal region), X does not obtain his goal.

X obtains his goal only if A, B, C, etc., obtains theirs.

A, B, C, etc., obtain their goals only if X obtains his.

Contriently Interdependent Goals

If A, B, or C, obtains his goal, Y does not obtain his goal.

Y obtains his goal only if A, B, C, etc., do not obtain theirs.

A, B, C, etc., do not obtain their goals if Y obtains his.

From the definitions of promotively and contriently interdependent goals, it appears to follow that: (a) Any person X who has promotively interdependent goals with persons A, B, C, etc., will come to have promotively interdependent locomotions in the direction of his goal[4] with persons A, B, C, etc.; (b) any person Y who has contriently interdependent goals with persons A, B, C, etc., will come to have contriently interdependent locomotions in the direction of his goal with persons A, B, C, etc.

[4] It should be emphasized that, at this point in the development, "locomotion in the direction of the goal" refers to locomotion in an objective social space, not to locomotion in the individual's life space. That is, as yet, no inference should be drawn as to whether the individual is aware of, or even affected by, his locomotion in objective social space. An example of locomotion in objective social space without immediate corresponding locomotion in the individual's life space, is the following: A student takes an exam., thinks he fails, and is afraid he will not graduate. The instructor corrects the exam., passes the student, the student is approved for graduation, etc., within a day after the student takes the exam. The student is not notified that he has passed; he worries, anticipates failure, and (to carry the example to its extreme) commits suicide. Objectively, socially, he has locomoted past the barrier of the exam., psychologically he has not. Being unaware of his objective social locomotion, his psychological position in relation to his goal is unaffected by his objective locomotion. As a consequence, he behaves as though still confronted by the barrier.

The above statements are based on the following considerations: Locomotion in the direction of the goal, from any point not in the goal region, may be thought of as a condition for entry into the goal region. Entry into the goal region may be thought of as a part of locomotion in the direction of the goal; entry being the final step in locomotion. It follows that a locomotion by X or Y in the direction of his goal can be considered to be promotively or contriently interdependent with the locomotions of A, B, C, etc. in the direction of their goals; the nature of the interdependence with respect to locomotions depending upon the nature of the interdependence with respect to goal regions.

Promotively Interdependent Locomotions in the Direction of the Goal

If A, B, or C, etc., does not locomote in the direction of his goal, X does not locomote in the direction of his goal.

If X locomotes in the direction of his goal, A, B, C, etc., will locomote in the direction of their goals.

If A, B, or C, etc., locomotes in the direction of his goal, X will locomote in the direction of his goal.

Contriently Interdependent Locomotions in the Direction of the Goal

If A, B, or C, etc., locomotes in the direction of his goal when Y is not locomoting in the direction of his goal (or locomotes at a more rapid rate than Y locomotes towards his goal), the rivalry ratio:—

$$\left(\frac{\text{Locomoting Person's Distance to his Goal}}{\text{Person Y's Distance to his Goal will decrease}} \right)$$

If Y locomotes in the direction of his goal, when A, B, or C, etc., is not locomoting in the direction of his goal (or locomotes at a more rapid rate than A, B, or C, etc., is locomoting toward his goal) the rivalry ratio described above will increase.

If A, B, or C, etc., does not locomote in the direction of his goal and Y does not locomote, the rivalry ratio will either remain constant or increase.

In addition to the above implications of statements 1 and 1a,[5] it seems to be possible to draw implications concerning locomotion which is in a direction away from the goal.[6]

From the statements about promotively and contriently interdependent locomotions it seems to be possible to draw further implications, if we accept the following additional statements:

1. Facilitating locomotion (i.e.—decreasing resistances to locomotion) in the direction of the goal makes it more likely that the goal will be obtained.
2. Hindering locomotion (i.e.—increasing resistances to locomotion) in the direction of the goal makes it less likely that the goal will be obtained.

Promotively Interdependent Locomotions in a Direction away from the Goal

If A, B, or C, etc., does not locomote in a direction away from his goal, X does not locomote in a direction away from his goal.

Contriently Interdependent Locomotion in a Direction away from the Goal

If A, B, or C, etc., locomotes in a direction away from his goal when Y is not locomoting in a direction away from his goal (or locomotes at a more rapid rate than Y does in such a direction), the rivalry ratio:—

$$\left(\frac{\text{Locomoting Person's Distance to his Goal}}{\text{Person Y's distance to his Goal will increase}} \right)$$

---

[5] See below, p. 138.
[6] For the definition of the direction "away from" see Lewin's monograph (7) "The Conceptual Representation and Measurement of Psychological Forces."

If X locomotes in a direction away from his goal, A, B, or C, etc., will locomote in a direction away from their goals.

If A, B, or C, etc., locomotes in a direction away from his goal, X will locomote in a direction away from his goal.

If Y locomotes in a direction away from his goal, when A, B, C, etc., is not locomoting in a direction away from his goal (or locomotes at a more rapid rate than A, B, or C, etc., in such a direction), the rivalry ratio will decrease.

If A, B, or C, etc., does not locomote in a direction away from his goal and Y does not locomote, the rivalry ratio will either remain constant or decrease.

Promotively Interdependent

If X facilitates the locomotion of A, B, or C, etc., in the direction of their goals, he facilitates his own locomotion in the direction of his goal.

If A, B, or C, etc., facilitate the locomotion of X toward his goal, their locomotion will be facilitated.

If X hinders the locomotion of A, B, or C, etc., toward their goals, he will hinder his own locomotion.

If A, B, or C, etc., hinder the locomotion of X, the locomotion of A, B, or C, etc., will be hindered.

Contriently Interdependent

If Y facilitates the locomotion of A, B, or C, etc., in the direction of their goals, the rivalry ratio is likely to decrease.

If A, B, or C, etc., facilitates the locomotion of Y towards his goal, Y's rivalry ratio is likely to increase.

If Y hinders the locomotion of A, B, or C, etc., toward their goals, he will be likely to increase his own rivalry ratio.

If A, B, or C, etc., hinder the locomotion of Y towards his goal, Y's rivalry ratio is likely to decrease.

Several major differences reveal themselves as inherent in the distinctions between the co-operative and competitive social situations. The analysis of the co-operative situation reveals that all the individuals in such a setting occupy the same relative positions with respect to their goals; if any one individual locomotes, the others must also locomote in the same direction. In the competitive situation, the various individuals may occupy the same or differing positions with respect to their goals; locomotion by any individual has no necessary effect on the locomotions of others, though it may affect the relative positions of the various individuals.

Step II: The Deduction of Psychological Implications from the Conceptualizations of the Co-operative and Competitive Situations

Up to this point we have been stating some of the consequences logically inherent in the conceptualizations of simple co-operative and competitive social situations. No statements have been made which have a direct psychological reference (i.e.—a reference in terms of individual life spaces). The statements have had reference only to an objectively defined social space.

The next step called for appears to be an attempt to derive psychological implications from these statements by introducing additional psychological assumptions which will somehow relate these statements about events in objective social space to events in individual life spaces. In the attempt to take this next step, many of the theoretical issues that are involved in the relationship of "objective facts" to "psychological facts" will be ignored. It is felt that it would be over-ambitious to try to deal with these issues in the scope of this article.

The problem to be solved in taking this next step is quite a difficult one. Essentially the question of "What psychological assumptions are necessary in order to derive psychological or perceived interdependence[7] from objective social interdependence?" or "Under what circumstances will individuals who, objectively, are in a co-operative or competitive social situation come to perceive that they are co-operatively or competitively inter-related with the others?"[8]

It is evident that the problem being raised here is in certain respects similar to the question Koffka raises of "Why do things look as they do?" Koffka, dealing with problems of the perception of physical objects, clearly points out the inadequacies of any answers solely in terms of the real properties of the objects or even in terms of the proximal stimulus properties of the object. Yet even so, for effective behavioral adjustment to its environment, an organism's perceptions and expectancies must be veridical to the entities and the relationships among those entities that compose its functional environment. To explain the behavioral adequacy of our perceptions, expectations, or cognitions one might say that the same kinds of laws govern both the organization of real entities and the organization of the perceptual field. Such an explanation could perhaps be accepted for the simpler perceptions, perceptions in which object-Ego relations do not influence the organization of the perceptual field (though even in the simpler cases there appear to be many exceptions to such an explanation). However, it is likely that all social perceptions and expectations involve Ego-forces in their organization. Thus, the explanation of the behavioral adequacy or inadequacies of our social perceptions and expectations requires an insight into the nature of object-Ego relationships and an understanding of how these relationships are acquired.

Without in any way attempting to detail an explanation of the reasons for the behavioral adequacy or inadequacy of our perceptions and expectations, it becomes apparent that learning principles, as well as principles of perceptual and cognitive organization, are basic to the explanation. Learning principles are necessary to bridge the gap between objects and relations, and percepts and expectations. (They are necessary but not efficient. It is clear that principles of cognitive organization, such as revealed by the work of Heider, as well as the more obvious factors of perceptual organization, are involved.) "Objective social facts," as well as "things" come to have "psychological" significance (i.e., significance in terms of the life-space) through learning. By assuming that all action is a process which is directed toward reduction or removal of need-tension, that some such principle as the "Principle of Least Action" (26) guides action, and that object significance is established in the course of action, it is possible to derive that the perceptions and expectations of an individual are likely to be veridical to his objective environment in direct proportion to the individual's capacities, to his amount of experience in the environment, and to the simplicity of the environment being perceived.

The preceding several paragraphs have been an excursus. It is hoped that this ex-

[7]The phrase "psychological or perceived interdependence" is not meant to be limited in meaning to only those psychological events which are "conscious," "verbalizable," or "mediated by a process of awareness."

[8]Another approach to the problem of the interrelationship between objective social interdependence and perceived social interdependence would be to postulate that psychological or perceived interdependence is a necessary condition for objective social interdependence. It seems apparent that such an approach would by-pass the problem and in by-passing the problem would ignore facts that indicate that an individual can locomote through an objective social space without, in any sense, being immediately aware that locomotion is taking place. Further, such an approach, by definition, would not be able to analyze why under varying social conditions there would be little or much psychological unity in groups that have the same objective social interdependence.

cursus has served two purposes. One purpose has been to demonstrate the very complex and shaky assumptions that exist at the base of any predictions about behavior in an objective social situation. The second purpose has been to provide the rationale for such predictions by offering an empirical co-ordination for hypotheses to be derived from the conceptualizations of the two objective social situations. In brief, the preceding sections were meant to provide the rationale for the following kind of statement: "If five reasonably well-adjusted college students, of fairly homogeneous abilities, are placed in a social situation in which they have, objectively, promotively interdependent goals (or contriently interdependent goals) and the clues to the situation are reasonably obvious, the five students will perceive themselves as having promotively interdependent goals (or contriently interdependent goals)." The rationale for the statement is the previously stated assumption that the perceptions and expectations of an individual are likely to be veridical to his environment if he has had enough experience with the situation, if he has intelligence, and if the situation is simple enough. The subjects in the experiment to be reported in a subsequent paper were all relatively intelligent. All of them had had experience with co-operative and competitive social situations. The experimental manipulations defining the two situations were simple and explicit.

The same psychologic can be applied to promotively (and contriently) interdependent locomotions and to promotively (and contriently) interdependent facilitations and hinderings so as to derive psychological or "perceived" interdependence from the objective social interdependence. However, it should be pointed out that in the experimental situation the tasks that the individuals were exposed to were of such a nature that the clues provided by objective locomotion were neither simple nor clear-cut. Thus, it can be assumed that the correspondence between objective and psychological locomotion was far from perfect. This lack of correspondence has, of course, its empirical consequences which one should be able to predict from theoretical considerations.[9] Fortunately, for the present purposes, the lack of perfect correspondence between "objective" and "perceived" interdependence can be disregarded since the hypotheses to be offered in the next pages are relative rather than quantitatively refined.

BASIC HYPOTHESES

Hypothesis 1. (a) Individuals who are exposed to the co-operative social situation (*Indiv co-op*) will perceive themselves to be more promotively interdependent (in relation to the other individuals composing their group) with respect to goal, locomotions, facili-

---

[9]In large measure, one should be able to explain the differences of behavior (individual or group) that occur in objective social situations as being due to lack of correspondence between the "perceived" and "objective" situation. Moreover, knowledge of the explicitness of cues provided by a given co-operative (or competitive) social situation should enable us "to predict" differences in kind and amount of co-operative (or competitive) behavior.

An individual is not "co-operative" even though objectively he stands in a co-operative relation to others, when he does not perceive this relationship. From this lack of correspondence, without too many additional psychological assumptions, one should be able to predict the following: how an individual will diverge from "co-operative" behavior; what happens when the "divergent" individual bumps up against the objective situation; and the effect of his divergence on others who are in a "co-operative" situation with him. The kind of prediction that would be made is the same order of prediction that one would make about a rat's behavior, knowing how much the rat's percept and expectations with respect to the maze he has to run diverge from the objective structure of the maze.

tations, etc., than will individuals who are exposed to the competitive social situation (*Indiv comp*).

(b) *Indiv comp* will perceive themselves to be more contriently interdependent (in relation to the other individuals composing their group) with respect to goal, locomotions, facilitations, etc., than will *Indiv co-op*.

For convenience sake, let us direct our attention to the psychological implications of locomotion in the co-operative or competitive situation. Let us analyze the following hypothetical instance with respect to locomotion in the direction of the goal: "A" locomotes in the direction of his goal and the other individuals in the social situation perceive that "A" is locomoting:

1. *In the co-operative situation* "X" would (be likely to) perceive that he has locomoted towards his goal as a consequence of "A's" actions. Several implications seem directly to follow, if we accept certain additional psychological assumptions:

(a) *Substitutability*—Since "X" has locomoted towards his goal as a consequence of "A's" actions, there is no longer any necessity for "X" to perform any action which is similar (functionally identical) to "A's". We can derive that "A's" action will be substitutable for "X's," if we assume any one of the following: a principle of "Least Action," a principle of "Efficiency," or that the force in a direction of a region is zero when the person is in that region.

(b) *Positive Cathexis*—If we make an assumption, which is rather widely accepted, that an entity will acquire positive valence or cathexis (become attractive) if that entity is seen to be promotively related to need satisfaction—it is possible to derive that "A's" action (which results in locomotion in the direction of the goal) will be positively cathected by "X." That is, "X" is likely to accept, like, or reward "A's" action.

(c) *Inducibility*—The assumption here is a little more complex: Let us assume that the relationship of inducibility derives from the fact that the inducible person perceives the inducing entity to be such that it stands in a causative relationship to the intensification, continued persistence, or lowering of need tension within himself. Positive inducibility[10] occurs when the inducing entity is seen to be promotive rather than contrient with respect to tension-reduction (or when the inducing entity is seen as more powerful—i.e., capable of producing even more tension than the tension existing to be reduced).

Making the above assumption, one can derive that "X" will stand in the relationship of positive inducibility to "A" insofar as "A's" action contributes towards "X's" locomotion in the direction of his goal.

2. *In the competitive situation* "Y" would (be likely to) perceive that his rivalry ratio with respect to "A" has decreased. The situation here is somewhat more complex than in co-operation. The amount of change in the rivalry ratio would depend upon the distances of both "A" and "Y" from their goals and also upon the distance locomoted by "A." Nevertheless several implications seem directly to follow, if we accept certain additional psychological assumptions (though, it may be that if the rivalry ratio is greater than a certain maximum, or lower than a certain minimum, a rivalry situation will no longer exist psychologically).

(a) *Substitutability*—It is evident that there will be no substitutability.

[10]Positive inducibility is meant to include two related phenomena: (*a*) The production of additional "own" forces in the direction induced by the inducing entity. (*b*) The channelizing of existing "own" forces in the direction induced by the inducing entity.

(b) *Negative Cathexis*—The assumption here is parallel to that made in deriving positive cathexis; an entity will acquire negative cathexis if that entity is seen to be contriently related to need satisfaction (therefore, is seen to decrease the probability of need satisfaction). The additional assumption here is that decreasing the rivalry ratio will be seen as decreasing the probability of success. (This additional assumption may only hold within minimum and maximum limits.) From these assumptions it is possible to derive that "A's" locomotions in the direction of his goal will be negatively cathected by "Y."

(c) *Negative Inducibility* [11] —Assuming that negative inducibility occurs when the inducing entity is seen as contrient with respect to tension reduction, one can derive that "Y" will stand in the relationship of negative inducibility to "A" insofar as "A's" actions lead to locomotions by "A" which decrease "Y's" probability of reaching his goal. However, another factor, cognitive in nature, may come into play making "Y's" relation to "B" one of ambivalence or non-inducibility—the cognition that "going in a direction opposite to or away from "A's" would be going in an opposite direction to or away from his own goal."

We can, with the same kinds of assumption, analyze a hypothetical instance in which "B" locomotes in a direction away from his goal. Without detailing the analysis, it is evident that in the co-operative situation, substitutability is not expected, but one would expect negative cathexis and negative inducibility. The competitive situation, again, is not so unequivocal as the co-operative situation. Here one would expect positive cathexis and ambivalent inducibility or non-inducibility.

Facilitations and Hinderings—One can make the same derivations that were made with respect to substitutability, cathexis, and inducibility for facilitations and hinderings, respectively, as those that were made for locomotions in the direction towards or away from the goal. Thus, it is possible to make statements about "helpfulness" and "obstructiveness"—defining "helpfulness" as the act of facilitating locomotion, and defining "obstructiveness" as the act of hindering locomotion.

In the *co-operative situation*, if "X" facilitates the locomotion of "A" in the direction of his goal, he also facilitates his own locomotion in the direction of this goal. Assuming that facilitation of locomotion makes locomotion more probable, it is evident that "X's" facilitations of others are likely to result in his own locomotion, and therefore, is also likely to result in tension-reduction with respect to that locomotion. His own actions of facilitation (*helpfulness*) will become positively cathected and will be likely to be manifested in appropriate situations (according to learning theory previously assumed). Using the same kind of analysis one can demonstrate that acts hindering locomotion in the direction of the goal (obstructiveness) will be negatively cathected and will be avoided. For "facilitations" and "hinderings" in a direction opposite to the goal, of course, the converse of the above statements would be true.

In the *competitive situation*, with respect to locomotions of others in the direction of the goal, "helpfulness" would become negatively cathected, "obstructiveness" positively cathected. The converse would be true for locomotion in a direction opposite to that of the goal.

[11] Negative inducibility is meant to include two related phenomena: (a) the production of additional "own" forces; (b) channelizing of existing "own" forces in the direction opposite to that desired by the inducer.

Up to this point, we have made some statements about substitutability, cathexis, inducibility, and helpfulness in each of the two social situations, co-operation and competition, under each of two different circumstances—locomotions, etc., in the direction of the goal and in the direction opposite to the goal. In each of the situations, under different conditions, there is positive and negative cathexis, helpfulness and obstructiveness. To test the theory it is necessary to know which of the conditions are operating. The assumption will be made that under the experimental conditions set up to test the theory there will be more locomotions in the direction of the goal than in a direction away from the goal in both instances. From this assumption and the foregoing analysis it is possible to assert the following hypotheses:

Hypothesis 2: There will be greater substitutability for similarly intended actions among *Indiv co-op* as contrasted with *Indiv comp*.

Hypothesis 3: There will be a larger percentage of actions by fellow members positively cathected by *Indiv co-op* than by *Indiv comp*.

Hypothesis 3a: There will be a larger percentage of actions by fellow members negatively cathected by *Indiv comp* than by *Indiv co-op*.

Hypothesis 4: There will be greater positive inducibility with respect to fellow members among *Indiv co-op* than among *Indiv comp*.

Hypothesis 4a: There will be greater internal (self) conflict among *Indiv comp* than among *Indiv co-op*.

Hypothesis 5: There will be more helpfulness towards each other among *Indiv co-op* than among *Indiv comp*.

Hypothesis 5a: There will be more obstructiveness towards each other among *Indiv comp* than among *Indiv co-op*.

Step III: The Applications of the Psychological Implications of Co-operative and Competitive Situations to Small, Face-to-Face Group Functioning

In this step an attempt will be made to apply some of the psychological implications of the hypotheses derived in the preceding section to the functioning of small face-to-face groups. To draw out these implications for group functioning, additional assumptions will be necessary; these assumptions will be stated when recognized and when feasible. The aspects of group functioning to be considered will for convenience sake be arbitrarily grouped under the following headings: (a) Organization, (b) Motivation, (c) Communication, (d) Orientation, (e) Productivity, (f) Interpersonal Relations, and (g) Individual Behavior. No attempt will be made to exhaust the implications to be drawn with respect to these aspects of group functioning; it should also be clear that an empirical test of all of these implications was not possible in the experimental study to be reported later.

(a) Organization

Several different aspects of "organization" appear to be relevant to the differences between co-operation and competition: (i) Interdependence; (ii) Homogeneity of Sub-Units; (iii) Specialization of Function; (iv) Stability of Organization; (v) Situational Flexibility of Organization.

(i) *Interdependence*—From Hypothesis 4 (re positive inducibility), it seems evident that one would expect greater co-ordination of effort, as well as more frequent inter-relationship of activity, among *Indiv co-op* than among *Indiv comp.*

Hypothesis 6: At any given time there will be more co-operation of efforts (working together, interrelation of activities) among *Indiv co-op* than among *Indiv comp.*

Hypothesis 6a: Over a period of time, there will be more frequent co-ordination of efforts among *Indiv co-op* than among *Indiv comp.*

(ii) *Homogeneity*—If we assume that the individuals composing the various groups, in both the co-operative and competitive situation, differ from one another with respect to ability or personal inclinations to contribute, etc., it is possible from the substitutability hypothesis (Hyp. 2) to derive:

Hypothesis 7: There will be more homogeneity with respect to amount of contributions or participations among *Indiv comp* than among *Indiv co-op.*

The above hypothesis follows from the consideration that the contribution of an *Indiv co-op* can be a substitute for similarly intended contributions by another *Indiv co-op;* this does not hold for *Indiv comp.* In the co-operative situation, if any individual has ability and contributes, there is less of a need for another individual to contribute—this factor is likely to produce heterogeneity in amount of contributions.

(iii) *Specialization of Function*—Making the same kinds of assumptions as above plus the additional ones that the individuals compromising the various groups differ in respect to ability and/or interest in performing the various functions (e.g.—"orienting," "elaborating," "co-ordinating," etc.), necessary for successful task completion (and are aware of these differences in aptitude or interest) it is possible to derive, from the substitutability hypothesis, the following:

Hypothesis 8: There will be greater specialization of function (i.e.— different individuals fulfilling different functions) among *Indiv co-op* than among *Indiv comp.*

If we assume some time or achievement pressure, from the substitutability hypothesis it is also possible to derive:

Hypothesis 9: There will be greater specialization with respect to content or activity (i.e—different individuals taking different aspects of the task and working on them simultaneously) among *Indiv co-op* than among *Indiv comp.*

The structure of certain kinds of tasks makes it extremely difficult for this type of specialization to take place. So that one would expect fewer differences between *Indiv co-op* and *Indiv comp* on some tasks and more on others.

(iv) and (v) *Stability and Situational Flexibility of Organization*—

If specialization of function occurs, and we assume that expectations are established as a result of this specialization and that these expectations act as a determinant of behavior, we would expect:

Hypothesis 10: There would be greater structural stability (from like situation to like situation) with respect to functions assumed among *Indiv co-op* than among *Indiv comp.* This difference should increase with time.

From the lack of substitutability among *Indiv comp* one can derive a rigidity, each individual always trying to fulfil all the functions. Stability of structure among *Indiv co-op* may result in some perseverance but there does not seem to be any reason to equate rigidity and stability.

Hypothesis 11: In the face of changing circumstance, more organizational flexibility (change of roles to adapt to circumstance) will be manifested among *Indiv co-op* than among *Indiv comp.*

(b) Motivation

There are three things to consider when making a force analysis: (i) direction of the force; (ii) strength of the force; and (iii) point of application of the force.

(i) *Direction of the Force*—From the hypothesis about positive inducibility it can be expected that:

Hypothesis 12: The direction of the forces operating on *Indiv co-op* would be more similar than the direction of the forces operating on *Indiv comp.*

This being the case, other things being equal, one would expect more rapid locomotions—i.e., more rapid decisions and reaching of agreements by co-operative groups. Another point to be considered here is that of the frame of reference with respect to locomotion in the co-operative and competitive situations. In the competitive situation the individual is oriented to locomotions relative to the locomotions of the other individuals with whom he is competing (the rivalry ratio); in the co-operative situation meaningful locomotion units are defined in relation to task completion. If this is the case it can be expected that:

Hypothesis 13: The directions of the forces operating on *Indiv co-op* would be more toward task closure than would be the directions of the forces operating on *Indiv comp*— i.e., there is more achievement pressure on the *Indiv co-op.*

(ii) *Point of Application of the Force*—From the hypothesis of positive inducibility we can assert that a force on any *Indiv co-op* is likely to be paralleled by a force on other *Indiv co-op.* This, if we define *group motivation* as some complex function of the strength of forces that operate simultaneously on all individuals as a function of their interrelationship with respect of positive inducibility, it follows that:

Hypothesis 14: The group force in the direction of the goal in a co-operative group will be stronger than such a group force in a competitive group. This hypothesis has somewhat the same operational significance as hypotheses 12 and 13.

(iii) *Strength of Force*—From positive inducibility we would expect more additional own forces to be induced on the *Indiv co-op* once he is exposed to induction by other members; in the competitive situation due to combined negative and positive induction one would also expect the production of more own forces. If to the concept of the sum of the strength of forces operating on an individual we co-ordinate "interest" or "involvement," there does not seem to be any clear-cut rationale for predicting differences between the situations.

Hypothesis 15: There will not be a significant difference in the total strength of the forces (interest, involvement) operating on the *Indiv co-op* and *Indiv comp* in their respective situations [12] (making the assumptions that situationally irrelevant ego-systems do not become involved).

---

[12]It may be argued that in our culture a competitive situation evokes more basic motives and would thus result in more ego involvement. This may well be true. However, in the present experimental situation, the co-operative groups were in a position of inter-group competition, thus possibly eliminating differential ego-involvement.

(c) Communication

The term "communication," in its widest sense, is used to cover any instance of the establishment of a commonage, that is, the making common of some property to a number of things. For the present purpose, we will follow Morris (19) and limit the word "communication" to mean "the arousing of common significata through the production of signs"; the establishment of a commonage other than that of signification, whether it be by signs or other means, again following Morris' usage, will be called "communization." From the communicator's point of view, communication may be considered a special case of exerted positive induction—i.e., the use of signs to induce in the communicatee sign-behavior similar to that of the communicator. Normally, for the communicator, the process of communication stands in a means relationship to some such purpose as informing, persuading, or being expressive of one's self.

There are three principal elements to the definition of communication: (i) "The production of signs," (ii) "the arousing of," (iii) "common significata". Let us see what implications our basic hypotheses have for these different aspects of the communication process.

(i) *"The Production of Signs"*—If we assume that in certain kinds of tasks (notably, tasks in which there are no clearly discernible "objective" criteria of locomotion—i.e., tasks in which the group itself provides the criteria for judging locomotion) the production of signs can be perceived as a means of locomotion, it is possible to make certain derivations (with additional assumptions) about the quantity of such production in the co-operative and competitive situations. First, it should be made clear that the production of signs by an individual within a group can be made with or without the intent to communicate to the other individuals in the group. Thus, an individual can produce signs under the assumption that "talking" is a means of locomoting, or an individual may produce signs with the intent of communicating with some one outside the group (for example, a "judge" or "observer").

From the substitutability hypothesis and the additional assumptions that: (a) it is perceived that locomotion takes place either through the utterance of many good ideas (i.e., the production of many signs that will be evaluated highly) or through the frequent persuasion or informing of others via communication; (b) quantitative efforts do not seriously interfere with qualitative efforts or that, if they do, quantity is seen to be as or more important than quality: and (c) the time space available per unit of time allows for more production of signs than are necessary for optimal solution of any problem—it is possible to derive:

Hypothesis 16: When the task-structure is such that production in quantity of observable signs is perceived to be a means for locomotion, there will be a greater total of signs produced per unit of time by the *Indiv comp* than by the *Indiv co-op.*

From the hypothesis about the co-ordination of effort (Hyp. 6 and 6a) in tasks one would expect that:

Hypothesis 17: When the task structure is such that locomotion is possible without the production of observable signs, there will be a greater total production of such signs per unit time by the *Indiv co-op* than by the *Indiv comp.*

(ii)*"The arousing of"*—If from the communicator's point of view, communication can be considered a locomotion or a means of locomotion, the state of receptivity (i.e., the readiness to be aroused) in the communicatee stands in a potential relation of facilitating or hindering the locomotions of the communicator. From the hypotheses re helpfulness and obstructiveness (Hyp. 5 and 5a), it can be derived that:

Hypothesis 18: There will be less attentiveness (readiness to be aroused) to each other's production of signs among *Indiv comp* than among *Indiv co-op*.

(iii) *"Common Significata"*—If one assumes that attentiveness is a condition for the arousing of common significata, it follows:

Hypothesis 19: The production of signs by *Indiv comp* will less frequently result in common significata among other *Indiv comp* than will be the case for the production of signs by *Indiv co-op*.

Even when attentiveness is present, there seems to be reason to believe that there is greater likelihood of distortion by communicatees in the competitive situation. This is a consequence of the fact that in the competitive situation, locomotion is likely to be perceived in terms of its effect on relative position (the rivalry ratio); in the co-operative situation the locomotion of any individual is likely to be perceived as resulting in the locomotion of the others. The consequence of this difference is that the expressive characteristics of the production of signs are likely to be more significant to *Indiv comp*. A sign is expressive if the fact of its production is itself a sign to its interpreter of something about the producer of a sign. Tolman's concept of sign-magic (doing to the sign what the organism is predisposed to do to the significata of that sign) combined with his concept of sign-gestalt (25) helps to explain why it is likely that:

Hypothesis 20: There will be more lack of common signification, even when attentiveness is optimal, among *Indiv comp* than among *Indiv co-op*.

From the hypothesis with respect to positive inducibility it follows directly that:

Hypothesis 21: There will be more common appraisals (mutual agreements and acceptances) of communications by communicators and communicatees among *Indiv co-op* than among *Indiv comp*.

(d) Orientation

There are several aspects of orientation: (i) Orientation of members to each other; (ii) Commonality of perceptions of goal, position, direction to goal, and steps in the path to the goal.

(i) *Orientation of Members to Each Other*—The question here is: How well do the members know each other's opinions, values, aptitudes, etc.? From the hypothesis with respect to communication, one can assert (a qualification must be added with respect to the *Indiv co-op* who communicate little, as per heterogeneity hypothesis) that:

Hypothesis 22: The *Indiv co-op* will have more knowledge about its active members than will the *Indiv comp*.

(ii) *Commonality of Perception*—We will define group orientation to exist to the extent that there is commonality of perception among the members. Group orientation can be assessed in relation to goals, position at a given time, direction to goal, or steps in path to the goal. From the communication hypothesis and from the hypothesis of positive inducibility one can derive that:

Hypothesis 23: There will be more group orientation among the *Indiv co-op* than among the *Indiv comp.*

(e) Group productivity

There are various possibilities of defining "group productivity." One could define it in terms of motivation reduction of the members, in terms of the entity produced, in terms of a group's realization of its potential, etc. For present purposes we shall consider group productivity in terms of the entity produced by the group, and, in terms of the learning of the individuals composing the groups.

From the hypothesis with respect to strength of group motivation (Hyp. 14), assuming that, other things being equal, locomotion will proceed more rapidly the stronger the motivation, one can derive that:

Hypothesis 24: The *Indiv co-op* (as a group) will produce more per unit of time than will the *Indiv comp* (as a group).

Hypothesis 24a: It will take less time for the *Indiv co-op* (as a group) to produce what the *Indiv comp* (as a group) produces.

If we assume that any or all of the following are negatively related to group productivity (in respect to quality of product): lack of co-ordination, communication difficulties, persisting internal conflict, lack of group orientation, we can derive that:

Hypothesis 25: The qualitative productivity of the *Indiv co-op* (as a group) will be higher than that of *Indiv comp* (as a group).

From the hypotheses about communication and the hypotheses with respect to positive inducibility, with the additional assumption that the individuals composing the various groups have information and a background of experience that could benefit the other individuals, it is possible to derive that:

Hypothesis 26: The *Indiv co-op* will learn more from each other than will the *Indiv comp.* (The more knowledgeable and experienced of the *Indiv co-op* would, of course, learn less than the not so well-informed *Indiv co-op*).

(f) Interpersonal relations

There are various things to be considered here: (i) Valence of the actions of fellow members, of the group, of the situation, and the extent of the generalization of this property; (ii) The occurrence of group or individual functions; (iii) The perception of effect on others; (iv) The incorporation of the attitude of the generalized other.

(i) *Valence or Cathexis of the actions of fellow members, etc.*—From the hypotheses with respect to cathexis (Hyp. 3 and 3a) we expect the actions of fellow members to be more positively cathected among *Indiv co-op* than among *Indiv comp.* We would also expect the perceived source of these actions to acquire, to some extent, a cathexis similar to that held with respect to the actions.

Hypothesis 27: There will be more friendliness among *Indiv co-op* than among *Indiv comp.*

The extent of generalization of the cathexis will be a function of the centrality for the person of the goals he has involved in the situation of cooperation or competition. Thus, if the situation is important to the person, we would expect his perceptions of the personalities of other members to be affected by the cathexis[13], we would also expect the friendliness or lack of it to generalize to other situations, etc.

Just as Hyp. 27 follows from the original cathexis hypothesis, it seems likely that the cathexis will be generalized to the products of the joint actions of fellow members and oneself—i.e., the group products.

Hypothesis 28: The group products will be evaluated more highly by *Indiv co-op* than by *Indiv comp*.

(ii) *The Occurrence of Group or Individual Functions*—If we define as "group functions" any actions which are intended to increase the solidarity of the group, or to maintain and regulate the group so that it functions "smoothly" and assert that "group functions" are seen to be "helpful" (i.e.—facilitate locomotion) it follows from the "helpfulness" hypothesis (Hyp. 5a) that:

Hypothesis 29: There will be a greater percentage of group functions among *Indiv co-op* than among *Indiv comp*.

If we define "individual functions" to include any actions of the individual which are not immediately directed toward task solution and which are not "group functions" (i.e., actions which are obstructive, blocking, aggressive, or self-defensive, etc., are "individual functions") it follows from the "obstructiveness" hypothesis (Hyp. 5a) that:

Hypothesis 30: There will be a greater percentage of individual functions among *Indiv comp* than among *Indiv co-op*.

(iii) *The Perception of Effect on Others*—There seem to be two questions here: (a) How realistic are the individual's perceptions of his effects on others? and (b) What kinds of effects are the individuals likely to have in the differing social situations?

From the communication hypothesis, it was developed (Hyp. 22) that over a period of time *Indiv co-op* should know more about the attitudes of (active) fellow members than is the case for *Indiv comp*. Using the same reasoning, and making the assumption that the communication difficulty with respect to this content is also greater for *Indiv comp*, it follows that:

Hypothesis 31: The perception of the attitudes of the others towards aspects of one's own functioning in the group, etc., by *Indiv co-op* should be more realistic than such perceptions by *Indiv comp*.

From the inducibility hypothesis, it also follows that:

Hypothesis 32: The attitudes of any individual with respect to his own functioning should be more similar to the attitudes of the others with respect to his functioning among *Indiv co-op* than among *Indiv comp*.

From Hyp. 31 and the cathexis hypothesis we can derive that *Indiv co-op* will tend to perceive that they have a favorable effect on the others in the group. If we make the assumption of "autistic hostility" (20)—that is, that hostile impulses under conditions of reduced communication tend to create the expectation of counter-hostility, we can demonstrate that:

Hypothesis 33: *Indiv co-op* will perceive themselves as having more favorable effects on fellow-members than will *Indiv comp*.

[13] See F. Heider (9).

(iv) *The Incorporation of the Attitude of the "Generalized Other"*[14]—The term "attitude of the generalized other" refers to an internalized structure which is developed as a result of introjecting the mutually interacting attitudes of those with whom one is commonly engaged in a social process. From our preceding development it is clear that the development of the "attitude of the generalized other" requires communication and positive inducibility. It follows then, that:

Hypothesis 34: Incorporation of the attitude of the generalized other will occur to a greater extent in *Indiv co-op* than in *Indiv comp*.

The operational implications of the preceding hypothesis are similar to those of the co-ordination and orientation hypothesis. It has further implications in terms of group development which will not be drawn here. For present purposes, the "feeling of responsibility" to other members will be taken as an operational definition of the degree of internalized attitude of the generalized other.

(g) Individual behavior

No attempt will be made in this study to derive how individuals with certain personality characteristics will behave nor what the reactions of other individuals to such behavior will be in the two different types of situation—co-operation and competition. Suffice it to say, that it is evident that one would expect more behavioral homogeneity in competitive situations than in co-operative situations. It is also apparent that the reactions of others to a "stupid" individual (one who hinders locomotion or locomotes in the wrong direction) or to a "bright" individual will vary significantly from one situation to another.

(h) The course of development with time

From our theory one would predict quite different developments in successful and unsuccessful co-operative groups. Similarly, important developmental differences would occur in competitive situations in which reward over a period of time was all accumulated by one individual as compared with competitive situations in which over a period of time different individuals were rewarded. The derivation of these predictions will not be attempted in this article.

SECTION C

The Concept of "Group"

In the introductory paragraphs of this article it was suggested that a linkage existed between the conceptualization of the co-operative situation and the concept of group and that this linkage provided the possibility for the derivation and empirical testing of group hypotheses. The task of this section will be to clarify the nature of the linkage and to define some group concepts. As a brief introduction, let us consider the questions: (i) "In

---

[14]The concept of "generalized other" plays a crucial role in the social psychology of G. H. Mead (17).

what sense, if any, do groups exist?"; (ii) "What are some of the existing formulations with respect to groups?"

(a) In what sense, if any, do groups exist?

Kurt Lewin (8) has emphasized the importance of the belief in the "existence" of something as a psychological prerequisite for the scientist's interest in that something as an object for scientific investigation. He suggests that "the taboo against believing in the existence of a social entity is probably most effectively broken by handling this entity experimentally." The pioneering works Lippitt (11) and French (3) have done much to shatter the scientific belief that groups do not exist—the belief, therefore, that the concept of "group" has no empirical reference.

The resistance to the acceptance of the belief in the "reality" of groups stems largely from what Whitehead (27) has called "The Fallacy of Misplaced Concreteness." The very words used in phrasing the question "In what *Sense* . . . " implied the acceptance of the fallacy that for anything to be real it must have "simple location" in physical space-time. It is clear that many groups do not have the property of simple location; that is, one cannot answer the question "Where?" in terms of a physical space. The lack of physical *locus* for a group has confused many people and has led them to react to the concept of group as though it could have no meaningful empirical co-ordinates. Yet it should be clear that many of these same people have unwittingly accepted concepts such as "the person" which a more than superficial analysis would reveal have no simple locations, fallaciously concretizing concepts which are quite "abstract."

Another related source of resistance to the acceptance of the "reality" of groups, has been the argument that we cannot scientifically speak of a group as deciding and acting, since it is the individuals that compose the group that decide and act. Child (2) has, in answer to such argument, pointed out that the same kind of objection could be raised with respect to considering the individual as a unit; it too is composed of sub-units, which in turn are composed of sub-units, etc. It is clear that this argument has to do with the size of unit that is most fruitful in the investigation of any scientific problem. This is a problem in the pragmatics of science. It is believed that the concept of "group" will have the same value for the study of social phenomena that the concept of the "individual" has had for the study of psychological phenomena (12). It is further believed that the concepts "individual" and "group" have two crucial similar attributes—the idea of organization or patterning of its sub-parts and the idea of motivation; organization being established in the course of purposeful striving in relation to the environment (23).

To sum up, the answer to the question "In what sense, if any, do groups exist?" is simply that groups exist as concepts that have empirical references. Their usefulness as concepts depends in part on the nature of the relationship of the concept "group" to other concepts and in part on the nature of the empirical co-ordinations.

(b) What are some of the existing formulations with respect to groups?

No attempt will be made here to make a thorough census of formulations with respect to groups. Wilson (28) has recently attempted such a summary of sociological formulations. From this summary it is apparent that the group concept is pivotal in the thinking of many sociologists. The works of such sociologists as Durkheim ("The Division of Labor"), Simmel (the effect of size upon group organization, interaction processes, etc.), Von Weise (a classificatory approach to groups), Cooley ("Social Process" and "Social Organization"), Brown ("Social Groups"), and Coyle ("Social Process in Organized Groups") have much to offer in the way of fruitful hypotheses for experimental research. Wilson, however, summarized his survey by asserting that there exists "a prevailing ambiguity of conceptualization and classification with reference to the group in the whole field of sociology."

Yet if we look carefully at the definitions used by sociologists we find a common core, based on the idea of "interaction." (Some sociologists use the word "group" to include also "categories" based on similarities, "aggregates" based on proximity, as well as "groups" based upon "psychic" interaction). In most usages it is not made explicit whether interaction is defined in terms of an objective, social interdependence or a psychological interdependence. In addition to the criterion of interaction some sociologists, e.g., Znaniecki (29) and Newstetter (21), have stated that the concept of group includes "a feeling of identification," or "realization of a selective bond." Sociologists have, in considering the relationship of the individual and the group, tended to emphasize the incompleteness of the individual without the group (Durkheim's concept of "anomie").

Koffka (6) makes a distinction between "sociological" (geographical) groups and "psychological" (behavioral) groups. He asserts that *sociological groups* are "gestalts" and as gestalts they have characteristics which are somewhat distinctive. In the first place the "strength" of the gestalt (the degree of interdependence) may differ over an enormously wide range; secondly, the individuals composing the group are not completely determined by the group. The reality of the *psychological group* is expressed in the pronoun "we," "we," implying here the feeling of unity in joint action. As used by Koffka the phrase "psychological group" refers to an individual life space, the phrase "sociological group" refers to a group space. He asserts that a sociological group of n members presupposes n psychological groups. Koffka has many stimulating suggestions to offer with respect to the conditions of group formation, group structure, and with respect to the relation of the individual to the group.

French states two criteria for the existence of a group: inter-dependence and identification. He defines "identification conceptually in terms of two dynamic factors: (a) belonging to the group has, for its members, a positive valence, (b) compared to the nonmembers, the members accept to a greater degree the forces induced by the group" (3, p. 275). Interdependence is the basic criterion; not all psychological groups presuppose identification.

One of the most stimulating contributions to the theory of groups and organization is presented in Barnard's "The Functions of the Executive" (1). This work, which must be considered a "basic work" in this field, is too pregnant with ideas to permit any concise summary. He suggests that the word "group" is most appropriately applied to the relationship of co-operation, which is a system of interactions. He also points out, as Koffka has done, (but in rather different terminology) that: (i) the group or organization as a system has properties independently of the persons composing the group; (ii) the persons composing a group possess some characteristics which may not be pertinent to the group and the group, of course, does not completely determine the person. In effect, Barnard uses the term "member" to apply to the group relevant aspects of the person. Any person may have many different memberships.

He asserts "an organization comes into being when (i) there are persons able to communicate with each other, (ii) who are willing to contribute action (iii) to accomplish a common purpose. These elements are necessary and sufficient conditions initially . . . For the continued existence either effectiveness or efficiency is necessary" (1, p. 82). That is, an organization cannot persist unless the individuals obtain more satisfaction than discomfort in the course of directly obtaining the specific objectives of the organization or unless they do it indirectly.

The conceptualization to be offered below, though not influenced by Barnard, is in many respects similar to his.

(c) A proposed formulation:

Basic definitions:

1. A sociological group[15] exists (has unity) to the extent that the individuals or sub-units composing it are pursuing promotively interdependent goals.

2. A psychological group[15] exists (has unity) to the extent that the individuals composing it perceive themselves as pursuing promotively interdependent goals.

3. A psychological group has cohesiveness as a direct function of the strength of goals perceived to be promotively interdependent and of the degree of perceived interdependence.

The following definitions are reformulations of the above definitions from the point of view of membership.

1a. Individual or sub-units belong in a sociological group to the extent that they are pursuing promotively interdependent goals.

2a. Individuals or sub-units possess membership in a psychological group to the extent that they perceive themselves as pursuing promotively interdependent goals.

3a. Individuals or sub-units possess membership motive in a psychological group as a direct function of the strength of goals perceived to be promotively interdependent and of the degree of perceived interdependence.

The conceptualization of the cooperative situation (see Section B) is, of course, identical with the definition of the sociological group. It follows that if *Indiv co-op* and *Indiv comp* are equated in other respects, *Indiv co-op* will possess more unity as a sociological group than will *Indiv comp*. From the logical and psychological consideration advanced in the preceding sections it would also follow that the *Indiv co-op* will possess more unity as a psychological group than will the *Indiv comp*. Since all the hypotheses in the preceding sections were relative statements, based on the assumption that the *Indiv co-op* and *Indiv comp* were equated in other respects, it is possible to substitute for "*Indiv co-op*" the phrase "a psychological group with greater unity," and to substitute for "*Indiv comp*" the phrase, "a psychological group with lesser unity."

Thus, in effect, through creation of a co-operative and a competitive situation it

---

[15]It should be noted that these terms are not being used as Koffka has used them.

becomes possible to test empirically the effect of variation in degree of unity or strength of membership motive of a psychological group upon the functioning of groups.

SUMMARY

In this article an attempt has been made to sketch out a theory of cooperation and competition and to apply this theory to the functioning of small groups. The development has proceeded by the following steps: (i) the social situations of co-operation and competition were defined; (ii) some of the logical implications inherent in the definitions were pointed to; (iii) with the introduction of psychological assumptions, some of the psychological implications of the definitions of the two objective social situations were then drawn; (iv) the psychological implications, with the aid of additional psychological assumptions, were then applied to various aspects of small-group functionings to develop a series of hypotheses about the relative effects of co-operation and competition upon group process; and (v) finally, the concept of group was defined and linked with the concept of co-operation, thus making all of the preceding theoretical development with respect to co-operation relevant to group concepts.

In a forthcoming article, an experimental study of the effects of cooperation and competition upon group process will be reported.

REFERENCES

1. Barnard, C. I. *The Functions of The Executive.* Harvard, 1938.
2. Child, C. M. *Physiological Foundations of Behavior.* Holt, 1924.
3. French, J. R. P. "Organized and Unorganized Groups Under Fear and Frustration." Studies in Topological and Vector Psychology, III, *Univ. Ia., Stud. Child Welf.*, 20.
4. Heider, F. "Attitudes and Cognitive Organization." *J. Psychol.*, 1946, 21, 107–112.
5. Hiller, E. T. *Principles of Sociology.* Harpers, 1933.
6. Koffka, K. *Principles of Gestalt Psychology.* Harcourt-Brace, 1935.
7. Lewin, K. "The Conceptual Representation and The Measurement of Psychological Forces." *Contr. Psychol. Theor.*, 1, No. 4, 1–207.
8. Lewin, K. "Frontiers in Group Dynamics." *Human Relations*, I, 1, 1947.
9. Lewis, H. B. "An Experimental Study of the Role of Ego in Work. I. The Role of the Ego in Co-operative Work." *J. Exp. Psychol.*, 34, 1944. 113–127.
10. Lewis, H. B., and Franklin, M. "An Experimental Study of the Role of Ego in Work: II. The Significance of Task-Orientation in Work." *J. Exp. Psychol.*, 34, 1944, 195–216.
11. Lippitt, R. "An Experimental Study of the Effect of Democratic and Authoritarian Group Atmospheres." Studies in Topological and Vector Psychology I., *Univ. Ia., Stud. Child. Welf.*, 16, No. 3.
12. Lundberg, G. A. *Foundations of Sociology.* Macmillan, 1939.
13. MacIver, R. M. *Society: A Textbook of Sociology.* Farrar & Rinehart, 1937.
14. Maller, J. B. "Co-operation and Competition: An Experimental Study in Motivation." *Teach. Coll., Contrib. to Educ.* No. 384, 1929.
15. May, N. A., and Doob, L. W. "Co-operation and Competition." *Soc. Sci. Res. Council Bull.* 125, 1937.
16. Mayo, E. *Social Problems of an Industrial Civilization.* Harvard, 1945.

17. Mead, G. H. *Mind, Self and Society*. Univ. of Chicago, 1934.
18. Mead, M. *Co-operation and Competition Among Primitive Peoples*. McGraw-Hill, 1937.
19. Morris, C. *Signs, Language, and Behavior*. Prentice-Hall, 1946.
20. Newcomb, T. M. "Autistic Hostility and Social Reality." *Human Relations*, I, 1, 1947.
21. Newstetter, et al. *Group Adjustment*.
22. Parsons, T. *The Structure of Social Action*. McGraw-Hill, 1937.
23. Russell, E. S. *The Directiveness of Organic Activities*. Cambridge Univ., 1945.
24. Spykman, N. A. *The Social Theory of George Simmel*. Univ. of Chicago, 1925.
25. Tolman, E. C. *Purposive Behavior in Animals and Men*. The Century Co., 1932.
26. Wheeler, R. H. *The Science of Psychology*. Crowell, 1940.
27. Whitehead, A. N. "Science and the Modern World." *Macmillan*, 1925.
28. Wilson, L. "Sociology of Groups" in *Twentieth Century Sociology* edited by Gurvitch, G., and Moore, W. E.
29. Znaniecki, F. "Social Groups as Products of Participating Individuals," *Am. J. Sociol.*, 44, 1939, 799–812.

— · — · — · — · — · — · — · — · — · —

ROBERT F. BALES

*Interaction Process Analysis**

In a recent review of the state of research in the field of small groups, Edward Shils makes some remarks which aptly point up the problem to which this paper is addressed:

> Because problems are dimly 'felt,' because they are neither related to a general theory of behavior on the one side, nor rigorously connected with the categories and indices to be chosen for observation on the other, the results of the research can very seldom become part of the cumulative movement of truth which constitutes the growth of scientific knowledge. When concrete indices (and classifications) are not clearly related to the variables of a general theory of human behavior in society, they tend to be *ad hoc*. Under these conditions they are only with difficulty, applicable, i.e., translatable into another concrete situation by an investigator who seeks to confirm, revise, or disconfirm the previously 'established' proposition.[1]

*Robert F. Bales, "A Set of Categories for the Analysis of Small Group Interaction," *American Sociological Review 15*, (1950): 257–263. Reprinted by permission of the publisher and the author.
[1] Edward Shils, *The Present State of American Sociology*, Glencoe, Illinois: Free Press, 1948, p. 45.

Probably most of us have some difficulty in thinking of a session between a psychiatrist and patient, a corner boy's gang in a political huddle, and a staff conference of business executives as comparable within a single frame of reference. It is probably more difficult, for example, than thinking of the social systems of China, of Bali, and the United States as legitimate objects for comparative analysis. At least the latter three constitute full scale, and in some sense, complete social systems.

What do the former three groups have in common? They are small face-to-face groups. If we call them social systems, we shall have to say that they are partial, as well as microscopic social systems. To place a slightly different emphasis, it can be said they they are systems of human interaction. At this degree of abstraction there is no necessary incongruity in comparing them with each other, or with full-scale social systems. Both small groups and complete societies can be viewed as types of interaction systems, even though one is tremendously more inclusive than the other. If this point of view turns out to be excessively formal or abstract, we may have to retreat to less generalized frames of reference.

To take the more hopeful view, it may very well be that one of the main contributions of the study of small groups will be an expanding of the range of available empirical data in such a way as to force our theory of social systems to a more general and powerful level of abstraction. If the theory of social systems has been generalized and strengthened by the necessity of making it applicable to a range of full-scale social systems, non-literate as well as literate, Eastern as well as Western, then there is at least the possibility that it will be further strengthened by the necessity of making it applicable up and down the scale from large to small.

However this may be, the present set of categories was developed with this hope, and took its initial point of departure from a body of theory about the structure and dynamics of full-scale social systems. This will not be immediately apparent in viewing the set of categories, nor can it be spelled out to any satisfactory degree in this article. A manual dealing with both the theoretical and practical aspects of the method for those who may wish to apply it in their own research has recently been published.[2] The present paper will give only a simplified introductory description of the method and some of its possible uses.

DESCRIPTION OF THE METHOD

The method is called interaction process analysis. It is a type of content analysis in the basic sense, but the type of content which it attempts to abstract from the raw material of observation is the type of problem-solving relevance of each act for the total on-going process. Hence it has seemed less confusing to refer to what we are doing as "process analysis" rather than as "content analysis."

The heart of the method is a way of classifying behavior act by act, as it occurs in small face-to-face groups, and a series of ways of analyzing the data to obtain indices

[2] Robert F. Bales, *Interaction Process Analysis; A Method For the Study of Small Groups*, Cambridge, Massachusetts: Addison-Wesley Press, 1950.

descriptive of group process, and derivatively, of factors influencing that process. The set of categories as it actually appears on the observation form is shown under the twelve numbers in Chart I. The outer brackets and labels do not appear on the observation form,

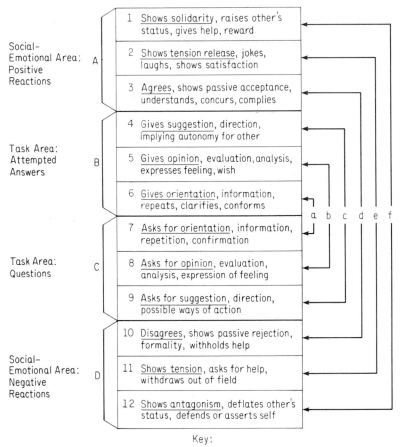

Key:

a. Problems of orientation   c. Problems of control   e. Problems of tension-management
b. Problems of evaluation   d. Problems of decision   f. Problems of integration

Chart I. The system of categories used in observation and their relation to major frames of reference.

but constitute a part of the mental set of the observer. The twelve observation categories are numbered from the top down, but are arranged in a series of complementary pairs proceeding from the center pair, 6 and 7, outward. The phrases and terms within the numbered categories are only catch-phrases designed to be concretely descriptive of the implied theoretical content of the categories in their usual forms. Actually there are extended definitions of each of the categories, and the central meaning of each is given by its position in the frames of reference to which they are all related as indicated by the labeled brackets on the Chart.

The set of twelve categories (and the actual behavior which is classified under them) are brought into working relation to other bodies of theory[3] in terms of the frame of reference. The key assumption which provides this articulation is the notion that all organized and at least partially cooperative systems of human interaction, from the smallest to the most inclusive, and of whatever concrete variety, may be approached for scientific analysis by abstracting from the events which go on within them in such a way as to relate the consequences of these events to a set of concepts formulating what are hypothetically called "functional problems of interaction systems."

For purposes of the present set of categories we postulate six interlocking functional problems which are logically applicable to any concrete type of interaction system. As indicated in Chart 1, these are in one-word terms: problems of orientation, evaluation, control, decision, tension-management, and integration. These terms are all related to a hypothetical conception of an over-arching problem-solving sequence of interaction between two or more persons. As a concrete first approximation we may find it helpful to think of the functional problems as related in an order of "stages" or "steps" in a problem-solving sequence, as their order suggests. Actually this is an over-simplified view. However, in order to illustrate the notion of stages as they may appear under certain conditions, let us take a short description of a fictional group meeting. The same example will serve to illustrate the method of scoring with the categories.

HOW THE SCORING IS DONE

Let us imagine we are observing a group of five persons who are meeting together to come to a decision about a point of policy in a project they are doing together. Three or four of the members have arrived, and while they wait they are laughing and joking together, exchanging pleasantries and "small talk" before getting down to business. The missing members arrive, and after a little more scattered conversation the chairman calls the meeting to order. Usually, though not necessarily, this is where the observer begins his scoring.

Stage 1. Emphasis on problems of orientation: (deciding what the situation is like). The chairman brings the meeting up to date with a few informal remarks. He says, "At the end of our last meeting we decided that we would have to consider our budget before laying out plans in greater detail." The observer, sitting with the observation form in front of him, looks over the list of twelve categories and decides that this remark is most relevant to the problem of orientation, and specifically that it takes the form of an "attempted answer" to this problem, and so he classifies it in Category 6, "Gives orientation, information, repeats, clarifies, confirms." The observer has already decided that he will designate the chairman by the number 1, and each person around the table in turn by the numbers 2, 3, 4, and 5. The group as a whole will be designated by the symbol 0. This remark was made by the chairman and was apparently addressed to the group as a whole, so the observer writes down the symbols 1–0 in one of the spaces following Category 6 on the observation form.

---

[3]More specifically, theory applying to larger social systems, and perhaps also theory applying to personality. There seems to be no particular incongruity in thinking of the personality as an interaction system, if we understand by this, not a system of "persons," but a system of interdependent acts or potential acts. This, in fact, seems to me to be the character of much of contemporary personality theory.

In this one operation, the observer has thus isolated a unit of speech or process which he considers a proper unit for classification, has classified it, identified the member who performed the act, and the person or persons to whom it was directed. If he were writing on a moving tape instead of a paper form, as we do for some purposes,[4] he would also have identified the exact position of the act in sequence with all others. In practice we find that we obtain from 10 to 20 scores per minute in keeping up with most interaction, and that this speed is not excessive for a trained observer.

As the chairman finishes his remark, Member 2 asks the chairman, "Has anybody gone over our expenditures to date?" The observer decides that this is a "question" indicating that a problem of orientation exists, and so should be classified in Category 7, "Asks for orientation, information, repetition, confirmation." He so records it by placing the symbols 2-1 in a box following this category. The chairman replies, "I have here a report prepared by Miss Smith on the expenditures to date." The observer marks down the symbols 1-2 under Category 6, as an "attempted answer" to the indicated problem of orientation. As the chairman goes over the report the observer continues to score, getting a good many scores in Categories 6 and 7, but also occasional scores in other categories.

Stage 2. Emphasis on problems of evaluation: (deciding what attitudes should be taken toward the situation). As the chairman finishes reviewing the items on the report he may ask, "Have we been within bounds on our expenditures so far?" The observer puts down a score under Category 8, "Asks for opinion, evaluation, analysis, expression of feeling." Member 3 says, "It seems to me that we have gone in pretty heavily for secretarial help." The observer puts down a score in Category 5, "Gives opinion, evaluation, analysis, expresses feeling." Member 4 comes in with the remark, "Well I don't know. It seems to me . . ." The observer puts down the symbols 4-3 in Category 10, "Disagrees, shows passive rejection, formality, withholds help," and continues with scores in Category 5 as Member 4 makes his argument. The discussion continues to revolve around the analysis of expenditures, with a good many scores falling in Category 5, but also in others, particularly Categories 10 and 3, and interspersed with a number in Categories 6 and 7 as opinions are explained and supported.

Stage 3. Emphasis on problems of control: (deciding what to do about it). Finally the chairman says, "Well a little more than half our time is gone." The observer scores 1-0 in Category 6. "Do you want to go ahead and decide whether we should buy that piece of equipment or . . ." The observer scores 1-0 in Category 9, "Asks for suggestion, direction, possible ways of action." Member 2 says, "I think we should get it." The observer scores 2-0 in Category 4, "Gives suggestion, direction, implying autonomy for other." As Member 2 begins to support his suggestion, Member 3 breaks in with a counter argument, and the discussion begins to grow more heated.

The observer begins to have trouble in keeping up as the members are talking more rapidly and some remarks are left unfinished. He does not forget to keep scanning the group, however, and presently he notices that Member 5, who has said little up to this point, sighs heavily and begins to examine his fingernails. The observer puts down a score under Category 11, "Shows tension, asks for help, withdraws out of field." He enters this score as 5-y, since he has decided ahead of time to use the symbol y to stand for "self,"

---

[4]Robert F. Bales and Henry Gerbrands, "The Interaction Recorder; An Apparatus and Check List for Sequential Content Analysis of Social Interaction," *Human Relations*, Vol. 1, No. 4, 1948.

and to use it when activity is directed toward the self, or is expressive and non-focal, that is, not directed toward other members.

Meantime, Member 3, the chronic objector, comes through with a remark directed at Member 2, "Well, I never did agree about hiring that deadhead secretary. All she's got is looks, but I guess that's enough for Joe." The others laugh at this. The observer scores the first and second remarks under Category 12, "Shows antagonism, deflates other's status, defends or asserts self." The laugh which follows is scored in Category 2, "Shows tension release, jokes, laughs, shows satisfaction." In this case the score is written 0-3, all to Member 3.

At this point Member 5 comes in quietly to sum up the argument, and by the time he finishes several heads are nodding. The observer scores both the nods and the audible agreements in Category 3, "Agrees, shows passive acceptance, understands, concurs, complies." The chairman says, "Then it looks like we are in agreement." The observer scores in Category 6, and scores the answering nods in Category 3. Member 3, the chronic objector, who is also the chronic joker, comes in with a joke at this point, and the joking and laughing continue for a minute or two, each member extending the joke a little. The observer continues to score in Category 2 as long as this activity continues. As the members pick up their things one of them says, "Well, I think we got through that in good shape. Old Bill certainly puts in the right word at the right time, doesn't he." The observer marks down two scores under Category 1, "Shows solidarity, raises other's status, gives help, reward," and after a few more similar remarks the meeting breaks up.

THE POSSIBILITY OF EMPIRICAL NORMS

The foregoing is a fictional example, designed to illustrate the nature of the scoring operation, as well as a kind of hypothetical sequence of stages which may occur under certain conditions. To summarize, we might say that during the course of this meeting there were a series of "phases" portrayed, during which one or more of the functional problems included in our conceptual framework received more than its usual share of attention. The temporal order of these phases in this fictional example follows in a rough way the logical order in which we arrange the categories on the observation form in pairs from the center line outward, that is, as dealing with problems of orientation, evaluation, control, and then in rapid order, a special emphasis on final decision, tension reduction, and reintegration. Each of the major functional problems has been made into an implicit "agenda topic."

The categories of activity as classified by the present system are assumed to bear a functional relation to each other similar to the relation of the phases in the meeting just portrayed. The example has been constructed so that in its phases the relations of the categories to each other are "written large," to borrow an idea from Plato. Hence it is relevant to ask what degree the notion of phases on the larger scale is actually to be taken as an empirical description rather than as a logical model. It is important to emphasize in answer to this question that we do not assume nor believe that all group meetings actually proceed in just this way. One of the thorniest problems in the history of thinking about the process of small groups is whether or not, or in what sense there may be a series of "steps" or "stages" in group problem solving. Data will later be published which indicate that under *certain conditions*, which must be carefully specified, a group problem-solving process essentially like that sketched above, does tend to appear. The data indicate that the sequence described is a kind of average sequence for problem-solving groups, that is, an empirical norm. It further appears that departures from the average picture can be used as diagnostic indicators of the nature of the conditions under which interaction takes place.

Similarly, it appears that there are empirical uniformities in the way activities are distributed between persons. We have some data which indicate that, on the average, if we rank order participants according to the total number of acts they originate, they will then also stand in rank order as to (1) the number of acts they originate to the group as a whole (to 0), (2) the number of acts they originate to specific other members of the group, and (3) the number of acts they receive from all other members of the group. In addition, (4) each person in the rank order series addresses a slightly larger amount of activity to the person just above him in the series than the person above addresses to him, with the top person addressing the group as a whole to a disproportionate degree. It seems likely that these uniformities can be tied together in a more comprehensive theory, and that departures from this average picture can be used as a diagnostic indicator of the nature of the conditions under which interaction takes place. Data on this problem will be published later.

Similarly, ignoring time sequence and the specific persons who initiate or receive acts, empirical uniformities appear in the gross frequency with each category of activity tends to occur. Preliminary data on these uniformities are given below.

FREQUENCY OF OCCURRENCE OF EACH TYPE OF ACTIVITY

We have available for this tabulation some 23,000 scores in terms of the present twelve categories, from observations of groups of different sizes and kinds, ranging through nursery school children, high school and college students, married couples, college faculty discussions, etc., on tasks of widely different kinds. We do not know how badly biased this collection of scores may be as a sample of something larger. They are simply all of the raw scores we have to date on all of the groups and tasks we happen to have observed for a variety of reasons. The scorings were made by the present author. The general problems of reliability are treated in the manual mentioned above.[5] Very briefly it may be said that satisfactory reliability has been obtained between observers, but requires intensive training which should be regarded as an integral part of the method.

Table 1 shows the raw scores and their percentage distribution (or rates) in the twelve categories. In order to have certain conventional limits for inspection of the variability of particular profiles we have employed an external criterion rather than utilize the variance of our samples, which are known to be quite heterogeneous. Our experience indicates that when the rate for a given category on a particular profile is outside the range suggested in Table 1, we are usually able to connect the deviation with some more or less obvious source of variation in the conditions under which the interaction took place. For example, we find that a profile of nursery school children at free play is over

[5] See footnote 2, above.

TABLE 1. RAW SCORES OBTAINED ON ALL INTER-
ACTION OBSERVED TO DATE, PERCENTAGE
RATES, AND SUGGESTED LIMITS, BY CATEGORIES

Category	Raw Scores	Per-centage	Suggested Limits for Inspection of Profiles* *	
			Lower	Upper
1	246	1.0	0.0	5.0
2	1675	7.3	3.0	14.0
3	2798	12.2	6.0	20.0
4	1187	5.2	2.0	11.0
5	6897	30.0	21.0	40.0
6	4881	21.2	14.0	30.0
7	1229	5.4	2.0	11.0
8	809	3.5	1.0	9.0
9	172	.8	0.0	5.0
10	1509	6.6	3.0	13.0
11	1009	4.4	1.0	10.0
12	558	2.4	0.0	7.0
	22970	100.0		

*Suggested limits shown have been established for each cate-
gory by use of binomial confidence limits given in Snedecor,
Statistical Methods, 1946, p. 4, with p equal "Percentage of total"
and n equal 100. This provides relatively wider ranges for the
smaller values and although such conventions do not properly reflect the multinomial character of the variation, they provide a
first approximation for present purposes.

the suggested limits on showing solidarity and showing antagonism, on giving direct
suggestions and on disagreement, and is under the limits on asking for opinion, giving
orientation, and giving opinion. A group of high school boys in group discussion is over
the limits on laughing and joking, and under the limits on giving orientation. A group of
faculty members planning a thesis problem with a graduate student is within the limits on
all categories. Pending the development of a satisfactory typology of groups, tasks, and
other sources of variation, and the accumulation of more experience, this arbitrary procedure for detecting "significant variations" may serve a useful purpose.

APPLICABILITY OF THE METHOD

Verbal interaction accounts for the largest part of the scores, but the categories apply
to non-verbal interaction as well. Groups of manageable size for the method fall in the
range between two and perhaps twenty, but there is no definitely established top limit—
the top manageable size depends upon the character of the interaction. The method is
most easily applied in groups where the attention of the members tends to focus in turn
on single speakers or members, as in most discussion groups. Hence it might be said to
apply to groups small enough so that each member potentially takes into account the
reactions of each of the others.

In concrete terms, the groups which one might be able to study with the method are
very diverse. They would include a series of groups concerned primarily with substantive
problems external to their own process, such as discussion groups, planning groups, policy
forming and executive committees, boards and panels, diagnostic councils in clinical

work, seminars and classroom groups, teams and work groups, certain kinds of problem-solving groups in experimental social psychology and sociology, etc. In addition, there are certain groups with a primary focus on their own procedure in an impersonal way, for training purposes, such as those formed for training in basic human relations skills, now an important branch of small group research. In a less impersonal way, there are large numbers of small groups which have the interaction or interpersonal relations of the members as a primary focus, whatever their concern with substantive external problems. These would include family and household groups, children's play groups, adolescent gangs, adult cliques, social and recreational clubs, and small associations of a great many kinds. Finally there are groups which might be said to have a primary focus on problems of personal content or experience of members, such as therapy or confessional groups of various kinds, and groups of two, such as therapist and patient, counselor and client, interviewer and interviewee, and a number of others in the general class of professional specialist and client.

Some of these types of groups have been studied with the present method or others similar to it. Some of them are unexplored as yet. Taken together, however, the total range of possible types of groups constitutes a challenging array. If interaction in groups of the diverse sorts mentioned can be brought within the range of a single frame of reference, and can be made to yield data by the same method of analysis, we should be some distance along toward meeting the difficulties which Shils indicates in the comments at the beginning of this paper.

— · — · — · — · — · — · — · — · — · — · —

RICHARD H. WILLIS

*Diamond Model of Social Response**

Much of what I am going to say tonight I have said before, but this time I am going to say it somewhat differently in order to clarify a frequently misunderstood point—*viz.*, my models of social response are not *psychological* models in the usual sense, even though they are intended for use by psychologists conducting psychological research.

On previous occasions I have used the term *descriptive* models to refer to what I am now calling *mapping* models. The adjective "descriptive" is, paradoxically, less descriptive than the adjective "mapping" because basically my models function as maps.

These mapping models of social response are not literally maps of the kind you find in an atlas. Rather, they map out the various possible patterns of responding in certain social situations and diagram the interrelations among these patterns.

*Richard H. Willis, "Mapping Models of Response to Social Influence." A paper delivered at the Eastern Psychological Association, 1969. Reprinted by permission of the author.

You can locate a person on the map of the United States, and chart changes in his location as he travels about. The map allows you to describe where he is at any time as he moves around, but it says nothing about *why* he moves as he does. In this sense maps are descriptive, not explanatory. However, accurate description often facilitates explanation. Thus, we may be better able to explain why someone goes from Minneapolis to Miami during Christmas vacation, assuming we have forgotten the locations of these cities, by consulting a map.

Perhaps these mapping models are contributions to psychological theory—but, if so, only in a rather unusual sense. Usually the term "psychological theory" implies some systematic treatment of psychological *processes* such as those of perception, motivation, or learning. My mapping models are not concerned directly with such underlying, inferred processes, but are nevertheless theoretical insofar as they provide a means of organizing data. They play a role on the response side analogous to that played by the color solid, which organizes and interrelates the three stimulus dimensions of hue, brightness, and saturation.

A survey of the literature on social influence and attitude change reveals that models for mapping the interrelations among dimensions of response are almost never made explicit. By reading between the lines one can see that the mapping model usually assumed in research on social influence is unidimensional, with one end labelled Conformity and the other Independence. In attitude change research, the Conformity-Independence model is sometimes extended into the region of negative change. Such negative changes are often referred to as boomerang effects. In other contexts terms such as *negativism, counterformity*, and *anticonformity* are used to refer to closely related effects.

The model with the region of negative change can handle boomerang or anticonformity reactions, but only so long as we consider changes one at a time. If we consider even two trials or occasions for change, this model could not differentiate between a subject showing no movement on either trial and one showing equal amounts of movement in opposite directions. In order to handle multi-trial situations involving movement in both directions, two dimensions of response must be differentiated.

Three two-dimensional mapping models that I have developed are diagrammed as shown. Shaded areas represent excluded regions, and subjects cannot behave in ways

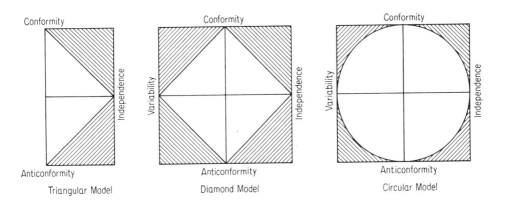

which would assign them to these regions. Here the map analogy breaks down, for cartographic maps do not possess absolutely inaccessible regions.

The first two models were developed within the following experimental context. On each trial the subject is required to make a binary response *prior* to exposure to social pressure and another *after*, both responses being made to the same stimulus. The social pressure is introduced via the interpolated response, also binary, attributed to a partner or other source. An error-choice technique is used. Subjects must respond either "longer" or "shorter."[1]

In the *triangular* model, on the left, the horizontal axis plots the total amount of movement over all trials. The more movement, the less independent the subject. On the vertical axis is plotted net directionality of movement. Positions above the mid-point represent instances of more conformity than anticonformity, while positions below the mid-point correspond to a balance of movement in the anticonformity direction. Each subject is assigned two scores, an *independence* score and a *net conformity* score.

If the subject exhibits no movement from pre-exposure to post-exposure positions, he will be located at the Independence vertex. If he shows movement in the conformity direction, he will be located somewhere along the upper edge of the triangle, the exact position being determined by the amount of movement. If he shows only anticonformity movement, he will be located at a position along the lower edge determined by the amount of movement. Movement in both directions locates the subject within the interior of the response space.

One advantage of the triangular model is that it can handle anticonformity tendencies in multi-trial situations. Another is that it graphically depicts the interrelations among the three basic response modes of conformity, independence, and anticonformity. It makes evident, for example, the fact that pure conformity behavior and pure anticonformity behavior are both instances of pure dependence behavior. This can be seen from the fact that both the conformity and anticonformity vertices are located to the left, at the dependence end of the horizontal axis. The anticonformist too, as well as the conformist, shows a large amount of movement even though in the opposite direction.

Individuals having a tendency to react negativistically, in a misguided effort to attain a greater degree of independence, might do well to consider this basic similarity between conformity and anticonformity.

The upper shaded area in the first figure is required because one cannot be both highly conforming and highly independent at the same time. The lower shaded area reflects the impossibility of being simultaneously highly anticonforming and highly independent. More generally, the more independent a subject, the narrower the range of net conformity scores that are possible. This is a basic feature of the scoring formulas, and was quite deliberately incorporated into them.

The second model, the diamond, is merely a refinement of the triangular model. Certain considerations relating to the experimental procedures, which I will not go into here, logically require that the horizontal axis be extended leftward so that the response space is doubled in size and gains another vertex labelled Variability. The Variability mode of response is the most difficult to interpret psychologically. We may accordingly

---

[1] Whereas the correct response is always equal.

say that the triangular model has the greater initial intuitive appeal, whereas the diamond model is constructed on sounder logical foundations. My own preference here is for refining one's psychological insights so as to make them compatible with the requirements of logic, rather than accommodating in the reverse direction.

Pure variability is another kind of complete independence, and a highly bizarre one. It is the antithesis of the no-movement kind of independence we have already considered. It implies, in fact, maximum movement, with a change in position on every trial. Because movement always occurs, it occurs independently of the interpolated responses, and the subject therefore gives no weight at all to the source of social pressure.

We are now prepared to consider another way of thinking about the axes of the diamond model. Each one measures its own brand of net conformity. The vertical axis, as we have seen, measures net conformity with respect to an external source of influence, while the horizontal axis reflects net conformity relative to an internal source—*viz*., the subject's own pre-exposure responses. Viewed in this light, the ends of the horizontal axis might be labelled Self-conformity and Self-anticonformity.

Knowing that variability is self-anticonformity makes it easier to understand, but one would probably conjecture that such self-anticonformity behavior is quite rare except in a highly attenuated form. Our experimental evidence to date lends support to this conjecture. Only very rarely does a subject behave in such a way as to be located on the left side of the diamond. Resorting again to the map analogy, one can compare the role of the left side of the response space to that part of a map of North America charting the northern latitudes of Canada. Not many people are located up there, but the picture would be incomplete without it.

The circular model is just a variant of the diamond model, differing only in the shape of the boundary. The axes and vertices are interpreted in the same way. The diamond model, it turns out, is the natural one when dealing with the *binary-response* experimental procedures already described. When dealing with certain *ranking* procedures with pre-, and post-, and interpolated measures, one is led to the circular model. It is possible to transform coordinates in one model to those of the other by means of a trigonometric transformation of scores. A choice between these models is primarily a matter of convenience.

It is possible to extend these two-dimensional models to three dimensions in various ways. Assume we switch to stimulus items that do have right answers. Then the third dimension can be used to plot the accuracy of the subject's responses, either pre-exposure, post-exposure, or both. Formally, the addition of a third orthogonal axis to the diamond produces an *octohedral* model. The diamond yields another model by rotation about its horizontal axis. This *biconical* model possesses a possible advantage over the octohedral one in that the correlation between interpolated and correct responses is represented by the angle of separation between the net conformity axis and the accuracy axis. As for the circular model, the natural extension is to a *spherical* one. These three-dimensional models have not yet been employed experimentally, and I will not comment on them further here.

A few comments may be in order about the research utility of the two-dimensional mapping models. On the positive side, they are tight and clean—especially the diamond and the circle. Behavior is neatly decomposed into two basic components, and each subject is assigned a pair of scores locating him precisely within a well-defined outcome space. There is a perfect one-to-one correspondence between possible score combinations and locations within and along the response space.

Still on the positive side, these models are easily utilized within the experimental paradigms for which they were developed, and within these paradigms are capable of considerable flexibility. It should be noted, however, that these more elaborate two-dimensional formulations are unnecessary if it is known in advance that negativistic response tendencies will be negligible. To illustrate, in the complete absence of anticonformity behavior, the diamond model placed subjects along the upper right edge, between the Conformity and Independence vertices. This means that the simpler unidimensional view is in this case fully adequate.

Turning now to a negative feature, attempts to generalize these mapping models, while at the same time retaining their tightness, leads rapidly to formidible complications. For example, in generalizing the diamond model scoring formulas from two response categories to three, one must first distinguish three cases depending upon assumptions made about interrelations among the categories. The case of unordered categories yields a reasonably solution quite easily. For the case of ordered categories with the mid-category defined as *Don't know*, no simple solution is available but a rather complicated one has been found which is in all other respects quite gratifying. For the remaining case, however, in which the mid-category reflects a confident judgment of an intermediate magnitude, no fully satisfactory solution has been devised. Going from two to three dimensions likewise produces an escalation of complexity, but no insoluble cases. Cases of more than three categories or more than three dimensions have not been examined, but there is no need to in order to see that extensive generalization will be possible only at the expense of formal elegance.

This by no means implies that we are anywhere near the end of interesting research applications of the models already developed, but it suggests strongly that it might be worthwhile to work out some less formal but more general models.

Consider the following scheme, which may be too loose to be called a model. The subject makes his pre-exposure response on each trial along a scale with any large number of categories—say 100 to be concrete. The interpolated responses attributed to the source of social pressure are distributed according to a predetermined rule over these 100 response categories. As usual, the subject makes a post-exposure response to each stimulus.

Two scores are computed for each subject. The first is the *total* movement score obtained by summing the distances between pre-exposure and post-exposure responses over all trials. This total movement score is directly analogous to the independence score of the models diagrammed in the hand-out. The less movement, the greater the independence. The second score is the net movement score, and is obtained by subtracting the amount of movement away from the interpolated responses from the amount of movement toward them. This net movement score is analogous to the net conformity score of the diagrammed models.

In order to make comparisons among subjects it would be necessary to introduce an adjustment based on the uncontrolled variation in congruence between each subject's pre-exposure responses and the interpolated responses. One can hope that this adjustment might often be small enough to ignore in practice. If so, inter-subject comparisons can be conveniently made. The highly dependent subject might exhibit the same level of net movement as a more independent subject, because his overconformity and anti-conformity cancel one another, but he would be revealed by his higher total movement score.

This procedure would not yield the sharply defined response space, invariant from one subject or occasion to another, which characterize the triangle, the diamond, and the circle. On the other hand, the freedom with respect to the number of categories should allow greater flexibility and sensitivity.

This concludes my remarks on the formal aspects of these mapping models, but I would like to repeat an important point. These mapping models are neutral with respect to underlying processes. They are bystanders or noncombatants, so to speak. Their proper function is to provide a more highly differentiated description of that which is to be explained. They impose no restrictions upon the type of explanation that might be advanced, and in fact they can suggest explanations that would otherwise be overlooked.

If time permitted, much could be said about relating descriptive analysis to psychological explanation, but under the circumstances my remarks on this point will be very brief indeed. Consider the concept of *reactance*, about which you have already heard tonight. Reactance consists of a particular kind of motivational arousal which is inferred from observed behavior and which in turn can be used to predict observable behavior. Much of the behavior that can be explained by or predicted from the process of reactance is best described as negativism or anticonformity. Thus, mapping models designed to accommodate negativistic response tendencies provide a tool for conceptualizing and investigating reactance, although there is nothing about these kinds of models which prejudges the issue of the nature of the underlying processes responsible for overt behavior.

— · — · — · — · — · — · — · — · — · —

STANLEY MILGRAM

*Experiments on Obedience**

The situation in which one agent commands another to hurt a third turns up time and again as a significant theme in human relations. It is powerfully expressed in the story of Abraham, who is commanded by God to kill his son. It is no accident that Kierkegaard, seeking to orient his thought to the central themes of human experience, chose Abraham's conflict as the springboard to his philosophy.

War too moves forward on the triad of an authority which commands a person to

*Stanley Milgram, "Some Conditions of Obedience and Disobedience to Authority," *Human Rèlations* 18 (1965): 57–75. Reprinted by permission.

destroy the enemy, and perhaps all organized hostility may be viewed as a theme and variation on the three elements of authority, executant, and victim.[1] We describe an experimental program, recently concluded at Yale University, in which a particular expression of this conflict is studied by experimental means.

In its most general form the problem may be defined thus: if X tells Y to hurt Z, under what conditions will Y carry out the command of X and under what conditions will he refuse. In the more limited form possible in laboratory research, the question becomes: if an experimenter tells a subject to hurt another person, under what conditions will the subject go along with this instruction, and under what conditions will he refuse to obey. The laboratory problem is not so much a dilution of the general statement as one concrete expression of the many particular forms this question may assume.

One aim of the research was to study behavior in a strong situation of deep consequence to the participants, for the psychological forces operative in powerful and lifelike forms of the conflict may not be brought into play under diluted conditions.

This approach meant, first, that we had a special obligation to protect the welfare and dignity of the persons who took part in the study; subjects were, of necessity, placed in a difficult predicament, and steps had to be taken to ensure their wellbeing before they were discharged from the laboratory. Toward this end, a careful, post-experimental treatment was devised and has been carried through for subjects in all conditions.[2]

TERMINOLOGY

If Y follows the command of X we shall say that he has obeyed X; if he fails to carry out the command of X, we shall say that he has disobeyed X. The terms *to obey* and to *disobey*, as used here, refer to the subject's overt action only, and carry no implication for the motive or experiential states accompanying the action.[3]

[1] Consider, for example, J. P. Scott's analysis of war in his monograph on aggression:
'. . . while the actions of key individuals in a war may be explained in terms of direct stimulation to aggression, vast numbers of other people are involved simply by being part of an organized society.
'. . . For example, at the beginning of World War I an Austrian archduke was assassinated in Sarajevo. A few days later soldiers from all over Europe were marching toward each other, not because they were stimulated by the archduke's misfortune, but because they had been trained to obey orders.' (Slightly rearranged from Scott (1958), *Aggression*, p. 103.)
[2] It consisted of an extended discussion with the experimenter and, of equal importance, a friendly reconciliation with the victim. It is made clear that the victim did not receive painful electric shocks. After the completion of the experimental series, subjects were sent a detailed report of the results and full purposes of the experimental program. A formal assessment of this procedure points to its overall effectiveness. Of the subjects, 83.7 per cent indicated that they were glad to have taken part in the study; 15.1 per cent reported neutral feelings; and 1.3 per cent stated that they were sorry to have participated. A large number of subjects spontaneously requested that they be used in further experimentation. Four-fifths of the subjects felt that more experiments of this sort should be carried out, and 74 per cent indicated that they had learned something of personal importance as a result of being in the study. Furthermore, a university psychiatrist, experienced in outpatient treatment, interviewed a sample of experimental subjects with the aim of uncovering possible injurious effects resulting from participation. No such effects were in evidence. Indeed, subjects typically felt that their participation was instructive and enriching. A more detailed discussion of this question can be found in Milgram (1964).
[3] *To obey* and *to disobey* are not the only terms one could use in describing the critical action of Y. One could say that Y is cooperating with X, or displays conformity with regard to X's commands. However, *cooperation* suggests that X agrees with Y's ends, and understands the relationship between his own behavior and the attainment of those ends. (But the experimental procedure, and, in particular, the experimenter's command that the subject shock the victim even in the absence of a response

To be sure, the everyday use of the word *obedience* is not entirely free from complexities. It refers to action within widely varying situations, and connotes diverse motives within those situations: a child's obedience differs from a soldier's obedience, or the love, honor, and *obey* of the marriage vow. However, a consistent behavioral relationship is indicated in most uses of the term: in the act of obeying, a person does what another person tells him to do. Y obeys X if he carries out the prescription for action which X has addressed to him; the term suggests, moreover, that some form of dominance-subordination, or hierarchical element, is part of the situation in which the transaction between X and Y occurs.

A subject who complies with the entire series of experimental commands will be termed an *obedient* subject; one who at any point in the command series defies the experimenter will be called a *disobedient* or *defiant* subject. As used in this report, the terms refer only to the subject's performance in the experiment, and do not necessarily imply a general personality disposition to submit to or reject authority.

SUBJECT POPULATION

The subjects used in all experimental conditions were male adults, residing in the greater New Haven and Bridgeport areas, aged 20 to 50 years, and engaged in a wide variety of occupations. Each experimental condition described in this report employed 40 fresh subjects and was carefully balanced for age and occupational types. The occupational composition for each experiment was: workers, skilled and unskilled: 40 per cent; white collar, sales, business: 40 per cent; professionals: 20 per cent. The occupations were intersected with three age categories (subjects in 20s, 30s, and 40s, assigned to each condition in the proportions of 20, 40, and 40 per cent respectively).

THE GENERAL LABORATORY PROCEDURE[4]

The focus of the study concerns the amount of electric shock a subject is willing to administer to another person when ordered by an experimenter to give the 'victim'

---

from the victim, preclude such understanding.) Moreover, cooperation implies status parity for the co-acting agents, and neglects the asymmetrical, dominance-subordination element prominent in the laboratory relationship between experimenter and subject. *Conformity* has been used in other important contexts in social psychology, and most frequently refers to imitating the judgements or actions of others when no explicit requirement for imitation has been made. Furthermore, in the present study there are two sources of social pressure: pressure from the experimenter issuing the commands, and pressure from the victim to stop the punishment. It is the pitting of a common man (the victim) against an authority (the experimenter) that is the distinctive feature of the conflict. At a point in the experiment the victim demands that he be let free. The experimenter insists that the subject continue to administer shocks. Which act of the subject can be interpreted as conformity? The subject may conform to the wishes of his peer or to the wishes of the experimenter, and conformity in one direction means the absence of conformity in the other. Thus the word has no useful reference in this setting, for the dual and conflicting social pressures cancel out its meaning.

In the final analysis, the linguistic symbol representing the subject's action must take its meaning from the concrete context in which that action occurs; and there is probably no word in everyday language that covers the experimental situation exactly, without omissions or irrelevant connotations. It is partly for convenience, therefore, that the terms *obey* and *disobey* are used to describe the subject's actions. At the same time, our use of the words is highly congruent with dictionary meaning.

[4] A more detailed account of the laboratory procedure can be found in Milgram (1963). A similar and independently evolved experimental procedure, employing a shock generator, victim, and learning

increasingly more severe punishment. The act of administering shock is set in the context of a learning experiment, ostensibly designed to study the effect of punishment on memory. Aside from the experimenter, one naïve subject and one accomplice perform in each session. On arrival each subject is paid $4.50. After a general talk by the experimenter, telling how little scientists know about the effect of punishment on memory, subjects are informed that one member of the pair will serve as teacher and one as learner. A rigged drawing is held so that the naïve subject is always the teacher, and the accomplice becomes the learner. The learner is taken to an adjacent room and strapped into an 'electric chair'.

The naïve subject is told that it is his task to teach the learner a list of paired associates, to test him on the list, and to administer punishment whenever the learner errs in the test. Punishment takes the form of electric shock, delivered to the learner by means of a shock generator controlled by the naïve subject. The teacher is instructed to increase the intensity of electric shock one step on the generator on each error. The learner, according to plan, provides many wrong answers, so that before long the naïve subject must give him the strongest shock on the generator. Increases in shock level are met by increasingly insistent demands from the learner that the experiment be stopped because of the growing discomfort to him. However, in clear terms the experimenter orders the teacher to continue with the procedure in disregard of the learner's protests. *Thus, the naïve subject must resolve a conflict between two mutually incompatible demands from the social field. He may continue to follow the orders of the experimenter and shock the learner with increasing severity, or he may refuse to follow the orders of the experimenter and heed the learner's pleas. The experimenter's authority operates not in a free field, but against ever-mounting countervailing pressures from the person being punished.*

A few technical points need to be considered before the findings of the study are described. For the purpose of delivering shock, a simulated shock generator is used, with 30 clearly marked voltage levels that range from 15 to 450 volts (and each activated by one of 30 individual lever switches set in a horizontal line). The naïve subject is given a sample shock of 45 volts to convince him of the authenticity of the instrument. The generator bears verbal designations that range from 'Slight Shock' to 'Danger: Severe Shock.'

The responses of the victim are standardized on tape, and each protest is coordinated to a particular voltage level on the shock generator. Starting with 75 volts the learner begins to grunt and moan. At 150 volts he demands to be let out of the experiment. At 180 volts he cries out that he can no longer stand the pain. At 300 volts he refuses to provide any more answers to the memory test, insisting that he is no longer a participant in the experiment and must be freed. In response to this tactic, the experimenter instructs the naïve subject to treat the absence of an answer as equivalent to a wrong answer, and to follow the usual shock procedure. The experimenter reinforces his demand with the statement: 'You have no other choice, you must go on!' (This imperative is used whenever the naïve subject tries to break off the experiment.) If the subject refuses to give the next higher level of shock, the experiment is considered at an end. A quantitative value is

---

task, was reported by Buss (1961). Buss used the technique for studying aggression, not obedience, and did not make use of the fundamental measure employed in the present study: break-off points. His investigation promises to be a useful complement to the present research.

assigned to the subject's performance based on the maximum intensity shock he administered before breaking off. Thus any subject's score may range from zero (for a subject unwilling to administer the first shock level) to 30 (for a subject who proceeds to the highest voltage level on the board). For any particular subject and for any particular experimental condition the degree to which participants have followed the experimenter's orders may be specified with a numerical value, corresponding to the metric on the shock generator.

This laboratory situation gives us a framework in which to study the subject's reactions to the principal conflict of the experiment. Again, this conflict is between the experimenter's demands that he continue to administer the electric shock, and the learner's demands, which become increasingly more insistent, that the experiment be stopped. The crux of the study is to vary systematically the factors believed to alter the degree of obedience to the experimental commands, to learn under what conditions submission to authority is most probable, and under what conditions defiance is brought to the fore.

PILOT STUDIES

Pilot studies for the present research were completed in the winter of 1960; they differed from the regular experiments in a few details: for one, the victim was placed behind a silvered glass, with the light balance on the glass such that the victim could be dimly perceived by the subject (Milgram, 1961).

Though essentially qualitative in treatment, these studies pointed to several significant features of the experimental situation. At first no vocal feedback was used from the victim. It was thought that the verbal and voltage designations on the control panel would create sufficient pressure to curtail the subject's obedience. However, this was not the case. In the absence of protests from the learner, virtually all subjects, once commanded, went blithely to the end of the board, seemingly indifferent to the verbal designations ('Extreme Shock' and 'Danger: Severe Shock'). This deprived us of an adequate basis for scaling obedient tendencies. A force had to be introduced that would strengthen the subject's resistance to the experimenter's commands, and reveal individual differences in terms of a distribution of break-off points.

This force took the form of protests from the victim. Initially, mild protests were used, but proved inadequate. Subsequently, more vehement protests were inserted into the experimental procedure. To our consternation, even the strongest protests from the victim did not prevent all subjects from administering the harshest punishment ordered by the experimenter; but the protests did lower the mean maximum shock somewhat and created some spread in the subject's performance; therefore, the victim's cries were standardized on tape and incorporated into the regular experimental procedure.

The situation did more than highlight the technical difficulties of finding a workable experimental procedure: it indicated that subjects would obey authority to a greater extent than we had supposed. It also pointed to the importance of feedback from the victim in controlling the subject's behavior.

One further aspect of the pilot study was that subjects frequently averted their eyes from the person they were shocking, often turning their heads in an awkward and conspicuous manner. One subject explained: 'I didn't want to see the consequences of what I had done.' Observers wrote:

> ... subjects showed a reluctance to look at the victim, whom they could see through the glass in front of them. When this fact was brought to their attention they indicated that it caused them discomfort to see the victim in agony. We note, however, that although the subject refuses to look at the victim, he continues to administer shocks.

This suggested that the salience of the victim may have, in some degree, regulated the subject's performance. If, in obeying the experimenter, the subject found it necessary to avoid scrutiny of the victim, would the converse be true? If the victim were rendered increasingly more salient to the subject, would obedience diminish? The first set of regular experiments was designed to answer this question.

IMMEDIACY OF THE VICTIM

This series consisted of four experimental conditions. In each condition the victim was brought 'psychologically' closer to the subject giving his shocks.

In the first condition (Remote Feedback) the victim was placed in another room and could not be heard or seen by the subject, except that, at 300 volts, he pounded on the wall in protest. After 315 volts he no longer answered or was heard from.

The second condition (Voice Feedback) was identical to the first except that voice protests were introduced. As in the first condition the victim was placed in an adjacent room, but his complaints could be heard clearly through a door left slightly ajar, and through the walls of the laboratory.[5]

---

[5]It is difficult to convey on the printed page the full tenor of the victim's responses, for we have no adequate notation for vocal intensity, timing, and general qualities of delivery. Yet these features are crucial to producing the effect of an increasingly severe reaction to mounting voltage levels. (They can be communicated fully only by sending interested parties the recorded tapes.) In general terms, however, the victim indicates no discomfort until the 75-volt shock is administered, at which time there is a light grunt in response to the punishment. Similar reactions follow the 90- and 105-volt shocks, and at 120 volts the victim shouts to the experimenter that the shocks are becoming painful. Painful groans are heard on administration of the 135-volt shock, and at 150 volts the victim cries out, 'Experimenter, get me out of here! I won't be in the experiment any more! I refuse to go on!' Cries of this type continue with generally rising intensity, so that at 180 volts the victim cries out, 'I can't stand the pain', and by 270 volts his response to the shock is definitely an agonized scream. Throughout, he insists that he be let out of the experiment. At 300 volts the victim shouts in desperation that he will no longer provide answers to the memory test; and at 315 volts, after a violent scream, he reaffirms with vehemence that he is no longer a participant. From this point on, he provides no answers, but shrieks in agony whenever a shock is administered; this continues through 450 volts. Of course, many subjects will have broken off before this point.

A revised and stronger set of protests was used in all experiments outside the Proximity series. Naturally, new baseline measures were established for all comparisons using the new set of protests.

There is overwhelming evidence that the great majority of subjects, both obedient and defiant, accepted the victims' reactions as genuine. The evidence takes the form of: (a) tension created in the subjects (see discussion of tension); (b) scores on 'estimated pain' scales filled out by subjects immediately after the experiment; (c) subjects' accounts of their feelings in post-experimental interviews; and (d) quantifiable responses to questionnaires distributed to subjects several months after their participation in the experiments. This matter will be treated fully in a forthcoming monograph.

(The procedure in all experimental conditions was to have the naïve subject announce the voltage level before administering each shock, so that—independently of the victim's responses—he was continually reminded of delivering punishment of ever-increasing severity.)

The third experimental condition (Proximity) was similar to the second, except that the victim was placed in the same room as the subject, and $1\frac{1}{2}$ feet from him. Thus he was visible as well as audible, and voice cues were provided.

The fourth, and final, condition of this series (Touch-Proximity) was identical to the third, with this exception: the victim received a shock only when his hand rested on a shockplate. At the 150-volt level the victim again demanded to be let free and, in this condition, refused to place his hand on the shockplate. The experimenter ordered the naïve subject to force the victim's hand onto the plate. Thus obedience in this condition required that the subject have physical contact with the victim in order to give him punishment beyond the 150-volt level.

Forty adult subjects were studied in each condition. The data revealed that obedience was significantly reduced as the victim was rendered more immediate to the subject. The mean maximum shock for the conditions is shown in Figure 1.

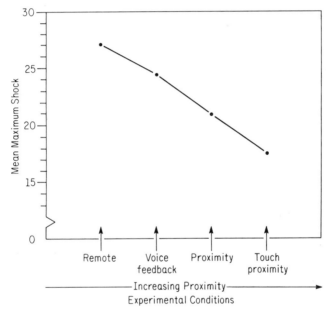

Figure 1. Mean maxima in proximity series.

Expressed in terms of the proportion of obedient to defiant subjects, the findings are that 34 per cent of the subjects defied the experimenter in the Remote condition, 37.5 per cent in Voice Feedback, 60 per cent in Proximity, and 70 per cent in Touch-Proximity.

How are we to account for this effect? A first conjecture might be that as the victim was brought closer the subject became more aware of the intensity of his suffering and regulated his behavior accordingly. This makes sense, but our evidence does not support the interpretation. There are no consistent differences in the attributed level of pain across the four conditions (i.e. the amount of pain experienced by the victim as estimated by the subject and expressed on a 14-point scale). But it is easy to speculate about alternative mechanisms:

Empathetic cues. In the Remote and to a lesser extent the Voice Feedback condition, the victim's suffering possesses an abstract, remote quality for the subject. He is aware, but only in a conceptual sense, that his actions cause pain to another person; the fact is apprehended, but not felt. The phenomenon is common enough. The bombardier can reasonably suppose that his weapons will inflict suffering and death, yet this knowledge is divested of affect, and does not move him to a felt, emotional response to the suffering resulting from his actions. Similar observations have been made in wartime. It is possible that the visual cues associated with the victim's suffering trigger empathic responses in the subject and provide him with a more complete grasp of the victims experience. Or it is possible that the empathic responses are themselves unpleasant, possessing drive properties which cause the subject to terminate the arousal situation. Diminishing obedience, then, would be explained by the enrichment of empathic cues in the successive experimental conditions.

Denial and narrowing of the cognitive field. The Remote condition allows a narrowing of the cognitive field so that the victim is put out of mind. The subject no longer considers the act of depressing a lever relevant to moral judgement, for it is no longer associated with the victim's suffering. When the victim is close it is more difficult to exclude him phenomenologically. He necessarily intrudes on the subject's awareness since he is continuously visible. In the Remote conditions his existence and reactions are made known only after the shock has been administered. The auditory feedback is sporadic and discontinuous. In the Proximity conditions his inclusion in the immediate visual field renders him a continuously salient element for the subject. The mechanism of denial can no longer be brought into play. One subject in the Remote condition said: 'It's funny how you really begin to forget that there's a guy out there, even though you can hear him. For a long time I just concentrated on pressing the switches and reading the words.'

Reciprocal fields. If in the Proximity condition the subject is in an improved position to observe the victim, the reverse is also true. The actions of the subject now come under proximal scrutiny by the victim. Possibly, it is easier to harm a person when he is unable to observe our actions than when he can see what we are doing. His surveillance of the action directed against him may give rise to shame, or guilt, which may then serve to curtail the action. Many expressions of language refer to the discomfort or inhibitions that arise in face-to-face confrontation. It is often said that it is easier to criticize a man 'behind his back' than to 'attack him to his face'. If we are in the process of lying to a person it is reputedly difficult to 'stare him in the eye'. We 'turn away from others in shame' or in 'embarrassment' and this action serves to reduce our discomfort. The manifest function of allowing the victim of a firing squad to be blindfolded is to make the occasion less stressful for him, but it may also serve a latent function of reducing the stress of the executioner. In short, in the Proximity conditions, the subject may sense that he has become more salient in the victim's field of awareness. Possibly he becomes more self-conscious, embarrassed, and inhibited in his punishment of the victim.

Phenomenal unity of act. In the Remote conditions it is more difficult for the subject to gain a sense of *relatedness* between his own actions and the consequences of these actions for the victim. There is a physical and spatial separation of the act and its consequences. The subject depresses a lever in one room, and protests and cries are heard from another. The two events are in correlation, yet they lack a compelling phenomenological unity. The structure of a meaningful act—*I am hurting a man*—breaks down because of the spatial arrangements, in a manner somewhat analogous to the disappearance of phi phenomena when the blinking lights are spaced too far apart. The unity is more fully achieved in the Proximity conditions as the victim is brought closer to the action that causes him pain. It is rendered complete in Touch-Proximity.

Incipient group formation. Placing the victim in another room not only takes him further from the subject, but the subject and the experimenter are drawn relatively closer. There is incipient group formation between the experimenter and the subject, from which the victim is excluded. The wall between the victim and the others deprives him of an intimacy which the experimenter and subject feel. In the Remote condition, the victim is truly an outsider, who stands alone, physically and psychologically.

When the victim is placed close to the subject, it becomes easier to form an alliance with him against the experimenter. Subjects no longer have to face the experimenter alone. They have an ally who is close at hand and eager to collaborate in a revolt against the experimenter. Thus, the changing set of spatial relations leads to a potentially shifting set of alliances over the several experimental conditions.

Acquired behavior dispositions. It is commonly observed that laboratory mice will rarely fight with their litter mates. Scott (1958) explains this in terms of passive inhibition. He writes: 'By doing nothing under . . . circumstances [the animal] learns to do nothing, and this may be spoken of as passive inhibition . . . this principle has great importance in teaching an individual to be peaceful, for it means that he can learn not to fight simply by not fighting.' Similarly, we may learn not to harm others simply by not harming them in everyday life. Yet this learning occurs in a context of proximal relations with others, and may not be generalized to that situation in which the person is physically removed from us. Or possibly, in the past, aggressive actions against others who were physically close resulted in retaliatory punishment which extinguished the original form of response. In contrast, aggression against others at a distance may have only sporadically led to retaliation. Thus the organism learns that it is safer to be aggressive toward others at a distance, and precarious to be so when the parties are within arm's reach. Through a pattern of rewards and punishments, he acquires a disposition to avoid aggression at close quarters, a disposition which does not extend to harming others at a distance. And this may account for experimental findings in the remote and proximal experiments.

Proximity as a variable in psychological research has received far less attention than it deserves. If men were sessile it would be easy to understand this neglect. But we move about; our spatial relations shift from one situation to the next, and the fact that we are near or remote may have a powerful effect on the psychological processes that mediate our behavior toward others. In the present situation, as the victim is brought closer to the man ordered to give him shocks, increasing numbers of subjects break off the experiment, refusing to obey. The concrete, visible, and proximal presence of the victim acts in an important way to counteract the experimenter's power and to generate disobedience.[6]

[6] Admittedly, the terms *proximity*, *immediacy*, *closeness*, and *salience-of-the-victim* are used in a loose sense, and the experiments themselves represent a very coarse treatment of the variable. Further experiments are needed to refine the notion and tease out such diverse factors as spatial distance, visibility, audibility, barrier interposition, etc.

The Proximity and Touch-Proximity experiments were the only conditions where we were unable to use taped feedback from the victim. Instead, the victim was trained to respond in these conditions as he had in Experiment 2 (which employed taped feedback). Some improvement is possible here, for it should be technically feasible to do a proximity series using taped feedback.

CLOSENESS OF AUTHORITY

If the spatial relationship of the subject and victim is relevant to the degree of obedience, would not the relationship of subject to experimenter also play a part?

There are reasons to feel that, on arrival, the subject is oriented primarily to the experimenter rather than to the victim. He has come to the laboratory to fit into the structure that the experimenter—not the victim—would provide. He has come less to understand his behavior than to *reveal* that behavior to a competent scientist, and he is willing to display himself as the scientist's purposes require. Most subjects seem quite concerned about the appearance they are making before the experimenter, and one could argue that this preoccupation in a relatively new and strange setting makes the subject somewhat insensitive to the triadic nature of the social situation. In other words, the subject is so concerned about the show he is putting on for the experimenter that influences from other parts of the social field do not receive as much weight as they ordinarily would. This overdetermined orientation to the experimenter would account for the relative insensitivity of the subject to the victim, and would also lead us to believe that alterations in the relationship between subject and experimenter would have important consequences for obedience.

In a series of experiments we varied the physical closeness and degree of surveillance of the experimenter. In one condition the experimenter sat just a few feet away from the subject. In a second condition, after giving initial instructions, the experimenter left the laboratory and gave his orders by telephone; in still a third condition the experimenter was never seen, providing instructions by means of a tape recording activated when the subjects entered the laboratory.

Obedience dropped sharply as the experimenter was physically removed from the laboratory. The number of obedient subjects in the first condition (Experimenter Present) was almost three times as great as in the second, where the experimenter gave his orders by telephone. Twenty-six subjects were fully obedient in the first condition, and only 9 in the second (Chi square obedient *vs.* defiant in the two conditions, 1 d.f. = 14.7; $p < 001$). Subjects seemed able to take a far stronger stand against the experimenter when they did not have to encounter him face to face, and the experimenter's power over the subject was severely curtailed.[7]

Moreover, when the experimenter was absent, subjects displayed an interesting form of behavior that had not occurred under his surveillance. Though continuing with the experiment, several subjects administered lower shocks than were required and never informed the experimenter of their deviation from the correct procedure. (Unknown to the subjects, shock levels were automatically recorded by an Esterline-Angus event recorder wired directly into the shock generator; the instrument provided us with an objective record of the subjects' performance.) Indeed, in telephone conversations some subjects specifically assured the experimenter that they were raising the shock level according to instruction, whereas in fact they were repeatedly using the lowest shock on the board. This form of behavior is particularly interesting: although these subjects acted in a way that clearly undermined the avowed purposes of the experiment, they found it

---

[7]The third condition also led to significantly lower obedience than this first situation, in which the experimenter was present, but it contains technical difficulties that require extensive discussion.

easier to handle the conflict in this manner than to precipitate an open break with authority.

Other conditions were completed in which the experimenter was absent during the first segment of the experiment, but reappeared at the point that the subject definitely refused to give higher shocks when commanded by telephone. Although he had exhausted his power via telephone, the experimenter could frequently force further obedience when he reappeared in the laboratory.

Experiments in this series show that the physical *presence* of an authority is an important force contributing to the subject's obedience or defiance. Taken together with the first experimental series on the proximity of the victim, it would appear that something akin to fields of force, diminishing in effectiveness with increasing psychological distance from their source, have a controlling effect on the subject's performance. As the victim is brought closer, the subject finds it harder to administer shocks to him. When the victim's position is held constant relative to the subject, and the authority is made more remote, the subject finds it easier to break off the experiment. This effect is substantial in both cases, but manipulation of the experimenter's position yielded the more powerful results. Obedience to destructive commands is highly dependent on the proximal relations between authority and subject.

TENSIONS

The description of final scores does not fully convey the character of the subjects' performance, and it would be useful to interrupt our reporting of quantitative relationships to remark on the subjects' general reaction to the situation.

One might suppose that a subject would simply break off or continue as his conscience and temperament dictated. Yet this is very far from what happened. There were powerful reactions of tension and emotional strain in a substantial proportion of the participants. Persons were observed to sweat, tremble, stutter, bite their lips, and groan as they found themselves increasingly implicated in the experimental conflict. Some sense of the subjects' mood can be gotten from a transcript of their remarks at break-off point. Here are the remarks of two defiant subjects:

> Is he banging? . . . Is he hurt out there? Well, I don't want to be responsible for anything that happens to him. No, I can't go on with it. I don't know whether he's all right or not. I mean he may have a heart condition or something; I wouldn't feel right doing it. He's banging for help. He's evidently in trouble or he wouldn't bang . . . I don't see any sense to this—to knocking him out or something. I just can't see it.

> *(Subject refuses to administer shocks)*   [*Subject 0108*]

> The man is banging. He wants to get out . . . I'm sorry. If the man wants to get out I'd just as soon stop . . . I don't want to administer any more [extremely excited] . . . I will gladly refund the check, but I will not harm this man . . . I'm sorry, I will not give him any more if he obviously wants to get out. There is no money in the world that will make me hurt another individual. [*Subject 010X*]

And here is a transcript from an obedient subject. He began the experiment calmly, but became increasingly tense as the experiment proceeded. After administering 150-volt shock, he began to address the experimenter in agitated tones:

150 volts delivered. You want me to keep going?
165 volts delivered. That guy is hollering in there. There's a lot of them here. He's liable to have heart condition. You want me to go?
180 volts delivered. He can't stand it! I'm not going to kill that man in there! You hear him hollering? He's hollering. He can't stand it. What if something happens to him? . . . I'm not going to get that man sick in there. He's hollering in there. You know what I mean? I mean I refuse to take responsibility. He's getting hurt in there. He's in there hollering. Too many left here. Geez, if he gets them wrong. There's too many of them left. I mean who is going to take responsibility if anything happens to that gentleman?
[*The experimenter accepts responsibility.*] All right.
195 volts delivered. You see he's hollering. Hear that. Gee, I don't know. [*The experimenter says: 'The experiment requires that you go on.'*]—I know it does, sir, but I mean—hugh—he don't know what he's in for. He's up to 195 volts.
210 volts delivered
225 volts delivered
240 volts delivered. Aw, no. You mean I've got to keep going up with the scale? No sir. I'm not going to kill that man! I'm not going to give him 450 volts! [*The experimenter says: 'The experiment requires that you go on.'*]—I know it does, but that man is hollering in there, sir . . .

Despite his numerous, agitated objections, which were constant accompaniments to his actions, the subject unfailingly obeyed the experimenter, proceeding to the highest shock level on the generator. He displayed a curious dissociation between word and action. Although at the verbal level he had resolved not to go on, his actions were fully in accord with the experimenter's commands. This subject did not want to shock the victim, and he found it an extremely disagreeable task, but he was unable to invent a response that would free him from *E*'s authority. Many subjects cannot find the specific verbal formula that would enable them to reject the role assigned to them by the experimenter. Perhaps our culture does not provide adequate models for disobedience.

One puzzling sign of tension was the regular occurrence of nervous laughing fits. In the first four conditions 71 of the 160 subjects showed definite signs of nervous laughter and smiling. The laughter seemed entirely out of place, even bizarre. Full-blown, uncontrollable seizures were observed for 15 of these subjects. On one occasion we observed a seizure so violently convulsive that it was necessary to call a halt to the experiment. In the post-experimental interviews subjects took pains to point out that they were not sadistic types and that the laughter did not mean they enjoyed shocking the victim.

In the interview following the experiment subjects were asked to indicate on a 14-point scale just how nervous or tense they felt at the point of maximum tension. Figure 2 shows the self-reports on 'tension and nervousness' for 137 subjects in the Proximity experiments. Subjects were given a scale with 14 values ranging from 'Not at all tense and nervous' to 'Extremely tense and nervous'. They were instructed: 'Thinking back to that point in the experiment when you felt the most tense and nervous, indicate just how you felt by placing an X at the appropriate point on the scale.' The results are shown in terms of mid-point values. The scale ranged from 'Not at all tense and nervous' to 'Extremely tense and nervous'. Self-reports of this sort are of limited precision, and at best provide only a rough indication of the subject's emotional response. Still, taking the reports for what they are worth, it can be seen that the distribution of responses spans the entire range of the scale, with the majority of subjects con-

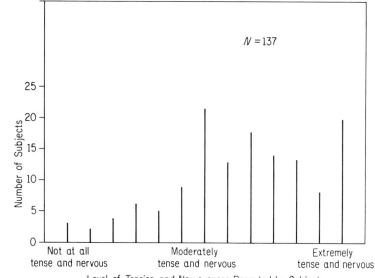

Figure 2. Level of tension and nervousness.

centrated at the center and upper extreme. A further breakdown showed that obedient subjects reported themselves as having been slightly more tense and nervous than the defiant subjects at the point of maximum tension.

How is the occurrence of tension to be interpreted? First, it points to the presence of conflict. If a tendency to comply with authority were the only psychological force operating in the situation, all subjects would have continued to the end and there would have been no tension. Tension, it is assumed, results from the simultaneous presence of two or more incompatible response tendencies (Miller, 1944). If sympathetic concern for the victim were the exclusive force, all subjects would have calmly defied the experimenter. Instead, there were both obedient and defiant outcomes, frequently accompanied by extreme tension. A conflict develops between the deeply ingrained disposition not to harm others and the equally compelling tendency to obey others who are in authority. The subject is quickly drawn into a dilemma of a deeply dynamic character, and the presence of high tension points to the considerable strength of each of the antagonistic vectors.

Moreover, tension defines the strength of the aversive state from which the subject is unable to escape through disobedience. When a person is uncomfortable, tense, or stressed, he tries to take some action that will allow him to terminate this unpleasant state. Thus tension may serve as a drive that leads to escape behavior. But in the present situation even where tension is extreme, many subjects are unable to perform the response that will bring about relief. Therefore there must be a competing drive, tendency, or inhibition that precludes activation of the disobedient response. The strength of this inhibiting factor must be of greater magnitude than the stress experienced, else the terminating act would occur. Every evidence of extreme tension is at the same time an indication of the strength of the forces that keep the subject in the situation.

Finally, tension may be taken as evidence of the reality of the situations for the subjects. Normal subjects do not tremble and sweat unless they are implicated in a deep and genuinely felt predicament.

BACKGROUND AUTHORITY

In psychophysics, animal learning, and other branches of psychology, the fact that measures are obtained at one institution rather than another is irrelevant to the interpretation of the findings, so long as the technical facilities for measurement are adequate and the operations are carried out with competence.

But it cannot be assumed that this holds true for the present study. The effectiveness of the experimenter's commands may depend in an important way on the larger institutional context in which they are issued. The experiments described thus far were conducted at Yale University, an organization which most subjects regarded with respect and sometimes awe. In post-experimental interviews several participants remarked that the locale and sponsorship of the study gave them confidence in the integrity, competence, and benign purposes of the personnel; many indicate that they would not have shocked the learner if the experiments had been done elsewhere.

This issue of background authority seemed to us important for an interpretation of the results that had been obtained thus far; moreover it is highly relevant to any comprehensive theory of human obedience. Consider, for example, how closely our compliance with the imperatives of others is tied to particular institutions and locales in our day-to-day activities. On request, we expose our throats to a man with a razor blade in the barber shop, but would not do so in a shoe store; in the latter setting, we willingly follow the clerk's request to stand in our stockinged feet, but resist the command in a bank. In the laboratory of a great university, subjects may comply with a set of commands that would be resisted if given elsewhere. *One must always question the relationship of obedience to a person's sense of the context in which he is operating.*

To explore the problem we moved our apparatus to an office building in industrial Bridgeport and replicated experimental conditions, without any visible tie to the university.

Bridgeport subjects were invited to the experiment through a mail circular similar to the one used in the Yale study, with appropriate changes in letterhead, etc. As in the earlier study, subjects were paid $4.50 for coming to the laboratory. The same age and occupational distributions used at Yale, and the identical personnel, were employed.

The purpose in relocating in Bridgeport was to assure a complete dissociation from Yale, and in this regard we were fully successful. On the surface, the study appeared to be conducted by RESEARCH ASSOCIATES OF BRIDGEPORT, an organization of unknown character (the title had been concoted exclusively for use in this study).

The experiments were conducted in a three-room office suite in a somewhat run-down commercial building located in the downtown shopping area. The laboratory was sparsely furnished, though clean, and marginally respectable in appearance. When subjects inquired about professional affiliations, they were informed only that we were a private firm conducting research for industry.

Some subjects displayed skepticism concerning the motives of the Bridgeport experimenter. One gentleman gave us a written account of the thoughts he experienced at the control board:

> ... Should I quit this damn test? Maybe he passed out? What dopes we were not to check up on this deal. How do we know that these guys are legit? No furniture, bare walls, no telephone. We could of called the Police up or the Better Business Bureau. I learned a lesson tonight. How do I know that Mr. Williams [the experimenter] is telling the truth ... I wish I knew how many volts a person could take before lapsing into unconsciousness ...
>
> [*Subject 2414*]

Another subject stated:

> I questioned on my arrival my own judgment [about coming]. I had doubts as to the legitimacy of the operation and the consequences of participation. I felt it was a heartless way to conduct memory or learning processes on human beings and certainly dangerous without the presence of a medical doctor.
>
> [*Subject 2440 V*]

There was no noticeable reduction in tension for the Bridgeport subjects. And the subjects' estimation of the amount of pain felt by the victim was slightly, though not significantly, higher than in the Yale study.

A failure to obtain complete obedience in Bridgeport would indicate that the extreme compliance found in New Haven subjects was tied closely to the background authority of Yale University; if a large proportion of the subjects remained fully obedient, very different conclusions would be called for.

As it turned out, the level of obedience in Bridgeport, although somewhat reduced, was not significantly lower than that obtained at Yale. A large proportion of the Bridgeport subjects were fully obedient to the experimenter's commands (48 per cent of the Bridgeport subjects delivered the maximum shock *vs.* 65 per cent in the corresponding condition at Yale).

How are these findings to be interpreted? It is possible that if commands of a potentially harmful or destructive sort are to be perceived as legitimate they must occur within some sort of institutional structure. But it is clear from the study that it need not be a particularly reputable or distinguished institution. The Bridgeport experiments were conducted by an unimpressive firm lacking any credentials; the laboratory was set up in a respectable office building with title listed in the building directory. Beyond that, there was no evidence of benevolence or competence. It is possible that the *category* of institution, judged according to its professed function, rather than its qualitative position within that category, wins our compliance. Persons deposit money in elegant, but also in seedy-looking banks, without giving much thought to the differences in security they offer. Similarly, our subjects may consider one laboratory to be as competent as another, so long as it *is* a scientific laboratory.

It would be valuable to study the subjects' performance in other contexts which go even further than the Bridgeport study in denying institutional support to the experimenter. It is possible that, beyond a certain point, obedience disappears completely. But that point had not been reached in the Bridgeport office: almost half the subjects obeyed the experimenter fully.

FURTHER EXPERIMENTS

We may mention briefly some additional experiments undertaken in the Yale series. A considerable amount of obedience and defiance in everyday life occurs in connexion with groups. And we had reason to feel in the light of many group studies already done in psychology that group forces would have a profound effect on reactions to authority. A series of experiments was run to examine these effects. In all cases only one naïve subject was studied per hour, but he performed in the midst of actors who, unknown to him, were employed by the experimenter. In one experiment (Groups for Disobedience) two actors broke off in the middle of the experiment. In another condition the actors followed the orders obediently; this strengthened the experimenter's power only slightly. In still a third experiment the job of pushing the switch to shock the learner was given to one of the actors, while the naïve subject performed a subsidiary act. We wanted to see how the teacher would respond if he were involved in the situation but did not actually give the shocks. In this situation only three subjects out of forty broke off. In a final group experiment the subjects themselves determined the shock level they were going to use. Two actors suggested higher and higher shock levels; some subjects insisted, despite group pressure, that the shock level be kept low; others followed along with the group.

Further experiments were completed using women as subjects, as well as a set of dealing with the effects of dual, unsanctioned, and conflicting authority. A final experiment concerned the personal relationship between victim and subject. These will have to be described elsewhere, lest the present report be extended to monographic length.

It goes without saying that future research can proceed in many different directions. What kinds of response from the victim are most effective in causing disobedience in the subject? Perhaps passive resistance is more effective than vehement protest. What conditions of entry into an authority system lead to greater or lesser obedience? What is the effect of anonymity and masking on the subject's behavior? What conditions lead to the subject's perception of responsibility for his own actions? Each of these could be a major research topic in itself, and can readily be incorporated into the general experimental procedure described here.

LEVELS OF OBEDIENCE AND DEFIANCE

One general finding that merits attention is the high level of obedience manifested in the experimental situation. Subjects often expressed deep disapproval of shocking a man in the face of his objections, and others denounced it as senseless and stupid. Yet many subjects complied even while they protested. The proportion of obedient subjects greatly exceeded the expectations of the experimenter and his colleagues. At the outset, we had conjectured that subjects would not, in general, go above the level of 'Strong Shock'. In practice, many subjects were willing to administer the most extreme shock available when commanded by the experimenter. For some subjects the experiment provides an occasion for aggressive release. And for others it demonstrates the extent to which obedient dispositions are deeply ingrained, and are engaged irrespective of their consequences for others. Yet this is not the whole story. Somehow, the subject becomes implicated in a situation from which he cannot disengage himself.

The departure of the experimental results from intelligent expectation, to some extent, has been formalized. The procedure was to describe the experimental situation in concrete detail to a group of competent persons, and to ask them to predict the performance of 100 hypothetical subjects. For purposes of indicating the distribution of break-off points judges were provided with a diagram of the shock generator, and recorded their predictions before being informed of the actual results. Judges typically underestimated the amount of obedience demonstrated by subjects.

In Figure 3, we compare the predictions of forty psychiatrists at a leading medical school with the actual performance of subjects in the experiment. The psychiatrists predicted that most subjects would not go beyond the tenth shock level (150 volts; at this point the victim makes his first explicit demand to be freed). They further predicted that by the twentieth shock level (300 volts; the victim refuses to answer) 3.73 per cent of the subjects would still be obedient; and that only a little over one-tenth of one per cent of the subjects would administer the highest shock on the board. But, as the graph indicates, the obtained behavior was very different. Sixty-two per cent of the subjects obeyed the experimenter's commands fully. Between expectation and occurrence there is a whopping discrepancy.

Why did the psychiatrists underestimate the level of obedience? Possibly, because their predictions were based on an inadequate conception of the determinants of human action, a conception that focuses on motives *in vacuo*. This orientation may be entirely

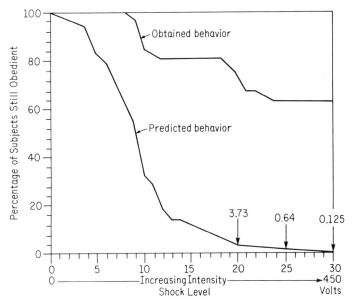

Figure 3. Predicted and obtained behavior in voice feedback.

adequate for the repair of bruised impulses as revealed on the psychiatrist's couch, but as soon as our interest turns to action in larger settings, attention must be paid to the situations in which motives are expressed. A situation exerts an important press on the individual. It exercises constraints and may provide push. In certain circumstances it is not so much the kind of person a man is, as the kind of situation in which he is placed, that determines his actions.

Many people, not knowing much about the experiment, claim that subjects who go to the end of the board are sadistic. Nothing could be more foolish as an overall character-ization of these persons. It is like saying that a person thrown into a swift-flowing stream is necessarily a fast swimmer, or that he has great stamina because he moves so rapidly relative to the bank. The context of action must always be considered. The individual, upon entering the laboratory, becomes integrated into a situation that carries its own momentum. The subject's problem then is how to become disengaged from a situation which is moving in an altogether ugly direction.

The fact that disengagement is so difficult testifies to the potency of the forces that keep the subject at the control board. Are these forces to be conceptualized as individual motives and expressed in the language of personality dynamics, or are they to be seen as the effects of social structure and pressures arising from the situational field?

A full understanding of the subject's action will, I feel, require that both perspectives be adopted. The person brings to the laboratory enduring dispositions toward authority and aggression, and at the same time he becomes enmeshed in a social structure that is no less an objective fact of the case. From the standpoint of personality theory one may ask: What mechanisms of personality enable a person to transfer responsibility to authority? What are the motives underlying obedient and disobedient performance? Does orientation to authority lead to a short-circuiting of the shame-guilt system? What cognitive and emotional defenses are brought into play in the case of obedient and defiant subjects?

The present experiments are not, however, directed toward an exploration of the motives engaged when the subject obeys the experimenter's commands. Instead, they examine the situational variables responsible for the elicitation of obedience. Elsewhere, we have attempted to spell out some of the structural properties of the experimental situation that account for high obedience, and this analysis need not be repeated here (Milgram, 1963). The experimental variations themselves represent our attempt to probe that structure, by systematically changing it and noting the consequences for behavior. It is clear that some situations produce greater compliance with the experimenter's com-mands than others. However, this does not necessarily imply an increase or decrease in the strength of any single definable motive. Situations producing the greatest obedience could do so by triggering the most powerful, yet perhaps the most idiosyncratic, of motives in each subject confronted by the setting. Or they may simply recruit a greater number and variety of motives in their service. But whatever the motives involved—and it is far from certain that they can ever be known—action may be studied as a direct function of the situation in which it occurs. This has been the approach of the present study, where we sought to plot behavioral regularities against manipulated properties of the social field. Ultimately, social psychology would like to have a compelling *theory of situations* which will, first, present a language in terms of which situations can be defined; proceed to a typology of situations; and then point to the manner in which definable properties of situations are transformed into psychological forces in the individual.

POSTSCRIPT

Almost a thousand adults were individually studied in the obedience research, and there were many specific conclusions regarding the variables that control obedience and disobedience to authority. Some of these have been discussed briefly in the preceding sections, and more detailed reports will be released subsequently.

There are now some other generalizations I should like to make, which do not derive in any strictly logical fashion from the experiments as carried out, but which, I feel, ought to be made. They are formulations of an intuitive sort that have been forced on me by observations of many subjects responding to the pressures of authority. The assertions represent a painful alteration in my own thinking; and since they were acquired only under the repeated impact of direct observation, I have no illusion that they will be generally accepted by persons who have not had the same experience.

With numbing regularity good people were seen to knuckle under the demands of authority and perform actions that were callous and severe. Men who are in everyday life responsible and decent were seduced by the trappings of authority, by the control of their perceptions, and by the uncritical acceptance of the experimenter's definition of the situation, into performing harsh acts.

What is the limit of such obedience? At many points we attempted to establish a boundary. Cries from the victim were inserted; not good enough. The victim claimed heart trouble; subjects still shocked him on command. The victim pleaded that he be let free, and his answers no longer registered on the signal box; subjects continued to shock him. At the outset we had not conceived that such drastic procedures would be needed to generate disobedience, and each step was added only as the ineffectiveness of the earlier techniques became clear. The final effort to establish a limit was the Touch-Proximity condition. But the very first subject in this condition subdued the victim on command, and proceeded to the highest shock level. A quarter of the subjects in this condition performed similarly.

The results, as seen and felt in the laboratory, are to this author disturbing. They raise the possibility that human nature, or—more specifically—the kind of character produced in American democratic society, cannot be counted on to insulate its citizens from brutality and inhumane treatment at the direction of malevolent authority. A substantial proportion of people do what they are told to do, irrespective of the content of the act and without limitations of conscience, so long as they perceive that the command comes from a legitimate authority. If in this study an anonymous experimenter could successfully command adults to subdue a fifty-year-old man, and force on him painful electric shocks against his protests, one can only wonder what government, with its vastly greater authority and prestige, can command of its subjects. There is, of course, the extremely important question of whether malevolent political institutions could or would arise in American society. The present research contributes nothing to this issue.

In an article titled 'The Dangers of Obedience', Harold J. Laski wrote:

> . . . civilization means, above all, an unwillingness to inflict unnecessary pain. Within the ambit of that definition, those of us who heedlessly accept the commands of authority cannot yet claim to be civilized men.
> . . . Our business, if we desire to live a life, not utterly devoid of meaning and significance, is to accept nothing which contradicts our basic experience

merely because it comes to us from tradition or convention or authority. It may well be that we shall be wrong; but our self-expression is thwarted at the root unless the certainties we are asked to accept coincide with the certainties we experience. That is why the condition of freedom in any state is always a widespread and consistent skepticism of the canons upon which power insists.

REFERENCES

Buss, Arnold H. (1961). *The psychology of aggression.* New York and London: John Wiley.

Kierkegaard, S. (1843). *Fear and trembling.* English edition, Princeton: Princeton University Press, 1941.

Laski, Harold J. (1929). The dangers of obedience. *Harper's Monthly Magazine 159*, June, 1-10.

Milgram, S. (1961). Dynamics of obedience: experiments in social psychology. Mimeographed report, *National Science Foundation*, January 25.

Milgram, S. (1963). Behavioral study of obedience. *J. abnorm. soc. Psychol. 67*, 371-8.

Milgram, S. (1964), Issues in the study of obedience: a reply to Baumrind. *Amer. Psychol. 19*, 848-52.

Miller, N. E. (1944). Experimental studies of conflict. In J. McV. Hunt (Ed.), *Personality and the behavior disorders.* New York: Ronald Press.

Scott, J. P. (1958). *Aggression.* Chicago: University of Chicago Press.

＿ ・ ＿ ・ ＿ ・ ＿ ・ ＿ ・ ＿ ・ ＿ ・ ＿ ・ ＿ ・ ＿

JOHN R. P. FRENCH, JR.

*Field Theory of Social Power**

This formal theory is a small part of the later stages of a program of empirical research on social influence.[1] It tries to integrate previous findings into a logically consistent theory from which one can derive testable hypotheses to guide future research.[2] The more specific purpose of the theory is to explore the extent to which the influence process in groups can be explained in terms of patterns of interpersonal relations.

In discussing the effects of the majority on conformity by the individual deviate, Asch states, "The effects obtained are not the result of a summation of influences

*John R. P. French, Jr., "A Formal Theory of Social Power," *Psychological Review* 63 (1956): 181-194. Copyright 1956 by the American Psychological Association, and reproduced by permission.

[1] The work reported in this paper was financed in part by a grant from the Rockefeller Foundation and by a contract with the Group Psychology Branch of the Office of Naval Research.

[2] Similar current attempts to construct mathematical theories of social influence include unpublished papers by Ardie Lubin, by Harold Guetzkow and Herbert Simon, and by Solomon Goldberg.

proceeding from each member of the group; it is necessary to conceive the results as being relationally determined" (15, p. 186). Both Heider (18) and Newcomb (29) have treated patterns of opinion and of interpersonal relations as a single system of relations, though they have discussed only two-person groups. The present theory reduces the process of influence in N-person groups to a summation of interpersonal influences which takes into account three complex patterns of relations: (a) the power relations among members of the group, (b) the communication networks or patterns of interaction in the group, and (c) the relations among opinions within the group. Thus prepositions which have been conceptualized at the group level (e.g., that the strength of group standards increases with increasing cohesiveness of the group) are deduced from concepts at the interpersonal level.

The deductive power and the internal consistency of a mathematical model stem from a set of explicit definitions and postulates stated with enough precision so that one can apply the rules of logic. But the construction of theory by coordinating mathematical definitions and postulates to psychological constructs and assumptions leads to a dilemma: the very precision which gives power to the theory also tends to oversimplify it. For reasons of mathematical convenience one tends to make simple assumptions which so restrict the theory that it may seem unrealistic compared to the complexity observed in social behavior. Game theory, for example, describes certain aspects of how "the rational economic man" ought to behave, but actual economic behavior often departs widely from this simple ideal (20).

The present theory deals with this dilemma partly by utilizing a kind of mathematics, the theory of directed graphs, which does not require the making of precise quantitative assumptions about empirical variables.[3] In addition, the basic concepts and postulates of this theory were chosen to conform to the results of experiments on social influence. Frequently, however, our present knowledge was not adequate for making these choices in precise detail. At these points we attempted to choose postulates which would be essentially correct in their main outlines even though some details would have to be changed as new empirical knowledge accumulates. It is not surprising, therefore, that many of the theorems are quite similar to previous findings about influence on opinions and attitudes, even though no research has been done specifically to test this theory. Nevertheless we have intentionally oversimplified the process of social influence by omitting many important determinants and by making very restrictive assumptions about others. It seemed wise to start by examining the implications of a small number of postulates before proceeding to more complex theories.

THE MODEL

Following the theory of quasi-stationary equilibria of Lewin (23), changes in opinion, attitude, or judgment are conceptualized in terms of forces operating along a

---

[3] The theory of directed graphs, which is an extension of graph theory (16), has been studied by Frank Harary and Robert Norman with a view toward utilization by social scientists. A publication of this work is planned for the near future (17). The author is indebted to these mathematicians for specific help in proving the theorems of this theory as well as for their work on the theory of digraphs upon which it is based.

unidimensional continuum (5, 12). Social influences are coordinated to force fields induced by person A on person B; and the strength of these forces is assumed to vary with the power of A over B. The potential force field corresponding to this power relation will be actualized only if A communicates to B or interacts with him. When A expresses his opinion or argues for it in a way that influences B, then the force field operating on B has a central position corresponding to A's position along the continuum of opinion. All the forces operating on B are directed toward this central position, so B will tend to change his opinion in a direction which brings him closer to A. Similarly, other members, C, D, E, etc., who communicate to B may set up force fields on him with central positions correspondng to their own opinions. The actual changes in B's opinion will be in accordance with the resultant force from all these induced forces plus a force corresponding to his own resistance.

In order to derive the exact amount of influence that each member will have on the opinion of every other, let us assume that we are dealing with a unidimensional continuum of opinion which can be measured with a ratio scale. We might think, for example, of the classic experiment on social norms by Sherif (32), where the members of the group were asked to state their opinions about how many inches the light moved as they viewed the autokinetic effect. We shall denote the members of the group by A, B, C, . . . and their initial opinions by a, b, c, . . . respectively, where a is the distance of A's opinion from the zero point on the scale. The abscissa of Figure 1 shows such a scale

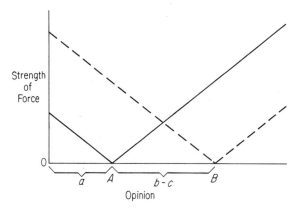

Figure 1. The force fields influencing opinion.

of opinion together with the initial opinions of A and B. The ordinate indicates the strength of the forces. The gradient of forces around A represents the forces he can induce on B to agree with his opinion, while the gradient of forces around B represents his tendency to resist changing his opinion. Where these two gradients intersect, a distance of $\frac{1}{2}(a + b)$ from the origin, there is an equilibrium point where the two forces are equal in strength and opposite in direction. At all points to the right of this equilibrium the forces induced by A are stronger than B's resistance, so B will move toward the point of equilibrium. Conversely, at all points to the left of the equilibrium, B's resistance forces are stronger than A's inductions, so B will still move toward the point of equilibrium. Similar calculations of the resultant force and consequent changes of opinion can be made for A and for groups with any number of members by placing all members on the same scale and by assuming that the gradient of forces around each member represents both forces he can induce on others and forces he can set up as resistance against others.

The process of influence in a group takes place gradually over a period of time. As one member changes his position and begins to influence others toward his new position, the force fields corresponding to his influence will also shift their central positions. It will be convenient, therefore, to divide the influence process into a sequence of units defined in terms of opinion change rather than in terms of physical time. A *unit* is defined as the time required for all members who are being influenced to shift their opinions to the point of equilibrium of all the forces operating at the beginning of that unit. At the end of the unit, after this shift has taken place, we assume that the members now start to argue for their new opinions. It should be noted that this definition implies that all members respond at the same rate to the forces impinging on them. One possible operational definition of a unit might be a single trial in an experiment such as Sherif's.

This conception of influence as a process over time implies a distinction between direct and indirect influence. In a typical organization the president usually influences indirectly a person at the bottom of the chain of command through orders which are handed down through several subordinates. *Direct* influence is exerted on another person by direct communication which is not channelled through a third person. *Indirect influence* is exerted on another through the medium of one or more other persons. Therefore the direct influence of A on B always occurs during the same unit, whereas indirect influence requires two or more units. For example, A influences B directly during the first unit, and B influences C toward his new opinion during the second unit. Thus A has indirectly influenced C by transmitting his opinion via B. In this model, the power structure and the communication channels of the group are translated into a process of influence over time. In the first unit any member, A, influences only those recipients of his communication over whom he has direct power; in the second unit A's influence is also transmitted to all those over whom these intermediaries have power; in the third unit A's influence is transmitted to those who are three steps removed from him in the power structure, etc.

THE POSTULATES

Three main postulates are involved in this model. The first is concerned with interpersonal power. The definition of *power* used in this postulate is the same as that given by Cartwright (6): the power of A over B (with respect to a given opinion) is equal to the maximum force which A can induce on B minus the maximum resisting force which B can mobilize in the opposite direction.

The *basis* of interpersonal power is defined as the more or less enduring relationship between A and B which gives rise to the power. French and Raven (in an unpublished manuscript) have discussed five bases: *attraction power* based on B's liking for A, *expert power* based on B's perception that A has superior knowledge and information, *reward power* based on A's ability to mediate rewards for B, *coercive power* based on A's ability to mediate punishments for B, and *legitimate power* based on B's belief that A has a right to prescribe his behavior or opinions. Any basis of power can vary in strength: there may be variations in how much B likes A, in how much B respects A's expertness, etc. Postulate 1 is general enough to refer to all bases of social power.

Postulate 1. For any given discrepancy of opinion between A and B, the strength of the resultant force which an inducer A can exert on an inducee B, in the direction of agreeing with A's opinion, is proportional to the strength of the bases of power of A over B.

Attraction as a basis for interpersonal influence has been demonstrated in experiments by Back (2) and by French and Snyder (13), and in field studies by Lippitt, Polansky, and Rosen (25). Expertness as a basis for interpersonal power has been demonstrated in the latter two studies as well as in many others (19, 27, 28). In unpublished experiments French and Raven and French, Levinger, and Morrison have demonstrated that legitimacy and the ability to punish are bases for social power. Heider (18) and Newcomb (29) state their theories in terms of "positive relations," a more general conception which combines several types of power. In most real groups the power relations probably do combine several of the bases discussed here and others too. Postulate 1 refers to all of these bases combined.

Resistance, as a part of the social power discussed in Postulate 1, has not been treated separately nor in detail in this model. In a further development it might be coordinated to such factors as "certainty of own opinion" (13), or as Kelman (21) and Mauser (26) call it, "prior reinforcement," and to various personality characteristics such as rigidity and authoritarianism (8).

Postulate 2. The strength of the force which an inducer A exerts on an inducee B, in the direction of agreeing with A's opinion, is proportional to the size of the discrepancy between their opinions.

This postulate combines two effects which have been demonstrated in previous research. (a) More influence is attempted toward the member who is more discrepant (10, 11, 30). These studies also show, however, that this effect holds only under conditions where the inducee is not rejected. Too great a deviation leads to changes in the attraction power structure of the group and hence to changes in the effects implied by Postulate 1. (b) If the amount of influence attempted is held constant, the amount of change in the inducee increases with increasing size of discrepancy. For this latter relation, French and Gyr (12) report correlations of .77, .62, .65, and .83 in different experimental groups. Goldberg (14) also reports a strong tendency for the amount of change to increase with increasing discrepancy, with the inducee moving 30 per cent of the way toward the inducer for discrepancies of all sizes. In a subsequent unpublished theoretical paper,[4] Goldberg also assumes that change in opinion is a direct function of discrepancy until the inducee rejects the credibility (expert power) of the inducer, after which it becomes an inverse function of discrepancy. Again the data support Postulate 2 within the range where the expert power structure of the group is not changed.

Postulate 2 is represented in Figure 1 by the two increasing gradients of forces around A's opinion and around B's opinion. The two gradients are assumed to be linear, though the evidence cited above would suggest that they are curvilinear. We have made

[4] S. C. Goldberg, Some cognitive aspects of social influence: a hypothesis. (Mimeographed.)

the more convenient assumption because it appears to be true as a first approximation and because it seems to be possible to revise the postulate later, if subsequent empirical data do show curvilinearity, with only minor quantitative changes in the theorems.

Postulate 3. In one unit, each person who is being influenced will change his opinion until he reaches the equilibrium point where the resultant force (of the forces induced by other members at the beginning of the unit and the resisting force corresponding to his own resistance to change) is equal to zero.

Postulate 3 is an application of a basic assumption of Lewin (22) that locomotion or restructuring will take place in the direction of the resultant force whenever that force is greater than zero. Though consistent with a great many empirical studies, this assumption is close to a conceptual definition which cannot be directly tested.

THEOREMS

For lack of space, no attempt will be made to state all the theorems which have been proven nor to give the formal proofs of those presented. Instead we will select some representative theorems and indicate informally the nature of the derivations. In making empirical predictions from these theorems, this theory, like any other, must always assume "other things being equal," including all extrasystem influences and the many factors within the group which are not part of the theory.

The Effects of the Power Structure of the Group

This section presents some theorems concerning the effects of the power structure of the group on the influence process and its outcome. These theorems illustrate how the present theory explains a well known proposition about groups in terms of concepts about interpersonal relations.

This proposition—that the strength of group standards increases with increasing cohesiveness of the group—has been substantiated in several studies (2, 4, 9, 30, 31). A group standard has been defined conceptually as group-induced pressures toward uniformity of behavior or belief, and it may be measured by the degree of conformity of members produced by these pressures. *Cohesiveness* has been defined conceptually as the resultant forces on members to belong to the group, but it has been operationalized in many of these experiments as the attraction of members for one another (7, 24). Festinger, Schachter, and Back (9) have shown that the hypothesized relation is stronger when cohesiveness is operationalized in a way which takes account of the pattern of the sociometric structure instead of a simple summation of choices. But each sociometric choice measuring the attraction of member *B* toward member *A* is, according to Postulate 1, a basis for *A*'s power over *B*. Thus the sociogram of a group can be transformed into the attraction power structure of the group by simply reversing the direction of each arrow. The attraction power structure of the group is a special type of power structure, and hence it is treated in these theorems about power structure and trends toward uniformity of opinion within the group.

The power structure of a group may be represented conceptually in terms of the mathematical theory of directed graphs, called "digraphs." A digraph is a finite set of points A, B, C, ... and a subset of the directed lines $\overrightarrow{AB}$, $\overrightarrow{BA}$, $\overrightarrow{AC}$, $\overrightarrow{CA}$, $\overrightarrow{BC}$, $\overrightarrow{CB}$, ... between distinct points. In representing power structures as digraphs, we shall coordinate points to members and directed lines to power relations between members. In this coordination we shall make only relatively crude distinctions in differences of power: if "A has power over B," there is a directed line $\overrightarrow{AB}$ in the digraph representing the power structure of the group; if "A does not have power over B," there is no such line.

Various properties of digraphs may be used to characterize power structures of groups. We shall be concerned here primarily with the "degree of connectedness" of power structures. In order to discuss this property we need two definitions: *complete digraph* and *directed path.* A digraph is complete if there exists a directed line from each point to every other point. A power structure would be complete, then, if each member had power over each other member. If we assume that when A chooses B sociometrically B has power over A, then it follows that when every member of a group chooses every other member, the digraph representing the power structure of the group will be complete (e.g., No. 5 in Figure 2). A *directed path* is a collection of distinct points A, B, C, ...,together with the lines $\overrightarrow{AB}$, $\overrightarrow{BC}$, ... If in the power structure of a group there is a directed path from A to C, it follows that A can exert influence on C even though A may not have direct power over C (there must be a sequence of directed lines originating at A and going to C even though there is no line $\overrightarrow{AC}$).

In their work on digraphs Harary and Norman (17) have defined four degrees of connectedness. Their definitions are as follows: (a) A digraph is *strongly connected* (or *strong*) if for every pair of distinct points, A and B, there exists a directed path from A to B *and* a directed path from B to A. It follows that every complete digraph is strong, but not every strong digraph is complete. (b) A digraph is *unilaterally connected* (or *unilateral*) if for every pair of points, A and B, there is a directed path from A to B *or* from B to A. (c) A digraph is *weakly connected* (or *weak*) if it is impossible to separate the points of the digraph into two classes such that no line of the digraph has one end point in one class and the other end point in the other class. Thus, for every possible separation of all of the points of a weak digraph into two disjoint, nonempty classes, there must be at least one line having one end point in one class and the other end point in the other class. (d) A digraph is *disconnected* if it is not weak. Thus a disconnected digraph may be separated into two (or more) disjoint classes of points such that no line goes from one class to the other. From these definitions it is clear that all strong digraphs are unilaterally and weakly connected and that all unilateral digraphs are weakly connected. It is also clear that all weak digraphs are *not* strongly connected. For this reason it is useful to define a digraph as *strictly unilateral* if it is unilateral but not strong, and to define a digraph as *strictly weak* if it is weak but not unilateral. In our discussion here, when we speak of unilateral or weak digraphs we shall mean "strictly unilateral" and "strictly weak."

In groups where each member communicates to all others over whom he has direct power during every unit of the influence process, the amount of uniformity and the speed of achieving it tend to vary with the degrees of connectedness of the power structure, except that no differences were proved for weak vs. disconnected graphs.

The effect is illustrated in Figure 2, and generalized later in the first four theorems. In Figure 2 five different types of structures (complete, strong, unilateral, weak, and

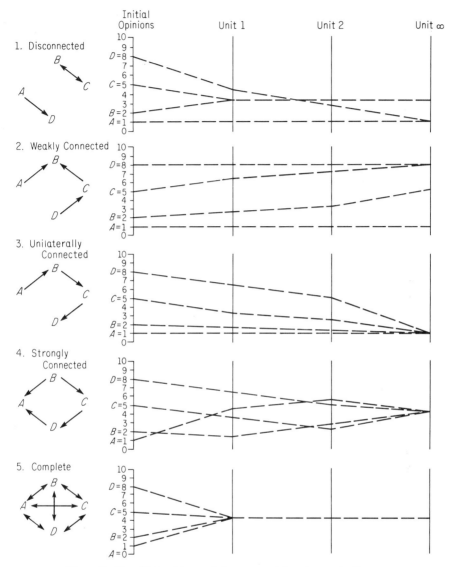

Figure 2. The effects of connectedness on opinion changes in the group.

disconnected) are illustrated by digraphs of four-person groups. To the right of each structure are curves showing some of the theoretically predicted changes of opinion. The ordinate gives the scale of opinion and, at the left, the initial opinion of members $A, B, C,$ and D. The line labeled "Unit 1" gives the distribution of opinion after the first unit; the line labeled "Unit 2" gives the distribution of opinion after the second unit; and the line labeled "Unit ∞" gives the equilibrium of opinions reached in an infinite number of units.

The disconnected structure is composed of two cliques, AD and BC. Between these two cliques there are no paths of influence, regardless of direction. Consequently neither clique can influence the other, and each will eventually end up with a different opinion. Within the *AD* clique, influence is all in one direction, so *A* will eventually swing *D* over to his opinion. Since *D* only moves half-way in each unit, however, he will require an infinite number of units to move all the way. Accordingly the dotted lines show *D*'s opinion converging to *A*'s at infinity while *A*'s opinion remains unchanged. Within the *BC* clique, influence is mutual, so in the first unit *B* will influence *C* to move half-way from 5 to 2 on the opinion scale, and likewise *C* will influence *B* to move half-way from 2 to 5. Therefore both *B* and *C* will arrive at $3\frac{1}{2}$ on the opinion scale in the first unit and will remain in agreement thereafter.

The weakly connected structure is more highly connected but still does not result in unanimous agreement. In this case there is no directed path, for example, between *A* and *D*, so neither can influence the other.

The unilaterally connected structure has a directed path in at least one direction between every possible pair of points. Because it has a higher degree of connectedness, it shows more convergence of opinion.

The strongly connected structure has directed paths in both directions between every possible pair of points. In this example the strongly connected digraph is a cycle, yielding a final common opinion which reflects more equal influence of all members.

The completely connected structure has direct, one-step paths in both directions between the members of every possible pair. It converges in only one unit to a final common opinion.

Theorem 1. For all possible patterns of initial opinion, in a completely connected power structure the opinions of all members will reach a common equilibrium level equal to the arithmetic mean of the initial opinions of all the members, and this final common opinion will be reached in one unit.

Under these conditions where the power and the resistance of all members is equal, we have already illustrated in Figure 1 that the new opinion of *A* is equal to $\frac{1}{2}(a + b)$, i.e., the arithmetic mean of the opinions of both members. *B*'s opinion at the end of the first unit b_1 is also equal to $\frac{1}{2}(a + b)$, according to Postulates 2 and 3. Thus this two-person group reaches agreement in one step. The proof of Theorem 1 for an *N*-person group is a simple extension of this example.

Theorem 2. In an *N*-person cycle (which is a strongly connected group) the members will reach a final common opinion at the arithmetic mean, $(1/N)(a + b + c + \ldots)$, in an infinite number of units.

If *A* has power over *B*, then $b_1 = \frac{1}{2}(a + b)$ and b_2, the opinion of *B* at the end of the second unit, $= \frac{1}{2}(a_1 + b_1)$. In general, *B*'s opinion at the end of any unit will be half-way between his own and *A*'s opinion at the beginning of the unit; so the general difference equation describing *B*'s change of opinion in any unit, *n*, is: $b_n = \frac{1}{2}(a_{n-1} + b_{n-1})$. Solving these general difference equations for all members constitutes a proof of Theorem 2.

Theorem 3. In a unilaterally connected group the opinions of all members will converge to a final common opinion in an infinite number of steps.

It is an obvious theorem of digraph theory that no strictly unilateral digraph can have more than one point of input zero, i.e., with no directed lines leading to it (because then these two or more points could not have a directed path between them—which violates the definition of a unilateral digraph). It follows that, during every unit, at least one of the two members at the extremes of the range of opinion will be subject to the power of another and will move toward the center, thus restricting the range of opinion still further. Eventually, therefore, all members will arrive at the same opinion. If there is one person in the group with input zero, then all members will eventually agree with his initial opinion, for he will influence the others but no one will influence him.

Theorem 4. In a weakly connected group the members will not reach common agreement except under special conditions in the distribution of initial opinions.

A (strictly) weak digraph contains at least one pair of points with no directed path between them. Thus there are at least two members who cannot influence each other either directly or indirectly.

The disconnected group. When the final equilibrium has been reached, a disconnected group will tend to have at least as many different opinions as there are cliques (i.e., disjoint classes of members), because no clique can influence any other. If all the cliques are themselves either completely connected, strongly connected, or unilaterally connected, it follows from Theorems 1, 2, and 3 that there will be uniformity of final opinions within each clique; but there will be differences among them except under special conditions in the distribution of initial opinion.

Summarizing the theorems illustrated in Figure 2, we can say that there is a "funnelling effect," a tendency for the opinions of individuals to converge toward one another, and the strength of this tendency increases with increasing connectedness in the power structure of the group. Since the power structure includes the special case of the attraction power of the group, we have a more general group of theorems consistent with the finding that the strength of group standards is determined by the cohesiveness of the group. Additionally the model predicts the exact level of the group standard as well as the precise degree of conformity at each unit. Thus we have rigorously derived a more differentiated statement of the empirically well-established relation between cohesiveness and group standards.

So far we have considered only all-or-none variations in the power of A over B; now we will illustrate the effect of continuous variation.

Theorem 5. The greater the bases of power of A over B (B's attraction to A, B's acceptance of A as an expert, etc.), the more influence A will have on B and subsequently on any other person P for whom there exists a directed path from B to P.

According to Postulates 1 and 3, increases in the basis of power of A over B will increase the strength of the resultant force exerted by A on B and therefore the amount of change produced in B. Similarly in subsequent units this influence will be transmitted, though in a weakened form, from B to P.

The Effects of Communication Patterns

In the preceding section we have dealt with the restricted case of groups of persons whose power is always utilized in every unit.[5] Earlier we noted that the head of an

---

[5]It is probable that B will respond partly to the *relationships* among successive influence attempts by A, for example to the consistency among his various arguments or to the simple fact of too much reiteration of the same influence attempt; these factors are omitted from the present model.

organization may not communicate to all those over whom he has direct power but will instead follow the established channels of communication. Likewise in a face-to-face group a member may remain silent or may attempt to influence some but not others over whom he has power. These patterns of interaction often become stabilized so that they may be treated as more or less consistent channels of communication. It is also clear that the strength of influence attempted can vary continuously, but we shall here treat the communication from A to B as an all-or-none variable so that we can utilize digraph theory.

Now if we reverse the conditions of Theorems 1 through 4 and consider only completely connected power structures with variations in the degree of connectedness of the communication channels, we can apply the same four theorems and proofs. For example:

Theorem 1a. For all possible patterns of initial opinion, in a completely connected communication network, the opinions of all members will converge to a common equilibrium level equal to the arithmetic mean of the initial opinions of all the members; and this final common opinion will be reached in one unit.

Similarly, theorems analogous to 2, 3, and 4 can be stated for strong, unilateral, and weak communication networks, respectively. All possible networks in experiments of the Bavelas type (3) are included in these theorems.

Even where stable communication channels do not exist, this model may be applied provided the interaction pattern is specified for each unit. Consider a strongly connected cycle of three persons. Theorem 2 states that opinions in this group will converge to a final common opinion equal to $\frac{1}{3}(a + b + c)$. In Theorem 6 we assume a particular communication pattern: A exerts influence in the first unit, B and C exert influence in the second unit, A exerts influence in the third unit, B and C in the fourth unit, and so on.

Theorem 6. In a group where the power structure is a three-person cycle in which A has power over B, B has power over C, and C has power over A, and the communication pattern is A, BC, A, BC, . . . , the final common opinion in the group equals $\frac{1}{5}(2a + b + 2c)$.

We note that a change in the interaction pattern changes the outcome considerably. Furthermore B and C no longer have equal influence, even though they have equal interaction patterns and similar positions in the power structure; it is the interaction of these two factors which produces the difference. A has more influence than B because he comes first in the sequence of interaction, but C has more influence than B because he has direct power over A whereas B's power over A is indirect. Intuitively it would appear that the "primary effect" shown in this theorem can be generalized: the sooner a person speaks the more influence he will have.

The Effects of Patterns of Opinion

In an experiment like Sherif's, each member communicates to every other and the members probably have relatively equal power. In such a completely connected power structure with completely connected communication channels, what happens to the opinion of a single deviate member?

Theorem 7. The amount of change of the deviate toward the opinions of the majority is proportional to the sum of the deviations of all other members from the deviate.

By Theorem 1 the amount of change by the deviate D equals $d_1 - d$ which is equal to $1/N(d + a + b + c + \ldots) - d$. Thus the more members in the group the more they will influence the deviate. Also the larger each deviation, the more D will change. Though these predictions are generally congruent with Asch's findings, they probably do not agree in detail (1, 15). However, the conditions of Asch's experiment do not fit the model very well.

Leadership

To a large extent leadership consists of a member's ability to influence others both directly and indirectly by virtue of his position in the power structure, including the structure of legitimate authority. Thus leadership may be distributed among many members or concentrated in a few; the pattern of leadership is a distribution which describes the whole group rather than an attribute of single individuals. Figure 2 illustrates the dependence of influence on the total structure of the group.

Compare the influence of member A in the weakly connected group with the influence of member A in the unilaterally connected group. Both groups start out with the same distribution of opinion, and in both groups A has direct influence over only B. However, A's influence is markedly different in the two cases; in the weakly connected group the opinions of others diverge more and more from his, whereas in the unilaterally connected group the opinion of all other members converges completely to A's opinion.

The complete distribution of direct plus indirect leadership in a group with any power structure and any communication network may be calculated by matrix multiplication.[6] We may represent the power structure of the group as a matrix where each row shows the power applied to a member and each column shows the power exerted by a member. A *zero* in the cell corresponding to the ath row and the bth column shows that B does not have power over A, wheras a *one* in the cell corresponding to the cth row and the dth column shows that D does have power over C. Thus the number in a cell represents the number of directed lines from the person in that column to the person in that row (under the conditions assumed in this paper, always *one* or *zero*). If this matrix M is multiplied by itself, then the resulting squared matrix M^2 shows in each cell the number of sequences consisting of two directed lines between the person in the column and the person in the row. The cubed Matrix M^3 shows the number of three-line sequences between each pair of persons. By raising the matrix to successively higher powers, we can thus determine the number of directed line sequences, of various lengths, from each member to every other. The matrix M gives the directed lines which will result in influence in the first unit; M^2 gives the two-line sequences through which influence will be exerted by the end of the second unit; M^3 gives the three-line sequences through which influence will be exerted by the end of the third unit; etc.

In order to apply this process to Group G in Figure 3, we construct a matrix of opinion M where the columns a, b, c, d represent influence exerted by the initial opinions a, b, c, d of persons A, B, C, D, respectively. The rows represent the influence received by these opinions from all the opinions in the group. Thus the cell entries must

---

[6] See Harary and Norman (16) for a brief review of some related applications of matrix algebra to sociometric data.

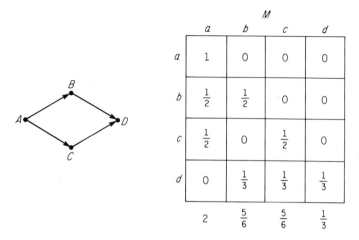

M

	a	b	c	d
a	1	0	0	0
b	$\frac{1}{2}$	$\frac{1}{2}$	0	0
c	$\frac{1}{2}$	0	$\frac{1}{2}$	0
d	0	$\frac{1}{3}$	$\frac{1}{3}$	$\frac{1}{3}$
	2	$\frac{5}{6}$	$\frac{5}{6}$	$\frac{1}{3}$

M^2

	a	b	c	d
a	1	0	0	0
b	$\frac{3}{4}$	$\frac{1}{4}$	0	0
c	$\frac{3}{4}$	0	$\frac{1}{4}$	0
d	$\frac{1}{3}$	$\frac{5}{18}$	$\frac{5}{18}$	$\frac{1}{9}$
	$2\frac{5}{6}$	$\frac{19}{36}$	$\frac{19}{36}$	$\frac{1}{9}$

M^3

	a	b	c	d
a	1	0	0	0
b	$\frac{7}{8}$	$\frac{1}{8}$	0	0
c	$\frac{7}{8}$	0	$\frac{1}{8}$	0
d	$\frac{11}{18}$	$\frac{19}{108}$	$\frac{19}{108}$	$\frac{1}{27}$
	$3\frac{13}{36}$	$\frac{65}{216}$	$\frac{65}{216}$	$\frac{1}{27}$

Figure 3. The distribution of leadership in a weakly connected group.

show the amount by which an opinion is changed by another opinion during one unit; and these values are given by the coefficients in the right hand side of the general difference equations. For Group G these equations are:

$$a_n = a_{n-1}, \tag{1}$$

$$b_n = \frac{1}{2}(a_{n-1} + b_{n-1}), \tag{2}$$

$$c_n = \frac{1}{2}(a_{n-1} + c_{n-1}), \tag{3}$$

$$d_n = \frac{1}{3}(b_{n-1} + c_{n-1} + d_{n-1}). \tag{4}$$

The cell a, a has an entry of 1, indicating that in any unit A's opinion is completely determined by his previous opinion; accordingly the remaining cells in row a have entries of zero, showing that opinions b, c, d do not influence a, since there are no directed paths from B, C, or D to A. Cells b, a, and b, b have entries of $\frac{1}{2}$ because b_n is a compromise half-way between the previous opinions of A and B, etc.

It will be noted that each row in M (and in M^2 and M^3) sums to 1 because it represents the total opinion of a member, and the fractions along the row represent the proportion of that opinion determined by each person. The sum of a column in M, on the other hand, represents the total influence of a person's opinion during the first unit on the opinions of all members (including the influence of his initial opinion on his second opinion—which we have called "resistance").

In M^2 the column sum shows the total influence of a person's initial opinion at the end of the second unit (including the changes produced in both the first and second units). Similarly M^3 shows the cumulative influence at the end of the third unit. The same procedure can obviously be extended to any number of units.

Thus the column totals of the successive powers of M give the distribution of leadership over time, as predicted by this theory. In Group G, we can see that A, the only member with input zero in the power structure, continuously increases his influence at the expense of the other members. B and C, having symmetrical positions in the structure, show the same curves of decreasing influence; but D, who is influenced by all other members, has the least influence.

CONCLUSIONS

This theory illustrates a way by which many complex phenomena about groups can be deduced from a few simple postulates about interpersonal relations. By the application of digraph theory we are able to treat in detail the *patterns of relations* whose importance has long been noted by the field theorists. Even if this treatment does not turn out to be empirically correct, it illustrates the need for some such conceptual and mathematical tools if we are to make progress toward the theoretical integration of psychology and sociology.

REFERENCES

1. Asch, S. E. *Social psychology*. New York: Prentice-Hall, 1952.
2. Back, K. W. Influence through social communication. *J. abnorm soc. Psychol.*, 1951, *46*, 9–23.
3. Bavelas, A. Communication patterns in task-oriented groups. In D. Cartwright & A. Zander (Eds.), *Group dynamics: research and theory.* Evanston: Row, Peterson, 1953.
4. Berkowitz, L. Group standards, cohesiveness, and productivity. *Hum. Relat.*, 1955, *7*, 509–519.
5. Biddle, B. J., French, J. R. P., Jr., & Moore, J. W. Some aspects of leadership in the small work group. *USAF Tech. Rep.* (Contract 33 [038] –14091), 1953.
6. Cartwright, D., *et al. Studies in social power.* Ann Arbor: Institute for Social Research, in press.
7. Cartwright, D., & Zander, A. *Group dynamics: research and theory.* Evanston: Row, Peterson, 1953.
8. Crutchfield, R. S. Conformity and character. *Amer. Psychologist*, 1955, *10*, 191–198.
9. Festinger, L., Schachter, S., & Back, K. *Social pressures in informal groups.* New York: Harper, 1950.
10. Festinger, L., & Thibaut, J. Interpersonal communication in small groups. *J. abnorm. soc. Psychol.*, 1951, *46*, 92–99.

11. Festinger, L., Gerard, H. B., Hymovitch, B., Kelley, H. H., & Raven, B. The influence process in the presence of extreme deviates. *Hum. Relat.*, 1952, *5*, 327–346.

12. French, J. R. P., Jr., & Gyr, J. Influence and role conformity. In D. Cartwright *et al.*, *Studies in social power.* Ann Arbor: Institute for Social Research, in press.

13. French, J. R. P., Jr., & Snyder, R. Leadership and interpersonal power. In D. Cartwright *et al.*, *Studies in social power.* Ann Arbor: Institute for Social Research, in press.

14. Goldberg, S. Three situational determinants of conformity to social norms. *J. abnorm. soc. Psychol.*, 1954, *49*, 325–329.

15. Guetzkow, H. (Ed.) *Groups, leadership and men.* Pittsburgh: Carnegie Press, 1951.

16. Harary, F., & Norman, R. Z. *Graph theory as a mathematical model in the social sciences.* Ann Arbor: Institute for Social Research, 1953.

17. Harary, F., Norman, R. Z., & Cartwright, D. *Introduction to digraph theory for social scientists.* Ann Arbor: Institute for Social Research, in press.

18. Heider, F. Attitudes and cognitive organization. *J. Psychol.*, 1946, *21*, 107–112.

19. Hovland, C., & Weiss, W. The influence of source credibility on communication effectiveness. *Publ. Opin. Quart.*, 1952, *15*, 635–650.

20. Katona, G. Rational behavior and economic behavior. *Psychol. Rev.*, 1953, *60*, 307–318.

21. Kelman, H. C. Effects of success and failure on "suggestibility" in the autokinetic situation. *J. abnorm. soc. Psychol.*, 1950, *45*, 267–285.

22. Lewin, K. The conceptual representation and measurement of psychological forces. *Contr. psychol. Theory*, 1938, *1*, 1–247.

23. Lewin, K. *Field theory in social science.* New York: Harper, 1951.

24. Libo, L. *The cohesiveness of groups.* Ann Arbor: Institute for Social Research, 1953.

25. Lippitt, R., Polansky, N., & Rosen, S. The dynamics of power. *Hum. Relat.*, 1952, *5*, 37–64.

26. Mausner, B. The effect of prior reinforcement on the interaction of observer pairs. *J. abnorm. soc. Psychol.*, 1954, *49*, 65–68.

27. Mausner, B. The effect of one partner's success or failure in a relevant task on the interaction of observer pairs. *J. abnorm. soc. Psychol.*, 1954, *49*, 557–560.

28. Moore, H. T. The comparative influence of majority and expert opinion. *Amer. J. Psychol.*, 1921, *32*, 16–20.

29. Newcomb, T. M. An approach to the study of communicative acts. *Psychol. Rev.*, 1953, *60*, 393–404.

30. Schachter, S. Deviation, rejection, and communication. *J. abnorm. soc. Psychol.*, 1951, *46*, 190–207.

31. Schachter, S., Ellertson, N., McBride, Dorothy, & Gregory, Doris. An experimental study of cohesiveness and productivity. *Hum. Relat.*, 1951, *4*, 229–238.

32. Sherif, M. A study of some social factors in perception. *Arch. Psychol.*, 1935, *27*, No. 187.

— · — · — · — · — · — · — · — · — · —

8 · ACHIEVEMENT MOTIVE

MAX WEBER

*Weber's Achievement Motive**

A glance at the occupational statistics of any country of mixed religious composition brings to light with remarkable frequency a situation which has several times provoked discussion in the Catholic press and literature, and in Catholic congresses in Germany, namely, the fact that business leaders and owners of capital, as well as the higher grades of skilled labour, and even more the higher technically and commercially trained person- nel of modern enterprises, are overwhelmingly Protestant. This is true not only in cases where the difference in religion coincides with one of nationality, and thus of cultural development, as in Eastern Germany between Germans and Poles. The same thing is shown in the figures of religious affiliation almost wherever capitalism, at the time of its great expansion, has had a free hand to alter the social distribution of the population in accordance with its needs, and to determine its occupational structure. The more freedom it has had, the more clearly is the effect shown. It is true that the greater relative participation of Protestants in the ownership of capital, in management, and the upper ranks of labour in great modern industrial and commercial enterprises, may in part be explained in terms of historical circumstances which extend far back into the past, and in which religious affiliation is not a cause of the economic conditions, but to a certain extent appears to be a result of them. Participation in the above economic functions usually involves some previous ownership of capital, and generally an expensive educa- tion; often both. These are to-day largely dependent on the possession of inherited wealth, or at least on a certain degree of material well-being. A number of those sections of the old Empire which were most highly developed economically and most favoured by natural resources and situation, in particular a majority of the wealthy towns, went over to Protestantism in the sixteenth century. The results of that circumstance favour the Protestants even to-day in their struggle for economic existence. There arises thus the historical question: why were the districts of highest economic development at the same time particularly favourable to a revolution in the Church? The answer is by no means so simple as one might think.

*Reprinted by permission of Charles Scribner's Sons from *The Protestant Ethic and the Spirit of Capitalism*, pp. 35-40 and 48-61, by Max Weber, translated by Talcott Parsons, 1958.

The emancipation from economic traditionalism appears, no doubt, to be a factor which would greatly strengthen the tendency to doubt the sanctity of the religious tradition, as of all traditional authorities. But it is necessary to note, what has often been forgotten, that the Reformation meant not the elimination of the Church's control over everyday life, but rather the substitution of a new form of control for the previous one. It meant the repudiation of a control which was very lax, at that time scarcely perceptible in practice, and hardly more than formal, in favour of a regulation of the whole of conduct which, penetrating to all departments of private and public life, was infinitely burdensome and earnestly enforced. The rule of the Catholic Church, "punishing the heretic, but indulgent to the sinner," as it was in the past even more than to-day, is now tolerated by peoples of thoroughly modern economic character, and was borne by the richest and economically most advanced peoples on earth at about the turn of the fifteenth century. The rule of Calvinism, on the other hand, as it was enforced in the sixteenth century in Geneva and in Scotland, at the turn of the sixteenth and seventeenth centuries in large parts of the Netherlands, in the seventeenth in New England, and for a time in England itself, would be for us the most absolutely unbearable form of ecclesiastical control of the individual which could possibly exist. That was exactly what large numbers of the old commercial aristocracy of those times, in Geneva as well as in Holland and England, felt about it. And what the reformers complained of in those areas of high economic development was not too much supervision of life on the part of the Church, but too little. Now how does it happen that at that time those countries which were most advanced economically, and within them the rising bourgeois middle classes, not only failed to resist this unexampled tyranny of Puritanism, but even developed a heroism in its defence? For bourgeois classes as such have seldom before and never since displayed heroism. It was "the last of our heroisms," as Carlyle, not without reason, has said.

But further, and especially important: it may be, as has been claimed, that the greater participation of Protestants in the positions of ownership and management in modern economic life may to-day be understood, in part at least, simply as a result of the greater material wealth they have inherited. But there are certain other phenomena which cannot be explained in the same way. Thus, to mention only a few facts: there is a great difference discoverable in Baden, in Bavaria, in Hungary, in the type of higher education which Catholic parents, as opposed to Protestant, give their children. That the percentage of Catholics among the students and graduates of higher educational institutions in general lags behind their proportion of the total population, may, to be sure, be largely explicable in terms of inherited differences of wealth. But among the Catholic graduates themselves the percentage of those graduating from the institutions preparing, in particular, for technical studies and industrial and commercial occupations, but in general from those preparing for middle-class business life, lags still farther behind the percentage of Protestants. On the other hand, Catholics prefer the sort of training which the humanistic Gymnasium affords. That is a circumstance to which the above explanation does not apply, but which, on the contrary, is one reason why so few Catholics are engaged in capitalistic enterprise.

Even more striking is a fact which partly explains the smaller proportion of Catholics among the skilled labourers of modern industry. It is well known that the factory has taken its skilled labour to a large extent from young men in the handicrafts; but this is much more true of Protestant than of Catholic journeymen. Among journeymen, in other words, the Catholics show a stronger propensity to remain in their crafts, that is they more often become master craftsmen, whereas the Protestants are attracted to a larger extent into the factories in order to fill the upper ranks of skilled labour and administrative positions. The explanation of these cases is undoubtedly that the mental and spiritual peculiarities acquired from the environment, here the type of education favoured by the religious atmosphere of the home community and the parental home, have determined the choice of occupation, and through it the professional career.

The smaller participation of Catholics in the modern business life of Germany is all the more striking because it runs counter to a tendency which has been observed at all times including the present. National or religious minorities which are in a position of subordination to a group of rulers are likely, through their voluntary or involuntary exclusion from positions of political influence, to be driven with peculiar force into economic activity. Their ablest members seek to satisfy the desire for recognition of their abilities in this field, since there is no opportunity in the service of the State. This has undoubtedly been true of the Poles in Russia and Eastern Prussia, who have without question been undergoing a more rapid economic advance than in Galicia, where they have been in the ascendant. It has in earlier times been true of the Huguenots in France under Louis XIV, the Nonconformists and Quakers in England, and, last but not least, the Jew for two thousand years. But the Catholics in Germany have shown no striking evidence of such a result of their position. In the past they have, unlike the Protestants, undergone no particularly prominent economic development in the times when they were persecuted or only tolerated, either in Holland or in England. On the other hand, it is a fact that the Protestants (especially certain branches of the movement to be fully discussed later) both as ruling classes and as ruled, both as majority and as minority, have shown a special tendency to develop economic rationalism which cannot be observed to the same extent among Catholics either in the one situation or in the other. Thus the principal explanation of this difference must be sought in the permanent intrinsic character of their religious beliefs, and not only in their temporary external historico-political situations.

If we try to determine the object, the analysis and historical explanation of which we are attempting, it cannot be in the form of a conceptual definition, but at least in the beginning only a provisional description of what is here meant by the spirit of capitalism. Such a description is, however, indispensable in order clearly to understand the object of the investigation. For this purpose we turn to a document of that spirit which contains what we are looking for in almost classical purity, and at the same time has the advantage of being free from all direct relationship to religion, being thus, for our purposes, free of preconceptions.

Remember, that *time* is money. He that can earn ten shillings a day by his labour, and goes abroad, or sits idle, one half of that day, though he spends but sixpence during his diversion or idleness, ought not to reckon *that* the only expense; he has really spent, or rather thrown away, five shillings besides.

Remember, that *credit* is money. If a man lets his money lie in my hands after it is due, he gives me the interest, or so much as I can make of it during that time. This amounts to a considerable sum where a man has good and large credit, and makes good use of it.

Remember, that money is of the prolific, generating nature. Money can beget money, and its offspring can beget more, and so on. Five shillings turned is six, turned again it is seven and threepence, and so on, till it becomes a hundred pounds. The more there is of it, the more it produces every turning, so that the profits rise quicker and quicker. He that kills a breeding-sow, destroys all her offspring to the thousandth generation. He that murders a crown, destroys all that it might have produced, even scores of pounds.

Remember this saying, *The good paymaster is lord of another man's purse.* He that is known to pay punctually and exactly to the time he promises, may at any time, and on any occasion, raise all the money his friends can spare. This is sometimes of great use. After industry and frugality, nothing contributes more to the raising of a young man in the world than punctuality and justice in all his dealings; therefore never keep borrowed money an hour beyond the time you promised, lest a disappointment shut up your friend's purse for ever.

The most trifling actions that affect a man's credit are to be regarded. The sound of your hammer at five in the morning, or eight at night, heard by a creditor, makes him easy six months longer; but if he sees you at a billiard-table, or hears your voice at a tavern, when you should be at work, he sends for his money the next day; demands it, before he can receive it, in a lump.

It shows, besides, that you are mindful of what you owe; it makes you appear a careful as well as an honest man, and that still increases your credit.

Beware of thinking all your own that you possess, and of living accordingly. It is a mistake that many people who have credit fall into. To prevent this, keep an exact account for some time both of your expenses and your income. If you take the pains at first to mention particulars, it will have this good effect: you will discover how wonderfully small, trifling expenses mount up to large sums, and will discern what might have been, and may for the future be saved, without occasioning any great inconvenience.

For six pounds a year you may have the use of one hundred pounds, provided you are a man of known prudence and honesty.

He that spends a groat a day idly, spends idly above six pounds a year, which is the price for the use of one hundred pounds.

He that wastes idly a groat's worth of his time per day, one day with another, wastes the privilege of using one hundred pounds each day.

He that idly loses five shillings' worth of time, loses five shillings, and might as prudently throw five shillings into the sea.

He that loses five shillings, not only loses that sum, but all the advantage that might be made by turning it in dealing, which by the time that a young man becomes old, will amount to a considerable sum of money.

It is Benjamin Franklin who preaches to us in these sentences, the same which Ferdinand Kürnberger satirizes in his clever and malicious *Picture of American Culture* as the supposed confession of faith of the Yankee. That it is the spirit of capitalism which here speaks in characteristic fashion, no one will doubt, however little we may wish to claim that everything which could be understood as pertaining to that spirit is contained in it. Let us pause a moment to consider this passage, the philosophy of which Kürnberger sums up in the words, "They make tallow out of cattle and money out of men." The peculiarity of this philosophy of avarice appears to be the ideal of the honest man of recognized credit, and above all the idea of a duty of the individual toward the increase of his capital, which is assumed as an end in itself. Truly what is here preached is not simply a means of making one's way in the world, but a peculiar ethic. The infraction of its rules is treated not as foolishness but as forgetfulness of duty. That is the essence of the matter. It is not mere business astuteness, that sort of thing is common enough, it is an ethos. *This* is the quality which interests us.

When Jacob Fugger, in speaking to a business associate who had retired and who wanted to persuade him to do the same, since he had made enough money and should let others have a chance, rejected that as pusillanimity and answered that "he (Fugger) thought otherwise, he wanted to make money as long as he could," the spirit of his statement is evidently quite different from that of Franklin. What in the former case was an expression of commercial daring and a personal inclination morally neutral, in the latter takes on the character of an ethically coloured maxim for the conduct of life. The concept spirit of capitalism is here used in this specific sense, it is the spirit of modern capitalism. For that we are here dealing only with Western European and American capitalism is obvious from the way in which the problem was stated. Capitalism existed in China, India, Babylon, in the classic world, and in the Middle Ages. But in all these cases, as we shall see, this particular ethos was lacking.

Now, all Franklin's moral attitudes are coloured with utilitarianism. Honesty is useful, because it assures credit; so are punctuality, industry, frugality, and that is the reason they are virtues. A logical deduction from this would be that where, for instance, the appearance of honesty serves the same purpose, that would suffice, and an unnecessary surplus of this virtue would evidently appear to Franklin's eyes as unproductive waste. And as a matter of fact, the story in his autobiography of his conversion to those virtues, or the discussion of the value of a strict maintenance of the appearance of modesty, the assiduous belittlement of one's own deserts in order to gain general recognition later, confirms this impression. According to Franklin, those virtues, like all others, are only in so far virtues as they are actually useful to the individual, and the surrogate of mere appearance is always sufficient when it accomplishes the end in view. It is a conclusion which is inevitable for strict utilitarianism. The impression of many Germans that the virtues professed by Americanism are pure hypocrisy seems to have been confirmed by this striking case. But in fact the matter is not by any means so simple. Benjamin Franklin's own character, as it appears in the really unusual candidness of his autobiography, belies that suspicion. The circumstance that he ascribes his recognition of the utility of virtue to a divine revelation which was intended to lead him in the path of righteousness, shows that something more than mere garnishing for purely egocentric motives is involved.

In fact, the *summum bonum* of this ethic, the earning of more and more money, combined with the strict avoidance of all spontaneous enjoyment of life, is above all completely devoid of any eudæmonistic, not to say hedonistic, admixture. It is thought of so purely as an end in itself, that from the point of view of the happiness of, or utility to, the single individual, it appears entirely transcendental and absolutely irrational. Man is dominated by the making of money, by acquisition as the ultimate purpose of his life. Economic acquisition is no longer subordinated to man as the means for the satisfaction of his material needs. This reversal of what we should call the natural relationship, so irrational from a naive point of view, is evidently as definitely a leading principle of capitalism as it is foreign to all peoples not under capitalistic influence. At the same time it expresses a type of feeling which is closely connected with certain religious ideas. If we thus ask, *why* should "money be made out of men," Benjamin Franklin himself, although he was a colourless deist, answers in his autobiography with a quotation from the Bible, which his strict Calvinistic father drummed into him again and again in his youth: "Seest thou a man diligent in his business? He shall stand before kings" (Prov. xxii. 29). The earning of money within the modern economic order is, so long as it is done legally, the result and the expression of virtue and proficiency in a calling; and this virtue and proficiency are, as it is now not difficult to see, the real Alpha and Omega of Franklin's ethic, as expressed in the passages we have quoted, as well as in all his works without exception.

And in truth this peculiar idea, so familiar to us to-day, but in reality so little a matter of course, of one's duty in a calling, is what is most characteristic of the social ethic of capitalistic culture, and is in a sense the fundamental basis of it. It is an obligation which the individual is supposed to feel and does feel towards the content of his professional activity, no matter in what it consists, in particular no matter whether it appears on the surface as a utilization of his personal powers, or only of his material possessions (as capital).

Of course, this conception has not appeared only under capitalistic conditions. On the contrary, we shall later trace its origins back to a time previous to the advent of capitalism. Still less, naturally, do we maintain that a conscious acceptance of these ethical maxims on the part of the individuals, entrepreneurs or labourers, in modern capitalistic enterprises, is a condition of the further existence of present-day capitalism. The capitalistic economy of the present day is an immense cosmos into which the individual is born, and which presents itself to him, at least as an individual, as an unalterable order of things in which he must live. It forces the individual, in so far as he is involved in the system of market relationships, to conform to capitalistic rules of action. The manufacturer who in the long run acts counter to these norms, will just as inevitably be eliminated from the economic scene as the worker who cannot or will not adapt himself to them will be thrown into the streets without a job.

Thus the capitalism of to-day, which has come to dominate economic life, educates and selects the economic subjects which it needs through a process of economic survival of the fittest. But here one can easily see the limits of the concept of selection as a means of historical explanation. In order that a manner of life so well adapted to the peculiarities of capitalism could be selected at all, i.e. should come to dominate others, it had to originate somewhere, and not in isolated individuals alone, but as a way of life common to whole groups of men. This origin is what really needs explanation. Concerning the doctrine of the more naïve historical materialism, that such ideas originate as a reflection or superstructure of economic situations, we shall speak more in detail below. At this point it will suffice for our purpose to call attention to the fact that without doubt, in the country of Benjamin Franklin's birth (Massachusetts), the spirit of capitalism (in the sense we have attached to it) was present before the capitalistic order. There were complaints of a peculiarly calculating sort of profit-seeking in New England, as distinguished from other parts of America, as early as 1632. It is further undoubted that capitalism remained far less developed in some of the neighbouring colonies, the later Southern States of the United States of America, in spite of the fact that these latter were founded by large capitalists for business motives, while the New England colonies were founded by preachers and seminary graduates with the help of small bourgeois, craftsmen and yeomen, for religious reasons. In this case the causal relation is certainly the reverse of that suggested by the materialistic standpoint.

But the origin and history of such ideas is much more complex than the theorists of the superstructure suppose. The spirit of capitalism, in the sense in which we are using the term, had to fight its way to supremacy against a whole world of hostile forces. A state of mind such as that expressed in the passages we have quoted from Franklin, and which called forth the applause of a whole people, would both in ancient times and in the Middle Ages have been proscribed as the lowest sort of avarice and as an attitude entirely lacking in self-respect. It is, in fact, still regularly thus looked upon by all those social groups which are least involved in or adapted to modern capitalistic conditions. This is not wholly because the instinct of acquisition was in those times unknown or undeveloped, as has often been said. Nor because the *auri sacra fames*, the greed for gold, was then, or now, less powerful outside of bourgeois capitalism than within its peculiar sphere, as the illusions of modern romanticists are wont to believe. The difference between the capitalistic and precapitalistic spirits is not to be found at this point. The greed of the Chinese Mandarin, the old Roman aristocrat, or the modern peasant, can stand up to any comparison. And the *auri sacra fames* of a Neapolitan cab-driver or *barcaiuolo*, and certainly of Asiatic representatives of similar trades, as well as of the craftsmen of southern European or Asiatic countries, is, as anyone can find out for himself, very much more intense, and especially more unscrupulous than that of, say, an Englishman in similar circumstances.

The universal reign of absolute unscrupulousness in the pursuit of selfish interests by the making of money has been a specific characteristic of precisely those countries whose bourgeois-capitalistic development, measured according to Occidental standards, has remained backward. As every employer knows, the lack of *coscienziosità* of the labourers of such countries, for instance Italy as compared with Germany, has been, and to a certain extent still is, one of the principal obstacles to their capitalistic development. Capitalism cannot make use of the labour of those who practise the doctrine of undisciplined *liberum arbitrium*, any more than it can make use of the business man who seems absolutely unscrupulous in his dealings with others, as we can learn from Franklin. Hence the difference does not lie in the degree of development of any impulse to make money. The *auri sacra fames* is as old as the history of man. But we shall see that those who submitted to it without reserve as an uncontrolled impulse, such as the Dutch sea-captain who "would go through hell for gain, even though he scorched his sails," were by no means the representatives of that attitude of mind from which the specifically modern capitalistic spirit as a mass phenomenon is derived, and that is what matters. At all periods of history, wherever it was possible, there has been ruthless acquisition, bound to no ethical norms whatever. Like war and piracy, trade has often been unrestrained in its relations with foreigners and those outside the group. The double ethic has permitted here what was forbidden in dealings among brothers.

Capitalistic acquisition as an adventure has been at home in all types of economic society which have known trade with the use of money and which have offered it opportunities, through *commenda*, farming of taxes, State loans, financing of wars, ducal courts and officeholders. Likewise the inner attitude of the adventurer, which laughs at all ethical limitations, has been universal. Absolute and conscious ruthlessness in acquisition has often stood in the closest connection with the strictest conformity to tradition. Moreover, with the breakdown of tradition and the more or less complete extension of free economic enterprise, even to within the social group, the new thing has not generally been ethically justified and encouraged, but only tolerated as a fact. And this fact has been treated either as ethically indifferent or as reprehensible, but unfortunately unavoidable. This has not only been the normal attitude of all ethical teachings, but, what is more important, also that expressed in the practical action of the average man of pre-capitalistic times, pre-capitalistic in the sense that the rational utilization of capital in a permanent enterprise and the rational capitalistic organization of labour had not yet become dominant forces in the determination of economic activity. Now just this attitude was one of the strongest inner obstacles which the adaptation of men to the conditions of an ordered bourgeois-capitalistic economy has encountered everywhere.

The most important opponent with which the spirit of capitalism, in the sense of a definite standard of life claiming ethical sanction, has had to struggle, was that type of attitude and reaction to new situations which we may designate as traditionalism. In this case also every attempt at a final definition must be held in abeyance. On the other hand, we must try to make the provisional meaning clear by citing a few cases. We will begin from below, with the labourers.

One of the technical means which the modern employer uses in order to secure the greatest possible amount of work from his men is the device of piece-rates. In agriculture, for instance, the gathering of the harvest is a case where the greatest possible intensity of labour is called for, since, the weather being uncertain, the difference between high profit and heavy loss may depend on the speed with which the harvesting can be done. Hence a system of piece-rates is almost universal in this case. And since the interest of the employer in a speeding-up of harvesting increases with the increase of the results and the intensity of the work, the attempt has again and again been made, by increasing the piece-rates of the workmen, thereby giving them an opportunity to earn what is for them a very high wage, to interest them in increasing their own efficiency. But a peculiar difficulty has been met with surprising frequency: raising the piece-rates has often had the result that not more but less has been accomplished in the same time, because the worker reacted to the increase not by increasing but by decreasing the amount of his work. A man, for instance, who at the rate of 1 mark per acre mowed $2\frac{1}{2}$ acres per day and earned $2\frac{1}{2}$ marks, when the rate was raised to 1.25 marks per acre mowed, not 3 acres, as he might easily have done, thus earning 3.75 marks, but only 2 acres, so that he could still earn the $2\frac{1}{2}$ marks to which he was accustomed. The opportunity of earning more was less attractive than that of working less. He did not ask: how much can I earn in a day if I do as much work as possible? but: how much must I work in order to earn the wage, $2\frac{1}{2}$ marks, which I earned before and which takes care of my traditional needs? This is an example of what is here meant by traditionalism. A man does not "by nature" wish to earn more and more money, but simply to live as he is accustomed to live and to earn as much as is necessary for that purpose. Wherever modern capitalism has begun its work of increasing the productivity of human labour by increasing its intensity, it has encountered the immensely stubborn resistance of this leading trait of pre-capitalistic labour. And to-day it encounters it the more, the more backward (from a capitalistic point of view) the labouring forces are with which it has to deal.

Another obvious possibility, to return to our example, since the appeal to the acquisitive instinct through higher wage-rates failed, would have been to try the opposite policy, to force the worker by reduction of his wage-rates to work harder to earn the same amount than he did before. Low wages and high profits seem even to-day to a superficial observer to stand in correlation; everything which is paid out in wages seems to involve a corresponding reduction of profits. That road capitalism has taken again and again since its beginning. For centuries it was an article of faith, that low wages were productive, i.e. that they increased the material results of labour so that, as Pieter de la Cour, on this point, as we shall see, quite in the spirit of the old Calvinism, said long ago, the people only work because and so long as they are poor.

— · — · — · — · — · — · — · — · — · — · — · —

DAVID C. McCLELLAND

*Key Hypothesis**

FORMING THE KEY HYPOTHESIS: THE EFFECTS OF THE PROTESTANT REFORMATION ON *n* ACHIEVEMENT (NEED ACHIEVEMENT)

While research findings of the sort just described might well have suggested our key hypothesis, it was actually a study by Winterbottom (1953) which first pointed to a possible link between achievement motivation and economic development. She was interested in trying to discover how parents, or more particularly mothers, produced a strong interest in achievement in their sons. She first obtained *n* Achievement scores on a group of 29 eight-year-old boys and then conducted interviews to determine if the mothers of the "highs" had different attitudes toward bringing up children. What she found was that mothers of the "highs" expected their sons to master earlier such activities as the following (see also Table 9.1):

> Know his way around the city
> Be active and energetic
> Try hard for things for himself
> Make his own friends
> Do well in competition

*From *The Achieving Society* by David C. McClelland, Copyright © 1961 by Litton Educational Publishing, Inc.

Furthermore, the mothers of the "lows" reported more restrictions: they did not want their sons to play with children not approved by the parents, nor did they want them to make important decisions by themselves. The picture here is reasonably clear. The mothers of the sons with high n Achievement have set higher standards for their sons: they expect self-reliance and mastery at an earlier age. (Winterbottom, 1958, pp. 468–472.)

An interesting historical parallel suggested itself. As we have seen, the German sociologist Max Weber (1904) described in convincing detail how the Protestant Reformation produced a new character type which infused a more vigorous spirit into the attitude of both workers and entrepreneurs and which ultimately resulted in the development of modern industrial capitalism. If the Protestant Reformation represented a shift toward self-reliance training and the new "capitalistic spirit" an increased n Achievement, then the relationship found by Winterbottom may have been duplicated at a societal level in the history of Western Europe. The accompanying diagram shows the parallel.

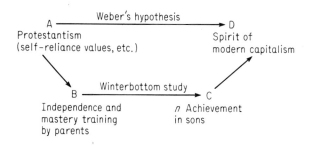

That is, the Winterbottom study suggests a psychological means by which the historical development described by Weber may have come about. The Protestant Reformation might have led to earlier independence and mastery training, which led to greater n Achievement, which in turn led to the rise of modern capitalism. Certainly, Weber's description of the kind of personality type which the Protestant Reformation produced is startlingly similar to the picture we have drawn of a person with high achievement motivation. He notes that Protestant working girls seemed to work harder and longer, that they saved their money for long-range goals, that Protestant entrepreneurs rose to the top more often in the business world despite the initial advantages of wealth many Catholic families on the Continent had. In particular, he points out that the early Calvinist businessman was prevented by his religious views from enjoying the results of his labors. He could not spend money on himself because of scruples about self-indulgence and display, and so, more often than not, he re-invested his profits in his business, which was one reason he prospered. What, then, drove him to such prodigious feats of business organization and development? Weber feels that such a man "gets nothing out of his wealth for himself, except the irrational sense of having done his job well." (Weber, 1904, p. 71.) This is exactly how we define the achievement motive in coding for it in fantasy.

In explaining how such men were produced more often by Protestantism, Weber felt that it was the intrinsic character of their religious beliefs that counted and not their particular political or economic circumstances, since these varied so much from country to country. In particular he stressed two factors: (1) the Protestant insistence on the importance of man's "calling" which meant that man's primary responsibility was to do his best at whatever God had assigned him in life, rather than to withdraw from the world and devote himself entirely to God, as the Catholic Church had taught as a counsel of perfection, and (2) the "rationalization" of all of life introduced into the Protestant ethic particularly by Calvin's notion of predestination. The early Protestants had been particularly offended by the sale of indulgences and had turned against the notion that "good works" could help a man "purchase" salvation. In his sermon *On Christian Liberty*, Luther thundered that a man could be good works from the top of his head to the tip of his toe and still not enter into heaven. Calvin argued that the decision as to who were the "elect" had already been made by God and that no amount of good works on earth could alter the decision. As Weber points out, this still left the practical problem for the ordinary believer of discovering whether he was one of the "elect" or not. Only by trying *in every particular* to be like someone in the Bible who was obviously one of the elect could he hope to get rid of the fear that he was damned forever. Thus, the average Protestant had to behave well in every respect, not, as Weber points out, as a "technical means of purchasing salvation, but of getting rid of the fear of damnation. . . . In practice this means that God helps those who help themselves. Thus the Calvinist, as it is sometimes put, himself creates his own salvation, or, as would be more correct, the conviction of it. But this creation cannot, as in Catholicism, consist in a gradual accumulation of individual good works to one's credit, but rather in a systematic self-control which at every moment stands before the inexorable alternative, chosen or damned." (Weber, 1904, pp. 338–339.) Such a rigid rationalization of all of conduct when combined with the emphasis on doing one's duty in one's station in life destroyed the leisureliness, in Weber's mind, with which capitalistic enterprise had been pursued up to this time. The entrepreneur worked harder—in fact he could not relax for a moment. The Protestant labor force he recruited worked harder, and none of them could enjoy the increased fruit of their labors for fear of losing the conviction that they were saved. So profits and savings were available to be plowed back into further expansion of business which in itself was a serious calling ordained by God.

From the standpoint of our present knowledge of and interest in achievement motivation, we can add to Weber's argument. Protestantism also involved a revolt against excessive reliance on the institutional church. Luther preached the "priesthood of all believers"; the individual did not have to depend exclusively on more learned experts, but should read his Bible for himself and find divine guidance directly. There was greater stress on literacy for exactly this reason among Protestants. It seems very probable, then, that Protestant parents would stress earlier self-reliance and mastery of at least reading skills so that their children could fulfill their religious duties better. Such training, as we have seen, may well have increased *n* Achievement in the children according to Winterbottom's findings.

Furthermore, Calvin's description of what Weber calls "rationalization" of life is written in terms of striving continually for perfection, which would be scored very high for *n* Achievement. Consider the following passage, for example:

> Let us every one proceed according to our small ability, and prosecute the journey we have begun. No man will be so unhappy but that he may every day make some progress, however small. Therefore, let us not cease to strive, that we may be incessantly advancing in the way of the Lord, nor let us despair on

account of the smallness of our success; for however our success may not correspond to our wishes, yet our labor is not lost, when this day surpasses the
preceding one; provided that with sincere simplicity we keep our end in view,
and press forward to the goal, not practicing self-adulation, nor indulging our
own evil propensities, but perpetually exerting our endeavors after increasing
degrees of amelioration, till we shall have arrived at a perfection of goodness,
which indeed, we seek and pursue as long as we live . . . (Calvin, I, pp. 775-776.)

In other words, the rationalization of conduct meant more than orderliness and
rigidity, it meant continual striving to improve one's self, to achieve. While the achievement was supposed to be in the religious sphere primarily, Calvin made it clear that this
did not imply monasticism or withdrawal from life. "Let us discard therefore that in-
human philosophy which, allowing no use of the creatures but what is absolutely necessary . . . malignantly deprives us of the lawful enjoyment of the Divine beneficence. . . ."
In other words, God provided the world and what was in it "not only for our necessity
but likewise for our pleasure and delight." Furthermore, we are given these earthly things
as stewards. "They are, as it were, deposits entrusted to our care, of which we must one
day give an account." Thus, as Weber points out, the striving to do one's best religiously
was readily interpreted to mean doing one's best in the "post assigned him by the Lord,"
namely, in his occupation. (Calvin, I, pp. 786-790.)

So it seems reasonable enough to interpret Weber's argument for the connection
between Protestantism and the rise of capitalism in terms of a revolution in the family,
leading to more sons with strong internalized achievement drives. The case is further
strengthened by the fact that the Protestant Church did away with the celibate priesthood and substituted what Troeltsch argues had far-reaching social consequences, namely
"the Protestant citizen-pastor and his household." (Troeltsch, 1958, p. 144.) The Protestant pastor could now give concrete examples of child-rearing practices that might be
emulated by his parishioners in a way that was formerly impossible under the celibate
priesthood. The social mechanism was provided by which the new religious world-view
could specifically affect socialization and thereby the motivation of the new generation.

PRELIMINARY EVIDENCE FOR LINKAGES BETWEEN PROTESTANTISM, n ACHIEVEMENT, AND ECONOMIC DEVELOPMENT

But logic and reasonableness are one thing. Evidence is another. Is there any factual
basis whatsoever for the linkages among the various events shown in the diagram above?
Let us begin with Weber's argument. What is the evidence that Protestantism is connected
with greater economic progress? It would be difficult, indeed, to arrive at a sound opinion
from the facts presented by historians and sociologists. The methods used are simply not
adequate for reaching a decision. Those who accept Weber's hypothesis point to the role
of Protestantism in the industrialization of England, Switzerland, Germany, and the
Scandinavian countries. Those who disagree with him point out that a Catholic country
like Belgium showed as strong an entrepreneurial spirit and as rapid an industrialization as
any of the Protestant countries. And what about Catholic Venice, which before the
Reformation reached a height of capitalistic enterprise seldom attained thereafter? It does
not help particularly to point out that though Belgium was over 99 per cent Catholic, it
was ruled by Protestant kings during its industrialization in the 19th century, or that

Venice, in fact, very nearly became Protestant during the Reformation. The matter simply cannot be settled by the battle of instance and counterinstance. A more sophisticated method is necessary.

Are Protestant countries more economically advanced today than Catholic countries matched for natural resources? Such a question can be answered fairly precisely, although of course it is not the only question that might be asked. Table 2.2 presents the relevant data. The measure of economic development used is consumption of electricity in kilowatt-hours per capita as of 1950. . . . The reasons for choosing such a measure are . . . basically: (1) that the figures are expressed in internationally comparable units, as contrasted with, for example, national income figures which are very difficult to translate into one another, and (2) that electricity is a form of energy on which modern industrial civilization is largely based. Anyway in 1950 kilowatt-hours per capita consumed correlated .87 with estimates of income per capita . . . The countries listed in the first column in Table 2.2 are all those for which data were available lying outside the tropical zone, i.e., lying between the Tropics of Cancer and Capricorn. Since advanced economies appear to be confined more or less to the temperate zone, it seemed unfair to include the many Caribbean and Latin American Catholic countries, which lie within the tropics.

The association between level of economic development and Protestantism appears very marked in the first column of Table 2.2, as was pointed out in a previous publication (McClelland, 1955). However, further research demonstrated that some correction for differences in natural resources must be made, since the two groups of countries are not very well equated for the water power and coal supplies used in the production of electricity.[2] The disparity is most striking in the usable water power resources (column 2) which appear to be about five times as great on the average in the Protestant as in the Catholic countries, and the correlation between water power resources and electrical output is highly significant (over .50). Furthermore since 72 per cent of the electricity produced in the world in 1950 was thermal in origin, it is also necessary to include coal resources as the chief means of producing heat. Unfortunately, "coal in the ground" is not a good measure because, unlike water resources, the amount available is not always accurately known. Therefore output of coal per capita was used as an estimate of coal resources (column 3), although it is a somewhat contaminated measure, since it may be higher in those very countries where people work harder and therefore reach a higher level of economic development. In predicting, for example, how much electricity should be produced per capita in England on the basis of her coal production, we may well overestimate, for the reason that coal production already includes the energy with which resources have been used. Another people living in the same country with the same coal resources might have produced less, and we would therefore predict less economic development and the country would appear to be less of an "underachiever" than Britain is in the table. The water power measure does not suffer from this defect since it represents what is available and not what is produced.

Nevertheless, some measure of available coal is necessary, since when it is combined in standard score terms with the water power reserves, the correlation of total reserves with electrical output is .75. In other words, the differences noted in column 1 might largely be due to greater natural resources in the Protestant than in the Catholic countries, since available natural resources correlate highly with production of electricity.

TABLE 2.2 AVERAGE PER CAPITA CONSUMPTION OF ELECTRIC POWER, CORRECTED FOR NATURAL RESOURCES, FOR PROTESTANT AND CATHOLIC COUNTRIES OUTSIDE THE TROPICS OF CANCER AND CAPRICORN

	Countries	Consumption of Electricity kwh/cap[1] (1950)	Usable Water Power hp/cap[2] (1947) (SD = 1.36)	Coal Produced tons/cap[3] (1951) (SD = .99)	Combined Natural Resources ($\Sigma \sigma$ scores)[4]	Predicted Output kwh/cap[5]	Difference (predicted-obtained)	Rank of Difference[6]
Protestant	Norway	5,310	4.182	.000	+2.73	3379	1931	1
	Canada	4,120	3.079	1.124	+2.49	3186	934	4
	Sweden	2,580	1.117	.026	− .35	908	1672	2
	United States	2,560	.388	3.431	+1.42	2328	232	9
	Switzerland	2,230	1.553	.000	+ .03	1253	977	3
	New Zealnad	1,600	1.405	.675	+ .42	1526	74	11
	Australia	1,160	.164	2.505	+ .51	1598	−438	20
	United Kingdom	1,115	.023	4.529	+1.86	2681	−1566	24
	Finland	1,000	.810	.000	− .67	652	348	6
	Union S. Africa	890	.203	2.165	+ .30	1430	−540	21
	Holland	725	.003	1.238	− .58	724	1	15
	Denmark	500	.011	.121	−1.39	74	426	5
	Average	*1,983*	*1.078*	*1.318*		*1645*	*338*	*10.1*

Catholic	Belgium	986	.004	3.335	+ .96	1959	-973	22
	Austria	900	.500	.379	- .71	620	280	8
	France	790	.289	1.293	- .25	989	-199	16
	Czechoslovakia	730	.085	2.837	+ .68	1734	-1004	23
	Italy	535	.265	.033	-1.20	227	308	7
	Chile	484	.676	.381	- .53	764	-280	18
	Poland	375	.059	3.338	+1.02	2007	-1632	25
	Hungary	304	.017	1.049	- .70	628	-324	19
	Ireland	300	.156	.061	-1.29	154	146	10
	Argentina	255	.318	.003	-1.17	251	4	14
	Spain	225	.271	.418	- .91	459	-234	17
	Uruguay	165	.204	.000	-1.29	154	11	13
	Portugal	110	.070	.052	-1.38	82	28	12
	Average	*474*	*.224*	*1.014*		*771*	*-298*	*15.7*

[1] From Woytinsky, W. S. and E. S. *World population and production.* New York: Twentieth Century Fund, 1953. Table 415, p. 972. A few of the values are for Thermo- or Hydroelectric power only but in all these cases, except Chile, which has been recomputed here, the alternative source is negligible.

[2] Computed from Woytinsky, *ibid.,* Table 407, p. 952. The figures are the sum of the capacity in horsepower of existing plants and undeveloped power (ordinary minimum flow) divided by the population.

[3] Computed from *World Energy Supplies,* United Nations Statistical papers, Series J. No. 2, New York, 1957, pp. 13*ff.*

[4] Sum of standard scores for water power and coal produced.

[5] Based on the regression equation computed for these 25 countries, i.e., $Y = 80.2(X + 2) - 41.5$, where Y is the predicted value in kwh/cap and X is the sum of the standard scores for water and coal resources.

[6] The probability that the higher ranks could be associated with Protestantism by chance is less than .03 (Mann-Whitney U test).

However, it is possible to remove the effect of natural resources by a regression analysis which predicts, as in column 4, what output could be expected from a country on the basis of its natural resources. Then by subtracting the predicted output from the actual output, one can determine whether a country has done better or worse than could be expected on the basis of its natural resources. As the last column on the right shows, 9 out of 12 of the Protestant countries, or 67 per cent, have done better than expected, whereas only 3 out of 13 of the Catholic countries (Austria, Italy, and Ireland) have done substantially better than expected. If the differences are ranked from those which have done best to those which have done least well, it is clear that the ranks of the Protestant countries are higher on the average and the difference is significant according to the Mann-Whitney U test ($p < 03$). It needs perhaps to be stressed again that the measures are approximate, particularly the adjustment for coal resources, but errors unless they are systematically biased in favor of Protestant or Catholic countries, can only serve to disguise a relationship, or weaken it, rather than actually to create it. So it may be concluded with reasonable confidence that, as of 1950, Protestant countries are economically more advanced on the average, even taking their differences in natural resources into account, than are Catholic countries. The question as to why the difference exists is another matter.

Granted that Weber's hypothesis has some basis in fact, what about the evidence for the other links in the key hypothesis? Do Protestants stress earlier independence and mastery training, as we have reasoned they should? Preliminary evidence suggested that they do (McClelland, Rindlisbacher and de Charms, 1955). Samples of Protestant, Irish-Catholic and Italian-Catholic mothers and fathers matched for socioeconomic status were interviewed in Connecticut using the same schedule as the one developed by Winterbottom to test various attitudes towards self-reliance training. (See Table 9.1.) Many of the parents were obtained through church groups, so that the sample perhaps included a larger number of religiously active individuals than would be obtained from a random sample. On the average, the Protestant parents expected their sons to do well in school, to know their way around the city, etc., at the age of about $6^1/_2$, the Irish parents at about $7^1/_2$, and the Italian parents at about $8^1/_2$. The differences were significant, although the number of cases in each sample varied only between 35 and 40. As predicted, the Protestant mothers stressed earlier self-reliance than the Catholic mothers. It should also follow that Protestant boys, on the average, equating for social class, should have higher n Achievement. Such a comparison proved impossible in the United States because of migration differentials. Catholics, at least on the East Coast, represent for the most part ethnic minorities which have settled in the country within the last few decades and have generally started at the bottom of the socioeconomic ladder. Those who rise to middle-class status may well have higher n Achievement, as a considerable amount of evidence indicated. Thus it would not be possible to draw any conclusions about religious influences from a comparison of middle-class Protestant boys with middle-class Italian boys, since the Italian boys would come from upwardly mobile families with higher n Achievement than the average among not-so-mobile Protestants. Furthermore, lower-class Protestants in New England represent a peculiar minority that have failed to rise and may not, therefore, be fairly compared with lower-class Italians, more of whom may have high n Achievement because they have not had time to rise into the middle class.

To avoid these difficulties, it seemed wise to go to a place where Protestants and Catholics had lived side by side for centuries, so that comparisons would not involve complications arising out of migration differentials. The data were available on a small sample of German boys from the city of Kaiserslautern (McClelland, Sturr, Knapp and Wendt, 1958) which confirmed the hypothesis, as Table 2.3 shows, that Protestant boys would have higher n Achievement on the average than Catholic boys where other factors

TABLE 2.3 MEAN n ACHIEVEMENT SCORES OF A SAMPLE OF GERMAN BOYS, AGED 17-19, CLASSIFIED BY RELIGIOUS AND SOCIOECONOMIC BACKGROUND, AND LEADERSHIP STATUS

Father's Educational Level		Protestant		Catholic		Mean
		Leaders	Nonleaders	Leaders	Nonleaders	
University	N	15	7	3	4	
	mean	3.33	3.29	1.00	2.25	2.93
Mittelschule	N	10	12	4	7	
	mean	1.70	3.42	1.25	2.71	2.48
Volksschule	N	9	4	4	3	
	mean	2.78	6.00	1.75	1.67	2.55

Protestant mean = 3.42   Catholic mean = 1.77
Leader mean = 1.97   Nonleader mean = 3.22

Analysis of Variance					
Source of Variance	df	Sum of Squares	Mean Square	F	p *
Total	11	20.19	—	—	—
Father's educational level	2	1.32	.66	.77	NS
Religion	1	8.15	8.15	9.48	<.05
Leadership status	1	4.72	4.72	5.49	~.05
Interactions	7	6.00	.86		

*Number of times in 100 that the F-value could have arisen by chance.

were equal. It should be stressed . . . that the sample is small and highly selected, consisting entirely of boys preparing for a university education in one part of Germany. The data are included because they constituted the evidence available at the time it was decided to investigate the problem on a larger scale. It was not possible to perform an analysis of variance using the individual scores because of the unevenness in subclass numbers, but the classification by father's educational level and by leadership or lack of it in the class provided enough variation to get an estimate of error from the interaction terms. Socioeconomic status as represented by the father's educational level does not contribute significantly to the variance here, probably because all the students are highly selected in the sense of aspiring to a university education. It is also interesting to note that leadership (here defined by peer nominations) is not associated with high n Achievement, but rather the reverse. The boys with high n Achievement are not regarded by their peers as likely to be future leaders. Such a finding is a healthy corrective to the view that n Achievement is a generally "good" characteristic to have, like intelligence, which leads to greater success in all spheres of life.

Finally so far as this sample is concerned significantly more of the Protestant than Catholic boys were attending a "modern language" as contrasted with a "classical language" school. That is, 67 per cent of the 60 Protestant boys and only 41 per cent of the 27 Catholic boys were attending the *neusprachliches Gymnasium* (X^2 = 5.10, p < .03), the remainder in both cases being in the *altsprachliches Gymnasium*. The finding is interesting because Weber argued on the basis of some data collected by Offenbacher on German school attendance in the 1890's that Protestants more often went to technical or modern schools which they found to be better preparation for business, while Catholics showed greater preference for classical humanistic studies (Merton, 1949, pp. 344 *ff.*). Thus we might infer that attending more "modern" schools becomes the means by which higher Protestant *n* Achievement becomes channeled into business activity in Germany. Samuelson has recently argued that Offenbacher's figures failed to take base rates into account (Lipset and Bendix, 1959, p. 54), but this criticism does not seem to apply to our figures in the 1950's. At any rate the whole problem deserves further investigation since it suggests a means by which values and motives may affect vocational choice and eventually economic development. It is discussed below in Chapters 8 and 9, in terms of more extensive data collected subsequently.

The final link in the key hypothesis is between *n* Achievement and economic development. Was there any evidence to support the belief that high *n* Achievement would predispose individuals toward business success? Some was available, but not much. Among a group of college freshmen, a search was made to see what occupations those with the highest *n* Achievement (top 20 per cent) liked significantly more than those with the lowest *n* Achievement (bottom 20 per cent of the class). Oddly enough, the only five occupations out of one hundred in the first part of the Strong Vocational Interest Blank preferred near-significantly more often (χ^2 > 3.74) by the "highs" than the "lows" were the following:

> Stock broker
> Real estate salesman
> Advertiser
> Buyer of merchandise
> Factory manager

While one could expect to get five significant differences in one hundred tests of significance by chance, it is at least interesting that the five particular ones turned out to be in the business area. Since only around one-quarter of the one hundred occupations listed in the Blank relate to business, it can be estimated that the chances of getting all of the differences in the business area purely by luck are less than 1 in 1,000. Furthermore, a check was available on the same group of Kaiserslautern boys to see whether the ones among them with high *n* Achievement also favored these particular five occupations significantly more than those among them with low *n* Achievement. Such turned out to be the case, despite the fact that the German boys on the whole were much less favorable to these items than the American boys. When the average favorableness of each German toward all five of the business occupations listed above was computed (Like = 2, Indifferent = 1, Dislike = 0), it was found that those with high *n* Achievement favored them slightly more on the average than those with low *n* Achievement (t = 2.12, p < .05). The difference, therefore, did not seem to be particularly restricted to American culture. Thus, boys with high *n* Achievement did appear to look with more favor on business occupations as predicted by the hypothesis, though of course there was as yet no evidence that they would be more likely to enter those occupations or to perform better in them after they had entered them.

The evidence so far presented summarizes what was available at the time the present study was initiated. In general, it seemed to support the key hypothesis in enough particulars to warrant a more detailed study of what was going on. But it raised almost as many questions as it answered and left many issues entirely untouched. For example, was it Protestantism as such that led to economic development and perhaps to an increase in achievement motivation, or was it certain values which happened to be associated with Protestantism in the West? What about Japan, whose economic development seemed quite rapid, but could in no way be attributed to the Protestant Reformation? Was it higher *n* Achievement that led to economic development in Japan and if so what parental values produced it there? The Winterbottom study was limited to only twenty-nine middle-class families in the Middle Western part of the United States. Does earlier independence and mastery training produce higher *n* Achievement everywhere, regardless of cultural differences? Are there alternative sources of *n* Achievement?

Above all, more work needs to be done on the hypothesized connection between *n* Achievement and economic development. Is the connection a completely general one that applies to all societies, primitive and modern, ancient and contemporary? If so, why? Does *n* Achievement somehow predispose young boys to look with favor on the entrepreneurial role, or does it have this effect only when business is generally looked on with favor in the society? One of the major problems involved here is whether *n* Achievement leads to better performance in all occupational roles—from artist to priest to businessman —or to greater success only in certain roles, somehow centering around economic or rationalized activities. What is needed is a very broad attack on the problem, in which the connection between achievement motivation and economic development could be checked in a variety of times and places. It appeared likely from the outset that Weber's hypothesis represents a special case of a more general relationship that ought to be investigated fully.

REFERENCES

Calvin, John. *Institutes of the Christian religion* (transl. by John Allen). Philadelphia: Presbyterian Board of Christian Education Edition. Volume 1.

Lipset, S. M., & Bendix R. *Social mobility in industrial society*. Berkeley and Los Angeles: Univer. of Calif. Press, 1959.

McClelland, D. C. Some social consequences of achievement motivation. In M. R. Jones (Ed.), *Nebraska symposium on motivation 1955*. Lincoln, Nebr.: Univer. Nebr. Press, 1955.

McClelland, D. C., Rindlisbacher, A., & deCharms, R. C. Religious and other sources of parental attitudes toward independence training. In D. C. McClelland (Ed.), *Studies in motivation*. New York: Appleton-Century-Crofts, 1955.

McClelland, D. C., Sturr, J. F., Knapp, R. H., & Wendt, H. W. Obligations to self and society in the United States and Germany. *J. abnorm. soc. Psychol.*, 1958, 56, 245–255.

Merton, R. K. *Social theory and social structure*. Glencoe, Ill.: Free Press, 1949.

Troeltsch, E. *Protestantism and progress*. (Transl. by W. Montgomery.) Boston: Beacon Press, 1958.

Weber, M. *The Protestant ethic and the spirit of capitalism*. 1904. (Transl. by T. Parsons.) New York: Scribner, 1930.

Winterbottom, Marian R. The relation of childhood training in independence to achievement motivation. Unpublished doctoral dissertation. Univer. Mich., 1953.

Winterbottom, Marian R. The relation of need for achievement to learning experiences in independence and mastery. In J. W. Atkinson (Ed.), *Motives in fantasy, action, and society*. Princeton, N. J. Van Nostrand, 1958. Pp. 453–478.

— · — · — · — · — · — · — · — · — · — · —

RALPH M. STOGDILL

*Group Achievement**

In summary, high group morale appears to be associated with high productivity. The greater the freedom from restraint, within limits, that a group exhibits in attacking its task, the more it is able to produce. Morale may be related either positively or negatively with integration. High cohesiveness is related to high morale when the group is actively engaged in operations upon a goal objective. However, high cohesiveness is related to low morale under conditions of continued threat and frustration. Integration and productivity tend to be related inversely. The time and effort spent on the maintenance of integration cannot be devoted at the same time to productivity. However, both productivity and integration may be high under conditions of high morale, task motivation, and effort. These findings appear to lend some support to the hypothesis that a group is a system which tends to maintain a continuous balance among its various achievement outputs. With inputs held constant, an increase in one achievement factor is accomplished at the cost of some other achievement element. A simultaneous increase in productivity, integration, and morale can only be accomplished at the expense of an increase in some form of input value or effort.

A rather exacting and laborious procedure has been followed in developing a theory of group achievement and examining it in reference to the pertinent experimental data. In order to construct a satisfactory system, it has been necessary to start with concepts that are firmly anchored in the scientific literature, to define them strictly, to examine the interrelationships among them, and to trace in systematic detail the effects generated by their interactions upon each other.

A group is regarded as an input-output system. The inputs are the performances, expectations, and interactions of the group members. These variables in combination account for the development of group structure and for the initiation and maintenance of group operations. The input behaviors, transformed into group structure and operations, result in outcomes which describe the achievement of the group. The logical development of the system has required that group achievement be analyzed in terms of productivity, integration, and morale. A group may be examined at any stage in its operations to evaluate its status in respect to these three aspects of achievement.

Various concepts used in the system are reviewed in the following sections.

CHARACTERISTICS OF INDIVIDUALS AND OF GROUPS

Performance and expectation are characteristics of individuals. Interaction is an interpersonal form of behavior. A group by definition involves interactions and performances (actions and reactions). A group also involves expectations. The structuring of positions in a group tends to confirm differential expectations relative to the predictable initiative of certain members and the predictable reactions of other members. In addition, the members tend to confirm for each other a normative set of values relative to the group purpose and member behavior affecting the group purpose. Not only do the members in interaction develop norms which define expected behavior, but they exert strong pressures upon each other to conform with the norms of the group. Purpose and norms represent mutually confirmed sets of expectations which must be regarded as characteristics of groups. Structure and operations are also characteristics of groups.

THE INPUT BEHAVIORS

The concepts *performance*, *interaction*, and *expectation* must be regarded as abstractions which refer to observed or inferred aspects of behavior that are recognized in general conversation as well as in the scientific literature. The concepts have been defined in the scientific literature by a variety of research operations. For this reason, we know more about the concepts and the behaviors to which they refer than we do about various other concepts that might have been used for the theory. The fact that several concepts have been redefined according to the demands of the theory and in order to bring them into closer conformity with research findings requires us to keep in mind the scientific rather than the cultural meanings of the terms.

Interaction is defined as an action-reaction sequence in which the reactions of each participant in the sequence are responses to actions initiated by other participants. A *group* is defined as an interaction system. It must be regarded as an open system because it gains and loses members, and exchanges values with its environment. The structure of a group is determined by the actions and reactions of its members. A position in a group is defined as a predictable sequence of actions by a member which elicits predictable reactions from other members of the system. Successive interactions and the gain or loss of members do not change the identity of the system. Although interaction is not self-perpetuating, the continuance of interaction, at least intermittently, is necessary to maintain the identity of the system. The degree of structure of a system determines the freedom of action permitted its members. The concept of interaction, as here developed, enables us to account for group structure, identity, and freedom of action, which are important concepts in a theory of groups.

Performance is defined as any action exhibited by an individual which identifies him as a member of a group. A performance may be an action initiated by a member or a reaction to the action of another member. Each action and each reaction is a performance. The nature or content of an interaction sequence is described in terms of the performances (actions and reactions) involved. The performances of the members, singly or in interaction, accomplish the work of the group and describe the operations of the group. The concept of performance increases our ability to explain group identity. It enables us to describe the nature of interaction. It provides a means of explaining group operations, or group task performance.

Expectation is defined as readiness for reinforcement. It is regarded in this theory as a function of drive, the estimated level of desirability of a possible outcome, and the estimated probability of the outcome. A reinforcing outcome confirms or disconfirms desirability estimates and probability estimates. A reinforcing outcome usually, but not always, reduces drive temporarily. Successive reinforcements increase expectation, but add progressively smaller increments of strength. Inconsistent schedules of reinforcement reduce freedom of action in that they mobilize drive and maintain the organism in a state of constant readiness for the reinforcement of a dominant expectation.

Motivation is regarded as a function of drive and confirmed desirability estimates. The confirmation of desirability estimates determines the value of an outcome in relation to a scale of value or previously confirmed desirability estimate. Secondary reinforcement and generalization account for the development of value systems, which may be regarded as sets of desirability estimates whose confirmation is not dependent upon the confirmation of probability estimates. Value systems provide the individual with stable reference scales for the evaluation and direction of behavior in an environment that exhibits a high degree of uncertainty and unpredictability. The concept of expectation enables us to account for the goal direction and continuity of behavior, as well as for prediction and value.

GROUP STRUCTURE AND OPERATIONS

Variance among the members in the initiation of behavior and in response to the initiative of others results in the differentiation of a structure of positions in a group. The mutual confirmation of expectation among the members that comes about in the process of establishing the structure of positions tends to define the contribution of each position to the accomplishment of the group purpose. These expectations, when mutually acknowledged and confirmed, define the function and status of each position in the system. Since function and status are defined in relation to the group purpose, they tend to remain unchanged even though a succession of different persons may occupy a given position.

In order to accomplish the group purpose, it is necessary for the members to act and interact in carrying out the tasks assigned to each position. These performances and interactions describe the operations of the group. Because of the impact of environmental pressures and changing operational requirements, and because of differences between individuals, function and status cannot define in detail the manner in which a member is expected to behave in a group. Successive occupants of the same position are not expected to act alike. The members in interaction develop mutually confirmed expectations relative to the role that each is expected to play as a participant in the changing group operations. A member's role defines the responsibility and authority he is expected to exercise by virtue of the functions and status of his position, the demands made upon him by changing group operations, and the kind of person he is perceived to be. The mutual acknowledgement and confirmation of positions and roles tends to legitimize these systems and to insure their stability. Both role definition and group norms tend to specify a set of sanctions which reward conformity and penalize nonconformity. The continued legitimation of a role depends on the correspondence between the behavior of a member and the specifications and norms pertaining to his role. A member may act in such a manner as to undermine the legitimacy of his role without affecting the legitimacy of the function and status defined for his position. Role conflict occurs when contradictory expectations are made upon the occupant of a position.

Groups are found to develop structures of positions and roles as means of subdividing the group task, controlling group operations, and insuring unity of goal direction. The provision for operations control gives some members greater access to power than is available to others. Conflict within groups tends to center around the legitimation of the uses of power. Power is defined as the differential right to control the reinforcement of expectation.

It is found that the concepts of performance, interaction, and expectation, when used in combination, are able to account for group structure and operations. They are also able to account for group achievement.

GROUP ACHIEVEMENT

Achievement is defined as the group outcome resulting from the member inputs, mediated through group structure and operations. The achievement of a group at any stage of its operations may be analyzed in terms of its productivity, morale, and integration. Productivity is defined as the degree of change in expectancy values resulting from group operations. Integration is a measure of capacity to maintain structure and function under stress. Morale is defined as freedom from restraint in action toward a group goal.

The three aspects of achievement are necessarily defined in terms of group capacity. The standards of reference for measuring group achievement involve time and capacity. Productivity measures the extent to which operational capability has been utilized with past performance as a standard of reference. Morale is a measure of the degree to which a group actually utilizes its potentiality for freedom of action at the time of observation. Integration has a future reference, in that it is a measure of capacity to maintain structure and function under conditions of stress.

Because of the fact that the achievement of a group is valued differently by different members as well as by observers who are not members, it is difficult to establish any absolute standards for evaluating different aspects of achievement. Nevertheless, both members and outside observers make evaluative judgments of group achievement and tend to accept such appraisals as valid.

An increase or decrease in inputs permits an increase or decrease in productivity, morale, and integration simultaneously. However, with inputs constant, an increase in productivity is accomplished at some expense to integration. An increase in integration involves some decrease in productivity. Morale is usually, but not always, related positively to productivity. Morale tends to be higher under medium degrees of integration than under extremely high or low degrees of integration.

BALANCE AND COUNTERBALANCE

Membership provides a means for the accomplishment of individual goals while aiding in the achievement of group goals. An organization is usually interested in the creation of specific productivity values which are defined in its declaration of purpose. The end values created by the performances of the members and the operations of the group are accomplished at a cost to the members and to the group. The cost to the members is reckoned in terms of the time and effort they devote to the group, the dues they pay, the illnesses and accidents they suffer in the performance of their duties, the frustrations and disappointments they experience, the freedom of self-determination they surrender, and the subordination of personal loyalties and goals to the welfare of the group. Such factors as these are costs to the members, even though they cannot all be measured in dollars and cents.

The group also must pay a cost of one sort or another for the participation of the members. It must create for the members such values as are necessary to reinforce their expectations. Groups, as collectivities of individuals, generally expect the contributions of the members to be related to the productive purpose of the group. In turn, they expect the members to be content with rewards that may be derived from the accomplishment of the group purpose. If it is the purpose of the group to produce material values, the members are expected to be satisfied with material rewards. In athletic groups the return to the members may be the fun of playing the game or of watching others play it. In religious groups it may be the reinforcement of personal value systems and perhaps the rendering of humanitarian services. In business groups it may be the financial reward for the effort and responsibility invested in task performance. In a social group it may be the pleasure of interaction, mutual stimulation, and emotional support. However, these primary values are not the only ones that the members expect to derive from a group. Some members value the pride that comes with membership in a high prestige organization. Others value the opportunity provided by a group to exercise responsibility and authority and to experience a sense of achievement. Some members value the sense of security provided by a group, while others derive satisfaction from the opportunity for innovation, advancement in status, and the exercise of power. The members of a group may differ widely among themselves depending upon differences in social background, training, and reference group identifications. The meeting of these various expectations takes time and effort which the group might otherwise devote to task performance, and thus represents a cost to the group.

All that is a cost to a member represents an input for the group. Some of the input may not be highly valued, but it will exert an effect someplace in the group. Although inputs that have a high positive or negative value are often recognized, groups as organized entities appear to exhibit little awareness of the total costs paid by their members. Thus, there is usually more invested in a group than is recognized as constituting individual and collective input. Correspondingly, the group creates outputs, such as integration and morale, which are seldom recognized as aspects of achievement.

Performance is regulated to a high degree by operational demands and subgroup norms which may bear no close relationship to the amount, nature, or relevance of the rewards for performance. Group structures, on the other hand, exhibit numerous mechanisms for their mutual reinforcement. Value systems are highly reinforcible. Although work decrement in response to dissatisfaction is to be observed, productive effectiveness may be maintained at high levels despite a state of extreme dissatisfaction among the members. Griping, hostility, absenteeism, accidents, separations, malco-ordination, and other evidences of low group integration are observed instead. It is the structural-functional integrity of the group that is most vulnerable to inadequate or inappropriate reinforcement.

A member tends to judge the outcomes he experiences as satisfying or unsatisfying in reference to his own expectations and in comparison with the outcomes he perceives other members to be experiencing in the group. If he perceives some members to be receiving excessive rewards, he sees the group as potentially able to increase his own rewards as well.

When the members permit the group to accumulate a surplus of values, they realize that this surplus gives the group a degree of power that the members could not exert individually if the surplus were divided equally among them. Therefore, all the members, except perhaps a few who are antagonistic to certain of its goals, are interested in seeing that the group has a sufficient reserve to insure its power to operate and to fulfill its purpose. The greater the extent to which their own welfare is perceived to be dependent upon, and served by, the activities of the group, the greater the interest of the members in the adequate reserve power of the group.

The decision by a group to play a game or perform a task involves much more than the accomplishment of the stated objective. It involves also the differentiation of function and status, a process which places different values on the contributions of the various members. Thus, the basic process of organizing creates a situation which is likely to reward certain members but to disappoint the expectations of certain others. Although this outcome may not be avoidable, the integration of the group may depend upon the extent to which the group sensitizes itself to the expectations of its members and succeeds in satisfying or else restructuring them.

Organization seeks to establish stable structures of expectations relative to interaction, performance, and outcomes. However, the model structure can never anticipate nor represent all the demands that the organization will be required to fulfill. Therefore, it is confronted by two extreme alternatives with a wide range of values in between. It can spend all its energy on the reinforcement of structural integrity, or it can devote all its energies to task achievement. The former solution represents little advantage over the primal group, for it merely formalizes the original struggle for structure in the form of a non-productive ritualism. The latter solution may be expected eventually to jeopardize integration and morale. Therefore, a realistic concern for the survival of the group demands a solution that lies between these two extremes.

In times of crisis, the members may sacrifice most, if not all, of their personal goals for the benefit of the organization. The internal problems of the group are likely to be simplified under these circumstances because it can devote most of its attention to maximizing productive effectiveness. Nevertheless, many groups that do not live under continued crisis, persist in operating under routine conditions as if crisis were ever present. Under continued pressure for productivity when no crisis exists, the members are likely to become wearied and disillusioned. When this occurs, the time has passed for the group to have sensitized itself to the expectations of its members and to its structural integrity and morale.

The real test of the integrity of a group is whether its members will support it in time of crisis. A member's loyalty to a group appears to be determined by some ratio between the personal cost he has to pay to support the group and the magnitude of the discrepancy between his expectations and the outcomes he experiences in the group. When this ratio becomes so unbalanced that the member feels cheaply valued or that his interests are betrayed, he may also feel inclined to let the organization suffer whatever reverses may be in store for it.

The formal organization does, or should, structure the expectations of the members. Correspondingly, it is the responsibility of the formal structure to fulfill the relevant expectations of the members. The integration of a group is founded on its formal structure and on the correspondence between individual goals and group goals. This mutual support is brought about by the clear definition of roles, by the careful structuring of expectations, and by the reinforcement of those expectations.

Not only the group as a system, but the members as individuals, are interested in the primary purpose of the group, its productive achievement. However, the necessity of maintaining operational balance, and the setting of limits upon the personal reward that can be achieved for increased effort tend to counteract the attempts made by the group to increase productivity through the use of various motivating measures. In addition, the subgroups tend to demand uniformity of performance and rewards, and the solution of problems by formula. For example, they may expect promotions to be based on seniority, technical ability, or some other standard formula. A group can hardly hope to devise a formula which will satisfy all the members. It is difficult for the group, even when it realizes the desirability of doing so, to sensitize itself to the expectations of the individual members with the aim of satisfying each in a maximum degree. In fact, the primary concern of the group is for the welfare and accomplishment of the group as a whole rather than for the satisfaction of the individual members, and it tends to reject those members who cannot conform to this concern.

High status members are found to experience a greater degree of personal freedom in the group, to enlarge the area of freedom of other members, and to be more tolerant and supportive of the deviate. Thus, there are some functions which neither the group as a whole nor the various subgroups can perform, but which the members will permit high status members to perform. It now becomes clear why group productivity is related to supervisory leadership rather than to satisfaction with the job or the group as a whole. The group is conservative by nature and necessity. It must maintain balance and control if it is to survive. Productivity among the various subgroups must be equalized in order to prevent a wastage of group resources, and the rewards to peers in the same subgroup must be equalized in order to prevent dissension. The members tend to produce more when they are given freedom to perform and interact in conformity with the demands of their tasks and roles. Excessive degrees of freedom are observed to result in indecision, confusion, and malco-ordination. The desirability of balancing responsibility and authority is more than a trite saying. It is a requirement for effective performance. The high status member provides freedom of action, definition of structure, and co-ordination control.

There are many balancing and counterbalancing factors at work in an organized group. An excess in any one factor may be accomplished at the cost of a deficiency in others. The exercise of a high degree of control over performance and interaction reduces satisfaction and productivity. Granting an optimum degree of freedom of action increases productivity and satisfaction but weakens co-ordination control. Under a maximum degree of freedom, co-ordination breaks down, production is reduced, and satisfaction is lowered. If disproportionate amounts of time and effort are devoted to the structuring and reinforcement of expectations, satisfaction tends to increase, but productivity suffers. On the other hand, if the member expectations relative to status and function, responsibility and authority, recognition and reward are disregarded, satisfaction and loyalty to the organization are depressed.

The subgroups develop norms which tend to regulate performance. On the other hand, the subgroups may exert pressures which induce conformity to the group standards. The subgroups may also provide support which enables members to resist the attempts of internal and external agents to alienate them from the group. It is equally true that an alienated subgroup may make life very difficult for a member who is loyal to the group. In the interests of survival, it is important for the group to structure and satisfy the legitimate expectations of its members. The development of structural integrity under normal operation conditions, even at the expense of productive effectiveness, strengthens the group for times of crisis.

If responsibility and authority are too rigidly structured and controlled, the members suffer a reduction in their freedom of action. Thus, a too rigid role structure may incapacitate the organization for coping with changing environmental demands. However, if roles are not clearly defined, the members may not know what they are expected to do in the way of task performance or interaction with other members. As a result, initiative is lowered, operations become disorganized, and dissatisfaction increases.

In order for an organization to cope with changing conditions, it is necessary that initiative and freedom of decision be permitted at the operative levels where technical problems are encountered first hand. This is true, not only for combat troops in the field, but for civilian organizations as well. Even when the technical details of task performance are strictly prescribed and controlled, there are always situations arising which demand technical knowledge and action on the spot. Lacking freedom to decide and act within his defined area of responsibility, the individual feels frustrated and distrusted in the performance of his task. Given too much freedom, the member may feel confused and inhibited lest he overstep his authority or make decisions which conflict with those made by other members.

Group productivity, as well as morale and integration, are dependent upon structure and control. All aspects of achievement are frustrated when structure is not firmly controlled. All are inhibited when structure is too rigid and operations control is too firm.

The maintenance of an optimum balance among the different elements of group achievement requires insightful attention to the problems involved in group structure and operations.

An organized group may be regarded as a complex system of overlapping and interacting input values, structures, operations, and output values. The various elements and subsystems of elements are in constant balance, change, and counterbalance. The theory that we have developed outlines the structure and functioning of a group as a generally conceptualized operating system. Although the theory cannot describe in detail the many specific variations to be found in different groups, it should be of value in specifying the important variables to be considered in analyzing the problems of groups in general.

CHANGE AND SURVIVAL

The survival of a group may depend upon the manner in which it responds to the demand for change. The problems created by the demand for change and those resulting from the requirement for stability are not identical. Neither are they entirely contradictory.

We have observed that function and status define the stable relationship of a position to the group purpose. The formal acknowledgment of function and status provides the formal structure of positions with a high degree of legitimation in the expectations of the members. This legitimation is attached to the position and is independent of the behaviors of different occupants of the position. The formal system tends to exhibit a profound degree of stability as long as group purpose remains unchanged.

Whereas function and status are defined in general terms, responsibility and authority are given flexible, detailed definitions which provide for a high degree of adaptation to changing operational demands. The role that a member can play in a group is determined not only by the extent to which his responsibility and authority are acknowledged by himself and others but also by the extent to which others knowingly or unknowingly exercise responsibilities and authority defined for his role or permit him to invade the boundaries of their roles. It is more difficult for a member to establish the legitimacy of his role behavior in a group than it is to establish the legitimacy of his position. A member in a high status position may be granted an enlarged or a restricted role in initiating and controlling group operations, depending on the contribution he is perceived to make to group productivity, morale, and integration. Role performance is expected to change as operations change and as the environment imposes forces which demand adaptation or resistance in order to cope with the problem of change.

An organized group contains structures which are well designed to preserve its stability and other structures which enable it to cope with change. The continued power of a group depends upon its ability to maintain the legitimation of these structures, to utilize them continuously, and to keep them in balance.

Continued change in a group is dependent upon a structure that exhibits stability. A structure that disintegrates under the influence of change cannot continue to change because it no longer exists. At the opposite extreme, a completely rigid structure may collapse under the impact of internal or external stresses. There appears to be a median range within which flexibility and stability optimize the capacity for survival.

Numerous factors operate to complicate the problem of change. The overlapping structures of a group are not easy to perceive. The more clearly defined the structures of a group, the greater the utility of the structures for rational decision and action on the part of all the group members. However, individuals differ in the extent to which they will acknowledge the legitimacy of structure not controlled by themselves or by reference groups with which they identify themselves. Group members also differ in the extent to which they value stability and change. Many persons feel threatened by change. Others appear highly motivated to promote group improvement and growth. Still others seem to thrive on turmoil and confusion. When active proponents of these differing ideologies begin operating in a group, both the group and its individual members have much at stake.

Reactions to proposals for change are likely to differ, depending on the part of the organization affected. Change in the formal structure of a group is likely to be accepted by the members if they perceive the change to be instrumental to more effective group achievement. They are likely to resist change in the formal structure when such change is perceived as a device for reinforcing the power available to individuals who seek to exploit the group. Members are also likely to resist change which results in lowering the status of their positions. A member feels devalued when he loses status in a legitimized status structure.

Changes in the role structure may affect a member's responsibility and authority directly, or indirectly by enlarging or restricting the responsibility and authority of associated roles. A member may welcome a change in role if it gives him a valued responsibility or relieves him of an unwanted burden. He may oppose role change if it takes away a valued responsibility or burdens him with a "dirty job." A member's reactions to marked changes in group operations and operational technologies are likely to be determined by his perception of the impact of the changes on his role.

Members in different status levels tend to react differently to the same proposal for change. Those in low status positions tend to be affected most seriously by change in operational technologies. Those in high status positions are more directly affected by change in formal structure. Changes in the occupancy of high status positions may affect all the members.

The readiness of individuals and subgroups to accept change may depend upon the origin of the proposal. Changes proposed by superiors, peers, subordinates, and outsiders are not viewed alike. Whether or not a proposal is regarded as potentially beneficial to the group or to its members as individuals tends to be determined by the members' perceptions of the motive behind the proposal. Both individuals and subgroups are likely to oppose a change which challenges the legitimacy of their roles, dislodges them from their positions, reduces the value of the outcomes they can experience in the group, imposes unnecessary hardships, or places them at a comparative disadvantage in relation to other individuals or subgroups.

Any effective disparagement of the formal system and the goal values it supports is most damaging to a group. Such action tends to undermine the legitimacy of the organization in the eyes of its members and reduces their capacity to support it as vigorously as they might otherwise do. Actions on the part of a member which cause others to challenge the legitimacy of his role, and power struggles between individuals or factions, are likely to be perceived by most members as threatening to the survival of a group. The direction in which the members throw their support may or may not be related to the objective merits of the issue being contested. Any action they take is likely to be determined by the extent to which the group has served as an effective medium for the reinforcement of their expectations.

We have observed that groups contain within themselves the structures necessary to preserve their stability and to cope with change. Granted a formal structure that is adequate to serve the group purpose, a group can best insure its survival by a continuously sensitive regard for the definition and utilization of its role system in conformity with the norm systems of the group. In concrete terms, this means that each member is permitted to perform near the outer bounds of his role as clearly defined by his responsibility and authority, and in conformity with the norms pertaining to his role. The more responsibly a member is engaged in the solution of operational problems defined for his role, the greater his opportunity to perceive the need for useful change. The more effectively he is involved in the planning and initiation of change, the greater his acceptance of it. The more adequate the authority of a member to carry out the responsibilities in which he is effectively involved, the greater his support of the role system which provides him with these satisfying outcomes. It must be admitted that these observations apply most directly to organizations that start out "right" and keep going that way. They are not necessarily invalid when applied to organizations with a less fortunate history, but they are certainly more difficult to put into effect.

APPLICATIONS

A theory need not define an applied technology. However, a useful theory may stimulate the development of a variety of technologies. Although a theory provides a set of concepts and hypotheses that may be used for analytical purposes, neither the theory nor the technologies derived from it can yield a solution to a problem until analytical operations have been performed. This fact is generally understood in regard to the physical sciences. However, a theory in the behavior sciences tends to be regarded as useful only if it provides answers and solutions to practical problems without the necessity of diagnosis and analysis. This misconception of the nature of theory in the social sciences has at times resulted in considerable disillusionment relative to the value of the sciences. In order to avoid the disappointment of expectation, it is necessary to regard a theory, both in the physical and the social sciences, as a systematic method for increasing our understanding rather than as a given solution to all problems that may arise.

The theory presented in this book is based upon, and incorporates, a variety of sub-theories, the validities of which are well documented. The integration accomplished by this system defines related sets of problems for the scientist and for the practitioner. For the scientist, it has shown the need for more clearly defined research on expectation, particularly in regard to the relationships between drive, desirability estimates, and probability estimates. It has suggested a new approach to the design of research on group achievement. It points out the strong need that exists for refinement of methods for measuring morale and integration. The current methods of measuring productivity are far from satisfactory. The set of hypotheses relative to the relationships between productivity, integration, and morale should be subjected to rigorous experimental testing. There is need for research in a wide variety of operating organizations to determine the exact conditions under which various remedial measures may be applied effectively.

Despite its research orientation, the theory here proposed has generated a number of hypotheses which are relevant to the administration of organized groups. These hypotheses challenge the viewpoint that productive effectiveness is the only value with which managerial leadership need concern itself. Group integration and morale are here shown to be achievement values which are equal in importance with productivity. If this theory is confirmed by the results of further systematic research, it will necessitate a new formulation of the basic responsibilities of managerial leadership.

The theory presented does not suggest any ready-make solutions to group problems. However, it defines a set of concepts that may be useful for the diagnosis of problems. Although the theory cannot relieve the members or the leadership of a group from the responsibility for continued analysis of their concrete situations, it can be counted a gain if it sensitizes them to the important factors that need to be considered in their efforts to understand the problems of organization structure, operations, and achievement.

— · — · — · — · — · — · — · — · —

ROBERT B. ZAJONC

*Social Facilitation (Motivation)**

Most textbook definitions of social psychology involve considerations about the influence of man upon man, or, more generally, of individual upon individual. And most of them, explicitly or implicity, commit the main efforts of social psychology to the problem of how and why the *behavior* of one individual affects the behavior of another. The influences of individuals on each others' behavior which are of interest to social psychologists today take on very complex forms. Often they involve vast networks of interindividual effects, such as one finds in studying the process of group decision-making, competition, or conformity to a group norm. But the fundamental forms of interindividual influence are represented by the oldest experimental paradigm of social psychology: social facilitation. This paradigm, dating back to Triplett's original experiments on pacing and competition, carried out in 1897 (*1*), examines the consequences upon behavior which derive from the sheer presence of other individuals.

Until the late 1930's, interest in social facilitation was quite active, but with the outbreak of World War II it suddenly died. And it is truly regrettable that it died, because

*Robert B. Zajonc, "Social Facilitation," *Science* 149, (July 16, 1965): 269–274. Copyright 1965 by the American Association for the Advancement of Science. Reprinted by permission of the publisher and author.

the basic questions about social facilitation—its dynamics and its causes—which are in effect the basic questions of social psychology, were never solved. It is with these questions that this article is concerned. I first examine past results in this nearly completely abandoned area of research and then suggest a general hypothesis which might explain them.

Research in the area of social facilitation may be classified in terms of two experimental paradigms: audience effects and co-action effects. The first experimental paradigm involves the observation of behavior when it occurs in the presence of passive spectators. The second examines behavior when it occurs in the presence of other individuals also engaged in the same activity. We shall consider past literature in these two areas separately.

AUDIENCE EFFECTS

Simple motor responses are particularly sensitive to social facilitation effects. In 1925 Travis (2) obtained such effects in a study in which he used the pursuit-rotor task. In this task the subject is required to follow a small revolving target by means of a stylus which he holds in his hand. If the stylus is even momentarily off target during a revolution, the revolution counts as an error. First each subject was trained for several consecutive days until his performance reached a stable level. One day after the conclusion of the training the subject was called to the laboratory, given five trials alone, and then ten trials in the presence of from four to eight upperclassmen and graduate students. They had been asked by the experimenter to watch the subject quietly and attentively. Travis found a clear improvement in performance when his subjects were confronted with an audience. Their accuracy on the ten trials before an audience was greater than on any ten previous trials, including those on which they had scored highest.

A considerably greater improvement in performance was recently obtained in a somewhat different setting and on a different task (3). Each subject (all were National Guard trainees) was placed in a separate booth. He was seated in front of a panel outfitted with 20 red lamps in a circle. The lamps on this panel light in a clockwise sequence at 12 revolutions per minute. At random intervals one or another light fails to go on in its proper sequence. On the average there are 24 such failures per hour. The subject's task is to signal whenever a light fails to go on. After 20 minutes of intensive training, followed by a short rest, the National Guard trainees monitored the light panels for 135 minutes. Subjects in one group performed their task alone. Subjects in another group were told that from time to time a lieutenant colonel or a master sergeant would visit them in the booth to observe their performance. These visits actually took place about four times during the experimental session. There was no doubt about the results. The accuracy of the supervised subjects was on the average 34 percent higher than the accuracy of the trainees working in isolation, and toward the end of the experimental session the accuracy of the supervised subjects was more than twice as high as that of the subjects working in isolation. Those expecting to be visited by a superior missed, during the last experimental period, 20 percent of the light failures, while those expecting no such visits missed 64 percent of the failures.

Dashiell, who, in the early 1930's, carried out an extensive program of research on social facilitation, also found considerable improvement in performance due to audience effects on such tasks as simple multiplication or word association (*4*). But, as is the case in many other areas, negative audience effects were also found. In 1933 Pessin asked college students to learn lists of nonsense syllables under two conditions, alone and in the presence of several spectators (*5*). When confronted with an audience, his subjects required an average of 11.27 trials to learn a seven-item list. When working alone they needed only 9.85 trials. The average number of errors made in the "audience" condition was considerably higher than the number in the "alone" condition. In 1931 Husband found that the presence of spectators interferes with the learning of a finger maze (*6*), and in 1933 Pessin and Husband (*7*) confirmed Husband's results. The number of trials which the isolated subjects required for learning the finger maze was 17.1. Subjects confronted with spectators, however, required 19.1 trials. The average number of errors for the isolated subjects was 33.7; the number for those working in the presence of an audience was 40.5.

The results thus far reviewed seem to contradict one another. On a pursuit-rotor task Travis found that the presence of an audience improves performance. The learning of nonsense syllables and maze learning, however, seem to be inhibited by the presence of an audience, as shown by Pessin's experiment. The picture is further complicated by the fact that when Pessin's subjects were asked, several days later, to recall the nonsense syllables they had learned, a reversal was found. The subjects who tried to recall the lists in the presence of spectators did considerably better than those who tried to recall them alone. Why are the learning of nonsense syllables and maze learning inhibited by the presence of spectators? And why, on the other hand, does performance on a pursuit-rotor, word-association, multiplication, or a vigilance task improve in the presence of others?

There is just one, rather subtle, consistency in the above results. It would appear that the emission of well-learned responses is facilitated by the presence of spectators, while the acquisition of new responses is impaired. To put the statement in conventional psychological language, performance is facilitated and learning is impaired by the presence of spectators.

This tentative generalization can be reformulated so that different features of the problem are placed into focus. During the early stages of learning, especially of the type involved in social facilitation studies, the subject's responses are mostly the wrong ones. A person learning a finger maze, or a person learning a list of nonsense syllables, emits more wrong responses than right ones in the early stages of training. Most learning experiments continue until he ceases to make mistakes—until his performance is perfect. It may be said, therefore, that during training it is primarily the wrong responses which are dominant and strong; they are the ones which have the highest probability of occurrence. But after the individual has mastered the task, correct responses necessarily gain ascendency in his task-relevant behavioral repertoire. Now they are the ones which are more probable—in other words, dominant. Our tentative generalization may now be simplified: audience enhances the emission of dominant responses. If the dominant responses are the correct ones, as is the case upon achieving mastery, the presence of an audience will be of benefit to the individual. But if they are mostly wrong, as is the case in the early stages of learning, then these wrong responses will be enhanced in the presence of an audience, and the emission of correct responses will be postponed or prevented.

There is a class of psychological processes which are known to enhance the emission of dominant responses. They are subsumed under the concepts of drive, arousal, and activation (8). If we could show that the presence of an audience has arousal consequences for the subject, we would be a step further along in trying to arrange the results of social-facilitation experiments into a neater package. But let us first consider another set of experimental findings.

CO-ACTION EFFECTS

The experimental paradigm of co-action is somewhat more complex than the paradigm involved in the study of audience effects. Here we observe individuals all simultaneously engaged in the same activity and in full view of each other. One of the clearest effects of such simultaneous action, or co-action, is found in eating behavior. It is well known that animals simply eat more in the presence of others. For instance, Bayer had chickens eat from a pile of wheat to their full satisfaction (9). He waited some time to be absolutely sure that his subject would eat no more, and then brought in a companion chicken who had not eaten for 24 hours. Upon the introduction of the hungry co-actor, the apparently sated chicken ate two-thirds again as much grain as it had already eaten. Recent work by Tolman and Wilson fully substantiates these results (10). In an extensive study of social-facilitation effects among albino rats, Harlow found dramatic increases in eating (11). In one of his experiments, for instance, the rats, shortly after weaning, were matched in pairs for weight. They were then fed alone and in pairs on alternate days. Figure 1 shows his results. It is clear that considerably more food was consumed by the

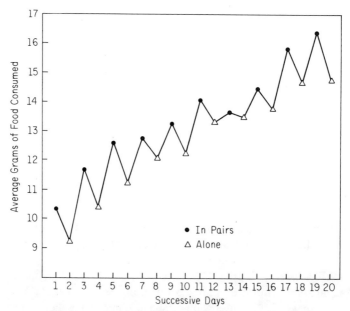

Figure 1. Data on feeding of isolated and paired rats.
[Harlow (11).]

animals when they were in pairs than when they were fed alone. James (*12*), too, found very clear evidence of increased eating among puppies fed in groups.

Perhaps the most dramatic effect of co-action is reported by Chen (*13*). Chen observed groups of ants working alone, in groups of two, and in groups of three. Each ant was observed under various conditions. In the first experimental session each ant was placed in a bottle half filled with sandy soil. The ant was observed for 6 hours. The time at which nest-building began was noted, and the earth excavated by the insect was carefully weighed. Two days afterward the same ants were placed in freshly filled bottles in pairs, and the same observations were made. A few days later the ants were placed in the bottles in groups of three, again for 6 hours. Finally, a few days after the test in groups of three, nest-building of the ants in isolation was observed. Figure 2 shows some of Chen's data.

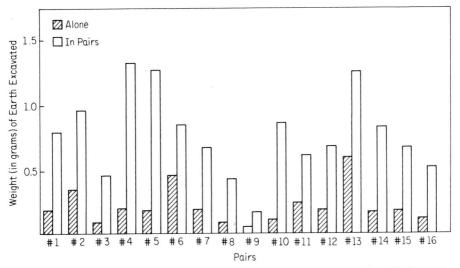

Figure 2. Data on net-building behavior of isolated and paired ants. [Chen (13).]

There is absolutely no question that the amount of work an ant accomplished increases markedly in the presence of another ant. In all pairs except one, the presence of a companion increased output by a factor of at least 2. The effect of co-action on the latency of the nest-building behavior was equally dramatic. The solitary ants of session 1 and the final session began working on the nest in 192 minutes, on the average. The latency period for ants in groups of two was only 28 minutes. The effects observed by Chen were limited to the immediate situation and seemed to have no lasting consequences for the ants. There were no differences in the results of session 1, during which the ants worked in isolation, and of the last experimental session, where they again worked in solitude.

If one assumes that under the conditions of Chen's experiment nest-building *is* the dominant response, then there is no reason why his findings could not be embraced by the generalization just proposed. Nest-building is a response which Chen's ants have fully mastered. Certainly, it is something that a mature ant need not learn. And this is simply an instance where the generalization that the presence of others enhances the emission of dominant and well-developed responses holds.

If the process involved in audience effects is also involved in co-action effects, then learning should be inhibited in the presence of other learners. Let us examine some literature in this field. Klopfer (14) observed greenfinches—in isolation and in hetero-sexual pairs—which were learning to discriminate between sources of palatable and of unpalatable food. And, as one would by now expect, his birds learned this discrimination task considerably more efficiently when working alone. I hasten to add that the subjects' sexual interests cannot be held responsible for the inhibition of learning in the paired birds. Allee and Masure, using Australian parakeets, obtained the same result for homo-sexual pairs as well (15). The speed of learning was considerably greater for the isolated birds than for the paired birds, regardless of whether the birds were of the same sex or of the opposite sex.

Similar results are found with cockroaches. Gates and Allee (16) compared data for cockroaches learning a maze in isolation, in groups of two, and in groups of three. They used an E-shaped maze. Its three runways, made of galvanized sheet metal, were sus-pended in a pan of water. At the end of the center runway was a dark bottle into which the photophobic cockroaches could escape from the noxious light. The results, in terms of time required to reach the bottle, are shown in Figure 3. It is clear from the data that the solitary cockroaches required considerably less time to learn the maze than the grouped animals. Gates and Allee believe that the group situation produced inhibition.

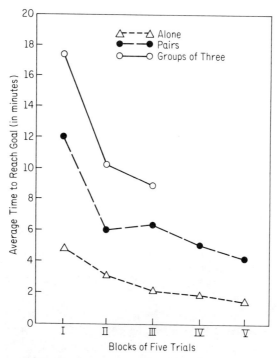

Figure 3. Data on maze learning in isolated and grouped cockroaches. [Gates and Allee (16).]

They add, however (*16*, p. 357): "The nature of these inhibiting forces is speculative, but the fact of some sort of group interference is obvious. The presence of other roaches did not operate to change greatly the movements to different parts of the maze, but did result in increased time per trial. The roaches tended to go to the corner or end of the runway and remain there a longer time when another roach was present than when alone; the other roach was a distracting stimulus."

The experiments on social facilitation performed by Floyd Allport in 1920 and continued by Dashiell in 1930 (*4, 17*), both of whom used human subjects, are the ones best known. Allport's subjects worked either in separate cubicles or sitting around a common table. When working in isolation they did the various tasks at the same time and were monitored by common time signals. Allport did everything possible to reduce the tendency to compete. The subjects were told that the results of their tests would not be compared and would not be shown to other staff members, and that they themselves should refrain from making any such comparisons.

Among the tasks used were the following: chain word association, vowel cancellation, reversible perspective, multiplication, problem solving, and judgments of odors and weights. The results of Allport's experiments are well known: in all but the problem-solving and judgments test, performance was better in groups than in the "alone" condition. How do these results fit our generalization? Word association, multiplication, the cancellation of vowels, and the reversal of the perceived orientation of an ambiguous figure all involve responses which are well established. They are responses which are either very well learned or under a very strong influence of the stimulus, as in the word-association task or the reversible-perspective test. The problem-solving test consists of disproving arguments of ancient philosophers. In contrast to the other tests, it does not involve well-learned responses. On the contrary, the probability of wrong (that is, logically incorrect) responses on tasks of this sort is rather high; in other words, wrong responses are dominant. Of interest, however, is the finding that while intellectual work suffered in the group situation, sheer output of words was increased. When working together, Allport's subjects tended consistently to write more. Therefore, the generalization proposed in the previous section can again be applied: if the presence of others raises the probability of dominant responses, and if strong (and many) incorrect response tendencies prevail, then the presence of others can only be detrimental to performance. The results of the judgment tests have little bearing on the present argument, since Allport gives no accuracy figures for evaluating performance. The data reported only show that the presence of others was associated with the avoidance of extreme judgments.

In 1928 Travis (*18*), whose work on the pursuit rotor I have already noted, repeated Allport's chain-word-association experiment. In contrast to Allport's results, Travis found that the presence of others decreased performance. The number of associations given by his subjects was greater when they worked in isolation. It is very significant, however, that Travis used stutterers as his subjects. In a way, stuttering is a manifestation of a struggle between conflicting response tendencies, all of which are strong and all of which compete for expression. The stutterer, momentarily hung up in the middle of a sentence, waits for the correct response to reach full ascendancy. He stammers because other competing tendencies are dominant at that moment. It is reasonable to assume that, to the extent that the verbal habits of a stutterer are characterized by conflicting response tendencies, the presence of others, by enhancing each of these response tendencies, simply heightens his conflict. Performance is thus impaired.

AVOIDANCE LEARNING

In two experiments on the learning of avoidance responses the performances of solitary and grouped subjects were compared. In one, rats were used; in the other, humans.

Let us first consider the results of the rat experiment, by Rasmussen (19). A number of albino rats, all litter mates, were deprived of water for 48 hours. The apparatus consisted of a box containing a dish of drinking water. The floor of the box was made of a metal grille wired to one pole of an electric circuit. A wire inserted in the water in the dish was connected to the other pole of the circuit. Thirsty rats were placed in the box alone and in groups of three. They were allowed to drink for 5 seconds with the circuit open. Following this period the shock circuit remained closed, and each time the rat touched the water he received a painful shock. Observations were made on the number of times the rats approached the water dish. The results of this experiment showed that the solitary rats learned to avoid the dish considerably sooner than the grouped animals did. The rats that were in groups of three attempted to drink twice as often as the solitary rats did, and suffered considerably more shock than the solitary subjects.

Let us examine Rasmussen's results somewhat more closely. For purposes of analysis let us assume that there are just two critical responses involved: drinking, and avoidance of contact with the water. They are clearly incompatible. But drinking, we may further assume, is the dominant response, and, like eating or any other dominant response, it is enhanced by the presence of others. The animal is therefore prevented, by the facilitation of drinking which derives from the presence of others, from acquiring the appropriate avoidance response.

The second of the two studies is quite recent and was carried out by Ader and Tatum (20). They devised the following situation with which they confronted their subjects, all medical students. Each subject is told on arrival that he will be taken to another room and seated in a chair, and that electrodes will be attached to his leg. He is instructed not to get up from the chair and not to touch the electrodes. He is also told not to smoke or vocalize, and is told that the experimenter will be in the next room. That is all he is told. The subjects are observed either alone or in pairs. In the former case the subject is brought to the room and seated at a table equipped with a red button which is connected to an electric circuit. Electrodes, by means of which electric shock can be administered, are attached to the calf of one leg. After the electrodes are attached, the experimenter leaves the room. From now on the subject will receive $1/2$ second of electric shock every 10 seconds unless he presses the red button. Each press of the button delays the shock by 10 seconds. Thus, if he is to avoid shock, he must press the button at least once every 10 seconds. It should be noted that no information was given him about the function of the button, or about the purpose of the experiment. No essential differences are introduced when subjects are brought to the room in pairs. Both are seated at the table and both become part of the shock circuit. The response of either subject delays the shock for both.

The avoidance response is considered to have been acquired when the subject (or pair of subjects) receives less than six shocks in a period of 5 minutes. Ader and Tatum report that the isolated students required, on the average, 11 minutes, 35 seconds to reach this criterion of learning. Of the 12 pairs which participated in the experiment, only two reached this criterion. One of them required 46 minutes, 40 seconds; the other, 68 minutes, 40 seconds! Ader and Tatum offer no explanation for their curious results. But there is no reason why we should not treat them in terms of the generalization proposed above. We are dealing here with a learning task, and the fact that the subjects are learning to avoid shock by pressing a red button does not introduce particular problems. They are confronted with an ambiguous task, and told nothing about the button. Pressing the button is simply not the dominant response in this situation. However, escaping is. Ader and Tatum report that eight of the 36 subjects walked out in the middle of the experiment.

One aspect of Ader and Tatum's results is especially worth noting. Once having learned the appropriate avoidance response, the individual subjects responded at considerably lower rates than the paired subjects. When we consider only those subjects who achieved the learning criterion and only those responses which occurred *after* criterion had been reached, we find that the response rates of the individual subjects were in all but one case lower than the response rates of the grouped subjects. This result further confirms the generalization that, while learning is impaired by the presence of others, the performance of learned responses is enhanced.

There are experiments which show that learning is enhanced by the presence of other learners (*21*), but in all these experiments, as far as I can tell, it was possible for the subject to *observe* the critical responses of other subjects, and to determine when he was correct and when incorrect. In none, therefore, has the co-action paradigm been employed in its pure form. That paradigm involves the presence of others, and nothing else. It requires that these others not be able to provide the subject with cues or information as to appropriate behavior. If other learners can supply the critical individual with such cues, we are dealing not with the problem of co-action but with the problem of imitation or vicarious learning.

THE PRESENCE OF OTHERS AS A SOURCE OF AROUSAL

The results I have discussed thus far lead to one generalization and to one hypothesis. The generalization which organizes these results is that the presence of others, as spectators or as co-actors, enhances the emission of dominant responses. We also know from extensive research literature that arousal, activation, or drive all have as a consequence the enhancement of dominant responses (*22*). We now need to examine the hypothesis that the presence of others increases the individual's general arousal or drive level.

The evidence which bears on the relationship between the presence of others and arousal is, unfortunately, only indirect. But there is some very suggestive evidence in one area of research. One of the more reliable indicators of arousal and drive is the activity of the endocrine systems in general, and of the adrenal cortex in particular. Adrenocortical functions are extremely sensitive to changes in emotional arousal, and it has been known for some time that organisms subjected to prolonged stress are likely to manifest substantial adrenocortical hypertrophy (23). Recent work (24) has shown that the main bio-chemical component of the adrenocortical output is hydrocortisone (17-hydroxy-corticosterone). Psychiatric patients characterized by anxiety states, for instance, show elevated plasma levels of hydrocortisone (25). Mason, Brady, and Sidman (26) have recently trained monkeys to press a lever for food and have given these animals unavoidable electric shocks, all preceded by warning signals. This procedure led to elevated hydro-cortisone levels; the levels returned to normal within 1 hour after the end of the experi-mental session. This "anxiety" reaction can apparently be attenuated if the animal is given repeated doses of reserpine 1 day before the experimental session (27). Sidman's conditioned avoidance schedule also results in raising the hydrocortisone levels by a factor of 2 to 4 (26). In this schedule the animal receives an electric shock every 20 seconds without warning, unless he presses a lever. Each press delays the shock for 20 seconds.

While there is a fair amount of evidence that adrenocortical activity is a reliable symptom of arousal, similar endocrine manifestations were found to be associated with increased population density (28). Crowded mice, for instance, show increased ampheta-mine toxicity—that is, susceptibility to the excitatory effects of amphetamine—against which they can be protected by the administration of phenobarbital, chlorpromazine, or reserpine (29). Mason and Brady (30) have recently reported that monkeys caged to-gether had considerably higher plasma levels of hydrocortisone than monkeys housed in individual cages. Thiessen (31) found increases in adrenal weights in mice housed in groups of 10 and 20 as compared with mice housed alone. The mere presence of other animals in the same room, but in separate cages, was also found to produce elevated levels of hydrocortisone. Table 1, taken from a report by Mason and Brady (30), shows plasma levels of hydrocortisone for three animals which lived at one time in cages that afforded them the possibility of visual and tactile contact and, at another time, in separate rooms.

TABLE 1. BASAL PLASMA CONCENTRATIONS OF 17-HYDROXYCORTICOSTERONE IN MONKEYS HOUSED ALONE (CAGES IN SEPARATE ROOMS), THEN IN A ROOM WITH OTHER MONKEYS (CAGES IN SAME ROOM). [Leiderman and Shapiro (35, p. 7)]

Subject	Time	Conc. of 17-Hydroxycorticosterone in Caged Monkeys (μg per 100 ml of plasma)	
		In Separate Rooms	In Same Room
M-1	9 a.m.	23	34
M-1	3 p.m.	16	27
M-2	9 a.m.	28	34
M-2	3 p.m.	19	23
M-3	9 a.m.	32	38
M-3	3 p.m.	23	31
Mean	9 a.m.	28	35
Mean	3 p.m.	19	27

TABLE 2. VARIATIONS IN URINARY CONCENTRATION OF HYDROCORTISONE OVER A 9-DAY PERIOD FOR FIVE LABORATORY MONKEYS AND ONE HUMAN HOSPITAL PATIENT. [LEIDERMAN AND SHAPIRO (35, p. 8)]

Subjects	Amounts Excreted (mg/24 hr)								
	Mon.	Tues.	Wed.	Thurs.	Fri.	Sat.	Sun.	Mon.	Tues.
Monkeys	1.88	1.71	1.60	1.52	1.70	1.16	1.17	1.88	
Patient		5.9	6.5	4.5	5.7	3.3	3.9	6.0	5.2

Mason and Brady also report urinary levels of hydrocortisone, by days of the week, for five monkeys from their laboratory and for one human hospital patient. These very suggestive figures are reproduced in Table 2 (*30*). In the monkeys, the low weekend traffic and activity in the laboratory seem to be associated with a clear decrease in hydrocortisone. As for the hospital patient, Mason and Brady report (*30*, p. 8), "he was confined to a thoracic surgery ward that bustled with activity during the weekdays when surgery and admissions occurred. On the weekends the patient retired to the nearby Red Cross building, with its quieter and more pleasant environment."

Admittedly, the evidence that the mere presence of others raises the arousal level is indirect and scanty. And, as a matter of fact, some work seems to suggest that there are conditions, such as stress, under which the presence of others may lower the animal's arousal level. Bovard (*32*), for instance, hypothesized that the presence of another member of the same species may protect the individual under stress by inhibiting the activity of the posterior hypothalamic centers which trigger the pituitary adrenal cortical and sympathetico-adrenal medullary responses to stress. Evidence for Bovard's hypothesis, however, is as indirect as evidence for the one which predicts arousal as a consequence of the presence of others, and even more scanty.

SUMMARY AND CONCLUSION

If one were to draw one practical suggestion from the review of the social-facilitation effects which are summarized in this article he would advise the student to study all alone, preferably in an isolated cubicle, and to arrange to take his examinations in the company of many other students, on stage, and in the presence of a large audience. The results of his examination would be beyond his wildest expectations, provided, of course, he had learned his material quite thoroughly.

I have tried in this article to pull together the early, almost forgotten work on social facilitation, and to explain the seemingly conflicting results. This explanation is, of course, tentative, and it has never been put to a direct experimental test. It is, moreover, not far removed from the one originally proposed by Allport. He theorized (*33*, p. 261) that "the sights and sounds of others doing the same thing" augment ongoing responses. Allport, however, proposed this effect only for *overt* motor responses, assuming (*33*, p. 274) that "*intellectual* or *implicit responses* of thought are hampered rather than facilitated" by the presence of others. This latter conclusion was probably suggested to him by the negative results he observed in his research on the effects of co-action on problem solving.

Needless to say, the presence of others may have effects considerably more complex than that of increasing the individual's arousal level. The presence of others may provide cues as to appropriate or inappropriate responses, as in the case of imitation or vicarious learning. Or it may supply the individual with cues as to the measure of danger in an ambiguous or stressful situation. Davitz and Mason (*34*), for instance, have shown that the presence of an unafraid rat reduces the fear of another rat in stress. Bovard (*32*) believes that the calming of the rat in stress which is in the presence of an unafraid companion is mediated by inhibition of activity of the posterior hypothalamus. But in their experimental situations (that is, the open field test) the possibility that cues for appropriate escape or avoidance responses are provided by the co-actor is not ruled out. We might therefore be dealing not with the effects of the mere presence of others but with the considerably more complex case of imitation. The animal may not be calming *because* of his companion's presence. He may be calming *after* having copied his companion's attempted escape responses. The paradigm which I have examined in this article pertains only to the effects of the mere presence of others, and to the consequences for the arousal level. The exact parameters involved in social facilitation still must be specified.

REFERENCES AND NOTES

1. N. Triplett, *Amer. J. Psychol. 9*, 507 (1897).
2. L. E. Travis, *J. Abnormal Soc. Psychol. 20*, 142 (1925).
3. B. O. Bergum and D. J. Lehr, *J. Appl. Psychol. 47*, 75 (1963).
4. J. F. Dashiell, *J. Abnormal Soc. Psychol. 25*, 190 (1930).
5. J. Pessin, *Amer. J. Psychol. 45*, 263 (1933).
6. R. W. Husband, *J. Genet. Psychol. 39*, 258 (1931). In this task the blindfolded subject traces a maze with his finger.
7. J. Pessin and R. W. Husband, *J. Abnormal Soc. Psychol. 28*, 148 (1933).
8. See, for instance, E. Dufy, *Activation and Behavior* (Wiley, New York, 1962); K. W. Spence, *Behavior Theory and Conditioning* (Yale Univ. Press, New Haven, 1956); R. B. Zajonc and B. Nieuwenhuyse, *J. Exp. Psychol. 67*, 276 (1964).
9. E. Bayer, *Z. Psychol. 112*, 1 (1929).
10. C. W. Tolman and G. T. Wilson, *Animal Behavior 13*, 134 (1965).
11. H. F. Harlow, *J. Genet. Psychol. 43*, 211 (1932).
12. W. T. James, *J. Comp. Physiol. Psychol. 46*, 427 (1953); *J. Genet. Psychol. 96*, 123 (1960); W. T. James and D. J. Cannon, *ibid. 87*, 225 (1956).
13. S. C. Chen, *Physiol. Zool. 10*, 420 (1937).
14. P. H. Klopfer, *Science 128*, 903 (1958).
15. W. C. Allee and R. H. Masure, *Physiol. Zool. 22*, 131 (1936).
16. M. J. Gates and W. C. Allee, *J. Comp. Psychol. 15*, 331 (1933).
17. F. H. Allport, *J. Exp. Psychol. 3*, 159 (1920).
18. L. E. Travis, *J. Abnormal Soc. Psychol. 23*, 45 (1928).
19. E. Rasmussen, *Acta Psychol. 4*, 275 (1939).
20. R. Ader and R. Tatum, *J. Exp. Anal. Behavior 6*, 357 (1963).
21. H. Gurnee, *J. Abnormal Soc. Psychol. 34*, 529 (1939); J. C. Welty, *Physiol. Zool. 7*, 85 (1934).
22. See K. W. Spence, *Behavior Theory and Conditioning* (Yale Univ. Press, New Haven, 1956).

23. H. Selye, *J. Clin. Endocrin. 6*, 117 (1946).
24. D. H. Nelson and L. T. Samuels, *ibid. 12*, 519 (1952).
25. E. L. Bliss, A. A. Sandberg, D. H. Nelson, *J. Clin. Invest. 32*, 9 (1953); F. Board, H. Persky, D. A. Hamburg, *Psychosom. Med. 18*, 324 (1956).
26. J. W. Mason, J. V. Brady, M. Sidman, *Endocrinology 60*, 741 (1957).
27. J. W. Mason and J. V. Brady, *Science 124*, 983 (1956).
28. D. D. Thiessen, *Texas Rep. Biol. Med. 22*, 266 (1964).
29. L. Lasagna and W. P. McCann, *Science 125*, 1241 (1957).
30. J. W. Mason and J. V. Brady, in *Psychobiological Approaches to Social Behavior*, P. H. Leiderman and D. Shapiro, Eds. (Stanford Univ. Press, Stanford, Calif., 1964).
31. D. D. Thiessen, *J. Comp. Physiol. Psychol. 57*, 412 (1964).
32. E. W. Bovard, *Psychol. Rev. 66*, 267 (1959).
33. F. H. Allport, *Social Psychology* (Houghton-Mifflin, Boston, 1924).
34. J. R. Davitz and D. J. Mason, *J. Comp. Physiol. Psychol. 48*, 149 (1955).
35. P. H. Leiderman and D. Shapiro, Eds., *Psychobiological Approaches to Social Behavior* (Stanford Univ. Press, Stanford, Calif., 1964).
36. The preparation of this article was supported in part by grants Nonr-1224(34) from the Office of Naval Research and GS-629 from the National Science Foundation.

— · — · — · — · — · — · — · — · —

9 · LEADERSHIP

KURT LEWIN
RONALD LIPPITT

Leadership: Authoritarian and Democratic *

If one hopes to investigate experimentally such fundamental socio-psychological problems as: group ideology; conflicts between and within groups; types of their spontaneous substructuring; the stability of various spontaneous group structures versus structures created by external authority; minority problems; renegade, scapegoat, double loyalty conflicts—one has to create a setup where group life might be studied under rather free but well defined conditions. Instead of utilizing the groups in schools, clubs, factories, one should create groups experimentally because only in this way the factors influencing group life will not be left to chance but will be in the hands of the experimenter.

However, one should break away from the rather narrow aspect of studying the effect of the group influence on the individual (e.g. the effect of various groups on the suggestibility of the individual) as the main problem; one should consider not only one effect of a given social situation (e.g. the influence on productivity). Rather one should try to approach an experimental procedure: (1) where group life can proceed freely; (2) where the total group behavior, its structure and development can be registered. Any specific problem such as group ideology should be approached in the experimental setup and in the analysis of the data as a part of this greater whole.

Such data might always be analyzed with a double frame of reference, that of the individual group member and of the group as a dynamic unity.

The main interest of the present preliminary study is to develop from this point of view techniques to investigate "democracy" and "autocracy" as group atmospheres.

Two experimental mask-making clubs of ten and eleven year old children were selected from a group of eager volunteers of the fifth and sixth grades of the University Elementary School. A preliminary sociometric survey, following Moreno's technique, was made of the affinities and rejections existing in the two classrooms. With a sociogram of

*Kurt Lewin and Ronald Lippitt, "An Experimental Approach to the Study of Autocracy and Democracy: A Preliminary Note," *Sociometry* 1 (1938): 292–300. Reprinted by permission.

each group at hand the groups were selected (one from each schoolroom) from the available volunteers so that the groups would be as nearly equated as possible on the number of potency of friendship and rejection relationships, and on general popularity and leadership characteristics of the members. Instead of choosing a clique of close friends five children were chosen in each case who had expressed little relationship with each other, either in the school situation or in playing together in non-school groupings. It was believed that any inter-personal relations that developed during the life of the club could then be more closely correlated to the common life space of the new group membership.

In a ten minute preliminary meeting with each group the leader made it clear that the aim of the club would be to make theatrical masks (a new activity for all of the children); that the masks would belong to the group as a whole; and that one mask would be made at a time rather than each individual making one by himself. Two half-hour meetings a week were held with each group, the same experimenter being the leader in both clubs.

It is methodologically meaningless in studying democracy and autocracy experimentally to be guided mainly by the question: What is "the" prototype of democracy and which is the "true" autocracy. One should realize from the start that there are many varieties of such atmospheres. The experimental approach can only try to attack one case at a time. What type of democracy should be chosen should be less guided by the tendency to copy some historically given case than by the attempt to realize those types of group atmospheres which promise the best insight into the underlying dynamics and laws. Only the insight into these laws, and not the search for a prototype, will enable us to answer the question of what are the common properties and individual differences of autocracies and democracies.

With such a point of view the experimenter attempted to differentiate the atmospheres of the two groups chiefly in the following ways:

AUTHORITARIAN	DEMOCRATIC
1. All determination of policy by the strongest person (leader).	1. All policies a matter of group determination, encouraged and drawn out by the leader.
2. Techniques and steps of attaining the goal (completed mask) dictated by the authority, one at a time, so that future direction was always uncertain to a large degree.	2. Activity perspective given by an explanation of the general steps of the process (clay mould, plaster paris, papier mache, etc.) during discussion at first meeting. Where technical advice was needed the leader tried to point out 2 or 3 alternative procedures from which choice could be made.
3. The authority usually structured autocratically the activities of each member—the task and whom to work with.	3. The members were free to work with whomever they chose and the division of tasks was left up to the group.
4. The dominator criticized and praised individual's activities and remained aloof from group participation. He was always impersonal rather than outwardly hostile or friendly (a necessary concession in method).	4. The leader attempted to be a group member in spirit but not in the actual work. He gave criticism and praise, generally in regard to the group as a whole.

It is obvious that with voluntary group participation, and with the cooperation of the school system radically autocratic methods would not be utilized. A congenial extra-group relationship was maintained with all of the children during the entire course of the experimental sessions. The attempt was to make the authoritarian atmosphere as much more autocratic than the schoolroom as the democratic one was freer than the school-room.

During the series of twelve meetings for each group four trained observers made observational records, synchronized in minute units, of a varied nature. These techniques are here described very briefly:

1. A quantitative running account of the social interactions of the five children and leader, in terms of symbols for ascendant, submissive, and objective (fact-minded) approaches and responses, including a category of purposeful refusal to respond to a social approach.

2. A quantitative group structure analysis minute by minute with running comments to give a record of: activity subgroupings (e.g. three of the children are busy mixing plaster of paris, one is tearing up paper towels for papier mache, and the fifth is working on the clay mould. This would be a 3-1-1 group structure with three subgroups. One individual may be a subgroup.); the activity goal of each subgroup; whether the subgroup was initiated by the leader or spontaneously formed by the children; and ratings on the degree of interest and unity of each subgroup.

3. Running comments and ratings indicating shifts of interest from minute to minute for each member (from complete involvement in the club activity to "out-of-the-field" preoccupations).

4. A stenographic record of conversation.

5. To the observers' records outlined above was added a post-meeting writeup by the leader of his impressions gathered from the more intimate contacts with the children.

Laid side by side these records give a rather complete minute by minute, meeting by meeting picture of the ongoing life of the group. A wide variety of quantitative and qualitative analyses are possible. Below are listed a few upon which we have already made some progress:

1. The total volume of social interactions broken down into ascendant, submissive, objective, and ignoring behavior.

2. The volume and types of social interactions between subgroups as compared to those within subgroups.

3. Analysis in terms of individual activity curves of these same data.

4. The stability of group structure and of specific subgroupings under varied conditions.

5. The influence on unity and stability of structure of leader-initiated and spontaneous subgroupings.

6. Analysis of stenographic records in terms of such categories as hostility, attention demands, resistant behavior, hostile and objective criticism, expression of competition and cooperation, amount of dependence on authority, expressions of "I-centeredness" (ego-centrism) versus "we-centeredness" (group spirit), etc.

7. Analysis of gradients of activity such as increase of hostility, and volume of total activity.
8. Changes of interest in terms of such related factors as group stability, outbreak of hostility, and standards of production.

The first purpose of this technique of observation is to record as fully and insightfully as possible the total behavior of the group. This is a distinct break away from the usual procedure of recording only certain symptoms which are determined in advance. It is an attempt to apply the same "total behavior" methodology in social psychology which has proven fruitful in a number of investigations into individual psychology (i.e. Dembo's study on anger, Karsten's of psychological satiation, and that of Dembo and Barker on frustration), and which is a logical procedure for the "field theoretical" approach in social psychology.

The second point we wish to stress is that exact quantitative records become valueless if one loses sight of the meaning which the single action had within the total setting. It is therefore most important to have some complete characterization of the atmosphere as a whole. The necessary quantitative analysis (choice of items, classification of items, and statistical combinations) should always be made in view of these larger wholes.

The comprehensiveness of these data makes it possible to follow up with re-analysis new clues which arise from time to time as to behavioral relationships. It is our belief at the present time that this "total behavior" technique, combining strands of all degrees of quantativeness and qualitativeness offers the most hopeful methodology yet developed for the experimental study of group life. The possibility of focusing numerous strands of evidence upon one or two focal points corrects to some extent the necessity of working with such a number of variables as the social situation presents.

An interesting set of problems has arisen in the statistical analysis of social interactions which has led to the development of an embryo "mathematics of group life." It became obvious that before statements could be made about the relative amount of interactions between members of in-groups under various circumstances or between members of out-groups, it was necessary to take into account the possibilities of in- and out-group communication in each type of group structure. For example, it is clear that if all members were working on isolated individual bits of activity there could be no in-group relationships for no subgroup would have more than one member. If all five children were united in one activity unity there would be no possibility of interactions with an out-group member. In case the total group were divided into two subgroups these possibilities are different in case the two subgroups contain 4 and 1 children, or 3 and 2 children.

It is necessary then to compute the possibilities of in- and out- group communication for each possible group structure. In case the total group contains 5 individuals the following 7 group structures are possible:

$$5, 4\text{-}1, 3\text{-}2, 3\text{-}1\text{-}1, 2\text{-}2\text{-}1, 2\text{-}1\text{-}1\text{-}1, 1\text{-}1\text{-}1\text{-}1\text{-}1$$

The formula for computing in-group interaction possibilities (*ip*) and out-group interaction possibilities (*op*) for any given group structure may be stated simply:

$$ip = a\,(a\text{-}1) + b\,(b\text{-}1) + \ldots r\,(r\text{-}1)$$
$$op = m\,(m\text{-}1) - ip$$

where a, b, . . . r are the number of members in the various subgroups coexisting in a particular group structure and where m is the total number of members in the group.

In our case we find the following interaction possibilities: Possible group structures

	5	4-1	3-2	3-1-1	2-2-1	2-1-1-1	1-1-1-1-1
ip	20	12	8	6	4	2	0
op	0	8	12	14	16	18	20

Weighting these possibilities by the time that each group structure existed we get an index with which to measure the relative in-group, out-group, and total social interactions in the authoritarian and democratic atmospheres. We can use the following formula for the total in-group interaction possibilities (Σip) during a given period of group life:

$$\Sigma ip = ip(A).t(A) + ip(B).t(B) + \ldots + ip(L).t(L)$$

where A, B, ..., L are the various types of group structure which came up during that period; $t(A)$, $t(B)$, . . . $t(L)$ the duration of each group structure; $ip(A)$, $ip(B)$, . . . $ip(L)$ their in-group interaction possibilities.

The total out-group possibilities (Σop) is:

$$\Sigma op = op(A).t(A) + op(B).t(B) + \ldots + op(L).t(L)$$

The total social interaction possibilities (Σsp) is:

$$\Sigma sp = \Sigma ip + \Sigma op$$

Ex: If, during a certain club meeting the structure was 4-1 for 5 minutes, 3-1-1 for 10 minutes, and 2-1-1-1 for 10 minutes the formulation of the index would demand this computation:

$$\Sigma ip = 12 \times 5 + 6 \times 10 + 2 \times 10 = 140$$
$$\Sigma op = 8 \times 5 + 14 \times 10 + 18 \times 10 = 360$$
$$\Sigma sp = 140 + 360 = 500$$

The computation of these interaction possibilities seems an essential step in the experimental treatment of group relationships. It makes possible also the correction for missing members now and then over a series of club meetings.

There is little space in this note for an adequate exposition of the analyses which have been completed on the lives of these two experimental clubs. In summary form the findings indicate that:

1. A higher state of tension existed in the atmosphere of the autocratic group. A number of findings focus on this point: (a) a much higher volume of social interactions (55% more) in spite of the fact that the ongoing activity demanded less communication than in the democratic group; (b) a less stable group structure was maintained; (c) more ascendance and less submissiveness and objectivity of members toward each other; (d) the development of two scapegoats during 12 meetings; (e) about 30 times as much hostility expressed between members as in the democratic group.

2. More cooperative endeavor emerged in the democratic group; (a) a much higher incidence of offering and asking for cooperation; (b) many more occurrences of praise and expressions of friendliness.

3. More expression of an objective attitude in the democratic group: (a) many more constructive suggestions offered; (b) more give and take of objective criticism without personal involvement.

4. Constructiveness was higher in the democratic group: (a) superiority of the group products; (b) more careless and unfinished work in the autocratic group; (3) greater incidence of constructive suggestions in the democratic group.

5. The feeling of "we'ness" was greater in democracy, and that of "I'ness" was greater in the authoritarian group as shown by test situations and by analysis of the stenographic records.

6. The group structure was more stable and tended to maintain a higher degree of unity in the democratic group. When the authority withdrew his influence on the situation the group structure tended toward disorganization in the autocratic group.

7. Twice in the autocratic group a situation arose where the group combined its aggression against one individual, making him a scapegoat. In both cases the scapegoat quit the group. No such lack of harmony existed in the democratic group.

8. The feeling for group property and group goals was much better developed in the democratic group as shown by test situations and the stenographic accounts.

9. Following the one exchange of group members which was made there was a decrease in dominating behavior for the child transferred to the democratic group and an increase in like behavior for the child changed to the authoritarian group.

It seems necessary to reiterate that a number of these specific results, which will be tabulated more fully when further analysis is completed, may be due to the particular types of autocratic and democratic atmospheres developed in these groups. For instance there would probably not be such an overt expression of hostility in most cases of authoritarian group atmosphere, for it would be suppressed. This "steam valve" of free expression was purposely left open however in this investigation because it was hoped it would prove a good measuring stick for the record of tension when it existed. This seems to have been the case. The thoughtful establishment of such test areas seems at the present to be a very fruitful procedure. Only further research, some of which is already under way, with a variety of groups and leaders will make possible a more assured statement as to the common factors in these dynamic relationships. These new experiments indicate, for example, that the dynamic differences between free and authoritarian atmospheres present quite a different picture in case the freedom of the group swings from democratic group determination to anarchic individualism.

A more sociological survey of the atmospheres of the other groups (e.g. family, school) in which the children have membership-character will also need to be made for clues as to the influence of overlapping group memberships upon the development of the experimental group ideology. New methods of experimental manipulation are also being developed as we become more oriented to the nature of the task.

— · — · — · — · — · — · — · — · — · — · —

FRED E. FIEDLER

Leadership Effectiveness *

THE GROUP

By this term we generally mean a set of individuals who share a common fate, that is, who are *interdependent* in the sense that an event which affects one member is likely to affect all (Campbell, 1958). Typically, the human group shares a common goal, and its members interact in their attempt to achieve this goal. Typically, also, the members are rewarded as a group for achieving their goal; they are punished or they feel that they have failed if their group does not perform as expected.

Task groups, which are our major concern, very rarely are isolated units. It is, therefore, not only unrealistic but often misleading to think of the task group as independent from the larger organization of which it is a part. While we shall return to this problem later on, it is well to emphasize at this point that almost all task groups are creatures of a larger organization and that the organization assigns members to the group, appoints the leader, and specifies the task. The organization, represented by higher management, evaluates task performance and rewards the group or its members for compliance and effective performance, and it penalizes the members or the entire group for noncompliance or poor performance. A group which fails to perform over extended periods of time may be disbanded and its members reassigned or discharged.

It is curious that the concept of group, which is extensively used in social psychology, should have such a wide range of definitions. Andrews (1955) has defined the group as "an association of people who meet face to face frequently; have certain common sentiments, attitudes and values; carry on activities together; have feelings of mutual identification and recognition; and normally, pursue a common goal."

Kretch and Crutchfield (1948) have defined the group as follows:

A group does not merely mean individuals characterized by some similar property. Thus, for example, a collection of Republicans or farmers or Negroes or blind men is not a group. These collections may be called classes of people. The term group, on the other hand, refers to *two or more people who bear an explicit psychological relationship to one another.* This means that for each member of the group the other members must exist in some more or less immediate psychological way so that their behavior and their characteristics influence him.

These are, by no means, the only definitions available. A perusal of the literature will unearth dozens more (see Bass, 1960a).

For purposes of discussing task groups, it is useful to draw attention to some further distinctions. A classification of groups can be made in terms of the work relations among its members and especially in terms of the leader's role in directing the group's activities.

---

*From *A Theory of Leadership Effectiveness* by F. E. Fiedler. Copyright ©1967 by McGraw-Hill, Inc. Used by permission of McGraw-Hill Book Company.

Will the leader need to coordinate the work of his members so that they will not fall over one another? Will he need to motivate his men? Or will he have to spend his time in arbitrating differences among his group members? We shall deal with this problem in the next chapter.

THE LEADER

This term has, if possible, even more definitions than the term "group." Several quoted by Andrews (1955) are here reproduced.

> Leadership is the exercise of authority and the making of decisions (Dubin, 1951).
> Leadership is the initiation of acts which result in a consistent pattern of group interaction directed toward the solution of a mutual problem (Hemphill, 1954).
> The leader is the man who comes closest to realizing the norms the group values highest; this conformity gives him his high rank, which attracts people and implies the right to assume control of the group (Homans, 1950).
> Leadership is an ability to persuade or direct men without use of the prestige or power of formal office or external circumstance (Reuter, 1941).
> The leader is one who succeeds in getting others to follow him (Cowley, in Hemphill, 1954).
> The leader is the person who creates the most effective change in group performance (Cattell, 1953).
> The leader is one who initiates and facilitates member interaction (Bales and Strodtbeck, 1951).
> Leadership, in group discussion, is the assumption of the tasks of initiating, organizing, clarifying, questioning, motivating, summarizing, and formulating conclusions; hence, the leader is the person who spends the most time talking to the group, since he carries out more of these verbal tasks (Bass, 1949).
> Leadership is the process of influencing group activities toward goal setting and goal achievement (Stogdill, 1950).
> The leader is that person identified and accepted as such by his followers (Sanford, 1949).

Various workers in this area have proposed still other definitions of the term "leader." In particular, there has been a distinction among emergent, elected, and appointed leaders, between leaders and headmen (Gibb, 1954), and between formal and informal leaders. Leadership has also been identified by some in terms of leadership acts, thus defining the leader as the person who behaves most like a leader at a given time (e.g., Hemphill 1949).

We shall here define the leader as *the individual in the group given the task of directing and coordinating task-relevant group activities or who, in the absence of a designated leader, carries the primary responsibility for performing these functions in the group.* We must take cognizance of the fact that leadership functions are frequently shared among group members and that one person may be most influential at one time and less influential at another (Berkowitz, 1953, Cattell, 1951). However, we shall here designate only one group member as leader, namely, the one who meets one of the following criteria: (1) he is appointed as the leader, supervisor, chairman, etc., by a representative of the larger organization of which the group is a part; (2) he is elected by the group; or (3) if there is neither an elected nor an appointed leader, or if such a leader is clearly only a figurehead, he is the individual who can be identified as most influential by task-relevant questions on a sociometric preference questionnaire.

LEADER'S EFFECTIVENESS

This also has been variously defined. Stogdill (1957) has proposed that group effectiveness be defined in terms of (1) the group's output, (2) its morale, and (3) the satisfactions of its members. A similar definition has been advanced by Bass (1960a). Some investigators have also gone on the assumption that any task performance can be utilized as a criterion. On the other hand, it seems at least equally reasonable to take the position that the group typically owes its very existence to the tasks it is supposed to perform and that it will be evaluated primarily on the basis of these task performances rather than on the satisfaction and morale of the members of the group. A group may have low morale or it may give little satisfaction to its members and yet perform well on its mission. However, a group which continually fails to complete its mission will disintegrate or it may be disbanded no matter how high the morale and member satisfactions.

We shall here evaluate leader effectiveness in terms of group performance on the group's primary assigned task, even though the group's output is not entirely the function of the leader's skills. Such events as personality clashes, bad luck, or unfavorable circumstances may affect the group output to a greater or lesser extent. So may member abilities, motivation, and organizational support. However, in terms of the statistical treatment of leadership research such factors manifest themselves as "error variance," which reduces the relationship between leader attributes and group performance. This research strategy errs thus in the conservative direction. Morale and member satisfaction, while certainly affected by the leader's behavior, are here seen as interesting by-products rather than as measures of task-group performance. An exception is, of course, the case where the building of morale, or the increase of member satisfaction, is the primary goal of the leader and is explicitly made the leader's task. (This occasionally occurs when, for example, a military commander or business executive is told to rebuild the morale of a unit.) Usually, however, the major organizational concern is with the effectiveness and performance of a group, be this over a period of hours, days, or weeks, or over a long period of years or decades.

★ ★ ★

Interest in empirical investigations of leadership style dates back to the classic studies by Lewin and Lippitt (1938) on the effect of democratic, autocratic, and laissez-faire leadership styles on the behavior of boys' clubs. These studies have had a far-reaching impact on the field. They have raised questions about the degree to which the leader should take major responsibility for the direction and administration of the group versus the degree to which the leader should be concerned primarily with personal relations; the degree to which the leader should permit and encourage participation by members of his group; and the degree to which he should share planning and decision making with his associates.

McGrath (1961) in his summary of the literature has pointed to two clusters of leadership behavior and attitudes which have been the focus of most psychological research in the area. These clusters have been variously labeled as autocratic, authoritarian, task-oriented, and initiating on the one hand versus democratic, equalitarian, permissive, group-oriented, and considerate on the other. The leader can either take the responsibility for making decisions and for directing the group members ("I make the plans and you carry them out") or he can, to a greater or lesser extent, share the decision-making and coordinating functions with the members of his group. He can use the proverbial stick or the equally proverbial carrot for motivating his members. All these methods, and any combination of them, have worked in some situations and not in others (Gibb, 1954; Hare, 1962). The problem of what constitutes the best leadership style has, in fact, been one of the major controversies in the area.

While this black and white categorization is grossly oversimplified, the orthodox viewpoint has been reflected in traditional supervisory and managerial training and practices as well as in military doctrine. It holds that the leader must be decisive, that he must think and plan for the group, and that the responsibility for directing, controlling, coordinating, and evaluating the group members' actions is primarily his and that it cannot be shifted to others.

The opposing viewpoint, represented by the human relations-oriented theorists, holds that the leader will be most effective when he can call out the creativity and willing cooperation of his men and that he can do this most effectively only when he can get his group members to participate in the decision-making processes and in the direction of group action. A number of investigators (e.g., Pelz, 1952) have pointed out that different leadership situations require different leadership styles. Generally, however, there have been few empirical tests to spell out the specific circumstances under which various leadership styles are most appropriate.

The theory presented in this book attempts to do this. In briefest outline and as a way of orienting the reader to the main problem with which we shall be concerned, the theory postulates two major styles of leadership. One of these is a leadership style which is primarily task-oriented, which satisfies the leader's need to gain satisfaction from

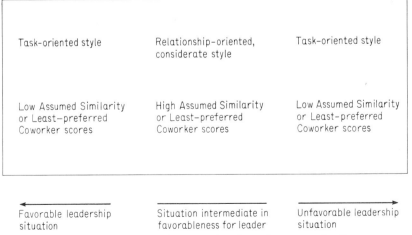

Figure 1-1. Leadership styles appropriate for various group situations.

performing the task. The other is primarily oriented toward attaining a position of prominence and toward achieving good interpersonal relations. In terms of promoting group performance, our data show that the task-oriented type of leadership style is more effective in group situations which are either very favorable for the leader or which are very unfavorable for the leader. The relationship-oriented leadership style is more effective in situations which are intermediate in favorableness. Favorableness of the situation is here defined as the degree to which the situation enables the leader to exert influence over his group. Leadership style is measured by means of interpersonal perception scores which ask the leader to describe his most and least preferred coworkers. The specific scores, the esteem for the Least-preferred Coworker (LPC) scores and the Assumed Similarity between Opposites (ASo) scores, are described in the third chapter.

Figure 1-1 presents a schematic picture of the major hypothesis. As Figure 1-1 indicates, the theory predicts that a task-oriented style will be maximally effective in favorable leadership situations, a relationship-oriented style will be effective in intermediate situations, and a task-oriented leadership style will again be most effective in unfavorable group situations.

★   ★   ★

The Contingency Model postulates that leadership effectiveness depends upon the appropriate matching of the individual's leadership style of interacting and the influence which the group situation provides. What are the implications of this theory and our findings for the selection and recruitment of leaders for training and for the management of organizations?

The major point of this theory is that leadership effectiveness—that is, effective group performance—depends just as much on the group situation as it does on the leader. If the theory is right this means that a personnel program that deals only with the personality aspects of the leader or only with the situational aspects of the organization is bound to fail. One style of leadership is not in itself better than the other, nor is one type of leadership behavior appropriate for all conditions. Hence, almost everyone should be able to succeed as a leader in some situations and almost everyone is likely to fail in others. If we want to improve organizational performance we must deal not only with the leader's style but also with the factors in the situation which provide him with influence. While one can never say that something is impossible, and while someone may well discover the all-purpose leadership style or behavior at some future time, our own data and those which have come out of sound research by other investigators do not promise such miraculous cures. And if leadership performance is in fact a product of both the individual's leadership style and the leadership situation then it is logically impossible that one leadership style could serve in every context. On the other hand, it also follows from this theory that we can improve group or organizational performance either by changing the leader to fit the situation or by changing the situation to fit the leader.

Industrial psychologists and personnel men typically view the executive's position as fixed and immutable and the individual as highly plastic and trainable. When we think of improving leadership performance we generally think first of training the leader. Yet, we know all too well from our experience with psychotherapy, our attempts to rehabilitate prison inmates, drug addicts, or juvenile delinquents—not to mention our difficulties with rearing our own progeny—that our ability to change personality has its limitations.

A person's leadership style, as we have used the term, reflects the individual's basic motivational and need structure. At best it takes one, two, or three years of intensive psychotherapy to effect lasting changes in personality structure. It is difficult to see how we can change in more than a few cases an equally important set of core values in a few hours of lectures and role playing or even in the course of a more intensive training program of one or two weeks.

On the other hand, executive jobs and supervisory responsibilities almost always can be modified to a greater or lesser extent both by the incumbent of the position and, even more readily, by his organization. In fact, organizations frequently change the specifications of a management job to make it more appealing to the executive whom the organization wishes to attract or whom it wishes to retain. If anything, many organizations change executive jobs and responsibilities more often than might be necessary.

Executives at higher echelons are well aware of the fact that they must take account of the strengths and weaknesses of their subordinate managers. One man may operate most effectively when his authority is strictly defined and circumscribed while another must be given considerable leeway and discretion. Some executives excel in staff work while others perform best in line positions; some are known as specialists in trouble-shooting who thrive on turmoil and crisis while others perform best as administrators of well-running subunits of the organization. Our theory provides a conceptual framework and a preliminary set of guidelines for determining how to match the leadership situation and the man. While cookbook prescriptions are still a task for the future we can indicate here some of the major directions which our theory indicates. The basic methods in managing executive and managerial talent has been by leadership recruitment and selection and by leadership training. We shall add to these an organizational engineering approach and discuss these three approaches in light of the theory and the data which this book has presented.

LEADERSHIP RECRUITMENT AND SELECTION

The classical and "time-tested" method for maintaining a cadre of executives calls for the recruitment of men who not only have the technical experience and background which the job requires but also the personality attributes and abilities which will make them effective leaders. Given a candidate who has the technical and intellectual qualifications, the recruiter then tries to predict the individual's leadership potential from his background and possibly from psychological tests.

However, previous leadership experience is likely to predict future performance only if the past leadership situation was nearly identical to the leadership situation for which the individual is to be selected. And all too frequently the recruiter knows very little about the leadership situation the individual is likely to face. He knows next to nothing about what he will do two or five years later. And no system of leadership selection is likely to work without this knowledge as long as leadership performance varies from situation to situation or from task to task. That this is the case has been amply demonstrated. To mention but a few studies, Knoell and Forgays (1952) showed that the same aircrew might perform excellently on one task and quite poorly on another. Flanagan's (1949) study of naval officer performance showed that highly rated naval officers did not necessarily obtain high ratings in officer candidate school and that officers' efficiency ratings for sea duty were uncorrelated with their efficiency ratings for shore duty. And our own data on bomber crews, tank crews . . . , and Belgian navy teams . . . further support this statement. If the performance of the same group can be excellent on one subtask and poor on another it is obvious that we cannot hope to predict how the leader will perform with a single leadership test. This is even less likely when neither his future group nor his future tasks are known.

Some studies have shown consistency of leadership performance. These include studies by Bass (1954), Carter (1953), Gibb (1947), and Bell and French (1955). However, all of these studies were conducted in highly controlled laboratory settings in which the leadership situations were quite similar from task to task. Where tasks differed, as they did in a study by Carter, leadership performance was similar within families of tasks but dissimilar from one task family to another. In Gibb's study, groups were given widely different tasks. However, leadership performance was assessed by members' ratings of their fellow members, and these ratings are likely to be highly influenced by halo effect.

Also worth mentioning are the important studies which indicate that peer ratings can be used to predict future leadership performance (for example, Anderhalter et al., 1952; Hollander, 1956). These demonstrate respectably high relations between peer ratings obtained in officer candidate school and subsequent efficiency ratings by superior officers several years later. Do these indicate that leadership ability is a personality attribute that remains constant over situations? Sociometric studies cannot be interpreted this way. These studies are important contributions in their own right. It should be noted, however, that the predictions are based on ratings of men who performed highly similar tasks as students in officer candidate school and as junior officers. The men were rated *as individuals* and not strictly in terms of the performance of their groups. The man who looks and acts like the stereotype of a good officer while in officer candidate school will probably still look and act this way several years later. This is not to say that ratings of this type may not be extremely useful for various purposes. In fact, leadership style measures make sense only if the basic personality remains constant over situations, but it is unlikely that these ratings can serve as generalized predictors of leadership ability as measured by group performance.

We must emphasize that management and administrative functions, or being a "good executive," are not identical with leadership. Management is more than leadership. It includes routine administration and the maintenance of communications with other departments or other agencies; it requires knowledge of organizational procedures and regulations. It usually involves negotiating and bargaining functions between the manager and his own superior or with others at his level to maintain the status of his department within the total organization (see for example Barnard, 1938; Katz and Kahn, 1965). It also requires the motivation to seek and accept executive responsibilities. Some of these factors of administrative skill may well be predictable by personality and achievement tests. Leadership ability—the knack of getting any group to perform in a highly efficient manner—is not currently predictable. Considering the fact that years of effort have failed to produce any generally valid leadership tests, and that these tests would fly in the face of all currently available evidence, it seems safe to say that they are not likely to appear in future.

If our theory is correct then the recruitment and selection of leaders can be effective only when we can also specify the relevant components of the situation for which the leader is being recruited. There is no reason to believe that this cannot be done, or that this should not be done in specific cases. Difficulties arise because leadership situations change over time. The organization must then be aware of the type of leadership situations into which the individual should be successively guided, but this is basically no different than seeing that an electrical engineer does not get assigned to bookkeeping duties.

LEADERSHIP TRAINING

Because the leader is seen as the key to organizational success, be this in government, in educational institutions, in sports, in the military, or in business and industry, it is not surprising that these organizations have unstintingly devoted substantial time and money to leadership training. These training programs, supervisory and leadership workshops, and residential courses have enjoyed widespread popularity for many years both in the United States and abroad.

These programs frequently provide instruction in administration procedures, in organizational policy, and such various other fields as accounting, cost control, and legal responsibilities of the organization. As before, our discussion deals only with leadership training per se, that is, with the skills that can be measured in terms of group and organizational effectiveness. We recognize that these training programs often provide a number of other benefits. These may range from giving the executive a welcome break from his routine or widening his intellectual horizon to raising his own morale and that of his subordinates. Whether or not an executive development program or a leadership training workshop can be justified in these terms is a matter of administrative judgment.

Of relevance is the fact that many of these programs are primarily designed to increase the individual's leadership skills. It might also be pointed out that the yearly amount expended for training programs of this sort in the United States is likely to stagger the imagination. It is all the more unfortunate, therefore, that the development of these programs, as well as the utilization of other leadership selection devices, has not been matched by an appropriate number of adequate evaluation studies. Organizations have been more than happy to spend money on training programs but they have been considerably less eager to find out whether the training really does any good. Moreover, personnel research has been severely handicapped by the fact that the criteria of group and departmental effectiveness are only vaguely spelled out and defined in many organizations, and even less frequently are they measured with any degree of reliability.

This is not to say that the problems in assessing the value of an executive training program or of a leadership workshop are minor. As Jaques (1961) and Martin (1959) have pointed out, the manager's job is necessarily one which requires a longer time perspective than does the job of the nonsupervisory employee. It takes longer, therefore, and it is correspondingly more difficult to obtain accurate measures on the effects of managerial training the higher we go up the executive ladder.

There are, in fact, very few studies which evaluate leadership training research under controlled conditions and with objective performance measures. Those which have been reported throw considerable doubt on the efficacy of these training programs for increasing organizational and group performance. Thus, Fleishman et al. (1955) compared the performance of a group of trained and untrained foremen in the International Harvester Company before and after training. While these authors reported some changes in attitudes and behaviors they found no evidence that the training program had increased departmental effectiveness. Similar findings have been reported by Carter (1953) and Tyler (1949). Newport (1963) recently surveyed a large number of major business organizations in the United States which conducted executive development programs for middle managers. While most of the companies reported themselves to be satisfied with the results of these programs, he found no objective evidence that the training programs had increased leadership performance.

Equally discouraging are the findings from our Belgian navy study . . . (Fiedler, 1966). We compared the groups led by forty-eight new and inexperienced navy recruits with a matched sample of forty-eight Belgian petty officers who had received two years of training in petty officer candidate school and who had an average of ten years of navy experience. The tasks were designed with the assistance of navy officers at the training center, and they were similar to tasks which a group of enlisted men might be expected to perform. Yet, the groups led by trained and experienced petty officers did not perform significantly better on any of the four tasks than did groups led by raw recruits who had had less than six weeks of experience in the navy. Moreover, when we correlated the group performance scores of petty officers with the number of years of navy leadership experience of these petty officers, the correlations were essentially zero. Thus, neither the leadership training nor the leadership experience, tantamount to on-the-job training, had enabled the men to perform more effectively in these leadership situations.

A relatively new method of leadership training was developed in the late 1940s. This method, variously called T-group, sensitivity, or laboratory training, is built around unstructured group situations which provide the participant an opportunity to explore his own motivations and reactions, and his relations with other participants in the group. Excellent descriptions of this method are now available, e.g., Schein and Bennis (1965); Blake and Mouton (1961), Bradford (1961); Argyris (1964). Here again, however, the evaluation research which deals with group performance leaves much to be desired. Schein and Bennis (1965) introduce their chapter on research on laboratory training outcomes by noting ". . . that the evidence is meager."

Unfortunately very few studies of laboratory training deal with group performance as the measure of outcome. Argyris (1962) found an increase in a top management team's decision-making processes although no evidence is available on the effect of these decisions on organizational performance. Blake and Mouton (1963) report an investigation to evaluate the effects of an idea laboratory. But here again the performance criteria consisted of measures indicating better listening ability, greater readiness to face conflict, and increased rejection of compromise as the basis for decision making. Research of this nature is important and these outcomes are intrinsically interesting and valuable as are the changes in individual values and attitudes. But this research does not indicate whether the work performance of groups with trained leaders was significantly greater or better than the work performance of groups with untrained leaders.

Laboratory training methods potentially provide one important avenue for introducing the individual to leadership situations in which he can perform well and to those in which he is likely to fail. Laboratory training might also provide the environment in which the individual can experiment with attempts to change the leader-member relations or his position power vis-à-vis his fellow group members. Whether laboratory training can effect changes in the individual's leadership style is considerably more doubtful.

While we can offer no more than speculation to account for the lack of positive results of leadership training programs, a few comments may be appropriate. There is, first of all, evidence that leadership training programs result in some behavioral and attitudinal changes (Shartle, 1956; Schein and Bennis, 1965) even though these may not be lasting unless the organizational climate is conducive to these new behaviors and attitudes. Likewise, the more elaborate T-group and laboratory training may assist the leader in developing a more favorable group climate and more positive member attitudes. Training, therefore, has some effect on the trainee and on his group.

Most leadership training programs are designed either to change the trainee's attitudes and behaviors in the direction which will make him more task-oriented, managing, and directive, or in the direction which will make him more human-relations oriented, permissive, and nondirective. If we assume that these training programs are effective in changing the behavior in the desired direction, and if the Contingency Model is an accurate mapping of reality, then about half the trainees would have come out with an inappropriate leadership style no matter which type of program they attended. Those trained to be directive, managing, and task-oriented would be well suited for leadership situations which are very favorable or else very unfavorable, but they would be unsuited for the situations intermediate in favorableness. Those trained to be relationship-oriented, permissive, and nondirective would be well suited for the situations intermediate in favorableness but poorly suited for the very favorable or the very unfavorable situations. This assumes, of course, that a training program actually can effect more than temporary modifications in the individual's leadership style and concomitant behavior, which still remains to be established.

If leadership training is to be successful, the present theory would argue that it should focus on providing the individual with methods for diagnosing the favorableness of the leadership situation and for adapting the leadership situations to the individual's style of leadership so that he can perform effectively. It should be relatively easy to develop methods which would indicate to the leader whether or not the situation fits his particular style. . . . Scales for measuring leader position power and task structure are already available. . . . It should also be possible to construct a measure which would indicate to the leader how good his relations are with his group members. We can then instruct the leader in making the necessary modifications in the leadership situation so that the situation will match his style. While this sounds simple in principle a number of difficulties will need to be resolved before a procedure of this type can be put into general practice.

REFERENCES

Anderhalter, O. F., W. L. Wilkins, and Marilyn K. Rigby, Peer ratings. Technical Report No. 2, St. Louis University, St. Louis, Mo., 1952. (Mimeograph)

Andrews, R. E. Leadership and supervision. U.S. Civil Service Commission, Personnel Management Series No. 9, Washington, D.C., 1955.

Argyris, C. *Integrating the individual and the organization.* New York: Wiley, 1964.

Argyris, C. *Interpersonal competence and organizational effectiveness.* Homewood, Ill.: Dorsey Press, 1962.

Bales, R. F., and F. L. Strodbeck. Phases in group problem solving. *Journal of Abnormal and Social Psychology*, 1951, *46*, 485–495.

Barnard, C. I. *The functions of the executive.* Cambridge, Mass.: Harvard, 1938.

Bass, B. M. An analysis of the leaderless group discussion. *Journal of Applied Psychology*, 1949, *33*, 527–533.

Bass, B. M. The leaderless group discussion. *Psychological Bulletin*, 1954, *51*, 465–492.

Bass, B. M. *Leadership, psychology, and organizational behavior.* New York: Harper & Row, 1960. (a)

Bell, G. B., and R. L. French. Consistency of individual leadership position in small groups of varying membership. In A. Hare, E. Borgatta, and R. Bales (eds.), *Small groups*, New York: Knopf, 1955.

Berkowitz, L. Sharing leadership in small, decision making groups. *Journal of Abnormal and Social Psychology*, 1953, *48*, 231–238.

Blake, R. R., and Jane S. Mouton. Improving organizational problem solving through increasing the flowing and utilization of ideas. *Training Directors Journal*, 1963, *17*, 48–57.

Bradford, L. P. *Group development, NTL, selected reading series no. 1.* Washington, D.C.: National Education Association, 1961.

Campbell, D. T. Common fate, similarity, and other indices of aggregates of persons as social entities. *Behavioral Science*, 1958, *3*, 14–25.

Carter, L. F. Leadership and small group behavior. In M. Sherif and M. O. Wilson (eds.), *Group relations at the crossroads.* New York: Harper & Row, 1953.

Cattell, R. B. New concepts for measuring leadership in terms of group syntality. *Human Relations*, 1951, *4*, 161–184.

Cattell, R. B., D. R. Saunders, and G. F. Stice. The dimensions of syntality in small groups. *Human Relations*, 1953, *6*, 331–356.

Dubin, R. *Human relations in administration; the sociology of organization, with readings and cases.* New York: Prentice-Hall, 1951.

Fiedler, F. D., and S. M. Nealey. *Second-level management: A review and analysis.* U.S. Civil Service Commission, Office of Career Development, Washington, D.C., March, 1966.

Flanagan, J. C. Critical requirements: A new approach to employee evaluation. *Personnel Psychology*, 1949, *2*, 419–425.

Fleishman, E. A., E. H. Harris, and H. E. Burtt. Leadership and supervision in industry. Educational Research Monograph No. 33, Ohio State University, Columbus, Ohio, 1955.

Gibb, C. A. Leadership. In G. Lindzey, *Handbook of social psychology*, vol. II. Cambridge, Mass.: Addison-Wesley, 1954.

Gibb, C. A. The principles and traits of leadership. *Journal of Abnormal and Social Psychology*, 1947, *42*, 267–284.

Hare, A. P. *Handbook of small group research.* New York: Free Press, 1962.

Hemphill, J. K. A proposed theory of leadership in small groups. *Second preliminary report.* Columbus, Ohio: Personnel Research Board, Ohio State University, 1954.

Hollander, E. P. Authoritarianism and leadership choice in a military setting. *Journal of Abnormal and Social Psychology*, 1954, *49*, 365–370.

Hollander, E. P. Conformity, status and idiosyncrasy credit. *Psychological Review*, 1958, *65*, 117–127.

Hollander, E. P. *Leaders, groups and influence.* New York: Oxford, 1964.

Homans, G. C. *The human group.* New York: Harcourt, Brace, 1950.

Jaques, E. *Equitable payment.* New York: Wiley, 1961.

Katz, D., and R. L. Kahn. *The social psychology of organizations.* New York: Wiley, 1966.

Knoell, Dorothy, and D. G. Fogays. Interrelationships of combat crew performance in the B-29. *Research Note,* CCT 52-1, USAF Human Resources Research Center, 1952.

Krech, D., and R. S. Crutchfield. *Theory and problems of social psychology.* New York: McGraw-Hill, 1948.

McGrath, J. E. Assembly of quasi-therapeutic rifle teams. Urbana, Ill.: Group Effectiveness Research Laboratory, University of Illinois, 1961. (Mimeograph)

Martin, N. H. The levels of management and their mental demands. In W. L. Warner and N. H. Martin (eds.), *Industrial man.* New York: Harper & Row, 1959, 276–294.

Pelz, D. C. Leadership within a hierarchical organization. *Journal of Social Issues,* 1951, 7, 49–55.

Reuter, E. B. *Handbook of sociology.* New York: Dryden Press, 1941.

Sanford, F. H. *ONR research on leadership.* Washington, D.C.: Office of Naval Research, 1949.

Schein, E. H., and W. G. Bennis. *Personal and organizational change through group methods: The laboratory approach.* New York: Wiley, 1965.

Shartle, C. L. *Executive performance and leadership.* Englewood Cliffs, N.J.: Prentice-Hall, 1956.

Stogdill, R. M., and A. E. Coons. Leader Behavior: Its description and measurement. Research Monograph No. 88, Ohio State University, Columbus Ohio, 1957.

Tyler, B. B. A study of factors contributing to employee morale. Unpublished M.A. thesis. Columbus, Ohio: Ohio State University, 1949.

— · — · — · — · — · — · — · — · — · —

RAYMOND B. CATTELL

*Leadership and Group Syntality**

I. FIRST THINGS FIRST IN SOCIAL PSYCHOLOGY

Now that social psychology has recognized its major concern to be the psychology of groups—in relation to one another and to individuals—the time is ripe to discuss research methods and concepts for arriving at *the description of group behavior.*

It is to be hoped that history will not repeat itself by recapitulating in social psychology the unnecessarily wayward and wasteful course of individual psychology. The development of an exact science of prediction in relation to individual personality required, as in other biological sciences, the prior provision of accurate description, measurement and

*Raymond B. Cattell, "Concepts and Methods in the Measurement of Group Syntality," *Psychological Review* 55. (1948): 48–63. Copyright 1948 by the American Psychological Association, and reproduced by permission.

classification of phenomena. Actually amateur speculation and incontinent 'explanation,' remote from actualities of measurement of observation, ran riot and sadly delayed progress by deflecting the attention of researchers, until recent years, from the basic and unescapable discipline of a true science of personality measurement.

This contribution to social psychology begins, therefore, with the challenge that the solution of the vital practical and theoretical social problems now clamoring for attention requires scientific workers to restrain themselves from superficial 'research' until a correct foundation for the meaningful description and measurement of groups has been achieved. It then proceeds to propound concepts, methods and experiments for this foundation. It asserts, as a logical premise, that to arrive at laws governing the development and interaction of groups, we must first have some accurate means of defining a group at a given moment.

We have, in short, to establish a branch of psychology concerned with the 'personality' of groups. 'Establish' is used advisedly; for at present—in spite of much talk about 'culture patterns'—methods and concepts simply do not exist. The sociologists, recognizing that a group cannot be defined in merely political or economic terms, have turned to the psychologist for a science of the living group entity, but, for reasons evident in the following section, they have yet done so in vain. Mannheim (24), typical of sociologists disappointed in constructive synthesis by the psychologists' impotence, well says "The main reason for our failure in this branch of human studies is that up till now we have had no historical or sociological psychology."

II. THE DIMENSIONS OF SYNTALITY

By 'personality,' in the individual, we mean "that which will predict his behavior in any given, defined situation" (8). Mathematically we take a pattern of indices which defines the personality and another set defining the situation, arriving therefrom at an estimate of the ensuing behavior. Psychologically we speak of the former—the personality indices—as a structure of traits—a set of more or less permanent 'readinesses,' which function behaviorally under the impact of a stimulus situation.

For the corresponding structure in the group an unambiguous term is needed. Examination of many possible verbal roots indicates *syntality* as best indicating the 'togetherness' of the group, while having sufficient suggestive parallelism to 'personality' and 'totality.' Further, we may perhaps speak appropriately of the syntality of a group as inferred from the 'synaction' of its members—the group action as defined below. Syntality covers dynamic, temperamental and ability traits of the group.[1]

The measurement of syntality can profit greatly from the technical advances gained in the measurement of personality. The early failures of personality study mentioned

---

[1] Apparently the only other use of syntality, a specialized and remote one, is in C. Morris's *Signs, Language and Behavior*, New York: Prentice Hall, 1946. The derived term, synergy, employed below, has been used (apart from its physiological use) in sociology by Lester Ward (37) but again in a far wider and less technical, defined sense than here. These contexts are so remote that no danger of confusion arises.

above came not only from an attempt to abort the descriptive phase of psychology, but from an inability, once the necessity of description was admitted, to find any better foundation for measurement than the numberless shifting sands of arbitrary 'traits' in poorly designed *ad hoc* 'tests.' All that has been altered, by the original work of Spearman, Burt (5), Thurstone (35) and many others, which made the concept of the unitary trait meaningful. Although this work has yet scarcely affected applied psychology it has, in the last fifteen years, delivered psychology already from a confused impasse. It first enlightened the measuring of abilities, and later, by the work of Guilford, Mosier, Reyburn and others on questionnaire response and the present writer's analyses of surface and source traits, was carried to those unitary traits which could complete the description of personality.

It is easy to see now that if factorial methods had been applied from the beginning to the description and measurement of personality, using R-technique for common traits and P-technique (8) for unique traits, a true perspective of the important dimensions would have been obtained much earlier than by the hit-or-miss methods of clinical 'intuition.' The measurement of abilities, for example, would have been saved many a discouraging, profitless circuit of 'philosophical' debate as to the nature of various abilities, as well as many acrimonious, ineffectual arguments as to the criteria against which measures should be validated. The disillusionment of students with overburdened lists of personality 'types'—each peculiar to the university at which he happened to be studying—would also have been avoided.

Social psychology now stands where the study of individual personality then stood. In effect psychologists have accumulated a few fragmentary aspects of group syntality from various isolated studies. They have chanced upon 'morale' (although the label probably covers such different variables as group persistence against difficulties and mean level of individual idealism), aggressiveness, authoritarian-democratic structure, isolationism, degree of freedom from internal dissension etc. Mostly these 'dimensions' of group behavior have been seized upon in response to the suggestion of some immediate practical problem, without regard to any over-all theory or to long-term scientific needs in social psychology. The slightest consideration of the whole natural history of groups would probably suggest more important variables than these for describing their total behavior.

An embarrassing harvest of muddle, moreover, is likely to be reaped if the application of large terms for small variables continues very long with respect to the labelling of group traits. Is it fitting, for example, to describe experimental groups as Totalitarian or Democratic (in science as distinct from journalism) when no proof is offered that these are unitary patterns or when the variables actually measured are perhaps the least important for defining that total pattern, if it exists as a single pattern?

It would seem better to stick to modest, less interpretive, more contingent labels for more completely definable experimental variables, until the true patterns emerge and are confirmed.

Social psychology, therefore, now awaits its foundation of accurately described syntalities, alike at the level of culture patterns, of institutional groups and of small committees. That foundation can be achieved *by factor analysis of a 'population' of groups, on a suitably chosen collection of group behavior variables*. Our purpose here is not to present particular results but to examine the promise and the limitations of this novel application of factorization and discuss the conditions under which it is valid. Nevertheless, the discussion will be guided at least by certain rough and qualitative observations already possible on the first two studies now proceeding in the field, and to be reported elsewhere (11, 12). The first is a study of 60 nations, factorizing 40 variables by R-technique, checked by two small sample studies employing Q- and P-techniques (8, 11). The second (12) factorizes a rich variety of group performances from 25 groups of six people each, *i.e.*, of 'committee size.' For effective exploration with the new method requires that it be brought to bear on widely different group sizes and forms.

A general requirement of the method is that the variables shall be chosen with the utmost catholicity to cover all aspects of group behavior. The application of this principle to individual personality in the 'personality sphere' concept (8) has already rewarded us with factors which not only clarify long familiar, previously foggy, clinical syndromes, but also reveal important dimensions which were never conceptualized. By attention to this principle in the realm of social psychology we can expect similarly to discover those factors which will describe most of the differences of groups in terms of relatively few unitary traits or meaningful dimensions. They may turn out to be familiar dimensions such as morale, democratic organization, industrialization, etc. or may open our eyes to functionally new 'wholes' or dimensions of groups. Thereafter, by assigning measurements on these primary dimensions to any given culture pattern we can accurately define its syntality, as the necessary basis for developmental and causal studies.

III. THE FACTORIZABLE CHARACTERISTICS OF GROUPS: LOGICAL ANALYSIS

As we concentrate on the choice of variables we run into certain problems of assortment which can perhaps be solved to a certain degree by armchair reflection. This and the following section constitute attempts thus to achieve the maximum clarity of experimental design and problem formulation, with the adoption of definite hypotheses.

Out of deference to majority opinion we ought perhaps to ask at the outset the supposedly devastating question whether such a thing as a group mentality exists at all. It is of historical if not of scientific importance that McDougall's penetrating pioneer analysis (25) of 'the group mind' was badly received by a certain section of American psychologists. In the descendants of this sectional opposition the allergic reaction to his expression is still so strong as to paralyze thought, and writers who pander[2] to irrationality have for years operated with McDougall's concept by circumlocutions. The rejection was not due to opposition to Hegelianism, for McDougall's able philosophical preamable explicitly refuted Hegelian mysticism and accepted Hobhouse's searching anti-idealist criticisms. The probably correct, but more trivial explanation was that this contribution to social psychology was launched at an unfortunate moment. For a large number of callow

---

[2]To the objection that many psychologists misconceive the term one must reply as Freud did to Max Eastman's similar objection to the precisely defined notion of the Unconscious, "Cannot they correct their misconceptions?"

students in psychology were unable at that time to recognize any manifestation of mind unless formally, or often actually, reduced to the twitching of a dog's hind leg. From the drouth of this sterile atomism they presently rushed, with undiminished lack of judgment, down a steep place into the sea of ineffable, unmeasurable—but far from inaudible—Gestalt.

Fortunately a steady nucleus of naturalistic observation and methodological constructiveness survived and developed, despite those local set-backs, and despite the disturbances from the clamorous medieval tournaments among the pseudo-philosophical 'isms' of psychology. Meanwhile the idea was further developed by Gurwitch (18) in sociology, and, in more vague terms, by Whitehead and by Roethlisberger in industrial psychology. Finally, the main line of development in pure psychology has given us better technical methods, notably factor analysis and its variants, for investigating behavioral wholes and dynamic patterns.

It could be argued that any study of total organisms, such as McDougall proposed, should have been postponed until new methods had been invented, but this is quite different from asserting (a) that reflexology is capable of explaining the behavior of organisms as such, or (b) that wholes do not exist. Of the difficulties of the social psychologist at that juncture McDougall wrote (25, p. x), " . . . to the obscure question of fact with which he deals, it is in the nature of things impossible to return answers supported by indisputable experimental proofs. In this field the evidence of an author's approximation towards truth can consist only in his success in gradually persuading competent opinion of the value of his views." His optimism about the existence of a large reservoir of competent opinion proved unjustified. But the vigor of prejudice has one virtue: that it forces the development of precision methods from the conclusions of which the prejudiced cannot escape.

McDougall himself, unfortunately, failed to develop the method here described, but many of his conclusions about group behavior are likely to prove correct, and his basic contention that it is rewarding to deal with groups as single entities remains the springboard whence we take off into new research fields. His arguments for treating the group as an organism or mind which have never been refuted, are set out below[3] together with

---

[3]The behavior of a group has more formal resemblance to the behavior of an individual organism than to any other natural entity, principally in the following respects:

(1) A group preserves characteristic behavior habits and structure despite the continual replacement of actual individuals.

(2) It shows memory for group experiences and learning.

(3) It is capable of responding as a whole to stimuli directed to its parts, *i.e.*, it tends to solve problems of individuals and sub-groups by group action.

(4) It possesses drives which become more or less integrated in executive functions of nutrition, acquisition, aggression, defence, etc. Groups vary in dynamic integration analogously to the variation of individuals in character.

(5) It experiences 'moods' of expansiveness, depression, pugnacity, etc. which modify characteristic behavior and energy output as do emotional states in the individual.

(6) It shows collective deliberation, a process highly analogous to the trial-and-error thinking of the individual, when held up in a course of action. Similarly the act of collective volition, through legislatures and executives, is closely analogous to the resolution of conflicting dynamic demands in the individual.

A group also tends to exercise some choice on admission or rejection of those who aggregate

certain new observations on the question. That some psychologists should ever have congratulated themselves on their 'realism' (rather than on mere concrete thinking and failure of abstraction) in rejecting the group as an organic entity, is still more surprising when one observes that hard-headed lawyers, politicians and statesmen deal operationally with groups *as* groups every day.

As to the behavior from which the group mentality is to be inferred, however, there runs alike through McDougall's and other psychologists' writings what we consider a rather serious confusion of characteristics. On grounds of logical analysis we suggest that there are *three* aspects or 'panels' to be taken into account in defining a group.

(1) *Syntality Traits* (Behavior of the group as a group). The group behavior recorded here concerns any effect the group has as a totality, upon other groups or its physical environment. Just as the individual may show more willed (conscious), and less organized (neurotic symptom, temperament) behavior, so the group behavior will range from action by (a) whatever organized will and executive agencies the group processes, to (b) less organized, uncontrolled elements and so to (c) unorganized mass action, expressing largely the average individual as under (3) below. For example, the sheer amount of food the group eats would be largely a function of this last kind.

A catalogue of syntality traits, analogous to the personality sphere, as advocated above, is not easy to obtain, since there is no dictionary as of personality traits. We have proceeded by (a) making an exhaustive study of the many incisive writings on group characteristics, *e.g.*, Benedict (1), Brogan (3), Cole (13), Keyserling (23), Mead (26), Siegfried (32) and Münsterberg (29), and of the characterizations found in history and (b) by using the *personality sphere* (8) as a guide to possibly important areas of behavior in syntality.

Most of these traits will be inferred from external behavior of the group, but the executive will of the group can manifest its properties also in *internal action*, *e.g.*, in deliberately changing internal organization, suppressing internal revolt. Examples of syntality traits are: aggressiveness against groups (*e.g.*, acts of declaration of war), efficiency in exploitation of natural resources, isolationism, energy in trading, reliability in commitments, proneness to trade cycles or to revolutions.

(2) *Characteristics of Internal Structure.* These concern the *relationships among the members of the group.* The character of unification and of government is primary, and this may vary from a practically unstructured crowd through horde leadership and the

---

towards it. This, like some few other basic characteristics of groups, has no analogy in the individual mind, except the remote one of selective learning and attention.

Against these it can be urged (1) that the grey matter or total nervous system is more dispersed than that associated with the single biological organism, and (2) that there is no group consciousness corresponding to individual consciousness. Both of these are doubtful objections, but in any case they are outside the realm of psychological observation. They *may* account for the systematic differences research will undoubtedly find between the 'group mind' and the individual mind; they do not jeopardize the aim of using the group as a behavioral unity and reference point in psychological research. A less bald outline of the theoretical arguments over the group mind has been set out by the present writer elsewhere (7). Extremely few 'experimental' (as distinct from historical) treatments of groups as unitary organisms yet exist to demonstrate the practicability of the hypothesis; but Thorndike's treatment of cities (34), showing them to have persistent characteristic traits, already offers some pragmatic proof. Characteristic (3) above—that all parts react adjustively (perhaps homeostatically) to stimuli affecting limited segments—will be taken as the primary definition of the group.

incipient democratic leadership in Moreno's (27) vague "tele or the movement of feeling toward leader individuals" to a highly organized legislature and executive. Internal structure characters issue in syntality traits but they are not themselves the behavior of the group.

Examples of structural characters are: all sorts of indices expressing degree of heterogeneity in various characteristics, indices of class structure, pattern of institutions and organs such as church, army, family, modes of government and communication.

(3) *Population Traits*. These are mere aggregate values—definitions of the personality of the *average* (or typical, modal) member of the group. It is noticeable that in the literature of group characteristics the bulk of observations actually concern the typical member of the population rather than the group syntality.

Examples of population characteristics are: average intelligence, crime incidence, attitudes on moral and religious questions and all that is usually gathered by population polls.

The probable relationship among these three[4] panels is that if we knew all the laws of social psychology we could predict the first from the second and third. Alternatively, if we knew the third and the environment of the group we could predict the second, *i.e.*, the type of group structure which would emerge, and therefore, ultimately, the first, *i.e.*, the group behavior. This is no denial of the principle that the mind of the group is fashioned by individuals and in turn fashions the individual mind. In the extreme instance of the second where we are dealing with a practically unstructured crowd, the first and third become practically identical.

From the interim observations available in our experiments we can already generalize the hypothesis that the changes in syntality traits produced by changes in population traits will be qualitatively as well as quantitatively different from the latter. For example, an increment in average intelligence may change character-like qualities in the group, while a difference between groups in average emotional stability of the population may appear as a difference in the ability of the group *per se* to solve cognitive complexities. This we shall call the *theory of emergents* (or syntal emergents).

IV. SEVEN THEOREMS ON THE DYNAMICS OF SYNTALITY

The implicit conception of group which most people unconsciously adopt in such discussions as the above is of an aggregate composed of a number of individuals whose *whole existence* is bound up with the group. Real groups are rarely of this kind and for the most profitable application of the new method to general group investigation it behooves us first to analyze as far as possible what the situation is with regard to varieties of groups and the modifications of method required to cope with them. This analysis turns principally on the dynamic relations within and between groups, for temperamental

---

[4]It may be objected that we overlook a fourth ingredient in the definition of the group—namely the group tradition. It is true that this 'momentum' of the group is as important as its material existence and that groups of any maturity are composed of the dead as much as of the living. These traditions, however, exist in the minds of the living—the constitution of the United States, for example, would be ineffective if no one knew about it—and are adequately included in all three panels above.

and ability characters do not differ in any systematic way, as far as we can see, from those known in individuals.

Sociologists have written a good deal about group classification and, more tangentially, about dynamics, and we must first glance at the evolution of opinion among outstanding representatives. Gumplowicz in his classical treatment (16) outdistanced most of the psychologists of a generation later by conceiving that laws can be formed about the behavior of groups ("The behavior of collective entities is determined by natural laws") but failed to agree with the present integrative psychological position by maintaining somewhat unnecessarily that this behavior had no relation to "the motives and natural qualities of (constituent) individuals." Ross (30) proceeded to carry the study of groups into a classificatory system which included 'Fortuitous groups' (crowds), 'Natural groups' (families, clans), 'Interest groups' (states, confederacies, guilds), and also, but less happily, 'Likeness groups' (professions, classes) in which presumably nothing dynamic but only a logical bond might hold the members together. Gillin and Gillin (15) adopt a somewhat similar classification, but descriptively and without implying fundamental psychological differences. To the psychologist a merely logical classification is untenable. *Every* group is an interest group—in the sense that its existence arises from a dynamic need—or else it is not, in any psychological sense, a group. Sorokin and Zimmerman's (33) distinction between 'systems' and 'congeries' seems to be a statement of this issue in other terms.[5]

Even when sociologists, however, have recognized that a group exists only because and so long as it satisfies psychological needs, they have failed to appreciate the nature of the ergic (10) and the metanergic needs that are involved in its support. Hayes (20), Hart (19), Von Wiese (36) and others stress or dwell wholly upon security, as if small groups form, and then aggregate into larger groups, only under threat. This may be a common motive—indeed fear and gregariousness may account for practically all association in the lower animals. But in man, with his power of learning ways of long-circuited satisfaction, the whole gamut of primary ergs—hunger, escape, self assertion, curiosity, sex, gregariousness, etc.—may participate in group formation. The sheer fact of groups needing to have adequate dynamic basis, obvious though it may now be, needs emphasis at this juncture in social psychology because the extension of group experiment of the present kind brings the risk that, in the artificial situation of experiments, groups will be employed which are not created by a real purpose of the participants.

Beyond this fundamental character the psychologist has next to recognize the fact of *dynamic specialization*, a phenomenon tied up with the almost universal occurrence of overlapping groups. For the simplification of a first experimental approach we have chosen, as described above, self-contained groups: nations, which have relatively shadowy loyalties beyond themselves, and committee groups in a control 'vacuum' situation in which no other loyalties of the members are brought into action or conflict. But the great majority of existing social groups, other than nations, are overlapping, in the sense that

[5]The satisfaction of a need through the physical existence of the group is the basic definition of existence of a psychological group. The definition that a group exists when there is 'internal interaction' of individuals seems less fundamental to the present writer, and indeed derivative from the above primary condition.

individuals belong simultaneously to several groups. This situation exists because, as Cole succinctly puts it (13), "an association (group) can always be made specific in function, while man can never be made so."

From this arise some intricate but important relations among groups and between group structure and the dynamic structure of the individual. For brevity and precision we shall formulate these relations in *seven theorems concerning the psychodynamics of groups*, the first of which will simply state the conclusion of the above few paragraphs' discussion.

Theorem 1. The Dynamic Origin of Groups: Definition of Synergy. Groups are devised for achieving individual satisfaction and exist only when they provide a means to the ends of individual ergic goals.

The interest, 'ergic investment,' or 'need satisfaction' tied up with the existence of the group must be clearly conceived as having three parts or modifications: (1) First there is the total individual energy going into the group—absorbed by its activities—which we have called the group *synergy*. (2) As Rousseau (31) pointed out, however, "the general will" is not the same as "the will of all." In Bosanquet's (2) phrase, the individual wills "cancel one another" resulting in "sovereignty." In our vectorial theory of dynamic traits certain components nullify one another, as shown by the difference between the resultant expressing the dynamic interest of the group and the non-vectorial sum of the individual interests. The unified attitude which emerges as the dynamic intention of the group *per se* we shall call the *effective synergy* or effective investment. It is the energy expressed in gaining the outside goals for which the group has come together. (3) The difference between the total synergy and the effective synergy is absorbed in internal friction and in maintaining cohesion of the group. This we may call the *intrinsic or group maintenance synergy*. It is a loss by internal friction and absorption. Without more space than can be given here it is not possible to analyze the rather complex transformations in group maintenance. This synergy absorbs not only selfish, anti-social and aggressive motivations, which 'cancel out,' but also the self-submissive and self assertive satisfactions of leader-follower activity and the needs of the gregarious drive. The latter is usually satisfied wholly in the group and does not pass on into effective synergy, though, like some other intrinsic synergy expenditures, it does 'effective' work in the sense of preserving group cohesion.

Though the magnitude of the intrinsic synergy normally has to be inferred from the difference of (1) and (2), it manifests itself directly as an active resistance when attempts are made to dissolve the group. Intrinsic synergy is *relatively* (not absolutely) great, in comparison with effective synergy, in a recreational club interested in sociability: effective synergy is relatively great in a political party, a scientific institute or a religious missionary society. However, in the special situation of an attempt to dissolve the group *all* the energy may be thrown back into cohesive activities, so that the last statement will no longer be true.

Theorem 2. The Vectorial Measurement of Group Synergy. To measure the total vectorial intrinsic and effective investment in a given group, *i.e.*, the total group *synergy*, we have to take account of (1) the number of people interested; (2) the intensity or strength of the satisfaction each gains; (3) the ergic quality (vector direction (10)) of the satisfactions, and (4) the subsidiation relations of these satisfactions with respect to other groups and other purposes of the individuals concerned.

The number of people interested in a group will depend partly on the demostatic level or percolation range (6) of the idea involved, from the point of view of intelligence level, and partly on the dynamic needs it sets out to satisfy. For the present we can set aside this mere number, as a multiplier of whatever other measurements we make.

The measurement of dynamic quantity and quality has been treated systematically elsewhere (10). An attitude is a vector quantity defined as to direction (quality) by: (aF_1) (bF_2) (cF_3) . . . etc., where F_1, F_2, etc. are coordinates corresponding to basic drives (ergs) or to general sentiment structures (and therefore common social institutions) and a, b, etc. are coefficients for the particular attitude, expressing the extent of its subsidiation to each of these common and basic goals. The strength of the attitude is expressed by

$$S = aF_1 + bF_2 + cF_3 \ldots \text{etc.,}$$

where a, b and c are as above, and F_1, F_2, etc. have satisfaction values specific for that group.

The synergy of the group is the vectorial resultant of the attitudes toward the group of all its members. Individual attitudes will vary slightly in direction and some of this deviation will be cancelled in the vectorial sum—in other words, it will be lost in the internal friction of the group. The rest will appear either as intrinsic investment, constituting the basic strength of cohesion of the group, or as effective investment, constituting the interest of the group as such.

The effective synergy of the group can finally be expressed as a vector quantity on the same coordinates as for individual attitudes.

Theorem 3. Syntal Subsidiation and the Dynamic Lattices of Groups. The effective synergy of any group goes out to purposes which are outside the group and consequently sets up habits of reacting which are subsidiary (10), with respect to some ultimate goal of the group's activity. The formation or partial support of other (mostly ancillary) groups is generally part of the subsidiation chain. For example, a nation sets up an army as a means to its goal of security or aggression (Diagram 1), and a country club may set up a committee to engineer a swimming pool as part of its synergic purpose of providing recreation. The use of group B as a tool by group A is not incompatible with the use of A by B, and, as in personal subsidiation (10), paths will form a complex, *dynamic lattice* with transflux and retroaction.

Some typical syntal subsidiations in the group and individual habits which form institutions are illustrated in the dotted lines in the following diagram. The nation supports universities because they are on its subsidiation chain to the goal of an educated democracy. It favors the family as maintaining population stability, while cities contribute to its desire for revenue and prestige. Both the family and the city, as groups, in turn have need of the nation, which satisfies their need for protection, etc. The army, in pursuit of its purposes, founds an Army Air Force and this in turn sets up a psychological Personnel Section. Although these latter accord with the will of the nation they are not directly in the subsidiary chain of the nation's purpose of self defence, but draw their

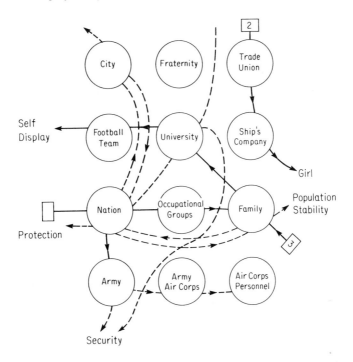

origin from separate successive synergies of Army and Army Air Force. The nation, as it were, delegates synergy to the army and, as a group, has no sense of these further purposes.

Syntal dynamic lattices are quite different and distinct from the dynamic lattice patterns of individuals, even of the particular individuals who happen to constitute chief executives of groups. (Compare dotted with continuous lines in the diagram.) This happens increasingly with the growth of specialized labor and of general currency. Nevertheless the two sets of dynamic lattices necessarily add up to the same activities and the same energy total—save for the loss between intrinsic and effective synergy.

Problems of relationship of syntal lattices and personal lattices will be different for overlapping and non-overlapping groups. Some groups, *e.g.*, nations, demand a sovereignty which will not permit members to belong to other, generally similar, groups, or to experience subjection to the purposes of other groups. Most groups, however, have overlapping personnel, and this creates dynamic problems in connection with syntal subsidiation more complex than for non-overlapping groups.

Syntal subsidiation chains will not normally end in ergic goals, as do those of individuals. The basic goals of the group concern the preservation and expansion of the group. They can be resolved into ergic goals, by analysis, but they are not individual biological goals in themselves.

Theorem 4. Personal Subsidiation of Groups in the Individual Dynamic Lattice. The subsidiation chains occurring in the dynamic lattice of the individual (10) often include groups as 'links.' For example, an emigré doctor may acquire citizenship (Group 1) in order that he may belong to his professional group (Group 2) in order that he may maintain his family (Group 3). (Chain 1 in the diagram.) Or a man may belong to a trade union (Group 2), in order to be able to join a ship's company (Group 2) in order to travel to see his girl. (Chain 2 in the diagram.) Or, to illustrate a different direction, a young man half in mind to leave the parental roof may maintain his belonging to the family in order to be sent to a university in order to get onto the university football team. (Chain 3 in the diagram.)

Naturally, the personal subsidiation chains, like the syntal chains, will not run wholly among groups ('girl' in 2), nor will they run in one direction, but will curve back on themselves. Also like subsidiary chains generally (10), they will split at frequent intervals. For example, the motivation to join a university will not be sustained wholly by the satisfactions in connection with joining the football team (even in this day and age!) but also by the prospect of joining a fraternity, acquiring professional standing, etc. Consequently calculation of the investment in any group, by the adding up of the dynamic energies of subsidiation chains, must heed the redistribution which occurs at each link.

Theorem 5. Patterns of Loyalty, Subsidiation and Subordination Determined by Law of Effect. Like any other pattern of dynamic behavior the habits of individuals with respect to groups are formed either by insightful or by trial and error behavior, in which the most rewarded reactions become stabilized.[6] The final pattern of syntal and personal subsidiation, as well as other characteristics discussed below, is, in other words, *settled by conditions of external reality*, in that it is the best pattern discovered for approaching maximum dynamic satisfaction.

Harmful or unnecessary group reactions tend to be removed. For example, a group which does not support (by its effective synergy) its necessary ancillary groups fails; a group which tolerates parasitic subgroups fails; a group which errs in establishing correct orders of loyalty, *e.g.*, family more important than country, fails—and these failures break down the corresponding faulty group habits of the population concerned.

How far it would be profitable to deal with syntal learning by the law of effect applied to groups as a whole remains to be seen. Two transformations between syntal and personal adjustments to reality can, however, be indicated. (1) The rewards and punishments of individuals in group modification are different in kind and magnitude from those of the group. For example, the defeat of a nation may mean death to some, economic loss to others, loss of self regard for all. The 'death' of a nation—its total disintegration—may mean no more than the necessity for the individual to acquire new language and other habits. (2) Not only are individual rewards different, but they are also often delayed, indirect and harder to associate, insightfully, with their group causes. Since group learning eventually takes place through this 'secondary' learning of individuals it is not surprising that the acquisition of intelligently adapted and integrated group behavior is a slower and more painful process than similar learning with respect to the purposes of individuals.

In referring to the group behavior that has to get adapted to reality we have spoken of a hierarchy of loyalty, as well as of the previously described personal subsidiation

[6]If any proof of this is needed, it is offered, for example, by Mowrer's neat experiments on the social behavior of the rat (28).

lattice and syntal subsidiation (or 'subordination') lattice. The relation of these to one another is tentatively discussed in the next section.

That personal, individual behavior shall fit in with the requirements of syntal subsidiation and integration is assured mainly by (a) the creation of forces in the individual super ego which augment personal subsidiation trends usually of a more purely ergic level, and (b) the shifting of rewards to 'artificial' points by money and other tokens exchangeable for dynamic satisfaction. Thus when many desire the defense of a country but few volunteer for the army an army of mercenaries may be made 'loyal' to the country by rewards transferred from the money representing and created by the dynamic attachments of others to their country. Money is thus one way, the principal way, of transferring dynamic energy from one point to another. This needs to be taken into account in any attempt at dynamic calculus and offers one of the bridges from psychology to economics.

Theorem 6. Synergic Constancy in a Closed System (Fixed Population) with Overlapping Groups. By reason of the principle of constancy of individual mental energy (on which we proceed in such matters of individual dynamics as learning or neurosis) certain relations follow in the synergies of overlapping groups.

Chief among these deduced relations is that of *constancy of total synergy in overlapping groups*, providing certain conditions are maintained. Not all of the individual's energy goes into groups, so condition (1) is that the non-group investment remain constant. Condition (2) is that the group activities remain on the same level with regard to long-circuiting (or goal distance). This is necessary for two reasons. First, the individual's energy becomes expressed more readily if he is permitted less long-circuited satisfaction. Since some groups occasion less suppression and internal conflict in individuals than others, releasing more of the individual's total energy for external expression, this condition is not easily satisfied. Secondly, new groups can be linked on to a personal subsidiation chain of groups without calling on fresh energy, provided the population has not reached its toleration limit for long circuiting. For example, if a man has interest in a golf club he may be induced to join a society for the preservation of the golf course, without drawing on any new springs of interest. But this long circuiting may strike him as a bore. There are probably further conditions related to his interest in golf which will only become evident when the principle of constancy of individual mental energy is more accurately worked out. For example, we are arguing on the condition of constancy of what psychoanalysts would call 'object libido investment,' not of total energy, and certain social changes might alter the ratio of object libido to the total energy.

A corollary on this theorem is that the liquidation of any group structure will then automatically create—for psychological reasons alone and without regard for social needs and real conditions—a readjustment among the synergies of the remaining overlapping groups. They must alter their patterns to give new qualities of satisfaction—or else the residue must be taken up by some new group, equivalent in synergy, if not in intellectual content, to the lost group. For example, the dissolution of football teams might result in the activities of political parties taking on the characteristics of street fighting. A calculus of group readjustment could thus be founded on the ergic mensuration of vectors of synergy.

Theorem 7. Isomorphism of Syntality Change and Personality Change. Although the structures and functions of groups, overlapping or non-overlapping, are always ultimately shaped by the conditions of reality (as in Theorem 5 above), their form at any moment depends also on the readiness of individual minds to learn quickly or to depart quickly from that structure which is, realistically, optimum.

There will thus be a close parallelism (modified by the nature of the intrinsic relations within the groups) between syntality traits and personality traits of the population, especially those concerned with learning and dynamic stability. For example, the immediate cause of stability of group structures is the stability of the corresponding attitudes and sentiments in the individual mind. Nothing prevents an army marching to the capital and taking charge of a nation except the higher loyalty of the patriotic sentiment, in relation to the army sentiment, in the minds of the individual soldiers. (In fact Roman legionnaires abroad sometimes experienced such a growth of the sentiment toward their army fellows that unscrupulous generals could use them to overpower the Republic. The 'realistic' checks ultimately make this unrewarding (to the army and to the nation), but the immediate check is only the inherent stability (disposition rigidity) of sentiments in the individual mind.

Among the chief parallel characteristics that may be suggested are syntal conservatism (resistance to gradual change) and personal, individual *disposition rigidity*; syntal integration and personal intelligence level; syntal freedom from fashions and boom-depression cycles and individual emotional maturity; syntal democratic political conflict and personal tolerance for internal mental conflict (since group conflict in overlapping groups brings parallel personal mental conflict), and so on. Some evidence that the first of these relations can be demonstrated in data already available has been set out by the present writer elsewhere (9). In so far as this theorem operates, the advance of social psychology as an exact science is limited by the advance of personality measurement.

V. SYNTALITY MEASUREMENT AND THE DYNAMIC RELATIONS OF GROUPS

The implications of the above theorems for the design of experiments directed to determining the dimensions of syntality are numerous and we have space to emphasize only a few.

In the first place, the dynamic makeup (synergy) of groups will vary far more than that of individuals, both in strength and quality. Consequently it may be profitable to sort groups into classes of more comparable kinds before starting experiments. Sorokin, Zimmerman and Galpin (33) have already proceeded with group classification essentially on this basis, into 'elementary groups' which satisfy a single need and 'cumulative groups' which hold their members by many ties. The dynamic vectorial methods suggested here simply carry this to greater quantitative meaning and exactness.

Secondly, group syntality will usually be far more narrow in dynamic content than the dynamic expression of individuals. Groups can fight, ally, acquire, fear, protect, submit, assert themselves, seek food, etc., but sexually directed behavior, for example, is rare (the rape of the Sabines, and matrimonial agencies, apart). The choice of dynamic variables for factorization therefore needs to aim at more dense representation in narrow ergic directions.

Theorem 2 above, that synergy can be expressed with regard to the ergic coordinates used for individuals leaves open the possibility that factorization may show synergy to be conveniently expressible also in terms of some relatively basic goals *per se*. For example, the interests of an insurance company or a library may be as intelligible, if not as apt for dynamic calculus, when expressed in terms of service to a few basic social institutions as of basic human ergs.

This remains to be clarified by our initial experiments, as also does the question whether any laws systematically relate syntal and personal dynamic lattices and the hierarchy of typical individual loyalty to groups discussed in Theorem 5. There are concepts here which can only be tentatively defined and inter-related. Is 'loyalty' to a group determined by 'duty' (super ego investment) or by total synergy? Is the order of loyalty the same as the order of 'social distance' (17) among people in the various groups, or, more likely, the same as the syntal subsidiation order? Can the correct order of syntal subsidiation be determined by asking "Could this group exist at all without that?" or must a situation always be arranged in which some conflict between the groups, from the standpoint of individual loyalties, exists? Is it possible that groups can only conflict in so far as their subsidiation paths are different? These questions will be dealt with elsewhere. Thirdly, because of the sensitive interdependence of groups, in regard to synergic quantity and quality, the synergy of most groups and especially the smaller, subordinate ones, will be much more liable to gross fluctuations than the total dynamic traits of the individual. So great a 'function fluctuation' makes factorization more difficult but no less worth while. It requires 'snapshot' measurement by R-technique, or the special use of P-technique. Measurement of the changing synergies of groups offers the true basis for discovery of the laws governing syntal subsidiation and other group inter-relationships.

The measurement of syntalities with respect to their dynamic make-up and subsidiation relationships offers the prospect not only of putting the description of group behavior on an altogether higher level of exactness, but of making possible a new branch of study employing a kind of 'dynamic bookkeeping' with respect to overlapping groups and the energy investments of individuals. From this 'bookkeeping' the data for a whole field of new laws regarding the psychodynamics of groups emerge. For example, many overlapping groups are approximately isomorphous (in the sense of mathematical group theory) so that their synergies would behave as approximately complementary.

Pursuit of measurable relationships in the dynamics of personalities and syntalities opens up also two extremely important developments of psychology—ethics and economics. A good deal of morality of individual behavior is admittedly weighed in terms of the effects of the latter on the welfare of groups (whether or not we accept the whole theoretical basis of Mill and Bentham). Indeed, the calculations of discrepancy between constituent individual attitudes and group synergies become in effect an estimation of individual morality—if the general position of Mill and Evolutionary Ethics (7) is accepted.

Similarly the key to the whole relationship of psychology and economics lies in these calculations. For groups to achieve their objects it is necessary to transmit interest energy from place to place. Transmission along a subsidiation chain takes place for groups and for individuals principally by tokens (money) but the process is perhaps clearer for groups. As frequently mentioned in sociology the most consistent characteristics of existing primary groups (other than behaving as a totality) are (1) order and (2) taxation. Synergy expresses itself most frequently through the latter. Members of a group tax themselves, proportionally to the strength of their interest in the existence of the group. This money is at once a measure of the strength of their individual attitudes and of the group synergy; for, generally it is not by work on the part of the members themselves that the group synergy expresses itself, but by the work of others paid for by the taxation of the group. That cost could be used as a measure of desire, thus uniting economic and psychodynamic measures, is not a new idea but an old one which was found wanting (8, 10). Only when it is considered in the total setting of group dynamics, apparently, can it be made workable.

These theoretical vistas in group dynamics can be glanced along but not followed, here. For the dynamic traits of groups are only one aspect of the total syntality and have been examined more analytically only because it appears that syntality differs from personality more in dynamic structure than in ability or temperament traits. However, the upshot of our examination is that dynamic characteristics, especially if they are sampled with proper regard to the nature of group synergies, can profitably be included in the same factorization with measures of group temperament and group abilities.

VI. SUMMARY

(1) Social psychological research can advantageously be centered on the behavior of groups as organic, functionally integrated entities. Group syntality has more resemblances than differences with regard to individual personality, suggesting profitable transfer of research methods from one to the other.

(2) Effective research on the development, abnormalities and inter-relations of groups can proceed only on a foundation of syntality measurement. The dimensions of syntality can be found by factor analysis.

(3) Factor analysis must rest on an even sampling of a wide range of group characteristics. The characteristics of groups have to be sought at three levels: (1) Syntality—the behavior of the group; (2) Structure—the relations of individuals in the group; (3) Population personality traits—the individual characteristics averaged.

(4) Groups differ from individuals most radically in their dynamic make-up or synergy, especially because of the structural possibilities of overlapping groups. This does not invalidate the factorization of group characteristics but it introduces complications requiring special attention to the design of investigation.

(5) The dynamic relationships which have to be heeded in the design of experiments to investigate group syntalities, and which require investigation in their own right as prime determiners of the behavior of groups, have been expressed in seven theorems. These theorems may be briefly labelled: (1) Dynamic origin of groups; (2) Vectorial measurement of synergy; (3) Subsidiation in the syntal lattice; (4) Subsidiation in the personal lattice; (5) Hierarchies of loyalty from the law of effect; (6) Synergic constancy

in a system of overlapping groups; and (7) Isomorphism of syntality change and personality change.

BIBLIOGRAPHY

1. Benedict, R. *Patterns of culture*. New York: Houghton, Mifflin, 1934.
2. Bosanquet, B. *The philosophical theory of the state*. London: Macmillan, 1910.
3. Brogan, D. W. *The American character*. New York: Knopf, 1945.
4. Buell, R. L. *International relations*. New York: Henry Holt, 1929.
5. Burt, C. *Factors of the mind*. London: University of London Press, 1940.
6. Cattell, R. B. Some changes in social life in a community with a falling intelligence quotient. *Brit. J. Psychol.*, 1938, 28, 430–450.
7. ———. *Psychology and the religious quest*. New York: Nelson, 1938.
8. ———. *The description and measurement of personality*. New York: World Book Co., 1946.
9. ———. The riddle of perseveration. II. Solution in terms of personality structure. *J. Person.*, 1946, 14, 239–268.
10. ———. The ergic theory of attitude and sentiment measurement. *Educ. & Psychol. Measurement*, 1947, 7, 221–246.
11. ———. The syntality of national culture patterns: I. R-technique on 63 nations. (Publication to be announced.)
12. ———, & Wispe, L. The dimensions of syntality in structured groups of six persons. (Publication to be announced.)
13. Cole, C. D. H., & Cole, M. *A guide to modern politics*. London: Gollancz, 1934.
14. Cole, G. D. H. *Social theory*. New York: Frederick Stokes, 1920.
15. Gillin, J. L., & Gillin, J. P. *Introduction to sociology*. New York: Macmillan, 1946.
16. Gumplowicz, L. *Outlines of sociology* (trans. by F. H. Moore). Philadelphia: American Academy of Political and Social Science, 1899.
17. Gurnee, H., & Baker, E. The social distances of some common social relationships. *J. abnorm. & soc. Psychol.*, 1938, 33, 265–269.
18. Gurwitch, A. *The sociology of law*. New York: Philosophical Library, 1942.
19. Hart, H. N. *Science of social relations*. New York: Holt, 1931.
20. Hayes, E. C. *Principles of sociology*. New York: D. Appleton Co., 1923.
21. Hobhouse, L. T. *The metaphysical theory of the state*. New York: Macmillan, 1918.
22. Jennings, H. Structure of leadership—development and sphere of interest. *Sociometry*, 1938, 1, 99–143.
23. Keyserling, H. *Das Spektrum Europas*. Berlin: Deutsche Verlags-Anstalt, 1928.
24. Mannheim, K. *Man and society*. New York: Harcourt, Brace, 1940.
25. McDougall, W. *The Group mind*. New York: Putnam, 1920.
26. Mead, M. *And keep your powder dry*. New York: Morrow, 1943.
27. Moreno, J. L., & Jennings, H. H. Statistics of social configurations. *Sociometry*, 1938, 1, 342–374.
28. Mowrer, O. H. *An experimentally produced "social problem."* (Film, obtainable Harvard Educ. Dept.), 1939.
29. Münsterberg, H. *The Americqus*. Garden City: Doubleday, 1914.
30. Ross, E. A. *Foundations of sociology*. New York: Macmillan, 1905.
31. Rousseau, J. J. *du contrat social*. Amsterdam: Rey, 1762.

32. Siegfried, A. *France, a study in nationality*. London: H. Milford, Oxford University Press, 1930.
33. Sorokin, R. A., Zimmerman, C. C., & Galpin, C. J. *A systematic source book in rural sociology*. Minneapolis: Univ. of Minnesota Press, 1930.
34. Thorndike, E. L. *Your city*. New York: Harcourt, Brace, 1939.
35. Thurstone, L. L. *The vectors of the mind*. Chicago: University of Chicago Press, 1935.
36. Von Weise, L. *Systematic sociology* (trans. by H. Becker). New York: John Wiley & Sons, 1932.
37. Ward, L. F. *Pure sociology*. New York: Macmillan, 1903.

10 · PSYCHOLOGY OF RUMOR, PREJUDICE, PROPAGANDA, AND PUBLIC OPINION

GORDON W. ALLPORT
LEO J. POSTMAN

*Psychology of Rumor**

Although the disadvantages of war far outweigh its advantages, yet we may reckon among its meagre benefits the powerful incentives and exceptional opportunities that war gives to scientists to advance their knowledge in fields which normally they neglect to explore or are wont to explore in a desultory fashion. Social psychology is one of the sciences whose work has been greatly stimulated during the recent conflict. Under the stress of wartime needs, it has made significant progress in several areas of investigation. Among them, we name propaganda analysis, morale studies, public opinion measurement, food habits, group therapy, situational tests for selecting personnel, minority group problems, the nature of prejudice, of re-education, and of rumor.[1] It is the last area of progress that we shall here explore.

RUMORS IN WARTIME

During the year 1942, rumor became a national problem of considerable urgency. Its first dangerous manifestation was felt soon after the initial shock of Pearl Harbor. This traumatic event dislocated our normal channels of communication by bringing into existence as unfamiliar and unwelcome, if at the same time a relatively mild censorship of

*_Transactions_ of The New York Academy of Sciences, Volume 8, Number 2, pages 61–81, G. W. Allport and L. J. Postman. Copyright©The New York Academy of Sciences; 1945. Reprinted by permission.

[1] For a review of civilian wartime investigations in these fields, see G. W. Allport & H. E. Veltfort, Social Psychology and the Civilian War Effort, J. Soc. Psychol. (S.P.S.S.I. Bulletin). 18:165–233, 1943: G. R. Schmielder & G. W. Allport, Social Psychology and the Civilian War Effort, May 1943–May 1944. J. Soc. Psychol. (S.P.S.S.I. Bulletin) 20: 145–180. 1944.

news, and it simultaneously dislocated the lives of millions of citizens whose futures abruptly became hostages to fortune.

This combination of circumstances created the most fertile of all possible soils for the propagation of rumor. We now know that *rumors concerning a given subject-matter will circulate within a group in proportion to the importance and the ambiguity of this subject-matter in the lives of individual members of the group.*

The affair of Pearl Harbor was fraught with both importance and ambiguity to nearly every citizen. The affair was important because of the potential danger it represented to all of us, and because its aftermath of mobilization affected every life. It was ambiguous because no one seemed quite certain of the extent of, reasons for, or consequences of the attack. Since the two conditions of rumor—importance and ambiguity—were at a maximum, we had an unprecedented flood of what became known as "Pearl Harbor rumors." It was said that our fleet was "wiped out," that Washington didn't dare to tell the extent of the damage, that Hawaii was in the hands of the Japanese. So widespread and so demoralizing were these tales that, on February 22, 1942, President Roosevelt broadcast a speech devoted entirely to denying the harmful rumors and to reiterating the official report on the losses.

Did the solemn assurance of the Commander-in-Chief restore the confidence of the people and eliminate the tales of suspicion and fear? It so happens that a bit of objective evidence on this question became available to us almost by accident. On the twenty-first of February, the day before the President's speech, we had asked approximately two-hundred college students whether they thought our losses at Pearl Harbor were "greater," "much greater," or "no greater" than the official Knox report had stated. Among these students, 68 per cent had believed the demoralizing rumors in preference to the official report, and insisted that the losses were "greater" or "much greater" than Washington admitted. Then came the President's speech. The next day, an equivalent group of college students were asked the same question. Among those who had not heard or read the speech the proportion of rumor-believers was still about two-thirds. But among those who were acquainted with the President's speech, the number of rumor-believers fell by 24 per cent. It is important to note that, in spite of the utmost efforts of the highest authority to allay anxiety, approximately 44 per cent of the college population studied were too profoundly affected by the event and by the resulting rumors to accept the reassurance.

The year 1942 was characterized by floods of similar fear-inspired tales. Shipping losses were fantastically exaggerated. Knapp records one instance where a collier was sunk through accident near the Cape Cod Canal. So great was the anxiety of the New England public that this incident became a fantastic tale of an American ship being torpedoed with the loss of thousands of nurses who were aboard her.[2]

Such wild stories, as we have said, are due to the grave importance of the subject for the average citizen and to the ambiguity to him of the objective situation. This ambiguity may result from the failure of communications, or from a total lack of authentic news, a condition that often prevailed in war-torn countries or among isolated bands of troops who had few reliable sources of news. Again, the ambiguity may be due to the receipt of conflicting news stories, no one more credible than another, or it may be due (as in the case of the Pearl Harbor rumors) to the distrust of many people in the candor of the

[2] R. H. Knapp, A Psychology of Rumor. Pub. Op. Quart. 8:22–37. 1944.

Administration and in the operation of wartime censorship. As the war progressed, a higher degree of confidence in our news services was rapidly achieved, and rumors concurrently subsided.

In addition to the fear-rumors of 1942, which persisted until the tide of victory commenced to turn, there was a still more numerous crop of hostility-rumors whose theme dealt always with the shortcomings, disloyalty, or inefficiency of some special group of co-belligerents. The Army, the Navy, the Administration, our allies, or American minority groups were the most frequent scapegoats in these rumors. We were told that the Army wasted whole sides of beef, that the Russians greased their guns with lend-lease butter, that Negroes were saving ice-picks for a revolt, and that Jews were evading the draft.

These hostility rumors were the most numerous of all. An analysis of 1000 rumors collected from all parts of the country in 1942,[3] revealed that they could be classified fairly readily as:

Hostility (wedge-driving) rumors =	66 per cent
Fear (bogey) rumors =	25 per cent
Wish (pipe-dream) rumors =	2 per cent
Unclassifiable rumors =	7 per cent
TOTAL	100 per cent

To be sure, the proportion of fear and wish rumors soon altered. As victory approached, especially on the eve of VE and VJ day, the whirlwind of rumors was almost wholly concerned with the cessation of hostilities, reflecting a goal-gradient phenomenon whereby rumor under special conditions hastens the completion of a desired event. But, throughout the war and continuing to the present, it is probably true that the majority of all rumors are of a more or less slanderous nature, expressing hostility against this group or that.

The principal reason why rumor circulates can be briefly stated. It circulates because it *serves the twin function of explaining and relieving emotional tensions felt by individuals.*[4]

The Pearl Harbor rumors, for example, helped to *explain* to the teller why he felt such distressing anxiety. Would his jitters not be justified if it were true that our protecting fleet was "wiped out" at Pearl Harbor? Something serious must have happened to account for his anxiety. Families deprived of sons, husbands or fathers, vaguely cast around for someone to blame for their privation. Well, the Jews, who were said to be evading the draft, were "obviously" not doing their share and thus the heavy burden falling on "good citizens" was explained. True, this draft-evasion charge did not last very

[3] R. H. Knapp, op. cit.:25.

[4] This brief formula leaves out of account only the relatively few rumors which seem to serve the purpose of "phatic communication,"–a form of idle conversation to facilitate social intercourse. When a lull occurs in a conversation, an individual may "fill in" with the latest bit of gossip that comes to mind, without being motivated by the deeper tensions that underlie the great bulk of rumor-mongering.

In this paper we cannot enter into a fuller discussion of the reasons why people believe some rumors and not others. This question is carefully studied by Z. H. Allport & M. Lopkin, Wartime Rumors of Waste and Special Privilege: Why Some People Believe Them, J. Abnorm. & Soc. Psychol. 40: 3–36. 1945.

long, owing, no doubt, to the inescapable evidence of heavy enlistments among Jews and of their heroic conduct in the war. But when shortages were felt, the traditional Jewish scapegoat was again trotted out as a convenient explanation of the privations suffered. Their operation of the black market "explained" our annoying experiences in the futile pursuit of an evening lamb-chop.

To blame others verbally is not only a mode of explanation for one's emotional distress, but is at the same time a mode of *relief*. Everyone knows the reduction of tension that comes after administering a tongue-lashing. It matters little whether the victim of the tongue-lashing is guilty or not. Dressing down *anyone* to his face or behind his back has the strange property of temporarily reducing hatred felt against this person or, what is more remarkable, of reducing hatred felt against any person or thing. If you wish to deflate a taut inner-tube you can unscrew the valve or you can make a puncture. Unscrewing the valve corresponds to directing our hostility toward the Nazis or Japanese, who were the cause of our suffering. Making a puncture corresponds to displacing the hostility upon innocent victims or scapegoats. In either case, the air will escape and relaxation follow. To blame Jews, Negroes, the Administration, brass hats, the OPA, or the politicians, is to bring a certain relief from accumulated feelings of hostility whatever their true cause. Relief, odd as it may seem, comes also from "bogey" rumors. To tell my neighbor that the Cape Cod Canal is choked with corpses is an easy manner of projecting into the outer world my own choking anxieties concerning my son or my friends in combat service. Having shared my anxiety with my friends by telling him exaggerated tales of losses or of atrocities, I no longer feel so much alone and helpless. Through my rumor-spreading, others, too, are put "on the alert." I therefore feel reassured.

That rumors were harmful to national morale was quickly recognized both by federal authorities and by civilian leaders of opinion. The efforts of the FBI to trace subversive rumors constitute a story yet to be told; the preventive campaign conducted by OWI and other federal agencies marks another chapter in the story; the establishment of "Rumor Clinics" in at least 40 newspapers in the United States and Canada is yet another. Lectures, pamphlets, movies, posters, and "rumor-wardens" all formed part of the campaign. This activity was at its peak during 1942–43. As victory became assured, the emotional insistency of anxiety and hate subsided, news services became more widely believed, rumor lessened, and the immediate crisis passed.

Though it was the darker days of the war that focused our attention upon rumor as a grave social problem, still the mischief of rumor and gossip is something we always have with us. At the present time, there is reason to suppose that we may be headed for another critical period of rumor-mongering, since we anticipate sharp clashes between minority groups of Americans and majority groups during the coming years of social readjustment. Records of the bitter race conflicts in Los Angeles, Beaumont, Harlem, Philadelphia, and Detroit have taught us what a close association exists between rumors and riot. The tie is so intimate that one of the best barometers we have of social strain lies in the analysis of rumors circulating in a tense community.[5]

[5] For an account of the relation of rumors to riots see A. McC. Lee & W. D. Humphrey, Race Riot. Dryden Press. New York. 1943: and J. B. Weckler & T. E. Hall, The Police and Minority Groups. Internat. City Managers Association, Chicago. 1944.

EXPERIMENTAL APPROACH

Leaving now the broader social setting of the problem, we ask ourselves what processes in the human mind account for the spectacular distortions and exaggerations that enter into the rumor-process, and lead to so much damage to the public intelligence and public conscience.

Since it is very difficult to trace in detail the course of a rumor in everyday life, we have endeavored by an experimental technique to study as many of the basic phenomena as possible under relatively well controlled laboratory conditions.

Our method is simple. A slide is thrown upon a screen. Ordinarily, a semi-dramatic picture is used containing a large number of related details. Six or seven subjects, who have not seen the picture, wait in an adjacent room. One of them enters and takes a position where he cannot see the screen. Someone in the audience (or the experimenter) describes the picture, giving about twenty details in the account. A second subject enters the room and stands beside the first subject who proceeds to tell him all he can about the picture. (All subjects are under instruction to report as "accurately as possible what you have heard.") The first subject than takes his seat, and a third enters to hear the story from the second subject. Each succeeding subject hears and repeats the story in the same way. Thus, the audience is able to watch the deterioration of the rumor by comparing the

Figure 1. A sample of pictorial material employed in the experiments. Here is a typical terminal report (the last in a chain of reproductions): "This is a subway train in New York headed for Portland Street. There is a Jewish woman and a Negro who has a razor in his hand. The woman has a baby or a dog. The train is going to Deyer Street, and nothing much happened."

successive versions with the stimulus-picture which remains on the screen throughout the experiment.

This procedure has been used with over forty groups of subjects, including college undergraduates, Army trainees in ASTP, members of community forums, patients in an Army hospital, members of a Teachers' Round Table, and police officials in a training course. In addition to these adult subjects, children in a private school were used, in grades from the fourth through the ninth. In some experiments, Negro subjects took part along with whites, a fact which, as we shall see, had important consequences when the test-pictures depicted scenes with a "racial angle."

All of these experiments took place before an audience (20–300 spectators). By using volunteer subjects, one eliminates the danger of stage fright. There was, however, a social influence in all the audience situations. The magnitude of this influence was studied in a control group of experiments where no one was present in the room excepting the subject and the experimenter.

At the outset, it is necessary to admit that in five respects this experimental situation fails to reproduce accurately the conditions of rumor-spreading in everyday life. (1) The effect of an audience is considerable, tending to create caution and to shorten the report. Without an audience subjects gave on the average twice as many details as with an audience. (2) The effect of the instructions is to maximize accuracy and induce caution. In ordinary rumor-spreading, there is no critical experimenter on hand to see whether the tale is rightly repeated. (3) There is no opportunity for subjects to ask questions of his informer. In ordinary rumor-spreading, the listener can chat with his informer and, if he wishes, cross-examine him. (4) The lapse of time between hearing and telling in the experimental situation is very slight. In ordinary rumor spreading, it is much greater. (5) Most important of all, the conditions of motivation are quite different. In the experiment, the subject is striving for *accuracy*. His own fears, hates, wishes are not likely to be aroused under the experimental conditions. In short, he is not the spontaneous rumor-agent that he is in ordinary life. His stake in spreading the experimental rumor is neither personal nor deeply motivated.

It should be noted that all of these conditions, excepting the third, may be expected to enhance the accuracy of the report in the experimental situation, and to yield far less distortion and projection than in real-life rumor spreading.

In spite of the fact that our experiment does not completely reproduce the normal conditions for rumor, still we believe that all essential changes and distortions are represented in our results. "Indoor" rumors may not be as lively, as emotionally-toned, or as extreme as "outdoor" rumors, and yet the same basic phenomena are demonstratable in both.

What happens in both real-life and laboratory rumors is a complex course of distortion in which three inter-related tendencies are clearly distinguishable.

LEVELING

As rumor travels, it tends to grow shorter, more concise, more easily grasped and told. In successive versions, fewer words are used and fewer details are mentioned.

The number of details *retained* declines most sharply at the beginning of the series of

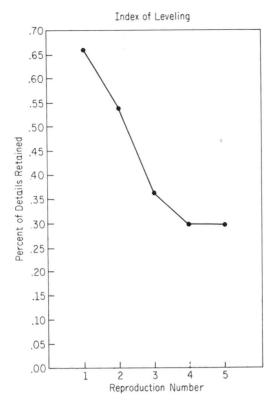

Figure 2. Percentage of details originally given which are retained in each successive reproduction.

reproductions. The number continues to decline, more slowly, throughout the experiment. Figure 2 shows the percentage of the details initially given which are retained in each successive reproduction.

The number of items enumerated in the description from the screen constitutes the 100 per cent level, and all subsequent percentages are calculated from that base. The curve, based on 11 experiments, shows that about 70 per cent of the details are eliminated in the course of five or six mouth-to-mouth transmissions, even when virtually no time lapse intervenes.

The curve is like the famous Ebbinghaus curve for decline in individual retention, though in his experiments the interval between initial learning and successive reproductions was not as short as under the conditions of our experiment. Comparing the present curve with Ebbinghaus's, we conclude that *social memory accomplished as much leveling within a few minutes as individual memory accomplishes in weeks of time.*

Leveling (in our experiments) never proceeds to the point of total obliteration. The stabilization of the last part of the curve is a finding of some consequence. It indicates (1) that a short concise statement is likely to be faithfully reproduced; (2) that when the report has become short and concise, the subject has very little detail to select from and the possibilities of further distortion grow fewer; (3) that the assignment becomes so easy that a virtually rote memory serves to hold the material in mind. In all cases, the terminal and the anteterminal reports are more similar than any two preceding reports.

The reliance on rote is probably more conspicuous in our experiments than in ordinary rumor-spreading, where accuracy is not the aim, where time interferes with rote retention, and where strong interests prevent literal memory. There are, however, conditions where rote memory plays a part in ordinary rumor-spreading. If the individual is motivated by no stronger desire than to make conversation, he may find himself idly repeating what he has recently heard in the form in which he heard it. If a rumor has become so crisp and brief, so sloganized, that it requires no effort to retain it in the literal form in which it was heard, rote memory seems to be involved. For example:

> The Jews are evading the draft
> The CIO is communist controlled
> Wallace believes in a pint of milk for every Hottentot

The importance of rote has been recognized by the writers of advertisements. They endeavor to make their slogans brief, concise, rhythmic and easy to remember:

> Lucky Strikes mean finer tobacco
> Smoke Chesterfields—they satisfy
> Duz does everything

Similarly, many legends and superstitions have been abbreviated to such an aphoristic point that it is almost impossible to forget them:

> Stuff a cold and starve a fever
> An apple a day keeps the doctor away
> A red sky at night, the sailor's delight
> Spare the rod and spoil the child
> Early to bed and early to rise makes a man healthy and wealthy and wise

We conclude that whenever verbal material is transmitted among a group of people whether as rumor, legend, or history, change will be in the direction of greater brevity and conciseness. Leveling is not a random phenomenon—we note in the following protocol how a group of soldier subjects tends to retain orientation throughout their series of reports.

Protocol A

Description from the screen: The scene is laid in France during wartime. Several men in uniform are obvious. Two of them are firing, one is on his back wounded, with a bandage around his knee. There is a Negro soldier standing, ready to throw a hand-grenade. Behind them there is a destroyed building with one doorway. There is a sign at the crossroads, reading "Cherbourg 21½ km., Paris 50 km." There is also a sign reading "Pain et Vin." There are shells at the sides of the wrecked building. Behind the building there is a church with a big roof hole. The church has a steeple, with the clock showing ten minutes to two. There are two aeroplanes behind the church, as there are explosions to be seen. There is an ambulance at the extreme right, with men coming out with shells. Sign, "Bread and Wine."
First Reproduction: The scene is laid in France. There are two soldiers in a trench, close behind them, is another, wounded. Nearby there is a wrecked house. A Negro soldier is throwing a grenade. There are signs reading "50 miles

to Cherbourg and 21 miles to Paris." There is a church with a steeple, showing ten minutes to two. The designation of shells bursting indicates that there is a battle going on. There is an ambulance somewhere in the picture. There is a sign "Bread and Wine."

Second Reproduction: The scene is in France. There is a trench with two men, one firing. A soldier is on his back, wounded. There is a signpost—"Paris 50 miles and Cherbourg 21 miles." There is an ambulance in the picture. There is a house or a barn behind a Negro soldier throwing a grenade. Behind the house is a church. On the steeple the time reads ten minutes to two. Behind the church there are some aeroplanes.

Third Reproduction: The scene is in France. There are two soldiers in a trench and a wounded soldier. There is an ambulance in the picture, and a house in the background, also a church with a steeple; the time is . . . I don't remember. There is a signpost "Cherbourg 21 miles, Paris 50 miles." There is a Negro soldier in the picture.

Fourth Reproduction: The scene takes place in France, 21 miles from Cherbourg, 50 miles from Paris. This information is given by a signpost. There are two soldiers in the picture and also a Negro soldier. In the distance there is a church, and also a house. There is an ambulance nearby.

Fifth Reproduction: The scene is in France, 21 miles from Cherbourg, 50 miles from Paris, as we can read on a signpost. There is a Negro soldier in the picture. There is a church nearby and also an ambulance.

Sixth Reproduction: The scene is in France, 21 miles from Cherbourg, and 50 miles from Paris, as a signpost indicates. There is a Negro soldier in the scene. An ambulance and a church are nearby.

Seventh Reproduction: The scene is in France, 21 miles from Cherbourg, and 50 miles from Paris. There is a Negro soldier in the scene, and also an ambulance.

Eighth Reproduction: The scene is in France, 50 miles from Cherbourg and at a distance from Paris, and in this scene is an ambulance and also a Negro soldier.

This protocol shows the continual shortening of the rumor, but, at the same time, the tendency of military subjects to preserve their orientation in space. The scene is always correctly laid in France, somewhere between Cherbourg and Paris. To be sure, kilometers are transposed into the more familiar measure of "miles," and the figure "50" gets attached to Cherbourg rather than Paris. Like every other rumor the report as received from hearsay is worthless, yet there is a selective type of retention that follows the occupational interest of the subject. Non-military subjects are much less likely to retain measures of distance or of time.

SHARPENING

We may define sharpening as the selective perception, retention, and reporting of a limited number of details from a larger context. In the military protocol just cited, geographical features are sharpened. Sharpening is inevitably the reciprocal of leveling. The one cannot exist without the other, for what little remains to a rumor after leveling has taken place is by contrast unavoidably featured.

Although sharpening occurs in every protocol, the items are not always emphasized. Sometimes, a trifling detail such as a subway advertising card becomes the focus of attention and report. Around it the whole rumor becomes structured. But, in most experiments, this same detail drops out promptly, and is never heard of after the first reproduction.

One way in which sharpening seems to be determined is through the retention of odd, or attention-getting words which, having appeared early in the series, catch the attention of each successive listener and are often passed on in preference to other details intrinsically more important to the story. An instance of this effect is seen in a series of protocols where the statement, "there is a boy stealing and a man remonstrating with him" is transmitted throughout the entire series. The unusual word "remonstrate" somehow caught the attention of each successive listener and was passed on without change.

Sharpening may also take a *numerical* turn, as in the experiments where emphasized items become reduplicated in the telling. For example, in reports of a picture containing the figure of a Negro, whose size and unusual appearance invite emphasis, we find that the number of Negroes reported in the picture jumps from one to "four" or "several."

There is also *temporal* sharpening manifested in the tendency to describe events as occurring in the immediate present. What happens *here* and *now* is of greatest interest and importance to the perceiver. In most instances, to be sure, the story is started in the present tense, but even when the initial description is couched in the past tense, immediate reversal occurs and the scene is contemporized by the listener. Obviously, this effect cannot occur in rumors which deal specifically with some alleged past (or future) event. One cannot contemporize the rumor that "the Queen Mary sailed this morning (or will sail tomorrow) with 10,000 troops abroad." Yet it not infrequently happens that stories gain in sharpening by tying them to present conditions. For example, a statement that Mr. X bought a chicken in the black market last week and paid $1.50 a pound for it may be (and usually is) rendered, "I hear they *are* charging $1.50 a pound on the black market for chicken." People are more interested in today than in last week, and the temptation, therefore, is to adapt (assimilate) the time of occurrence, when possible, to this interest.

Sharpening often takes place when there is a clear implication of *movement*. The flying of airplanes and the bursting of bombs are frequently stressed in the telling. Similarly, the falling flower pot in one picture is often retained and accented. Indeed, the "falling motif" may be extended to other objects such as the cigar which a man in the picture is smoking. In one rumor, it is said to be falling (like the flower pot), though in reality it is quite securely held between his teeth.

Sometimes sharpening is achieved by ascribing movement to objects which are really stationary. Thus, a subway train, clearly at a standstill at a subway station, is frequently described as moving.

Relative size is also a primary determinant of attention. Objects that are prominent because of their size tend to be retained and sharpened. The first reporter calls attention to their prominence and each successive listener receives an impression of their largeness. He then proceeds to sharpen this impression in his memory. The large Negro may, in the telling, become "four Negroes," or may become "a gigantic statue of a Negro."

There are verbal as well as physical determinants of attention. Thus, there is a pronounced tendency for *labels* to persist, expecially if they serve to set the stage for the story. One picture is usually introduced by some version of the statement, "This is a battle scene," and this label persists throughout the series of reproductions. Another story usually opens with the statement, "This is a picture of a race riot."

To explain this type of sharpening, we may invoke the desire of the subject to achieve some spatial and temporal schema for the story to come. Such orientation is essential in ordinary life and appears to constitute a strong need even when imaginal material is dealt with.

An additional factor making for preferential retention of spatial and temporal labels is the *primacy* effect. An item that comes first in a series is likely to be better remembered than subsequent items. Usually, the "label" indicating place and time comes at the beginning of a report and thus benefits by the primacy effect.

Sharpening also occurs in relation to familiar symbols. In one series of reports, a church and a cross are among the most frequently reported items, although they are relatively minor details in the original picture. These well known symbols "pack" meaning and are familiar to all. The subject feels secure in reporting them because they have an accustomed concreteness that the other details in the picture lack. Retention of familiar symbols advances the process of conventionalization that is so prominent an aspect of rumor-embedding. In two of our pictures are a night stick, symbol of police authority, and a razor, stereotyped symbol of Negro violence. These symbols are always retained and sharpened.

Explanations added by the reporter to the description transmitted to him comprise a final form of sharpening. They represent a tendency to put "closure" upon a story which is felt to be otherwise incomplete. They illustrate the "effort after meaning" which customarily haunts the subject who finds himself in an unstructured situation. Such need for sharpening by explanation becomes especially strong when the story has been badly distorted and the report contains implausible and incompatible items. As an example, one subject who received a badly confused description of the subway scene Figure 1 inferred that there must have been "an accident." This explanation seemed plausible enough to successive listeners and so was not only accepted by them but sharpened in the telling.

In everyday rumors, sharpening through the introduction of specious explanations is very apparent. Indeed, as we have said, one of the principle functions of a rumor is to explain personal tensions. To accept tales of army waste or special privilege among OPA officials could "explain" food shortages and discomfort. Such stories, therefore, find wide credence.

Here, perhaps, is the place to take issue with the popular notion that rumors tend to expand like snowballs, become over-elaborate, and verbose. Actually, the course of rumor is toward brevity, whether in the laboratory or in everyday life. Such exaggeration as exists is nearly always a sharpening of some feature resident in the original stimulus-situation. The distortion caused by sharpening is, of course, enormous in extent; but we do not find that we need the category of "elaboration" to account for the changes we observe.

ASSIMILATION

It is apparent that both leveling and sharpening are selective processes. But what is it that leads to the obliteration of some details and the pointing-up of others; and what accounts for all transpositions, importations, and other falsifications that mark the course of rumor? The answer is to be found in the process of *assimilation*, which has to do with the powerful attractive force exerted upon rumor by habits, interests, and sentiments existing in the listener's mind.

Assimilation to Principal Theme

It generally happens that items become sharpened or leveled to fit the leading motif of the story, and they become consistent with this motif in such a way as to make the resulting story more coherent, plausible, and well rounded. Thus, in Protocol A, the war theme is preserved and emphasized in all reports. In some experiments using the same picture, a chaplain is introduced, or people (in the plural) are reported as being killed, the ambulance becomes a Red Cross station, demolished buildings are multipled in the telling; the extent of devastation is exaggerated. All these reports, false though they are, fit the principle theme—a battle incident. If the reported details were actually present in the picture, they would make a "better" *Gestalt.* Objects wholly extraneous to the theme are never introduced—no apple pies, no ballet dancers, no baseball players.

Besides importations, we find other falsifications in the interest of supporting the principal theme. The original picture shows that the Red Cross truck is loaded with explosives, but it is ordinarily reported as carrying medical supplies which is, of course, the way it "ought" to be.

The Negro in this same picture is nearly always described as a soldier, although his clothes might indicate that he is a civilian partisan. It is a "better" configuration to have a soldier in action on the battlefield than to have a civilian among regular soldiers.

Good Continuation

Other falsifications result from the attempt to complete incompleted pictures or to fill in gaps which exist in the stimulus field. The effort is again to make the resulting whole coherent, and meaningful. Thus, the sign, "Loew's Pa . . .," over a moving picture theater is invariably read and reproduced as "Loew's Palace" and Gene *Antry* becomes Gene *Autry.* "Lucky Rakes" are reported as "Lucky Strikes."

All these, and many instances like them, are examples of what has been called, in *Gestalt* terms, "closures." Falsifications of perception and memory they are, but they occur in the interests of bringing about a more coherent, consistent mental configuration. Every detail is assimilated to the principal theme, and "good continuation" is sought, in order to round out meaning where it is lacking or incomplete.

Assimilation by Condensation

It sometimes seems as though memory tries to burden itself as little as possible. For instance, instead of remembering two items, it is more economical to fuse them into one. Instead of a series of subway cards, each of which has its own identity, reports sometimes refer only to a "billboard," or perhaps to a "lot of advertising" (Figure 1). In another picture, it is more convenient to refer to "all kinds of fruit," rather than to enumerate all the different items on the vendor's cart. Again, the occupants of the car come to be described by some such summary phrase as "several people sitting and standing in the car." Their individuality is lost.

Assimilation to Expectation

Just as details are changed or imported to bear out the simplified theme that the listener has in mind, so too many items take a form that supports the agent's habits of thought. Things are perceived and remembered the way they *usually* are. Thus, a drug-store in one stimulus-picture, is situated in the middle of a block; but, in the telling, it moves up to the corner of the two streets and becomes the familiar "corner drugstore." A Red Cross ambulance is said to carry medical supplies rather than explosives, because it "ought" to be carrying medical supplies. The kilometers on the signposts are changed into miles, since Americans are accustomed to having distances indicated in miles.

The most spectacular of all our assimilative distortions is the finding that, in more than half of our experiments, a razor moves (in the telling) from a white man's hand to a Negro's hand (Figure 1). This result is a clear instance of assimilation to stereotyped expectancy. Black men are "supposed" to carry razors, white men not.

Assimilation to Linguistic Habits

Expectancy is often merely a matter of fitting perceived and remembered material to pre-existing verbal clichés. An odd example is found in the case of a clock tower on a chapel. In the telling, the chapel becomes a "chaplain" and the clock, having no place to go, lands on a fictitious mantelpiece.

Sixth Reproduction: This is a picture of a battlefield. There is a chapel with a clock which says ten minutes to two. A sign down below gives the direction to Paris and Paris is 50 miles, and Cherbourg 21 miles away. People are being killed on the battlefield.

Seventh Reproduction: This is a picture of a battlefield. There is a chaplain, and a clock on the mantelpiece says ten minutes to two. There is a sign, so many miles to Cherbourg.

The powerful effect that words have in arousing images in the listener and fixing for him the categories in which he must think of the event is, of course, a major step in the conventionalization of rumor. A "zoot-suit sharpie" arouses a much more compelling image (capable of assimilating all details to itself) than more objective words, such as "a colored man with pegged trousers, wide brimmed hat, etc." (Figure 1). Rumors are commonly told in terms of verbal stereotypes. Over and over again, they include prejudicial judgment, such as "draft dodger," "Japanese spy," "brass-hat," "dumb Swede," "long-haired professor," and the like.

MORE HIGHLY MOTIVATED ASSIMILATION

Although the conditions of our experiment do not give full play to emotional tendencies underlying gossip, rumor, and scandal, such tendencies are so insistent that they express themselves even under laboratory conditions.

Assimilation to Interest

It sometimes happens that a picture containing women's dresses, as a trifling detail in the original scene, becomes, in the telling, a story exclusively about dresses. This sharpening occurs when the rumor is told by groups of women, but never when told by men.

A picture involving police was employed with a group of police officers as subjects. In the resulting protocol, which follows, the entire reproduction centers around the police officer (with whom the subjects undoubtedly felt keen sympathy or "identification"). Furthermore, the nightstick, a symbol of his power, is greatly sharpened and becomes the main object of the controversy. The tale as a whole is protective of, and partial to the policeman.

Protocol B

Description from the screen: This is an excerpt from a motion picture that appeared in a national magazine. The scene is Detroit during the colored-white riot. There is a crowd around a police officer with a riot stick in his right hand and a Negro sitting on the ground, holding to his leg. On the right a boy is running away. On the left, facing the officer is a man who looks hostile but is afraid to go nearer because of the riot stick. The crowd comprises approximately 100 people.

First Reproduction: The picture on the screen is an excerpt from a motion picture taken at the time of the Detroit riot. In the picture, a police officer with a stick in his right hand is standing over a man on the ground. On the right, is a small boy; on the left, is a man who wants to interfere but is afraid of the policeman's stick.

Second Reproduction: This is an excerpt from a movie taken at the time of the Detroit riot. There is an officer with a stick in his hand and a man on the ground. There is a small boy and a man who wants to interfere but is afraid.

Third Reproduction: Picture was taken during the Detroit riot. There is a man in the picture, also a police officer. The man has a stick in his hand and wants to interfere, but does not for some reason. There is also a child.

Fourth Reproduction: This is a picture of the Detroit riot showing a policeman and a civilian. The policeman has a billy in his hand and the man wants to take it away from him.

Fifth Reproduction: A picture of the Detroit riot. There is a police officer with a club. Somebody wants to take it away from him.

Protocols based on the same picture, taken from a group of subjects who were not policemen, show how, in a different group, the focus of interest and direction of sympathy may be quite different. Only the police tell rumors that favor the police.

Assimilation to Prejudice

Hard as it is in an experimental situation to obtain distortions that arise from hatred, yet we have in our material a certain opportunity to trace the hostile complex of racial attitudes.

We have spoken of the picture which contained a white man holding a razor while arguing with a Negro. In over half of the experiments with this picture, the final report indicated that the Negro (instead of the white man) held the razor in his hand, and several times he was reported as "brandishing it wildly" or as "threatening" the white man with it (Figure 1).

Whether this ominous distortion reflects hatred and fear of Negroes we cannot definitely say. In some cases, these deeper emotions may be the assimilative factor at work. And yet the distortion may occur even in subjects who have no anti-Negro bias. It is an unthinking cultural stereotype that the Negro is hot-tempered and addicted to the use of razors as weapons. The rumor, though mischievous, may reflect chiefly an assimilation of the story to verbal-clichés and conventional expectation. Distortion in this case may not mean assimilation to hostility. Much so-called prejudice is, of course, a mere matter of conforming to current folkways by accepting prevalent beliefs about an out-group.

Whether or not this razor-shift reflects deep hatred and fear on the part of white subjects, it is certain that the reports of our Negro subjects betray a motivated type of distortion. Because it was to their interest as members of the race to de-emphasize the racial caricature, Negro subjects almost invariably avoided mention of color. One of them hearing a rumor containing the phrase, "a Negro zoot-suiter," reported "There is a man wearing a zoot suit, *possibly* a Negro."

For one picture, a Negro reporter said that the colored man in the center of the picture "is being maltreated." Though this interpretation may be correct, it is likewise possible that he is a rioter about to be arrested by the police officer. White and Negro subjects are very likely to perceive, remember, and interpret this particular situation in quite opposite ways.

Thus, even under laboratory conditions, we find assimilation in terms of deep-lying emotional predispositions. Our rumors, like those of everyday life, tend to fit into, and support, the occupational interests, class or racial memberships, or personal prejudices of the reporter.

CHILDREN

Our findings showed a striking lack of interest among children in the racial identity of characters in the picture. A "Negro" was often reported simply as a "man." In the case of pictures disclosing racial identity, 85 per cent of our adult protocols mentioned this identity, while only 43 per cent of protocols taken from children did so.

Though we do not have extensive data from different age levels, it appears certain that the younger the child, the less he is likely to report ethnic character. One is reminded of the case of Tommy, aged six, who asked his mother if he might bring his schoolmate Sam home to lunch next day. Knowing that Tommy was in a "mixed" school, his mother asked if Sam was a Negro. Tommy replied, "I didn't notice, but I'll look and tell you tomorrow."

Our experiment offers an opportunity to study the growing importance of ethnic identity in word of mouth stories told by children of successive ages.

CONCLUSION: THE EMBEDDING PROCESS

Leveling, sharpening, and assimilation, are not independent mechanisms. They function simultaneously, and reflect a singular subjectifying process that results in the autism and falsification which are so characteristic of rumor. If we were to attempt to summarize what happens in a few words we might say:

Whenever a stimulus field is of potential importance to an individual, but at the same time unclear, or susceptible of divergent interpretations, a subjective structuring process is started. Although the process is complex (involving, as it does, leveling, sharpening, and assimilation), its essential nature can be characterized as an effort to reduce the stimulus to a simple and meaningful structure that has adaptive significance for the individual in terms of his own interests and experience. The process begins at the moment the ambiguous situation is perceived, but the effects are greatest if memory intervenes. The longer the time that elapses after the stimulus is perceived the greater the threefold change is likely to be. Also, the more people involved in a serial report, the greater the change is likely to be, until the rumor has reached an aphoristic brevity, and is repeated by rote.

Now, this three-pronged process turns out to be characteristic not only of rumor but of the individual memory function as well. It has been uncovered and described in the experiments on individual retention conducted by Wulf, Gibson, Allport,[6] and, in Bartlett's memory experiments carried out both on individuals and on groups.[7]

Up to now, however, there has been no agreement on precisely the terminology to use, nor upon the adequacy of the three functions we here describe. We believe that our conceptualization of the three-fold course of change and decay is sufficient to account, not only for our own experimental findings and for the experiments of others in this area, but also for the distortions that everyday rumors undergo.

For lack of a better designation, we speak of the three-fold change as the *embedding* process. What seems to occur in all our experiments and in all related studies is that each subject finds the outer stimulus-world far too hard to grasp and retain in its objective character. For his own personal uses, it must be recast to fit not only his span of comprehension and his span of retention, but, likewise, his own personal needs and interests. What was outer becomes inner; what was objective becomes subjective. In telling a rumor, the kernel of objective information that he received has become so embedded into his own dynamic mental life that the product is chiefly one of projection. Into the rumor, he projects the deficiencies of his retentive processes, as well as his own effort to engender meaning upon an ambiguous field, and the product reveals much of his own emotional needs, including his anxieties, hates, and wishes. When several rumor-agents have been involved in this embedding process, the net result of the serial reproduction reflects the lowest common denominator of cultural interest, of memory span, and of group sentiment and prejudice.

One may ask whether a rumor must always be false. We answer that, in virtually every case, the embedding process is so extensive that no credibility whatever should be ascribed to the product. If a report does turn out to be trustworthy, we usually find that secure standards of evidence have somehow been present to which successive agents could refer for purposes of validation. Perhaps the morning newspaper or the radio have held the rumor under control, but when such secure standards of verification are available, it is questionable whether we should speak of rumor at all.

There are, of course, border-line cases where we may not be able to say whether a given tidbit should or should not be called a rumor. But if we define rumor (and we herewith propose that we should), as *a proposition for belief of topical reference, without secure standards of evidence being present*—then it follows from the facts we have presented that rumor will suffer such serious distortion through the embedding process, that *it is never under any circumstances a valid guide for belief or conduct.*

[6]Conveniently summarized in K. Koffka, Principles of Gestalt Psychology. Harcourt Brace & Co. New York. 1935.
[7]P. O. Bartlett, Remembering. Cambridge University Press. 1932.

LEONARD W. DOOB

*Public Opinion and Propaganda**

This book seeks to analyze public opinion and propaganda from the viewpoint of modern social science. Instead of calling public opinion wise or foolish, it makes an effort to identify and explain the segment of human behavior known as public opinion, to describe how people react in social situations, and to assay the importance of public opinion in the modern world. Instead of presenting examples of the exotic or mundane results obtained from measuring public opinion, it utilizes such information incidentally and only to indicate the difficulties and the techniques of measurement. Instead of maintaining that propaganda is evil and tricky, it suggests that propaganda cannot be easily labeled and it focuses attention upon how propaganda functions. Instead of displaying grief or joy when the modern media of communication are contemplated, it tries faithfully to describe their accomplishments and potentialities as well as the reasons therefor.

The writer has only one thesis to advocate: public opinion and propaganda are intimately related because they both involve phases of human behavior. An understanding of human behavior, it is therefore contended, can provide insight into public opinion and propaganda. The reaction of public opinion to an atomic bomb or some propaganda fluff can be viewed in similar terms because the same principles of behavior are operating. In almost every paragraph an attempt is made to phrase the discussion in terms of human beings and thus to reduce apparently bewildering complexity to a common denominator.

Few people like principles, and principles can become unintelligible if they remain on an abstract level. To facilitate the analysis, consequently, specific illustrations of public opinion and propaganda are given at frequent intervals. On the whole these have been drawn from three fields: politics, business, and war. The selection is somewhat arbitrary, but seems justified because the fields are diverse and also important.

Social science, like all science, strives to be neutral. Facts are collected, collated, and fitted into theory. Or else theory in the first place demands their collection and collation. The utilization of social science is another problem—and, in this instance, the concluding chapter argues that the problem cannot be completely avoided. The argument is withheld from this preface: it is not an underlying motif of the book.

It must be said, however, that this volume aims to be useful to both the producer and the consumer of public opinion and propaganda. The producer is a fancy name for the individual who seeks to affect, measure, or control other people—and he may have the title of leader, politician, advertiser, public relations counsel, pollster, analyst, or journalist. Consumer refers to an individual in the group whose opinions are being affected, measured, or controlled—and he is either a student or a citizen. Specifically, for example, it is possible to learn how to conduct or to understand a public opinion poll; to plan or dissect an advertising campaign, to spray propaganda upon an enemy or to help immunize

*Leonard W. Dobb, *Public Opinion and Propaganda*, 2nd ed. (Hamden, Conn.: Archon Books, 1966), pages iii-iv, 240, 558–566. Copyright 1948 by Holt, Rinehart and Winston.

oneself from enemy propaganda. Let each reader decide for himself whether he is a producer or consumer.

★　★　★

THE NATURE OF PROPAGANDA

In short, the "right" kind of education consists of learning facts and theories which can be verified or of subscribing to points of view which are considered "good," "just," "beautiful," or "necessary" in the society. The "wrong" kind promotes unverified or unverifiable facts and theories as well as "bad," "unjust," "ugly," or "unnecessary" points of view. The educator has prestige in our society because it is presumed that he teaches what people want and need to be taught, in order to be socialized according to our standards. If he mixes radicalism with arithmetic or exposés with civics, he is branded a propagandist by the majority of people in the United States. If he mixes imperialism with geography or capitalism with economics, he is likewise angrily labeled a propagandist certainly not by the majority but by the radical-minded minority. Pick your science or the values you consider important in your society, and then you can decide what education is.

THE SCOPE OF PROPAGANDA

Propaganda is not education as education has been here defined. Propaganda can be called *the attempt to affect the personalities and to control the behavior of individuals toward ends considered unscientific or of doubtful value in a society at a particular time.* What has been said of education applies to propaganda but in a reverse manner. The imparting knowledge which has not reached the scientific stage is propaganda, as is the teaching of a skill which is not adapted to the situation at hand. The dissemination of a viewpoint considered by a group to be "bad," "unjust," "ugly," or "unnecessary" is propaganda in terms of that group's standards.

This severe distinction between education and propaganda on the basis of science and survival value does not mean that the influence of an individual upon his contemporaries is clearly either one or the other. What almost always occurs is a combination of the two.

★　★　★

THE BOUNDARIES OF COMMUNICATION[1]

Who attends political meetings, the candidate's friends or his opponents? What kinds of people depend upon television and radio rather than newspapers as their primary source of news? How can the leaders of one country communicate with the people of another? Questions of this type focus upon variables involving the attraction of an audi-

[1] This chapter is based almost completely upon quotations from the author's *Communication Africa* (1961) and upon the schema of analysis elaborated and illustrated therein. Permission to embed my own words and ideas in the present context has been graciously granted by the publisher, the Yale University Press.

ence to various forms of communication and not upon people's reactions when once they appear at the meeting, turn on their radio set, or come in contact with information originating abroad.

If several arguments are to be advanced, should the most important one come first or last? Should you try to win people's cooperation by making them anxious? Is it better for a communicator to state bluntly what he wishes to achieve than to conceal his objective? Here the presence of an audience is assumed, and the questions point to people's reactions.

Obviously both kinds of problems are important. Before a communication can possibly be effective, it must be perceived by an audience, but if perception may be assumed, attention can then be paid to psychological reactions. Ordinarily a particular investigation or analysis concentrates either upon the audience-getting or the audience-reacting part of the communication process, and deliberately neglects the other part by stating that other things must be equal.

Both parts of the process must obviously be taken into account if all aspects of a communication are to be analyzed or if communication between people is actually going to take place. A more inclusive frame of reference, therefore, is required, which is here delineated by means of a dozen variables. The task of analysis and understanding begins before a communication reaches its audience. First, there is the communicator and his goals.

I. The Communicator

The origin of virtually every communication is a human being, and usually more than one person is involved in the transmission. The teacher in the classroom is the last in a series of communicators. Other people have given him information: the writer of the textbook he uses, the principal determining the curriculum, the school board sanctioning the school and perhaps deliberately affecting the content and manner of teaching, etc.

Obviously the communicator or communicators must be identified and their status within the society determined. Are they, for example, insiders or outsiders? Since people interact, communicators are part of a network: sometimes they may be said to initiate a communicator (which is a pragmatic statement, since in a sociological sense no one ever originates anything completely), at other times they may mechanically transmit information (a teletype operator), and at others transmit and alter what they receive (a gossip).

The communicator can be analyzed in his own right. His attitudes toward his potential audience, the prestige he accords them as people, may affect the communication he produces; thus, if he thinks them morons, he is likely to pitch his message at a correspondingly low level. He himself has certain capabilities which can be conceptualized in terms of the resources he commands, his experience as a communicator with similar or dissimilar audiences, and the role which the motive to communicate plays within his personality.

II. The Goal

The communication would achieve some kind of goal which can involve virtually every aspect of human activity. People communicate in order to survive: the cultivator tells his son how to plant the crop or how to protect himself from disease or wild animals.

On a less basic level they also communicate to achieve social goals: the cultivator instructs the boy not only because he would obtain enough food for his family but also because he desires him to learn appropriate farming techniques at an early age. Even less biological but just as crucial are emotive communications where the aim seems to be not to achieve a specific goal or to influence people but to express oneself.

The consequence of attaining or not attaining a goal may itself be a form of communication. The well cultivated field of grain yields both a good crop and also information about the ability or character of the cultivator. In fact, the information actually communicated may or may not be in accord with what the communicator himself has intended. Or he may not be completely aware of the goal that he is seeking. On the conscious level the teacher would have his students learn arithmetic but, without appreciating his own intention, he may simultaneously be asserting his superiority in front of them by displaying greater knowledge.

The goal of the communicator is sought or attained by means of media of communication which can be considered basic or extending. One or both are utilized at a given moment or over a period of time.

III. Basic Media

The communicator expresses himself through media which flow directly from his body or personality and which are perceived by the audience in his presence. The teacher talks to his students, he listens to them, he praises and punishes them with words and also by moving his eyebrows and wrinkling his forehead. The last illustration would emphasize that basic media consist of more than speech and language, inasmuch as information can be communicated directly in a large variety of ways. The catalogue is long: nonspeech sounds (such as a belch, cough, cry, sob, yodel, etc.); the appearance of the human body whether genetically determined (skin color, somatotype, aging, etc.) or environmentally acquired (calloused hands, wrinkles, posture, etc.); body movements whether involuntary (ticks, jerks, sweating, blushing, etc.) or voluntary (in addition to gestures: posture, contrived facial expressions, spitting, etc.); dancing and other creative forms. It is not only what the communicator says, in short, which conveys information but also how he expresses himself and what he simultaneously does.

IV. Extending Media

The communicator is able to affect his audience at a distance or when absent. Students study outside the classroom by consulting notes or textbooks; or audio-visual aids, such as closed-circuit television, are invoked. Some of these media reach people instantaneously either without altering the basic form of the original communication (amplifiers, electronic channels) or after considerable encoding (bells, drums, horses, beacons, flags, etc.). Others preserve the communication, again either with little or no modification (motion pictures, recordings) or with considerable change (drawings, posters, statues, footprints). In addition activities that sustain and protect the body, tools of any kind, physical objects such as tombs and flags, attributes of objects (e.g., color, shape, size, and texture), money, and the presence of other people can convey information. Finally, natural phenomena (like dark clouds heralding a storm) become extending media when people attach significance to them.

The medium or media of communication function at some location and are to some extent subject to regulations.

V. Site

The characteristics of the site at which people receive the communication may well affect their reactions. Students hear the teacher in a classroom that has good or bad acoustics and ventilation; they are seated in rows or around a table; their number is large or small—what or how well they learn depends upon what they are taught as well as upon such extraneous factors. The site influences the size of the audience which may be attracted; for example, it may be located amid a dense or sparse population, it is accessible to few or many people or communicators. Attendence is regulated: some people are encouraged to join the audience, others are prohibited from doing so. At the site itself people's reactions to a communication may be influenced by how they feel toward one another; and that feeling in turn may be influenced by whether, from a sociological viewpoint, they are homogeneous or heterogeneous. People's interaction at the site may be intimate and intricate or distant and uncomplicated. Relevant, too, may be mechanical features of the site (ranging from physical comfort to aesthetic qualities) and the flexible or inflexible rules governing behavior, as a glib reference to the different atmosphere of a dance hall or a funeral parlor melodramatically suggests.

VI. Restrictions

For many reasons conditions exist which inhibit or facilitate the transmission of a communication. The teacher rejects what he considers to be a promising pedagogical technique because his students are too immature or the school too conservative. The perfect textbook remains unsold when the distributing facilities of the publisher break down.

Analysis or control of communication demands careful consideration of natural forces. Significant are meteorological factors (climate, including its effect upon disease, as well as weather and electrical disturbances), terrain, and physical resources. In addition, each medium has its own limitations—scars on people's faces may signify tribal identification, but this technique cannot be utilized to record the tribe's history. Human beings have their own limitations: intelligence, attention span, aging, etc. The training of personnel and the purchase of transmitting and receiving equipment are costs which can impose severe limitations. Social factors also may play a significant role: some form of censorship exists in any society, people may or may not be adequately literate, and communication between the various strata or groups of the community or the nation may be relatively easy or difficult.

At this point the psychology of communicating, the main theme of the propaganda sections of this volume, is finally relevant: the communication—delivered by a communicator to achieve a goal through a medium at a particular site—can be considered in its own right.

VII. The Communication

The actual contents of the communication as determined by some informal or formal method of analysis elicit responses in the audience. In the classroom, the same sentences, whether they are spoken by the teachers or appear in a textbook, do or would convey identical information which perhaps can be specified independently of the potential or actual audience. What is in the textbook, the school board asks, before it is adopted for use?

Probably the most standardized modes of analysis concern language rather than the other basic media of communication. There is likely to be, for example, greater agreement concerning the contents of a sentence than the message of a dance or a sonata. Each language possesses more or less distinctive attributes (vocabulary and structure) which, in ways not adequately understood, may affect people's perception of, and reaction to the outside world. Details of linguistic style may also be influential: figures of speech, allusions, temporal factors (e.g., position of a theme within a communication, repetition, etc.), and rhetoric.

VIII. Mood

Prior conditions produce temporary feelings and responses in the potential audience. Before or after an important holiday, for example, students are likely to be excited and hence not in an especially propitious learning mood. The time a teacher feels he must devote to a topic in order to transmit what he considers essential can affect the mood of the students: they become bored, excited, or indifferent.

Some of the factors affecting mood can be made explicit. First of all, consideration must be given to the time of communicating: people's reactions fluctuate with the time of the day, the day of the week, the season, and the period of life at which they receive the communication. Unusual conditions affecting mood include weather, food and drink (e.g., no vs. many cocktails), diseases, and crises within a group (e.g., death, war). The position of the communication, with relation to other communications or other themes, can likewise be critical. People react to the actual length of a communication, a reaction that depends in part upon their attitude toward time. The degree to which members of an audience actively participate in appraising a communication as they receive it—for example, by refuting it or committing themselves to the action it implies—affects not only their mood vis-à-vis the rest of the message but also, often, the ensuing behavior.

At last, it may now be presumed, people are exposed to a communication whose communicator (I) seeks to achieve a goal or set of goals (II) through a medium or media (III, IV) at a particular site (V), in spite of certain restrictions or in their absence (VI), by means of a message (VII) that reaches them in a specified mood (VIII). What happens then? As already indicated in this volume, certain psychological processes may be differentiated.

IX. Perception

The contents of the communication are perceived. The basic problem here is to account for perception by means of attributes of the communication, the ongoing drives of the recipients, or both. Ordinarily, many forces or groups compete for people's attention. Then, after attention has been gained, there are likely to be slips 'twixt the goal or the content of the communication and the comprehension of the audience.

The communicator may employ certain devices to ensure perception: he literally compels an audience to pay attention or else suffer a meaningful punishment; he employs stimuli so penetrating—because they are intense, because they are redundant, because they are part of traditional living, because they are novel—that people cannot avoid some contact with his communication. Members of the audience can provide their own impetus: they perceive the communication incidentally as they satisfy other drives or deliberately as they reduce their own frustrations; or in some instances they develop an interest in communicating as such. Comprehension of the communication is almost always a problem, but misunderstandings can be reduced by repeating or simplifying the communication; by pointing out, literally or figuratively, its salient features; or by seeking to diminish the ego- and ethnocentrism of the audience.

X. Reactions

After perceiving a communication and after comprehending its contents more or less accurately, people respond to their new percepts. Predisposition from the past are aroused, and the audience may then grow disturbed or pleased. What is the origin of these predispositions, how can the ensuing internal responses and processes best be described and analyzed?

The evoked predispositions pertain to all preliminary aspects of the communication from the communicator to the site. As a result, people find themselves in a more or less distinctive atmosphere which, among others, causes them to judge themselves and their behavior by reference to the values of one group rather than another. In addition, the form and content of the communication also elicit responses. The predispositions themselves can be charted as reflections of the culture or subculture of the audience and of individual personalities; and they can be considered as being expressed privately or publicly. The actual arousal of the preexisting tendencies represents an interplay involving dimensions of harmony-disharmony and comfort-discomfort.

XI. Changes

The effects of the communication range from zero to a profound change in overt behavior. In-between the gradations of change that are covert and that may have momentary or subsequent effects upon action.

The audience's information and values may change nonovertly without any noticeable effect upon behavior, like the evoked predisposition, the content thereof may pertain to any aspect of the communication. Overt action may never occur or the external effect of the communication may simply be unascertainable. If there is an effect, it may be immediate or delayed, and it may represent the achievement or the nonachievement of the communicator's original goal. The drives which may have led to the perception of the communication and which certainly were evoked by it may then be satisfactorily or unsatisfactorily reduced by the nonovert or overt changes.

One variable remains. So far, the communication, as it were, has been cast upon an audience by a communicator and that audience responds or fails to respond in some specified way. To what extent are those reactions communicated to the original communicator?

XII. Feedback

In general, the reaction of the audience to the communication is or is not conveyed to the communicator and, if conveyed, is or is not transmitted adequately. If there is feedback, it may occur while the communication is in progress (the speaker notes that his audience is restive), subsequently (the editor receives letters from his readers) or even antecedently (the results of one advertising campaign are used in planning the next one). In any case, feedback varies in frequency and may be sporadic or continuing. The information that is fed back may be general (people seem content) or it may be related to specific aspects of the communication, such as how many or what kinds of people perceive the message, how they react, whether they change, etc. The collector of the information may be the communicator himself or an intermediary. The information can be obtained from intuition, direct observation, interviewing (and the interview in turn may involve the entire audience, a sample, or critical members), or indices.

After feedback, the circle usually begins all over again. A communicator acts upon the information, in order to achieve certain goals through particular media, and so on. Human communication, in brief, cannot be analyzed or controlled speedily: the many interacting factors which must be taken into account keep whirling.

— · — · — · — · — · — · — · — · — · — · — · —

OTTO KLINEBERG

Prejudice*

The English term "prejudice" and its equivalents in many other European languages (French *préjugé;* German *Vorurteil*; Portugese *preconceito*) refer primarily to a prejudgment or a preconcept reached *before* the relevant information has been collected or examined and therefore based on inadequate or even imaginary evidence. In contemporary social science this notion has been retained but is usually regarded as constituting only one aspect of the complex phenomenon of prejudice, namely the conceptual, or cognitive, aspect—the ideas or opinions we have about those individuals or groups who are the objects of such prejudgment. (The term "stereotype" is usually applied to this aspect.) Prejudice also involves an attitude *for* or *against*, the ascription of a positive or negative value, an affective, or *feeling*, component. Usually there is in addition a readiness to express in action the judgments and feelings which we experience, to behave in a manner which reflects our acceptance or rejection of others: this is the conative, or behavioral, aspect of prejudice. (The resulting actions are also described as representing

*"Prejudice: I The Concept" by Otto Klineberg. Reprinted with permission of the publisher from *The International Encyclopedia of the Social Sciences*, David L. Sills, Editor. Volume 12, pp. 439–448. Copyright ©1968 by Crowell Collier and Macmillan, Inc.

varying degrees of *discrimination*.) Prejudice may therefore be defined as an unsubstanti-ated prejudgment of an individual or group, favorable or unfavorable in character, tending to action in a consonant direction.

Social science research has joined with popular usage in introducing two limitations to this concept. In the first place, favorable prejudices, although they undoubtedly exist, have attracted relatively little attention, perhaps on the principle that they do good rather than harm. It might, however, legitimately be argued that even favorable prejudices should be discouraged, since they too represent unwarranted generalizations, often of an irrational nature. Second, although prejudice may extend far and wide to apply to objects as disparate as trade-union leaders, women, or exotic foods, in practice it has been considered as dealing primarily—if not exclusively—with populations or ethnic groups distinguished by the possession of specific inherited physical characteristics ("race"), or by differences in language, religion, culture, national origin, or any combination of these. This article, therefore, will be primarily concerned with ethnic prejudice. The Italian anthropologist Tentori takes approximately this position when he defines prejudice as the "negative perception of human groups culturally different from ourselves" (1962, p. 14); but the limitation to perception on the one hand and to cultural differences on the other makes the concept considerably narrower than that which is here proposed.

The term "ethnic group" is used in preference to the more popular "race" as the object of prejudice, first because of the difficulty of adequately defining the latter term so that it may safely be applied to human populations, and second because of the even more important fact that the populations against whom prejudice may be directed do not usually satisfy the criteria of "race" proposed by physical anthropologists and geneticists. The phenomenon here being considered can be interpreted in terms of "race" in the case of the apartheid policy of the South African government, although even here the exten-sion of the same attitudes and the same degree of discrimination to Africans, to the mixed "Coloureds," and to Indians (usually classed by anthropologists with Caucasians) indicates the lack of consistency in this respect. American attitudes toward the Negro diverge from "race" relations in the true sense to the extent that persons who are genetically almost completely "white" may not be so considered if they have any degree of Negro admixture. Elsewhere other criteria of differentiation may play the dominant role. In Canada, Belgium, and India hostilities appear to follow mainly linguistic lines; in Malaysia the demarcation is due primarily to national origin, and comparable situations are found in many other regions where immigration has been extensive. In Lebanon, Nigeria, and the Sudan, religious differences are also important, as they are in part at least in the case of anti-Semitism; in Brazil and Mexico cultural (and class) factors predomi-nate, so that the word *indio* is restricted to those who have remained culturally Indian, and there appears to be complete acceptance of those Indians who have become "accul-turated." To speak of "race relations" in such contexts is clearly incorrect, and use of the expression "sociological races" to cover these cases—because the groups concerned are treated as if they were "races"—simply perpetuates an unfortunate and misleading termi-nology.

In his valuable treatment of the nature of prejudice, G. W. Allport states that "*Prejudgments become prejudices only if they are not reversible when exposed to new knowledge*" (1954, p. 9). This criterion of prejudice appears to go too far. Granted that prejudice is difficult to remove, it surely cannot be assumed that if and when it has been removed by new knowledge it could not really have been prejudice in the first place. The question of the use of information to reduce prejudice will be discussed below as part of the wider problem of determining what methods and techniques are most effective in this connection.

It would be difficult to overestimate the importance of prejudice as a problem for the social sciences. The hostility which prejudice engenders and the discrimination to which it may lead on the part of the dominant population toward other ethnic groups or minorities have caused so much human damage (the Nazi period represents perhaps the most drastic example) that it is hardly surprising that so many specialists in these disciplines have directed their energies toward understanding and control of this form of social pathology. Particularly but by no means exclusively in the United States, the problem has not only aroused general concern but has also been seen as a research challenge by psychologists, psychiatrists, sociologists, anthropologists, political scientists, lawyers, educators, and others whose professional activities are concerned with human behavior. This has been not only out of humanitarian motives but also out of conviction that the very life of a community may be at stake. The concern has been deepened by the realization that what happens inside a country may also have significant international repercussions. The apartheid policy has implications far outside the confines of South Africa; the American treatment of Negroes affects the image and the leadership of the United States throughout the world.

Nor is prejudice a monopoly of the whites. The emergence of new nations has to a certain degree brought with it what has sometimes been called *racism in reverse*, an antiwhite attitude on the part of darker-skinned peoples. The philosophy of *négritude*, developed by French-speaking Africans and West Indians, has stressed the values inherent in African culture, but it has by no means always been free of aggressive overtones (Thomas 1963). Prejudice and ethnic hostilities constitute a major danger to peace both within a nation and among nations.

THE CAUSES OF PREJUDICE

The fact that prejudice is so widespread has led to a popular belief that it is inevitable and universal. Even among social scientists the view has occasionally been expressed that human nature involves a "dislike of the unlike," although what is "unlike" has never been adequately defined: or it has been suggested that "in-group" feelings are invariably accompanied by dislike of the "out-group," but this, too, has never been demonstrated. A German social psychologist, Hofstätter, has suggested (1954) that one must accept the fact that prejudice against members of other groups represents a "normal" phenomenon of human social life and that no one is free from this attitude. This appears to be an extreme and unjustified conclusion. Individuals and groups vary so tremendously in the extent to which they show prejudice that any attempt to explain it in terms of a universal human nature fails to carry conviction. The full acceptance of Orientals by most whites in Hawaii and their relative rejection in California or British Columbia is difficult to reconcile with such a theory. The further fact that the most intimate degrees of association, including intermarriage or miscegenation have occurred to such an extent that most anthropologists deny the existence of "pure races" argues that prejudice cannot be universal. Finally, its absence in young children, even though they may acquire it relatively early in life from their social environment, argues that learning rather than nature plays the dominant role in its development (Harding et al. 1954).

Derivations from Psychoanalysis

One view of the universality of prejudice seems to derive from an erroneous interpretation of psychoanalytic theory. This theory, particularly in its orthodox form, regards hostility or aggression (Freud's Thanatos) as instinctive and universal; prejudice would then be simply one manifestation of this instinct. Not all psychoanalysts would add that although aggression must manifest itself *in some form*, there is *no one form* (for example, prejudice) which must be regarded as inevitable. There is still considerable argument as to whether hostile aggression is universal, but in any case it can be expressed in so many ways that inference to the universality of prejudice remains exceedingly doubtful.

Frustration-aggression theory. A variant of this view is found in the well-known frustration-aggression theory (Dollard et al. 1939), which in its original formulation argued that frustration always leads to aggression and that aggression is always due to frustration. An impressive array of clinical and experimental evidence was marshaled in favor of this position, and there can be no doubt that it has contributed to an understanding of the problem. The fact remains, however, that even if aggression is reactive rather than primary, the same objection holds—namely, that no one manifestation of aggression is necessarily implied and that the specific phenomenon of prejudice requires some further explanation. There is, therefore, circularity in the argument which holds that hostility must be expressed and that when a group like the Negroes is indicated by society as a legitimate object for such hostility, it can then be safely directed by the whites in this accepted fashion. The circularity occurs by taking for granted the very phenomenon that the theory sets out to explain: if society indicated that hostility may with impunity be directed against the Negro, that hostility must have been there to start with. It is not surprising that in later formulations of the theory the role of *learning* is given a prominent place (Miller & Dollard 1941) in determining the specific nature of the behavior that follows frustration.

Prejudice As a Learned Behavior

Prejudice may certainly be learned, it is through (mainly unconscious) learning that a child acquires and incorporates the prejudices prevalent in his society. Research has shown that in the early years there is a close relation between the ethnic attitudes of parents and children; somewhat later the correspondence is rather between teachers and their pupils. The representation of minority groups in the mass media may also play a part in reinforcing, if not in creating, the current attitudes. Most significant, in all probability, is the role of social factors and institutions which emphasize lines of demarcation between ethnic groups—segregation, whether *de jure* as in South Africa or *de facto* as in many North American cities, in connection with housing and education; "exclusive" clubs or resorts; churches limited to one ethnic group; restrictions on enrollment in certain colleges or universities, limitations on advancement to executive positions in industry; and discrimination in employment generally. These and similar phenomena serve as constant reminders that *they* are not like *us*. It is in this sense that discrimination causes prejudice as well as the other way around. As Myrdal pointed out in connection with the American Negro, the relation is a circular one: "White prejudice and discrimination keep the Negro low in standards of living, health, education, manners and morals. This, in turn, gives support to White prejudice. White prejudice and Negro standards thus mutually 'cause' each other . . . " (1944, p. 75).

Unimportance of contact. One form of learning turns out to be less important in causing prejudice or hostile attitudes than is usually believed, namely, that resulting from actual contact with other ethnic groups. It may of course happen that an extremely dramatic or traumatic experience—such as being attacked on a lonely street or being saved from drowning by a member of a particular ethnic group—may result in a generalization regarding the characteristics of the group concerned; it may also happen that repeated experiences of a similar nature may create, and even appear to justify, such a generalized attitude. Research has shown, however, that such experiences are not necessary for prejudices to develop. In one study, students showed a high degree of "social distance" from Turks, even though most of them had never seen a Turk. Other students rejected imaginary groups, such as the Wallonians, Danireans, and Pirenians, even though no one could have had any unpleasant experiences with any representatives of these nonexistent populations (Hartley 1946). Contact and experience *may* cause prejudice to develop, but they probably play no important role in many cases.

Role of language. It has been suggested that prejudices may also be learned through the linguistic habits of a community. The common association in many parts of the world between "white" and purity or honor ("that is white of you") and between "black" and dirt or evil ("he has a black heart") may create attitudes that are difficult to overcome. Less clear in their impact are expressions such as "to jew him down"; "nigger in the woodpile"; the Chinese reference to Europeans as "foreign devils"; the French *ivre comme un polonais*; or the Italian *fare il portoghese*, said when one enters a streetcar or a theater without paying.

Roots of the Tradition

All of these aspects of learning are important, but they are limited in their implications to the acquisition of attitudes already current in the community. They help us to understand the development of prejudice in children as they become "socialized" and absorb the prevailing cultural traditions. They leave open the question (as in connection with the frustration-aggression hypothesis discussed above) as to how the tradition of prejudice arose in the first place.

Fear of the stranger. Ethnological accounts of preliterate peoples have indicated with some frequency a fear of the stranger and the development of hostility as a consequence. This is by no means universal, however; Hooton even considered it relatively rare. He wrote: "Primitive people are probably not race conscious to the deplorable or laudable extent which is characteristic of civilized populations. I mean that they are rather naively free from race prejudice until they have learned it from bitter experience. The American Indian was ready to take the European literally to his arms until he found out that a civilized embrace was inevitably throttling" (1937, p. 143).

Historical factors. In the form in which prejudice is found in contemporary cultures, many different contributing influences may be recognized, all of which have a relatively long history. From the viewpoint of the whites, the facts of slavery and colonization must at least have reinforced—if they did not create—the notion of a racial hierarchy, with the darker peoples occupying an inferior position. Sometimes this went so far, as in the case of certain Spanish writers during the conquest of America, as to deny to American Indians the same humanity as that of their conquerors; more mildly, but with somewhat the same consequences, the British spoke of the "white man's burden" and the French of their *mission civilisatrice*, often expressed with the utmost sincerity but clearly implying the superiority of white culture and white people.

Historical factors are of great importance in this connection, and the contribution of the historian is needed at various points in this analysis. In some parts of the world relations between ethnic groups have taken a much more favorable turn, and prejudice has played only a minor role. In Hawaii, for example, Adams (1937) indicates that when white men served as advisers to the king, they were occasionally honored by receiving permission to marry ladies of the court. This set a pattern of ethnic friendliness which was later extended to other groups as well. It became impossible to set up any strict "racial" line because so many members of prominent families had intermarried. In the case of Brazil, where there is some degree of prejudice that tends to follow class lines but only a fraction of that found elsewhere, Freyre (1933) suggests a number of reasons for the relatively more friendly attitude. In the first place, the Portuguese who settled in Brazil had had centuries of contact with darker-skinned conquerors, namely the Moors, which predisposed them to a friendly and even respectful attitude. They developed an attraction for the "enchanting Mooress" which was extended to other women of darker complexion, thus encouraging intermarriage with Indian and later with Negro women. This was facilitated by the fact that Portuguese men migrated to Brazil for the most part without their families, in contrast to the settlers in most of North America. In addition, the fact that Brazil liberated its slaves peaceably and not as a consequence of civil war undoubtedly contributed to an earlier and smoother transition to a new relationship. Clearly, the history of ethnic contacts within a particular country helps to account for the pattern of aacceptance or rejection prevalent today.

Religious factors. In the case of one variety of prejudice which in recent times has been exhibited in the most virulent and extreme form, namely anti-Semitism, it seems clear that in its origins religious considerations have played a dominant role. (Negro slavery, too, has been justified by an appeal to the Bible.) The story of the New Testament as told to succeeding generations of children has left an imprint of ancient Jewish wickedness which has frequently been extended to the Jewish group as a whole (Glock & Stark 1966). This is true to some extent even in religious teaching today, although many attempts are being made to present a less biased and more objective picture (Olson 1963).

Religious identification may be relatively less significant to most people now than it was in the Middle Ages, but the climate of opinion created by past teaching is removed with difficulty even when circumstances have changed. Here, as elsewhere, the strength of "social lag"—the continuance of institutions and traditions even when they are no longer appropriate—is not to be discounted.

Nationalism. Another significant factor associated with prejudice is the growth of nationalism and feelings of national identity. Huxley and Haddon wrote: "A 'nation' has been cynically but not inaptly defined as a 'society united by a common error as to its origin and a common aversion to its neighbors' " (1936, p. 5). This aversion may be directed to different objects, and as has already been indicated social identity may be attached to a variety of characteristics, including language, religion, or any other symbol of demarcation. National identification is glorified as a means to social solidarity, to participation in a common enterprise, and to "belonging." Unfortunately, however, a "healthy" nationalism easily moves into an exaggerated chauvinism which is not only *for* "us" but *against* "them." Considerable research has indicated that this kind of hyper-nationalism is usually accompanied by ethnocentric prejudice (Adorno et al. 1950). Why it has developed in certain regions and at certain times, and why it has taken one form rather than another, are questions difficult to answer.

Economic factors. The analysis of the causes of prejudice has so far stressed the historical process related to ideas of "race," religion, and nationalism and to the manner in which the resulting patterns of prejudice and hostility are "taught" to individuals. Research clearly indicates, however, that learning occurs most readily and most efficiently when it is motivated and when it is accompanied by certain satisfactions which reinforce the learning process. In the case of prejudice, perhaps the most important reinforcement comes from the gains that appear to result, the practical ends to which prejudice and discrimination may lead. Among these ends, it is highly probably that economic gain plays a dominant role; for some theorists (Marxists or economic determinists) it constitutes the single significant factor. Prejudice and discrimination enable the dominant group to maintain others in a state of subservience, to exploit them, to treat them as slaves or serfs, to reduce their power to compete on equal terms for jobs, and to keep them "in their place." Gains and advantages other then economic may also enter, however. There may be a gain in status or prestige, permitting the humblest member of the dominant group to feel superior to the most successful among those who belong to the minority or to rejoice, through identification with his nation, in the subjugation of others through colonization, even when the consequence is economic loss rather than profit. There may be a gain from the point of view of self-image when, in times of misfortune or adversity, the blame can be placed on outsiders who serve as scapegoats; it is *they*, not *we*, who are responsible. Finally, less important today then in the past, there may be a sexual gain, when men of the dominant group have access to women of the minority, often with severely enforced taboos against the reverse relationship.

Rationalization. One of the striking aspects of the use of prejudice and discrimination as means toward these practical goals is that the underlying motive is so rarely recognized. Psychoanalysis has made us all familiar with the mechanism of rationalization, which in this context is characterized by the tendency to persuade ourselves that our actions stem from the loftiest ethical and even religious considerations rather than from anything as base as the desire for gain. This was briefly mentioned above in connection with the "white man's burden" and similar formulations. *They*, whom we keep in an inferior position, are happier than they would be otherwise, *they*, whom we persecute because of their beliefs, can be saved only if they accept the true (that is to say, *our*) religion; *they*, whom we destroy, are planning to destroy *us*, and we are simply exercising the right to protect ourselves. It is arguments like these, presented in all sincerity, which so often in the past, and not so rarely in the present, have given to men the conviction that what they are doing is somehow noble and beautiful and that, in Hooton's telling phrase, they "can rape in righteousness and murder in magnanimity" (1937, p. 151).

Personality Structure

The fact remains that under the same cultural conditions, surrounded by the same institutions and tempted by the same desire for gain, some people show prejudice and others do not. This has suggested that the key to the development of prejudice may be found in personality, and an extensive amount of research has been directed toward this aspect of the problem. The most important single study is undoubtedly *The Authoritarian Personality* (Adorno et al. 1950). One major finding was a verification of the results of earlier research indicating that prejudices tend to go together: those individuals who disliked Jews were also likely to dislike Negroes, Mexicans, and "foreigners" in general. The use of a series of scales or questionnaires demonstrated a positive correlation between ethnocentrism and (a) politico-economic conservatism, (b) chauvinism (labeled "pseudo-patriotism"), and (c) "fascism" as measured by the *F*-scale. The *F*-scale has been widely used in subsequent research, and some serious methodological questions have been raised about its application—for example, the failure to take into account the tendency of certain subjects to answer the question in an "acquiescent" direction, the fact that higher education and socioeconomic status are negatively correlated with the scale, and so on. On the whole however, the *F*-scale is considered to have made a valuable contribution toward the understanding of the prejudiced personality. It has also been applied with interesting results in countries other than the United States (Christie & Cook 1958).

The ethnocentric personality. More intensive analysis of prejudiced individuals, conducted as part of the same study, has indicated the following pattern of characteristics: the ethnocentric person is a conformist, he sees the world as menacing and unfriendly; he exalts his own group, he is fundamentally anxious and insecure; he blames others for his own faults and misfortunes; he appears to worship his parents but has strong repressed hostility toward them; he divides the world into the weak and the strong, has a well-developed concern for status, and is willing to obey those above him in the status hierarchy but demands obedience from those below. (Some aspects of this description suggest that the prejudiced person is pathological. This interpretation is justified in some cases but certainly not in all; it is only when authoritarianism is extreme that the inference of psychological maladjustment becomes reasonable.)

A major criticism of this important study is its relative neglect of social and cultural factors. Research has shown that groups may be high in ethnocentrism if their culture includes lines of demarcation strictly enforced by custom or by law, as in South Africa or the southern United States, without being particularly "authoritarian" (Pettigrew 1958). The fact remains that personality does exert an important influence, even though it must be seen as acting in conjunction with the historical and sociological factors mentioned above. Prejudice is multidimensional (Klineberg 1964; Williams 1964). Different individuals may develop prejudice for different reasons and frequently for more than one reason. Nor should these various possible causes be considered as independent: they interact, are interrelated, and influence one another. The search for a single, all-embracing origin for prejudice is chimerical.

VARIETIES OF PREJUDICE

It follows that prejudice is not a unitary phenomenon and that it will take varying forms in different individuals. Socially and psychologically attitudes differ depending on whether they are the result of deep-seated personality characteristics, sometimes of a pathological nature, or of a traumatic experience, or whether they simply represent conformity to an established social norm. No adequate typology of forms of prejudice is yet available, and since there will always be intervening and transitional varieties, perhaps no such typology will ever be fully acceptable.

Earlier it was indicated that three aspects of prejudice must be distinguished in the definition: the cognitive or ideational, the affective, and the conative or behavioral. The frequent lack of consistency among these three aspects or components has suggested one typology of attitudes (including prejudice). Katz and Stotland (1959), for example, distinguish between (1) affective associations, (2) intellectualized attitudes, and (3) action-oriented attitudes. In the case of the first two, no accurate prediction regarding behavior is possible; in the third, both the cognitive and affective elements may be absent. In addition there are (4) balanced attitudes, which show consistency among the three components. This is helpful as far as it goes, but it leaves out a number of the dimensions identified above as contributing to the development of prejudice and consequently to the forms which it takes in different individuals.

THE EFFECTS OF PREJUDICE

In his discussion of the place of the American Negro—or, as he prefers to say, the Negro American—in contemporary society, one social psychologist (Pettigrew 1964) speaks of the role and *its burdens*. There is much evidence that these burdens are varied and heavy. They are revealed in a pattern of objective life conditions that include considerable poverty and overcrowding, a shorter life expectancy, poorer education, inferior facilities for recreation, more family disorganization, and other related characteristics described in the *Dark Ghetto* (Clark 1965). On the subjective side, it is difficult to overestimate the effects on personality of belonging to a group which is generally regarded as inferior and so treated. A series of investigations has revealed the frequency with which Negro children show their preference for white over black (as, for example, in the dolls they choose to play with) and the emotional shock which may accompany an experience that requires them to become openly aware of their own skin color. Although this shock may become somewhat attenuated with the years, the damage done to the self-image and self-esteem of such children must be viewed as exceedingly serious (Clark 1955; Pettigrew 1964). It is precisely this damage that was referred to in the unanimous Supreme Court decision of May 17, 1954 as one justification for finding that enforced school segregation violated the rights of Negro children and was therefore contrary to the principles of the American constitution. (A study in São Paulo, Brazil, indicated a moderate preference by Negro children for white dolls, but with none of the emotional reactions so frequent among children in the United States; see Ginsberg 1955.)

The expression "self-hatred" has occasionally been applied to the reaction of Negroes, Jews, and other minorities who attempt in one form or another to reject their ethnic identity. In its most extreme form, accompanied by a dislike of every reminder of such identity and by hostility which echoes that shown by the dominant group, the term "self-hatred" may possibly be applicable, except that it is the group rather than the self that is hated. There is a whole range of reactions, however, which may result from being identified with a group that is stigmatized as not only different but inferior; it is inappropriate to speak of "hatred" in the case of these who may more legitimately be described as reaching for identification with the larger community. The phenomenon is too complex to be adequately described as "self-hatred," but the underlying psychological processes relating to rejection undoubtedly constitute great hazards to normal personality development. The relative frequency of Negro aggressive crime and the occasional outbursts of group violence are not too difficult to understand against this background of rejection.

The effects of prejudice on the dominant group are also clear, although more indirect. If one criterion of mental health is an adequate perception of reality (Jahoda 1958), free from distortions due to needs and wishes and including sensitivity in the understanding of other people, then prejudice obviously interferes with mental health. In any case, the economic and social waste consequent upon prejudice has a harmful effect on the whole community, majority and minority alike. The apparent gains resulting from prejudice and discussed above among its causes are more than offset by its real costs (Rose 1951).

THE REDUCTION OF PREJUDICE

The problem of the reduction of prejudice is part of the whole issue of attitude change and therefore involves the techniques of persuasion and propaganda, the effects of the mass media and of education, and other related phenomena. The present discussion will be limited to certain aspects which touch directly on prejudice, even though it must be recognized that in many cases these need to be seen against the background of attitude change in general.

Effects of Information

A great deal of thought and a substantial amount of research have been directed toward the question of whether informatin about minority groups contributes toward the reduction of prejudice. Since, as was indicated earlier, prejudice contains a cognitive component, it is reasonable to expect that improving the accuracy of that component should have a salutary effect. On the other hand, it is argued that purely informational campaigns will necessarily fail, since the target audience will select, accept, ignore, or even distort the meaning of the available content in order to keep it consonant with preconceptions. This is more likely to occur when the content is presented through the mass media and is somewhat less likely in the case of a "captive audience," although even in the latter case there will by no means be a passive acceptance of what is offered. Research in this area is equivocal in its findings but appears to justify the conclusion that information is indeed useful to a limited degree (Allport 1954; Klineberg 1950). It has been suggested that although cultural differences among ethnic groups should not be neglected in the information presented, particular stress should be laid on cultural similarities and on the common aspects of human experience.

Scientific evidence. It has also been urged that special attention be given to the position, held by the overwhelming majority of biological and social scientists, that there is no acceptable proof of the inherent genetic inferiority of any ethnic group. Myrdal (1944) has called for an "educational offensive" to reduce the gap between the scientific and the popular position in this regard. There has in fact been a marked change in this direction in recent years. A trend study of public opinion in the United States analyzed answers to the question "In general, do you think that Negroes are as intelligent as white people—that is, can they learn things just as well if they are given the same education and training?" In 1942, 50 per cent of Northern whites answered "yes"; in 1963, the figure had risen to 80 per cent. In the South, 21 per cent said yes in 1942 and 60 per cent in 1963. This degree of change may well be described as revolutionary (Hyman & Sheatsley 1964).

Effects of Religious Training

A special problem is posed by the relation of religious education to prejudice. The paradoxical situation arises that although in many areas the leaders in the attack on prejudice have a religious motivation or are identified with religion as an institution, in general there appears to be slightly more prejudice among those who are "religious" than among those who are not (Allport 1954, Adorno et al. 1950). This probably indicates that religion means different things to different people—in certain cases a true involvement, in others an outward, superficial expression. The problem for religious educators is to instill loyalty to one's faith while also emphasizing the brotherhood of man. It is not surprising that in the light of this difficult task the results of such education have so far been equivocal as far as prejudice is concerned.

Effects of Contact and Cooperation

Contact between members of different ethnic communities has also had a positive effect under certain conditions. The earlier, rather naïve expectation that if only people came to know members of other ethnic groups friendlier relations would automatically result has given way to a more sophisticated understanding of the factors involved. It seems clear, first, that best results are obtained when contact occurs between persons of equal status, no amount of contact between a white boss and Negro workers will alter the prevailing stereotype or prepare the way for better understanding. When status is equal, on the other hand, a salutary effect may usually be expected. This was demonstrated in a series of investigations of attitude change consequent upon integrated housing in a number of Northern communities. A second important condition is that the two groups work together toward the realization of a common goal and that they depend upon each other for its realization. This was the case in the U.S. Army during the Korean War. When the two ethnic groups were mixed in the same military outfits, the attitudes of white soldiers and noncommissioned officers toward Negroes became much more favorable.

It is important to note that in these cases the contact was not deliberately chosen or even necessarily welcomed; it was imposed in the one case by housing authorities and in the other by the military command. The participants were presented with a *fait accompli*. It appears that this procedure works successfully in other situations as well, including school desegration, the hiring of Negro sales personnel in department stores, and so forth (Saenger 1953). It may at first sight seem paradoxical that in a democratic society such techniques should work in spite of the expression of contrary opinion. One could hazard a guess that the *fait accompli* is effective in those cases in which the attitudes are held with some degree of ambivalence, so that those involved are *almost* as willing to be pushed in the liberal as in the reactionary direction. The opposition to acceptance of Negroes in these situations is not so strong as to inhibit adaptation to a new *status quo* when that is introduced by respected authorities.

The value of creating opportunities for two hostile groups to work together in a cooperative enterprise has also been demonstrated in a series of important experiments (Oklahoma, University of . . . 1961). An investigation in a boys' camp showed that the introduction of common or "superordinate" goals which could be attained only through joint activity, in which each group depended on the other for success, had a significant effect in reducing hostility. It seems highly probable that similar techniques would work on a wider scale and not only within the microcism of the experimental situation. What is not entirely clear is what would happen if the superordinate goal could not be reached. Would each group blame the other, with a consequent increase in tension? Or would the sympathy produced as a result of the common enterprise improve relations even in the case of failure? Further research is required in order to answer these questions.

Sociometry and Psychotherapy

In the case of conflicts between small groups or individuals, certain techniques used in group dynamics and sociometry have frequently been found to be effective. Among these, taking the role of the other—putting oneself in the "enemy's" place and attempting to see the problem from his viewpoint—represents a mechanism which may contribute to better understanding. A number of investigations, some of them specifically related to prejudice, indicate the value of this approach (Krech et al. [1948] 1962. pp. 259-261).

Much has also been written about prejudice as a form of pathology and therefore not susceptible to cure except by the methods of psychotherapy and psychoanalysis. Such methods are probably the only ones that could reach the extreme bigots but they can hardly be regarded as very practical, since bigots are unlikely to consider themselves ill and in need of treatment by a psychiatrist. It seems highly probable, however, that a system of child care which produces secure and mentally healthy individuals would reduce the frequency of bigots in the population.

Institutional Change

Earlier it was indicated that prejudice and discrimination are causally related in circular fashion, each contributing to the origin and growth of the other. It would follow that prejudice can be reduced through an attack on discrimination and that a change in institutions would inevitably mean, in time, a change in attitudes. In the United States, at least, from this point of view the legal approach has constituted the major source of improvement in the position of the Negro, affecting his access to more adequate education, housing, transportation, employment, recreation, and political rights. The frequently heard objection "you can't legislate against prejudice" becomes irrelevant, since one *can* legislate against discrimination, one of the causes of prejudice; in the case of decisions by the courts, the same effect can be produced not by new legislation but by so interpreting existing laws as to safeguard human rights. Not only in the United States but in many other countries as well, the rights of minorities have been expressly protected in national constitutions, and the full weight of the United Nations and of its specialized agencies, such as UNESCO, has been thrown into the campaign for the reduction of prejudice and discrimination, through both education and the law.

Institutions change as the result of many factors not necessarily legal in character. The recent history of the United States has been marked by a rapid transformation through the pressure of "sit-ins," nonviolent resistance, protest meetings, a march on Washington, the impact of the international scene, and even by outbreaks of violence which, although they must be deplored, may still function as reminders of "the unfinished business of democracy." Not least in its influence has been the development of a new climate of opinion and a reaffirmation of the democratic belief in the rights of all human beings.

These occurrences do not mean that the problem of prejudice has been solved. The social lag referred to above will mean a continuation of the prejudiced attitudes of many long after the law and the collective conscience have declared them obsolete. There is, however, some ground for optimism as far as the United States is concerned. To the question "Do you think white students and Negro students should go to the same schools or to separate schools?", a representative sample of American whites in 1942 included fewer than a third who favored school integration; in 1956 approximately one half favored it; in 1963, three-fourths. In the South, the proportion was 2 per cent in 1942, 14 per cent in 1956, and 30 per cent in 1963 (Hyman & Sheatsley 1964). The trend is clear. There is reason to hope that it will continue and that it is symbolic of a slow but certain change in attitude. There is hope, too, in the fact that "authoritarians" are conformist. If prejudice becomes unfashionable, even the hard core of resistance to change may give way to progress.

BIBLIOGRAPHY

Adams, Romanzo 1937 *Interracial Marriage in Hawaii*. New York: Macmillan.

Adorno, T. W. et al. 1950 *The Authoritarian Personality*. American Jewish Committee, Social Studies Series, No. 3, New York: Harper.

Allport, Gordon W. 1954 *The Nature of Prejudice*. Reading, Mass.: Addison-Wesley. → An abridged paperback edition was published in 1958 by Doubleday.

Christie, Richard; and Cook, Peggy A. 1958 A guide to Published Literature Relating to *The Authoritarian Personality* Through 1956. *Journal of Psychology* 45: 171–199.

Clark, Kenneth B. 1955 *Prejudice and Your Child*. Boston: Beacon.

Clark, Kenneth B. 1965 *Dark Ghetto*. New York: Harper.

Dollard, John et al. 1939 *Frustration and Aggression*. Yale University, Institute of Human Relations. New Haven: Yale Univ. Press. → A paperback edition was published in 1961.

Freyre, Gilberto (1933) 1956 *The Masters and the Slaves (Casa-grande & senzala): A*

Study in the Development of Brazilian Civilization. 2d English-language ed., rev. Translated from the 4th, definitive Brazilian edition. New York: Knopf. → First published in Portuguese. An abridged edition was published in 1964 by Knopf.

Ginsberg, Aniela M. 1955 Pesquisas sôbre as atitudes de um grupo de escolares de São Paulo em relação com as crianças de côr. Pages 311–361 in Roger Bastide and Florestan Fernandes (editors), *Relacões raciais entre negros e brancos em São Paulo.* São Paulo (Brazil): Anhembi.

Glock, Charles; and Stark, Rodney 1966 *Christian Beliefs and Anti-Semitism.* New York: Harper.

Harding, John S. et al. 1954 Prejudice and Ethnic Relations. Volume 2, pages 1021–1061 in Gardner Lindzey (editor), *Handbook of Social Psychology.* Cambridge, Mass.: Addison-Wesley.

Hartley, Eugene L. 1946 *Problems in Prejudice.* New York: King's Crown Press.

Hofstätter, Peter R. (1954) 1963 *Einführung in die Sozialpsychologie.* 3d ed., rev. Stuttgart (Germany): Kröner.

Hooton, Earnest A. 1937 *Apes, Men, and Morons.* New York: Putnam.

Huxley, Julian; and Haddon, Alfred Cort 1936 *We Europeans: A Survey of "Racial" Problems.* New York and London: Harper.

Hyman, Herbert H.; and Sheatsley, Paul B. 1964. Attitudes Toward Desegregation. *Scientific American* 211, July: 16–23.

Jahoda, Marie 1958 *Current Concepts of Positive Mental Health.* New York: Basic Books.

Katz, Daniel; and Stotland, Ezra 1959 A Preliminary Statement to a Theory of Attitude Structure and Change. Volume 3, pages 423–475 in Sigmund Koch (editor), *Psychology: A Study of a Science.* New York: McGraw-Hill.

Klineberg, Otto 1950 *Tensions Affecting International Understanding: A Survey of Research.* Social Science Research Council, Bulletin No. 62. New York: The Council.

Klineberg, Otto 1964 *The Human Dimension in International Relations.* New York: Holt.

Krech, David; Crutchfield, Richard S.; and Bellachey, Egerton L. (1948) 1962 *Individual in Society: A Textbook of Social Psychology.* New York: McGraw-Hill. → A revision of *Theory and Problems of Social Psychology,* by David Krech and Richard S. Crutchfield.

Miller, Neal E.; and Dollard, John 1941 *Social Learning and Imitation.* New Haven: Yale Univ. Press; Oxford Univ. Press.

Myrdal, Gunnar (1944) 1962 *An American Dilemma: The Negro Problem and Modern Democracy.* New York: Harper. → A paperback edition was published in 1964 by McGraw-Hill.

Oklahoma, University of, Institute of Group Relations 1961 *Intergroup Conflict and Cooperation: The Robbers Cave Experiment,* by Muzafer Sherif et al. Norman, Okla.: University Book Exchange.

Olson, Bernhard E. 1963 *Faith and Prejudice.* New Haven: Yale Univ. Press.

Pettigrew, Thomas F. 1958 Personality and Sociocultural Factors in Intergroup Attitudes: A Cross-national Comparison. *Journal of Conflict Resolution.* 2:29–42.

Pettigrew, Thomas F. 1964 *A Profile of the Negro American.* Princeton, N.J.: Van Nostrand.

Rose, Arnold (1951) 1961 The Roots of Prejudice. Pages 393–421 in United Nations Educational, Scientific and Cultural Organization, *The Race Question in Modern Science: Race and Science.* New York: Columbia Univ. Press.

Saenger, Gerhart 1953 *The Social Psychology of Prejudice.* New York: Harper.

Tentori, Tullio 1962 *Il pregiudizio sociale.* Rome: Studium.

Thomas, Louis-Vicent 1963 Une idéologie moderne: La négritude; Essai de synthèse psycho-sociologique. *Revue de psychologie des peuples* 18:246-272, 367-398.

Williams, Robin M. Jr. 1964 *Strangers Next Door: Ethnic Relations in American Communities*. Englewood Cliffs, N.J.: Prentice-Hall.

— · — · — · — · — · — · — · — · — · —

EUGENE HARTLEY

*Attitudes Toward Minority Groups**

It is very unlikely that attitude toward a single group represents a unitary characteristic within the individual holding the attitude. Not only is there difference within attitude toward Jews which separates European Jews from American Jews, Jews in general and Jews you know, the corner grocer and Albert Einstein, but there are the general attitudes of right and wrong, attitudes concerning personal relationships, employer-employee relationships, and so on, which influence the social expressions of an individual in this realm. This point of view can be supported not only by generalization of psychological theory based on empirical study; but by studies such as those of Minard (11), LaPiere (7), and Horowitz, (6) on race attitudes. Considerable study still needs to be done concerning the psychological organization of the individual and the nature of attitudes.

For purposes of the present study, a single realm of inquiry was defined and questionnaire approach was made to college students. Within the framework of the questionnaire, prejudices could be displayed toward several different ethnic groups. Within this framework it was found that tolerance-intolerance toward these ethnic groups represented a fairly generalized unitary function. Though we cannot predict from this particular framework to others, the evidence suggests that within a defined framework we may expect intolerance of some one group to be accompanied by intolerance of others, and relative tolerance of one group to be accompanied by tolerance of others. The general tolerance-intolerance function is unitary and its degree varies from individual to individual, and from group to group. The generalized nature of this attitude was sufficient to cause relatively high correlation between expressions of attitude toward existing groups and toward non-existing groups. This correlation was sufficiently high and sufficiently prevalent among the widely different samples studied to suggest that in order to understand attitudes toward a particular group we must first have more insight into the generalized tolerance attitudes. We might almost consider the attitude expressed toward some one group a particularization, a differentiation out from this generalized approach to peoples. Analysis of the details related to the response of an individual towards any one

*Eugene Hartley, *Problems in Prejudice* (New York: King's Crown Press: Division of Columbia University Press, 1946), pp. 117-121.

group would probably be obscured by the many individual and "chance" determinants. Our approach to the generalized tolerance seemed more likely to lead us along the trail of a psychological fundamental.

In addition to the generalized intolerance-tolerance fundamental, more careful examination revealed a patterning of preference for different ethnic groups which was uniform throughout the samples studied. This pattern was not related to the actual contact an individual may have had with the members of the groups included in the pattern, but seemed to represent part of the general United States culture pattern. This hierarchy of preferences is relatively constant and is to be found among practically all sections of the populations; its roots spread downward through the age scale, manifesting itself even among relatively young children. This pattern is based upon the historical background of our country, its original settlers and later immigrants. This pattern is illustrated in a codified form in our present immigration restrictions.

Members of minority groups that rank relatively low in the hierarchy tend to incorporate the prevailing pattern as a whole into their value system, with the unique exception of their own group. "Own group" is placed at the top of the list and the rest of the pattern tends to remain intact. Concrete experience with the members of the groups in the hierarchy may cause minor variation in the pattern of preferences, but the effect of such experience must be considered a decidedly unimportant factor when considering race prejudice as it is manifested on the contemporary social scene. Preferences are built up and attitudes toward groups are developed relatively independently of personal contact with the group in question or its members.

Although the pattern of preferences is predetermined in this country, there are distinct differences between the levels of tolerance within which this pattern is ordered. Tolerance for nations and races may be considered with reference to some arbitrary social scheme for evaluation. When studied in this fashion, groups are found to vary greatly in the level of tolerance which might be used to describe their responses to ethnic groups in spite of the fact that hierarchies of preferences are the same. Thus, we found that students at one school, ranking Jews toward the bottom of their schedule of preferences, were objectively responding toward this religious minority more favorably than the students of another school were responding toward Danes, though in the latter school Danes ranked toward the top of the list of preferences. These differences in the levels of tolerance manifested by groups were observed in the present study, but it was not deemed feasible to pursue the analysis of the factors determining such group differences on the basis of college samples available. It did seem feasible, however, to attempt to explore factors associated with individual differences.

To what is the generalized tolerance level related? First, it must be remembered that it is determined by those general laws which govern the differences among groups. With reference to individuals, Murphy and Likert studied generalized tolerance and demonstrated that it is positively correlated with higher grades in courses in college. They showed it to be correlated positively with the tendency toward "dissatisfaction" with some relatively general aspects of the American scene. Also it is positively correlated with a tendency toward "radicalism" as defined in their study. These three general findings were reported on the basis of independent analyses of students at the University of Michigan and Columbia University (12).

From the present study, we note that individuals who consider members of different national and religious groups similar tend toward tolerance. Individuals with more flexibility in regard to ways of doing things may be more tolerant. College students, with relatively good parental relationships appear more tolerant. These suggestions are very tentatively offered, with no implications of causality involved. They seem sufficiently fruitful to warrant presentation, though it is recognized that the correlations on which they are based are too low to justify generalization.

When the problem of individual differences was approached with the methodology of clinical analysis, constellations emerged of the generally tolerant and the generally intolerant personalities within the sample selected for such study.

The relatively tolerant personality seemed likely to exhibit some combination of the following characteristics: a strong desire for personal autonomy, associated with a lack of need for dominance, a strong need for friendliness, along with a personal seclusiveness, fear of competition; a tendency to placate others along with lack of general conformity to the culturally dominant mores. He appeared to be fairly serious, to be interested in current events, to have ideas about bettering society, to be a member of a political group and to have great need for personal achievement in the vocational area. He showed himself to be an accepting personality, disliking violence, able to appreciate the contributions of others, conscious of feeling that people tend to be more or less alike and adopting a nurturant rather than a dominant attitude toward those younger than he. He manifested conscious conflicts concerning loyalties and duties and was very seriously concerned about moral questions. His interests centered about what are commonly called the social studies, and about reading and journalism. Although personally seclusive, he showed great need to be socially useful.

The relatively intolerant personality was found to combine in varying degrees the following characteristics: unwillingness to accept responsibility; acceptance of conventional mores; a rejection of serious groups, rejection of political interests, and desire for groups formed for purely social purposes and absorption with pleasure activities; a conscious conflict between play and work; emotionality rather than rationality; extreme egocentrism; interest in physical activity, the body, health. He was likely to dislike agitators, radicals, pessimists. He was relatively uncreative, apparently unable to deal with anxieties except by fleeing from them. Often his physical activity had in it a compulsive component. (It may be that this compulsion to be on the move, that is, constantly occupied with sports, motoring, traveling, etc. served for him the same function as did study and activities with social significance for the individual with high tolerance.)

In evaluating the summaries of the personality characteristics of the tolerant and intolerant individuals, it must be remembered that these students were selected as extremes within a group which is not particularly representative either of the general population or, for that matter, of "typical college students." There is no particular reason to believe without evidence that the results do not apply to others, but until evidence is produced we must be very careful about extending these findings beyond the sample studied. Attention should be called, too, to the fact that we are referring here to the generalized tolerance function, not to the specific attitude toward any one group.

Though many studies of actual abilities and potentialities of different racial, national and religious groups have demonstrated that there are no necessary generalizations concerning individuals which can be made solely on the basis of the ethnic group background of an individual, nevertheless, *judgments* are made in terms of ethnic background in a variety of situations. The tendency to emphasize ethnic group affiliation was investigated in the present study and discussed as a definite attitude variable. This variable is designated "salience." An approach to its measurement on a sociological level was indicated and demonstrated analyses prepared. Further study of this factor as a variable related to the behavior of the individual was made. These analyses demonstrated that we may consider the tendency to make ethnic references a psychological characteristic of the respondent. Individual differences in ethnic salience were evident. Variability in ethnic salience did not seem to be clearly correlated with tolerance. A significant relationship was found in a limited sample between presence of ethnic salience and restriction of the outgoingness of the individual.

While every effort was made to conduct the study in such fashion that the results might be applied to other samples of the general population, we must again call attention to the fact that most of the studies of the personality correlates of the attitudes of tolerance-intolerance were made on students representing one type of community. Only further study can determine the limitations which must be imposed upon our findings as a result of this selection. Meanwhile, we may accept them as a possible orientation for consideration of the general community and we can consider them, to the extent that the statistical evaluation permits, as representative of at least one segment of the community.

APPENDIX

TABLE A. DATE OF ADMINISTRATION OF ATTITUDE TESTS AT THE DIFFERENT COLLEGES AND WHETHER SIGNATURES WERE ELICITED

Name of School	Date Given	Signature
"A" - Teachers College	Dec. 14, 1938	Optional
Bennington College	Dec. 20, 1938	Signed
College of the City of New York, Arts. (1st test*)	Dec. 9, 1938	Signed
College of the City of New York Business	March 1, 1939	Signed
Columbia	Nov. 30, 1938	Signed
Howard	Dec. 21, 1938	Optional
"B" - Normal School	Dec. 16, 1938	Optional
Princeton	March 22, 1939	Optional

*Re-test, Jan. 6, 1939 - Signed.

REFERENCES

6. Horowitz, E. L. "The Development of Attitude toward the Negro," *Archives of Psychology*, XXVIII, No. 194 (1936).

7. LaPiere, R. T. "Attitudes vs. Actions," *Social Forces*, XIII (1934) 230–237.

11. Minard, R. D. "Race Attitudes of Iowa Children," *University of Iowa Studies in Character*, IV, No. 2 (1931).

12. Murphy, G. and Likert, R. Public Opinion and the Individual. New York: Harper and Brothers, 1938.

E. FRENKEL-BRUNSWIK
D. J. LEVINSON
R. N. SANFORD

*The Authoritarian Personality**

INTRODUCTION

The present research was guided by the conception of an individual whose thoughts about man and society form a pattern which is properly described as antidemocratic and which springs from his deepest emotional tendencies. Can it be shown that such a person really exists? If so, what precisely is he like? What goes to make up antidemocratic thought? What are the organizing forces within the person? If such a person exists, how commonly does he exist in our society? And what have been the determinants and what the cause of his development?

Although the antidemocratic individual may be thought of as a totality, it is nevertheless possible to distinguish and to study separately (a) his ideology and (b) his underlying personality needs. Ideology refers to an organization of opinions, attitudes and values. One may speak of an individual's total ideology or of his ideology with respect to different areas of social life: politics, economics, religion, minority groups, and so forth. Ideologies have an existence independent of any single individual, those existing at a particular time being results both of historical processes and of contemporary social events. These ideologies, or the more particular ideas within them, have for different individuals different degrees of appeal, a matter that depends upon the individual's needs and the degree to which these needs are being satisfied or frustrated. The pattern of ideas that the individual takes over and makes his own will in each case be found to have a function within his over-all adjustment.

Although ideological trends are usually expressed more or less openly in words, it is important to note that, in the case of such affect-laden questions as those concerning minority groups, the degree of openness with which a person speaks will depend upon his situation. At the present time, when antidemocratic sentiments are officially frowned upon in this country, one should expect an individual to express them openly only in a guarded way or to a limited extent. This most superficial level of expression would afford a poor basis for estimating the potential for fascism in America. We should know, in addition, what the individual will say when he feels safe from criticism, what he thinks but will not say at all, what he thinks but will not admit to himself, and what he will be disposed to think when this or that appeal is made to him. In short, it is necessary to know the individual's *readiness* for antidemocratic thought and action, what it is that he will express when conditions change in such a way as to remove his inhibitions. Anti-

*Else Frenkel-Brunswik, Daniel J. Levinson, and R. Nevitt Sanford, "The Antidemocratic Personality." From *Readings in Social Psychology*, 3rd edition, edited by Eleanor E. Maccoby, Theodore M. Newcomb, and Eugene L. Hartley, pages 636–646. Copyright ©1947, 1952, 1958 by Holt, Rinehart and Winston, Inc. Reprinted by permission of Holt, Rinehart and Winston, Inc.

democratic propaganda, though it makes some appeal to people's real interests, addresses itself in the main to emotional needs and irrational impulses, and its effectiveness will depend upon the susceptibility existing in the great mass of people.

To know that antidemocratic trends reside in the personality structure is to raise the further question of how this structure develops. According to the present theory, the major influences upon personality development arise in the course of child training as carried forward in a setting of family life. The determinants of personality, in other words, are mainly social; such factors as the economic situation of the parents, their social, ethnic, and religious group memberships, and the prevailing ideology concerning child training might be factors of crucial significance. This means that broad changes in social conditions and institutions will have a direct bearing upon the kinds of personalities that develop within a society. It does not mean, however, that such social changes would appreciably alter the personality structures that already exist.

It was necessary to devise techniques for surveying surface expression, for revealing ideological trends that were more or less inhibited, and for bringing to light unconscious personality forces.[1] Since the major concern was with *patterns* of dynamically related factors, it seemed that the proper approach was through intensive individual studies. In order to gauge the significance and practical importance of such studies, however, it was necessary to study groups as well as individuals and to find ways and means for integrating the two approaches.

Individuals were studied by means of (a) intensive clinical interviews and (b) a modified Thematic Apperception Test; groups were studied by means of questionnaries. It was not hoped that the clinical studies would be as complete or profound as some which have already been performed, primarily by psychoanalysts, nor that the questionnaires would be more accurate than any now employed by social psychologists. It was hoped, however —indeed it was necessary to our purpose—that the clinical material could be conceptualized in such a way as to permit its being quantified and carried over into group studies, and that the questionnaires could be brought to bear upon areas of response ordinarily left to clinical study. The attempt was made, in other words, to bring methods of traditional social psychology into the service of theories and concepts from the newer dynamic theory of personality, and in so doing to make "depth psychological" phenomena more amenable to mass-statistical treatment, and to make quantitative surveys of attitudes and opinions more meaningful psychologically.

In order to study antidemocratic individuals, it was necessary first to identify them. Hence a start was made by constructing a questionnaire and having it filled out anonymously by a large group of people. This questionnaire contained, in addition to numerous questions of fact about the subject's past and present life, and a number of open-answer ("projective") questions, several opinion-attitude scales containing a variety of antidemocratic (anti-Semitic, ethnocentric, reactionary, profascist) statements with which the subjects were invited to agree or disagree. A number of individuals (identified by indirect means) who showed the greatest amount of agreement with these statements were then studied by means of clinical techniques, and contrasted with a number of individuals

---

[1] E. Frenkel-Brunswik and R. N. Sanford, "Some Personality Correlates of Antisemitism," *J. Psychol.*, 1945, XX, 271-291; D. J. Levinson and R. N. Sanford, "A Scale for the Measurement of Antisemitism." *ibid.*, 1944, XVII, 339-370.

showing strong disagreement. On the basis of these individual studies, the questionnaire was revised, and the whole procedure repeated. The study began with college students as subjects, and then was expanded to include a variety of groups from the community at large. The findings are considered to hold fairly well for non-Jewish, white, native-born, middle-class Americans.

THE STUDY OF IDEOLOGY

Anti-Semitism was the first ideological area studied. Anti-Semitic ideology is regarded as a broad system of ideas including: *negative opinions* regarding Jews (e.g., that they are unscrupulous, dirty, clannish, power-seeking); *hostile attitudes* toward them (e.g., that they should be excluded, restricted, suppressed); and *moral values* which permeate the opinions and justify the attitudes.

In what senses, if any, can anti-Semitic ideology be considered irrational? What are the main attitudes in anti-Semitism—segregation, suppression, exclusion—for the solution of "the Jewish problem"? Do people with negative opinions generally have hostile attitudes as well? Do individuals have a general readiness to accept or oppose a broad pattern of anti-Semitic opinions and attitudes?

These questions led to and guided the construction of an opinion-attitude scale for the measurement of anti-Semitic ideology. This scale provided a basis for the selection of criterion groups of extreme high and low scorers, who could then be subjected to intensive clinical study. The source material for the scale included: the writings of virulent anti-Semites; technical, literary, and reportorial writings on anti-Semitism and fascism; and, most important, everyday American anti-Semitism as revealed in parlor discussion, in the discriminatory practices of many businesses and institutions, and in the literature of various Jewish "defense" groups trying vainly to counter numerous anti-Semitic accusations by means of rational argument. In an attempt to include as much as possible of this type of content in the scale, certain rules were followed in its construction.

Each item should be maximally rich in ideas, with a minimum of duplication in wording or essential content. In order to reflect the forms of anti-Semitism prevalent in America today, the statements should not be violently and openly anti-democratic, rather, they should be pseudodemocratic, in the sense that active hostility toward a group is somewhat tempered and disguised by means of a compromise with democratic ideals. Each statement should have a familiar ring, should sound as it had been heard many times in everyday discussions and intensive interviews.

The 52-item scale contained five subscales—not statistically pure dimensions but convenient and meaningful groupings of items—the correlations among which should provide partial answers to some of the questions raised above. (a) Subscale "Offensive" (12 items) deals with imagery (opinions) of Jews as personally unpleasant and disturbing. Stereotypy is most explicit in the item: "There may be a few exceptions, but in general Jews are pretty much alike." To agree with this statement is to have an image of "the Jew" as a stereotyped model of the entire group. (b) Subscale "Threatening" (10 items) describes the Jews as a dangerous, dominating group. In various items the Jews are regarded as rich and powerful, poor and dirty, unscrupulous, revolutionary, and so on. (c) Subscale "Attitudes" (16 items) refers to programs of action. The specific hostile attitudes vary in degree from simple avoidance to suppression and attack, with intermediate actions of exclusion, segregation, and suppression. The social areas of discrimination covered included employment, residence, professions, marriage, and so on. (d) and (e) Subscales "Seclusive" and "Intrusive" deal with opposing stands on the issue of assimilation. The "Seclusive" subscale accuses the Jews of being too foreign and clannish; it implies that Jews can themselves eliminate anti-Semitism (a problem of their own making, so to speak) by greater assimilation and conformity to American ways. The "Intrusive" subscale, on the other hand, accuses the Jews of overassimilation, hiding of Jewishness, prying, seeking power and prestige. These items imply that Jews ought to keep more to themselves and to develop a culture, preferably even a nation of their own.

The total scale is intended to measure the individual's readiness to support or oppose anti-Semitic ideology as a whole. This ideology is conceived as involving stereotyped negative opinions describing Jews as threatening, immoral, and categorically different from non-Jews, and of hostile attitudes urging various forms of restriction. Anti-Semitism is conceived, then, not as a specific attitude (jealousy, blind hate, religious disapproval, or whatever) but rather as a general way of thinking and feeling about Jews and Jewish-Gentile relations.

For two groups, the reliabilities were at least .92 for the total A–S scale, and between .84 and .94 for all subscales ("Intrusive," second group only), except for "Seclusive," for which .71 was obtained (second group only). The correlations among the subscales "Offensive," "Threatening," and "Attitudes" are .83 to .85, while each of these correlates .92 to .94 with the total scale.

These correlations seem to reveal that each person has a rather general tendency to accept or reject anti-Semitic ideology as a whole. The correlations of subscale "Seclusive" with "Intrusive" (.74) and with "Attitudes" (also .74) reveal basic contradictions in anti-Semitic ideology. (All the raw coefficients, if corrected for attenuation, would be over .90.) Most anti-Semites are, apparently, willing to criticize both Jewish assimilation and Jewish seclusion. This is further testimony to the irrationality of anti-Semitism. Also irrational is the stereotyped image of "the Jew" (the item about Jews being all alike was very discriminating), an image which is intrinsically self-contradictory, since one person cannot be simultaneously rich and poor, dirty and luxurious, capitalistic and radical.

The question then presents itself: Are the trends found in anti-Semitic ideology—its generality, stereotyped imagery, destructive irrationality, sense of threat, concern with power and immorality, and so on—also expressed in the individual's social thinking about group relations generally? Can it be that what was found in anti-Semitism is not specific to prejudice against Jews but rather is present in prejudice against all groups?

Considerations such as these led to the study of ethnocentrism, that is, ideology regarding in-groups (with which the individual identifies himself), out-groups (which are "different" and somehow antithetical to the in-group), and their interaction. A 34-item Ethnocentrism scale was constructed along lines similar to those employed for the A–S scale. There were three subscales: (a) A 12-item subscale deals with Negroes and Negro-white relations. The items refer to Negroes as lazy, good-natured, and ignorant; also aggressive, primitive, and rebellious, and so on. (b) Minorities. These 12 items deal with various groups (other than Jews and Negroes), including minority political parties and religious sects, foreigners, Oklahomans (in California), zoot-suiters, criminals, and so on. (c) "Patriotism." These 10 items deal with America as an in-group in relation to other nations as out-groups. The items express the attitude that foreign, "inferior" nations should be subordinate, they include a value for obedience and a punitive attitude toward value-violators, and, finally, they express regarding permanent peace a cynicism which is rationalized by moralistic, hereditarian theories of aggressive, threatening out-group nations.

The reliabilities for the subscales ranged from .80 to .91; and for the total E scale .91. These figures, considered together with the correlations of .74 to .83 among the subscales, and the subscale Total E scale correlations of .90 to .92, indicate a generality in ethnocentric ideology that is almost as great as and even more remarkable than that found in A–S.

The correlations of A–S with E complete the picture. The A–S scale correlates .80 with the E scale, and from .69 to .76 with the subscales. Through successive revisions there finally emerged a single E scale of 10 items (including 4 A–S items) which had reliabilities of .7 to .9 in different groups of subjects. It is clear that an attempt to understand prejudice psychologically must start with the total pattern of ethnocentric thinking, including both general out-group rejection and in-group submission-idealization.

Space does not permit a detailed discussion of the study of politics and religion. Ethnocentrism is related, though not very closely, to political conservatism ($r = .5$) and to support of the more conservative political groupings. In the responses of individuals scoring high on the conservatism scale, two patterns could be distinguished: a traditional, *laissez-faire* conservatism as opposed to "pseudoconservatism" in which a profession of belief in the tenets of traditional conservatism is combined with a readiness for violent change of a kind which would abolish the very institutions with which the individual appears to identify himself. The latter appeared to contribute more to the correlation between E and conservatism than did the former. The nonreligious are less ethnocentric on the average than the religious, although such sects as the Quakers and Unitarians made low E scale means (nonethnocentric).

THE STUDY OF PERSONALITY

The main variables underlying the various ideological areas above represent personality trends expressed in ideological form. A primary hypothesis in this research is that an individual is most receptive to those ideologies which afford the fullest expression to his over-all personality structure. Thus, a person clinically described as strongly authoritarian, projective, and destructive is likely to be receptive to an antidemocratic ideology such as ethnocentrism—ultimately fascism as the total social objectification of these trends— because it expresses his needs so well.

The attempt at a quantitative investigation of personality variables underlying ethnocentric ideology led to the construction of a personality scale. It was called, for convenience, the F scale because it was intended to measure some of the personality trends which seemed to express a predisposition or deep-lying receptivity to fascism. The items are statements of opinion and attitude in nonideological areas (not dealing with formal groups or social institutions) such as self, family, people in general, sex, personal values, and so on; they are not tied by official statement or surface meaning to items in the other scales. Any consistency in response to the F and E scales, as indicated by the correlation between them, must be due primarily to the fact that both scales express the same underlying trends, since their surface content is quite different. The main difference between the scales is that the F items are less openly ideological.

Ten main variables guided scale construction, each variable being represented by a cluster of several items. The clusters were partially overlapping, since several items were intended to express more than a single variable. In three successive forms the scale contained 38, 34, then 30 items, but the 10 main variables were always represented.

The cluster variables were as follows: conventional values, authoritarian submission, authoritarian aggression, anti-intraception, superstition-stereotypy, pseudotoughness, power, cynicism, projectivity, and sex.

Three of these clusters may be discussed to illustrate the general approach. "Authoritarian submission" refers to an inability seriously to criticize, reject, or actively rebel against one's main in-group (particularly the family) figures and values. There is a highly moralized and idealized conception of authority-representatives and a submissive relation to them. Examples: "No sane, normal, decent person could ever think of hurting a close friend or relative"; "Every person should have complete faith in some supernatural power whose decisions he obeys without question."

"Anti-intraception" involves opposition to a psychological, insightful view of people and oneself. This includes a rejection of emotion and of attempts to look into one's deeper motives and conflicts. Personal inquiries tend to be regarded as prying, and there is often an exaggerated idea of how much prying is going on. Work and keeping busy are emphasized as ways of "not thinking about yourself." Examples: "When a person has a problem or worry, it is best for him not to think about it but to keep busy with more cheerful things"; "Nowadays more and more people are prying into matters that should remain personal and private."

"Projectivity" refers to the disposition to imagine strange, evil, dangerous, destructive forces at work in the outer world; these imaginings have only the smallest basis in reality but can be understood as projections of the individual's deep-lying sexual and aggressive strivings. Examples: "Wars and social troubles may someday be ended by an earthquake or flood that will destroy the whole world"; "Nowadays when so many different kinds of people move around and mix together so much, a person has to protect himself especially carefully against catching an infection or disease from them"; "The wild sex life of the old Greeks and Romans was tame compared to some of the goings-on in this country, even in places where people might least expect it."

The successive forms of the F scale involved elimination, modification, and addition of items, based on both statistical considerations and on theoretical requirements of richness and ideas and over-all inclusiveness. The reliability of the scale increased from an average of .74 for the first form to .85 on the last. Each high quartile scorer is high on most items and clusters; on each item and cluster the difference between high scorers (total scale) and low scorers is statistically significant.

Correlations of F with A–S and E increased from an average of about .6 to about .75 in later forms, that is, higher than the correlation of .50 with the conservatism scale. This correlation, in conjunction with the clinical findings reported below, gives evidence of the functional role of personality trends in organizing and giving meaning to surface attitudes, values, and opinions.

Does ethnocentrism help the individual avoid conscious ambivalence toward his family by displacing the hostility onto out-groups (the morally "alien") and thus leave in consciousness exaggerated professions of love toward family and authority? Do high scores on the F scale (who are usually also ethnocentric) have an underlying anticonventionalism, in-group- and family-directed hostility, a tendency to do the very things they rigidly and punitively oppose in others? What impels an individual to feel, for example, that aggression against his family is unthinkable and yet to agree that "homosexuals should be severely punished" and (during the war) that the "Germans and Japs should be wiped out"? Such contradictions suggest that the deeper personality trends of high scorers are antithetical to their conscious values, opinions, and attitudes. The clinical studies reported below investigate further these and other questions.

The so-called "projective questions" are intermediate between the scales and the intensive clinical techniques. As part of the questionnaire they are used in group studies in order to determine how common in larger populations were the relationships discovered in clinical studies. They are open questions to be answered in a few words or lines; each question deals with events or experiences which are likely to have emotional significance for the individual. The original set of about 30 questions was gradually reduced to 8, which were both statistically differentiating and theoretically inclusive. These deal with "what moods are unpleasant," "what desires are hard to control," "what great people are admired," "what would drive a person nuts," "what are the worst crimes," "what moments are embarrassing," "how to spend your last six months," "what is most awe-inspiring."

The responses of the entire high and low quartiles on the A-S (later the total E) scale were contrasted. For each question "high" and "low" scoring categories were made; a "high" category expresses a personality trend which seems most characteristic of ethnocentrists and which can be expected significantly to differentiate the two groups. A scoring manual, giving the specific categories (usually two to six) for each item, was the basis on which two independent raters scored each response (not knowing the actual A-S or E score of the subjects). Each response was scored "high," "low," or "neutral"—the neutral category being used when the response was omitted, ambiguous, or when it contained "high" and "low" trends equally. Less than 10 percent of the responses received neutral scores.

The scoring agreement for the battery of items averaged 80 to 90 percent on a variety of groups (total, 200 to 300). The high quartiles received an average of 75-90 percent "high" scores, as compared with 20-40 percent "high" scores for the low quartiles. Almost never was an individual ethnocentrist given more than 50 percent low scores, and conversely for the anti-ethnocentrists. For each item the difference between the two groups was always significant at better than the 1 percent level.

The differences between the ethnocentric and anti-ethnocentric groups may be illustrated by the scoring of the item "What experiences would be most awe-inspiring for you?" The "low" categories are: (a) Values which refer to personal achievement (intellectual, esthetic, scientific), contribution to mankind, the realization of democratic goals by self and society, and so on. (b) "Power," as exemplified in man's material-technological achievements and in nature. (c) Intense nature experiences in which there are clear signs of esthetic, sensual-emotional involvement.

The "high" categories for this item, in contrast, are: (a) "Power" in the form of deference and submission toward powerful people; emphasis on a generally authoritarian and ritualized atmosphere (military, superficial religious, patriotic, etc.). (b) Personal power in self, with others playing a deferent role. (c) Destruction-harm of people (e.g., "death of a close relative"; no open hostility). (d) Values which refer to conventionalized sex, material security, ownership, vague sense of virtue, and so on. (e) Dilute nature experiences which differ from those of the low-scorers in that they are matter-of-fact, unspecific, surface descriptions with no indication of sensual-emotional involvement.

Some other general differences between these two groups were found. Deeplying trends such as hostility, dependency, sexuality, curiosity, and the like exist in both groups, but in the unprejudiced group they are more ego-integrated, in the sense of being more focal, more tied to other trends, more complex affectively, and with fewer defenses. This group is also more aware of inner conflicts, ambivalence, and tendencies to violate basic values. Their inner life is richer if more troubled; they tend to accuse themselves of faults, while the prejudiced group externalizes and engages more in idealization of self and family.

CLINICAL ANALYSIS OF INTERVIEW MATERIAL

As mentioned above, those scoring extremely high or extremely low on the overt ethnocentrism scale of the questionnaire were further subjected to clinical interviews and to projective tests.

The interviews covered the following major fields: vocation, income, religion, politics, minority groups, and clinical data. The directives given to the interviewer listed in each field both the kinds of things it was hoped to obtain from the subject and suggestions as to how these things might indirectly be ascertained by questioning. The former were the "underlying questions"; they had reference to the variables by means of which the subject was eventually to be characterized. The "manifest questions," those actually put to the subject, were framed in such a way as to conceal as much as possible the real purpose of the interview and yet elicit answers that were significant in terms of over-all hypotheses. The manifest questions used to obtain material bearing on a given underlying question were allowed to vary greatly from subject to subject, depending in each case on the subject's ideology, surface attitudes, and defenses. Nevertheless a number of manifest questions, based on general theory and experience, were formulated for each underlying question. Not all of them were asked each subject.

Examples of manifest questions, taken from the area of Income are: "What would you do with (expected or desired) income?" and "What would it mean to you?" The corresponding underlying issues are the subject's aspirations and phantasies as to social status, as to power as a means to manipulate others, as to (realistic or neurotic) striving for security, as to lavish and exciting living, the readiness really to take chances, and so forth.

It was the task of the interviewer subtly to direct the course of the interview in such a way that as much as possible would be learned about these underlying attitudes without giving away to the subject the real foci of the inquiry.

In attempting to achieve a crude quantification of the interview material, so that group trends might be ascertained, there was developed an extensive set of scoring categories, comprising approximately a hundred headings. An attempt was made to encompass as much as possible of the richness and intricacy of the material. The complexity of the categories introduced inferential and subjective elements, but, as it turned out, this did not prevent adequate inter-rater reliability and validity. The categories were arrived at on the basis of a preliminary study of the complete interviews and of all the other available material pertaining to the same subjects. These categories represent, in fact, the hypotheses as to which clinical characteristics go with presence or absence of prejudice.

In order to test all the categories, passages of the interview protocols referring directly to political or social issues and all other data that might indicate the subject's identity or ideological position were carefully removed before two clinically trained scorers undertook the evaluation of the protocols.

Interviews of 40 women were thus evaluated. (A later report will present results from a group of men.) Three kinds of judgments were used for each category: (1) whether the interview revealed attitudes tentatively classified as "high" or as "low"; (2) whether no decision could be reached; or, more often, (3) whether no material was available on the issue in question. A number of categories proved nondiscriminating either because "high" and "low" statements appeared with equal frequency in the interviews of those found "high" and of those found "low" on the questionnaire, or because of a large proportion of "neutral" responses.

Some of the most discriminating categories included the following. Of the fifteen interviewed womon who were extremely low on ethocentrism, 0 (none) displayed a conventional "idealization" of the parents, the variable previously assumed to be characteristic of ethnocentrism, whereas 12 showed an attitude of objective appraisal of the parents.[2] On the other hand, of the 25 women interviewees extremely high on ethnocentrism, 11 clearly displayed the "high" and only 6 the "low" variant (the remaining 8 being "neutral"). This distribution of attitudes toward parents is in line with the general glorification of and submission to in-group authority, on the surface at least, by the high scorers on ethnocentrism. In fact, the corresponding figures on the category "submission to parental authority and values (respect based on fear)" vs. "principled independence" are 1 to 7 for the "low" as against 9 to 0 for the "high" subjects.

The "high" women emphasize sex as a means for achieving status; they describe their conquests and—as they do in other fields as well—rationalize rather than admit failures and shortcomings, whereas the "lows" do not shrink from open admission of inadequacies in this respect (8 to 3 for "highs"; 1 to 8 for "lows"). In the same vein we find in

[2] In view of the small number of cases (40 and the frequency of the neutral categories (about 30 percent), these differences between the high and low scorers must be regarded as tentative. However, there is additional evidence that these differences would be found in a large sample. (1) Even with this small number of cases the differences are very striking. (2) The data on men appear to reveal similar differences. This not only provides an independent confirmation, but it will provide a sample twice as large as the present one. (3) The variables considered here are similar to those found to be differentiating in the ideological material, the Thematic Apperception Test, and the projective questions.

"highs" underlying disrespect and resentment toward the opposite sex, typically combined with externalized, excessive and counteractive "pseudoadmiration," *vs.* "genuine respect and fondness for opposite sex" in the "lows" (11 to 4 for "highs"; 2 to 7 for "lows"). Similarly, the attitude toward the opposite sex in the "high" women is power-oriented, exploitative, manipulative, with an eye on concrete benefits hiding behind superficial submission as contrasted with a warm, affectionate and love-seeking attitude on the part of the "lows." Thus, the traits desired in men by "high" women are: hard-working, energetic, go-getting, moral, clean-cut, deferent, "thoughtful" toward the woman; the desiderata mentioned by the "low" women, on the other hand, are: companionship, common interests, warmth, sociability, sexual love, understanding, and liberal values. (For the entire pattern just described the figures are 14 to 4 for the "highs" and 2 to 10 for the "lows.")

As to attitudes toward people in general, the "highs" tend to assume an attitude of "moralistic condemnation" *vs.* the "permissiveness" shown toward individuals by the lows (14 to 3 for the "highs," 2 to 10 for the "lows"). Of special importance for the problem discussed here is the "hierarchical conception of human relations" in the "highs" as compared with an "equalitarianism and mutuality" in the "lows" (13 to 2 in the "highs" and 1 to 10 in the "lows").

All through the material it was frequently observed that the difference between the high and low subjects does not lie so much in the presence or absence of a basic tendency but rather in the way of dealing with such tendencies. As an illustration from the field of interpersonal relationships, we may refer to the category of Dependence. Whereas the dependence of the high subjects tends to be diffuse, ego-alien, and linked to an infantile desire to be taken care of, the dependence of the lows is focal and loveseeking as can be expected in cases where a real object relationship has been established (11 to 1 in the highs; 1 to 7 in the lows). The traits desired in friends are in many ways similar to those desired in the opposite sex (see above); we find emphasis on status, good manners, and so forth in the highs as compared with intrinsic values in the lows (9 to 2 for highs, 0 to 10 for lows.)

In the high scorer's attitude toward the Self, we find self-glorification mixed with feelings of inferiority which are not faced as such, conventional moralism, the belief in a close correspondence between what one is and what one wishes to be, and the "denial of genuine causality" (e.g., an explanation of one's traits or symptoms in terms of hereditary or accidental factors), as contrasted to opposite attitudes in the lows, with figures generally as discriminatory or better than those mentioned above for the other fields.

In the case of more general categories pertaining to personality dynamics an unusually large proportion were found to be discriminating. This might be due to the fact that the scoring of these categories was based on the over-all impression of the subject rather than on a specific piece of information. High-scoring women tend to give particular evidence of "rigid-moralistic anal reaction-formations" as ends in themselves, e.g., totalitarian-moralistic conceptualization of two kinds of people—"clean and dirty"—and overemphasis on propriety and kindliness, often with underlying aggression. The women with low scores show more evidence of "oral character structure"; and when such values as cleanliness and kindliness are present they are of a more functional nature.

As far as aggression is concerned, the high-scoring women tend toward a diffuse, depersonalized, moralized, and punitive type of aggression, whereas the aggression of the low-scoring women is more focal and personalized, and more often it seems to be elicited by violation of principles or as a response to rejection by a loved object.

Ambivalence, e.g., toward the parents, is not admitted into consciousness by the "high" subjects but is rather solved by thinking in terms of dichotomies and by displacement onto out-groups. The ambivalence of the "lows" is more often expressed against the original objects (e.g., parents) or representatives, in reality, of the original objects, e.g., real authority.

There is a strong tendency in the high-scoring women to display "femininity" exclusively, whereas the low-scoring women are more ready to accept and to sublimate their masculine traits.

Some of the categories scored under the tentative assumption of their relevance to prejudice did not prove discriminating. Among these are various "childhood events," e.g., death or divorce of parents, number of siblings, and order of birth. The conception of one's own childhood, e.g., image of father and mother, proved only slightly discriminating, mostly because of the great number of neutral scores due often to lack of information in these categories. The fact that some of the categories were not discriminating may be taken as evidence that the raters were at least partially successful in their attempt to eliminate halo effect.

As was mentioned above, the over-all contrast between the highly prejudiced and the tolerant women hinges less than originally expected on the existence or absence of "depth" factors such as latent homosexuality, but rather, as seen here again, on the way they are dealt with in the personality: by acceptance and sublimation in our tolerant extremes, by repression and defense measures in our prejudiced extremes.

It was because of their repressions, it may be supposed, that the high scorers are found to be outstanding on such formal characteristics as rigidity, anti-intraception, pseudoscientific thinking, and so forth.

The differences between high and low scorers revealed by the several independent techniques of the study reported here are consistent one with another and suggest a pattern which, embracing as it does both personality and ideology, may be termed the "antidemocratic personality."

— · — · — · — · — · — · — · — · — · —

11 · SOCIAL LEARNING AND SOCIAL PSYCHOLOGY OF LANGUAGE

B. F. SKINNER

Operant Behavior: Social and Verbal Behavior*

Social behavior may be defined as the behavior of two or more people with respect to one another or in concert with respect to a common environment. It is often argued that this is different from individual behavior and that there are "social situations" and "social forces" which cannot be described in the language of natural science. A special discipline called "social science" is said to be required because of this apparent break in the continuity of nature. There are, of course, many facts—concerning governments, wars, migrations, economic conditions, cultural practices, and so on—which would never present themselves for study if people did not gather together and behave in groups, but whether the basic data are fundamentally different is still a question. We are interested here in the methods of the natural sciences as we see them at work in physics, chemistry, and biology, and as we have so far applied them in the field of behavior. How far will they carry us in the study of the behavior of groups?

Many generalizations at the level of the group need not refer to behavior at all. There is an old law in economics, called Gresham's Law, which states that bad money drives good money out of circulation. If we can agree as to what money is, whether it is good or bad, and when it is in circulation, we can express this general principle without making specific reference to the use of money by individuals. Similar generalizations are found in sociology, cultural anthropology, linguistics, and history. But a "social law" must be generated by the behavior of individuals. It is always an individual who behaves, and he behaves with the same body and according to the same processes as in a nonsocial situation. If an individual possessing two pieces of money, one good and one bad, tends to spend the bad and save the good—a tendency which may be explained in terms of reinforcing contingencies—and if this is true of a large number of people, the phenomenon described by Gresham's Law arises. The individual behavior explains the group phe-

*Reprinted with permission of The Macmillan Company from *Science and Human Behavior* by B. F. Skinner, pp. 297–312. Copyright 1953 by The Macmillan Company.

nomenon. Many economists feel the need for some such explanation of all economic law, although there are others who would accept the higher level of description as valid in its own right.

We are concerned here simply with the extent to which an analysis of the behavior of the individual which has received substantial validation under the favorable conditions of a natural science may contribute to the understanding of social phenomena. To apply our analysis to the phenomena of the group is an excellent way to test its adequacy, and if we are able to account for the behavior of people in groups without using any new term or presupposing any new process or principle, we shall have revealed a promising simplicity in the data. This does not mean that the social sciences will then inevitably state their generalizations in terms of individual behavior, since another level of description may also be valid and may well be more convenient.

THE SOCIAL ENVIRONMENT

Social behavior arises because one organism is important to another as part of its environment. A first step, therefore, is an analysis of the social environment and of any special features it may possess.

Social Reinforcement

Many reinforcements require the presence of other people. In some of these, as in certain forms of sexual and pugilistic behavior, the other person participates merely as an object. We cannot describe the reinforcement without referring to another organism. But social reinforcement is usually a matter of personal mediation. When a mother feeds her child, the food, as a primary reinforcer, is not social, but the mother's behavior in presenting it is. The difference is slight—as one may see by comparing breast-feeding with bottle-feeding. Verbal behavior always involves social reinforcement and derives its characteristic properties from this fact. The response, "A glass of water, please," has no effect upon the mechanical environment, but in an appropriate verbal environment it may lead to primary reinforcement. In the field of social behavior special emphasis is laid upon reinforcement with attention, approval, affection, and submission. These important generalized reinforcers are social because the process of generalization usually requires the mediation of another organism. Negative reinforcement—particularly as a form of punishment—is most often administered by others in the form of unconditioned aversive stimulation or of disapproval, contempt, ridicule, insult, and so on.

Behavior reinforced through the mediation of other people will differ in many ways from behavior reinforced by the mechanical environment. Social reinforcement varies from moment to moment, depending upon the condition of the reinforcing agent. Different responses may therefore achieve the same effect, and one response may achieve different effects, depending upon the occasion. As a result, social behavior is more extensive than comparable behavior in a non-social environment. It is also more flexible, in the sense that the organism may shift more readily from one response to another when its behavior is not effective.

Since the reinforcing organism often may not respond appropriately, reinforcement is likely to be intermittent. The result will depend upon the schedule. An occasional success may fit the pattern of *variable-interval* reinforcement, and the behavior will show a stable intermediate strength. We might express this by saying that we respond to people with less confidence than we respond to the inanimate environment but are not so quickly convinced that the reinforcing mechanism is "out of order." The persistent behavior which we call teasing is generated by a *variable-ratio* schedule, which arises from the fact that the reinforcer responds only when a request has been repeated until it becomes aversive—when it acquires nuisance value.

The contingency established by a social reinforcing system may slowly change. In teasing, for example, the mean ratio of unreinforced to reinforced responses may rise. The child who has gained attention with three requests on the average may later find it necessary to make five, then seven, and so on. The change corresponds to an increasing tolerance for aversive stimulation in the reinforcing person. Contingencies of positive reinforcement may also drift in the same direction. When a reinforcing person becomes harder and harder to please, the reinforcement is made contingent upon more extensive or highly differentiated behavior. By beginning with reasonable specifications and gradually increasing the requirements, very demanding contingencies may be made effective which would be quite powerless without this history. The result is often a sort of human bondage. The process is easily demonstrated in animal experimentation where extremely energetic, persistent, or complicated responses which would otherwise be quite impossible may be established through a gradual change in contingencies. A special case arises in the use of piecework pay. As production increases, and with it the wages received, the piecework scale may be changed so that more work is required per unit of reinforcement. The eventual result may be a much higher rate of production at only a slight increase in pay—a condition of reinforcement which could not have become effective except through some such gradual approach.

We have already noted another peculiarity of social reinforcement: the reinforcing system is seldom independent of the behavior reinforced. This is exemplified by the indulgent but ambitious parent who withholds reinforcement when his child is behaving energetically, either to demonstrate the child's ability or to make the most efficient use of available reinforcers, but who reinforces an early response when the child begins to show extinction. This is a sort of combined ratio-and-interval reinforcement. Educational reinforcements are in general of this sort. They are basically governed by ratio schedules, but they are not unaffected by the level of the behavior reinforced. As in piecework pay, more and more may be demanded for each reinforcement as performance improves, but remedial steps may be needed.

Schedules of reinforcement which adjust to the rate of the behavior reinforced do not often occur in inorganic nature. The reinforcing agent which modifes the contingency in terms of the behavior must be sensitive and complex. But a reinforcing system which is affected in this way may contain inherent defects which lead to unstable behavior. This may explain why the reinforcing contingencies of society cause undesirable behavior more often than those apparently comparable contingencies in inanimate nature.

The Social Stimulus

Another person is often an important source of stimulation. Since some properties of such stimuli appear to defy physical description, it has been tempting to assume that a special process of intuition or empathy is involved when we react to them. What, for example, are the physical dimensions of a smile? In everyday life we identify smiles with considerable accuracy and speed, but the scientist would find it a difficult task. He would have to select some identifying response in the individual under investigation—perhaps the verbal response, "That is a smile"—and then investigate all the facial expressions which evoked it. These expressions would be physical patterns and presumably susceptible to geometric analysis, but the number of different patterns to be tested would be very great. Moreover, there would be borderline instances where the stimulus control was defective or varied from moment to moment.

That the final identification of the stimulus pattern called a smile would be much more complicated and time-consuming than the identification of a smile in daily life does not mean that scientific observation neglects some important approach available to the layman. The difference is that the scientist must identify a stimulus with respect to the behavior of someone else. He cannot trust his own personal reaction. In studying an objective pattern as simple and as common to everyone as "triangle," the scientist may safely use his own identification of the pattern. But such a pattern as "smile" is another matter. A social stimulus, like any other stimulus, becomes important in controlling behavior because of the contingencies into which it enters. The facial expressions which we group together and call "smiles" are important because they are the occasions upon which certain kinds of social behavior receive certain kinds of reinforcement. Any unity in the stimulus class follows from these contingencies. But these are determined by the culture and by a particular history. Even in the behavior of a single individual there may be several groups of patterns all of which come to be called smiles if they all stand in the same relation to reinforcing contingencies. The scientist may appeal to his own culture or history only when it resembles that of the subject he is studying. Even then he may be wrong, just as the layman's quick practical reaction may be wrong, especially when he attempts to identify a smile in a different culture.

This issue is far reaching because it applies to many descriptive terms, such as "friendly" and "aggressive," without which many students of social behavior would feel lost. The nonscientist working within his own culture may satisfactorily describe the behavior of others with expressions of this sort. Certain patterns of behavior have become important to him because of the reinforcements based upon them: he judges behavior to be friendly or unfriendly by its social consequences. But his frequent success does not mean that there are objective aspects of behavior which are as independent of the behavior of the observer as are such geometrical forms as squares, circles, and triangles. He is observing an objective event—the behavior of an organism; there is no question here of physical status, but only of the significance of classificatory terms. The geometrical properties of "friendliness" or "aggressiveness" depend upon the culture, change with the culture, and vary with the individual's experience within a single culture.

Some social stimuli are also frequently set apart because a very slight physical event appears to have an extremely powerful effect. But this is true of many nonsocial stimuli as well; to one who has been injured in a fire a faint smell of smoke may be a stimulus of tremendous power. Social stimuli are important because the social reinforcers with which they are correlated are important. An example of the surprising power of an apparently trivial event is the common experience of "catching someone's eye." Under certain circumstances the change in behavior which follows may be considerable, and this has led to the belief that some nonphysical "understanding" passes from one person to another. But the reinforcing contingencies offer an alternative explanation. Our behavior may be very different in the presence or absence of a particular person. When we simply see such a person in a crowd, our available repertoire immediately changes. If, in addition, we catch his eye, we fall under the control of an even more restrictive stimulus—he is not only present, he is watching us. The same effect might arise without catching his eye if we saw him looking at us in a mirror. When we catch his eye, we also know that he knows that we are looking at him. A much narrower repertoire of behavior is under the control of this specific stimulus: if we are to behave in a way which he censures, it will now be not only in opposition to his wishes but brazen. It may also be important that "we know that he knows that we know that he is looking at us" and so on. . . . In catching someone's eye, in short, a social stimulus suddenly arises which is important because of the reinforcements which depend upon it. The importance will vary with the occasion. We may catch someone's eye in a flirtation, under amusing circumstances, at a moment of common guilt, and so on—with an appropriate degree of control in each case. The importance of the event is seen in the use we make of the behavior of "looking someone in the eye" as a test of other variables responsible for such characteristics of behavior as honesty, brazenness, embarrassment, or guilt.

Social stimuli are important to those to whom social reinforcement is important. The saleman, the courtier, the entertainer, the seducer, the child striving for the favor of his parents, the "climber" advancing from one social level to another, the politically ambitious—all are likely to be affected by subtle properties of human behavior, associated with favor or disapproval, which are overlooked by many people. It is significant that the novelist, as a specialist in the description of human behavior, often shows an early history in which social reinforcement has been especially important.

The social stimulus which is least likely to vary from culture to culture is that which controls the imitative behavior described in Chapter VII. The ultimate consequences of imitative behavior may be peculiar to the culture, but the correspondence between the behavior of the imitator and that of the imitatee is relatively independent of it. Imitative behavior is not entirely free of style or convention, but the special features of the imitative repertoire characteristic of a group are slight. When a sizable repertoire has once been developed, imitation may be so skillful, so easy, so "instinctive," that we are likely to attribute it to some such special mode of interpersonal contact as empathy. It is easy to point to a history of reinforcement, however, which generates behavior of this sort.

THE SOCIAL EPISODE

We may analyze a social episode by considering one organism at a time. Among the variables to be considered are those generated by a second organism. We then consider the behavior of the second organism, assuming the first as a source of variables. By putting the analyses together we reconstruct the episode. The account is complete if it embraces all the variables needed to account for the behavior of the individuals. Consider, for example, the interaction between predator and prey called "stalking." We may limit ourselves to that behavior of the predator which reduces the distance between itself and its prey and that behavior of the prey which increases the distance. A reduction in the distance is positively reinforcing to the predator and negatively reinforcing to the prey; an increase is negatively reinforcing to the predator and positively reinforcing to the prey. If the predator is stimulated by the prey, but not vice versa, then the predator simply reduces the distance between itself and the prey as rapidly as possible. If the prey is stimulated by the predator, however, it will respond by increasing the distance. This need not be open flight, but simply any movement sufficient to keep the distance above a critical value. In the behavior called stalking the predator reduces the distance as rapidly as possible without stimulating the prey to increase it. When the distance has become short enough, the predator may break into open pursuit, and the prey into open flight. A different sort of interaction follows.

A similar formulation may be applied where "distance" is not so simple as in movement in space. In conversation, for example, one speaker may approach a topic from which another moves away uneasily. The first may be said to stalk the second if he approaches the topic in such a way as to avoid stimulating the second to escape. We eliminate the figure of speech in "approaching a topic" by analyzing the reinforcing and aversive properties of verbal stimuli.

Another example of a social episode is leading and following. This generally arises when two or more individuals are reinforced by a single external system which requires their combined action—for example, when two men pull on a rope which cannot be moved by either one alone. The behavior of one is similar to that of the other, and the interaction may be slight. If the timing is important, however, one man will pace the other. The first sets a rhythmic pattern relatively independent of the second; the second times his behavior by that of the first. The first may facilitate this by amplifying the stimuli which affect the second—as by saying, "All together now, one, two, three, *pull!*" Collateral behavior with a marked temporal pattern—for example, a sea chanty—may reduce the importance of the leader but will not eliminate it.

The nature of leading and following is clearer when the two kinds of behavior differ considerably and the contingency of reinforcement is complex. A division of labor is usually then required. The leader is primarily under the control of external variables, while the follower is under the control of the leader. A simple example is ballroom-dancing. The reinforcing consequences—both positive and negative—depend upon a double contingency: (1) the dancers must execute certain sequences of steps in certain directions with respect to the available space and (2) the behavior of one must be timed to correspond with that of the other. This double contingency is usually divided between the dancers. The leader sets the pattern and responds to the available space; the follower is controlled by the movements of the leader and responds appropriately to satisfy the second contingency.

It is easy to set up cooperative situations with two or more experimental organisms and to observe the emergence of leading and following. In a demonstration experiment two pigeons are placed in adjacent cages separated by a glass plate. Side by side near the glass are two vertical columns of three buttons each, one column being available to each pigeon. The apparatus is set to reinforce both pigeons with food but only when they peck corresponding buttons simultaneously. Only one pair of buttons is effective at any one time. The situation calls for a rather complicated cooperation. The pigeons must explore the three pairs to discover which is effective, and they must strike both buttons in each pair at the same time. These contingencies must be divided. One bird—the leader—explores the buttons, striking them in some characteristic order or more or less at random. The other bird—the follower—strikes the button opposite whichever button is being struck by the leader. The behavior of the follower is controlled almost exclusively by the behavior of the leader, whose behavior in turn is controlled by the apparatus which randomizes the reinforcements among the three pairs of buttons. Two followers or two leaders placed together can solve the problem only accidentally. The function of leader may shift from one bird to another over a period of time, and a temporary condition may arise in which both are followers. The behavior then resembles that of two people who, meeting under circumstances where the convention of passing on the right is not strongly observed, oscillate from side to side before passing.

Between such an experiment and the relation of leader to follower in politics, for example, there is more than a simple analogy. Most cultures produce some people whose behavior is mainly controlled by the exigencies of a given situation. The same cultures also produce people whose behavior is controlled mainly by the behavior of others. Some such division of the contingencies in any cooperative venture seems to be required. The leader is not wholly independent of the follower, however, for his behavior requires the support of corresponding behavior on the part of others, and to the extent that cooperation is necessary, the leader is, in fact, led by his followers.

Verbal Episodes

Verbal behavior supplies many examples in which one person is said to have an effect upon another beyond the scope of the physical sciences. Words are said to "symbolize" or "express" ideas or meanings, which are then "communicated" to the listener. An alternative formulation would require too much space here, but a single example may suggest how this sort of social behavior may be brought within range of a natural science. Consider a simple episode in which A asks B for a cigarette and gets one. To account for the occurrence and maintenance of this behavior we have to show that A provides adequate stimuli and reinforcement for B and vice versa. A's response, "Give me a cigarette," would be quite ineffective in a purely mechanical environment. It has been conditioned by a verbal community which occasionally reinforces it in a particular way. A has long since formed a discrimination by virtue of which the response is not emitted in the absence of a member of that community. He has also probably formed more subtle discriminations in which he is more likely to respond in the presence of an "easy touch." B has either reinforced this response in the past or resembles someone who has. The first interchange between the two is in the direction of B to A: B is a discriminative stimulus in the presence of which A emits the verbal response. The second interchange is in the direction A to B: the response generates auditory stimuli acting upon B. If B is already disposed to give a cigarette to A—for example, if B is "anxious to please A" or "in love with A," the auditory pattern is a discriminative stimulus for the response of giving a cigarette. B does not offer cigarettes indiscriminately; he waits for a response from A as an occasion upon which a cigarette will be accepted. A's acceptance depends upon a condition of deprivation in which the receipt of a cigarette is reinforcing. This is also the condition in which A emits the response, "Give me a cigarette," and the contingency which comes to control B's behavior is thus established. The third interchange is A's receipt of the cigarette from B. This is the reinforcement of A's original response and completes our account of it. If B is reinforced simply by evidence of the effect of the cigarette upon A, we may consider B's account closed also. But such behavior is more likely to remain a stable part of the culture if these evidences are made conspicuous. If A not only accepts the cigarette but also says, "Thank you," a fourth interchange takes place: the auditory stimulus is a conditioned reinforcer to B, and A produces it just because it is. B may in turn increase the likelihood of future "Thank you's" on the part of A by saying, "Not at all."

When B's behavior in responding to A's verbal response is already strong, we call A's response a "request." If B's behavior requires other conditions, we have to reclassify A's response. If "Give me a cigarette" is not only the occasion for a particular response but also a conditioned aversive stimulus from which B can escape only by complying, then A's response is a "demand." In this case, B's behavior is reinforced by a reduction in the threat generated by A's demand, and A's "Thank you" is mainly effective as a conspicuous indication that the threat has been reduced.

Even such a brief episode is surprisingly complex, but the four or five interchanges between A and B can all be specified in physical terms and can scarcely be ignored if we are to take such an analysis seriously. That the complete episode occupies only a few seconds does not excuse us from the responsibility of identifying and observing all its features.

Unstable Interaction

Although many of these interlocking social systems are stable, others show a progressive change. A trivial example is the behavior of a group of people who enter an unfamiliar room containing a sign which reads, "Silence, please." Such a verbal stimulus is generally effective only in combination with the behavior of other members of the group. If many people are talking noisily, the sign may have little or no effect. But let us assume that our group enters silently. After a moment two members least under the control of the sign begin to whisper. This slightly alters the situation for other members so that they also begin to whisper. This alters the situation for the two who are least under the control of the sign, and they then begin to speak in a low voice. This further changes the situation for the others, who also begin to speak in low voices. Eventually the conversation may be quite noisy. This is a simple "autocatalytic" process arising from a repeated interchange between the members of the group.

Another example is a practice common on sailing ships in the eighteenth century. Sailors would amuse themselves by tying several boys or younger men in a ring to a mast by their left hands, their right hands remaining free. Each boy was given a stick or whip and told to strike the boy in front of him whenever he felt himself being struck by the boy behind. The game was begun by striking one boy lightly. This boy then struck the boy ahead of him, who in turn struck the boy next ahead, and so on. Even though it was clearly in the interest of the group that all blows be gentle, the inevitable result was a furious lashing. The unstable elements in this interlocking system are easy to identify. We cannot assume that each boy gave precisely the kind of blow he received because this is not an easy comparison to make. It is probable that he underestimated the strength of the blows he gave. The slightest tendency to give a little harder than he received would produce the ultimate effect. Moreover, repeated blows probably generate an emotional disposition in which one naturally strikes harder. A comparable instability is seen when two individuals engage in a casual conversation which leads to a vituperative quarrel. The aggressive effect of a remark is likely to be underestimated by the man who makes it, and repeated effects generate further aggression. The principle is particularly dangerous when the conversation consists of an exchange of notes between governments.

SUPPORTING VARIABLES IN THE SOCIAL EPISODE

Although the interchange between two or more individuals whose behavior is interlocked in a social system must be explained in its entirety, certain variables may remain obscure. For example, we often observe merely that one person is predisposed to act with respect to another in certain ways. The mother caring for her child is a familiar case in point. The social emotions are by definition observed simply as predispositions to act in ways which may be positively or negatively reinforcing to others. Such terms as "favor" and "friendship" refer to tendencies to administer positive reinforcement, and love might be analyzed as the mutual tendency of two individuals to reinforce each other, where the reinforcement may or may not be sexual.

Sometimes a reciprocal interchange explains the behavior in terms of reinforcement. Each individual has something to offer by way of reinforcing the other, and once established, the interchange sustains itself. We may detect mutual reinforcement in the case of mother and child. Instead of tendencies to behave in certain ways, they may illustrate tendencies to be reinforced by certain social stimuli. Aside from this, the group may manipulate special variables to generate tendencies to behave in ways which result in the reinforcement of others. The group may reinforce the individual for telling the truth, helping others, returning favors, and reinforcing others in turn for doing the same. The Golden Rule is a generalized statement of the behavior thus supported by the group. Many important interlocking systems of social behavior could not be maintained without such conventional practices. This is an important point in explaining the success of the cultural practices characteristic of a group.

To the extent that prior reinforcement by the group determines the suitability of the behavior of the individual for an interlocking system, the system itself is not wholly self-sustaining. The instability is demonstrated when an individual who is not adequately controlled by the culture gains a temporary personal advantage by exploiting the system. He lies, refuses to return a favor, or breaks a promise, but this exploitation of the system eventually leads to its deterioration. The boy in the fable cries, "Wolf!" because certain patterns of social behavior have been established by the community and he finds the resulting behavior of his neighbors amusing. The aggressive door-to-door salesman imposes upon the good manners of the housewife to hold her attention in the same way. In each case the system eventually breaks down: the neighbors no longer respond to the cry of "Wolf!" and the housewife slams the door.

The behavior of two individuals may be related in a social episode, not primarily through an interchange between them, but through common external variables. The classic example is competition. Two individuals come into competition when the behavior of one can be reinforced only at the cost of the reinforcement of the other. Social behavior as here defined is not necessarily involved. Catching a rabbit before it runs away is not very different from catching it before someone else does. In the latter case, a social interchange may occur as a by-product if one individual attacks the other. Cooperation, in which the reinforcement of two or more individuals depends upon the behavior of both of them, is obviously not the opposite of competition, for it appears to require an interlocking system.

THE GROUP AS A BEHAVING UNIT

It is common to speak of families, clans, nations, races, and other groups as if they were individuals. Such concepts as "the group mind," "the instinct of the herd," and "national character" have been invented to support this practice. It is always an individual who behaves, however. The problem presented by the larger group is to explain why many individuals behave *together*. Why does a boy join a gang? Why does a man join a club or fall in with a lynching mob? We may answer questions of this sort by examining the variables generated by the group which encourage the behavior of joining and conforming. We cannot do this simply by saying that two individuals will behave together cooperatively if it is "in their common interest to do so." We must point to specific variables affecting the behavior of each of them. From a practical point of view, as in setting up cooperative behavior in the pigeon demonstration just described, an analysis of the relevant variables is also essential. The particular contingencies controlling the behavior of the cooperators must be carefully maintained.

Some progress toward explaining participation in a group is made by the analysis of imitation. In general, behaving as others behave is likely to be reinforcing. Stopping to look in a store window which has already attracted a crowd is more likely to be reinforced than stopping to look in store windows which have not attracted crowds. Using words which have already been used by others, rather than strange terms, is more likely to be reinforced positively or to be free of aversive consequences. Situations of this sort multiplied a thousandfold generate and sustain an enormous tendency to behave as others are behaving.

To this principle we must add another of perhaps greater importance. If it is always the individual who behaves, it is nevertheless the group which has the more powerful effect. By joining a group the individual increases his power to achieve reinforcement. The man who pulls on a rope is reinforced by the movement of the rope regardless of the fact that others may need to be pulling at the same time. The man attired in full uniform, parading smartly down the street, is reinforced by the acclaim of the crowd even though it would not be forthcoming if he were marching alone. The coward in the lynching mob is reinforced when his victim writhes in terror as he shouts at him—regardless of the fact that a hundred others are, and must be, shouting at him also. The reinforcing consequences generated by the group easily exceed the sums of the consequences which could be achieved by the members acting separately. The total reinforcing effect is enormously increased.

The interchanges within a group and the heightened effect of the group upon the environment may be studied within the framework of a natural science. They need to be explored further before we accept the proposition that there are social units, forces, and laws which require scientific methods of a fundamentally different sort.

— · — · — · — · — · — · — · — · — · — · —

NEAL E. MILLER
JOHN DOLLARD

*Social Learning and Imitation**

A PATTERN CASE OF IMITATION

Imitative behavior has attracted the attention of humanists and social psychologists for centuries. The small child sits in father's chair, scuttles around in his carpet slippers, or wants her hair done up like mother's. "Copy-cat" is a well-known reproach to the socially aspiring. Explanations of imitative behavior have varied from time to time, but each serious attempt has leaned heavily upon a particular psychological theory. The analysis proposed here is no exception. It rests upon a psychology which may be called, in brief, a reinforcement theory of social learning. It derives from the work of Pavlov (1927), Thorndike (1911; 1914; 1940), and Watson (1919), although it should not be confused with the detailed position of any one of these writers. Its best current statement and synthesis have been made by Hull (1943). The basic position has already been outlined. The present object is to see its relevance in a restatement of the nature of imitative behavior.

Common speech has already directed attention to imitative acts. Language, being a folk creation, would not be expected to provide a very exact discrimination of the forms of action which it lumps under the general term "imitation." It is, indeed, this inclusiveness of common speech which poses the scientific problem and demands that the scientist make further and more exact distinctions. The authors have decided to use three phases to indicate the sub-mechanisms which seem to account for all or most of the cases for which the term "imitation" is ordinarily used. These mechanisms are: *same* behavior; *matched-dependent* behavior; and *copying*. The authors agree with Faris (1937) that no single sub-mechanism will adequately account for all cases of imitation, but disagree with

*Neal E. Miller and John Dollard, *Social Learning and Imitation* (New Haven: Yale University Press, 1941), pp. 91–97, 119–121, 146–148, 152, 165, 181–182, 183, 272–273. Reprinted by permission.

him in that they hold that the three sub-mechanisms, derived from a single general learning theory, suffice to account for all cases.

Same behavior does not require the detailed analysis which will be given to the other two types of imitation. The characteristic fact is that two people perform the same act in response to independent stimulation by the same cue, each having learned by himself to make the response. Two persons, for instance, may take the same bus because each reads the card indicating its destination. Similarly, the crowd at a football game resolves itself into an ordered unit, each group of individuals presenting their tickets at the proper gate, each independently discriminating the letters above the proper doors and making similar adaptive responses. *Same* behavior may be learned with or without imitative aids.

Copying also will be mentioned only briefly at this point. In the characteristic case, one person learns to model his behavior on that of another. It is crucial that the copier know when his behavior is the same; the essential learning in copying centers around this knowledge. The copier must have criteria for the sameness and difference of the acts he performs. He must be aware that his copy falls within the band of tolerance as a match for the model act. Training to copy often begins with an external critic who rewards similarity and punishes dissimilarity; in the end the copier must be able to respond independently to the cues of sameness and difference.

The third mechanism, that of matched-dependent behavior, will be discussed in detail in the present chapter. It is extremely important in social life. It tends to occur whenever one person is older, shrewder, or more skilled than another. Younger people match behavior with, and are dependent upon, older people. Stupid children must, perforce, follow their more intelligent associates. Householders prepare for an ice storm when their scientists (meteorologists) give the sign. Social climbers must follow their status superiors through an intricate routine of watching and imitating. Learners of a foreign language must learn the appropriate situations in which to use certain words by following those who already speak the foreign tongue. The study of socialization in children offers innumerable examples where children match behavior with their elders and are dependent on them for cues as to when to do so. It will be useful and perhaps interesting to discuss one full-bodied example of such dependence matching as it was recorded by a gifted child observer. Such examples force us to fit theory to the actualities of social life. Since imaginary examples often lead to imaginary solutions, the authors have insisted that every example presented have an actual location in space and time and that they be able to give names and circumstances in further elaboration if necessary.

The following case is instructive just because the imitative behavior was maladaptive. Two boys—Jim, aged six, and Bobby, aged three—were playing a game with their father in the living room of their house. The father explained that he would hide two pieces of candy while the children were out of the room. When he gave the signal, they were to return and look for the sweets. When each child found his piece of candy, he could eat it. The father put one piece of candy under a pillow on the davenport and the other beside the radio cabinet. The older child came into the room, followed by his younger brother. The older boy, Jim, looked in the fireplace. The younger brother, Bobby, followed and looked there also. Jim looked inside the piano bench; so also did Bobby. Then Jim looked under the pillow on the davenport and found his piece of candy. Thereupon he stopped looking. Bobby was now helpless. He went again and looked under the pillow where his older brother had found his candy, but of course had no success. Finally, Bobby's candy was produced and given to him.

On a succeeding trial of the same game, exactly the same thing happened. The younger brother would look only in the places already examined by his older brother. He could not respond to place cues by looking for himself.

This behavior, comical when it occurred, is nevertheless worthy of attention. It could not have been acquired in previous situations of the identical kind since this occasion was the first when the game was played. Perhaps it was acquired in other but, in some respects, similar situations. A search of the life histories of the children proved that the latter was the correct surmise. The younger child had been rewarded for matching behavior with the older in a large number of situations which had cue elements in common with that of the game. It appears, therefore, that the tendency to match had generalized in this case from other similar cues to the cues of the new game. Out of the many rewarded examples of dependence matching discovered as the "background" for the game, one is selected for exposition. It is not advanced as proof of our theory. Such proof can come only from the better controlled conditions and the more exact communication of the experiments to be subsequently reported. The example, however, is intimately related to the structure of the experiments which follow. It shows, pattern perfect, the crucial elements in one type of imitative behavior.

A CASE OF MATCHED-DEPENDENT BEHAVIOR

The same two children, each a year younger, were playing in their bedroom, which was adjacent to the family kitchen. The kitchen opened upon a back stairway. It was six o'clock in the evening, the hour when father usually returned home, bearing candy for the two children. While playing in the bedroom, Jim heard a footfall on the stairs; it was the familiar sound of father's return. The younger child, however, had not identified this critical cue. Jim ran to the kitchen to be on hand when father came in the back door. Bobby happened on this occasion to be running in the direction of the kitchen and behind Jim. On many other occasions, probably many hundreds, he had not happened to run when Jim did. He had, for instance, remained sitting, continued playing with his toys, run to the window instead of the door, and the like; but on this occasion, he was running behind his brother. Upon reaching the kitchen, Jim got his candy and Bobby his.

On subsequent nights with similar conditions, the younger child ran more frequently at the mere sight of his older brother running. When he ran, he received candy. Eventually, the behavior, under pressure of continued reward, became highly stabilized, and the younger child would run when the older ran, not only in this situation but in many others where time and place stimuli were different. He had learned in this one respect to *imitate* his older brother, but he had not learned to run at the sound of his father's footfall.

Apparently, learning in this and other similar situations, in which responding imitatively was rewarded, generalized to the game and was the source of the maladaptive imitation observed there. Since imitation was not rewarded in the game, we should expect a discrimination eventually to be established; the younger child should learn not to imitate in such a situation.

ANALYSIS OF THE BEHAVIOR OF THE IMITATOR CHILD

Bobby's behavior can be analyzed in the form of a learning paradigm, as follows:

Imitator

Drive . . . . Appetite for candy
Cue . . . . Leg-twinkle of brother
Response . . . . Running
Reward . . . . Eating candy

ANALYSIS OF LEADER'S BEHAVIOR

The leader's problem is slightly different; his behavior parses out as follows:

Leader

Drive . . . . Appetite for candy
Cue . . . . Father's footfall
Response . . . . Running
Reward . . . . Eating candy

The leader in this case is reacting to the stable environmental cue provided by culture, i.e., the father's footfall on the stair, but otherwise his problem is identical with that of the imitator, or follower. Jim had obviously completed his learning of the connection between footfall and the running response before Bobby had commenced his. It might be added that it is not essential in every analysis of this type of imitation to know all of the factors operating to determine the leader's act. It is enough actually to be sure that he is following a cue which the imitator cannot discriminate.

COMPLETE PARADIGM OF MATCHED-DEPENDENT BEHAVIOR

The relationship between the acts of leader and imitator can be put together into one diagram as follows:

	Leader		*Imitator*
Drive	Appetite for candy		Appetite for candy
Cue	Father's footfall	____ dependent ___ ➤	Leg-twinkle of leader
Response	Running ========== matched ___ ➤		Running
Reward	Eating candy		Eating candy

It will be noted above that the responses are *matched*, thus fulfilling one important condition of imitative behavior. It is further clear that the response of the imitator is elicited by cues from the act of the leader. His behavior is therefore *dependent* on that of the leader. Simple, or simple-minded, as an analysis so detailed of an incident so humble may seem, it represents, nevertheless, a large class of cases of social behavior which is called imitative. Such cases are frequently encountered when the history of the act is not known, and therefore the observer cannot be certain that the imitative act was learned. Every case ought at least to be examined to see whether the variables called for by the learning hypothesis are not in fact present.

In order to emphasize the crucial rôle of learning principles in the behavior of the imitator child above, one can look at the elements of the paradigm from another standpoint. If Bobby had had no drive—that is, if he had not been hungry for candy—it would have been impossible for reinforcement to occur, and the connection between the response and the cue of the leg-twinkle would not have been fixed. If he had been unable to perceive his brother's cue—if, say, he had been blind—it would have been impossible for the learning to occur. If he had been unable to make the response of running—if, for instance, he had been kept in the room by a barrier which only his brother could leap—it would have been impossible to learn the imitative response. If he had not be rewarded on the occasions when he did follow his brother, he could not have learned to imitate. This example should indicate, therefore, that imitative acts of this type follow the laws of learning. What is crucial about them is that the cue from the leader's behavior is often more stable than other cues provided by the environment. If the leader child is, for instance, responding to the cue of the hands of a clock, he can make his response more regularly and discriminatingly than can the imitator child, who must depend on the cue of the leader's action. If, for example, the leader is gone for the day, the imitator child will be unable to make his response at all.

In social life, individuals are constantly being placed in situations analogous to the one above. The young, the stupid, the subordinate, and the unskilled must depend on the older, the brighter, the superordinate, and the skilled to read cues which they cannot themselves discriminate. They can respond only in the wake of those better instructed. Society, as will be shown, is so organized that the situation diagrammed above occurs over and over again. Imitative responses are not confined to childhood. They can and do appear at any time along the life line where the situation calls for them. They can be outgrown and abandoned when the need for them disappears; or they can be a permanent feature of the life of every individual, as in the case of dependence upon the skill of the political leader, the scientist, or the expert craftsman.

★ ★ ★

LEARNING OF IMITATION

In this series of experiments, albino rats that had been living together in a conventional type of wire cage were first tested to see if they had any initial tendency to perform a very simple type of imitative response. The response selected was that of turning in the same direction as a leader at the junction of a T-maze. It was found that animals raised under these conditions had no marked initial tendency either to imitate by going in the same direction as the leader or to non-imitate by going in the opposite direction. Then the animals were divided into two groups. One group was rewarded for going in the same direction as a leader; the other group was rewarded for going in the opposite direction. Under these conditions, it was found that the two groups gradually learned to imitate and to non-imitate, respectively.

In order to make the situation more parallel to many of the social situations in which imitation would be expected to be learned, the responses of the leaders were guided by black and white cards which they had learned to use as cues. Control tests, in which the cards were removed and leaders were used that had been trained to make either right or left turns, indicated that under the conditions of the experiment the animals learned to use the response of the leader as their cue.

After this simple type of imitation had been learned in one situation, tests indicated that it generalized, that is, appeared without additional training in other similar situations. The two groups trained to imitate and non-imitate white leaders showed a highly reliable tendency, respectively, to imitate and non-imitate black leaders. After the two groups had learned to imitate and non-imitate when motivated by hunger, they showed a highly reliable tendency to imitate and non-imitate when motivated by thirst. After learning to imitate and non-imitate on the long, narrow runway of the T-maze, they showed a tendency, which, however, was not statistically reliable, to imitate and non-imitate in stepping off a small, square starting platform onto one of four adjacent square platforms.

That animals can learn the response of imitating (or non-imitating) under appropriate conditions of drive, cue, and reward, and that this response learned in one situation generalizes to other similar situations, confirms the theoretical analysis made in the preceding chapter. The next step is to determine experimentally whether or not such learning also occurs in human subjects, then to proceed further with an analysis of the extent to which the conditions under which one would expect imitation to be learned are actually present in our society.

Before this analysis, however, the relevance of this work to further animal experimentation may be briefly examined. Previous experiments (referred to in more detail in Appendix 2 on the history of imitation) have tested animals to see whether or not they start imitating when first introduced into a test situation. The experimenters have not, however, deliberately set up specific conditions in which the animal could be observed to learn to imitate. Relatively often, different experimenters have secured contradictory results. If one assumes that imitation is wholly an instinctive matter, such contradictory results are somewhat puzzling. If one assumes that imitation can be learned, it might be expected that experimenters would secure different results provided that the past environment of some animals had happened to reward imitation, while that of others had not.

More consistent results are to be expected when experimenters are more careful to test separately for the following different factors:

1. An innate, or instinctive, tendency to imitate the response in question;
2. An innate capacity to learn to imitate the response in question;
3. Environmental conditions which have rewarded the animal for learning to imitate under conditions similar enough to the experimental set-up so that generalization can occur.

In the present experiment, the second and third of these factors were found to be of crucial importance. Since the life history of the animals was not rigorously controlled from birth, one cannot certainly conclude whether or not innate tendencies to imitate had ever been present. The remote possibility that they had been present but had been overridden before the start of the experiment by uncontrolled rewards for non-imitating cannot entirely be ruled out. Though the evidence against instinct is not conclusive, the evidence for the influence of learning is overwhelming. In the presence of such definite evidence that even an animal as lowly as the rat can learn to imitate, the burden of further proof would seem to rest with anyone wishing to claim that any specific act of imitation is not learned.

SECONDARY DRIVES OF IMITATION AND RIVALRY

Mary, at three and a half, has been playing in the snow with her friend Jean, who is about the same age. The mother puts Bill in his Taylor-tot (a small cart which can be pulled by a handle). Mary had previously paid no attention to Bill in this situation. The record reads:

> Jean said, "I want to pull Bill."
> Mary immediately said, "No, I want the first turn."
> I said, "Well, you can take turns at it. Mary, you can take the first turn, and then Jean." Mary pulled Bill for about fifteen feet and then dropped the handle and asked me to pull him. I said, "Now it is Jean's turn." Jean pulled him up the driveway.

The situation is not clear as concerns Jean's motive. Her history is virtually unknown, and we cannot, therefore, offer any convincing presumptions as to how she had learned to want to pull a little boy in a Taylor-tot. It must be accepted as a matter of fact, for the purpose of this analysis, that she did. It seems likely that she had learned to carry out such behavior with her own little sister under pressure of parental approval. This being conceded for the sake of the discussion, the imitative analysis would proceed as follows:

	Jean		*Mary*
Drive	Secondary–desire for approval		Rivalry
Cue	Boy in Taylor-tot, mother, etc.	dependent ----►	Jean's request to pull boy
Response	Request to pull boy	matched ----►	Request to pull boy
Reward	Unknown		Success in rivalry

It would seem that Mary's tendency to match behavior with another has here become a secondary drive, which can be called a drive to imitate. Its history is very clear from the record of her previous behavior. She had learned that acts that other people carry out are very likely to be fun (that is, tension reducing). Examples would be eating, drinking, and carrying through the various appetitive drives based upon these. She had also learned that this fun occurred very frequently when she matched her acts with another's. She had repeatedly eaten, for instance, with other children, so that their eating behavior tended to become a cue stimulus for her own. The imitative drive by itself, however, carried her only to the point of stimulating her to do what the other child was already doing. Mary has further learned that there are some situations in which only one person at a time can make a desired response, and that the other person must wait. This applies, for example, to getting the first piece of birthday cake, to being picked up first by a parent, to being swung by an adult. There is also operative in the situation a cultural "first come first served" principle, in which the parents grant favors to those who make the first demand for them. Verbalized for Mary, the attitude would read like this: "If I get there first, I will get the most gratifying result the quickest." Actually, Mary's reactions were probably more direct than such a formulation might imply. In many different situations she had been rewarded for striving to be first; hence in this situation she doubtless strove to be first without additional stimulation from thoughts about the probability of reward.

In families where there is an actual shortage of food, this rivalry factor frequently leads children to learn to eat very rapidly. The reward for quick eating is more of the scarce food.

★ ★ ★

These cases, it is hoped, suggest that complex social acts are susceptible to analysis from the standpoint of the principles and conditions of learning. They supplement the simpler cases where drive is direct and biological, reward is a reduction or primary drive, the cues are distinctive, and the response is of a gross muscular type. The possibilities of effective social analysis are greatly increased when it is realized that drive and reward can be acquired and complex, that cue patterns may be very intricate, and that responses may include verbal or other cue-producing types such as those involved in foresight and reasoning. Every principle and theorem of learning theory is doubtless involved at some time in some example of imitation. Mechanisms ranging from simple, almost reflex responses to the more elaborate responses which produce strong drives and distinctive cues all appear in examples of imitative behavior. Future expansions of learning theory will probably contribute to the analysis of examples of imitation which are now obscure. A theory of imitation, or of any other form of social behavior, can be no more effective than the general psychological and social theory from which it is derived. If the foregoing interpretations have been cogent for imitation, it seems likely that a similar pattern of analysis could be successfully undertaken for such phenomena as sympathy, suggestion, prestige, coöperation, and other social attitudes.

★ ★ ★

PRESTIGE MODELS

From the analysis of examples it has been found that one of the important conditions for the learning of imitation is the presence in our own society of hierarchies of individuals who differ greatly in the degree to which they have learned to make independently those responses which are most likely to be rewarded. Children of different ages form such a hierarchy. Because an older child knows better when, where, and how to respond independently to difficult cues in the environment, younger children are often rewarded for learning to imitate or copy older children.

★ ★ ★

These experiments have confirmed the deduction from learning theory that an individual can learn to discriminate between leaders as good and bad models. He learns to copy the leader whom he is rewarded for copying and to non-copy the leader whom he is rewarded for non-copying. Once such learning occurs, it generalizes to new leaders, so that there is a tendency to copy the new leaders who are similar to those whom the individual has been rewarded for copying and to non-copy the new leaders who are similar to others whom he has been rewarded for non-copying. If a leader has acquired prestige as a good model for several responses, he is likely to be copied in other new responses; and if he has acquired "negative prestige" as a bad model for several responses, he is likely to be non-copied in other new responses.

There seem to be at least four classes of persons who are imitated by others. They are: (1) superiors in an age-grade hierarchy, (2) superiors in a hierarchy of social status, (3) superiors in an intelligence ranking system, and (4) superior technicians in any field. Each of these groups will be discussed in detail in its turn.

COPYING AND DIFFUSION

Diffusion takes place by means of the copying mechanism. Copying is expedient because it produces the to-be-rewarded response rapidly as compared with trial-and-error learning. Copying, like all learning, takes place under the pressure of drive. The presence of relevant sub-responses in the copying society is a great convenience in diffusion. The absence of such responses lengthens or prevents learning. Copying can become an acquired drive, providing copying behavior has been rewarded. Conditions of social contact offer the best opportunity for rapid copying, since they bring the learner into contact with the model and critic who can rapidly elicit the correct response. The prestige of the model is the crucial matter in mobilizing the copying drive and setting in motion the attempt to match responses. Copying is rarely exact, owing to various circumstances, chief among them the pressure put on the incoming habit by the preëxisting matrix of the receiving culture.

REFERENCES

Faris, E. (1937.) The nature of human nature. New York, McGraw-Hill.

Hull, C. L. (1943.) *Principles of behavior.* New York: Appleton-Century-Crofts.

Pavlov, I. P. (1927.) Conditioned reflexes. London, Humphrey Milford, Oxford University Press.

Thorndike, E. L. (1911.) Animal intelligence. New York, Macmillan.

———— (1914.) Educational psychology. New York, Columbia University, Bureau of Publications of Teachers College.

Watson, J. B. (1919.) Psychology from the standpoint of a behaviorist. Chicago, J. B. Lippincott.

ALBERT BANDURA

*Vicarious Learning and Modeling Theory**

SOCIAL LEARNING ANALYSIS OF OBSERVATIONAL LEARNING

Social learning theory assumes that modeling influences produce learning principally through their informative functions, and that observers acquire mainly symbolic representations of modeled activities rather than specific stimulus-response associations (Bandura, 1969a; 1971a). In this formulation, modeling phenomena are governed by four interrelated subprocesses.

Attentional Processes

A person cannot learn much by observation if he does not attend to, or recognize, the essential features of the model's behavior. One of the component functions in learning by example is therefore concerned with attentional processes. Simply exposing persons to models does not in itself ensure that they will attend closely to them, that they will necessarily select from the model's numerous characteristics the most relevant ones, of that they will even perceive accurately the aspects they happen to notice.

Among the numerous factors that determine observational experiences, associational preferences are undoubtedly of major importance. The people with whom one regularly associates delimit the types of behavior that one will repeatedly observe and hence learn most thoroughly. Opportunities for learning aggressive behavior obviously differ markedly for members of delinquent gangs and of Quaker groups.

Within any social group, some members are likely to command greater attention than others. The functional value of the behaviors displayed by different models is highly influential in determining which models will be closely observed and which will be ignored. Attention to models is also channeled by their interpersonal attraction. Models who possess interesting and winsome qualities are sought out, whereas those who lack pleasing characteristics tend to be ignored or rejected, even though they may excel in other ways.

Some forms of modeling are so intrinsically rewarding that they can hold the attention of people of all ages for extended periods. This is nowhere better illustrated than in televised modeling. Indeed, models presented in televised form are so effective in capturing attention that viewers learn the depicted behavior regardless of whether or not they are given extra incentives to do so (Bandura, Grusec & Menlove, 1966).

Retention Processes

A person cannot be much influenced by observation of a model's behavior if he has no memory of it. A second major function involved in observational learning concerns

---

*Reprinted by permission of the publisher from *Social Learning Theory* by Albert Bandura, General Learning Press, New York City 10016, 1971.

long-term retention of activities that have been modeled at one time or another. If one is to reproduce a model's behavior when he is no longer present to serve as a guide, the response patterns must be represented in memory in symbolic form. By this means past influences can achieve some degree of permanence.

Observational learning involves two representational systems—an imaginal and a verbal one. During exposure modeling stimuli produce, through a process of sensory conditioning, relatively enduring, retrievable images of modeled sequences of behavior. Indeed, under conditions where stimulus events are highly correlated, as when a name is consistently associated with a given person, it is virtually impossible to hear the name without experiencing imagery of the person's physical characteristics. Similarly, reference to activities (e.g., golfing, skiing), places (e.g., San Francisco, Paris), and things (e.g., one's automobile, Washington Monument) that one has previously observed immediately elicits vivid imaginal representations of the absent physical stimuli.

The second representational system, which probably accounts for the notable speed of observational learning and long-term retention of modeled contents by humans, involves verbal coding of observed events. Most of the cognitive processes that regulate behavior are primarily verbal rather than visual. The route traversed by a model can be acquired, retained, and later reproduced more accurately by verbal coding of the visual information into a sequence of right-left turns (e.g., RLRRL) than by reliance upon visual imagery of the itinerary. Observational learning and retention are facilitated by such codes because they carry a great deal of information in an easily stored form.

After modeled activities have been transformed into images and readily utilizable verbal symbols, these memory codes serve as guides for subsequent reproduction of matching responses. That symbolic coding can enhance observational learning is shown by studies conducted with both children (Bandura, Grusec & Menlove, 1966; Coates & Hartup, 1969) and adults (Gerst, 1969). Observers who code modeled activities into either words, concise labels, or vivid imagery learn and retain the behavior better than those who simply observe or are mentally preoccupied with other matters while watching the performance of others.

In addition to symbolic coding, rehearsal serves as an important memory aid. People who mentally rehearse or actually perform modeled patterns of behavior are less likely to forget them than those who neither think about nor practice what they have seen. Some of the behaviors that are learned observationally cannot be easily strengthened by overt enactment either because they are socially prohibited or because the necessary apparatus is lacking. It is, therefore, of considerable interest that mental rehearsal of modeled activities can increase their retention (Michael & Maccoby, 1961).

Some researchers (Gewirtz & Stingle, 1968) have been especially concerned about the conditions that produce the first imitative responses on the assumption that they help explain observational learning at later stages of development. There is some reason to question whether initial and later imitations have equivalent determinants. In early years imitative responses are evoked directly and immediately by models' actions. In later periods, imitative responses are usually performed in the absence of the models long after their behavior has been observed. Immediate imitation does not require much in the way of cognitive functioning because the behavioral reproduction is externally guided by the model's actions. By contrast, in delayed imitation, the absent modeled events must be internally represented, and factors such as symbolic transformation and cognitive organization of modeling stimuli, and covert rehearsal, which facilitate retention of acquired contents, serve as determinants of observational learning. The difference between physically prompted and delayed imitation is analogous to drawing a picture of one's automobile when it is at hand, and from memory. In the latter situation, the hand does not automatically sketch the car; rather, one must rely on memory guides, mainly in the form of mental images.

Motoric Reproduction Processes

The third component of modeling is concerned with processes whereby symbolic representations guide overt actions. To achieve behavioral reproduction, a learner must put together a given set of responses according to the modeled patterns. The amount of observational learning that a person can exhibit behaviorally depends on whether or not he has acquired the component skills. If he possesses the constituent elements, they can be easily integrated to produce new patterns of behavior, but if the response components are lacking, behavioral reproduction will be faulty. Given extensive deficits, the subskills required for complex performances must first be developed by modeling and practice.

Even though symbolic representations of modeled activities are acquired and retained, and the subskills exist, an individual may be unable to coordinate various actions in the required pattern and sequence due to physical limitations. A young child can learn observationally the behavior for driving an automobile, and be adept at executing the component responses, but if he is too short to operate the controls he cannot maneuver the vehicle successfully.

There is a third impediment at the behavioral level to skillful reproduction of modeled activities that have been learned observationally. In most coordinated motor skills, such as golf and swimming, performers cannot see the responses that they are making; hence, they must rely on ill-defined proprioceptive cues or verbal reports of onlookers. It is exceedingly difficult to guide actions that are not easily observed or to identify the corrective adjustments needed to achieve a close match of symbolic model and overt performance. In most everyday learning, people usually achieve rough approximations of new patterns of behavior by modeling, and refine them through self-corrective adjustments on the basis of informative feedback from performance.

Reinforcement and Motivational Processes

A person can acquire, retain, and possess the capabilities for skillful execution of modeled behavior, but the learning may rarely be activated into overt performance if it is negatively sanctioned or otherwise unfavorably received. When positive incentives are provided, observational learning, which previously remained unexpressed, is promptly translated into action (Bandura, 1965). Reinforcement influences not only regulate the overt expression of matching behavior, but they can affect the level of observational learning by controlling what people attend to and how actively they code and rehearse what they have seen.

For reasons given above, the provision of models, even prominent ones, will not automatically create similar patterns of behavior in others. If one is interested merely in producing imitative behavior, then some of the subprocesses included in the social learning analysis of modeling can be disregarded. A model who repeatedly demonstrates desired responses, instructs others to reproduce them, physically prompts the behavior when it fails to occur, and then administers powerful rewards, will eventually elicit matching responses in most people. It may require 1, 10, or 100 demonstration trials, but if one persists the desired behavior will eventually be evoked. If, on the other hand, one wishes to explain why modeling does or does not occur, then a variety of determinants must be considered. In any given instance lack of matching behavior following exposure to modeling influences may result from either failure to observe the relevant activities, inadequate coding of modeled events for memory representation, retention decrements, motoric deficiencies, or inadequate conditions of reinforcement.

LOCUS OF RESPONSE INTEGRATION IN OBSERVATIONAL LEARNING

New patterns of behavior are created by organizing constituent responses into certain patterns and sequences. Theories of modeling differ on whether the response integration occurs mainly at central or at peripheral levels. Operant conditioning formulations (Baer & Sherman, 1964; Gewirtz & Stingle, 1968) assume that response elements are selected out of overt performances by providing appropriate antecedent stimuli and by rewarding actions that resemble the modeled behavior and ignoring those that do not. The response components presumably thus extracted are sequentially chained by the influence of reinforcement to form more complex units of behavior. Since, in this view, behavior is organized into new patterns in the course of performance, learning requires overt responding and immediate reinforcement.

According to social learning theory, behavior is learned, at least in rough form, before it is performed. By observing a model of the desired behavior, an individual forms an idea of how response components must be combined and temporally sequenced to produce new behavioral configurations. The representation serves as a guide for behavioral reproduction. Observational learning without performance is abundantly documented in modeling studies using a nonresponse acquisition procedure (Bandura, 1969a; Flanders, 1968). After watching models perform novel modes of response, observers can later describe the entire pattern of behavior with considerable accuracy and, given the appropriate conditions, they often achieve errorless behavioral reproductions on the first test trial.

It is commonly believed that controversies about the locus of learning cannot be satisfactorily resolved because learning must be inferred from performance. This may very well be the case in experimentation with animals. To determine whether a rat has mastered a maze one must run him through it. With humans, there exists a reasonably accurate index of learning that is independent of motor performance. To measure whether a human has learned a maze by observing the successful performances of a model, one need only ask him to describe the correct pattern of right-left turns. Such an experiment would undoubtedly reveal that people can learn through modeling before they perform.

ROLE OF REINFORCEMENT IN OBSERVATIONAL LEARNING

Another issue in contention concerns the role of reinforcement in observational learning. As previously noted, reinforcement-oriented theories (Baer & Sherman, 1964; Miller & Dollard, 1941; Gewirtz & Stingle, 1968) assume that imitative responses must be reinforced in order to be learned. Social learning theory, on the other hand, distinguishes between learning and performances of matching behavior. Observational learning, in this view, can occur through observation of modeled behavior and accompanying cognitive activities without extrinsic reinforcement. This is not to say that mere exposure to modeled activities is, in itself, sufficient to produce observational learning. Not all stimulation that impinges on individuals is necessarily observed by them, and even if attended to, the influence of modeling stimuli alone does not ensure that they will be retained for any length of time.

Anticipation of reinforcement is one of several factors than can influence what is observed and what goes unnoticed. Knowing that a given model's behavior is effective in producing valued rewards or averting negative consequences can enhance observational learning by increasing observers' attentiveness to the model's actions. Moreover, anticipated reinforcement can strengthen retention of what has been learned observationally by motivating people to code and to rehearse modeled responses that have high value. Theories of modeling primarily differ in the manner in which reinforcement influences observational learning rather than in whether reinforcement may play a role in the acquisition process. As shown in the schematization below, the issue in dispute is whether reinforcement acts backwards to strengthen preceding imitative responses and their association to stimuli, or whether it facilitates learning through its effects on attentional, organizational, and rehearsal processes. It would follow from social learning theory that a higher level of observational learning would be achieved by informing observers in advance about the payoff value for adopting modeled patterns of behavior than by waiting until observers happen to imitate a model and then rewarding them for it.

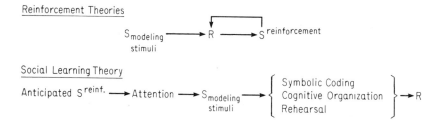

In social learning theory reinforcement is considered a facilitative rather than a necessary condition because there are factors other than response consequences that can influence what people will attend to. One does not have to be reinforced, for example, to hear compelling sounds, or to look at prominent visual displays. Hence, when people's attention to modeled activities can be gained through physical means, the addition of positive incentives does not increase observational learning (Bandura, Grusec & Menlove,

1966). Children who intently watched modeled actions on a television screen in a room darkened to eliminate distractions later displayed the same amount of imitative learning regardless of whether they were informed in advance that correct imitations would be rewarded or given no prior incentives to learn the modeled performances. Anticipated reinforcement would be expected to exert greatest influence on observational learning under self-selection conditions where people can choose whom they will attend to and how intensively they observe their behavior.

Both operant conditioning and social learning theories assume that whether or not people choose to perform what they have learned observationally is strongly influenced by the consequences of such actions. In social learning theory, however, behavior is regulated not only by directly experienced consequences from external sources, but also by vicarious reinforcement, and self-reinforcement.

THE MODELING PROCESS AND TRANSMISSION OF RESPONSE INFORMATION

A major function of modeling stimuli is to transmit information to observers on how to organize component responses into new patterns of behavior. This response information can be conveyed through physical demonstrations, through pictorial representation, or through verbal description.

Much social learning occurs on the basis of casual or studied observation of exemplary models. As linguistic skills are developed, verbal modeling is gradually substituted for behavioral modeling as the preferred mode of response guidance. By performing sequences of actions as described in instructional manuals people can learn how to assemble and operate complicated mechanical equipment, how to behave in a variety of unfamiliar social situations, and how to perform vocational and recreational tasks in a skillful manner. Verbal modeling is used extensively because one can convey through words an almost infinite variety of complex behaviors that would be exceedingly difficult and time-consuming to portray behaviorally.

Another influential source of social learning is the abundant and varied symbolic modeling provided in television, films, and other pictorial displays. There is a large body of research evidence showing that both children and adults can acquire atittudes, emotional responses, and new patterns of behavior as a result of observing filmed or televised models (Bandura, 1969a; Flanders, 1968; Lumsdaine, 1961). Considering the large amount of time that people spend watching televised models, mass media may play an influential role in shaping behavior and social attitudes. With further developments in communication technology, it will be possible to have almost any activity portrayed on request at any time on remote televison consoles (Parker, 1969). As such forms of symbolic modeling are increasingly used, parents, teachers, and other traditional role models may assume a less prominent role in social learning.

The basic modeling process is the same regardless of whether the desired behavior is conveyed through words, pictures, or live actions. Different forms of modeling, however, are not always equally effective. It is frequently difficult to convey through words the same amount of information contained in pictorial or live demonstrations. Some forms of modeling may also be more powerful in commanding attention than others. Children, or adults for that matter, rarely have to be compelled to watch television, whereas verbal characterizations of the same activities would fail to hold their attention for long. One might also expect observers who lack conceptual skills to benefit less from verbal modeling than from behavioral demonstrations.

Scope of Modeling Influences

In many instances the behavior displayed by exemplary models must be learned in essentially the same form. For example, driving automobiles or performing surgical operations permit little, if any, departure from established practices. In addition to transmitting fixed repertoires of behavior, modeling influences can, contrary to common belief, create generative and innovative behavior as well.

In studying more complex forms of modeling, persons observe models respond to different stimuli in accordance with a pre-selected rule or principle. Observers are subsequently tested under conditions where they can behave in a way that is stylistically similar to the model's disposition, but they cannot mimic his specific responses. To take an example, a model constructs from a set of nouns sentences containing the passive voice. Children are later instructed to generate sentences from a different set of nouns with the model absent, and the incidence of passive constructions is recorded. In this higher form of modeling, observers must abstract common features exemplified in diverse modeled responses and formulate a rule for generating similar patterns of behavior. Responses performed by subjects that embody the observationally derived rule are likely to resemble the behavior that the model would be inclined to exhibit under similar circumstances, even though observers had never witnessed the model's behavior in these new situations.

A number of studies have been conducted demonstrating how response-generative rules can be transmitted through modeling. Young children who had no formal grammatical knowledge altered their syntactic style in accord with the rules guiding the modeled verbal constructions (Bandura & Harris, 1966; Liebert, Odom, Hill & Huff, 1969; Rosenthal & Whitebrook, 1970). In addition, modeling influences have been successful in modifying moral judgmental orientations (Bandura & McDonald, 1963; Cowan, Langer, Heavenrich & Nathanson, 1969), delay of gratification patterns (Bandura & Mischel, 1965; Stumphauzer, 1969), and styles of information seeking (Rosenthal, Zimmerman, & Durning, 1970). Researchers have also begun to study how modeling influences alter cognitive functioning of the type described by Piaget and his followers (Rosenthal & Zimmerman, 1970; Sullivan, 1967).

The broader effects of modeling are further revealed in studies employing several models who display different patterns of behavior. Observers may select one or more of the models as the primary source of behavior, but they rarely restrict their imitation to a single source, nor do they adopt all of the characteristics of the preferred model. Rather, observers generally exhibit relatively novel responses representing amalgams of elements from different models (Bandura, Ross, & Ross, 1963a). Paradoxical as it may seem, innovative patterns can emerge solely through modeling. Thus, within a given family same-sex siblings may develop distinct personality characteristics as a result of adopting different combinations of parental and sibling attributes. A succession of modeling influences, in which observers later become sources of behavior for new members, would most likely produce a gradual imitative evolution of novel patterns that might bear little resemblance to those exhibited by the original models. In homogeneous cultures, where all models display similar modes of response, imitative behavior may undergo little or no change across successive models. It is diversity in modeling that fosters behavioral innovation.

The discussion thus far has been concerned solely with the process of learning through modeling. A second major function of modeling influences is to strengthen or to weaken inhibitions of responses that observers have previously learned (Bandura, 1971b). The effects that models have on behavioral restraints is largely determined by observation of rewarding and punishing consequences accompanying models' responses. As a result of seeing a model's actions punished, observers tend to inhibit behaving in a similar way. Conversely, observing models engage in threatening or prohibited activities without experiencing any adverse consequences can reduce inhibitions in observers. Such disinhibitory effects are most strikingly revealed in recent therapeutic applications of modeling principles (Bandura, 1971a). In these studies, people who dread and avoid certain activities are able to perform them in varying degrees after observing others perform the feared behaviors repeatedly without any harmful effects.

The actions of others can also serve as social cues that influence how others will behave at any given time. Response facilitation by modeling can be distinguished from observational learning and disinhibition by the fact that the model's actions neither teach new behaviors nor reduce inhibitions because the behavior in question, which already exists, is socially sanctioned and, therefore, is unencumbered by restraints. Inhibitory and disinhibitory effects of modeling are examined later in the context of vicarious reinforcement, while social facilitation effects are given detailed consideration in the discussion of stimulus control of behavior.

Modeling influences can have additional effects, though these may be of lesser importance. The behavior of models directs observers' attention to the particular objects used by the performer. As a result, observers may subsequently use the same objects to a greater extent, though not necessarily in an imitative way. In one experiment, for example, children who had observed a model pummel a large doll with a mallet not only imitated this specific aggressive action, but they spent more time pounding other things with a mallet than those who did not see a person handle this particular instrument (Bandura, 1962). Research findings, considered together, disclose that modeling influences can serve as teachers, as inhibitors, as disinhibitors, as response elicitors, as stimulus enhancers, and as emotion arousers.

— · — · — · — · — · — · — · — · — · —

ROGER BROWN

*Communication and Linguistic Phenomena**

The ten chapters that follow are concerned with such very old problems as the nature of meaning, the language of animals, the relation between language and thought, the character of primitive language, the possibility of phonetic symbolism, and the techniques of persuasion through language. In short, a set of real chestnuts, most of them either given up for dead, or demonstrated to be pseudo questions, or officially proscribed by scholarly societies. While I admit to believing that the old questions are the best, it is not merely antiquarian interest that causes me to discuss them now. The pleasant surprise is that there is a lot of new evidence on these matters, evidence derived from psychology, descriptive linguistics, and anthropology. The questions are alive and moving toward solution in the behavior sciences.

Chapter I. The Analysis of Speech. We begin, as Itard did, by leaving meaning aside while the sounds of speech are studied. The science of descriptive linguistics has found that all human languages are built on the same general plan. Most of the variations that occur in speech are not used to distinguish one referent from another. Only a very limited set of acoustic distinctions is used in this way. However, languages do not all recognize the same distinctions and so a person learning a second language has serious difficulty "hearing" that language as it is intended to be heard and pronouncing it as it is intended to be pronounced. The Frenchman is likely to say *zis and zat* for *this and that*, and we are likely to say *tu* as if it were *two*, and at first neither of us will hear anything wrong with his own pronunciation. The cause and remedy of this sort of difficulty become clearer when the results of descriptive linguistics are translated into the category metalanguage as they are in this first chapter.

Chapter II. The History of Writing and a Dispute About Reading. We continue Itard's sequence by moving next to the written language. It is a curious fact that the contemporary American dispute about whether Johnny can read and why not is closely connected with the history of writing systems. The earliest (pre-alphabetic) written symbols directly represented objects but for various reasons this kind of writing was not adequate for the needs of complex societies. There are great psychological economies in a phonetic writing such as our alphabet, economies that have caused phonetic writings to prevail over the older representational writings. However, the alphabet used for writing English has come to be a very irregular phonetic system. Some say that its irregularities are so exasperating that children ought to be taught to read English without any direct tuition in the sound values of the alphabet. Others say that this is tantamount to returning us to a hieroglyphic writing since it deprives children of the advantages that inhere in a phonetic writing. The question is whether the letters of our alphabet have sufficiently constant sound values to make knowing them worthwhile. If it is worthwhile knowing the usual sounds of the letters, should they be taught through explicit drill or ought exercises to be devised that will lead a child to induce the rules for himself?

Chapter III. Reference and Meaning. Itard undertook to teach the meanings of words by showing Victor examples of the things named and this is one of the ways in which meanings are commonly learned. What happens to a person when he experiences word and referent in association? Many psychologists and philosophers have reported that they form a mental image of the referent which thereafter comes to mind whenever the word is spoken and is the meaning of the word. However, we know that words name categories, and it is difficult to see what sorts of image would go with books-in-general or with keys-in-general and when it comes to animal-in-general most of us give up. We may even report, as have many before us, that we have no images at all for any words. What images, for example, have you had in connection with the last sentence? But if meaning is not an image, what is it?

Chapter IV. Phonetic Symbolism and Metaphor. What is the nature of the associations between words and referents? It is almost axiomatic with modern semantics that there is nothing natural or appropriate in such associations. They are supposed to be altogether arbitrary. Except for the trivial case of onomatopoeic or sound-imitative words it is even difficult to understand what "appropriateness" to a referent could mean. The whole notion of sound symbolism is generally taken to be a delusion of hyperaesthetical literary people. Metaphor is acknowledged to be real enough but of limited interest since it is chiefly a device of poetry. If all this is true how does it happen that *tumba* seems such a good word for a mound or swelling and *ongololo* so appropriate a name for the centipede? How is it possible for more than 90 per cent of native English speakers who know nothing of Chinese to guess that *ch'ing* means light and *ch'ung* means heavy? If metaphor is limited to poetry what do we mean when we say that a person has a "cold" manner, a "dry" wit, and "narrow" interests? Why, finally, do corporations pay a psychological consulting firm to find them a "good" name for a new product?

Chapter V. The Comparative Psychology of Linguistic Reference. It is common to cite man's ability to use language as a distinctive ability setting him off from the other animals. But is the break so absolute? Can we not find some phyletic continuity? Are there not animal communications that deserve to be called language? Certain birds are said to talk; the bees are reported to have an elaborate instinctive language; chimpanzees appear to produce sounds very like our vowels and consonants. The first four chapters have described the essential properties of human language and have put us in a position to judge whether or not animal communications are also languages. Even if the communications various animal species use among themselves are not languages, it is still possible that a gifted animal, given careful training, might learn to use a human language. What would happen, for instance, if a chimpanzee were from birth to be given more intensive and skillful training in the use of English than any child receives? Can the ape become a language-using animal? The interesting complement of this question is to ask how much of language can be learned by a human being like Victor who has in his early years been deprived of social contacts.

Chapter VI. The Original Word Game. This is the game of linguistic reference that Victor played with Itard and all children play with their parents. The rudiments of the game are the perception of speech categories, the pronunciation skill, and the identification of referent categories. This third process could also be called cognitive socialization since it involves learning to structure experience and thought as they are structured by the social group. The perception of speech in terms of a small set of distinctive features is the key to the larger and more important business of cognitive socialization. In this chapter we enjoy the benefits of our preliminary study of descriptive linguistics, for it is linguistic analysis that exposes the vital functions of speech in the socialization of the child. The Original Word Game is not given up after childhood. To be sure, the first two rudiments, speech perception and pronunciation, will have reached a level of automatic perfection but the categorizing and recategorizing of reality goes on as long as we continue to learn. All advanced education, all professional studies are in part problems of linguistic reference.

Chapter VII. Linguistic Relativity and Determinism. How do languages differ from one another? Obviously they make their words from different sound sequences. The Frenchman says *chien*, the German *Hund*, the American *dog*. In this case the words differ, but the referent seems to be the same. Is this always true? Are the languages of the world a set of alternative codes for the same concepts? If so, it is a pity that the world cannot agree on a single code and so save us all the trouble of boning up on a second or third language in preparation for a trip abroad or the reading of a foreign journal or a diplomatic mission. Of course, if the referents are different, as well as the words, then each language would embody a unique point of view and the loss of any one language would mean the loss of an insight into reality.

How is thought related to language? According to the usual view language does not come into play until thoughts are formulated. If the thinker wants to communicate, he uses language as a medium, as the passive carrier of thought. There is a contrary view which holds that language is an active determinant of thought. According to this view the structure of a man's native language is a kind of mold fixing the general form of his cognitive functions. This problem of the connection between language and thought is closely related to the nature of the differences between languages.

Chapter VIII. Progressions and Pathologies. Is there a direction of advance in linguistic reference? Does impairment of language function through brain injury or schizophrenia cause a regression in reference? The authorities say that the direction of advance is from "concrete" to "abstract" reference. Aphasic patients and schizophrenics are supposed to function concretely, as do animals, primitive peoples, and children, whereas the healthy, civilized adult is said to be capable of abstract reference. Using the category meta-language, it is possible to give precise definition to the notions of "concrete" and "abstract" reference and to examine the evidence for the doctrine of progressions and pathologies.

Chapter IX. Persuasion, Expression, and Propaganda. We hear, nowadays, that the science of propaganda has developed to the point where great masses of people can be persuaded to believe what is untrue and to perform what is immoral. This science is supposed to have swept several nations into totalitarian slavery and is said to be a potent threat to the American people. There is also some indignation at present over the unscrupulous use of advertising to manipulate consumer choices and even electoral choices. In general, modern man as a target of propaganda and advertising is pictured as a helpless dupe. This chapter argues that there is in human psychology something that checks the efforts of the unscrupulous propagandist. It is not any sort of sophisticated learning or higher education in propaganda analysis but simply our lifelong practice in learning to discern the true motives of people who try to influence us. We make a beginning at this business as children in the running propaganda warfare that goes on between children and adults. Essentially what is involved is learning to "read" behavior, and especially speech, as an expression of character. In numerous inadvertencies the propagandist is likely to "give away" his intentions and so deprive his message of persuasive power. The expressive function of language proves to be a varient of reference and susceptible of description in our metalanguage.

Chapter X. Linguistic Reference in Psychology. What are the special qualities of the language of science? Presumably it should be unequivocal and non-evaluative. The language of science ought to be purged of the ambiguities and implicit judgments that plague ordinary language. More than any other science, psychology uses terms that are close to popular parlance. Sometimes the professional borrows from colloquial speech; sometimes the professional's term is taken up by colloquial speech. The concepts and propositions of psychology are themselves psychological and social forces. Ideas about human nature and national character, for instance, though formed within the science are bound to have an influence in the world at large. As a consequence, the psychologist has an especially difficult time using language as a trustworthy instrument. In this last chapter we twist around and apply what we have learned about the psychology of language to the language of psychology.

12 · CULTURAL DETERMINANTS OF PERSONALITY

WILLIAM C. SCHUTZ

FIRO: A Three-Dimensional Theory of Need Complementarity (Interpersonal Behavior)*

The general reaction to the appearance of FIRO in 1958 was one of skeptical optimism. Most reviewers remarked on the ambitiousness of undertaking to evolve a theory of interpersonal behavior. The potential value of such a system was acknowledged, along with the need for more research to establish the soundness of the theory.

The past years have seen a slow, steady increase in the publication of articles and dissertations testing the FIRO concepts and using the questionnaires presented in the book. Because the field of interpersonal behavior is so ubiquitous, research on FIRO has taken place in a wide variety of fields, including:

1) The use of FIRO-B in marriage counseling and in selection of marital partners.
2) Study of the effect of compatibility on the outcome of several real-life dyads such as doctor-patient, experimenter-subject, teacher-student, salesman-customer. The studies have indicated that there is generally a positive effect as a result of compatibility—that is, patients seem to improve more, subjects do better, etc.
3) Evaluation of human relations workshops, such as the T-groups or sensitivity training groups of the National Training Laboratories. The FIRO-B questionnaire has been used often to measure changes in interpersonal relations during and following such workshops.
4) In clinical work, exploration of inclusion, control, and affection as possible dimensions for psychiatric classification. The relation between FIRO categories

*Reprinted by permission of the publisher. Schutz, William C., *The Interpersonal Underworld*, pp. v-vii and pp. 189–200. Science and Behavior Books, Palo Alto, California, 1966.

and standard psychiatric classifications—schizophrenic, neurotic, psychopathic, etc.—has also been investigated with some success.

5) Exploration of the relation of the FIRO dimensions of interpersonal needs—inclusion, control, and affection—to other dimensions such as birth order, need affiliation, social-class variables, scientific creativity, and differences among occupational groups.

6) Use of the FIRO techniques of compatibility as a method of group composition for teaching teams, therapy and training groups, task groups, and even string quartets!

In addition to these investigations the author has been engaged for the past several years in a large study of the applicability of the FIRO theory to the educational context, particularly the relation of the school administrator to the school board members, teachers, and parents. This study, soon to be published, attempts to use the hypotheses of the theory to understand and predict the success of an administrator under particular social conditions. It also extends the theory to incorporate cognitive and sociological factors more adequately than before.

Another important development in the theory is the construction of several tests previewed in the book. Since the original presentation of FIRO-B in 1958, the following tests have been developed:

FIRO-F (for Feelings), a measure of an individual orientation toward expressed and wanted feelings in the areas of inclusion, control, and affection. These feelings are respectively, importance, competence, and lovability.

COPE (Coping operations preference enquiry), when involved with an interpersonal anxiety the respondent's preference for using the defense mechanisms of denial, isolation, projection, regression, or turning-against-self.

LIPHE (Life interpersonal history enquiry), a measure of the respondent's interpersonal behavior and feelings toward his parents when he was a child.

VAL-ED (Educational values), the values a person holds about the relations among teacher, student, school administrator, and community, in the school situation.

All of these tests are derived from the FIRO theory. Under development at the present time are MATE (Marital attitudes evaluation), an evaluation of interpersonal satisfaction in marriage, and VAL-DOC (Doctor-patient values), an assessment of values governing the relations between doctor and patient.

Development of these questionnaires is a key effort in advancing the theory since they represent precise definitions of the theoretical concepts, and they allow for extensive testing of the theory. Further, to have a series of tests covering a wide variety of phenomena at different levels and in different areas of interaction, but generated from the same theoretical structure, provides the basis for a wide variety of studies interrelating distant areas of investigation. Data relevant to one questionnaire have implications for all the others since they are connected by the same theory.

Looking back on the theory after seven years, I find that one area in particular is unresolved, that of the relation of task-oriented behavior (also called "work," "competence," "creativity," or the "conflict-free ego sphere") to the three interpersonal needs. I vacillate between a need-reduction notion that asserts that work is simply one way of trying to gratify interpersonal needs, and an ego psychology approach stating a separate autonomous energy source (as in Maslow's deficiency motivation and being motivation). I have tried to deal with this problem, leaning toward the second conception, but I still feel dissatisfied with the formulation.

★ ★ ★

A THEORY OF INTERPERSONAL BEHAVIOR

In the preceding pages a theory was presented. As each element was introduced it was dutifully labeled and discussed. At this time a closer look will be taken at the theory as a theory. All the theoretical elements are assembled, commented on, and elevated. References are made throughout to the chapters where fuller discussions of particular points may be found.

What is to follow constitutes a formal theory of interpersonal behavior. . . . That is, it is an approximation to a formal theory within the limitations of our present embryonic knowledge of human behavior. There are several purposes served by presenting this theory in this quasi-formal fashion. Some of these purposes follow.

1. *To achieve conceptual clarity.* The necessity to state ideas explicitly leads to the identification of contradictions, omissions, repetitions, and confusions. Formalization fosters clear statements, explicit definitions, and clear logical sequences.

2. *To detect hidden assumptions.* Formalization requires that all steps leading to the statement of a theorem be made explicit. If the chain of reasoning is incomplete, a hidden assumption may be revealed.

3. *To gain from indirect verification.* If the relations between theorems are made explicit, then the verification of one theorem may indirectly verify the other, since they are parts of a logically interconnected system.

4. *To specify the range of conceptual relevance.* Formalization makes clear which aspects of a theory are affected by particular data. It makes explicit which theorems follow from which postulates and therefore which thoerems and postulates are affected by a particular experimental result.

5. *To identify equivalent theories and theorems.* If theorems are explicitly stated in two theories, it is possible to see in what respects they are similar and in what respects different.

6. *To achieve deductive fertility.* By the verifying of a small number of postulates, many theorems are verified. Deductions from the postulates may lead to many unexpected results. Although deductive fertility is probably the primary aim of a formal theory, it is not yet realizable in the present theory, a fact that is unfortunate but hardly unexpected for a theory about behavior at the present state of knowledge. However, as stated in the introduction, the approach to theory building taken here explicitly aims at approximating a formal theory as closely as possible, in order to achieve whatever deductive fertility is available.

The method of presentation of this theory is relatively informal. The primitive terms are introduced and briefly described. The defined terms and the postulates (except the first) are all stated in relatively precise mathematical or logical terms. Theorems following from the postulates are stated only in words, with no attempt made to symbolize them.

Throughout the presentation, explanatory comments are included to aid in the understanding of the theory.

RANGE OF THE THEORY

The phenomena which the theory is intended to cover are encompassed by the term "interpersonal," .... Briefly, behavior of people in which participants take account of one another is called interpersonal behavior. More specifically, interpersonal behavior encompasses three types of relations: (a) *prior:* relations between previous experience and present interpersonal behavior . . . (b) *present:* relations between elements of the interpersonal situation . . . (c) *consequent:* relations between elements of the interpersonal situation and other behavior and attitudes.

PRIMITIVE TERMS

These are the terms that are formally undefined within the theory, and from which all defined terms and postulates are formed. There are no logical requirements for the introduction of primitive terms, since they are undefined. However, the present system is an interpreted one; that is, the logical terms are given empirical meaning. Therefore the primitive terms must be made sufficiently clear to the reader.

An assumption underlying the selection of these terms as primitives, and of the definitions of the defined terms to follow, will now be made explicit. The assumption is that it is fruitful, with respect to the predictive and explanatory aim of this theory, to select *these specific* terms as primitive and to introduce *these particular* definitions for the defined terms. This assumption is important, because it specifies a possible source of inadequacy in the theory. If the theory does not predict well, it may be not only because of incorrect theorems and postulates but also because of a poor choice of definitions or of primitives.

The process of interpreting the primitive terms is called providing semantic rules. The primitive terms and their meanings follow:

1. *Interpersonal need.* A requirement for a person to establish a satisfactory relation between himself and other people. "Relation" refers to the amount of interchange between himself and others, and the degree to which he originates and receives behavior.

2. *Inclusion behavior (I).* Behavior directed toward the satisfaction of the interpersonal need for inclusion, the need to maintain and establish a satisfactory relation with people with respect to association. This term is used synonymously with *behavior in the area of inclusion.* For individuals two aspects of inclusion behavior (e^1 and w^1; see below) are measured by FIRO-B.

3. *Control behavior (C).* Behavior directed toward the satisfaction of the interpersonal need for control, the need to maintain and establish a satisfactory relation with people with respect to control and power. This term is used synonymously with *behavior in the area of control.* For individuals two aspects of control behavior (e^C and w^C; see below) are measured by FIRO-B.

4. *Affection behavior (A).* Behavior directed toward the satisfaction of the interpersonal need for affection, the need to maintain and establish a satisfactory relation with

people with respect to affection and love. This term is used synonymously with *behavior in the area of affection*. For individuals, two aspects of affection behavior (e^A and w^A; see below) are measured by FIRO-B.

For group interaction, behavior during any time interval may be described as behavior predominantly in one of the three interpersonal need areas; that is, either I, C, or A behavior. This behavior is measured by the FIRO Content Questionnaire. Relations may also be described as occurring predominantly in a particular area depending on the most characteristic type of behavior required by the relation. For example, "sweetheart" may be considered predominantly an affectional relation; "officer, enlisted man," predominantly control; and "fraternity man, pledge," predominantly inclusion.

 5. *Expressed behavior (e)*. Actions taken by a person.

 6. *Wanted behavior (w)*. Behaviors from other people that a person feels will satisfy an interpersonal need.

 7. *Feared behavior (f)*. Behavior from other people that a person feels will not satisfy or would increase an interpersonal need.

 8. *Goal achievement (g)*. Degree to which optimal performance toward a goal is achieved. The goal must be acknowledged by the group or individual as one they wish to achieve. "Optimal performance" means, under the best possible circumstances, the maximal performance of which the group or individual is capable. Some examples of group goals are productivity (measured by specific criteria appropriate to the task), cohesion (measured by the Cohesion questionnaire), and mutual liking (measured by responses to various types of sociometric questions).

These primitive terms are introduced for the purpose of forming the defined terms and postulates introduced in the next sections. In addition to the terms listed above, the theory assumes the language of logic, mathematics, and grammatical expressions. These languages include such terms as "individual," "toward," "time," "statistical significance," and "correlation," and logical signs, especially "$\in$," which means "is a member of"; for example, "$b \in A$" is read, "b is a member of class A." If any term is used which has not been defined, it is to be understood in its usual meaning.

DEFINED TERMS

These are terms useful for formulating postulates and theorems, which are defined by using only the primitive terms and the logical languages assumed. Although they are all adequately defined by mathematical expressions, a brief description of each is provided.

Def. 1. *Compatibility* (K). Compatibility is a property of a relation between two or more persons, between an individual and a role, or between an individual and a task situation, that leads to mutual satisfaction of interpersonal needs, and harmonious coexistence.

 (a) $K = rK + oK + xK$,

   where rK = reciprocal compatibility,
     oK = originator compatibility,
     xK = interchange compatibility.

An alternate formulation is somewhat more useful for demonstrating the relation of compatibility to the Postulate of Group Development.

(b) $K = \theta_I K^I + \theta_C K^C + \theta_A K^A$,

where K^I, K^C, K^A = compatibility in the areas of inclusion, control, and affection,

$\theta_I, \theta_C, \theta_A$ = coefficients which vary with the area in which the group is interacting in the following way

$$(e_h I): \theta_I > \theta_C \text{ and } \theta_I > \theta_A,$$
$$(e_h C): \theta_C > \theta_A \text{ and } \theta_C > \theta_I,$$
$$(e_h A): \theta_A > \theta_I \text{ and } \theta_A > \theta_C,$$

where e^h = the behavior of the group h.

This specification of θ embodies the idea that each area (I, C, A) of compatibility is most pertinent when the group is interacting in the corresponding need area. The values of θ cannot yet be determined beyond the inequality stated above. Very likely another set of coefficients should be assigned to rK, oK, and xK, perhaps to reflect differences in situational factors. However, for now these coefficients are assumed to be equal to one.

Def. 1a. *Area Compatibility* (K^I, K^C, K^A). Compatibility in an interpersonal need area (Chapter 6).

$$K^I = rK^I + oK^I + xK^I,$$
$$K^C = rK^C + oK^C + xK^C,$$
$$K^A = rK^A + oK^A + xK^A,$$

where rK = reciprocal compatibility,
oK = originator compatibility,
xK = interchange compatibility.

Def. 1b. *Reciprocal Compatibility* (rK). Compatibility based on reciprocal need satisfaction; primarily applicable to dyads.

(a) $rK = \theta_I rK^I + \theta_C rK^C + \theta_A rK^A$,

(b) $rK^I = |e_i I - w_j I| + |e_j I - w_i I|$,

(c) $rK^C = |e_i C - w_j C| + |e_j C - w_i C|$,

(d) $rK^A = |e_i A - w_j A| + |e_j A - w_i A|$,

where rK^I, rK^C, rK^A = reciprocal compatibility in the areas of inclusion, control, affection.

$e_i I, e_i C, e_i A$ = behavior of individual i in the areas of inclusion, control, affection (subscripts indicating individuals on rK symbol are always assumed).

$w_j I, w_j C, w_j A$ = behavior individual j wants from other in the areas of inclusion, control and affection.

Def. 1c. *Originator Compatibility* (oK). Compatibility based on differences in tendencies to originate or initiate behavior. Primarily applicable to dyads.

(a) $oK = \theta_I oK^I + \theta_C oK^C + \theta_A oK^A$,

(b) $oK^I = (e_i{}^I - w_i{}^I) + (e_j{}^I - w_j{}^I)$,

(c) $oK^C = (e_i{}^C - w_i{}^C) + (e_j{}^C - w_j{}^C)$,

(d) $oK^A = (e_i{}^A - w_i{}^A) + (e_j{}^A - w_j{}^A)$,

> where oK^I, oK^C, oK^A = originator compatibility in the areas of inclusion, control, and affection.

Def. 1d. *Interchange Compatibility* (xK). Compatibility based on desired amount of interchange between self and others. Primarily applicable to groups (Chapter 7).

(a) $xK = \theta_I xK^I + \theta_C xK^C + \theta_A xK^A$,

(b) $xK^I = \left| (e_i{}^I + w_i{}^I) - (e_j{}^I + w_j{}^I) \right|$,

(c) $xK^C = \left| (e_i{}^C + w_i{}^C) - (e_j{}^C + w_j{}^C) \right|$,

(d) $xK^A = \left| (e_i{}^A + w_i{}^A) - (e_j{}^A + w_j{}^A) \right|$.

> where xK^I, xK^C, xK^A = interchange compatibility in the areas of inclusion, control, and affection.

A summary of the definitions of compatibility may clarify the relations between the various aspects of compatibility (Table 6-1).

TABLE 6-1. RELATIONS BETWEEN COMPATIBILITY
MEASURES

		Areas of Compatibility			
		I	C	A	Row Sums
Types of	r	$\theta_I rK^I$	$\theta_C rK^C$	$\theta_A rK^A$	rK
Compatibility	o	$\theta_I oK^I$	$\theta_C oK^C$	$\theta_A oK^A$	oK
	x	$\theta_I xK^I$	$\theta_C xK^C$	$\theta_A xK^A$	xK
Column Sums		$\theta_I K^I$	$\theta_C K^C$	$\theta_A K^A$	K Total

Hence the sums of rows define rK, oK, and xK, while the sums of columns define $\theta_I K^I$, $\theta_C K^C$, $\theta_A K^A$. Both the sum of all rows and the sum of all columns add to K, and constitute the two definitions of K given above. The θ coefficients are included in the terms that include rK, oK, and xK, while they are the multipliers for K^I, K^C, and K^A. Although the two definitions are mathematically equivalent they have interesting psychological differences: one deals with compatibility within need areas, and the other deals with types of compatibility.

Def. 2. *Role Definition.* The behavior which the other group members express toward the role player, and the behavior they want from him.

> Role Definition = e_h(obs), w_h(obs),
> where h = other group members,
> > obs = from the standpoint of outside observers.

Def. 3. *Role Expectation.* The role player's perception of the behavior which the other group members express toward him, and his perception of the behavior which they want from him.

> Role Expectation = e_h(rol), w_h(rol)
> where rol = from the standpoint of the role player.

Def. 4. *Enacted Role.* The behavior the role player expresses toward other group members, and the behavior he wants them to express toward him.

> Enacted Role = e_r(obs), w_r(obs),
> where r = role player.

Def. 5. *Perceived Role Performance.* The role player's perception of his own expressed behavior toward other group members, and his perception of the behavior he wants from the group.

> Perceived Role Performance = e_r(rol), w_r(rol)

Def. 6. *Norm.* The behavior the members of a group (that is, the group) want from any person who is a member of that group.

> Norm = $w_{h.a}$(obs),
> where $w_{h.a}$ = behavior h wants from any group member a.

Def. 7. *Sanction.* The behavior expressed by group members (that is, the group) toward an expressed or wanted behavior of a particular group member.

> Sanction = e_h(obs), in response to e_r(obs) or w_r(obs).

The five definitions above are summarized in Table 8–8.

TABLE 8–8. EXPLICATION OF "ROLE," "NORM," AND "SANCTION"

		Perception of Role Player	*Perception of Observer*		
Behavior of Group	e_h w_h	Role expectation	Role definition	←	Norm (for role player = average group member)
Behavior of Role Player	e_r w_r	Perceived role performance	Enacted role	← ←	Sanction = response e_h to previous e_r, w_r

All values used for defining the above terms are derived from FIRO-B scales adapted to this purpose. Each definition consists of a set of numbers, representing scores on the appropriate FIRO-B scales. . . . Definition 2 through definition 7 are not required for the statement of the postulates. However, they are important concepts used in the study of interpersonal relations that are expected to be useful for formulating new postulates for the system. It is helpful, too, to demonstrate the approach to conceptualizing situational factors from the standpoint of interpersonal behavior. All seven of the above definitions provide semantic rules for the use of certain terms in the logical system. Logically, it is sufficient merely to define them in terms of the basic terms. Empirically, however, it is important to provide meaning for these terms beyond formulas. These definitions form a part of the explication process. Thus it is assumed that these terms successfully render old concepts into new. Carnap gives four criteria for an adequate explicatum: (1) similarity to the explicandum, (2) exactness, (3) fruitfulness. (4) simplicity. The third criterion, fruitfulness, must be judged in part by the adequacy of the theorems in which the explicatum is used, and the new theorems to which it leads.

POSTULATES

These are the propositions expressing what are taken to be the most fundamental ideas embodied in the theory. In the ideal instance, all theorems in the system are derivable from these postulates. In the present instance, they represent the best estimate of the most basic ideas in the theory presented.

Postulate 1. *The Postulate of Interpersonal Needs.*
(a) Every individual has three interpersonal needs: inclusion, control, and affection.
(b) Inclusion, control, and affection constitute a sufficient set of areas of interpersonal behavior for the prediction and explanation of interpersonal phenomena.

This statement means that there are some important areas of interpersonal behavior for which failure to consider any of the interpersonal need areas leads to a poor correlation between prediction and outcome, and the addition of any further variables will yield at best a small increment in predictive power. . . . This postulate is stated with sufficient clarity that further specificity is unnecessary.

Theorem 1-1. If a representative battery of measures of interpersonal behavior is factor-analyzed, the resulting factors will reasonably fall into the three need areas, inclusion, control, and affection.

"Reasonably fall" may be made more specific by including measures of the three areas in the battery, and by predicting that each area measure will be heavily loaded on one factor, and that no interpersonal factor will not include a highly loaded I, C, or A scale.

Postulate 2. *The Postulate of Relational Continuity.* An individual's expressed interpersonal behavior will be similar to the behavior he experienced in his earliest interpersonal relations, usually with his parents, in the following way:

Principle of Constancy. When he perceives his adult position in an interpersonal situation to be similar to his own position in his parent-child relation, his adult behavior positively covaries with his childhood behavior toward his parents (or significant others).
Principle of Identification. When he perceives his adult position in an interpersonal situation to be similar to his parent's position in his parent-child

relation, his adult behavior positively covaries with the behavior of his parents (or significant others) toward him when he was a child.

This postulate may be made more precise by repeating Figure 5-1 here.

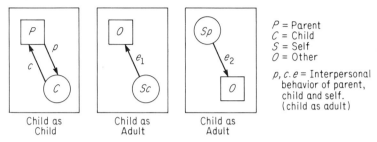

Child as Child	Child as Adult	Child as Adult	

P = Parent
C = Child
S = Self
O = Other

p, c.e = Interpersonal behavior of parent, child and self. (child as adult)

Figure 5-1. Schema for postulate of relational continuity.

The first diagram schematizes the relation of the parent and child. In the second diagram the child-become-adult occupies a role similar to the one he had as a child (*Sc*). In the third diagram he occupies a role similar to the one his parent occupied toward him (*Sp*). The Postulate of Relational Continuity specifies the relations between e_1, e_2, p, and c. To demonstrate the postulate, all possibilities for e_1, and e_2 (the term e will be used to designate both e_1 and e_2) are enumerated:

1. e covaries positively with c.
2. e covaries negatively with c.
3. e does not covary with c.
4. e covaries positively with p.
5. e covaries negatively with p.
6. e does not covary with p.

The term "covaries" means "varies concomitantly in a statistically significant sense." It is to be interpreted as a statistical concept measured by the appropriate statistical measure, for example, product-moment correlation, chi-square, rank-order correlation. The Principle of Constancy asserts that for e_1, possibility (1) is true; that is, e_1 covaries positively with c. The Principle of Identification asserts the truth of (4) for e_2; that is, e_2 covaries positively with p. It should be noted that the Principle of Constancy implies that (2) and (3) are false but is noncommittal about (4), (5), and (6). Similarly, the Principle of Identification implies that (5) and (6) are false, and is noncommittal about (1), (2), and (3). Thus the Postulate of Relational Continuity is formulated as follows:

1. Principle of Constancy

$$P(e_1, c) > s$$

2. Principle of Identification

$$P(e_2, p) > s,$$

where P = an appropriate measure of covariance,
    s = the level required for statistical significance.

Postulate 3. *The Postulate of Compatibility.* If the compatibility of one group, h, is greater than that of another group, m, then the goal achievement of h will exceed that of m.

In mathematical terms this postulate is simply stated:

$$\text{If } K_h > K_m, \text{ then } g_h > g_m.$$

The definition of compatibility introduced earlier is fully utilized in this postulate. Since the definition of K includes the coefficients, θ, the Postulate of Compatibility incorporates the notion that different areas of compatibility are more pertinent during different kinds of interaction; for example, if the group is interacting in the affection area, or if the interpersonal relation is primarily affectional, as "sweetheart," then K^A is the most important ingredient of K in determining the compatibility of the group.

Also utilized in the statement of the postulate is the definition of "goal achievement." This term was defined as the degree to which the group approaches its optimal performance on a goal it desires to achieve. The theorems specify various aspects of the postulate.

Theorem 3-1. If the compatibility of one dyad, y_1, is greater than the compatibility of another dyad, y_2, then the members of y_1 are more likely to prefer each other for continued personal interchange.

Theorem 3-2. If the compatibility of one group, h, is greater than the compatibility of another group, m, then the productivity goal achievement of h will exceed that of m.

Theorem 3-3. If the compatibility of one group, h, is greater than the compatibility of another group, m, then h will be more cohesive than m.

Theorems 3-4, 3-5, and 3-6 were not confirmed in further testing; therefore they are not included here....

Theorem 3-7. In the compatible groups, those predicted to be focal persons and those predicted to be main supporting members should rank one another very high on the relation "work well with."

Theorem 3-8. In all the groups focal persons will be chosen as group leaders by the group members.

Theorem 3-9. The effect of compatibility on productivity (the C-P effect) increases as the task situation requires more interchange in the three need areas.

Postulate 4. *The Postulate of Group Development.* The formation and development of two or more people into an interpersonal relation (that is, a group) always proceed in the same sequence, as follows:

Principle of Group Integration. For the time period starting with the group's beginning until three intervals before the group's termination the predominant area of interpersonal behavior begins with inclusion, is followed by control, and finally by affection. This cycle may recur.

Principle of Group Resolution. The last three intervals prior to a group's anticipated termination follow the opposite sequence in that the predominant area of interpersonal behavior is first affection, then control, and finally inclusion.

The postulate may be specified more precisely.

The Principle of Group Integration

when $t_1 < t_i < t_n - 2$,

$$e_h(t_i)\epsilon I, \text{ for } i = 3m + 1,$$
$$e_h(t_i)\epsilon C, \text{ for } i = 3m + 2,$$
$$e_h(t_i)\epsilon A, \text{ for } i = 3m + 3,$$

where m = any integer,

$t_1, t_2, \ldots t_n$ = time intervals of an interpersonal relation.

They are successive, exhaustive intervals which change when, and only when, the predominant area of interpersonal behavior (I, C, A) changes, measured by FIRO Content Questionnaire.

h = any group or interpersonal relation, including a small training group, an infant and parent, and the like.

The Principle of Group Resolution

when $t_i > t_n - 1$,

$$e_h(t_i)A, \text{ for } i = n - 2,$$
$$e_h(t_i)C, \text{ for } i = n - 1,$$
$$e_h(t_i)I, \text{ for } i = n$$

This principle states that the last three intervals of a group's existence follow the opposite sequence from the integration phase. With impending separation, first comes affection, then control, and finally inclusion. This is the period of "decathecting" the group, or withdrawing investment. This postulate states that investment is withdrawn in the opposite order from that in which it was placed in the group. . . . If the two parts of Postulate 4 are put together, the sequence of interaction for any interpersonal relation of group is

I	C	A	I	C	A	...	A	C	I
t_1	t_2	t_3	t_4	t_5	t_6		$t_n - 2$	$t_n - 1$	t_n

Theorem 4-1. (1) If a group is high on inclusion compatibility (K^I), but low on K^C and K^A, group members will be most compatible during the initial stages of their relation.

(2) If a group is high on K^C, but low on K^I and K^A, group members will be most compatible during the middle stages of their relation.

(3) If a group is high on K^A, but low on K^I and K^C, group members will be most compatible during the last stages of their relation prior to the separation sequence.

SUMMARY OF THEORY

There are three interpersonal need areas, inclusion, control, and affection, sufficient for the prediction of interpersonal behavior. Orientations which an individual acquires toward behavior in these areas are relatively invariant over time. Compatibility of two or more persons depends on (a) their ability to satisfy reciprocally each other's interpersonal needs, (b) their complementarity with respect to originating and receiving behavior in each need area, (c) their similarity with respect to the amount of interchange they desire with other people in each need area. "Roles" may be defined in terms of interpersonal requirements in such a way that a measurement can be made of the compatibility of an individual and a role. Compatibility varies with the type of interaction being experienced. If, for example, individuals are engaged in inclusion behavior, or involved in a primary inclusion relation, then compatibility in the inclusion area (K^1) is the most important determinant of their compatibility in the situation itself. Areas and degrees of compatibility are therefore distinguishable which are roughly comparable to personal relations that flourish under one set of circumstances but cannot withstand the stress of a different type of relation.

Every interpersonal relation follows the same general developmental sequence. It starts with inclusion behavior, is followed by control behavior and, finally, affection behavior. This cycle may recur. When the relation approaches termination it reverses direction, and investment from the relation is withdrawn in the order affection, control, and inclusion.

From these postulates it is theoretically possible to predict the course of a relation, if we know the interpersonal orientations of the individual members of the relation and the interpersonal description of the circumstances under which they will interact.

— · — · — · — · — · — · — · — · — · — · — · —

MARGARET MEAD

*Culture in Shaping Human Behavior**

Upon the solution of the Oedipus situation will depend a great deal of the way in which a boy or a girl accepts primary sex membership. But it is not enough for a child to decide simply and fully that it belongs to its own sex, is anatomically a male or a female, with a given reproductive rôle in the world. For growing children are faced with another problem: "*How male*, how female, am I?" He hears men branded as feminine, women condemned as masculine, others extolled as real men, and as true women. He hears occupations labelled as more or less manly, for a man, or more or less likely to derogate her womanhood, for a women. He hears types of responsiveness, fastidiousness, sensitiv-

*Margaret Mead, *Male and Female* (New York: William Morrow, 1949), pp. 128–142. Reprinted by permission of William Morrow and Company, Inc. Copyright 1949 by Margaret Mead.

ity, guts, stoicism, and endurance voted as belonging to one sex rather than the other. In his world he sees not a single model but many as he measures himself against them; so that he will judge himself, and feel proud and secure, worried and inferior and uncertain, or despairing and ready to give up the task altogether.

In any human group it is possible to arrange men and women on a scale in such a way that between a most masculine group and a most feminine group there will be others who seem to fall in the middle, to display fewer of the pronounced physical features that are more characteristic of one sex than of the other. This is so whether one deals entirely in secondary sex characters, such as arrangement of pubic hair, beard, layers of fat, and so on, or whether one deals with such primary sex characters as breasts, pelvic measurements, hip-torso proportions and so on. These differences are even more conspicuous when one considers such matters as skin sensitivity, depth of voice, modulation of movement. Also, one finds in most groups of any size that there are very few individuals who insist on playing the rôle of the opposite sex in occupation or dress or interpersonal sex activities. Whether full transvestitism will occur seems to be a question of cultural recognition of this possibility. Among many American Indian tribes the *berdache*, the man who dressed and lived as a woman, was a recognized social institution, counterpointed to the excessive emphasis upon bravery and hardiness for men. In other parts of the world, such as the South Pacific, although a large number of ritual reversals of sex on ceremonial occasions may occur, there are many tribes where there is no expectation that any single individual will make the complete shift. Peoples may provide sex-reversal rôles for both sexes—as among the Siberian aborigines, where sex reversal is associated with shamanism; they may permit it to men but deny it to women; or they may not provide any pattern at all. But between the conspicuous transvestitism of the Mohave Indians[1] —where the transvestite men mimic pregnancy and child-birth, going aside from the camp to be ceremonially delivered of stones—and the Samoans—who recognize no transvestitism, but among whom I found one boy who preferred to sit among the women and weave mats— the contrast is clearly one of social patterning. A society can provide elaborate rôles that will attract many individuals who would never spontaneously seek them. Fear that boys will be feminine in behaviour may drive many boys into taking refuge in explicit femininity. Identification of a little less hairiness on the chin, or a slightly straighter bust-line, as fitting one for membership in the opposite sex may create social deviance. If we are to interpret these experiences, which all children have, we look for some theory of what these differences mean.

We strip away all this superstructure when we have invoked the presence or absence, the recognition and toleration, of transvestite social institutions, or the explicit suppression of homosexual practice, but we still find differences that need explanation. After we have gathered together the insights from detailed case-histories in Western society that show how accidents of upbringing, faulty identifications with the wrong parent, or excessive fear of the parent of the opposite sex may drive both boys and girls into sexual inversion, still we are left with a basic problem. Set end to end, standing in a line, the men of any group will show a range of explicit masculinity of appearance as well as masculinity of behaviour. The females of any group will show a comparable variety, even more, in

[1] Devereux, George, "Institutionalized Homosexuality of the Mohave Indians," *Human Biology*, Vol. 9 (1937), pp. 498–527.

fact, if we have X-ray pictures to add to their deceptive pelvic profiles, which do not reveal their feminine reproductive capacities accurately.[2] Is this apparent range to be set down to differences in endocrine balance, set against our recognition that each sex depends for full functioning upon both male and female hormones and the interaction between these hormones and the other endocrines? Has every individual a bisexual potential that may be physiologically evoked by hormone deficit or surplus, which may be psychologically evoked by abnormalities in the process of individual maturation, which may be sociologically invoked by rearing boys with women only, or segregating boys away from women entirely, or by prescribing and encouraging various forms of social inversion? When human beings—or rats—are conditioned by social circumstances to respond sexually to members of their own sex as adults and in preference to members of the opposite sex, is this conditioning playing on a real bisexual base in the personality, which varies greatly in its structure as between one member of a group and another?

At first blush, it seems exceedingly likely that we have to advance some such hypothesis. If one looks at a group of little boys, it would seem fairly obvious that it would be easier to condition those who now appear "girlish" to an inverted rôle, and that from a group of little girls, the "boyish" girl would be the easiest to train into identification with the opposite sex. And does not "easiest" here mean the greatest degree of physical bisexuality? Yet the existing data make us pause. The most careful research has failed to tie up endocrine balance with actual homosexual behaviour. Those rare creatures who have both male and female primary sex organs present of course major anomalies and confusions, but so far they have thrown little light on the general problem. The extraordinary lack of correlation between physique that can be regarded as hypermasculine and hyperfeminine and successful reproductivity is marked in every group. The man who shows the most male characteristics may have no children, while some pallid, feminine-looking mouse of a man fathers a large brood. The woman with ample bosom and wide hips may be sterile, or if she bears children she may be incapable of suckling them. Yet we are still continually confronted with what looks like a correlation between the tendency towards sexual inversion of the men and women who deviate most towards the expected physique of the opposite sex. In the primitive tribe that does not recognize inversion, the boy who decides to make mats will look more like the female type for that tribe, the woman who goes out hunting will tend to look more like the male. Does this apparent physical correspondence mean nothing, is it sheerly an accident within a normal range of variation? If the tribe sets hairiness up as a desirable male characteristic, will the less hairy become confused about their sex rôle, while if the tribesmen think that hairiness is simply a brutish characteristic, the very hairy may be almost sexually ostracized and the most hairless will not thereby be regarded as less male? This would be the extreme environmental answer, while the invocation of some very subtle, as yet unplumbed structural and functional variation in the biological basis of sex membership would be the extreme genetic answer.

I suggest another hypothesis that seems to me to fit better the behaviour of the seven South Seas peoples whom I have studied. A Balinese male is almost hairless—so hairless that he can pluck his whiskers out one by one with pincers. His breasts are considerably

---

[2]Gruelich, William Walter, and Thoms, Herbert, with collaboration of Ruth Christian Twaddle, "A Study of Pelvic Type and Its Relationship to Body Build in White Women," *Journal of American Medical Association*, Vol. 112 (1939), pp. 485–93.

more developed than are a Westerner's. Almost any Balinese male placed in a series of western-European males would look "feminine." A Balinese female, on the other hand, has narrow hips and small high breasts, and almost any Balinese female placed among a group of western-European women would look "boyish." Many of them might be suspected of being unable to suckle children, perhaps accused of having infantile uteruses. But should these facts be interpreted to mean that the Balinese is more bisexual, less sexually differentiated than the western European, that the men are less masculine, the women less feminine, or simply that the Balinese type of masculinity and feminity is different? The extreme advocates of a varying bisexual balance would claim that in some races the men are less differentiated, are more feminine and so on, than in others, and might also apply the same argument to the women. But on the whole, it would be agreed that at least some of the respects in which a Balinese male would seem feminine are matters that do not really affect his masculinity at all: his height, girth, hairiness, and the like. So it might be fairly readily admitted that as between racial strains that vary as greatly as Balinese and northern Europeans, Andamanese pygmies and Nubian giants, not only would certain of the criteria for masculinity and femininity be inoperative, but also that actual cross-correspondence might occur, as all Andamanese males would fall within the height range for females in some much taller group.

But all human groups of which we have any knowledge show evidence of considerable variation in their biological inheritance. Even among the most inbred and isolated groups, very marked differences in physique and apparent temperament will be found, and despite the high degree of uniformity that characterizes the child-rearing practices of many primitive tribes, each adult will appear as more or less masculine, or more or less feminine, according to the standards of that particular tribe. There will be, furthermore, orders of variation that seem, at least on inspection—for we have no detailed records—to apply from one group to another. Although almost every Balinese would fall within the general configuration that might be classified technically as asthenic, yet the asthenic Balinese continues to contrast with the Balinese who is heavier in bony structure, or shorter and plumper. Within the limits set by the general type, these same differences occur, in both men and women. Not until we have far more delicate methods of measurement, which allow not only for individual constitution but for ancestral strains, will we have any way of knowing whether there is any genuine correspondence, on a behavioural level, among the slender, narrow-bodied of the Arapesh, Tchambuli, Swede, Eskimo, and Hottentot, or whether their behaviour, although possibly in some way constitutionally based, is still in no way referable to something they may be said to have in common. Until such measures are developed, and such studies made, one can only speculate on the basis of careful observation, with no better instrument for comparison than the human eye. But use of this instrument on seven different peoples has suggested to me the hypothesis that within each human group we will find, probably in different proportions and possibly not always in all, representatives of the same constitutional types that we are beginning to distinguish in our own population. And I further suggest that the presence of these contrasting constitutional types is an important condition in children's estimate of the completeness of their sex membership.

If we recognized the presence of comparable ranges of constitutional types in each human society, any single continuum that we now construct from the most masculine to the least masculine can be seen to be misleading, especially to the eye of the growing child. We should instead define a series of continuums, distinguishing between the most masculine and the least sexually differentiated male within each of these several types. The slender little man without beard or muscle who begets a whole brood of children would not then seem such an anomaly, but could be regarded as the masculine version of a human type in which both sexes are slender, small, and relatively hairless. The tall girl whose breasts are scarcely discernible, but who is able to suckle her baby perfectly satisfactorily as her milk seems to spread in an almost even line across her chest, will be seen not as an imperfectly developed female—a diagnosis that is contradicted by the successful way in which she bears and suckles children, and her beautiful carriage in pregnancy—but as the female of a particular constitutional type in which women's breasts are much smaller and less accentuated. The big he-man with hair on his chest, whose masculinity is so often claimed to be pallid and unconvincing, will be seen to be merely a less masculine version of a type in which enormous muscularity and hairiness are the mode. The woman whose low fertility contrasts so strangely with her billowing breasts and hips may be seen as only one of a type of woman with very highly emphasized breasts and hips—her low fertility only conspicuous because most of the women with whom she is compared have smaller bosoms and less full hips. The apparent contradiction between pelvic X-rays and external pelvic measurements might also be resolved if it were considered from this point of view.

And as with physical type, so with other aspects of personality. The fiery, initiating woman would be classified only with fiery, initiating men of her own type, and might be found to look like not a lion, but merely like a lioness in her proper setting. When the meek little Caspar Milquetoast was placed side by side not with a prize-fighter, but with the meekest female version of himself, he might be seen to be much more masculine than she. The plump man with soft breast-tissue, double chin, protruding buttocks, whom one has only to put in a bonnet to make him like a woman, when put beside the equally plump woman will be seen not to have such ambiguous outlines after all; his masculinity is still indubitable when contrasted with the female of his own kind instead of with the male of another kind. And the slender male and female dancers, hipless and breastless, will seem not a feminine male and a boyish female, but male and female of a special type. Just as one would not be able to identify the sex of a male rabbit by comparing its behaviour with that of a lion, a stag, or a peacock as well as by comparing rabbit buck with doe, lion with lioness, stag with doe, and peacock with peahen—so it may well be that if we could disabuse our minds of the habits of lumping all males together and all females together and worrying about the beards of the one and the breasts of the other, and look instead for males and females of different types, we would present to children a much more intelligible problem.

A great number of very puzzling theoretical questions would fall into place also. Take for instance the question of degree of sex activity, and the greater activity reported by men who mature early. Are such men more masculine, or simply another type? Take the women who even among a people like the Arapesh, who have no concept of orgasm for the female, are actively demanding in sex, and specific in their sexual appetites. Or take the women who among peoples like the Mundugumor, who cast women as sexually specific and unmaternal, are still diffusively responsible and maternal. These deviations would no longer be regarded as signs of greater or less femininity, but of different types of women, types so biologically rooted that all the apparatus of cultural conditioning is insufficient to mould them completely to the type which that particular culture has come to regard as really feminine or masculine.

The growing child in any society is confronted then by individuals—adults and adolescents and children—who are classified by his society into two groups, males and females, in terms of their most conspicuous primary sex characters, but who actually show great range and variety both in psysique and in behaviour. Because primary sex differences are of such enormous importance, shaping so determinatively the child's experience of the world through its own body and the responses of others to its sex membership, most children take maleness or femaleness as their first identification of themselves. But once this identification is made, the growing child then begins to compare itself not only in physique, but even more importantly in impulse and interest, with those about it. Are all of its interests those of its own sex? "I am a boy," but "I love colour, and colour is something that interests only women." "I am a girl," but "I am fleet of foot and love to run and leap. Running and leaping, and shooting arrows, are for boys, not girls." "I am a boy," but "I love to run soft materials through my fingers; an interest in touch is feminine, and will unsex me." I am a girl," but "My fingers are clumsy, better at handling an axe-handle than at stringing beads; axe-handles are for men." So the child, experiencing itself, is forced to reject such parts of its particular biological inheritance as conflict sharply with the sex stereotype of its culture.

Moreover, a sex stereotype that decrees the interests and occupations of each sex is usually not completely without a basis. The idea of the male in a given society may conform very closely to the temperament of some one type of male. The idea of the female *may* conform to the female who belongs to the same type, or instead to the female of some other type. For the children who do not belong to these preferred types, only the primary sex characters will be definitive in helping them to classify themselves. Their impulses, their preferences, and later much of their physique will be aberrant. They will be doomed throughout life to sit among the other members of their sex feeling less a man, or less a woman, simply because the cultural ideal is based on a different set of clues, a set of clues no less valid, but different. And the small rabbit man sits sadly, comparing himself with a lionlike male beside whom he is surely not male, and perhaps for that reason alone yearning forever after the lioness woman. Meanwhile the lioness woman, convicted in her inmost soul of lack of femininity when she compares herself with the rabbity little women about her, may in reverse despair decide that she might as well go the whole way and take a rabbity husband. Or the little rabbity man who would have been so gently fierce and definitely masculine if he had been bred in a culture that recognized him as fully male, and quite able to take a mate and fight for her, may give up altogether and dub himself a female and become a true invert, attaching himself to some male who possesses the magnificent qualities that have been denied him.

Sometimes one has the opportunity to observe two men of comparable physique and behaviour, both artists or musicians, one of whom has placed himself as fully male, and with brightly shining hair and gleaming eye can make a roomful of women feel more feminine because he has entered the room. The other has identified himself as a lover of men, and his eye contains no gleam and his step no sureness, but instead an apologetic adaptation when he enters a group of women. And yet, in physical measurement, in tastes, in quality of mind, the two men may be almost interchangeable. One, however, has been presented, for example, with a frontier setting, the other with a cosmopolitan European one; one with a world where a man never handles anything except a gun, a hunting-knife, or a riding-whip, the other with a world where men play the most delicate musical instruments. When one studies a pair such as this, it seems much more fruitful to look not at some possible endocrine difference, but rather at the discrepancy, so much more manifest to one than to the other, between his own life preferences and those which his society thinks appropriate for males.

If there are such genuine differences among constitutional types that maleness for one may be so very different from maleness for another, and even appear to have attributes of femaleness—as found in some other type—this has profound implications not only for interpretation of variation within each sex, and for the forms of inversion and sex failure that occur in any society, but also for the pattern of inter-relationships between the sexes. Some simple societies, and some castes within complex societies seem to have chosen their sex ideals for both sexes from the same constitutional type. The aristocracy, or the cattle-men, or the shopkeeper class may cherish as the ideal the delicate, small-boned, sensitive type for both males and females, or the tall, fiery, infinitely proud, specifically nervously sexed man and woman, or the plump, placid man and woman. But we do not know whether the male and female ideals of a given culture complement each other in this way. When the ideals for the two sexes do seem to be consistently interrelated, it is probable that a more finely meshed, more biologically direct relationship can be established as the ideal marriage, and the marriage forms will have a greater consistency. When those men and women who do not conform to the ideal type try to use the marriage forms—the delicate interwoven ballet, or the fierce proud reserve, or the comfortable post-prandial hot milk, which have become the appropriate and developed forms for that ideal type—they are at least faced with a consistent though alien pattern, which it may be easier to learn.

Let us imagine for instance an aristocracy in which for both men and women the ideal is tall, fiery-tempered, proud, specifically and very sensitively sexed. Into such an aristocratic household is born a boy who is plump, easy-going, fond of eating, diffusely sexed. All through his childhood he will be trained in the behaviour appropriate to a type very different from himself, and this will include accepting as his feminine ideal a girl who is fiery-tempered, reserved, specifically sexed. If he marries such a girl, he will have learned a good part of his proper rôle, which she in turn will have learned to expect of him. If he marries a girl who deviates as much as he from the expected standards, each will nevertheless have learned a consistent rôle, he to treat her as if she were sensitive and proud, she to treat him as if he were sensitive and proud. Their life may have more artificiality in it than that of those who actually approximate the types for which the cultural rôles are designed, but the very clarity of the pattern of male and female rôles may make them rôles that can be played. In every such tightly patterned picture there will be some who will rebel, will commit suicide—if suicide is a culturally recognized way out—will become promiscuous or frigid or withdrawn or insane, or, if they are gifted, will become innovators of some variation in the pattern. But most of them will learn the pattern, alien though it be.

So in each of the societies I have studied it has been possible to distinguish those who deviated most sharply from the expected physique and behaviour, and who made different sorts of adjustment, dependent upon the relationship between own constitutional type and cultural ideal. The boy who will grow up into a tall, proud, restive man whose very pride makes him sensitive and liable to confusion suffers a very different fate in Bali, Samoa, Arapesh, and Manus. In Manus, he takes refuge in the vestiges of rank the Manus retain, takes more interest in ceremonial than in trading, mixes the polemics of acceptable trading invectives with much deeper anger. In Samoa such a man is regarded as too violent to be trusted with the headship of a family for many, many years; the village waits until his capacity for anger and intense feeling has been worn down by years of erosive soft resistance to his unseemly over-emphases. In Bali, such a man may take more initiative than his fellows only to be thrown back into sulkiness and confusion, unable to carry it through. Among the Maori of New Zealand, it is probable that he would have been the cultural ideal, his capacity for pride matched by the demand for pride, his violence by the demand for violence, and his capacity for fierce gentleness also given perfect expression, since the ideal woman was as proud and fiercely gentle as himself.

But in complex modern societies, there are no such clear expectations, no such perfectly paired expectancies, even for one class or occupational group or rural region. The stereotyped rôles for men and for women do not necessarily correspond, and whatever type of man is the ideal, there is little likelihood that the corresponding female type will also be the ideal. Accidents of migration, of cross-class marriage, of frontier conditions, may take the clues for the female ideal from quite another type from which the male ideal is taken. The stereotype may itself be blurred and confused by several different expectations, and then split again, so that the ideal lover is not the ideal brother or husband. The pattern of inter-relationships between the sexes, of reserve or intimacy, advance or retreat, initiative and response, may be a blend of several biologically congruent types of behaviour instead of clearly related to one. We need much more material on the extent to which this sort of constitutional types may actually be identified and studied before we can answer the next questions about the differential strength and stability and flexibility of cultures in which ideals are a blend, or a composite, or a single lyric theme, ideals that are so inclusive that every male and female finds a rather blurrily defined place within them, or so sharp and narrow that many males and females have to develop counterpointed patterns outside them.

A recognition of the possibilities would change a great deal of our present-day practices of rearing children. We would cease to describe the behaviour of the boy who showed an interest in occupations regarded as female, or a greater sensitivity than his fellow, as "on the female" side, and could ask instead what kind of male he was going to be. We would take instead the primary fact of sex membership as a cross-constitutional classification, just as on a wider scale the fact of sex can be used to classify together male rabbits and male lions and male deer, but would never be permitted to obscure for us their essential rabbit, lion, and deer characteristics. Then the little girl who shows a greater need to take things apart than most of the other little girls need not be classified as a female of a certain kind. In such a world, no child would be forced to deny its sex membership because it was shorter or taller, or thinner or plumper, less hairy or more hairy, than another, nor would any child have to pay with a loss of its sense of its sex membership for the special gifts that made it, though a boy, have a delicate sense of touch, or, though a girl, ride a horse with fierce sureness.

If we are to provide the impetus for surmounting the trials and obstacles of this most difficult period in history, man must be sustained by a vision of a future so rewarding that no sacrifice is too great to continue on the journey towards it. In that picture of the future, the degree to which men and women can feel at home with their own bodies, and at home in their relationships with their own sex and with the opposite sex, is extremely important.[3]

[3] Our obligations in the choice of hypotheses about mankind are deep and binding. As scientists pledged to a search for the best hypotheses, we have certain clear obligations. As members of human society in the year 1948, we also have clear obligations to explore actively those hypotheses which would seem to open up the most important next fields of research. Hypotheses of constitutional type are two-edged swords. To the degree that they emphasize that there may be deep and inalienable differences between individuals, they lend themselves to dangerous extensions to racial groups. It is so very easy to identify a certain type of human being and confuse that type with some localized group, such as northern Europeans, and because type A is tall and lean as an individual type, to attribute his characteristics to some people who as a group happen to be taller and leaner than some other group. The next step to such fallacious reasoning is a recrudescence of racism of a new sort, with all the usual attendant dangers of racism, when the direction of order at this period in history seems far better by emphasizing man's modifiable rather than his unmodifiable characteristics. The student of constitutional types has only to make two errors—to confuse the cultural institution of the behavior congruent with a particular type with the innate temperament and confuse relative physique within a group with relative position within the human race—and we have been landed in a very parlous state of inadmissible racism. In fact this danger is so great that in a choice of research lines, the pursuit of the implications of constitutional differences must be undertaken with an extra sense of responsibility.

— · — · — · — · — · — · — · — · — · — · —

SIGMUND FREUD

*Culturally Induced Conscience (Superego)**

I cannot tell whether the same thing will happen to you as to me. Ever since, under the powerful impression of this clinical picture, I formed the idea that the separation of the observing agency from the rest of the ego might be a regular feature of the ego's structure, that idea has never left me, and I was driven to investigate the further characteristics and connections of the agency which was thus separated off. The next step is quickly taken. The content of the delusions of being observed already suggests that the

*Reprinted from *New Introductory Lectures on Psycho-Analysis* by Sigmund Freud. Translated and edited by James Strachey. By permission of W. W. Norton & Company, Inc. Copyright © 1965, 1964 by James Strachey. Copyright 1933 by Sigmund Freud. Copyright renewed 1961 by W. J. H. Sprott. Also by permission of Sigmund Freud Copyrights, Ltd., The Institute of Psycho-Analysis, and The Hogarth Press, Ltd.

observing is only a preparation for judging and punishing, and we accordingly guess that another function of this agency must be what we call our conscience. There is scarcely anything else in us that we so regularly separate from our ego and so easily set over against it as precisely our conscience. I feel an inclination to do something that I think will give me pleasure, but I abandon it on the ground that my conscience does not allow it. Or I have let myself be persuaded by too great an expectation of pleasure into doing something to which the voice of conscience has objected and after the deed my conscience punishes me with distressing reproaches and causes me to feel remorse for the deed. I might simply say that the special agency which I am beginning to distinguish in the ego is conscience. But it is more prudent to keep the agency as something independent and to suppose that conscience is one of its functions and that self-observation, which is an essential preliminary to the judging activity of conscience, is another of them. And since when we recognize that something has a separate existence we give it a name of its own, from this time forward I will describe this agency in the ego as the '*super-ego*'.

I am now prepared to hear you ask me scornfully whether our ego-psychology comes down to nothing more than taking commonly used abstractions literally and in a crude sense, and transforming them from concepts into things—by which not much would be gained. To this I would reply that in ego-psychology it will be difficult to escape what is universally known; it will rather be a question of new ways of looking at things and new ways of arranging them than of new discoveries. So hold to your contemptuous criticism for the time being and await further explanations. The facts of pathology give our efforts a background that you would look for in vain in popular psychology. So I will proceed.

Hardly have we familiarized ourselves with the idea of a super-ego like this which enjoys a certain degree of autonomy, follows its own intentions and is independent of the ego for its supply of energy, than a clinical picture forces itself on our notice which throws a striking light on the severity of this agency and indeed its cruelty, and on its changing relations to the ego. I am thinking of the condition of melancholia,[1] or, more precisely, of melancholic attacks, which you too will have heard plenty about, even if you are not psychiatrists. The most striking feature of this illness, of whose causation and mechanism we know much too little, is the way in which the super-ego—'conscience', you may call it, quietly—treats the ego. While a melancholic can, like other people, show a greater or lesser degree of severity to himself in his healthy periods, during a melancholic attack his super-ego becomes over-severe, abuses the poor ego, humiliates it and ill-treats it, threatens it with the direst punishments, reproaches it for actions in the remotest past which had been taken lightly at the time—as though it had spent the whole interval in collecting accusations and had only been waiting for its present access of strength in order to bring them up and make a condemnatory judgement on their basis. The super-ego applies the strictest moral standard to the helpless ego which is at its mercy; in general it represents the claims of morality, and we realize all at once that our moral sense of guilt is the expression of the tension between the ego and the super-ego. It is a most remarkable experience to see morality, which is supposed to have been given us by God and thus deeply implanted in us, functioning [in these patients] as a periodic phenomenon. For after a certain number of months the whole moral fuss is over, the criticism of the super-ego is silent, the ego is rehabilitated and again enjoys all the rights of man till the

---

[1] [Modern terminology would probably speak of 'depression.']

next attack. In some forms of the disease, indeed, something of a contrary sort occurs in the intervals; the ego finds itself in a blissful state of intoxication, it celebrates a triumph, as though the super-ego had lost all its strength or had melted into the ego; and this liberated, manic ego permits itself a truly uninhibited satisfaction of all its appetites. Here are happenings rich in unsolved riddles!

No doubt you will expect me to give you more than a mere illustration when I inform you that we have found out all kinds of things about the formation of the super-ego—that is to say, about the origin of conscience. Following a well-known pronouncement of Kant's which couples the conscience within us with the starry Heavens, a pious man might well be tempted to honour these two things as the masterpieces of creation. The stars are indeed magnificent, but as regards conscience God has done an uneven and careless piece of work, for a large majority of men have brought along with them only a modest amount of it or scarcely enough to be worth mentioning. We are far from overlooking the portion of psychological truth that is contained in the assertion that conscience is of divine origin; but the thesis needs interpretation. Even if conscience is something 'within us', yet it is not so from the first. In this it is a real contrast to sexual life, which is in fact there from the beginning of life and not only a later addition. But, as is well known, young children are amoral and possess no internal inhibitions against their impulses striving for pleasure. The part which is later taken on by the super-ego is played to begin with by an external power, by parental authority. Parental influence governs the child by offering proofs of love and by threatening punishments which are signs to the child of loss of love and are bound to be feared on their own account. This realistic anxiety is the precursor of the later moral anxiety.[2] So long as it is dominant there is no need to talk of a super-ego and of a conscience. It is only subsequently that the secondary situation develops (which we are all too ready to regard as the normal one), where the external restraint is internalized and the super-ego takes the place of the parental agency and observes, directs and threatens the ego in exactly the same way as earlier the parents did with the child.

The super-ego, which thus takes over the power, function and even the methods of the parental agency, is however not merely its successor but actually the legitimate heir of its body. It proceeds directly out of it, we shall learn presently by what process. First, however, we must dwell upon a discrepancy between the two. The super-ego seems to have made a one-sided choice and to have picked out only the parents' strictness and severity, their prohibiting and punitive function, whereas their loving care seems not to have been taken over and maintained. If the parents have really enforced their authority with severity we can easily understand the child's in turn developing a severe super-ego. But, contrary to our expectation, experience shows that the super-ego can acquire the same characteristic of relentless severity even if the upbringing had been mild and kindly and had so far as possible avoided threats and punishments. We shall come back later to this contradiction when we deal with the transformations of instinct during the formation of the super-ego.

I cannot tell you as much as I should like about the metamorphosis of the parental relationship into the super-ego, partly because that process is so complicated that an

---

[2] ['*Gewissensangst*', literally conscience anxiety.' Some discussion of the word will be found in an Editor's footnote to *Inhibitions, Symptoms and Anxiety*, Standard Ed., *20*, 128.]

account of it will not fit into the framework of an introductory course of lectures such as I am trying to give you, but partly also because we ourselves do not feel sure that we understand it completely.   So you must be content with the sketch that follows.

The basis of the process is what is called an 'identification'—that is to say, the assimilation of one ego to another one,[3] as a result of which the first ego behaves like the second in certain respects, imitates it and in a sense takes it up into itself. Identification has not been unsuitably compared with the oral, cannibalistic incorporation of the other person. It is a very important form of attachment to someone else, probably the very first, and not the same thing as the choice of an object. The difference between the two can be expressed in some such way as this. If a boy identifies himself with his father, he wants to *be like* his father; if he makes him the object of his choice, he wants to *have* him, to possess him. In the first case his ego is altered on the model of his father; in the second case that is not necessary. Identification and object-choice are to a large extent independent of each other; it is however possible to identify oneself with someone whom, for instance, one has taken as a sexual object, and to alter one's ego on his model. It is said that the influencing of the ego by the sexual object occurs particularly often with women and is characteristic of femininity. I must already have spoken to you in my earlier lectures of what is by far the most instructive relation between identification and object-choice. It can be observed equally easily in children and adults, in normal as in sick people. If one has lost an object or has been obliged to give it up, one often compensates oneself by identifying oneself with it and by setting it up once more in one's ego, so that here object-choice regresses, as it were, to identification.[4]

I myself am far from satisfied with these remarks on identification; but it will be enough if you can grant me that the installation of the super-ego can be described as a successful instance of identification with the parental agency. The fact that speaks decisively for this view is that this new creation of a superior agency within the ego is most intimately linked with the destiny of the Oedipus complex, so that the super-ego appears as the heir of that emotional attachment which is of such importance for childhood. With his abandonment of the Oedipus complex a child must, as we can see, renounce the intense object-cathexes which he has deposited with his parents, and it is as a compensation for this loss of objects that there is such a strong intensification of the identifications with his parents which have probably long been present in his ego. Identifications of this kind as precipitates of object-cathexes that have been given up will be repeated often enough later in the child's life; but it is entirely in accordance with the emotional importance of this first instance of such a transformation that a special place in the ego should be found for its outcome. Close investigation has shown us, too, that the super-ego is stunted in its strength and growth if the surmounting of the Oedipus complex is only incompletely successful. In the course of development the super-ego also takes on the influences of those who have stepped into the place of parents—educators, teachers, people chosen as ideal models. Normally it departs more and more from the original parental figures; it becomes, so to say, more impersonal. Nor must it be forgotten that a

---

[3] [I.e. one ego coming to resemble another one.]

[4] [The matter is in fact only very briefly alluded to in the *Introductory Lectures* (see the later part of Lecture XXVI, *Standard Ed.*, *16*, 427–8). Identification was the subject of Chapter VII of *Group Psychology* (1921c), ibid., *18*, 150 ff. The formation of the super-ego was discussed at length in Chapter III of *The Ego and the Id* (1923b), ibid., *19*, 28 ff.]

child has a different estimate of its parents at different periods of its life. At the time at which the Oedipus complex gives place to the super-ego they are something quite magnificent; but later they lose much of this. Identifications then come about with these later parents as well, and indeed they regularly make important contributions to the formation of character; but in that case they only affect the ego, they no longer influence the super-ego, which has been determined by the earliest parental imagos.[5]

I hoped you have already formed an impression that the hypothesis of the super-ego really describes a structural relation and is not merely a personification of some such abstraction as that of conscience. One more important function remains to be mentioned which we attribute to this super-ego. It is also the vehicle of the ego ideal by which the ego measures itself, which it emulates, and whose demand for every greater perfection it strives to fulfil. There is no doubt that this ego ideal is the precipitate of the old picture of the parents, the expression of admiration for the perfection which the child then attributed to them.[6]

[5][This point was discussed by Freud in a paper on 'The Economic Problem of Masochism' (1924c), Standard ed., 19, 168, where, incidentally, an Editorial footnote deals with Freud's use of the term 'imago.']

[6][There is some obscurity in this passage, and in particular over the phrase 'der Träger des Ichideals', here translated 'the vehicle of the ego ideal.' When Freud first introduced the concept in his paper on narcissism (1914c), he distinguished between the ego ideal itself and 'a special psychical agency which performs the task of seeing that narcissistic satisfaction from the ego ideal is ensured and which, with this end in view, constantly watches the actual ego and measures it by that ideal' (Standard ed., 14, 95). Similarly in Lecture XXVI of the Introductory Lectures (1916–17), Standard Ed., 16, 429, he speaks of a person sensing 'an agency holding sway in his ego which measures his actual ego and each of its activities by an ideal ego that he has created for himself in the course of his development.' In some of Freud's later writings this distinction between the ideal and the agency enforcing it became blurred. It seems possible that it is revived here and that the super-ego is being identified with the enforcing agency. The use of the term 'Idealfunktion' three paragraphs lower down (p. 66) raises the same question. The whole subject was discussed in the Editor's Introduction to The Ego and the Id (1923b) (ibid., 19, 9–10).]

— · — · — · — · — · — · — · — · — · — · —

ERIK ERIKSON

Psychosocial Identity*

When we wish to establish a person's *identity*, we ask what his name is and what station he occupies in his community. *Personal identity* means more; it includes a subjective sense of continuous existence and a coherent memory. *Psychosocial identity* has even more elusive characteristics, at once subjective and objective, individual and social.

*"Identity, Psychosocial" by Erik Erikson. Reprinted with permission of the publisher from *The International Encyclopedia of the Social Sciences*, David L. Sills, Editor. Volume 7, pp. 61–65. Copyright © 1968 by Crowell Collier and Macmillan, Inc.

A subjective sense of identity is a sense of sameness and continuity as an individual—but with a special quality probably best described by William James. A man's character, he wrote in a letter, is discernible in the "mental or moral attitude in which, when it came upon him, he felt himself most deeply and intensely active and alive. At such moments there is a voice inside which speaks and says: '*This* is the real me!' " Such experience always includes "an element of active tension, of holding my own, as it were, and trusting outward things to perform their part so as to make it a full harmony, but without any guaranty that they will" (1920, vol. 1, p. 199). Thus may a mature person come to the astonished or exuberant awareness of his identity.

What underlies such a subjective sense, however, can be recognized by others, even when it is not expecially conscious or, indeed, self-conscious: thus, one can observe a youngster "become himself" at the very moment when he can be said to be "losing himself" in work, play, or company. He suddenly seems to be "at home in his body," to "know where he is going," and so on.

The social aspects of identity formation were touched upon by Freud when in an address he spoke of an "inner identity" that he shared with the tradition of Jewry and which still was at the core of his personality, namely, the capacity to live and think in isolation from the "compact majority" ([1926] 1959, p. 273). The gradual development of a mature psychosocial identity, then, presupposes a community of people whose traditional values become significant to the growing person even as his growth assumes relevance for them. Mere "roles" that can be "played" interchangeably are obviously not sufficient for the social aspect of the equation. Only a hierarchical integration of roles that foster the vitality of individual growth as they represent a vital trend in the existing or developing social order can support identities. Psychosocial identity thus depends on a complementarity of an inner (ego) synthesis in the individual and of role integration in his group [*see* Erikson 1959].

In individual development, psychosocial identity is not feasible before and is indispensable after the end of adolescence, when the grown-up body grows together, when matured sexuality seeks partners, and when the fully developed mind begins to envisage a historical perspective and seeks new loyalties—all developments which must fuse with each other in a new sense of sameness and continuity. Here, persistent (but sometimes mutually contradictory) infantile identifications are brought in line with urgent (and yet often tentative) new selfdefinitions and irreversible (and yet often unclear) role choices. There ensues what we call the *identity crisis*.

Historical processes in turn seem vitally related to the demand for identity in each new generation; for to remain vital, societies must have at their disposal the energies and loyalties that emerge from the adolescent process: as positive identities are "confirmed," societies are regenerated. Where this process fails in too many individuals, a *historical crisis* becomes apparent. Psychosocial identity, therefore, can also be studied from the point of view of a complementarity of life history and history (Erikson 1958; 1964, chapter 5).

In its individual and collective aspects, psychosocial identity strives for ideological unity; but it is also always defined by that past which is to be lived down and by that potential future which is to be prevented. Identity formation thus involves a continuous conflict with powerful negative identity elements. In times of aggravated crises these come to the fore to arouse in man a murderous hate of "otherness," which he judges as evil in strangers—and in himself. The study of psychosocial identity thus calls also for an assessment of the hierarchy of positive and negative identity elements present in an individual's stage of life and in his historical era.

These are dimensions which will prove indispensable to the study of identity in the variety of disciplines now to be listed. In the meantime, I hope to have disposed of the faddish contemporary "definition" of identity as the question, "Who am I?"

INTERESTS AND APPROACHES

Psychiatry and Social Psychiatry

Intricate life processes often reveal themselves first in epidemiological states of dysfunction. Thus, in our time the significance of the identity process first became apparent to psychopathologists who recognized psychosocial factors in severe disturbances of the individual sense of identity (alienation, identity confusion, depersonalization) and to diagnosticians of social upheavals who found psychosocial phenomena at work (role conflict, anomie).

As the theoretical focus of psychoanalysis shifted from "instincts" to "ego," from defensive to adaptive mechanisms, and from infantile conflict to later stages of life, states of acute ego impairment were recognized and treated. A syndrome called *identity confusion* ("identity diffusion" proved a somewhat ambiguous term) was recognized as characterizing neurotic disturbances resulting from traumatic events, such as war, internment, and migration (Erikson [1950] 1964, pp. 38–45). But it also proved to be a dominant feature in developmental disturbances in adolescence (Erikson 1959, pp. 122–146). Identity crises aggravated by social and maturational changes can evoke neurotic or psychotic syndromes but are found to be diagnosable and treatable as transitory disturbances (Blaine & McArthur 1961). Identity confusion, furthermore, can also be recognized in pervert—delinquent and bizarre—extremist behavior, which can assume epidemiological proportions as a result of technological changes and population shifts (Witmer & Kotinsky 1956). Thus theory, therapy, and prevention are seen to lack the proper leverage if the need for psychosocial identity is not understood, and especially if instead the young deviant or patient is "confirmed" as a born criminal or a lifelong patient by correctional or therapeutic agencies (Erikson & Erikson 1957; K. T. Erikson 1957).

Child Development and Anthropology

The study of a variety of dysfunctions thus threw light on identity formation as the very criterion of psychosocial functioning at, and after, the conclusion of one critical stage of development: adolescence. Identity, to be sure, does not originate (and does not end) in adolescence: from birth onward the child learns what counts in his culture's space time and life plan by the community's differential responses to his maturing behavior. He learns to identify with ideal prototypes and to develop away from evil ones. But identity formation comes to a decisive crisis in youth—a crisis met, alleviated, or aggravated by different societies in different ways (Lichtenstein 1961; Erikson 1950).

History and Sociology

Historical considerations lead back into man's prehistory and evolution. Only gradually emerging as one mankind conscious of itself and responsible to and for itself, man has been divided into pseudospecies (tribes and nations, castes and classes), each with its own overdefined identity and each reinforced by mortal prejudice against its images of other pseudospecies.

In history, identifications and identities are bound to shift with changing technologies, cultures, and political systems. Existing or changing roles thus must be reassimilated in the psychosocial identity of the most dominant and most numerous members of an organization. Large-scale irreconcilabilities in this ongoing assimilation result in *identity panic* that, in turn, aggravates irrational aversions and prejudices and can lead to erratic violence on a large scale or to widespread self-damaging malaise (Stein et al. 1960; Wheelis 1958).

The fact that the remnants of "tribalism" in an armed and industrialized species can contribute to conditions of utmost danger to the survival of the species itself is leading to a new consciousness of man's position in his own ongoing history.

Religion and Philosophy

While projecting evil otherness on enemies and devils, man has habitually assigned a supreme "identity" to deities who guarantee, under revealed conditions, his chances for individual immortality or rebirth. This tendency is a proper subject for psychoanalytic and psychosocial investigation only insofar as it reveals the psychological and cultural variations of man's projection of his striving for omnipotent identity on the "Beyond" (Erikson 1958).

Finally, man's psychosocial identity has been related philosophically to his striving to attain and to transcend *the pure "I"* that remains each individual's existential enigma. Old and new wisdom would suggest that man can transcend only what he has affirmed in a lifetime and a generation. Here, clinical and social science will concern themselves with the demonstrable, and philosophy with the thinkable (Lichtenstein 1963).

Out of this multiplicity of approaches we will now select a few converging themes for more coherent presentation.

A THEORY OF PSYCHOSOCIAL IDENTITY

The Identity Crisis

In some young people, in some classes, at some periods in history, the identity crisis will be noiseless; in other people, classes and periods, the crisis will be clearly marked off as a critical period, a kind of "second birth," either deliberately intensified by collective ritual and indoctrination or spontaneously aggravated by individual conflict.

In this day of psychiatric overconcern, it must be emphasized that crisis here does not mean a fatal turn but rather (as it does in drama and in medicine) a crucial time or an inescapable turning point for better *or* for worse. "Better" here means a confluence of the constructive energies of individual and society, as witnessed by physical grace, mental alertness, emotional directness, and social "actualness." "Worse" means prolonged identity confusion in the young individual as well as in the society which is forfeiting the devoted application of the energies of youth. But worse can ultimately lead to better: extraordinary individuals, in repeated crises, create the identity elements of the future (Erikson 1958).

Identity Closure and "Ideology"

In the individual, the normative identity crisis is brought about by contemporaneous and indivisible developments that have received uneven attention in various fields of inquiry. The "growing together" of late adolescence results in increasingly irreversible configurations of physical and sexual type, of cognitive and emotional style, and of social role. Sexual maturation drives the individual toward more or less regressive, furtive, or indiscriminate contact; yet the fatefulness of a narrowing choice of more permanent partners becomes inescapable. All of this is strongly related to maturing patterns of cognition and judgment. Inhelder's and Piaget's studies (1955) suggest that only in adolescence can man "reverse" in his mind a sequence of events in such a way that it becomes clear why what *did* happen *had* to happen. Thus, the irreversibility of consequences (more or less intended, more or less "deserved") becomes painfully apparent. With such cognitive orientation, then, the young person must make or "make his own" a series of personal, occupational, and ideological choices.

At the same time, an unconscious integration of all earlier identifications must take place. Children have the nucleus of a separate identity early in life; often they are seen to defend it with precocious self-determination against pressures which would make them overidentify with one or both of their parents. In fact, what clinical literature describes as identification is usually neurotic overidentification. The postadolescent identity must rely, to be sure, on all those earlier identifications that have contributed to a gradual alignment of the individual's instinctual make-up with his developing endowment and the tangible promise of future opportunities. But the wholeness of identity is more than the sum of all earlier identifications and must be supported by a communal orientation which we will call ideological. A living ideology is a systematized set of ideas and ideals which unifies the striving for psychosocial identity in the coming generation, and it remains a stratum in every man's imagery whether it remains a "way of life" or becomes a militant "official" ideology [*see* IDEOLOGY]. An ideological world view may be transmitted in dogmatic from by special rites, inductions, or confirmations; or society may allow youth to experiment for specified periods (I have called them *psychosocial moratoria*) under special conditions (*Wanderschaft*, frontier, colonies, service, college, etc.).

Fidelity

Sooner or later, the young individual and the functioning society must join forces in that combination of loyalty and competence which may best be termed *fidelity* (Erikson 1963). This may be realized by the involvement of youth as beneficiaries and renewers of tradition, workers and innovators in technology, critics and rejuvenators of style and logic, and rebels bent on the destruction of hollow form in such experience as reveals the essence of the era. For contemporaries, it is often difficult to discern the vital promise of a new and more inclusive identity or to assess the specific alienation inherent in a historical period: there are prophetic voices in all eras which make a profession of ascribing man's existential self-estrangement to the sins of the time.

Obviously, an era's identity crisis is least severe in that segment of youth which is able to invest its fidelity in an expanding technology and thus evolves new and competent types and roles. Today, this includes the young people in all countries who can fit into and take active charge of technical and scientific development, learning thereby to identify with a life-style of invention and production. Youth which is eager for such experience but unable to find access to it will feel estranged from society until technology and nontechnical intelligence have come to a certain convergence.

Male and Female Identity

Do male and female identities differ? The "mechanisms" of identity formation are, of course, the same. But since identity is always anchored both in physiological "givens" and in social roles, the sex endowed with an "innerbodily space" capable of bearing offspring lives in a different total configuration of identity elements than does the fathering sex (Erikson 1965). Obviously also, the childhood identifications to be integrated differ in the two sexes. But the realization of woman's optimal psychosocial identity (which in our day would include individuality, workmanship, and citizenship, as well as motherhood) is beset with ancient problems. The "depth," both concretely physical and emotional, of woman's involvement in the cycle of sexual attraction, conception, gestation, lactation, and child care has been exploited by the builders of ideologies and societies to relegate women to all manner of life-long "confinements" and confirming roles. Psychoanalysis has shown feminine identity formation to be prejudiced by what a woman cannot be and cannot have rather than by what she is, has been, and may yet become. Thus the struggle for legal and political equality is apt to be accompanied by strenuous attempts to base woman's identity on the proof that she is (almost) as good as man in activities and schedules fashioned by and for men. However, the flamboyant brinkmanship of technological and political men in matters now of vital concern to the whole species has revived the vision of a new identity of womanhood, one in which the maternal orientation is not at odds with work and citizenship but gives new meaning to both. But here as elsewhere new inventions will not suffice as long as deep-seated negative identities prevail.

Negative Identity and Totalism

As pointed out, a negative identity remains an unruly part of the total identity. In addition, man tends to "make his own" the negative image of himself imposed on him by superiors and exploiters (Erikson 1959, pp. 31–38). To cite a contemporary issue, a colored child's identity may have gained strength from his parent's melodious speech, and yet he may come to suspect this speech as the mark of submission and begin to aspire to the harsh traits of a superiority from which the "master race" tries by every means to exclude him. A fanatical segregationist, in turn, may have learned to reinforce regional identity with the repudiation of everything colored and yet may have experienced early associations with colored people for which he remains nostalgic. He will, therefore, protect his superiority with a narrow-mindedness so defensive that it fails to provide a reliable identity in an enlightened society.

Two phenomena further complicate these inner rifts. For one, negative images become tightly associated with one another in the individual's imagery. The reinforced defense against a negative identity may make a pronounced he-man despise in himself and others everything reminiscent of female sentimentality, colored passivity, or Jewish braininess and at the same time make him fear that what is thus held in contempt may take over his world. This kind of reaction is the source of much human hate. In the event of aggravated crises, furthermore, an individual (or a group) may despair of his or its ability to contain these negative elements in a positive identity. This can lead to a sudden surrender to total doctrines and dogmas (Lifton 1961) in which the negative identity becomes the dominant one. Many a young German, once sensitive to foreign criticism, became a ruthless Nazi on the rebound from the love for a *Kultur* which in post-Versailles Germany seemed at odds with a German identity. His new identity, however, was based on a totalism marked by the radical exclusion of dangerous otherness and on the failure to integrate historically given identity elements also alive in every German. What differentiates such totalism from conversions promising a more inclusive wholeness is the specific rage that is aroused wherever identity development loses the promise of a traditionally assured wholeness. This latent rage is easily exploited by fanatic and psychopathic leaders. It can explode in the arbitrary destructiveness of mobs, and it can serve the efficient violence of organized machines of destruction.

HISTORICAL CONSIDERATIONS

As predicted, developmental considerations have led us to examine historical processes, for identity and ideology seem to be two aspects of the same psychosocial process. But identity and ideology are only way stations on the route to further individual and collective maturation; new crises work toward those higher forms of social identification in which identities are joined, fused, renewed, and transcended.

There are, however, periods in history which are relative identity vacuums and in which three forms of human apprehension aggravate each other: fears aroused by discoveries and inventions (including weapons) which radically expand and change the whole world image, anxieties aggravated by the decay of institutions which had been the historical anchor of an existing ideology, and the dread of an existential vacuum devoid of spiritual meaning. In the past, ideological innovators evolved vital new identity ingredients out of their own prolonged and repeated adolescent conflicts (Erikson 1958; 1964, pp. 201–208). Today, however, the ideology of progress has made unpredictable and unlimited change itself the "wave of the future." In all parts of the world, therefore, the struggle now is for anticipatory and more inclusive identities. Revolutionary doctrines promise the new identity of "peasant-and-worker" to the youth of countries which must overcome their tribal, feudal, or colonial orientation. At the same time, new nations attempt to absorb regions, and new markets attempt to absorb nations; the world space is extended to include outer space as the proper locale for a universal technological identity.

Functioning societies can reconfirm their principles, and true leaders can create significant new solidarities only by supporting the development of more inclusive identities; for only a new and enlightened ethics can successfully replace dying moralisms. Nehru said that Gandhi had given India an identity; and, indeed, by perfecting an active mode of nonviolence, Gandhi had transformed a divisive and negative identity (the "passive" Indian) into an inclusive and militant claim on unified nationhood. In other parts of the world, youth itself has shown that when trusted to do so, it can provide patterns for new elites. One thinks here of Israel's "kibbutzniks," the U.S. Peace Corps, and the American students committed to the dislodgement of racial prejudice. In such developments, young men and women can be seen to develop new forms of solidarity and new ethics.

In conclusion, however, we must remind ourselves that the complementarity and relativity of individual identity and collective ideology (which no doubt has emerged as part of man's sociogenetic evolution) also bestows on man a most dangerous potential, namely, a lastingly immature perspective on history. Ideologies and identities, it is true, strive to overcome the tyranny of old moralisms and dogmatisms; yet, they often revert to these, seduced by the righteousness by which otherness is repudiated when the conditions supporting a sense of identity seem in danger. Old ideologists equipped with modern weaponry could well become mankind's executioners. But a trend toward an all-inclusive human identity, and with it a universal ethics, is equally discernible in the development of man, and it may not be too utopian to assume that new and world-wide systems of technology and communication may serve to make this universality more manifest.

BIBLIOGRAPHY

Blaine, Graham B.; and McArthur, Charles (editors) 1961 *Emotional Problems of the Student.* New York: Appleton.

Erikson, Erik H. (1950) 1964 *Childhood and Society.* 2d ed., rev. & enl. New York: Norton.

Erikson, Erik H. (1958) 1962 *Young Man Luther.* New York: Norton.

Erikson, Erik H. 1959 Identity and the Life Cycle. *Psychological Issues* 1, no. 1.

Erikson, Erik H. (editor) 1963 *Youth: Change and Challenge.* New York: Basic Books.

Erikson, Erik H. 1964 *Insight and Responsibility.* New York: Norton.

Erikson, Erik H. 1965 Inner and Outer Space: Reflections on Womanhood. Pages 1-26 in Robert Lifton, *The Woman in America.* New York: Houghton Mifflin.

Erikson, Erik H. 1966 The Concept of Identity in Race Relations: Notes and Queries. *Daedalus* 95:145-171.

Erikson, Erik H.; and Erikson, Kai T. 1957 The Confirmation of the Delinquent. *Chicago Review* 10:15-23.

Erikson, Kai T. 1957 Patient Role and Social Uncertainty. *Psychiatry* 20:263-274.

Freud, Sigmund (1926) 1959 Address to the Society of B'nai B'rith. Volume 20, pages 272-274 in Sigmund Freud, *The Standard Edition of the Complete Psychological Works.* London: Hogarth.

Inhelder, Bärbel; and Piaget, Jean (1955) 1958 *The Growth of Logical Thinking From Childhood to Adolescence.* New York: Basic Books. → First published as *De la logique de l'enfant à la logique de l'adolescent.*

James, William 1920 *Letters.* Volume 1. Boston: Atlantic Monthly Press.

Lichtenstein, Heinz 1961 Identity and Sexuality: A Study of Their Interrelationship in Man. *Journal of the American Psychoanalytic Association* 9:179-260.

Lichtenstein, Heinz 1963 The Dilemma of Human Identity. *Journal of the American Psychoanalytic Association* 11:173–223.

Lifton, Robert J. 1961 *Thought Reform and the Psychology of Totalism: A Study of "Brainwashing" in China.* New York: Norton.

Stein, Maurice R.; Vidich, Arthur; and White, David M. (editors) 1960 *Identity and Anxiety.* New York: Free Press.

Wheelis, Allen 1958 *The Quest for Identity.* New York: Norton.

Witmer, Helen L.; and Kotinsky, Ruth (editors) 1956 *New Perspectives for Research on Juvenile Delinquency.* Washington: U.S. Children's Bureau.

— · — · — · — · — · — · — · — · — · — · —

JEAN PIAGET

*Moral Judgment of the Child**

We find that the notions of justice and solidarity develop correlatively as a function of the mental age of the child. In the course of this section, three sets of facts have appeared to us to be connected together. In the first place, reciprocity asserts itself with age. To hit back seems wrong to the little ones because it is forbidden by adult law, but it seems just to the older children, precisely because this mode of retributive justice functions independently of the adult and sets "punishment by reciprocity" above "expiatory punishment." In the second place, the desire for equality increases with age. Finally, certain features of solidarity, such as not cheating or not lying between children, develop concurrently with the above tendencies. . . .

DEVELOPMENT OF THE IDEA OF JUSTICE

We asked the children, either at the end or at the beginning of our interrogatories, to give us themselves examples of what they regarded as unfair.[1]

The answers we obtained were of four kinds: 1) Behavior that goes against commands received from the adult—lying, stealing, breakages, etc; in a word, everything that is forbidden. 2) Behavior that goes against the rules of a game. 3) Behavior that goes against equality (inequality in punishment as in treatment). 4) Acts of injustice connected with adult society (economic or political injustice). Now, statistically, the results show very clearly as functions of age:

---

*Reprinted with permission of the Macmillan Company from *The Moral Judgment of the Child* by Jean Piaget. First published 1932. Also by permission of Routledge & Kegan Paul Ltd.

[1] As a matter of fact this term is not understood by all, but it can always be replaced by "not fair" (Fr. *pas juste*).

	Forbidden	Games	Inequality	Social Injustice
6-8	64%	9%	27%	. . .
9-12..........	7%	9%	73%	11%

Here are examples of the identification of what is unfair with what is forbidden:

AGE 6: *"A little girl who has a broken plate,"* *"to burst a balloon,"* *"children who make a noise with their feet during prayers,"* *"telling lies,"* *"something not true,"* *"it's not fair to steal,"* etc.

AGE 7: *"Fighting,"* *"disobeying,"* *"fighting about nothing,"* *"crying for nothing,"* *"playing pranks,"* etc.

AGE 8: *"Fighting each other,"* *"telling lies,"* *"stealing,"* etc.

Here are examples of inequalities:

AGE 6: *"Giving a big cake to one and a little one to another."* *"One piece of chocolate to one and two to another."*

AGE 7: *"A mother who gives more to a little girl who isn't nice."* *"Beating a friend who has done nothing to you."*

AGE 8: *"Someone who gave two tubes* [to two brothers] *and one was bigger than the other"* [taken from experience, this!] *"Two twin sisters who were not given the same number of cherries"* [also experienced].

AGE 9: *"The mother gives a* [bigger] *piece of bread to someone else."* *"The mother gives a lovely dog to one sister and not to the other."* *"A worse punishment for one than for the other."*

AGE 10: *"When you both do the same work and don't get the same reward."* *"Two children both do what they are told, and one gets more than the other."* *"To scold one child and not the other if they have both disobeyed."*

AGE 11: *"Two children who steal cherries: only one is punished because his teeth are black."* *"A strong man beating a weak one."* *"A master who likes one boy better than another, and gives him better marks."*

AGE 12: *"A referee who takes sides."*

And some examples of social injustice.

AGE 12: *"A mistress preferring a pupil because he is stronger, or cleverer, or better dressed."*

"Often people like to choose rich friends rather than poor friends who would be nicer."

"A mother who won't allow her children to play with children who are less well dressed."

"Children who leave a little girl out of their games, who is not so well dressed as they are."

These obviously spontaneous remarks, taken together with the rest of our enquiry, allow us to conclude, in so far as one can talk of stages in the moral life, the existence of three great periods in the development of the sense of justice in the child. One period, lasting up to the age of 7-8, during which justice is subordinated to adult authority; a period contained approximately between 8-11, and which is that of progressive equalitarianism; and finally a period which sets in towards 11-12, and during which purely equalitarian justice is tempered by considerations of equity.

The first is characterized by the non-differentiation of the notions of just and unjust from those of duty and disobedience: whatever conforms to the dictates of the adult authority is just. As a matter of fact even at this stage the child already looks upon some kinds of treatment as unjust, those, namely in which the adult does not carry out the rules he has himself laid down for children (*e.g.*, punishing for a fault that has not been committed, forbidding what has previously been allowed, etc.). But if the adult sticks to his own rules, everything he prescribes is just. In the domain of retributive justice, every punishment is accepted as perfectly legitimate, as necessary, and even as constituting the essence of morality: if lying were not punished, one would be allowed to tell lies, etc. In the stories where we have brought retributive justice into conflict with equality, the child belonging to this stage sets the necessity for punishment above equality of any sort. In the choice of punishments, expiation takes precedence over punishment by reciprocity, the very principle of the latter type of punishment not being exactly understood by the child. In the domain of immanent justice, more than three-quarters of the subjects under 8 believe in an automatic justice which emanates from physical nature and inanimate objects. If obedience and equality are brought into conflict, the child is always in favour of obedience: authority takes precedence over justice. Finally, in the domain of justice between children, the need for equality is already felt, but is yielded to only where it cannot possibly come into conflict with authority. For instance, the act of hitting back, which is regarded by the child of 10 as one of elementary justice, is considered "naughty" by the children of 6 and 7, though, of course, they are always doing it in practice. (It will be remembered that the heteronomous rule, whatever may be the respect in which it is held mentally, is not necessarily observed in real life.) On the other hand, even in the relations between children, the authority of older ones will outweigh equality. In short, we may say that throughout this period, during which unilateral respect is stronger than mutual respect, the conception of justice can only develop on certain points, those, namely, where cooperation begins to make itself felt independently of constraint. On all other points, what is just is confused with what is imposed by law, and law is completely heteronomous and imposed by the adult.

The second period does not appear on the plane of reflection and moral judgment until about the age of 7 or 8. But it is obvious that this comes slightly later than what happens with regard to practice. This period may be defined by the progressive development of autonomy and the priority of equality over authority. In the domain of retributive justice, the idea of expiatory punishment is no longer accepted with the same docility as before, and the only punishments accepted as really legitimate are those based upon reciprocity. Belief in immanent justice is perceptibly on the decrease and moral action is sought for its own sake, independently of reward or punishment. In matters of distributive justice, equality rules supreme. In conflicts between punishment and equality, equality outweighs every other consideration. The same holds good *a fortiori* of conflicts with authority. Finally, in the relations between children, equalitarianism obtains progressively with increasing age.

Towards 11-12 we see a new attitude emerge, which may be said to be characterized by the feeling of equity, and which is nothing but a development of equalitarianism in the direction of relativity. Instead of looking for equality in identity, the child no longer thinks of the equal rights of individuals except in relation to the particular situation of each. In the domain of retributive justice this comes to the same thing as not applying the same punishment to all, but taking into account the attenuating circumstances of some. In the domain of distributive justice it means no longer thinking of a law as identical for all but taking account of the personal circumstances of each (favouring the younger ones, etc.). Far from leading to privileges, such an attitude tends to make equality more effectual than it was before.

Even if this evolution does not consist of general stages, but simply of phases characterizing certain limited processes, we have said enough to try to elucidate now the psychological origins of the idea of justice and the conditions of its development. With this in view, let us distinguish retributive from distributive justice, for the two go together only when reduced to their fundamental elements, and let us begin with distributive judgment, whose fate in the course of mental development seems to indicate that it is the most fundamental form of justice itself.

★ ★ ★

TWO MORALITIES OF THE CHILD

The analysis of the child's moral judgments has led us perforce to the discussion of the great problem of the relations of social life to the rational consciousness. The conclusion we came to was that the morality prescribed for the individual by society is not homogeneous because society itself is not just one thing. Society is the sum of social relations, and among these relations we can distinguish two extreme types: relations of constraint, whose characteristic is to impose upon the individual from outside a system of rules with obligatory content, and relations of cooperation whose characteristic is to create within people's minds the consciousness of ideal norms at the back of all rules. Arising from the ties of authority and unilateral respect, the relations of constraint therefore characterize most of the features of society as it exists, and in particular the relations of the child to its adult surrounding. Defined by equality and mutual respect, the relations of cooperation, on the contrary, constitute an equilibrial limit rather than a static system. Constraint, the source of duty and heteronomy, cannot, therefore, be reduced to the good and to autonomous rationality, which are the fruits of reciprocity, although the actual evolution of the relations of constraint tends to bring these nearer to cooperation.

— · — · — · — · — · — · — · — · — · —

AUGUST B. HOLLINGSHEAD
FREDRICK C. REDLICH

*Relation of Social Class to Mental Illness**

Americans prefer to avoid the two facts of life studied in this book: social class and mental illness. The very idea of "social class" is inconsistent with the American ideal of a society composed of free and equal individuals, individuals living in a society where they have identical opportunities to realize their inborn potentialities. The acceptance of this facet of the "American Dream" is easy and popular. To suggest that it may be more myth than reality stimulates antagonistic reactions.

Although Americans, by choice, deny the existence of social classes, they are forced to admit the reality of mental illness. Nevertheless, merely the thought of such illness is abhorrent to them. They fear "mental illness," its victims, and those people who cope with them: psychiatrists, clinical psychologists, social workers, psychiatric nurses, and attendants. Even the institutions our society has developed to care for the mentally ill are designated by pejorative terms, such as "bug house," "booby hatch," and "loony bin," and psychiatrists are called "nutcrackers" and "head shrinkers."

Denial of the existence of social classes and derisive dismissal of the mentally ill may salve the consciences of some people. The suggestion that different social classes receive different treatment for mental illness may come as a shock, but to repress facts because they are distasteful and incongruent with cherished values may lead to consequences even more serious than those we are trying to escape by substituting fantasy for reality.

MENTAL ILLNESS

Our attitudes toward mental illness are also a product of our cultural heritage. Historical evidence indicates that mental "disturbances" have been known in all civilized societies. The severe disturbances of kings, generals, religious leaders, and other personages have been recorded since ancient times. Persons who were not important enough to have their mental aberrations written into the human record undoubtedly also were afflicted, even though their ailments and their numbers have been lost in the mists of time. Although man's mental and emotional maladjustments are not new, the public is more clearly aware of them now than in the past, and responsible leaders have become increasingly concerned with their alleviation.

In the last decade mental illness has been recognized as one of the most serious unsolved health problems facing our society. A few figures will indicate its magnitude. The approximately 750,000 persons who are currently hospitalized in mental institutions

*August B. Hollingshead and Fredrick C. Redlich, *Social Class and Mental Illness* (New York: John Wiley & Sons, Inc., 1958), pp. 3-6, 84-85, 94-95, 103-104, 113-114, 198-199, 216-217, 225-229. Reprinted by permission.

occupy some 55 percent of all hospital beds in the United States. Hundreds of thousands of other mentally ill persons are treated by psychiatrists in clinics and in private practice, but the number of hospitalized cases increases year by year. During World War II, 43 percent of all discharges (980,000) from the Armed Forces were granted on psychiatric grounds, and 865,000 young men were rejected for psychiatric reasons in Selective Service examinations. Moreover, some 16,000 to 17,000 persons commit suicide each year and, according to the best estimates, there are about 3,800,000 alcoholics in the adult population. We are certain that patients hospitalized in mental institutions in addition to those cared for by psychiatrists in private practice and in clinics represent only a portion of those who are mentally ill. Estimates indicate that there are from seven to eight million other Americans who are less seriously disturbed but who could benefit from psychiatric care if it were available.[1]

SOCIAL CLASS AND MENTAL ILLNESS

Is the presence of mental illness in the population related to class status? Is the treatment received by a mentally ill member of our society an effect of his class position? These questions are crucial to the research reported here. They are even more important from the viewpoint of their scientific meaning and their implications for social policy.

Detailed evidence will be presented in this book to support the answers we have reached. If our answers support American ideals of equality, class status should have no effect upon the distribution of mental illness in the population. Neither should it influence the kind of psychiatric treatment mentally ill patients receive. However, the reader should remember that our ideals and our behavior are two different things.

Both social class and mental illness may be compared to an iceberg; 90 percent of it is concealed below the surface. The submerged portion, though unseen, is the dangerous part. This may be illustrated by recalling what happened when an "unsinkable" trans-Atlantic luxury liner, the *Titanic*, rammed an iceberg on her maiden voyage in 1912. In that crisis, a passenger's class status played a part in the determination of whether he survived or was drowned. The official casualty lists showed that only 4 first class female passengers (3 voluntarily chose to stay on the ship) of a total of 143 were lost. Among the second class passengers, 15 of 93 females drowned; and among the third class, 81 of 179 female passengers went down with the ship. The third class passengers were ordered to remain below deck, some kept there at the point of a gun.[2]

The idea that stratification in our society has any bearing on the diagnosis and treatment of disease runs counter to our cherished beliefs about equality, especially when they are applied to the care of the sick. Physicians share deeply ingrained egalitarian ideals with their fellow citizens, yet they, too, may make subtle, perhaps unconscious, judgments of the differential worth of the members of our society. Physicians, among them psychiatrists, are sensitive to statements that patients may not be treated alike; in fact there is strong resistance in medical circles to the exploration of such questions. But

[1] Kenneth Appel, "Present Challenge of Psychiatry," *American Journal of Psychiatry*, Vol. III, No. 1 (July 1954), pp. 1-12; J. M. A. Weiss, "Suicide: An Epidomiological Analysis," *Psychological Quarterly*, Vol. 28 (1954), pp. 225-252.
[2] Walter Lord, *A Night to Remember* (New York: Henry Holt and Company, 1955), p. 107.

closing our eyes to facts or denying them in anger will help patients no more than the belief that the *Titanic* was "unsinkable" kept the ship afloat after it collided with an iceberg.

CLASS STATUS AND CULTURAL CHARACTERISTICS

Class I

Class I is composed of the community's business and professional leaders. Its members live in those areas of the community generally regarded as the "best"; the male heads are college graduates, usually from famous private institutions; their wives have completed from one to four years of college. Incomes are the highest of any stratum, and many families are wealthy; often their wealth is inherited. This is true particularly of a core group of interrelated families who have lived in the area for several generations. Members of the core group are descendants of the pioneers who settled in New England three centuries ago. These families dominate the private clubs that play so prominent a part in this group's use of leisure time. The core group family is stable, secure, and, from the viewpoint of its values, socially responsible for its members and the welfare of the community.

★ ★ ★

Class II

Almost all adults in the class II stratum have had some formal education beyond high school. The males occupy managerial positions; many are engaged in the lesser ranking professions. The class II members live in one-family houses in the better residential areas. These families are well-to-do, but there is no substantial inherited or acquired wealth. Class II persons are sensitive to status factors perhaps as a consequence of the fact that four in five are upward mobile. The aspirations of these people have taken them away from their parental families and in many cases from their home communities. Upward mobility is closely linked with ethnic heterogeneity and religious affiliation. About one half of the families are Protestants; the remainder are divided rather equally between Roman Catholics and Jews. The nuclear family is composed predominantly of married adults and their minor children. Only 5 percent of the families with children under 17 years of age are broken or have an aged relative, usually a grandparent, in the home. Family members of all ages are "joiners." Their memberships include neighborhood clique groups, associations for mutual protection against "undesirables," local church organizations, political clubs, fraternal societies, business associations, the Boy Scouts, the Girl Scouts, and Parent Teacher Associations. In addition, about half of these families belong to lesser ranking private clubs in the area.

Tension points in class II generally revolve around the striving for success—economic, educational, and social. The younger adults are oriented toward the future, the time when they will "reach the top." Middle-aged men and women are more aware that they have not quite "made it." Older persons know they will not "make it"; they are resigned to things as they are, but there is an underlying fear that sickness, war, or depression will impair their ability to "hold on."

★ ★ ★

Class III

Significantly more men and women are dissatisfied with their present living conditions and less optimistic about the future than are the class II's. However, the majority have a positive view of the future. They look forward to the time when the home will be paid for or their income higher, and things will be easier. Some two out of three husbands and wives under 50 years of age believe that their chances of achieving a desired standard of living within the next ten years are "almost certain" or "very good." They expect to double their income within 15 years.

Men and women over 40 years of age are concerned about the maturing of their children, the maintenance of their neighborhood, and their health. Many are disturbed by reports of corruption in business and government, especially at the local level. Others are disturbed by the encroachment of Negroes into their neighborhoods; the feeling that people do not recognize moral responsibilities to their children, their neighbors, and their associates disturbs others; many middle-aged persons wonder about their "place" in life.

The realization of the gulf between what they think life might be and what it is for them is a point of stress for many beyond the middle years. Years of striving for their ideals has taught them to forego pleasures of the day for spiritual, moral, and social gains of tomorrow. As the years pass, and the realization that hoped-for goals have slipped away, or moved farther into the future, many adults have become resigned to the realization that they must adjust to things as they are.

★ ★ ★

Class IV

The modal family may be summarized in general terms. The husband who is 44 and the wife who is 42 years of age are members of an ethnic group—if Italian, second generation; if Irish, third. They were married after an engagement of five months in a Roman Catholic church when the husband was 21 and the wife was 19 years of age. When the couple married, they moved into a "rent" of their own in the dwelling owned by the husband's family. They now live in a two-family home, are satisfied with their housing, but hope to buy a single-family home in the suburbs some day. They have 4 or 5 children; the younger ones are in elementary and high school; the oldest one has finished school and is working on the production line of a local factory, or, if a male, is in the armed services. The husband and father has been working since the age of 17. He worked at his first job for about a year and a half, then changed to one he though was better; however, he is still a semiskilled worker on a production line. His wife, too, began to work in the factory when she was 17 years of age, but she many have tried sales or clerical jobs as well. She was working when she was married and continued to work until her first pregnancy was well advanced.

The recreation of the parents consists of "working around the place," viewing television, occasionally listening to the radio, some reading, and family visiting. The children spend more time with television, the radio, and the movies than do their parents. In addition, they go to local athletic events and visit the amusement park two or three times during the season. The husband belongs to "the union" but no other organization. The wife belongs to no formal organizations, but she is a member of an informal neighborhood women's group.

Their effective family income after withholding taxes, union dues, social security, and hospital insurance is approximately $65 a week, and they are able to save about $5 of it. Their savings are used periodically to pay for emergencies or the purchase of desired consumer goods. At present they feel economically secure, but they are not wholly satisfied with their living conditions; the children are dissatisfied. The parents believe that their marriage has been a "good one" and it has been aided by the cooperation and mutual interest they have held through the years. The parents look forward to a happy future, especially to when they will be able to save enough to buy their "dream house." They believe that their chances of obtaining it are "good" now that the children are "out from underfoot." The husband expects to continue to earn a "good income." He thinks his "best years" will come in his "late fifties" when he will be earning "about $100 a week."

★ ★ ★

Class V

Occupationally, class V adults are overwhelmingly semiskilled factory hands and unskilled laborers. Educationally, most adults have not completed the elementary grades. Individuals and families are concentrated in the "tenement" and "cold-water flat" areas of New Haven and in semirural "slums" in two of the suburban towns. Immigrants from southern and eastern Europe, their children, grandchildren, and great-grandchildren compose the vast majority of this stratum, but about 4 percent are swamp Yankees; and 25 percent are descendants of the "old immigrants" from northern and western Europe.

Five types of family constellations exist in class V: the nuclear family of father, mother, and children, the three- or four-generation stem family, the broken nuclear family of one parent and minor children, residual families consisting of widows, widowers, or elderly couples whose children have left home, mixed families of one parent, children, roomers and/or boarders, and common-law groups. Forty-one percent of the children under seventeen years of age live in broken homes. There are a few more separated or divorced adults in Class V than there are widows and widowers. Family ties are more brittle in class V than in the higher classes.

Only a small minority of the family members belong to and participate in organized community institutions. Their social life takes place in the household, on the street, or in neighborhood social agencies. Leisure time activities vary with the several age groups, but in all ages they tend to be informal and spontaneous. Reading either for information or pleasure is not a prominent feature of their activities. Television viewing is a major activity at all ages. Out-of-the-home recreations involve commercial amusements or trips to public places. Adolescent boys, in particular, tend to roam the streets and highways in search of adventure. This often brings them into contact with the police and the courts.

The struggle for existence is a meaningful reality to these people. Their level of skill is low, their jobs are poorly paid, and they have no savings to carry them over a crisis. Adults are resentful of the way they have been treated by employers, clergymen, teachers, doctors, police, and other representatives of organized society. They express their resentments freely in the home and in other primary groups. Children hear them, believe them, and react to the targets of the parents' hostility in ways that are generally approved by the parents. This means that the children fit into the mold provided for them by their parents. Their own experiences with representatives of the higher class reinforce the attitudes they bring into the situation. As a consequence, hostility breeds more hostility; but in order to survive the class V child or adult must repress his feelings and attitudes. These, however, tend to be expressed by acting out against society, members of the family, or the self. The psychopathological implications of the class V subculture should become clearer as we present data on the psychiatric side of the picture.

★ ★ ★

CLASS STATUS AND PREVALENCE OF DISORDERS

The first test of a possible interrelation between class status and mental illness is presented in Table 10.1. A glance at the percentages in Table 10.1 will show that class I has only one third as many patients as might be expected if class I individuals were distributed in the same proportion in the patient population as class I individuals are in the general population. Likewise, class II, III, and IV individuals are under-represented in the patient column, but not to the same extent as class I individuals. On the other hand, the percentage of patients in class V is more than double the percentage of class V individuals in the general population. The distribution of patients in comparison with nonpatients by class is significant.

TABLE 10.1. CLASS STATUS AND THE DISTRIBUTION OF PATIENTS AND NONPATIENTS IN THE POPULATION

Class	Population, %	
	Patients	Nonpatients
I......................	1.0	3.0
II.....................	7.0	8.4
III....................	13.7	20.4
IV....................	40.1	49.8
V.....................	38.2	18.4
	$n = 1891$	236,940

$$X^2 = 509.81, 4 \ df, p < .001$$

This indicates that there is foundation in fact for our assumption that class status is a factor conditioning whether or not a member of the community is a psychiatric patient. However, we are not content to accept the apparent relationship between class status and treatment or nontreatment for a mental disorder without a systematic examination of the influences age, sex, religion, and marital status may have on the data. If it should occur that, when these factors are included in the analysis, the significant association between class status and the prevalence of treated disorders in the population shown in Table 10.1 disappears, then we should modify the theoretical position posited in this research. If, however, the inclusion of these factors does not efface the differences between class status and the prevalence of patients in the different classes, then we may conclude *Hypothesis I* is tenable. Control of the five factors, in addition to class, will tell us whether the relationship we have found between class status and mental illness can be attributed to these factors.

★ ★ ★

The series of analyses we have presented in this chapter have been focused on a step-by-step examination of the tenability of the first hypothesis around which this research was designed. This hypothesis was premised on the assumption that the prevalence of psychiatric patients in the population of the community studies is related significantly to social class. The search for a clear-cut answer to this proposition was carried through six progressively more difficult steps. The first involved a direct comparison of the patients with the general population. This comparison revealed three things:

(1) A definite association exists between class position and being a psychiatric patient.

(2) The lower the class, the greater the proportion of patients in the population.

(3) The greatest difference is between classes IV and V in that class V has a much higher ratio of patients to population that class IV.

To assure ourselves that the strong association between class status and mental illness is not produced by variables other than class, the data were analyzed, in the second step, with selected factors controlled—sex, age, race, religion, and marital status. When each of these factors were held constant, the association between class status and mental illness reappeared. We next held two factors constant, and the association of mental illness with class continued to reappear with one exception: No significant difference was found between mental disorder and class position for individuals aged 15 through 24. The fourth analytical step entailed holding three factors constant. Once again the association between class and the prevalence of mental illness reappeared with few exceptions. The fifth step was taken when the previously demonstrated relationship between class and the prevalence of mental illness was viewed in terms of rates. The sixth step was taken when the components in prevalence were analyzed by class: incidence, re-entry into treatment, and continuous treatment. The rates for each of these components in the general picture of treated mental illness are linked in significant ways to class status.

The several procedures followed enable us to conclude that *Hypothesis 1* is true. Stated in different terms, a distinct inverse relationship does exist between social class and mental illness. The linkage between class status and the distribution of patients in the population follows a characteristic pattern; class V, almost invariably, contributes many more patients than its proportion of the population warrants. Among the higher classes there is a more proportionate relationship between the number of psychiatric patients and the number of individuals in the population.

★ ★ ★

CLASS POSITION AND TYPES OF MENTAL ILLNESS

Class Status and the Neuroses

We are now ready to present the crucial *internal* test we made of the proposition that class status is related to neurotic illnesses. The data essential for the examination of this proposition are summarized in Table 10.2.

TABLE 10.2. PERCENTAGE OF PATIENTS IN EACH DIAGNOSIS CATEGORY OF NEUROSIS–BY CLASS
(Age and Sex Adjusted)

Diagnostic Category of Neurosis	Class			
	I-II	III	IV	V
Antisocial and immaturity reactions	21	32	23	37
Phobic-anxiety reactions	16	18	30	16
Character neuroses	36	23	13	16
Depressive reactions	12	12	10	8
Psychosomatic reactions	7	9	13	11
Obsessive-compulsive reactions	7	5	5	0
Hysterical reactions	1	1	6	12
	n = 98	119	182	65

$$X^2 = 53.62, df\ 18, p < .001$$

The data in Table 10.2 demonstrate that a significant relationship does exist between class position and the kind of diagnoses psychiatrists place upon their patients. Anti-social and immaturity reactions are concentrated in classes III and V, whereas phobic and anxiety reactions cluster in class IV. Character neuroses focus in classes I and II; relatively few character neuroses are found in classes IV and V. The depressive reactions are scattered, but classes I and II have 50 percent more depressives than class V.

Psychosomatic reactions, by way of contrast, are related inversely to class. The class IV's and the class V's somatize their complaints to a greater extent than class I, II, and III patients. On the other hand, obsessive-compulsive reactions are directly related to class position. The obsessive-compulsives are concentrated in classes I and II. The gradient for hysterical patients runs in the opposite direction; in this illness there is an extreme concentration in class V.

Class Position and the Psychoses

Now that we have described the five diagnostic categories established for the psychoses, we are ready to test the applicability of *Hypothesis 2* to these several mental disorders. The essential data for this examination are summarized in Table 10.3.

TABLE 10.3. PERCENTAGE OF PATIENTS IN EACH DIAGNOSTIC CATEGORY OF PSYCHOSIS–BY CLASS
(Age and Sex Adjusted)

Diagnostic Category	Class			
	I-II	III	IV	V
Affective psychoses..............................	21	14	14	7
Psychoses resulting from alcoholism and drug addiction	8	10	4	8
Organic psychoses	5	8	9	16
Schizophrenic psychoses	55	57	61	58
Senile psychoses...................................	11	11	12	11
	n = 53	142	584	672

$$X^2 = 48.23, df\ 12, p < .001$$

The figures given in Table 10.3 reveal a significant association between the five types of psychotic disorders and class status. The effective disorders are linked directly to class position: The higher the class, the larger the proportion of patients who are affective psychotics. The proportion of affective psychotics in classes I and II is three times greater than in class V, but the percentage is the same in class III and class IV. The alcoholic and addictive psychotics show few class differences except in class IV where the percentage is only half that in classes I and II and class V. The organics exhibit a reverse of the distribution observed among the affective psychotics. Only 5 percent of the class I and II patients have an organic disorder, whereas 16 percent of the class V's suffer from one. The schizophrenic and senile psychotics show *no* appreciable percentage differences from class to class. We believe that this is a very important finding. In all classes schizophrenics make up well over half the patients. The senile psychotics represent a relatively small proportion, but this proportion is also constant from class to class.

In all classes schizophrenia is the predominant psychotic disorder. The next most frequent group is the affective one, but it tends to be concentrated more highly in classes I and II than in the other strata. The two functional psychotic groups, affectives and schizophrenics, make up well over two thirds of the patients in the four higher classes; but in class V these disorders total only 65 percent of the patients.

INDEXES

NAME INDEX

SUBJECT INDEX